Lecture Notes in Computer Science 13089

More information about this subseries at https://link.springer.com/bookseries/7409

Weijia Jia · Yong Tang ·
Raymond S. T. Lee · Michael Herzog ·
Hui Zhang · Tianyong Hao ·
Tian Wang (Eds.)

Emerging Technologies for Education

6th International Symposium, SETE 2021
Zhuhai, China, November 11–12, 2021
Revised Selected Papers

Springer

Editors
Weijia Jia
Beijing Normal University-Hong Kong Baptist University United International College
Zhuhai, China

Raymond S. T. Lee
Beijing Normal University-Hong Kong Baptist University United International College
Zhuhai, Guangdong, China

Hui Zhang
Beijing Normal University-Hong Kong Baptist University United International College
Zhuzai, China

Tian Wang
Beijing Normal University-Hong Kong Baptist University United International College
Zhuhai, China

Yong Tang
South China Normal University
Guangzhou, China

Michael Herzog
Hochschule Magdeburg-Stendal
Magdeburg, Germany

Tianyong Hao
South China Normal University
Guangzhou, China

ISSN 0302-9743 ISSN 1611-3349 (electronic)
Lecture Notes in Computer Science
ISBN 978-3-030-92835-3 ISBN 978-3-030-92836-0 (eBook)
https://doi.org/10.1007/978-3-030-92836-0

LNCS Sublibrary: SL3 – Information Systems and Applications, incl. Internet/Web, and HCI

This Springer imprint is published by the registered company Springer Nature Switzerland AG
The registered company address is: Gewerbestrasse 11, 6330 Cham, Switzerland

Preface

SETE 2021, the Sixth Annual International Symposium on Emerging Technologies for Education was held in conjunction with ICWL 2021 and jointly organized by Beijing Normal University-Hong Kong Baptist University United International College (UIC) and the Hong Kong Web Society.

Fueled by ICT technologies, the e-learning environment in the education sector has become more innovative than ever before. Diversified emerging technologies containing various software and hardware components provide the underlying infrastructure needed to create an enormous range of potential educational applications incorporated with proper learning strategies. These prevalent technologies might also lead to changes in the educational environment and thus in learning performance. Moreover, new paradigms are also emerging with the purpose of bringing these innovations to a certain level where they are widely accepted and sustainable. Therefore, the SETE symposium aims at serving as a meeting point for researchers, educationalists, and practitioners to discuss the state-of-the-art and in-progress research, exchange ideas, and share experiences about emerging technologies for education. This symposium also provides opportunities for the cross-fertilization of knowledge and ideas from researchers in diverse fields that make up this interdisciplinary research area. We hope that the implications of the findings of each work presented at this symposium can be used to improve the development of educational environment.

This year's event was held in Zhuhai, a prefecture-level city located on the west bank of the Pearl River estuary on the central coast of southern Guangdong province and in a sector of the Guangdong-Hong Kong-Macau Greater Bay Area of China. This year we received 58 submissions from authors in seven countries and/or regions worldwide. Following a strict double-blind review process, 33 full papers and 10 short papers were selected, yielding acceptance rate of 74%. These contributions covered the latest findings in areas such as digital technology for education, ICT for education, and the application of various AI-related research and technology for education.

SETE 2021 featured 1) the Guangdong-Hong Kong-Macau Bay Area Artificial Intelligence Summit Forum and 2) the Internet of Things Enter UIC event with over 20 renowned academicians as guest speakers. For the SETE 2021 presentations, in addition to the General Track on Emerging Technologies for Education, we had organized four special tracks and two workshops, namely, Track 1: Digital Technology, Creativity, and Education; Track 2: Education Technology (Edtech) and ICT for Education; Track 3: Education + AI; Track 4: Adaptive Learning, Emotion and Behaviour Recognition and Understanding in Education; Workshop 1: The 5th International Symposium on User Modeling and Language Learning (UMLL 2021) and Workshop 2: The 4th International Workshop on Educational Technology for Language Learning (ETLL 2021).

Last but not least, we would like to express our thanks to the Organizing Committee and particularly to the local organizing co-chairs for their time and efforts contributing to the success of the conference. We would also like to express our gratitude to members of the Program Committee for their timely reviews and professionalism. However, above all else, we would like to express our sincere thanks to all the diligent, hardworking authors for their outstanding contributions and continual support to devise emerging technologies for education.

November 2021

Weijia Jia
Yong Tang
Raymond Lee
Michael A. Herzog
Hui Zhang
Tianyong Hao
Tian Wang

Organization

General Co-chairs

Weijia Jia — Beijing Normal University-Hong Kong Baptist University United International College, China
Yong Tang — South China Normal University, China

Program Committee Co-chairs

Raymond Lee — Beijing Normal University-Hong Kong Baptist University United International College, China
Michael A. Herzog — Magdeburg-Stendal University of Applied Sciences, Germany
Hui Zhang — Beijing Normal University-Hong Kong Baptist University United International College, China

Steering Committee Representatives

Ralf Klamma — RWTH Aachen University, Germany

Treasurer

Goliath Li — Beijing Normal University-Hong Kong Baptist University United International College, China

Publicity Co-chairs

Tian Wang — Beijing Normal University-Hong Kong Baptist University United International College, China
Yingshan Shen — South China Normal University, China
Zhe Xuan Yuan — Beijing Normal University-Hong Kong Baptist University United International College, China
Zongwei Luo — Beijing Normal University-Hong Kong Baptist University United International College, China

Publication Chair

Raymond Lee — Beijing Normal University-Hong Kong Baptist University United International College, China

Track Co-chairs

Ping Li	Hong Kong Polytechnic University, Hong Kong, China
Guisong Yang	University of Shanghai for Science and Technology, China
Dapeng Qu	Liaoning University, China
Bo Sun	Beijing Normal University, Zhuhai, China

Workshop Co-chairs

Tianyong Hao	South China Normal University, China
Shili Ge	Guangdong University of Foreign Studies, China
Haoran Xie	Lingnan University, Hong Kong, China

Local Organizing Co-chairs

Jing Zhao	Beijing Normal University-Hong Kong Baptist University United International College, China
Xin Feng	Beijing Normal University-Hong Kong Baptist University United International College, China
Jefferson Fong	Beijing Normal University-Hong Kong Baptist University United International College, China
Yanyan Ji	Beijing Normal University-Hong Kong Baptist University United International College, China
Shuhong Chen	Beijing Normal University-Hong Kong Baptist University United International College, China

Web Chair

Jing He	Beijing Normal University-Hong Kong Baptist University United International College, China

Program Committee

Marie-Helene Abel	HEUDIASYC - Université de Technologie de Compiègne
Jeff Au Yeung	HKU SPACE Community College
Jorge Luis Bacca Acosta	University of Girona
Silvia Margarita Baldiris Navarro	Fundación Universitaria Tecnológico Comfenalco
Li Baoping	Beijing Normal University
Yi Cai	South China University of Technology
Ben Chang	National Central University
Maiga Chang	Athabasca University
Cheng-Te Chen	Far East University
Chih-Hung Chen	National Taichung University of Education

Depeng Chen	Anhui University
Fei Chen	Shenzhen University
Gaowei Chen	University of Hong Kong
Guanliang Chen	Monash University
Haiming Chen	Ningbo University
I-Hua Chen	National Cheng-Kung University
Jun-Ming Chen	National Taiwan University
Qiuxia Chen	Shenzhen Polytechnic
Siqi Chen	Tianjin University
Zhi-Hong Chen	National Taiwan Normal University
Tosti H. C. Chiang	National Taiwan Normal University
Chih-Yueh Chou	Yuan Ze University
Pao-Nan Chou	National Pingtung University of Science and Technology
Irene-Angelica Chounta	University of Duisburg-Essen
Hui Chun Chu	Soochow University
Xiaowen Chu	Hong Kong Baptist University
Hong-Ning Dai	Lingnan University
Fisnik Dalipi	Linnaeus University
Maria-Iuliana Dascalu	University Politehnica of Bucharest
Tania Di Mascio	DISIM, University of L'Aquila
Ping-Lin Fan	National Taipei University of Education
Jeffrey Gamble	National Chiayi University
Li Gao	University of Shanghai for Science and Technology
Gabriela Grosseck	West University of Timisoara
Peidi Gu	Beijing Normal University, Zhuhai
Xiaolei Han	Shanghai Business School
Preben Hansen	Stockholm University
Tianyong Hao	South China Normal University
Jun He	Beijing Normal University
Liu Hongzhi	Liaoning Technical University
Che-Jen Hsieh	Cheng Shiu UNIVERSITY
Min Chai Hsieh	Tainan University of Technology
Ting-Chia Hsu	National Taiwan Normal University
Xiaoyan Hu	Beijing Normal University
Chester Huang	National Kaohsiung University of Science and Technology
Gwo-Haur Hwang	National Yunlin University of Science and Technology
Heisawn Jeong	Hallym University
Jinyuan Jia	Tongji University
Weijia Jia	Beijing Normal University-Hong Kong Baptist University United International College
Morris Jong	Chinese University of Hong Kong
Tai-Chien Kao	National Dong Hwa University
Branko Kaučič	INITUT, Institute of Information Technology
Heng-Yu Ku	University of Northern Colorado

Theresa Kwong	Hong Kong Baptist University
Raymond Lee	Beijing Normal University-Hong Kong Baptist University United International College
Yow-jyy Joyce Lee	National Taichung University of Science and Technology
Fuliang Li	Northeastern University
Ping Li	Hong Kong Polytechnic University
Chang-Yen Liao	National Central University
Chia-Ching Lin	National Kaohsiung Normal University
Chiu-Pin Lin	National Tsing Hua University
Hao-Chiang Koong Lin	National University of Tainan
Alpha Ling	The Education University of Hong Kong
Man Ho Ling	The Education University of Hong Kong
Chao Liu	Ocean University of China
Dennis Y. W. Liu	Hong Kong Polytechnic University
Pei-Lin Liu	National Chiayi University
Qingtang Liu	Central China Normal University
Shiguang Liu	Tianjin University
Xiaofeng Liu	Hohai University
Xiaojun Liu	University of Macau
Yi-Chun Liu	Chia Nan University of Pharmacy and Science
Yong Liu	Beijing University of Chemical Technology
Hanjiang Luo	Shandong University of Science and Technology
George Magoulas	Birbeck, University of London
Chengying Mao	Jiangxi University of Finance and Economics
Anna Mavroudi	Norwegian University of Science and Technology
Alexander Mikroyannidis	The Open University
Iosif Vasile Nemoianu	University Politehnica of Bucharest
Yuichi Ono	University of Tsukuba
Kuo-Liang Ou	National Tsing Hua University
Kyparissia Papanikolaou	University of Athens
Luc Paquette	University of Illinois at Urbana-Champaign
Shaodong Peng	Hunan Normal University
Elvira Popescu	University of Craiova
Dapeng Qu	Liaoning University
Huiyan Qu	Jilin Agricultural University
Rubingong Rubin	Zhi Tech Ltd
Rainer Rubira-García	King Juan Carlos University
Demetrios Sampson	Curtin University
Flippo Sciarrone	Roma Tre University
Rustam Shadiev	Nanjing Normal University
Qing Shao	University of Shanghai for Science and Technology
Maria Grazia Sindoni	University of Messina
Sean Siqueira	Federal University of the State of Rio de Janeiro
Bo Sun	Beijing Normal University
Daner Sun	The Education University of Hong Kong

Jerry Chih-Yuan Sun	National Yang Ming Chiao Tung University
Zeyu Sun	Luoyang Institute of Science and Technology
Zhiyuan Sun	National Yang Ming Chiao Tung University
Davide Taibi	Italian National Research Council
Feng Tao	Anhui University of Technology
Shu-Yuan Tao	Takming University of Science and Technology
Marco Temperini	Sapienza University of Rome
Vladimir Trajkovik	Ss. Cyril and Methodius University of Skopje
Georgi Tuparov	New Bulgarian University
Gang Wang	PCTEL, Inc.
Jingyun Wang	Durham University
Na Wang	University of Shanghai for Science and Technology
Shan Wang	University of Macau
Shaoming Wang	University of Macau
Wei Wang	China Resources Group
Yi Hsuan Wang	Tamkang University
Chun-Wang Wei	Kaohsiung Medical University
Laixiang Wen	Jilin Animation Institute
Tak-Lam Wong	Douglas College
Jiun-Yu Wu	National Yang Ming Chiao Tung University
Sheng-Yi Wu	National Pingtung University
Yubao Wu	Georgia State University
Yongkang Xiao	Beijing Normal University
Junchang Xin	Northeastern University
Luyan Xu	Renmin University of China
Shuang Xu	Taiyuan University of Technology
Zichuan Xu	Dalian University of Technology
Fengting Yan	Tongji University
Euphony Yang	National Central University
Guisong Yang	University of Shanghai for Science and Technology
Yu-Ren Yen	Far East University
Shen Yingshan	South China Normal University
Titus Yiu	HKU SPACE Community College
Shelley Young	National Tsing Hwa University
Ran Yu	GESIS - Leibniz Institute for the Social Sciences
Yan Yu	Tianjin Normal University
Jian Yuan	Shanghai University of Science and Technology
Li Yuan	Beijing Normal University
Sergej Zerr	L3S Research Center
Amy Zhang	Beijing Normal University-Hong Kong Baptist University United International College
Bingxue Zhang	University of Shanghai for Science and Technology
Yi Zhang	Central China Normal University
Yinghui Zhang	Beijing Normal University
Hongwei Zhao	Shenyang University
Liang Zhao	Shenyang Aerospace University

Yin Zhaoxia	Anhui University
Boxin Zheng	University of Macau
Baichang Zhong	Nanjing Normal University
Wanlei Zhou	City University
Wen Zhou	Anhui Normal University
Zhiguo Zhou	Northeast Normal University
Jian Zhu	Guangdong University of Technology
Zhiming Zhu	National Ilan Universitys

Contents

Emerging Technologies for Education

Mind Map Based Computer Network Knowledge Graph Visualization Research and Application

Ming Tao(✉) and Renping Xie

School of Computer Science and Technology, Dongguan University of Technology, Dongguan 523808, People's Republic of China
ming.tao@mail.scut.edu.cn, renping.xie@whu.edu.cn

Abstract. As an effective knowledge visualization tool, mind map has unique advantages in knowledge representation and organization, and has been widely used in the field of education. Computer network as a required course of computer science has the following obvious characteristics, e.g., so many knowledge topics, the content is too abstract to comprehend, strong theoretical and practical. To improve the teaching effect of computer network course and arouse students' enthusiasm for learning, on the basis of summing up years of teaching experience, mind map is introduced into classroom teaching, and a mind map based knowledge graph visualization teaching mode is designed for computer network. Concretely, the drawing of mind map for pre-class preview, the design of mind map for classroom teaching process, and the design of mind map for review mode after class are all involved. The practical application results show that the teaching quality of the computer network course is improved and the students' interest in learning is motivated.

Keywords: Mind map · Knowledge graph · Visualization · Computer network

1 Introduction

As a central major course of computer science, computer network has the following obvious characteristics, e.g., so many scattered and extensive knowledge topics, the content is too abstract to comprehend, strong theoretical and practical. In the teaching process, students generally believe that the concepts of this course are too many to understand, and it is difficult to memorize and understand theoretical knowledge topics, and to establish a clear knowledge structure system. Additionally, most colleges and universities adopt the traditional classroom teaching mode. Typically, the teacher mainly teaches, and the students listen passively with little participation in class. However, the Engineering Accreditation Standards jointly issued by the Higher Education Teaching Evaluation Center of the Ministry of Education and the China Association for Accreditation of Engineering Education clearly put forwards the teaching effect that the course needs to achieve [1–4]. Therefore, how to mobilize the learning enthusiasm of students and enhance the classroom teaching effect, and how to let the

W. Jia et al. (Eds.): SETE 2021, LNCS 13089, pp. 3–12, 2021.
https://doi.org/10.1007/978-3-030-92836-0_1

students take the initiative to participate in teaching activities, have been challenging issues.

As a tool of knowledge visualization, mind map organically combines abstract thought with imaginal thinking in the form of combining words and images, which provides a new perspective and technical support for optimizing teaching activities [5–8]. On the one hand, the schematic characteristics of mind map make the abstract knowledge concepts be visible, facilitate the processing of the learned knowledge, which is helpful to improve the learners' understanding and memory, and improve their interest in learning. On the other hand, the application of mind map not only can improve the learners' understanding of the teaching content and the learning efficiency, but also can help motivate students to participate in teaching activities actively, which is helpful to realize the joint construction of the learned knowledge. Overall, mind map plays a positive role in improving the teaching effect, motivating the students' divergent and innovative thinking, as well as enhancing the ability of cooperation and communication, which not only can help students improve learning efficiency, but also help teachers improve teaching efficiency.

To this end, on the basis of summing up years of teaching experience, mind map is introduced into classroom teaching, and a mind map based knowledge graph visualization teaching mode is designed for computer network course. Concretely, the drawing of mind map for pre-class preview, the design of mind map for classroom teaching process, and the design of mind map for review mode after class are all involved. The quantitative analysis of the achievement of curriculum objectives finally has been shown to demonstrate the practical application effectiveness in improving the teaching quality and motivating the students' interest in learning.

The rest of this paper is organized as follows. In Sect. 2, an overview of computer network course is introduced. In Sect. 3, the designed mind map based knowledge graph visualization teaching mode is thoroughly introduced. In Sect. 4, combining the analysis of the achievement of the curriculum objectives, the practical application effectiveness of the designed teaching mode is demonstrated. In Sect. 5, this paper is summarized and concluded.

2 Overview of Computer Network Course

Computer course is a core course of related majors of computer science and technology, and it is a required course. As a basic course in the computer network course system, it plays a connecting role in the talent training program and curriculum system. In this course, it aims to introduce those involved knowledge topics in computer network design and implementation, e.g., the basic concepts, basic principles, architecture, Internet protocols and applications, as well as TCP/IP network programming methods [9].

According to the Engineering Accreditation Standards jointly issued by the Higher Education Teaching Evaluation Center of the Ministry of Education and the China Association for Accreditation of Engineering Education, the teaching objectives of the course and the supporting relationship to the graduation requirements are designed as follows [10] (Table 1).

Table 1. The teaching objectives of the course and the supporting relationship to the graduation requirements.

Teaching objectives	Graduation requirements	Indicator points
Knowledge: to train students to systematically master the basic principles of computer network	2: Problem analysis: applying the basic principles of mathematics, natural science and computer science to identify, express and analyze complex computer engineering problems	2-1: applying basic concepts from the natural sciences to appropriate represent the complex computer engineering problems
Ability: to cultivate students' ability to analyze, design, develop and use computer network systems	3: Design/develop solutions: the ability to analyze and solve computer engineering problems by combining basic theories and technical approaches 5: Using modern tools: the ability to develop, select and use appropriate technologies, resources, modern engineering tools and information technology tools for complex computer engineering problems	3-1: designing solutions for computer engineering problems and designing related experiments and solutions to obtain and analyze data 5-3: correctly collecting and sorting out the experimental data, carrying on the correlation analysis processing to the experimental results, and obtaining the reasonable and effective conclusion
Quality: cultivate students learning attitude and ideological consciousness with active participation, positive enterprising, advocating scientific and inquiry scientific	12: Lifelong learning: the consciousness of independent learning and lifelong learning, and the ability to continuously learn and adapting development	12-2: Possessing the knowledge foundation of lifelong learning, mastering the methods of self-learning, and understanding the ways to expand knowledge and ability 12-3: adapting to the development of society and industry by self-learning with appropriate methods according to personal or professional development needs

Accordingly, in the classroom teaching process, we focus on problem-based learning and cultivate students' comprehensive analysis and high-level thinking ability to solve complex problems, such as reflection, questioning, criticism and decision making. Taking the basic principle of CSMA/CD protocol introduced in "Link Layer" as an example. We firstly introduce the channel sharing technology of broadcast link in multiple access protocol, so that students can fully understand the background of the problems that need to be solved in link layer. Subsequently, we introduce the typical random access protocols including ALOHA protocol, pure ALOHA protocol, Carrier Sense Multiple Access Protocol (CSMA) and Carrier Sense Multiple Access Protocol with Collision Detection (CSMA/CD), so that students can understand the evolution of CSMA/CD protocol, and reflect on the strengths and weaknesses of these protocols and the scope of their application [11, 12]. Finally, based on mastering the basic principles of the protocol, we require the students to programming implementation of CSMA/CD protocol and further deeply think the protocol implementation logic and detailed reasoning. Accordingly, students' comprehensive abilities of process thinking, practice, reflection, criticism and decision making are cultivated. Generally, the teaching process fully integrates the realization of the three predetermined teaching objectives: knowledge, ability and quality.

3 Mind Map Based Knowledge Graph Visualization Teaching Mode

The predetermined teaching objectives of the course and the supporting relationship to the graduation requirements clearly show the evaluation standard of teaching effect of this course. To achieve the teaching efficiency, a mind map based knowledge graph visualization teaching mode is designed for computer network course. Concretely, the drawing of mind map for pre-class preview, the design of mind map for classroom teaching process, the design of mind map for review mode after class, and the mind map for evaluation of learning process are all involved [13].

3.1 Mind Map Based Pre-class Preview

In the current university classroom teaching, few students can take the initiative to preview the knowledge topics. Therefore, it is very necessary for teachers to provide students with teaching objectives, teaching priorities and difficulties, and the main teaching content before teaching the new lesson, and let students draw a preview outline based on mind map, so that students can find out what they do not understand or doubt. In this way, students will take the problems encountered in the preview process to attend the class. The learning process is more targeted, and the enthusiasm of students will be improved [14]. An illustration of mind map drawn by students after previewing media sharing techniques in the data link layer is shown in Fig. 1.

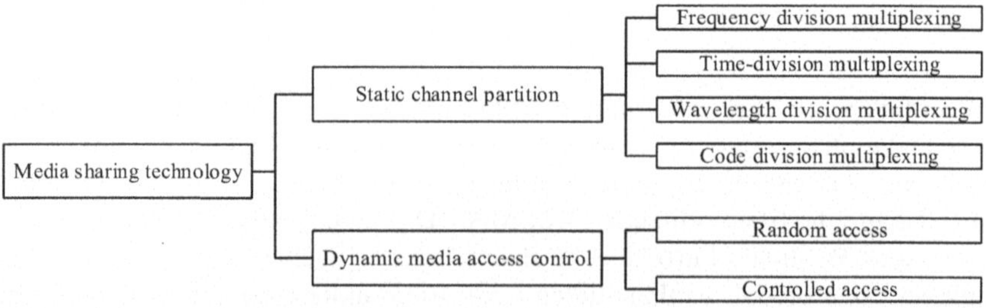

Fig. 1. An illustration of mind map drawn by students after previewing media sharing techniques in the data link layer.

It can be seen from the preview mind map drawn by students that students only give a general preview framework, and the knowledge cannot be better classified at this time.

3.2 Mind Map Based Classroom Teaching

The traditional classroom teaching often adopts the teacher-oriented indoctrination mode, which often ignores the principal position of students. Students' learning enthusiasm and participation are not enough, and they are in a passive learning state. To improve the teaching quality and motivate the students' interest in learning, classroom teaching based on mind mapping divides the teaching process into the following stages. An illustration of mind map based outline of teaching media sharing techniques in the data link layer is shown in Fig. 2.

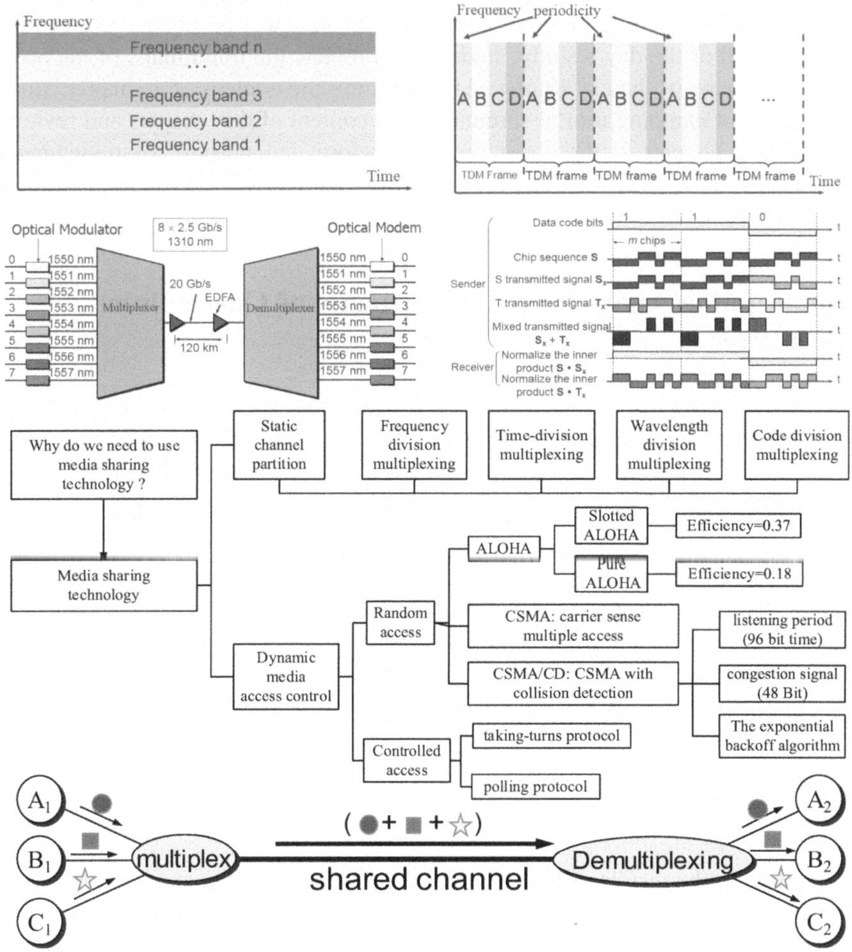

Fig. 2. An illustration of mind map based outline of teaching media sharing techniques in the data link layer.

First, the teacher presents the knowledge topics to the students in the form of diagrams with the help of the mind map. At the same time, the students are asked to take notes in the manner of mind map to form a mind map based notes. In the teaching process, the teacher puts forward preset questions according to students' responses in time for students to think. Under the guidance of the teacher, students can form their own knowledge structure system and complete the knowledge construction process.

On the basis of the mind map based pre-class preview, students re-summarize and reorganize the knowledge in combination with the content taught by the teacher in class, and draw a perfect mind map. This stage is helpful for students to construct knowledge, which can cultivate students' ability of summarizing and promote their understanding of knowledge [15].

3.3 Mind Map Based After-Class Review

Timely review is helpful to improve the effect of memory, enhance the understanding and mastery of knowledge, improve academic performance, and better use of knowledge. At the end of the day's study, students can review the mind maps of the preview and the mind maps of the class notes. After learning the content of a chapter, students can use the mind mapping tool to summarize the content of this chapter and review the content of this chapter at the same time. Therefore, the purpose of reviewing and consolidating knowledge is achieved through the process of arranging knowledge several times by using mind map.

4 Quantitative Analysis of Achievements of Curriculum Objectives

In order to evaluate the teaching quality of this semester, a questionnaire was designed to evaluate the teaching quality of Computer Network through questionnaire star, and the achievement degrees of the course objectives were evaluated. The indirect evaluation results are shown in Table 2.

Table 2. Achievement degrees of course objectives in indirect evaluation.

Objectives	Achieved levels					
	1 (Totally agree)	0.8 (Relatively match)	0.6 (General)	0.4 (Relatively not match)	0.2 (Not match)	Achievement degrees
Knowledge	79.63%	20.37%	0	0	0	0.96
Ability	77.78%	18.52%	3.7%	0	0	0.93
Quality	72.22%	24.08%	3.7%	0	0	0.94

According to the results of the questionnaire survey, students generally believe that the achievement degree of the course goal is above 0.90, which shows that the content design, teaching methods, evaluation mechanism and other course teaching design of this course can help students achieve the expected goals.

In practical, the actual evaluation results are obtained based on the students' grades and final exams. The course score of computer network consists of four parts: final exam score (70%) + usual homework score (10%) + experimental assessment (11%) + midterm exam (9%). The detailed course evaluation method is shown in Table 3.

Table 3. Course assessment and evaluation methods.

Objectives	Indicator points	Evaluation basis & score ratio (%)				Weight (%)
		Usual homework	Experimental assessment	Midterm exam	Final exam	
Knowledge	2-1	6	4	6	46	62
Ability	3-1 5-3	3	3	2	16	24
Quality	12-2 12-3	1	4	1	8	14
Aggregate		10	11	9	70	100

According to the "Implementation Measures for the Evaluation of Course Objective Achievement Degree of Dongguan University of Technology (Trial)", the target value of students' graduation requirements is 0.65. Taking Class 1–2 of Computer Science (including 100 students) in the first semester of 2020–2021 academic year as an example, the quantitative comparisons of the achievement of predetermined curriculum objectives are shown in Fig. 3. The achievements of predetermined curriculum objectives include average achievement of course objectives, achievement of course objective "Knowledge", achievement of course objective "Ability", achievement of course objective "Quality" [16]. From Fig. 3, we can clearly see that the evaluation values of the three predetermined curriculum objectives are equal or greater than 0.65, which indicate that the course objectives have been achieved well with the help of mind map based pre-class preview, classroom teaching process and after-class review.

The comparisons between the indirect evaluation results and the actual evaluation results show that there are big differences in the achievement degrees, which are mainly caused by the low final examination scores (the average score: 64.35, the pass rate: 85.42%, the standard deviation: 9.44, the highest score: 82.0, the lowest score: 38.0). The main reasons are summarized as follows.

(1) Students seem to be in a concentrated state in class, but they do not have a high degree of absorption and mastery of the course content, especially the poor completion of homework. Generally, they simply refer to the supporting instructions for exercises after class, lacking in-depth understanding and mastery of relevant knowledge points.
(2) In practical teaching, the comprehensive design experiments designed in this course are mainly combined with the theoretical knowledge points in theoretical teaching, focusing on students' ability to understand, master, program and solve problems on the knowledge points. In the process of experimental practice,

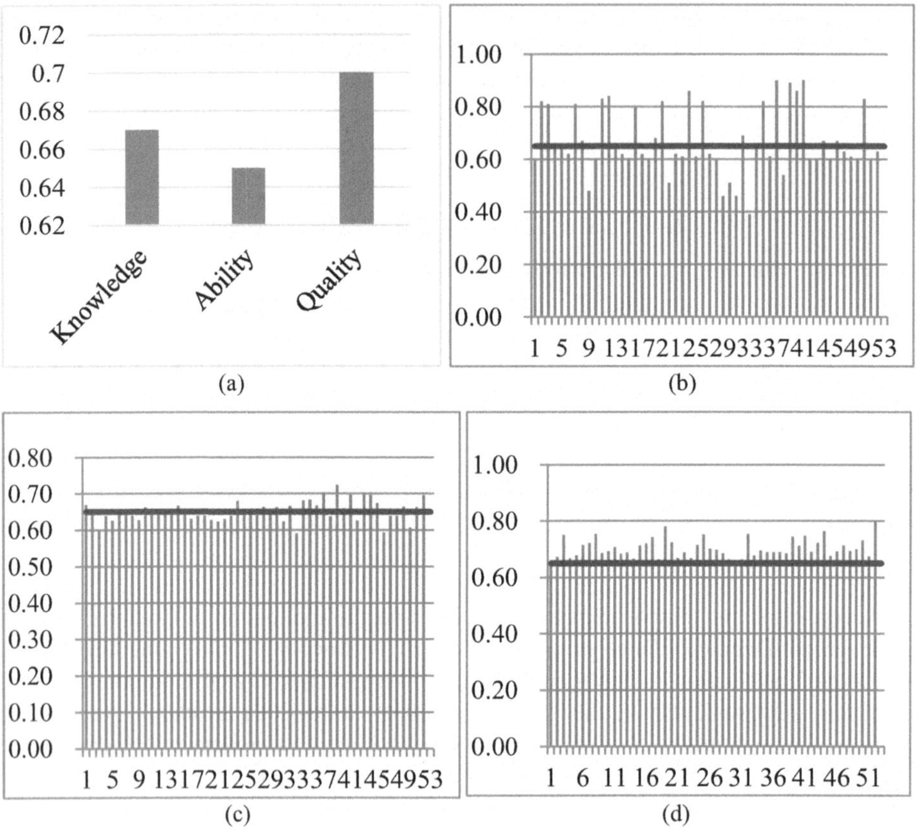

Fig. 3. The quantitative comparisons of the achievements of predetermined curriculum objectives. (a) Average achievements of course objectives. (b) Achievement of course objective "Knowledge". (c) Achievement of course objective "Ability". (d) Achievement of course objective "Quality".

students did not have a clear understanding of the principles of the relevant algorithms involved in the computer system, and their attitude was not correct and too perfunctory in the implementation of programming, resulting in serious loss of scores in the "experimental analysis questions" in the exam.

(3) Teachers' analysis of learning situation is not enough. In the course of teaching, students did not have a thorough understanding of the basic knowledge, especially some concepts related to the periphery of the computer network, such as the Internet of Things, big data, cloud computing, 5G, etc., which resulted in students' half-understanding of relevant content in the course of teaching.

According to the above list of existing problems, the following improvement measures are proposed.

(1) Strengthening the analysis of students' learning situation. Master students' understanding of some peripheral concepts of computer network through questionnaire survey.
(2) Strengthening the integration of "ideological and political elements". Through case analysis, the role of curriculum in professional personnel training is clarified, and students' interest in learning and determination to devote themselves to their major is stimulated.
(3) The achievement degree of "Knowledge" is low. The key lies in the fact that the selected textbooks are equipped with instructions for exercises after class. Students' attitude is not correct in daily exercises such as homework, so they should strengthen exercises after class in future teaching.
(4) "Ability" has been basically achieved, but students can exercise ability in the experiment and practice link is too elaborate, understand the principle of computer system algorithms involved is not clear, the programming to realize attitude is not correct, when in the process of experiment and practice in the future, will further strengthen management, enable the students to the active participation of comprehensive, positive enterprising, Cultivate the learning attitude and ideological consciousness of exploring science.
(5) "Quality" has been basically achieved, but students still have negative feelings towards "course ideology and politics". In the future teaching process, the assessment forms and standards of "course ideology and politics" will be diversified to improve the effect of "course ideology and politics" in educating students.
(6) From the analysis of the teaching process and exam results, the exam results of the students with correct attitude and serious study at ordinary times are within the expected range. However, most students still do not master the basic knowledge of this course and cannot apply it flexibly. Moreover, students' thoughts are loose, their learning motivation is insufficient, they spend less time after class, and they do not have enough review before the exam. Therefore, they need to correct their learning attitude and strengthen the construction of learning style.

5 Conclusion

In this paper, according to the Engineering Accreditation Standards jointly issued by the Higher Education Teaching Evaluation Center of the Ministry of Education and the China Association for Accreditation of Engineering Education, we firstly design the teaching objectives of computer network course and the supporting relationship to the graduation requirements. Subsequently, to further improve the teaching effect and arouse students' enthusiasm for learning, a mind map based knowledge graph visualization teaching mode is designed, which involves several parts in the teaching process, e.g., pre-class review, classroom teaching and after-class review. Finally, the quantitative analysis of the achievement of predetermined curriculum objectives are shown to demonstrate the practical application effectiveness in improving the teaching quality and motivating the students' interest in learning.

Acknowledgments. This work was supported in part by the Natural Science Foundation of Guangdong Province (Grant Nos. 2021A1515010656 & 2018A030313014), the Guangdong University Key Project (2019KZDXM012), and the research team project of Dongguan University of Technology (Grant No. TDY-B2019009).

References

1. Liu, S., Ba, L.: Countermeasures for local engineering colleges to deal with engineering education professional accreditation. In: 4th International Conference on Distance Education and Learning, pp. 194–199 (2019)
2. Qu, Z., Huang, W., Zhou, Z.: Applying sustainability into engineering curriculum under the background of "new engineering education" (NEE). Int. J. Sustain. High. Educ. **21**(6), 169–1187 (2020)
3. Zhao, Y.: Construction of engineering education professional certification system. In: 4th International Conference on Education and Training, Management and Humanities Science, vol. 5, pp. 262–265 (2018)
4. Chen, Y., Liu, Z.: Teaching reform of engineering graphics education in terms of engineering education professional certification in Guangzhou, China. In: IEEE International Conference on Teaching, Assessment, and Learning for Engineering, pp. 596–601 (2018)
5. González, J.M.M., Requena, B., Ariza, M.: Difficulties and expectations of future education professionals in the learning of the mind map. Mind Brain Educ. **14**(4), 341–350 (2020)
6. Eppler, M.J.: A comparison between concept maps, mind maps, conceptual diagrams, and visual metaphors as complementary tools for knowledge construction and sharing. Inf. Vis. **5** (3), 202–210 (2006)
7. Stokhof, H., De Vries, B., Bastiaens, T., et al.: Mind map our way into effective student questioning: a principle-based scenario. Res. Sci. Educ. **49**(2), 347–369 (2019)
8. Rezapour-Nasrabad, R.: Mind map learning technique: an educational interactive approach. Int. J. Pharmac. Res. **11**(11593), 1–5 (2019)
9. Fava-De-Moraes, F., Simon, I.: Computer networks and the internationalization of higher education. High Educ. Pol. **13**(3), 319–324 (2000)
10. Santos, G., Mandado, E., Silva, R., et al.: Engineering learning objectives and computer assisted tools. Eur. J. Eng. Educ. **44**(4), 616–628 (2019)
11. Kim, Y., Park, S.: Performance analysis and fair coexistence of heterogeneous radio networks for multiple devices with different channel access schemes. IEEE Access **8**, 73398–73419 (2020)
12. Khalifa, A.B., Stanica, R.: Performance evaluation of channel access methods for dedicated IoT networks. In: IEEE Wireless Days (WD), pp. 1–6 (2019)
13. Selvi, R.T., Chandramohan, G.: Case study on effective use of mind map in engineering education. In: IEEE Ninth International Conference on Technology for Education (T4E), pp. 205–207 (2018)
14. Sari, R., Sumarmi, S., Astina, I., et al.: Increasing students critical thinking skills and learning motivation using inquiry mind map. Int. J. Emerg. Technol. Learn. **16**(3), 4–19 (2021)
15. Rosba, E., Zubaidah, S., Mahanal, S.: Digital mind map assisted group investigation learning for college students' creativity. Int. J. Interact. Mob. Technol. **15**(5), 4–23 (2021)
16. Luna, M., Cruz, C., Arce, J.O.: Achievement, engagement and student satisfaction in a synchronous online course. In: IEEE Global Engineering Education Conference (EDUCON), pp. 124–132 (2019)

Student Experiences on Using Process-Centric Thesis Management Tool

Juha P. Lindstedt(✉), Altti Lagstedt, and Raine Kauppinen

Haaga-Helia University of Applied Sciences, Helsinki, Finland
juha.lindstedt@haaga-helia.fi

Abstract. We are in the middle of rapid change in the fields of digitalization and automation. The Covid-19 pandemic accelerated the industry 4.0 work revolution by shifting people to a remote mode at work wherever it is possible. At the same time, the younger generations entering higher degree studies demand more personalized solutions in their learning paths. Haaga-Helia University of Applied Sciences has been developing a digitalized edtech tool Wihi to support students' personalized thesis process and help supervisors to monitor multiple thesis projects. Wihi represents new kind of process-centric philosophy where a student's learning process and a supervisor's process are combined. While used two academic years so far, it was time to review what has been achieved, and especially, how students perceive the support of the system and the approach it represents. To find that out, we conducted a survey with structured and open-ended questions. The target group was the students who were in the thesis writing process or had recently completed it. The results reveal that Wihi supports students' thesis project and enables personalized learning approach. However, Wihi's features are used in different efficacy and there are also some challenges to be taken into account in further development and research.

Keywords: Digitalization · Personalized learning · Digitalized teaching processes · Thesis · Survey · Educational technology

1 Introduction

The world is constantly changing and one of the biggest drivers for the change is digitalization and automation, sometimes called industry 4.0 work revolution [1, 2]. Paradoxically, digitalization and automation are seen as one of the most effective tools to respond to the challenges and pressure coming from the change of world and work. Digitalization generates disruptive solutions, also forcing the most reluctant parties to react, and no industrial sector is safe from this [3, 4]. Education is not an exception [5].

However, this revolution of work is not only an organizational or ecosystem level change. The biggest changes and pressures are on individuals. Due the change of work (industry 4.0), many old jobs vanish and some new, more challenging, ones are generated [2, 6, 7]; and individuals must learn new skills and competencies. Education must be able to answer all the time faster changes or new requirements. Thus, the need for a change in the education sector is even bigger than in other industry sectors: if

W. Jia et al. (Eds.): SETE 2021, LNCS 13089, pp. 13–24, 2021.
https://doi.org/10.1007/978-3-030-92836-0_2

education sector is not able to adapt to change quickly enough, all other sectors will suffer a lack of skilled workforce, and the whole society will run into difficulties [2].

Although the need for the change is understood, and lot of discussion is done, for example, about personalized learning, there are not much examples of a holistic approach to the change in teacher's work processes supporting personalized learning in changing environment and digitalization. This kind of support is especially important in thesis phase, where students are already integrating to work life.

In our previous study [8] we presented a new educational technology solution Wihi. In Wihi development, we saw it important to combine the needs of supervisors and students together and to develop a tool to support both user groups' processes. Wihi is a working platform that keeps record of each thesis process and gives an overview of all or selected processes. It contains all the conversation and files related to thesis projects. In addition, it is a project management tool for students allowing students to assign tasks for themselves. Supervisors can make notes for their own use.

Often, when new edtech solutions are developed, only teaching situation or student's learning process are taken into account, solutions are in their own silos and the teacher or supervisor processes including the tasks and responsibilities outside of classroom are neglected [5]. In Wihi development, we followed expert oriented digitalization (EXOD) approach [8] and developed a personalized thesis management system to inline students and supervisors processes. Thus, on one hand, it is a tool for teachers to supervise thesis processes, but on the other hand, it is a tool helping the thesis-writing students to organize their work in individual level. Thus, it is important to evaluate Wihi from both of these aspects. The organizational level digitalization and change process has been analysed earlier [8], and now it was seen important to study how Wihi's features were serving the thesis process from the students' perspective. In our previous study, we presented some preliminary observations of Wihi's usage [9], but now, after the system has been in use almost two academic years, it was possible to collect real usage data.

To find out how students have experienced the new system, we formulated the following questions:

RQ1: *How students perceive Wihi's usefulness and usability?*
RQ2: *Which of the old practices, used in thesis process before the introduction of Wihi, are still in use?*

To answer these questions, we conducted a survey for students who were doing their thesis or had just graduated in fall 2020.

2 Theoretical Background

From a student's perspective, a thesis is as an example of a problem-solving project. According to [10, 89] a learner constructs one's own understanding by selecting and transforming information (past and present) in order to gain new personal knowledge and understanding. In the thesis process, students may even need technologies they have not met before.

Since teachers are familiar with the process, they may use new technologies only as a substitute for manual tasks, or they can take new digitalized processes in use [11]. As personalized learning requires the latter approach, it is important to evaluate the effects of students and teachers actions. Especially students in higher education institutes (HEI) are allowed, and required, to construct their own study paths, i.e. personalize their learning. A HEI itself defines the nature and scope of the thesis. The HEI sets, e.g., reporting standards, the format and gives the assessment criteria. Otherwise, a student has a lot of freedom to design and perform the project.

When education is considered from the student's point of view, motivation and self-directedness are easily emphasized, as well as the role of supervisor and the feedback and assessment system in use. However, the used IS (information system) has a great impact on the afore mentioned, and if the users do not perceive the IS useful and easy to use, it won't be used [12]. Thus, it is important that digital transformation in HEIs is done in a controlled manner.

2.1 The Digital Transformation in HEIs

There are several challenges to utilize digitalization effectively in HEIs. As [5] pointed out, many HEIs do not have a strategic vision how develop their business to fit digital age. Without strategic vision, there is no management commitment and different solutions are being tried in siloes, without coordination and mutual interaction [5]. Good practices are not shared, challenges are not discussed and no further steps are taken. Often, only digital quick fixes are sought and the wider role of digitalization across the institution is not understood [5].

It seems that the available edtech tools support this approach. A remarkable share of the solutions are intended for a very limited use and are mainly aimed at students, supporting a specific phase of specific pedagogy. If processes are mentioned, students' learning processes are emphasized. Teachers' or supervisors' processes, if considered at all, concentrate on teaching situation, that is, on how lectures should be organized and how ICT can support the teaching situation [see e.g., 13]. Although teaching is in the core of teachers' work, teachers' process include other tasks not visible for student. To be successful in digitalization, these tasks should be supported as well [5].

Another challenge are the assumed capability needs in digitalization. Overall picture of teachers' processes is seldom emphasized when teachers' capability for digital change is discussed. For example, the TPACK model [14] highlights three different areas of expertise teachers need to have to make education digital transformation possible: technological, pedagogical and content knowledge. Although the knowledge areas pointed out are essential for digital change, the teaching processes must be understood as well. If lecture-centeredness is the prevailing approach in teacher capability discussion, the risk is that the tasks outside of lectures are neglected. Thus, each teacher copes the situation according to their abilities, that is, processes are not harmonized and they include a lot of manual work.

In addition to lecture-centeredness in education processes discussion, most of the work related to analytics in the education has been on the actions and results of students [15–17]. Normally, the data are collected in the learning environment and analyzed to track the learning and the progress of the student [18, 19]. However, education can be analysed from study, learning, teaching and process points of views [20], and processes of all relevant stakeholders should be taken into account. Analysis should not focus only on student's processes, but more holistic perspective is needed [20], and a strategic level vision for digital transformation is essential in that.

If there is no strategic level vision for digital transformation in HEI and if teachers' situation as a whole is not understood, there is risk that the ISs used are in silos and do not support data collection in users' daily actions [5, 21]. In these cases, wrongly designed IS not only causes extra work and produce insufficient data, but in the worst cases also reduces the autonomy of experts (teachers). This easily leads into the situation where an IS is not used, or it is used only ostensibly to fulfill the given orders [21].

Having no understanding about the changed situation, lack of trust in digital services, digital illiteracy and burden of culture are mentioned as main barriers to digital transformation of HEIs [5, 8]. One reason for limited discussion of teachers' processes and the small number of systems supporting teaching processes might be that the teachers are considered as individual experts, which have quite a bit mechanical work but strong opinions and expertise combined with high autonomy [8]. Nonetheless, as [22] pointed out, it is possible to digitalize also the work of experts, and guidelines and recommendations for university processes digitalization have been studied as well [21, 23].

2.2 From Autoregulation to Self-directedness in Thesis Writing

Thesis is considered as a sample of the student's learning, and often the independency also affects the evaluation of thesis. When planning, scheduling and progress of thesis writing is responsibility of the student, the IS supporting thesis writing must help students to manage their thesis writing process.

Self-regulation or autoregulation [see 24, p. 94], explains the mechanisms that regulate human behaviour. In the context of pedagogy, this can be formulated as self-directedness. According to Breed [25, p. 3], self-directed learning requires student to figure out the learning needs and strategies to learn in order to meet the goals. Breed continues that some other researchers, e.g. Guglielmino; Brockett and Hiemstra, put more weight on the learners' characteristics.

During a thesis project, a student should schedule the project phases. The schedule cannot always be kept, but a student should still have a feeling that the project is under control. Otherwise, the feeling of failure may lead to anxiety and worsen the situation, possibly leading to halting the project and dropping out [see also 26].

2.3 Feedback and Assessment

Even if behavioural learning theories are mostly superseded by cognitive psychology and constructivism, the reinforcement appears in motivation theories [e.g. 27]. Immediate feedback is the most efficient. The challenge of the thesis is that the feedback is often directed to faults and deficits leading to demotivation if not to anxiety. Based on the feedback of graduating students [28], some students do not get constructive feedback or the feedback is given too late in the project's final stage.

Some students are highly independent with high self-esteem. Some may even get irritated if a supervisor is too keen on giving feedback [see also 27]. Illeris [29, p. 16] mentions mental resistance, which may block or distort learning. In a thesis work, a student may have already put all the effort into the report and feedback requiring major changes may be too much to deal with. The other extreme are the students who are so unsure about their decisions that they continuously want detailed feedback. Without the response from the supervisor, a student may halt the process. Therefore, it is important for a supervisor to manage the feedback and keep it at optimal level.

2.4 The Role of the Supervisor

Despite the Internet and modern libraries, there is still a need for traditional thesis tutoring in order to gain intellectual and cognitive growth [see 10, p. 14]. While this is easy for teachers used to interacting directly with the students, the systematic follow-up of every thesis project (with unique schedules) is challenging. Thesis supervisors need to use emails, spreadsheets and calendar applications to handle the situation.

One supervisor may have over 40 thesis in different phases to supervise at the same time. If no supporting IS is in use, communication is scattered in the supervisor's mailbox, with intermediate versions of thesis either as attachments or saved in supervisors' folders. In this kind of situation, certain (silent) students who might need help are easily forgotten. This may lead to delayed projects, anxiety or even to the students' dropping the project or their studies altogether. As a solution, all data should be kept in one database that can be accessed via a portal or user-tailored interface [21].

The roles of the thesis supervisor and the student resemble the apprenticeship where the knowledge and skills are transferred from a master (supervisor) to an apprentice (student) [10]. Kegan [30, pp. 42–44] uses terms informative and transformative learning. In informative learning, only the knowledge changes, but in transformative learning, there is an awareness of methods on developing knowing. This requires interaction, and it is most efficient in contact situations.

3 Research Method

This research can be classified as a small-scale survey having quantitative approach. The data was collected in Haaga-Helia University of Applied Sciences (HH) via Webropol application, and the e-mail addresses of the students were retrieved from Wihi. The electronic form contained 18 questions, 16 structured and two open-ended (one about the key benefits in using Wihi and one about the additional features that should be implemented). The questionnaire was bi-lingual (Finnish/English). As e.g. [31 pp. 301–350] suggests, the form was designed for multiple devices. The survey was open between November 30 and December 14 of 2020. One reminder was sent (as suggested in [31 pp. 301–350]) increasing N from 19 to 36.

The survey request was sent by e-mail to 695 bachelor students, who had recently completed or were about to complete the thesis. However, since the time window between completing the thesis and the graduation is very narrow, the ratio of graduated students was high in the sample. Consequently, the request did not reach all of the graduates because their HH e-mail addresses were expired. As an estimation, this cut out approximately 60% of the requests. In addition, graduated students may feel that they have not any responsibility nor reason to answer. As a reference, HH students' current response ratio to the course feedback is between 10 to 15% indicating general survey fatigue. The analysis of the data was done using SPSS statistical program. The answers to the open-ended questions were analysed by identifying their relevance to the research questions RQ1 and RQ2. From answers, representative ones are used as examples where applicable illustrating students' views as results are discussed.

4 Results

The findings are based on the answers of 36 thesis students. The majority of the students (N = 22) had already completed the process and for the rest (N = 14) the process was ongoing at the time of answering.

4.1 Perceived Usefulness and Usability (RQ1)

The usefulness was measured with a structured question "*Which of the following functions in Wihi have you used?*" having four preset choices. In addition, pedagogy related propositions and the two open-ended questions about the key benefits were related to usefulness and usability.

The structured question had "yes", "no" and "no answer" choices for *comments, files, media files* and *tasks*. The *comments* feature offers messaging between the student and the supervisor so that all messages are in one platform under student's project. It was used by 22 (61%) students while 10 (28%) had not used it and 4 (11%) did not reply. This reveals that one third of the communication bypasses Wihi or that there was no communication at all. Still, the feature was the second most often mentioned key benefit ("*all messaging with the supervisor is saved*"), although improvements were also proposed ("*make it easier to use and have a better nested messaging*") and due to perceived difficulties in using the feature, one student commented about using alternative means ("*this is why we have used e-mail instead*").

The *files* feature is used to keep all the thesis report versions, forms and other material in one place under the student's project. The feature was used by 29 (90%) students. It was also the most often mentioned key benefit ("*an easy way to send files*").

In comparison, the utilization of *media files* (other type of files than e.g. Word or pdf) and *tasks* was minimal. With the tasks feature, a student can set specified duties for him/her self and mark them done when completed. Tasks were used by less than 10% of the students indicating very modest self-directedness towards utilization of new type of information and keeping the work systematically organized and scheduled. There were no requests for additional features apart from recordings ("*online recorded seminars*"). Instead, some comments on additional features requested more comprehensive instructions for Wihi (for example, "*overall information on where to find and what is*" and "*instructions on the use*") and few comments noted little or no perceived benefit ("*I would have completed my thesis successfully without it*").

A pedagogical goal of Wihi is to support personalized learning and make the process more understandable. This was measured by propositions a–g with scale 0–10 (Table 1). The best results were achieved in a) *The division of the thesis process in stages at Wihi, has increased my confidence to achieve the goal.* The average 5,5 partially supports a student's self-esteem and increase in motivation. In addition, there were several comments about the benefit of division to stages ("*it did not feel so big when it was divided into smaller stages*").

Table 1. Descriptive statistics of the pedagogical propositions of the survey (a–h, scale 0–10, high values are positive results whereas in f low values are wished).

Propositions	N	Min	Max	Mean	S. E. mean	Std. dev.
a) The division of the thesis process in stages at Wihi, has increased my confidence to achieve the goal	30	0	9	5,50	,573	3,138
b) Wihi, as a tool for managing files and messaging, has improved to keep the focus in the thesis project	28	0	9	4,43	,607	3,214
c) Working in the Wihi platform has helped me to understand the core elements of the thesis, hence improved the overall comprehension	28	0	9	4,29	,563	2,980
d) The Wihi scheduling and monitoring has helped me to achieve the intermediate goals	28	0	9	4,68	,617	3,267
e) The Wihi scheduling and monitoring has increased my motivation	26	0	10	4,35	,574	2,925
f) The Wihi scheduling and monitoring has caused me negative feelings of pressure	22	0	8	2,86	,519	2,436
g) The interactive commentation between me and the supervisor in Wihi has helped to advance and complete the thesis	26	0	9	4,31	,632	3,222
h) Meetings (face to face/phone/video) with the supervisor have helped to advance and complete the thesis	15	3	10	6,93	,547	2,120

Proposition b) *Wihi, as a tool for managing files and messaging, has improved to keep the focus in the thesis project.* The average 4,4 is low to argue that the goal would have been reached, although the distribution is polarized meaning that some students have benefited of the feature. Also, as seen earlier, managing documented (*files*) and messaging (*comments*) were seen as the key benefits in open questions.

Since Wihi is a tool for thesis project managing and the comprehension is more up to the materials elsewhere, the average 4,3 of proposition c) *Working in the Wihi platform has helped me to understand the core elements of the thesis, hence improved the overall comprehension* is understandable. The students did not expect this either, since there was only one comment asking for instructions on core elements of the thesis ("*instructions on the progress of the thesis*"). More was expected of d) *The Wihi scheduling and monitoring has helped me to achieve the intermediate goals.* There are three 5-credit phases in thesis project, assuming rewards during the project to motivate the students. Average 4,7 is a slight low although highest standard deviation indicates that opinions are scattered and some students have benefitted from the intermediate credits. This is supported by the open questions ("*intermediate goals*").

Proposition e) *The Wihi scheduling and monitoring has increased my motivation* estimates if automatic monitoring can foster motivation to keep the schedule. In Wihi, the student sets the dates for project stages and Wihi indicates if dates are not met or no advancement has been detected in a certain period of time. Average 4,4 shows that there is no significant impact although some comments show that this is seen as a benefit ("*constant tracking of the progress made*"). In related variable f) *The Wihi scheduling and monitoring has caused me negative feelings of pressure,* low average was wanted and attained, since it was 2,9. There were no related comments.

Proposition g) *The interactive commentation between me and the supervisor in Wihi has helped to advance and complete the thesis* did not get high average, as it was 4,3. The distribution is polarized, indicated also in open questions, since the messaging (*comments*) was often mentioned as benefit, but also as a feature that could be improved. This may refer to the lack of perceived interactivity in messaging or that messaging took place in other media.

The opinions on usability were measured by two questions (Fig. 1) related to visual clarity and overall usability. The scale here was 4–10 (used in Finland and familiar to the students; it matches D-A scale approximately as follows: 4 = F, 5 = D, 6–7 = C, 8–9 = B, 10 = A). The average in both was 7 which is satisfactory. There were also several negative comments about the appearance (for example, "*boring*" and "*scarce*") and several suggestions for improving it or the usability (for example, "*more appealing looks*" and "*reminders featuring next planned events*").

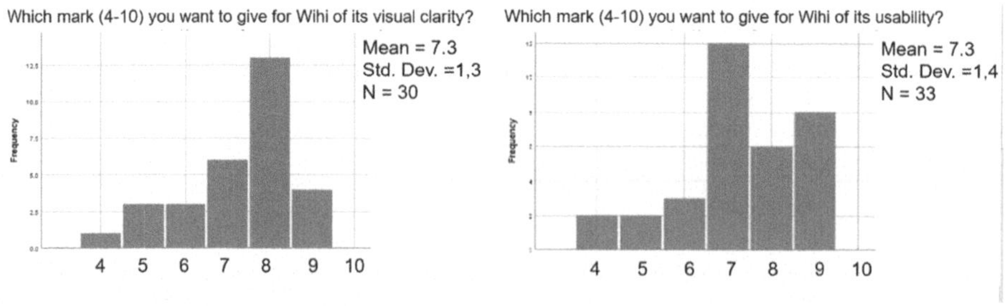

Fig. 1. Which mark (4–10) you want to give for Wihi of its visual clarity? (left); Which mark (4–10) you want to give for Wihi of its usability? (right).

4.2 The Use of Old Practices (RQ2)

It was assumed that some old practices still exist due the resistance to change or because all features in Wihi have not yet been fully comprehended [see also 32]. This was measured with two structured questions "*Which of the following have you needed/used in your thesis process?*" and "*Meetings (face to face/phone/video) with the supervisor have helped to advance and complete the thesis*" (proposition h in Table 1).

The first of these structured questions had "yes", "no" and "no answer" (=missing answer. i.e. "yes" or "no" not selected) choices for five preset options *email, phone, video meetings, face to face meetings* and *thesis workshops or camps. E-mail* had been used by 32 (89%) students and only 4 (11%) replied that they had not used e-mail. Although it may be a coincidence that the same number of students did not answer the earlier question about using *comments*, this emphasizes that the feature has not been fully understood. An important benefit of Wihi is that messaging between the student and the supervisor is in one place so that a student can find all the thesis-related messages from Wihi, instead of filtering them from e-mail. This feature is even more important for the supervisors, since one supervisor may have up to 40 ongoing thesis at a time.

Since Wihi does not have a chat or video meetings, it is understandable that 9 (25%) had used *phone* and 28 (78%) *video meetings* (Teams/Zoom/Skype) with their supervisor, especially taking into account Covid-19 preventing face-to-face meetings at the time of the survey. Still, because some students had started their thesis before Covid-19, 16 students (44%) reported having had face-to-face meetings (consultation), and 9 (25%) had joined thesis workshops or camps.

The second structured question was presented as a slider (0 = not at all, 10 = significantly). It is related to the live, phone and video meetings representing the traditional face-to-face meetings, since regardless of the introduction of Wihi, they remain as a pedagogical method. Although the numerus 15 is low partly due to the Covid-19, the average 6,9 tells that face-to-face contact cannot be ignored and there is still room for "analogue" techniques and human contact.

Related to the key benefits, there were also several comments illustrating that Wihi was not utilized to its full extend (for example, "*I did not use it that much*" and "*it was not actively used by the supervisor*"). This emphasises the importance of making the benefits (usefulness) clear to students and the importance of the supervisors' example.

5 Discussions and Conclusions

The student thesis management system Wihi was developed for a helpful tool for thesis coordinators, thesis supervisors and students. The students are the largest and the fastest changing user group with the shortest usage time of the system. There are 2000 new students per year, each student using the system only for one semester.

Based on the answers of the survey, we can conclude as an answer to RQ1: *How students perceive Wihi's usefulness and usability?,* that in general student are rather pleased for the system. Even though some criticism was levelled at the dullness of the interface, the system was considered clear and reasonably usable. Because students are a constantly changing group of users with limited time and guiding resources, the interface has been deliberately kept scarce and its functionalities at a minimum. Against this background, the results are good. Wihi supports students' thesis project and enables personalized learning by helping students to plan and schedule their thesis project, giving a communication channel and increasing students' confidence to achieve their goals. However, as Wihi's features are used in variable efficacy, the results also point out the need for more guidance. It was find out that not all students have understood the features correctly. The guidance can be improved by embedding guidelines within Wihi, by external guidelines, guidance by supervisor or general guidance given by thesis coordinators. Based on the answers, there is need to improve all these in some level.

One measure for the success of a new IS, and the new process it supports, is how many old practices are still used after the implementation of the IS. If perceived usefulness and usability by the users is one side of the coin, the replacement of the old practices is another. This was explored in RQ2: *Which of the old practices, used in thesis process before the introduction of Wihi, are still in use?* Based on the answers, we can conclude that old practices are still used in parallel with Wihi. In some cases, it is understandable (or even encouraged). For example, due to the Covid-19 situation, video meetings and phone are obvious tools to synchronous communication between the student and the supervisor, especially since Wihi is not planned for synchronous (live) communication (originally, in the process, the synchronous communication was done in face-to-face meetings). Wihi was planned for asynchronous communication to substitute emails. It seems that this objective is not fully successful, since email is still rather widely uses. After this finding, active measures have been taken to shift the conversations from email to Wihi. Further progress has been detected, but it seems that old practises vanish slowly.

The volatility of the student user group makes it difficult to have a system pleasing all, as 2000 new users per year is a challenge for any system. The features of the system, as well as the user interface must be kept as scarce as possible, and it seems that there Wihi has succeeded rather well. However, there is an identified need for more guidance, which is in line with the observations of the use of old practices, especially email, parallel to using Wihi. The students' use of the system is also unique compared, for example, to the supervisors who repeat the process with different students while individual student does a thesis once. Thus, it is crucial to provide support for the personalized process and based on the results, Wihi is a platform that already enables this very well and has even more underlying potential that to be realized when its capabilities are fully understood and used by both the students and their supervisors.

In future studies, it is good to note that the students are not using Wihi by themselves, but with close interaction and guidance from supervisors. Therefore, it is important to examine supervisors' use and experiences of Wihi as well: do they find the system useful, and do they require students to fully utilize it. In this study, we asked students opinions and experiences, but in order to get more comprehensive picture, it is important to also examine the real usage data from the Wihi system logs.

We see that the findings of this study are not important only for the further development of Wihi and the guidance supporting it, but also for the development of other similar kind of IS with high user turnover, which is rather typical situation in education. Instead of more common lecture-centric approach, the developed thesis management system, Wihi, represents a new kind of process-centric approach to education IS, and as such, has shown to be a useful tool for all parties. We see that these results are important to be considered when other process-centric solutions are developed. The personalized needs of users must be understood and supported in different situations and balanced between simplicity and usefulness.

References

1. Drath, R., Horch, A.: Industrie 4.0: Hit or Hype? IEEE Ind. Electron. Mag. **8**, 56–58 (2014)
2. Frey, C.B., Garlick, R., Friedlander, G., et al.: Technology at Work v2.0. CityGroup and University of Oxford (2016)
3. Bharadwaj, A., El Sawy, O., Pavlou, P., Venkatraman, N.: Digital business strategy: toward a next generation of insights. MIS Q. **37**, 471–482 (2013)
4. Borg, M., Wernberg, J., Olsson, T., et al.: Illuminating a blind spot in digitalization - software development in Sweden's private and public sector. In: IEEE/ACM 42nd International Conference on Software Engineering Workshops (ICSEW 2020) (2020)
5. McCusker, C., Babington, D.: The 2018 Digital University Staying Relevant in the Digital Age, pp. 1–20. Pricewaterhouse Coopers (2018)
6. Wike, R., Stokes, B.: In advanced and emerging economies alike, worries about job automation. Pew Res. Cent. 1–13 (2018)
7. Wilson, H.J., Daugherty, P.R., Morini-Bianzino, N.: The jobs that artificial intelligence will create. MIT Sloan Manag. Rev. **58**, 14–16 (2017)
8. Lagstedt, A., Lindstedt, J.P., Kauppinen, R.: An outcome of expert-oriented digitalization of university processes. Educ. Inf. Technol. **25**(6), 5853–5871 (2020). https://doi.org/10.1007/s10639-020-10252-x
9. Lindstedt, J.P., Kauppinen, R., Lagstedt, A.: Personalizing the learning process with wihi. In: Proceedings of 33rd Bled eConference, pp 305–318 (2020)
10. Pritchard, A., Woollard, J.: Psychology for the Classroom: Constructivism and Social Learning. Routledge, Florence (2010)
11. Jude, L., Kajura, M., Birevu, M.: Adoption of the SAMR model to asses ICT pedagogical adoption: a case of makerere university. Int. J. e-Educ. e-Bus. e-Manag. e-Learn. **4** (2014). https://doi.org/10.7763/ijeeee.2014.v4.312
12. Davis, F.D., Bagozzi, R.P., Warshaw, P.R.: User acceptance of computer technology: a comparison of two theoretical models. Manag. Sci. **35**, 982–1003 (1989). https://doi.org/10.1287/mnsc.35.8.982
13. Nikolić, V., Petković, D., Denić, N., et al.: Appraisal and review of e-learning and ICT systems in teaching process. Phys. A Stat. Mech. Appl. **513**, 456–464 (2019). https://doi.org/10.1016/j.physa.2018.09.003
14. Mishra, P., Koehler, M.J.: Technological pedagogical content knowledge: a framework for teacher knowledge. Teach. Coll. Rec. **108**, 1017–1054 (2006)
15. Greller, W., Drachsler, H.: Translating learning into numbers: a generic framework for learning analytics. Educ. Technol. Soc. **15**, 42–57 (2012)
16. Ferguson, R.: Learning analytics: Drivers, developments and challenges. Int. J. Technol. Enhanc. Learn. **4**, 304–317 (2012). https://doi.org/10.1504/IJTEL.2012.051816
17. Sclater, N., Peasgood, A., Mullan, J.: Learning Analytics in Higher Education. A Review of UK and International Practice. Bristol, Jisc (2016)

18. Chatti, M.A., Dyckhoff, A.L., Schroeder, U., Thüs, H.: A reference model for learning analytics. Int. J. Technol. Enhanc. Learn. **4**, 318–331 (2012). https://doi.org/10.1504/IJTEL.2012.051815
19. Siemens, G.: Learning analytics: the emergence of a discipline. Am. Behav. Sci. **57**, 1380–1400 (2013). https://doi.org/10.1177/0002764213498851
20. Kauppinen, R., Lagstedt, A.: Towards minimum viable education analytics. In: 15th annual International Technology, Education and Development Conference, INTED 2021 (2021)
21. Kauppinen, R., Lagstedt, A., Lindstedt, J.: Digitalizing Teaching Processes – How to Create Usable Data with Minimal Effort. Eur. J. High. Educ. IT **1** (2020)
22. Davenport, T.H.: Process management for knowledge work. In: vom Brocke, J., Rosemann, M. (eds.) Handbook on Business Process Management 1. IHIS, pp. 17–35. Springer, Heidelberg (2015). https://doi.org/10.1007/978-3-642-45100-3_2
23. Kauppinen, R., Lagstedt, A., Lindstedt, J.P.: Expert-oriented digitalization of university processes. In: The 4th International Symposium on Emerging Technologies for Education, SETE 2019 (2019)
24. Leontiev, D.A.: Why we do what we do: the variety of human regulations. In: Leontiev, D. A. (ed.) Motivation, Consciousness, and Self-Regulation, pp 93–103. Nova Science Publishers (2012)
25. Breed, B.: Exploring a cooperative learning approach to improve self-directed learning. High. Educ. J. New Gener. Sci. **14**, 1–21 (2016)
26. Vitasari, P., Abdul Wahab, M.N., Othman, A., Awang, M.G.: The use of study anxiety intervention in reducing anxiety to improve academic performance among university students. Int. J. Psychol. Stud. **2**, 89–95 (2010)
27. Keller, J.M.: Development and use of the ARCS model of instructional design. J. Instr. Dev. **10**, 2–10 (1987). https://doi.org/10.1007/BF02905780
28. The Ministry of Education and Culture and the Finnish National Agency for Education. AVOP 2020. The education administration's reporting portal "Vipunen" (2020)
29. Illeris, K.: A comprehensive understanding of human learning. In: Illeris, K. (ed.) Contemporary Theories of Learning: Learning Theorists … in Their Own Words, pp. 7–20. Routledge, Abingdon (2009)
30. Kegan, R.: What "form" transforms? A constructive-developmental approach to transformative learning. In: Contemporary Theories of Learning: Learning Theorists ... in Their Own Words, pp. 43–60. Routledge (2009)
31. Dillman, D.A., Smyth, J.D., Christian, L.M.: Internet, Phone, Mail, and Mixed-Mode Surveys: The Tailored Design Method. Wiley, Hoboken (2014)
32. Goh, E., Sigala, M.: Integrating information & communication technologies (ICT) into classroom instruction: teaching tips for hospitality educators from a diffusion of innovation approach. J. Teach. Travel Tour. **20**, 156–165 (2020)

AI-Based Language Chatbot 2.0 – The Design and Implementation of English Language Concept Learning Agent App

Rui Liu, Xin Shu, Peishan Li, Yinong Xu, Philip Yeung, and Raymond Lee(✉)

Beijing Normal University-Hong Kong Baptist University United International College, Zhuhai, China
raymondshtlee@uic.edu.cn

Abstract. In this paper, we propose an English Language Concept Learning App by combining English concept learning and AI technologies such as automatic options generation and speech recognition analysis. The application is based on WeChat mini-program aimed at assisting and conducting English learning by providing various exercises such as multiple-choice and phonetic questions. To generate wrong options for multiple-choice questions, we used new words from WordNet, a large English lexical database with collocations detected by using statistical natural language processing and neural network models such as CBOW in Word2vec or BERT. User voice input is embedded in voice interaction for recognition and analysis. Based on the framework, this application is expected to be combined with other Artificial Intelligence (AI) technologies to analyze users' performance and adjust subsequent teaching curriculum accordingly.

Keywords: English language chatbot · Concept learning · WordNet · Word2vec · BERT

1 Introduction

Teaching and learning in higher education is a popular topic, especially so since the emergence of coronavirus which makes in-person teaching difficult all over the world. Internet, mobile Internet-based information technology, big data and artificial intelligence (AI) applications are called into service to make continuous education possible.

English is a complex language. In this project, we have developed an AI application based on English Concept Learning developed by a language professional. English concept learning is a method that simplifies the complexity of English for users. It is a way to learn English by concepts which connect the dots, linguistically and culturally, and they apply them to the learning process. From the information technology perspective, it is a method to understand the patterns of usage, and decode the DNA of the English language to achieve a better comprehension and communication e with foreigners without barriers.

W. Jia et al. (Eds.): SETE 2021, LNCS 13089, pp. 25–35, 2021.
https://doi.org/10.1007/978-3-030-92836-0_3

This new learning approach is developed from an insider-outsider perspective, in that it came from the insights of a professional writer and teacher who happens to learn English as a non-native speaker. In this sense, while he is an insider as a professional writer, he is also an outsider as English is not his mother tongue. Through this paradoxical combination, this approach has been successful in turning the English native speaker's subconscious knowledge into conscious knowledge for the benefit of second language learners. This conversion of the subconscious into the conscious solves the mystery of why Chinese learners of English are often trapped in a learning bottleneck. This is a big breakthrough from the one-dimensional traditional grammar-led approach dampens student interest and hinders further progress in mastering the language. Conceptual learning is able to bridge the many gaps in the cultural and functional aspects of the language.

The main contributions and originality of this paper include:

A concept learning method for users to learn idiomatic English without losing interest. Also, a WeChat mini-program based application is built to promote and facilitate English concept learning, targeting college users and teachers who have a foundation in English and want to learn authentic English and raise their levels of proficiency in English. The application will be evaluated by a group of students who are taking the offline English concept learning course. Adjustment and improvement will be conducted basing on the learning outcomes of the students. For the future, the application will be combined with AI to analyze users' performance as well as provide them with user-friendly learning exercises and strategies.

This paper is presented as follows: Sect. 2 is the literature review on collocations in Statistical Natural Language Processing and word prediction with deep learning. Section 3 outlines the framework and methodology used in the program, which includes automatic wrong options generation, application data storage and voice recognition and analysis. Section 4 presents the implementation of application. The last section is focused on future research to improve mini-program function with other AI technologies.

2 Literature Review

Natural language processing (NLP) is a branch of AI concerned with interactions between human natural language and computers. In this application, NLP technologies is mainly utilized to predict the missing words in the sentence. Related models will be discussed from statistical natural language processing models to deep learning models.

2.1 Collocation in Statistical Natural Language Processing

Collocations are expressions of multiple words that commonly co-occurred [1]. In statistical natural language processing, there are statistical natural language processing models like frequency-based model or mean and variance-based model combined with null hypothesis testing available for collocation detection.

This frequency-based model counts the frequency of two contiguous words. The bigrams frequently occurring are considered as collocations. Justeson and Katz [2] promote the integration of a part-of-speech filter with the model which only allows patterns that are likely to be phrases, for example, a verb followed by a noun.

A drawback of the above model is that it is not suitable for collocations that consist of two words in a more flexible relationship to one another. In this case, a mean and variance-based model is used to define the pattern of distance variance between two words appearing in the same window. The pairs with low variance are considered as collocations since high randomness in the distance between two words leads to an increase of variance. Further, an additional constraint is applied by Smadja to filter out "flat" peaks in the position histogram [3]. Moreover, Null hypothesis with t-testing is combined with this model to prove that high frequency and low variance of the distance do not occur by chance and the t-value calculated can be used as a way to rank the possibility of collocation.

Collocations have been applied in many fields including natural language generation to ensure the output sounds natural, computational lexicography for automatic identification of the important collocations to be listed in a dictionary entry, parsing, and the corpus linguistic research like the study of social phenomena [4].

2.2 Word Prediction with Deep Learning

Language model (LM) assigns probabilities to a certain sequence of words by continuously gaining the probability to each next possible word [5]. Computer technologies development enhanced several neutral networking models are formed to build language model from traditional statistical way. Neural Network based Language Model (NNLM) is proposed in 2003 to calculate the appearance probability of the given word depending on its previous words [6]. Later, many models gain the word embedding through predicting the missing word. Continuous Bag-of-Words (CBOW) in the Word2vec is used to guess the output using its neighboring words which took the words behind into consideration compared with NNLM (see Fig. 1) [7]. Also, in a Bidirectional Encoder Representations from Transformers (BERT) model when the training sequence are inputted a certain percentage of words are replaced by a [MASK] token, the model then tries to predict the masked original word based on the context of other unmasked words in the sequence [8].

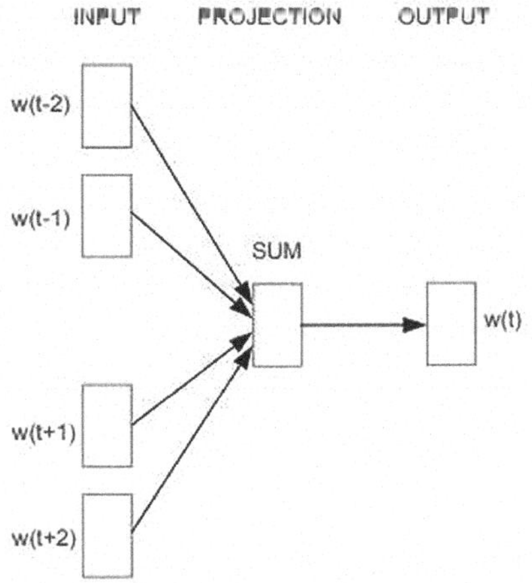

Fig. 1. The structure of CBOW.

3 Methodology

All teaching materials, that is the concepts of each unit and its introduction, sub-concepts, and corresponding examples will be stored in Excel files. Both English and Chinese explanations are given for each example to ensure the understanding by users (see Fig. 2). Considering that different concepts have different features and not all are suitable for the same type of questions, each example will be classified to show which type of question is appropriate according to the advice of an experienced English tutor. Then, examples that are suitable for multiple-choice questions will generate wrong options automatically and store all these data in the application database (see Fig. 3).

Concept	Sub-Concept 1	Sub-Concept 2	Example	Meaning	Meaning（中文）
Ellipsis			I need to go	I have to go to the toilet	我要去洗手间
Ellipsis			Dogs are territorial	Dogs protect their own area	狗是有地盘意识的。
Ellipsis			Trump refused to concede	Trump refused to admit defeat in the election	Trump拒绝承认败选
Ellipsis			I am not quite 100%	My body is not all healed yet.	我的身体还没好全。
Ellipsis			There is a window for his opponent	His opponent has a chance to beat him.	他的对手有机会击败他。

Fig. 2. The format of examples stored in Excel files.

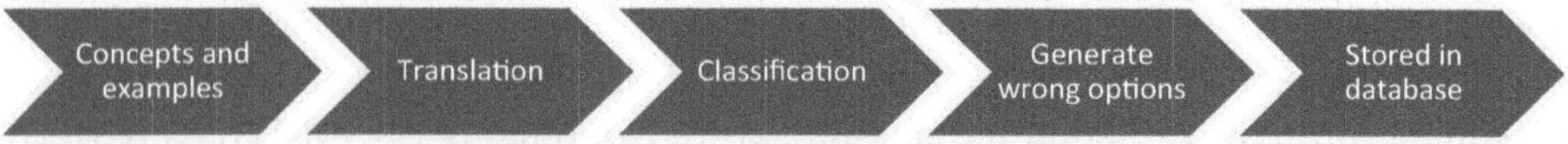

Fig. 3. Flow chart of the data processing.

The techniques used in the application is focused on automatic wrong options generation concerning the implementation of meaning questions as well as voice recognition and analysis for phonetic questions.

3.1 Automatic Generation of Wrong Options

There are four plans to generate wrong options: negation, literal meaning, replacement using words in same field, and collocations. This project is focused to achieve negation and collocations.

Negation. Attributes such as negation of auxiliary verbs, be verbs, and modal verbs are added to generate a new system with opposite meaning. For some sentences, replacing key words with its antonymy were also functional (see Fig. 4). These antonymies are offered in lexical database WordNet.

	Example	Meaning	Wrong Option
Verb	She is good behind the wheel	She is good at driving	She is not good at driving
	He is good under the hood	He can repair cars	He cannot repair cars
Antonym	**Example**	**Meaning**	**Wrong Option**
	Her hair is unfashionably short	He looks unfashionable in short hair	He looks fashionable in short hair
	She is short on looks and short on brains	She is ugly and stupid	She is beautiful and smart

Fig. 4. Examples of negation

Literal Meaning. Key words' usual meanings instead of specialized meanings in sentence are used to generate the options (see Fig. 5).

Example	Meaning	Wrong Option
He is good under the hood	He can repair cars	He's fine under the hood

Fig. 5. The example of literal meaning

Replacement Using Words in Same Field. This is a method to generate numbers of wrong options. Key word related closely to understanding of the example is replaced by the word that describes the same type of entity (see Fig. 6).

Words describing some type of thing	Example	Meaning	Obfuscated Options			Kinds of words
	He was literally spitting	He was very angry	happy	tired	sad	Adjectives related to human emotions
	He is snap-happy	He likes to take pictures	draw	ride a bike	swim	Adjectives related to hobbies

Fig. 6. Examples of replacement using words in same field

Collocations. As for collocations, we replace the key word with other words that can fit in the context. Statistical natural language processing models like frequency-based model or mean and variance-based model combined with null hypothesis testing can be used to get the collocations of the keywords' collocations. Meanwhile, given the two words before and behind the key words, Continuous Bag-of-Words (CBOW) in the Word2vec can tell the possible word that used to replace the key wording and keep the sentence sensible at the same time. In terms of BERT model, we replace the key word by the [MASK] token and send the marked sentence to the model (Fig. 7).

Example	Meaning	Obfuscated Options
They are dragging his name through the mud	They are saying or writing things that will harm his reputation	They are saying or writing things that will establish his reputation

Fig. 7. The example of collocation

3.2 Voice Recognition and Analysis

After a device records the input voice, the sentence will be converted into text, which is called answer text in this case. This is done with the voice recognition service provided by Google. Then, both answer text and the correct answer will be processed to remove punctuations and reduce noise that may interfere with accuracy. Then, the next step is tokenization. It is a technique to separate a piece of text into words. The fourth step is union and creation of word vectors. After obtaining the union from tokenization result, the tokenization result of each sentence will be mapped onto the union and generate two-word vectors which indicate the relationship between union and the composition words of each sentence. The percentage of identical words is compared rather than how close their meanings are. Thus, the cosine similarity is used to identify the similarity is between answer text and the correct answer (see Fig. 8).

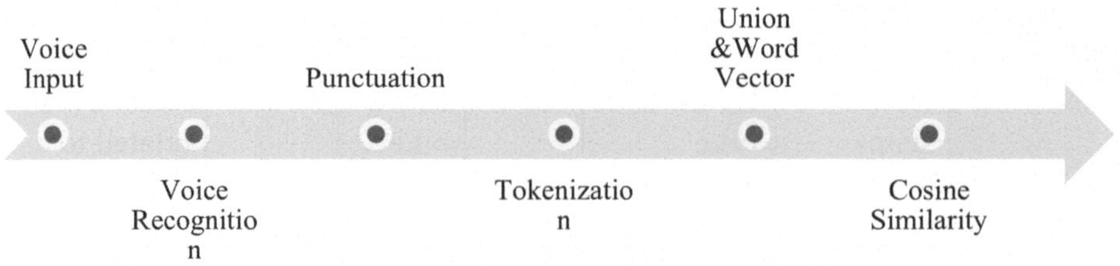

Fig. 8. The phases of voice recognition and analysis

Cosine similarity of the word vectors $\boldsymbol{u}$ and $\boldsymbol{v}$ is calculated as follows:

$$cosine(\boldsymbol{u}, \boldsymbol{v}) = \frac{\boldsymbol{u} \cdot \boldsymbol{v}}{\|\boldsymbol{u}\| \times \|\boldsymbol{v}\|} \quad (1)$$

4 System Design and Implementation

4.1 Design of the System

The target users of this application are university students, teachers and others that have fundamental proficiency in English and a professional or academic requirement in communicative competence. This application is designed to provide users with an interesting method in terms of usability and practicality to learn English authentically, so various patterns such as exercises and ranking are included to stimulate users' enthusiasm of using the app to learn English. Apart from practices on literary skills, the application offers voice output for every question to demonstrate pronunciations as well as questions that require voice input as answers, which forms the interaction between the application and users, embodying the characteristics of "Chatbot".

Figure 9 shows what users can operate with the app. Apart from the patterns mentioned above, it has 4 extra sections which includes corrections, planning daily tasks, check-in, and exercise collections. In addition, there are four types of exercises for users to learn. The use of each feature will be discussed in the following section.

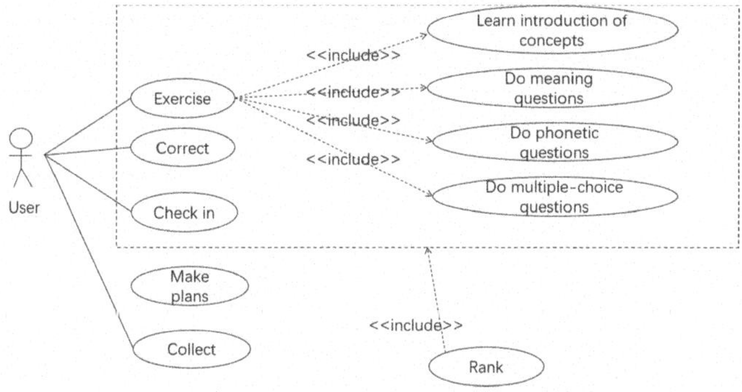

Fig. 9. Use case diagram.

4.2 Implementation

English Language Concept Learning Agent App was developed on WeChat Developer and established as a WeChat Mini Program. The Mini Program provides developers with a simple and efficient app development framework and a wide range of components and APIs [9].

This application can be divided into four parts according to its different functions in its implementation.

Task Plan and Ranking. To motivate users to persist in learning and to maintain enthusiasm, the first page contains a check-in button, a daily planning, and a link to the ranking list. Users are allowed to set how many exercises and corrections they want to do in a day at the lower part of the page. The total number of exercises will also be shown to indicate progress. Once the task is finished, the number will change to a check mark, indicating accomplishment.

Ranking function is based on grouping. Every user has his or her own points gained from doing exercises and corrections. Some users may want to study with their fellow learners i.e. students in a class. Thus, users are allowed to create a group or join in an existing group so that they can see all users' rankings in this learning community. Those who do not have a group can only see their points and titles, and do not participate in any rankings. On the other hand, the ranking list displays user names, points, and titles and all the users are categorized in an order from the highest to the lowest points.

Exercises. There are four levels of exercises that are currently implemented.

Level 1: Concept Introduction. This level requires users to learn concepts first before exercises. To provide users with simple overviews of concepts, an introduction and explanation of each concept are given in level 1.

Level 2: Concept Questions. This level allows users to do multiple-choice questions by selecting the correct concept for further understanding on concepts. Question pages contain a 10-s count down bar, a question, four options, a button directing to the next page, a collection button, and a Chinese meaning of the sentence after the users answer the question. After a user selects an option, the correct answer will turn green. If the user gives a wrong answer, the one selected will turn red. A user can gain 10 points from each question if the answer is correct. Figure 10 shows an example when a user selected a correct answer and a wrong answer in Level 2.

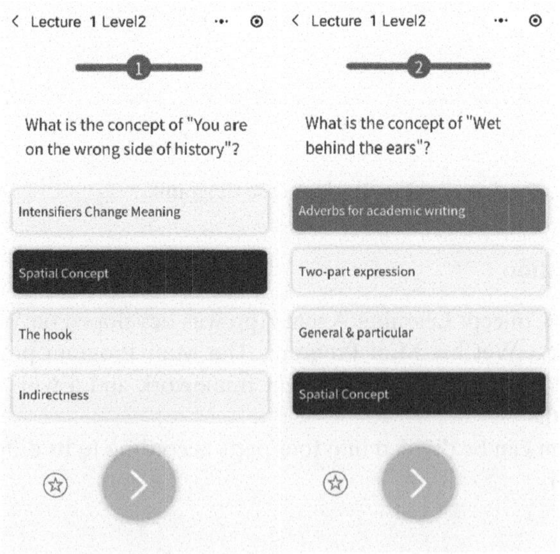

Fig. 10. Concept questions in Level 2

Level 3: Meaning Questions. This level also requires users to select an option from multiple-choice questions, but questions call for giving the meaning of examples. Except for the content of questions and options, all other components are identical to Level 2. Figure 11 shows an example that a user selected a correct answer and a wrong answer in Level 3.

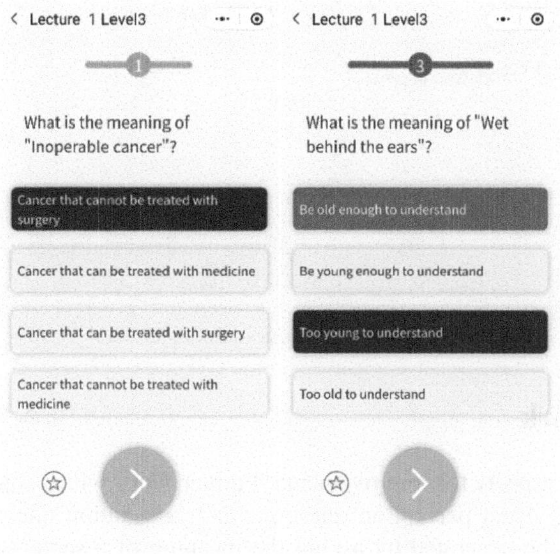

Fig. 11. Meaning questions in Level 3

Level 4: Phonetic Questions. This level is a verbal enquiry level that invites for users to practice what they have learnt from previous levels. It requires users to answer in English for a Chinese spoken sentence. It contains a 10-s count down, a question, a record button, a collection button, and an area for answers on a page. Figure 12 shows the questions and time out example in Level 4.

Corrections. This feature allows users to redo the questions that they have failed to answer correctly. Questions are identical to the ones they did wrongly in the previous levels. A user can gain 8 points from each corrected answer to a question.

Collections. This section allows users to mark questions that are important and worth being reviewed. A question can be collected by clicking the star icon at the end of each question.

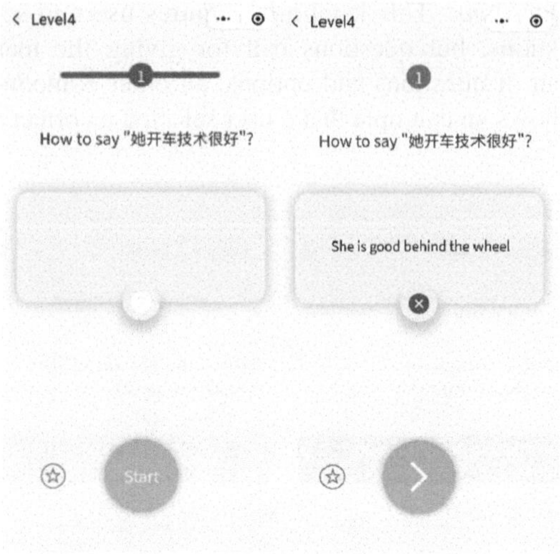

Fig. 12. Phonetic questions in Level 4

5 Future Work

There are several aspects for improvements. Further work will include two additional levels for users – visual perception questions and association questions. Visual perception level will be generated by asking the meaning of a sentence with visual elements and allows users to use a verbal response. Association level will mainly focus on word root usage. Therefore, a question will provide a Chinese meaning of a word and ask for the English meaning of a word with a change of root for this project.

The evaluation among students who are taking the offline English concept learning course will be conducted to quantify the effects of the mini-application on students' English learning outcomes. Refinement on functions, operations, and contents will be made basing on feedback from students.

Further, it is hoped that AI features will be adopted in this application to assist users in exercising reinforcement learning based on competences to achieve self-learning with mobile devices effectively. With this refined application, we can analyze their knowledge according to the answers selected by users, and automatically generate corresponding questions.

Acknowledgement. The authors would like to express great gratitude towards Yi-nong Xu, Ziting Xiao, Yuhan Zheng, Dingwen Xiao, Hanqi Zeng, Runlin Huang, Zhuoheng Ma for helping to develop the application. This paper was supported by Research Grant R202008 of Beijing Normal University-Hong Kong Baptist University United International College (UIC) and Key Laboratory for Artificial Intelligence and Multi-Model Data Processing of Department of Education of Guangdong Province.

References

1. Manning, C., Schütze, H.: Foundations of Statistical Natural Language Processing. The MIT Press, Cambridge (1999)
2. Justeson, J., Kat, S.: Technical terminology: some linguistic properties and an algorithm for identification in text. Nat. Lang. Eng. **1**(1), 9–27 (1995)
3. Smadja, F.: Retrieving collocations from text: xtract. Comput. Linguist. **19**(1), 143–177 (1993)
4. Stubbs, M.: Text and Corpus Analysis: Computer-Assisted Studies of Language and Culture. Blackwell Publishers, Hoboken (1996)
5. Jurafsky, D., Martin, J.H.: Speech and Language Processing. Prentice Hall, Hoboken (2008)
6. Bengio, Y., Ducharme, R., Vincent, P., Jauvin, C.: A neural probabilistic language model. J. Mach. Learn. Res. **3**, 1137–1155 (2003)
7. Chen, K., Dean, J., Mikolov, T., Corrado, G.: Efficient estimation of word representations in vector space. In: ICLR 2013 Conference (2013)
8. Devlin, J., Chang, M., Lee, K., Toutanova, K.: BERT: pre-training of deep bidirectional transformers for language understanding. In: NAACL 2019, pp. 4171–4186. Association for Computational Linguistics, Minneapolis (2019)
9. "Overview | Weixin public doc" Tencent (2021). https://developers.weixin.qq.com/miniprogram/en/dev/devtools/devtools.html

The Application of Virtual Simulation Technology in Law Teaching Practice

Haotian Li and Juan Xu(✉)

School of Bigdata and Law, School of Law and Public Affairs, Nanjing University of Information Science and Technology, Nanjing, China
{20191240004,003068}@nuist.edu.cn

Abstract. Virtual simulation technology has been increasingly applied to education including teaching. This paper conducts a systematic review of the application of virtual simulation technology in law teaching practice. Findings include that virtual simulation platforms in law teaching should contain five types of topics, including negotiation and mediation, litigation documents, case analysis, moot court, and the expert testimony of evidence. Main problems associated with the development of virtual simulation platforms are also discussed including the dilemma of the choice of teaching methods, the difficulty of unifying teaching assessment criteria, the neglect of legal knowledge in the simulation process, the lack of system modules, the high cost of equipment and training, and the lack of hardware realism. Action recommendations in teaching and platform construction are discussed by classifying the major problems, respectively.

Keywords: Practical teaching of law · Virtual simulation technology · Theme

1 Introduction

With the development of modern information technology, software programs can design and simulate various scenarios of relevant legal processes. Students and teachers can continuously add materials to the teaching of law practice, making it diverse, derivative and have its own characteristics [1]. In addition, immersive simulations by virtual simulation technology can improve teachers' self-efficacy and skills [2, 3]. Virtual simulation of practical teaching of law is a teaching mode that relies on information technology such as virtual reality, multimedia, human-computer interaction, database and network communication to build a highly simulated virtual experimental environment and experimental objects [4, 5], allowing students to carry out practice in a virtual environment. This teaching mode has been widely used. Law classes are often taught by creating teaching situations. If VR is used to restore these scenarios, learners can not only watch and listen, but also experience them directly [6]. In the related literature, virtual simulation of law has been described by various concepts and terms, such as virtual simulation class of law, VR experiment of law, virtual reality teaching of law, and VR simulation practice of law [7, 8].

W. Jia et al. (Eds.): SETE 2021, LNCS 13089, pp. 36–47, 2021.
https://doi.org/10.1007/978-3-030-92836-0_4

Nevertheless, many of these terms are intended to denote similar situations and share the same theoretical basis, which can be demonstrated by the following four points. First, a great deal of research is based on the classical theory of audiovisual technology in education, namely the "tower of experience" [9]. This theory states that students should first learn the bottom level "experience of doing", and then gradually move to the top level "abstract experience" and eventually form theories [10–12]. Virtual simulation in law teaching can enable students to gain the "experience of doing" as the foundation of the "tower of experience". Parsons argues that learning how to reflect on one's experiences is critical to developing the capacity for self-criticism and improvement, which is especially valuable for the legal profession [13]. Second, virtual simulation teaching in law is a teaching method that simulates or creates legal scenarios under controllable conditions. Through studying human behavior in legal scenarios, this method can study the deterministic connection between legal theory and legal reality [14]. Third, as stated by Zhu [14] and Yao [15], the key for the virtual simulation teaching of law to be established or not is whether it can simulate real life and legal scenes. Only by simulating life and legal scenes that are consistent with or the same as reality, can the conclusions drawn from the experiments on human jurisprudence be scientific. Fourth, it is widely believed that virtual simulation teaching in law is conducive to the cultivation of thinking and learning, especially to the deep processing of knowledge [16]. As a pedagogical approach, virtual simulation in law is an approach used by teachers in teaching activities to enable students to obtain knowledge, form skills, acquire interest, and master learning [17].

The publications on virtual simulation teaching and learning in law have been increasing dramatically, with the growing interest in research and practical applications of virtual simulation teaching and learning in law around the world [18, 19]. The virtual simulation teaching platform makes full use of multimedia technology to combine pictures, text and video so as to vividly and intuitively show the experimental content and the whole process of experiment [20]. Currently, a variety of software, tools, and specific platforms have been developed by major universities around the world, making cross-sectional research more difficult and preventing the field from exerting greater influence on policy and practice. Therefore, it is necessary to systematically review virtual simulation technology used in law teaching practice. By summarizing typical patterns and themes in this technology, scholars and practitioners can be assisted in designing or selecting virtual simulation teaching platforms.

2 Related Work

This systematic evaluation follows the guidelines in Kitchenham and Charters [21] on systematic evaluation in software engineering research. Following these guidelines, this research methodology consists of three main phases: planning the review, conducting the review, and reporting the results. The review began with the identification of relevant underlying research. The searched databases were electronic and focused on the fields of education and technology/computer science. In general, this search covered seven of the most commonly used digital libraries for similar studies that contain a mixture of social science and technical literature, specifically: Springer Link, IEEE Xplore, Heinonline, Springer Ebook, CNKI, SSRN, Google Scholar.

A key issue is the definition of the three search elements. A few sets of key-words were used: "jurisprudence" and its associated word "law", "educational practice" and "practice teaching", "virtual simulation", "virtual simulation" and its associated words "VR", "simulation experiment", "virtual reality", "simulation", "simulation teaching", "simulation experiment" [22]. Because of the small scope of the analysis, these three sets of search conditions given are broadly explained as follows: (1) "Jurisprudence" is interpreted as any heuristic method involving the study of any aspect of the law and the theory or practice in legal education. (2) "Education" is defined as university education or higher education related to law. The vast majority of items in the dataset describe simulations con-ducted in higher education, with a few in the workplace. The few secondary school programs found during the search were removed. (3) "Virtual Simulation" is defined as the practice of any form of digital technology used in design and/or discussion of the implementation, evaluation or analysis of simulation. Digital technologies include video, photographs and graphics, and text. The search re-strictions above were used to search each database on May 3, 2021, and all searches were conducted upon article titles and abstracts. Based on these definitions and search criteria, search filters on the databases were used to focus on articles that met the three search criteria.

Table 1. Literature selection criteria

Selection criteria	Exclusion criteria
Research on virtual simulation in teaching practices	Not focusing on keyword research
A study focusing on virtual simulation in law/legal teaching	Research focusing on virtual simulation in other educational teaching
Research published in peer-reviewed journals or conference proceedings	Non-peer-reviewed materials (audio/video files, web pages, etc.)

After an initial search, 218 potentially relevant items were identified from titles and abstracts. Then each document was read in its entirety, publications examined, and those showed complete or partial virtual simulation teaching in law based on the inclusion and exclusion criteria listed in Table 1 were kept. Ultimately 32 papers were retained for the study. Then the following information were systematically reviewed: the name of the platform, the main technology of the platform, the context in which the platform was used (i.e., cultural context and disciplinary context), and the experimental approach of the platform.

3 Theme Analysis of Virtual Simulation Teaching Platform of Law

The virtual practice teaching platform of law is a platform constructed and established based on the special needs of practice teaching of law majors and the general rules of online virtual teaching platform design. [23] This platform can not only promote the reform of new experimental teaching methods, but also build an open and compatible virtual simulation experimental teaching management and sharing platform. It mainly includes two teaching links of theory and practice [24], and the specific process can be divided into: (1) abstracting the corresponding experimental process; (2) designing and loading experimental projects; (3) imparting knowledge of substantive law and procedural law; (4) explaining the relevant operating procedures of the virtual simulation experimental system; (5) completing the virtual simulation experimental project of law and the experimental reports.

As an entrance and a breakthrough for the transformation of the teaching mode of law practice, the construction of virtual platform for law practice teaching has formed some typical models with various characteristics [25]: (1) the virtual platform construction model centered on role simulation experiment. Based on the basic principle of participatory experience teaching, this model establishes a role simulation experiment teaching platform covering the whole process of rule of law operation, and provides students with a variety of different online role experiences and interaction channels [26, 27]. (2) A virtual platform construction model centered on curriculum system reform [28]. By combinateing teaching online and offline, this model can provide students with a comprehensive learning experience. (3) The virtual platform construction model centered on the development of micro-course APP [29]. This model provides a platform for teachers and students to participate in a more convenient and faster way [30]. Based on the literature, the technical equipment, experimental approaches and the resource categories of virtual simulation platforms in these three models have summarized and categorized (Table 2 and Fig. 1).

Table 2. Technical equipment, experimental methods and their resource categories of virtual simulation platforms.

Modes	Main equipments	Experiment methods	Resource categories
Role simulation experiment mode	Virtual reality	Role simulation experiments	Video, electronic teaching material, courseware, software, experimental platform, simulation system, virtual lab
Curriculum reform mode	Virtual reality interactive multimedia	The experiments of course with integrated design	Video, electronic teaching material, courseware, software, software, experimental platform, intelligent instrument, test system, course
Micro-class APP mode	Mobile application	The independent experiments of micro-course	Video, electronic teaching material, courseware, software, virtual lab, mobile terminal, course

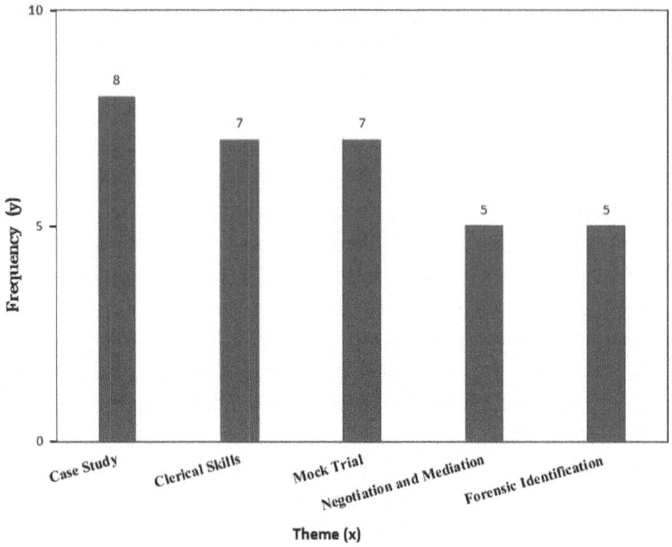

Fig. 1. Frequency statistics of the topic of virtual simulation teaching platform of law.

The literature reveals several platforms that are currently using virtual simulation technology, all with similar but slightly differentiated pedagogical motivations. After the use of virtual simulation platforms in law teaching have been reviewed, five themes have been included in their categories for virtual simulation teaching practice in law.

The first theme is the exercise of negotiation and mediation, which guides students through controlled experimental process to become familiar with the legal negotiation process in litigation disputes, master basic negotiation skills and learn to formulate negotiation plans. The software system enables students to enter the negotiation scenario step by step, independently formulate negotiation strategies, and independently complete the experiment through virtual reality cases, supplemented by multimedia means such as text, sound, and interactive interfaces [31]. Simulated negotiations and mediations of hypothetical or real disputes in this platform provide students with a more comprehensive under-standing of the realities of the negotiation and dispute resolution process [26, 32]. In mock arguments, students are found to have improved their advocacy, case analysis, and legal reasoning skills [33].

The second theme is writing skills, in which students can cultivate their skills of writing litigation documents such as indictments and pleadings. The "lawsuit writs" module can be called "Legal Lego Blocks" because each question raised by the experimental platform corresponds to a text of a legal instrument template. The experimental platform can fill in the gaps in the template with the students' answers to the questions, creating a completed "text block". The experimental platform then sorts out the necessary questions for the focus of the dispute according to the logical order of the questions and the position of the branches in the neural net diagram of legal relations, so as to sort out the "text blocks" corresponding to the questions, and finally combine the blocks one by one to form a complete set of litigation documents [34].

The third theme is case study. Take a typical case in judicial practice as a reference. The platform creates a litigation case, divides the experimental projects according to the trial process, and enables students to choose a role among the demandant, the defendant's commission agent, the judge, and the expert. By doing this, students are trained to understand and apply the rules of relevant litigation procedures, the burden of proof and cross-examination, especially the questioning skills of the expert and the examination and judgment of the expert opinion through the operation in 3D virtual environment. Through the analysis of typical cases, students can better grasp the rules and skills of cross-examination and review of expert opinions in litigation on the basis of the relevant rules of litigation [35, 36]. For example, in the analysis of criminal law cases, the crime scenario of indecent act is restored through virtual simulation technology as a way to explore and grasp the limits of criminal law intervention [37].

The fourth theme is trial simulation. The trial is essentially a process in which legal practitioners reconstruct real-life events or situations and apply certain relevant statutory rules [38]. Students can use VR, through visual, auditory, and tactile senses, to understand the teaching content and the whole story of the case comprehensively [40]. For example, the interactive control enables the court information to be transmitted instantly, and each character can receive timely feedback from the other. At the same time people's understanding is no longer limited to the trial stage, and they can understand the investigation after the incident through VR technology. Through the interactive experience of various legal procedure scenes after the case such as meeting the litigants, students can fully contact and understand the legal procedure after the case, supplement and improve the legal procedure after the trial preparation and the trial, so as to truly master the whole process of legal trial through practice [41]. In terms of the potential impact of VR technology on the court trial, this technology is still in the process of development and advancement, and its application in mock court teaching has both advantages and challenges [42].

The fifth them is the expert testimony of evidence. Traditionally, there are always some problems, such as limited teaching hours, heavy teaching tasks, painful course selection for students, and overlapped courses for students. Virtual simulation of specific experimental projects in the expert testimony of evidence includes four major types: forensic identification (including forensic clinical identification, forensic material evidence identification, forensic toxicology identification, forensic pathology identification, forensic psychiatry identification), physical evidence identification (including trace inspection identification, document inspection identification, trace physical evidence identification), audio-visual data identification (including audio-visual data identification, electronic data identification), and environmental damage identification. Virtual simulation teaching through three-dimensional simulation technology can reproduce the crime scene and restore the investigation technology, physical evidence technology, interrogation and other aspects. The teaching method can break through the limitations of long-term classroom teaching, integrate the teaching content directly into the virtual operation and simulation case scene teaching, show the abstract theoretical knowledge in practice, get feelings and inspiration in practical operation, thus it can effectively solve the problems in the current teaching.

As a non-case law country, China's Ministry of Education has approved the establishment of several "national virtual simulation experimental teaching pro-jects".

These projects are centered on virtual simulation laboratories of various law disciplines, and some of them have formed a multi-module integrated training mechanism of "virtual network attack and defense, crime investigation and examination, simulation teaching system, and real case file reading simulation" [44]. These platforms feature five themes: negotiation and mediation, litigation documents, case analysis, mock court, the expert testimony of evidence with the aim of cultivating students' innovative spirit and practical ability, which has comprehensively improved the experimental teaching and cultivated a great number of excellent law talents (Table 3).

Table 3. Statistical table of topic types of national virtual simulation teaching platform of law.

Themes	Platforms	Institutions
Negotiation& mediation	Virtual simulation experiment of legal negotiation	Hunan Normal University
	Virtual simulation mediation training of difficult and complex disputes	Xiangtan University
Litigation documents	Expert testimony of document authenticity in litigation	Nanjing Normal University
	Simulation of real case files	China University of Political Science and Law
Case study	Virtual simulation practice teaching of justifiable defense	University of Electronic Science and Technology of China
	Identification and prevention of legal risks in international technology trade	Northwestern Polytechnic University
	"Online data integrated processing" for road traffic accident disputes	Sichuan University
	Intervention of students' drug abuse	Yunnan University
Mock trial	Virtual simulation experimental teaching of mock trials	Shaoguan University
	Experimental teaching project of virtual simulation court of international law	Tianjin University
	Simulation experiment of Yangtze River ecological environment protection litigation	Zhongnan University of Economics and Law
Evidence	Virtual simulation experiment teaching of cross-examination of expert opinions in civil action	Fujian Normal University
	Virtual simulation training of expert testimony	Liaoning University
	Virtual simulation experiment of legal responsibility affirmatio	Wuhan University
	Virtual experiment of computer forensics	Renmin University of China

Note: The above virtual simulation platforms of law are "national virtual simulation experimental teaching projects" approved by the Chinese Ministry of Education

4 Discussions

People's views on several major issues are controversial, which has resulted in the diversification of forms and functions of virtual simulation teaching plat-forms. However, not all technology is effective, and technology must be implemented in conjunction with purposeful and well-planned learning objectives. In the following, the problems of virtual simulation platforms in law are analyzed from teaching methods and platform construction, and provide corresponding countermeasures.

4.1 Problems in the Use of Virtual Simulation Platform in Teaching

Generally speaking, concentrated experiments are conducive to raise students' experimental enthusiasm and regarded as the main way of experimental teaching. The experimental results can be as follows: either the experiment is completed ahead of schedule, or the experiment cannot be completed within the given time, or the completed experiment does not meet the realistic requirements. Therefore, it is necessary to set generous deadlines as a supplementary type of experiment. To be specific, when the results of the concentrated experiment are not satisfactory, the experiment needs to be reconducted and completed within the given time. To sum up, the way of practical teaching of law can be a flexible teaching method with concentrated experiments as the main and decentralized experiments as the supplement.

There is a great difference between legal experiments and experiments in other disciplines – the uncontrollable time, because it takes much time to find laws, regulations and precedents, and to make necessary amendments and supplements. Therefore, it is difficult to have a fully formalized document as the basis for the final grade evaluation in the virtual teaching platform. It is reasonable and possible to make a discretionary evaluation according to students' personal contributions and the process of document formulation.

At present, there is a consensus in implementing mock court simulation teaching: mock court only needs to ensure the smooth implementation of the trial process, and there is no need to pay too much attention to the substantive content of the trial case. Based on this understanding, mock court simulation teaching focuses on how to make the trial process smoother, and does not seriously study the substantive rights and obligations of the simulated case [45]. However, only by effectively combining procedural and substantive simulations can mock court simulation teaching truly serve the purpose of boosting students' ability to solve legal problems in real life.

4.2 Difficulties in the Construction of Virtual Simulation Teaching Platforms

Theoretically, the experimental simulation project can break through the limitations of time and space, so that students are no longer constrained by it. However, in reality, the virtual simulation teaching system of law needs to be improved in numerous ways. The evaluation showed that there is no course introduction and equipment introduction and even the experiment permission in some front-end systems of the virtual imitation teaching platform of law. The same virtual simulation project should be open to students from different schools and different regions, so as to achieve the sharing of teaching resources among universities. Meanwhile, the front-end system should contain the complete introduction and experimental guidance of simulation experiments, [45] and the back-end management system can build a management system with five modules as the core: teachers management, experimental teaching, reservation management, system administrator, course selection and experiments (Fig. 2).

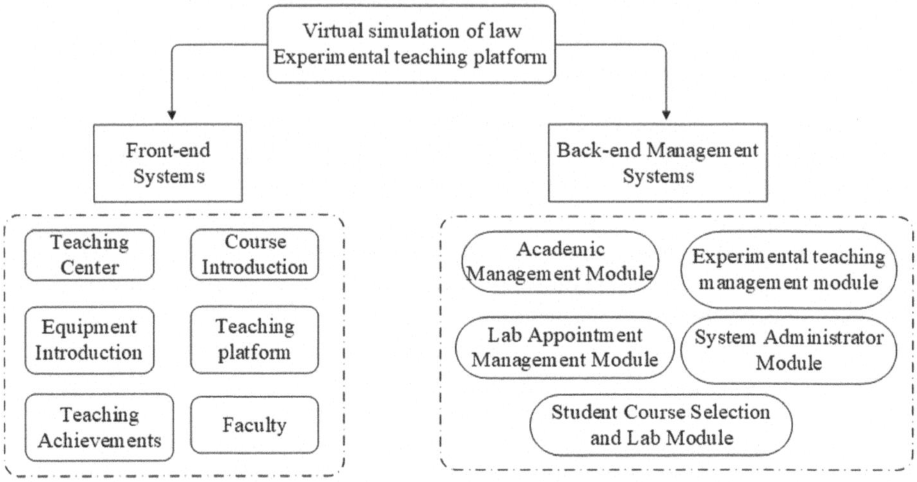

Fig. 2. Module system diagram of virtual simulation platform of law.

Despite the recent reduction in the cost of using VR [46], this remains an important issue. Many studies have commented on the large financial investment in the initial purchase of equipment [47, 48], as well as its ongoing costs for maintenance and support [49]. It may be difficult for new users to operate the hardware, so time must be spent training students and teachers [48, 50]. In addition, Yeh and Wan [51] warn that workload must be expected when using VR as a teaching device. In conclusion, it is important to refine construction projects ac-cording to the goals of teaching reduce unnecessary inputs.

Although VR technology has made substantial progress, the research suggests that the current hardware lacks realism due to its physical limitations [52] which may lead to a lack of engagement [50]. Limited hardware inevitably affects the design of VR environments in learning. According to the consistency principle, excessive use of unnecessary technology may produce irrelevant cognitive processing in the learner's brain, thus interrupting the cognitive learning process [57]. Therefore, it is important to design legal education VR with clear learning objectives [58].

5 Conclusions

This as an emerging teaching technology, virtual simulation teaching platform has attracted widespread interest worldwide, and publications in this field are increasing. In the practice of virtual simulation teaching of law, the choice of topic is crucial. This paper conducts a systematic review of virtual simulation plat-forms in law teaching. It is believed that six problems in simulation teaching and platform construction are closely related to the development of virtual simulation teaching or platform selection in law including the dilemma of the choice of teaching methods, the difficulty of unifying teaching assessment criteria, the neglect of legal knowledge in the simulation process, the lack of system modules, the high cost of equipment and training, and the lack of hardware realism. By summarizing the main issues, targeted suggestions have been put forward for the difficulties encountered in teaching and platform construction respectively. In addition, the review highlights that the virtual simulation teaching platform should contain five themes, namely negotiation and mediation, litigation documents, case analysis, moot court, and the expert testimony of evidence. The findings can be applicable to comparisons across educational and cultural backgrounds, which enables the field to have a greater impact on policy making and practice.

Acknowledgements. This work was supported by National Social Science Foundation of China (19BFX127).

References

1. Robin, W., Michael, A., Tom, A.: Computer simulation in legal education. Int. J. Law Inf. Technol. **5**, 279–307 (1997)
2. Badiee, F., Kaufman, D.: Design evaluation of a simulation for teacher education. SAGE Open **5**(2), 1–10 (2015)
3. Gilbert, K., Voelkel, R., Johnson, C.: Increasing self-efficacy through immersive simulations: Leading professional learning communities. J. Leadersh. Educ. **17**(3), 154–174 (2018)
4. Liu, M.: Experimental teaching system of law based on LETS software. Law Educ. Res. 71–85 (2015)
5. Maharg, P., Nicol, E.: Simulation and technology in legal education: a systematic review and future research programme. Legal Educ.: Simul. Theory Pract. (2014)
6. Gao, H.: Review of VR (virtual reality) educational applications. Inf. Comput. (Theory Edn.) **420**(2), 231–232 (2019)
7. Wang, S.: The promotion and change of "artificial intelligence + law" model on China's legal education. Western J. **123**(18), 113–115 (2020)
8. Shan, Z., Tang, Y.: The feasibility of the new platform of legal education in the field of simulation mimicry: an example of moot court teaching in Changchun Normal University. Legal Expo 183–184 (2021)
9. Tinker, M.A.: Review of audio-visual methods in teaching: review of the book audio-visual methods in teaching. J. Educ. Psychol. **38**(3), 191–192 (1947)
10. Wang, Y., Sun, C., Zhong, Z., Liang, H., Guo, R., Wang, Y.: The practice of virtual reality technology in university teaching. Educ. Observ. **7**(17), 67–70 (2018)

11. Zhu, H.: Design and implementation of simulation teaching environment based on virtual reality technology. Mod. Inf. Technol. **2**, 88–91 (2018)
12. Gao, D., Wang, S.: The impact of virtual reality technology development on the reform of university experimental teaching and response strategies. China High. Educ. Res. 56–59 (2016)
13. Parsons, L.: Competitive mooting as clinical legal education: can real benefits be derived from an unreal experience? Aust. J. Clin. Educ. **1**(1), 1–22 (2017)
14. Zhu, Q.: An outline of legal experimentation. Comparat. Law Stud. **128**(4), 24–34 (2013)
15. Yao, M.: The construction of virtual practice platform for university law majors under the perspective of online teaching. J. Anhui Radio Telev. Univ. **191**(4), 39–43 (2020)
16. Li, Y.: The theory and practice of virtual simulation experimental teaching in the construction of law majors in ethnic local universities. Educ. Observ. **8**(27), 65–67 (2019)
17. McBride, N.J.: Legal education: simulation in theory and practice. Surrey: Ashgate Publishing Co. Camb. Law J. **74**(03), 637–639 (2015)
18. Cho, J., Jung, T., Macleod, K., Swenson, A.: Using virtual reality as a form of simulation in the context of legal education. In: tom Dieck, M.C., Jung, T.H., Loureiro, S.M.C. (eds.) Augmented Reality and Virtual Reality. PI, pp. 141–154. Springer, Cham (2021). https://doi.org/10.1007/978-3-030-68086-2_11
19. Sun, Y.: Research on the application of virtual simulation technology in experimental teaching of law in the context of education informatization. Legal Expo **784**(32), 211–213 (2019)
20. Zhu, J.: Development and breakthrough of legal education in the age of intelligence. J. Huaiyin Norm. Coll. (Nat. Sci. Edn.) **19**(4), 370–372 (2020)
21. Kitchenham, B., Charters, S.: Guidelines for performing systematic literature reviews in software engineering. EBSE Technical report EBSE-2007-01. IEEE Computer Society (2007)
22. Stacy, K., Liz, R.: Teaching in virtual worlds: opportunities and challenges. Issues Inf. Sci. Inf. Technol. (2008)
23. Wang, N., Zhang, Y.: Research on the construction path of intelligent law virtual simulation laboratory based on effective teaching. Exp. Technol. Manag. **37**(4), 24–27 (2020)
24. Wang, S.: The application of virtual reality technology in law education. Teach. Educ. (High. Educ. Forum) **730**(36), 92–93 (2020)
25. Chen, Z.: Model: effect and prospect of virtual teaching platform construction in law. Law Educ. Res. 189–204 (2017)
26. Waters, B.: "A part to play": the value of role-play simulation in undergraduate legal education. Law Teach. **50**(2), 172–194 (2016)
27. Liu, Y.: Exploration and research on the construction of law laboratory in the context of strengthening practical teaching. Sci. Technol. Inf. **13**(8), 198 (2015)
28. Shang, S., Li, X.L.: Application and role simulation recommendation based on law experiment software. Teach. Educ. (High. Educ. Forum) **535**(21), 88–89 (2015)
29. Mc, F.H., Fitzgerald, E.: A realist evaluation of student use of a virtual reality smartphone application in undergraduate legal education. Br. J. Educ. Technol. **51**, 572–589 (2020)
30. Ji, F.: Exploration on the construction of a virtual simulation experimental teaching center for liberal arts. Exp. Technol. Manag. **34**(4), 14–17 (2017)
31. Jiang, X.M.: Virtual simulation experiment of legal negotiation (2019). http://fltpxn.hunnu.edu.cn/
32. Byrnes, R., Lawrence, P.: Bringing diplomacy into the classroom: Stimulating student engagement through a simulated treaty negotiation. Legal Educ. Rev. **26**(12), 19–46 (2016)
33. Daly, Y., Higgins, N.: The place and efficacy of simulations in legal education: a preliminary examination. All Ireland J. High. Educ. (2011)

34. Wang, Z.C., Chen, L., Zhou, D.L., et al.: Design and implementation of a virtual experimental teaching platform for law in the context of new liberal arts. Lab. Res. Explor. **38**(12), 208–215 (2019)
35. Yang, Y.H.: Virtual simulation "golden class" to spread the wings of law education. China Soc. Sci. J. (2020)
36. Mentzelopoulos, M., et al.: REVR-law: an immersive way for teaching criminal law using virtual reality. In: Allison, C., Morgado, L., Pirker, J., Beck, D., Richter, J., Gütl, C. (eds.) iLRN 2016. Communications in Computer and Information Science, vol. 621, pp. 73–84. Springer, Cham (2016). https://doi.org/10.1007/978-3-319-41769-1_6
37. Hansen, J.: Virtual indecent assault: time for the criminal law to enter the realm of virtual reality. Victoria Univ. Wellington Law Rev. **50**(1), 57 (2019)
38. Leonetti, C., Bailenson, J.: High-tech view: the use of immersive virtual environments in jury trials (2010)
39. Wang, Y.: Analysis of the application and countermeasures of VR in the practical teaching of legal professional education. Legal Expo **822**(34), 149–150 (2020)
40. Li H. l.: Exploring the application of VR simulation technology in mock court teaching. Law Soc. (29), 163–164 (2020)
41. An, N., Dang, W.P.: The application of virtual reality technology in courtroom trial. J. Tianjin Univ. (Soc. Sci. Edn.) **23**(2), 151–155 (2021)
42. Ding, C.L.: The use of virtual simulation experimental platform in the practical training course of forensic identification in law. Legal Expo **823**(35), 182–184 (2020)
43. Gao, Y.Q.: Discussion on the reform of mock courtroom simulation teaching under the concept of training applied legal talents. Times Econ. Trade **29**, 97–99 (2020)
44. Gao, X.X., Jin, Y., Ma, J.Q., et al.: Discussion on the construction of Internet virtual simulation teaching training system. Exp. Technol. Manag. **34**(1), 140–143 (2017)
45. Merchant, Z., Goetz, E.T., Cifuentes, L., et al.: Effectiveness of virtual reality-based instruction on students' learning outcomes in K-12 and higher education: a meta-analysis. Comput. Educ. **70**, 29–40 (2014)
46. Baxter, G., Hainey, T.: Student perceptions of virtual reality use in higher education. J. Appl. Res. High. Educ. (2019)
47. Kavanagh, S., Luxtonreilly, A., Wuensche, B., et al.: A systematic review of virtual reality in education. Themes Sci. Technol. Educ. **10**(2), 85–119 (2017)
48. Ludlow, B.L., Hartley, M.D.: Using second life for situated and active learning in teacher education. In: Emerging Tools and Applications of Virtual Reality in Education (2016)
49. Pantelidis, V.S.: Reasons to use virtual reality in education and training courses and a model to determine when to use virtual reality. Themes Sci. Technol. Educ. **2**(1–2), 59–70 (2009)
50. Yeh, E., Wan, G.: The use of virtual worlds in foreign language teaching and learning. In: Emerging Tools and Applications of Virtual Reality in Education (2016)
51. Kavanagh, S., Luxton-Reilly, A., Wuensche, B., et al.: A systematic review of virtual reality in education. Themes Sci. Technol. Educ. **10**(2), 85–119 (2017)
52. Parong, J., Mayer, R.E.: Learning science in immersive virtual reality. J. Educ. Psychol. **110** (6), 785–797 (2018)

The Effect of Online Collaborative Prewriting via DingTalk Group on EFL Learners' Writing Anxiety and Writing Performance

Xin Huang[1], Xiaobin Liu[1(✉)], Yiya Hu[2], and Qingsheng Liu[2]

[1] South China Normal University, Guangzhou, Guangdong, China
liuxiaobin@m.scnu.edu.cn

[2] The Affiliated Liwan School of Guangdong Experimental High School, Guangzhou, Guangdong, China

Abstract. This study aims at investigating the effects of online collaborative prewriting via DingTalk, a social software based on computer-mediated communication (communication across two or more networked computers), on EFL (English as a Foreign Language) learners' writing anxiety and writing performance. A total of 60 junior high school students were involved in the experiment. During the treatment, one class was required to adopt online collaborative prewriting in DingTalk, while the other class was asked to brainstorm alone. Written texts in pre-test and post-test were collected to analyze in detail. Meanwhile, second language writing anxiety inventory was administered in pre-test and post-test to examine the change of participants' writing anxiety. A post-study survey and an interview were conducted to investigate participants' attitudes and perceptions towards online collaborative prewriting. The results revealed that (1) online collaborative prewriting facilitates junior high school students' overall writing performance, (2) online collaborative prewriting helps to reduce overall writing anxiety, (3) students generally hold positive attitudes on online prewriting activity.

Keywords: Prewriting · Computer-mediated communication · Writing anxiety · Writing performance

1 Introduction

Writing is a key skill in comprehensive language ability, and it serves an essential role in second language learning as well. However, writing is regarded as one of the most challenging part in English learning. One of the main obstacles in writing is that at the beginning of writing, writers do not know how to start writing [1]. Moreover, some learners may encounter different degrees of writing anxiety when facing different writing tasks. Writing anxiety is an obstacle of success in second language writing, and personal reason is the largest factor that may cause writing obstacles and writing anxiety [2], which mainly involves prewriting anxiety and avoidance behavior.

As an important source of writing anxiety, prewriting is an important factor to ensure the writing quality [3]. For Chinese L2 learners (English as Second Language), one of the main problems in English writing is the lack of content [4]. Collaborative

W. Jia et al. (Eds.): SETE 2021, LNCS 13089, pp. 48–60, 2021.
https://doi.org/10.1007/978-3-030-92836-0_5

prewriting is believed to have a potential in promoting L2 writer's writing performance [5, 6], prewriting conducting in groups is considered more effective as it helps L2 writers better prepare for the writing tasks. However, most studies have investigated its effectiveness on writing performance, while few focuses on its effects of collaborative prewriting supported by technology on writing performance and writing anxiety. With the advent of Web 2.0, computer-mediated communication (CMC) have realized many-to-many communication, which helps promote meaningful communication [7] and support language learning [8]. Thus, the current study is intended to investigate the effectiveness of collaborative prewriting based on CMC.

2 Literature Review

2.1 Prewriting

Writing, a productive skill, is regarded as a difficult task as it involves a series of complex psychological activities. Hayes and Flower [9] divided the writing process into three subordinate processes: planning, translating and reviewing. From the perspective of process writing, the prewriting stage is an crucial part in the whole writing process [10]. For Chinese L2 learners, one of the main problems in English writing is the lack of content [4], which can be improved by preparation before writing because prewriting is an important factor to ensure the writing quality [3].

Some scholars proposed that strategy training before writing is very important [11], like brainstorming, which can help students better organize the text and improve the writing quality. Prewriting is proved effective in positively affecting the writing performance, such as complexity and fluency [5, 12]. In Cheng's [11] study, from participants' perspective, of all writing strategies, the most useful kind of strategy was prewriting strategy, which proves the importance of prewriting as it helps stimulate thinking.

2.2 Writing Anxiety

Anxiety is one of the biggest obstacles to the success of foreign language learning [13]. Daly and Miller [14] first put forward the term 'writing apprehension' for native speakers. They mentioned that there might exist a general anxiety about writing, and individuals with high writing apprehension would fear evaluation of their writing and avoid writing when possible. Faigley et al. [15] give a widely acceptable definition that writing anxiety 'is associated with the tendency of people to approach or avoid writing, which reflect in the behaviors they display as they write, in the attitudes they express about their writing, and in their written products'.

Krashen [16] noted that foreign language writing may generate more anxiety. Hong & Lim [17] examined the interrelationships among writing anxiety, writing strategy use and writing performance in Korean English learners. The results indicated that prewriting strategy uses exert positive effects on writing performance. Besides, collaborative work has the potential to lower learning anxiety and avoidance behavior [18]. However, As a popular CMC tool, few studies was conducted on the effect of technology-supported L2 writing on writing anxiety.

2.3 Computer-Mediated Communication and Collaborative Prewriting

Students living in the modern world are often called digital natives [19]. They can easily access to a variety of technologies in daily life, and computer-mediated communication (CMC) has been used in a wide variety of contexts. CMC can be divided into synchronous CMC and asynchronous CMC. Synchronous CMC realizes real-time communication, while asynchronous CMC provides a time lag that allows users to read or revise. An increasing number of scholars have explored the effectiveness of CMC-based systems in L2 writing, like wiki [20], Facebook [21], Blogs [22] and so on. During the COVID-19 pandemic, DingTalk, as an emerging tool, became the most popular CMC system for teachers and students from mainland China. Some scholars conduct studies on DingTalk and its affordances on learning, which have proved it a useful tool [23]. Generally, CMC-based systems provide online learning platforms that promote meaningful communication and cooperation.

Collaborative prewriting is rooted in Vygotsky's [24] sociocultural theory as communication and interaction can provide a scaffolding for language learning, making it easy and successful to communicate and interact with others using target language. CMC is facilitated by computers and online social medias, so CMC has a natural connection with sociocultural theory [25]. Given the support of CMC, the prior empirical studies exploring the effect of planning on writing performance provide diverse findings that different kinds of prewriting have different effects on writing performance. Besides, as an important online platform, it is necessary to testify whether DingTalk can facilitate prewriting and reduce writing anxiety. Thus, the research questions of the present study are as follows:

(1) Does online collaborative prewriting discussion via DingTalk improve EFL Learners' writing performance?
(2) Does online collaborative prewriting discussion via DingTalk relieve EFL Learners' writing anxiety?
(3) What are EFL Learners' perceptions and attitudes toward online collaborative prewriting discussion via DingTalk?

3 Method

3.1 Participants

Sixty junior high school students (Junior Three) in Guangzhou China were involved in the present study. Taking feasibility into consideration, the experiment was conducted in two classes, a total of 60 students. There are 30 students in experimental group (EG) and control group (CG) respectively. These students are all second language learners who have been learning English since primary school with similar learning experience. No significant difference was found between the two classes in terms of their writing scores and English test scores, suggesting that the two classes have the similar language proficiency.

3.2 Instruments

Tasks. To assess the effectiveness of DingTalk-based collaborative prewriting, pre-test and post-test were administered. Argumentative writing was designed as the writing task type in the study as making a good argument is essential in today's society. Taking junior high school students' language proficiency into account, the topics of argumentative writing tasks in the present study are closely related to students' daily life, including after-class training, school uniform, pet dog, Internet, mobile phone and so on (Fig. 1). The topics in the pre-test and post-test are different but similar in terms of task difficulty.

DingTalk. Online collaborative prewriting was conducted in DingTalk, which is a smart phone-based online workplace developed by Alibaba. During the COVID-19 pandemic, DingTalk was used by many schools due to its pedagogical affordances, such as, live streaming, homework submission and correction and so on (Fig. 1), making it one of the most popular online education tools during the special period.

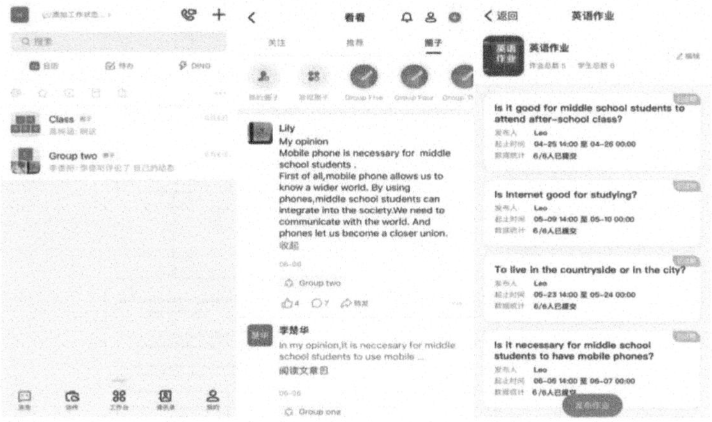

Fig. 1. DingTalk & DingTalk groups

Table 1. Target measures of syntactic complexity

Aspects	Items	Analysis tools
Fluency	Average number of words per text (W)	L2SCA
	Average number of T-units per text (T)	
	Average number of clauses per text (C)	
Complexity	Proportion of clauses to T-units (C/T)	L2SCA
	Proportion of dependent clauses to total clauses (DC/C)	
Accuracy	Percentage of error-free T-units	1 Checker
	Percentage of error-free clauses	

Target Measures. The tests adopted the scoring of senior high school entrance examination (Zhongkao). The full score of the writing part in Zhongkao is 15 marks, marked mainly from content and language. Apart from overall ratings, the following measures of syntactic complexity (Table 1) [26] were examined. Complexity and fluency was analyzed by L2 Syntactic Complexity Analyzer (L2SCA) [27], while in terms of accuracy, 1 Checker, an online tool, was used to find out the errors in participants' writings, and additional check was made to confirm the results. Besides, to measure participants' writing anxiety, Cheng's [28] Second Language Writing Anxiety inventory (SLWAI) was used in the present study. The scale consists of 22 items, including three types of writing anxiety: somatic anxiety, cognitive anxiety and avoidance behavior.

3.3 Procedures

The experiment lasted for 9 weeks, and the procedures are presented as follows. Participants were supposed to finish one argumentative task in every two weeks. The pre-test was arranged in week 1, and the post-test was arranged in week 9, including second language writing anxiety inventory and a writing task.

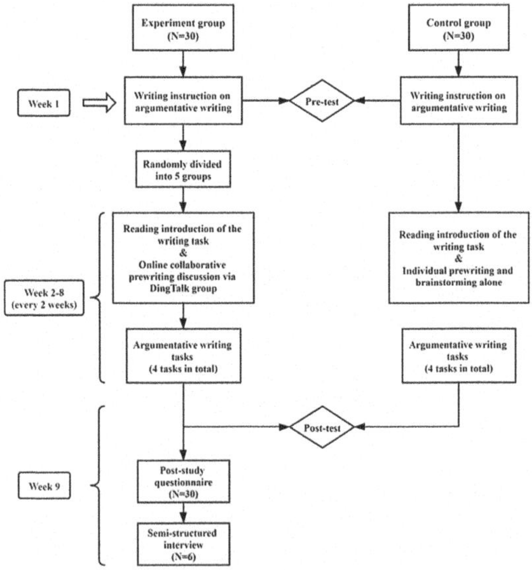

Fig. 2. Research procedures

In week 1, all participants received instructions on how to write an argumentation, and participants from EG were also taught how to use DingTalk group. During the treatment, from week 2 to 8, thirty participants in EG were randomly divided into five groups, while participants in CG were not divided. Following the groups, participants in EG logged in DingTalk and entered DingTalk groups respectively. Before prewriting, the researcher issued the topic of the task, related instructions to guide students to start prewriting. First, students needed to choose the perspective they supported, and they were required to use English in discussion. The prewriting activity mainly focuses on words/phrases, opinions and outline (Fig. 3). As for CG, they were informed to conduct prewriting planning in blank paper in terms of words/phrases, opinions and outline. All participants were given 30 min for prewriting and 30 min to finish an argumentative writing with no less than 100 words. Participants in EG submitted their writing texts online in DingTalk groups, while participants in CG handed in their writing in the form of paper. After the treatment, participants in EG were supposed to finish a post-study survey, and six participants were randomly chosen to take part in the interview, focusing on their overall experience.

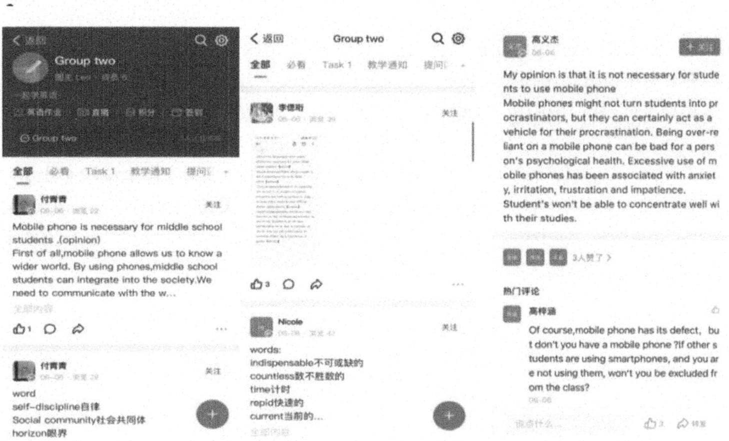

Fig. 3. Students' participation in DingTalk groups

4 Results

4.1 The Impact of Online Collaborative Prewriting on Writing Performance

Table 2 and 3 illustrate the results of overall ratings. Concerning the pre-test, no significance difference was found between EG and CG ($p = 0.400 > 0.05$), indicating that writing performance of two groups were equivalent before the treatment. As for the post-test, EG scored significantly higher than CG ($p = 0.006 < 0.05$), which confirmed the effectiveness of DingTalk-based collaborative prewriting.

Table 2. Results of independent samples T-tests of overall writing performance

	Groups	N	M	SD	t	p
Pre-test	EG	30	8.62	1.67	−.848	.400
	CG	30	8.96	1.53		
Post-test	EG	30	11.05	1.50	2.847	.006**
	CG	30	9.85	1.74		

Besides, displayed in Table 3, as for EG, there was a statistically significant difference (p = 0.000) in the comparison of pre-test and post-test, while no significant difference (p = 0.067) was found in CG. The value of significance in CG was quite close to the significant difference value 0.05, which indicated that the argumentative writing training and individual prewriting might, to some extent, improve the overall writing performance.

Table 3. Results of paired samples T-tests of overall writing performance

Groups		M	SD	SEM	t	p
EG	Pre-test - Post-test	−2.433	1.755	.321	−7.592	.000**
CG	Pre-test - Post-test	−.833	2.545	.465	−1.901	.067

Apart from overall writing performance, the results of target measures were shown in Table 4. Participants in EG scored significantly higher than those in CG in all measures of fluency, including average number of words (p = 0.022), average number of clauses (p = 0.013) and average number of T-units (p = 0.029). This indicated that the fluency of participants' writing from EG scored significantly higher than that from CG. After collaborative prewriting, students in EG produced longer texts, more clauses and T-units. However, as for complexity and accuracy, no significant difference was found between two groups.

Table 4. Results of independent samples T-tests for target measures of CG and EG

Measure		EG		CG		t	p
		M	SD	M	SD		
Fluency	W	151.500	29.383	133.333	23.554	2.359	.022*
	C	19.500	3.192	17.367	3.325	2.552	.013*
	T	12.733	2.490	11.200	2.797	2.243	.029*
Complexity	C/T	1.555	.229	1.560	.261	−.929	.977
	DC/C	.317	.098	.281	.092	1.476	.107
Accuracy	PEFT-U	.394	.126	.403	.128	−.286	.776
	PEFC	.498	.142	.462	.168	.945	.344

Note. *W = average number of words; C = average number of clauses; T = average number of T-units; C/T = proportion of clauses to T-units; DC/C = proportion of dependent clauses to total clauses; PEFT-U = percentage of error-free T-units; PEFC = percentage of error-free clauses*

4.2 The Impact of Online Collaborative Prewriting on Writing Anxiety

As shown in the Table 5, in pre-test, no significant difference was found between EG and CG (p = 0.446), while there existed statistically significant difference in post-test (p = 0.04), writing anxiety of EG (M = 56.70) was significantly lower than that of CG (M = 59.87).

Table 5. Results of independent samples T-tests of SLWAI

	Groups	N	M	SD	t	p
Pre-test	EG	30	60.27	7.64	−.767	.446
	CG	30	61.73	7.17		
Post-test	EG	30	56.70	5.90	−2.133	.04*
	CG	30	59.87	6.03		

Apart from overall writing anxiety, detailed items in writing anxiety scale were also compared. Regarding pre-test, no significant difference existed in any items. Table 7 displayed the items of significant differences in post-test. Significant differences existed in item 5 (p = 0.039), 9 (p = 0.029), 10 (p = 0.022) and 13 (p = 0.021). According to Cheng's [28] classification of SLWAI (Table 6), item 5 and 10 were about avoidance behavior, item 9 belonged to cognitive anxiety and item 13 went with somatic anxiety. Besides, the value of item 11 (p = 0.09), from somatic anxiety subscale, was quite close to the value of significant difference.

Table 6. Subscales of SLWAI

Subscale	Item
Somatic anxiety	2, 6, 8, 11, 13, 15, 19
Cognitive anxiety	1, 3, 7, 9, 14, 17, 20, 21
Avoidance behavior	4, 5, 10, 12, 16, 18, 22

Table 7. Results of independent samples T-tests of items in post-test

Item		Sig	t	p
...		×	–	–
5	I usually do my best to avoid writing English compositions	√	−2.110	.039*
...		Y	–	–
9	If my English composition is to be evaluated, I would worry about getting a very poor grade	√	v2.242	.029*
10	I do my best to avoid situations in which I have to write in English	√	−2.358	.022*
11	My thoughts become jumbled when I write English compositions under time constraint	×	−1.725	.09
...		×	–	–
13	I often feel panic when I write English compositions under time constraint	√	−2.369	.021*
...		×	–	–

*Note. √: there is a significant difference; ×: there is no significant difference; * p < .05; ** p < .01*

4.3 Participants' Attitudes

Table 8. Descriptive statistics of the questionnaire

Item	N	Min	Max	M	SD
Q1	30	3	5	4.17	.834
Q2	30	4	5	4.20	.610
Q3	30	3	5	4.40	.621
Q4	30	2	5	4.30	.750
Q5	30	1	5	2.50	1.042
Q6	30	3	5	4.33	.758
Q7	30	2	5	4.30	.794
Q8	30	2	5	3.97	.850
Q9	30	2	5	3.77	.898
Q10	30	3	5	4.20	.610
Q11	30	3	5	3.97	.718
Q12	30	3	5	4.43	.626

The post-study questionnaire is a Likert 5-level scale, including 12 items, which mainly focuses on the feasibility of DingTalk, anxiety change, the effectiveness of collaborative prewriting and their attitudes towards it. The value of Cronbach's α coefficient of the questionnaire is 0.86, indicating that the questionnaire is reliable. Table 8 presents the results of the questionnaire.

The results reveal that item 12 reached the highest mean score 4.43, which showed that 90% of the participants agreed that more ideas were shared and generated in CMC-based collaborative prewriting. Item 3, 4, 6 and 7 also scored high value, indicating that students considered DingTalk-based prewriting an useful and interesting project and they generally hold positive attitudes towards it. Item 8 represented that near 70% of the participants reported that lower writing anxiety after treatment, which was mainly in line with what participants answered in the interview. Besides, only 60% of the participants found it not difficult to discuss in English (item 5), which was in line with several students mentioned in the interview that discussing in English might be a bit difficult.

5 Discussion

From the analysis of the results presented above, it proved that compared with individual prewriting, online collaborative prewriting via DingTalk is more effective in improving students' overall writing performance. In accord with the results of other relevant studies on collaborative prewriting [29, 30], the present study reveals that DingTalk-based collaborative prewriting promotes overall writing performance. In DingTalk group, participants are given relaxing discussion atmosphere, and ideas can be shared conveniently in DingTalk groups, allowing participants to make full use of group resources to obtain the language form they need [31].

As for target measures, significant differences exist in several measures, namely average number of words, average number of clauses, average number of T-units. This results support Amiryousefi's [5] study which stated collaborative prewriting positively affect the fluency of participants' written texts. Besides, consistent with some prior studies [33], in pretask planning, students tended to pay more attention on the provision of thoughts and ideas, leading to the improvement in fluency. Prewriting via DingTalk provide social contexts where students assist each other in groups to explore more freely and generate diverse language patterns and ideas. The distinct difference in fluency of written texts proves that DingTalk-based collaborative prewriting facilitates L2 writers' ideas on the given topics and the enriches the content of their compositions.

However, no distinct difference was found in two measures of complexity, which is in line with the previous studies [32]. The present study failed to find any significant improvement in accuracy. The explanation may be, in accord with VanPatten's [34] Trade-off Hypothesis, which stated that L2 learners has a limited attentional capacity, participants cannot pay attention to all aspects of language. As various ideas were shared in DingTalk groups, participants tended to pay more attention on the content (e.g. fluency) instead of language form (e.g. accuracy and complexity).

From the statistical analysis of the SLWAI, collaborative prewriting via DingTalk can reduce writing anxiety. This finding is in line with Wu and Gu [18] who noted that cooperative learning can significantly reduce L2 writers' overall writing anxiety and somatic anxiety. Further analysis on detailed items in SLWAI reveals that collaborative prewriting is beneficial to relieve participants' somatic anxiety and cognitive anxiety and moderate the avoidance behavior as well. It may due to the scaffolding and language input DingTalk-based collaborative prewriting offered. In DingTalk, participants are given a less anxious writing experience, and it cultivates learners' positive writing attitude and improve students' sense of responsibility for writing tasks. Besides, the results also provide evidence for some studies on social technologies [22, 35], which claimed that social technologies have several advantages for L2 writing such as promoting meaningful interaction and communication and increasing L2 writers' confidence etc.

Participants generally hold a positive view on the argumentative writing tasks, usability and effectiveness of collaborative prewriting. It helps create a less stressful environment for discussion and provide comprehensible language input. Besides, DingTalk-based collaborative prewriting was believed to help generate and collect ideas better as well as offer support to writing task. These results are consistent with some studies on collaborative prewriting [36].

6 Conclusion

Based on the results, the major findings of the current study are presented as follows. Firstly, online collaborative prewriting help to facilitate junior high school students' writing performance. Apart from overall ratings, online collaborative prewriting exerts a positive effect on the fluency of the students' written texts. It can be concluded that during online collaborative prewriting, students can better share and generate their ideas and thoughts, so that they might pay much attention on the fluency and produce longer texts. Secondly, online collaborative prewriting can help junior high students reduce their writing anxiety. Online collaborative prewriting positively affects the writing anxiety, especially the fear and panic of writing as well as the avoidance behavior. Thirdly, students generally hold positive attitudes on online collaborative prewriting via DingTalk. They perceived it as an interesting and helpful group project, and they admitted the advantages of online collaborative prewriting, such as providing a less stressful discussion environment, helping generating ideas and offering support to subsequent writing task.

Acknowledgments. This work is supported by the Center for Language Cognition and Assessment, South China Normal University. It's also the result of Guangdong "13th Five-Year" Plan Project of Philosophy & Social Science (GD20WZX01–02).

References

1. Lan, Y.-J., Sung, Y.-T., Cheng, C.-C., Chang, K.-E.: Computer-supported cooperative prewriting for enhancing young EFL learners' writing performance. Lang. Learn. Technol. **19**(2), 134–155 (2015). http://dx.doi.org/10125/44421
2. Qin, X.Q., Yang, J.J., Bi, J.: EFL writer's block and writing apprehension: constructs and sources. Foreign Lang. Lit. Res. (01), 97–106 (2015). https://doi.org/10.16651/j.cnki.fllr.2015.01.014
3. Li, Z.X.: Quantitative analysis of the effects of English majors' planning variables on their writing performance. Foreign Lang. Teach. Res. (Bimonthly) (3), 178–183 (2008)
4. Wang, L.F.: Empirical studies on L2 writing in China: a review. Foreign Lang. China (01), 50–55 (2005)
5. Amiryousefi, M.: The differential effects of collaborative vs. individual prewriting planning on computer-mediated L2 writing: transferability of task-based linguistic skills in focus. Comput. Assist. Lang. Learn. **30**(8), 766–786 (2017). https://doi.org/10.1080/09588221.2017.1360361
6. Neumann, H., McDonough, K.: Exploring student interaction during collaborative prewriting discussions and its relationship to L2 writing. J. Second. Lang. Writ. **27**, 84–104 (2015). https://doi.org/10.1016/j.jslw.2014.09.009
7. Andujar, A., Salaberri-Ramiro, M.S.: Exploring chatbased communication in the EFL class: computer and mobile environments. Comput. Assist. Lang. Learn. (2019). https://doi.org/10.1080/09588221.2019.1614632
8. Yen, Y.-C., Hou, H.-T., Chang, K.E.: Applying role-playing strategy to enhance learners' writing and speaking skills in EFL courses using Facebook and Skype as learning tools: A case study in Taiwan. Comput. Assist. Lang. Learn. **28**(5), 383–406 (2015). https://doi.org/10.1080/09588221.2013.839568
9. Hayes, J.R., Flower, L.S.: Identifying the organization of writing processes. In: Gregg, W., Steinberg, R. (eds.) Cognitive Processes in Writing, pp. 3–30. Erlbaum, Hillsdale (1980)
10. Hyland, K.: Second Language Writing. Cambridge University Press, Cambridge (2003). https://doi.org/10.1017/CBO9780511667251
11. Cheng, C.M.: An empirical study on writing strategy teaching. A Chinese perspective on English writing teaching and research. In: Proceedings of the Fourth International Symposium on English writing teaching and research in China: College of English, University of international business and Economics, 7 (2008)

12. Ellis, R., Yuan, F.: The effects of planning on fluency, complexity, and accuracy in second language narrative writing. Stud. Second. Lang. Acquis. **26**, 59–84 (2004)
13. Oxford, R.L.: Anxiety and the language learner: new insights. In: Anold, J. (ed.) Affect in Language Learning. Cambridge University Press, Cambridge (1999)
14. Daly, J.A., Miller, M.D.: The empirical development of an instrument to measure writing apprehension. Res. Teach. Engl. **9**(3), 242–249 (1975)
15. Faigley, L., Daly, J.A., Witte, S.P.: The role of writing apprehension in writing performance and competence. J. Educ. Res. **75**(1), 16–21 (1981)
16. Krashen, S.: Second Language Acquisition and Second Language Learning, p. 151. Pergamon Press, Oxford (1982)
17. Hong, J., Lim, H.: Interrelations among writing anxiety, writing strategy use, and writing performance in Korean English learners. Engl. Lang. Lit. Teach. **20**(4), 85–106 (2014)
18. Wu, Y.H., Gu, W.X.: An empirical study on the effects of cooperative learning in reducing non-English majors' English writing anxiety. Foreign Lang. Their Teach. (06), 51–55 (2011)
19. Prensky, M.: Digital natives, digital immigrants part 2: do they really think differently? On Horiz. **9**(6), 1–6 (2001). https://doi.org/10.1108/10748120110424843
20. Hsu, H.C.: Wiki-mediated collaboration and its association with L2 writing development: an exploratory study. Comput. Assist. Lang. Learn. **32**(8), 945–967 (2019)
21. Dizon, G.: A comparative study of Facebook vs. paper-and-pencil writing to improve L2 writing skills. Comput. Assist. Lang. Learn. **29**(5–8), 1–10 (2016)
22. Recep, Ş.: Arslan & Aysel Şahin-Kızıl: How can the use of blog software facilitate the writing process of English language learners? Comput. Assist. Lang. Learn. **23**(3), 183–197 (2010)
23. Xiao, C., Cai, H., Su, Y., Shen, L.: Online teaching practices and strategies for inorganic chemistry using a combined platform based on DingTalk, Learning@ZJU, and WeChat. J. Chem. Educ. (2020). https://doi.org/10.1021/acs.jchemed.0c00642
24. Vygotsky, L.S.: Mind in Society: The Development of Higher Psychological Processes. Harvard University Press, Cambridge (1978)
25. Wang, J.Q.: Review on the application of computer-mediated communication in foreign language teaching. Foreign Lang. Teach. Res. (05), 775–783 (2012)
26. Wigglesworth, G., Storch, N.: Pair versus individual writing: effects on fluency, complexity and accuracy. Lang. Test. **26**(3), 445–466 (2009)
27. Lu, X.: Automatic analysis of syntactic complexity in second language writing. Int. J. Corpus Linguist. **15**(4), 474–496 (2010)
28. Cheng, Y.: A measure of second language writing anxiety: scale development and preliminary validation. J. Second. Lang. Writ. **4**, 313–335 (2004)
29. Kessler, M., Polio, C., Xu, C., Hao, X.: The effects of oral discussion and text chat on L2 Chinese writing. Foreign Lang. Ann. 1–20 (2020). https://doi.org/10.1111/flan.12491
30. Mazdayasna, G., Zaini, A.: The effect of collaborative prewriting discussions on L2 writing development and learners' identity construction. Iran. J. Appl. Linguist. **18**(2), 141–164 (2015)
31. Wen, Q.F.: A Theoretical Study of English Learning Strategies. Shaanxi Normal University Press, Xi'an (2004)
32. McDonough, K., De Vleeschauwer, J.: Comparing the effect of collaborative and individual prewriting on EFL learners' writing development. J. Second Lang. Writ. (2019). https://doi.org/10.1016/j.jslw.2019.04.003
33. Adams, R., Nik, N.: Prior knowledge and second language task production in text chat. In: Gonzalez-Lloret, M., Ortega, L. (eds.) Technology-Mediated TBLT: Researching Technology and Tasks, pp. 51–78. John Benjamins, Amsterdam (2014)

34. VanPatten, B.: Attending to content and form in the input: an experiment in consciousness. Stud. Second Lang. Acquis. **12**, 287–301 (1990)
35. Bikowski, D., Vithanage, R.: Effects of web-based collaborative writing on individual L2 writing development. Lang. Learn. Technol. **20**(1), 79–99 (2016)
36. Chang, B., Lu, F.C.: Social media facilitated English prewriting activity design and evaluation. Asia-Pac. Educ. Res. **27**(1), 33–42 (2018)

Evaluation of Distance Learning from the Perspective of University Students - A Case Study

Vaclav Zubr(✉) and Marcela Sokolova

University of Hradec Kralove, Rokitanskeho 62, 500 03 Hradec Kralove, Czech Republic
vaclav.zubr@uhk.cz

Abstract. The COVID-19 pandemic has had a significant impact on education. Almost overnight, it basically halted teaching at most educational institutions, and has gradually affected all educational levels. This situation was unprecedented. Educational institutions had to switch to a new form of education urgently. The pandemic affected the means as well as the methods of learning. It affected all stakeholders, i.e., teachers, students/pupils and institutions. The aim of this paper is to present the research results of a questionnaire that was focused on the distance learning experience of students. The questionnaire provided student feedback about the distance form (remote modality) of teaching they had experienced. The research was carried out at the Faculty of Informatics and Management (FIM) at the University of Hradec Králové. The surveyed students studied during the 2020/2021 academic year using distance learning. Overall, 122 students took part in the research. Results show that online tools such as Microsoft Teams and BlackBoard are most often used at FIM. Students indicated that the BlackBoard Learning Management System (LMS) was the most beneficial tool. Overall, respondents are equally satisfied with distance learning and face-to-face learning. It cannot be unequivocally determined whether students prefer distance learning or face-to-face learning.

Keywords: BlackBoard · Distance learning · Face-to-face learning

1 Introduction

The COVID-19 pandemic significantly affected education. Within a few months, almost all countries implemented distance learning, either online (online applications, television, radio) or offline (printed books, modules). Nobody had any experience with education during widespread lockdowns. Educational institutions had to switch to a new form of education urgently. The pandemic affected the means as well as the methods of learning. It affected all stakeholders (teachers, students/pupils, institutions).

Distance learning can take different forms, and use different tools such as synchronous and asynchronous tools. Synchronous learning is a form of learning with direct interactions between students and teachers, while using online forms such as conferencing and online chat, which are synchronous communication tools. Meanwhile, asynchronous learning is a form of indirect learning (not simultaneously)

W. Jia et al. (Eds.): SETE 2021, LNCS 13089, pp. 61–68, 2021.
https://doi.org/10.1007/978-3-030-92836-0_6

through an independent approach to learning. Some subjects are designed and displayed in a LMS such as Moodle or BlackBoard, or in Email systems, blogs, online discussions, Wikipedia, videos, articles and other asynchronous communication platforms [1–4]. Students have access to the teacher synchronously, asynchronously, or both [5–7].

Almaiah et al. addressed the factors influencing the introduction of e-learning in universities during the pandemic [8]. Their identified several challenges associated with the adoption of an e-learning system. They divided these challenges into four categories, namely (1) technology challenges, (2) individual challenges, (3) cultural challenges, and (4) course challenges. They also found that these challenges vary greatly from country to country due to different cultures, contexts, and preparedness [8].

It should be noted that in the context of the pandemic, we are talking about emergency remote learning (ERL), which is the rapid transition from the classic forms of learning to a completely remote setting. Consequently, the transition is unplanned and sudden. ERL is different from classic online learning especially in the assessment tools and in terms of the course design [9].

Due to the difference between classic distance learning and ERL, it is important to evaluate the ERL results during pandemic. Some authors published studies focused on evaluating the distance learning results. For example, Orlov et al. conducted a standardised assessment of knowledge at the end of the course to examine students' learning during the changes caused by the COVID-19 pandemic [10].

The FIM at the University of Hradec Kralove, like many other institutions, reacted flexibly to the conditions imposed by the COVID-19 pandemic and transferred the face-to-face learning to the a distance form. In order to obtain student feedback regarding attendance, activity during online learning, fulfilment of tasks and an overall evaluation of a course, a questionnaire survey was created. Ultimately, the results of the questionnaire would provide teachers adequate feedback from students, and thus the opportunity to improve online learning in the future.

2 Methodology

The aim of this study was to find out the students' opinion about the ongoing distance learning in comparison with the traditional face-to-face learning. A questionnaire survey focused on students at FIM was conducted during May 2021. The questionnaire was distributed to the respondents online through BlackBoard. Overall, 270 students were addressed, 122 valid questionnaires were evaluated (response rate 45.2%). Both, full-time students, and combined students were addressed as well as students of all three years of Bachelor programme. The questionnaire contained 20 questions. The first part of questionnaire was focused on demographic data. Furthermore, the questions focused on the tools supporting online teaching, which are used at the FIM (e.g. Microsoft Teams, BlackBoard, and Email). Microsoft Teams is used for online lecture delivery, and as an LMS; BlackBoard is usedonly as an LMS; Email is used as a channel for questions and answers. In the second section of the questionnaire, respondents expressed themselves in 10 statements in relation to distance learning. These statements were based on the authors' personal experiences with distance learning and on the basis of studies already carried out [8, 11]. To determine the degree of agreement with the statements, a 5-point Likert scale was chosen, where 1 = strongly disagree and 5 = strongly agree. The exact wording of the individual statements is shown in Table 1.

Table 1. Claims related to online learning

Claim 1	Distance learning is a benefit in times of pandemic in terms of the possibility of continuing education
Claim 2	The use of online tools allows students more flexibility than face-to-face teaching
Claim 3	During the lessons, the teacher receives sufficient feedback from students
Claim 4	Distance learning sufficiently supports student activity
Claim 5	Recording lectures allows easier understanding of the issue thanks to the possibility of replay, pause
Claim 6	Turning on the cameras would be beneficial during the synchronous teaching of the exercises
Claim 7	Students do not respond as flexibly in online teaching as in face-to-face teaching
Claim 8	During the lessons, students receive sufficient feedback from teachers
Claim 9	Students are more likely to lose concentration during online lessons
Claim 10	Distance learning suits me more than face-to-face learning

Using the IBM SPSS Statistics Version 26, the Cronbach coefficient of reliability was calculated. The highest value of Alpha coefficient was 0.659. Overall, the coefficient value was 0.618 (lower values of Alpha due to 122 respondents).

Based on a search of previously published studies [12–15], the following research questions were identified:

RQ1: How do students evaluate online teaching as compared to face-to-face? Is there a difference in the attitude of full-time and combined study students?
RQ2: What tools did the students use in distance learning? How do they evaluate their contribution?

The obtained data was evaluated in the following programmes Microsoft Excel 2016 and IBM SPSS Statistics version 26 using descriptive statistics and Pearson correlation.

3 Results

In total, 122 respondents participated in our study. Women were predominantly represented (57.4%). Mostly, first-year students participated (86.9%), which corresponds to the respondents age representation (dominant age group 18–30 years old, 93.4%). Almost 70% of respondents are full-time students. The most represented study programmes were Tourism Management (45.9%), Information Management (38.5%) and

Economics and Management (14.8%). Only one respondent (0.8%) studied in the Applied Informatics programme. The detailed demographic data are showed in Table 2.

Table 2. Respondents' demographic data (n = 122)

Gender	n	%
Male	52	42.6
Female	70	57.4
Age		
18–30	114	93.5
31–40	7	5.7
41–50	1	0.8
Form of study		
Full-time study	85	69.7
Combined study	37	30.3
Study programme		
Applied informatics	1	0.8
Economics and management (financial management)	18	14.8
Information management	47	38.5
Tourism management	56	45.9
Year of study		
First	106	86.8
Second	8	6.6
Third	8	6.6

The tools most used to support online learning are Microsoft Teams (121 respondents), BlackBoard (120 respondents) and Email (87 respondents). Respondents mostly use a combination of the three mentioned tools (86 respondents). In total, 34 respondents use the Microsoft Teams-BlackBoard or BlackBoard-Email tools combination. Only two respondents use Microsoft Teams separately. BlackBoard (55.7%) was rated as the most beneficial tool (5 points on a scale from 1 to 5), then Microsoft Teams (47.5%). In terms of benefits, overall, email was the worst rated.

Most respondents consider distance learning during a pandemic to be beneficial because it is possible to continue education. Respondents also agree that recording lectures makes it easier to understand the issue. At the same time, according to most respondents, online teaching allows students more flexibility compared to face-to-face teaching. However, at the same time, results show that students are more prone to lose concentration during online teaching and do not react as flexibly in online teaching as in face-to-face teaching. According to the respondents, students receive sufficient feedback from teachers during online teaching, but teachers often do not receive feedback from students. Based on the results, it is not possible to unequivocally tell whether students are more comfortable with distance or with face-to-face learning (see Table 3).

Table 3. Level of agreement with the claims

	Likert scale				
	1	2	3	4	5
Claim 1	1	9	21	39	52
Claim 2	1	5	13	47	56
Claim 3	11	42	46	19	4
Claim 4	7	55	39	13	8
Claim 5	2	3	10	41	66
Claim 6	5	35	47	27	8
Claim 7	3	12	22	42	43
Claim 8	3	10	21	53	35
Claim 9	5	9	10	45	53
Claim 10	16	18	29	29	30

Table 4 shows a significant correlation ($\alpha = 0.01$) between many statements. Claim 6 shows the lowest correlation rate: Turning on the cameras would be beneficial during the synchronous teaching of the exercises. Claim 7 shows a negative correlation at the level of significance $\alpha = 0.01$: Students do not respond as flexibly in online teaching as in face-to-face teaching. At the level of significance $\alpha = 0.01$ correlates the most with other claims of claim 10: Distance learning suits me more than face-to-face learning.

Table 4. Pearson correlation

	Claim1	Claim2	Claim3	Claim4	Claim5	Claim6	Claim7	Claim8	Claim9	Claim10
Claim 1	1	.296**	.203*	.364**	.393**	0.174	−0.086	.296**	−0.161	.330**
Claim 2	.296**	1	.292**	.341**	.323**	0.133	0.026	.264**	0.04	.422**
Claim 3	.203*	.292**	1	.569**	0.114	-0.005	−.264**	.264**	−.183*	.367**
Claim 4	.364**	.341**	.569**	1	.348**	0.099	−.277**	.323**	−.356**	.447**
Claim 5	.393**	.323**	0.114	.348**	1	0.165	0.003	.415**	-0.12	.235**
Claim 6	0.174	0.133	-0.005	0.099	0.165	1	.221*	0.143	.181*	−0.047
Claim 7	−0.086	0.026	−.264**	−.277**	0.003	.221*	1	−0.065	.532**	−.294**
Claim 8	.296**	.264**	.264**	.323**	.415**	0.143	-0.065	1	-0.074	.238**
Claim 9	−0.161	0.04	−.183*	−.356**	−0.12	.181*	.532**	−0.074	1	−.374**
Claim 10	.330**	.422**	.367**	.447**	.235**	−0.047	−.294**	.238**	−.374**	1

**Correlation is significant at the 0.01 level (2-tailed).
*Correlation is significant at the 0.05 level (2-tailed).

The average evaluation of claims between genders does not differ significantly, some claims are evaluated a little better by women (claims 1, 2, 5, 10). Men and women rated claims 4, 6, 8 and 9 with almost maximum agreement.

When comparing the average evaluation of statements in terms of the study form, 7 statements are evaluated slightly better by face-to-face study students. However, in general the average values are very similar.

The average evaluation of individual statements differs very little between individual fields. The highest average rating was given by respondents in the field of

Economics and Management (the highest average rating for 7 statements). Claims 3 and 10 were rated the worst by one respondent representing the field of Applied Informatics (see Table 5).

Table 5. Average evaluation of statements according to the studied field

	Claim 1	Claim 2	Claim 3	Claim 4	Claim 5	Claim 6	Claim 7	Claim 8	Claim 9	Claim 10
Applied Informatics	4.00	5.00	1.00	2.00	5.00	3.00	5.00	4.00	5.00	1.00
Economics and Management	4.33	4.56	2.94	2.78	4.61	3.06	3.44	4.17	3.39	3.94
Information Management	4.00	4.11	2.68	2.70	4.30	2.83	3.87	3.96	4.23	3.36
Tourism Management	4.07	4.25	2.66	2.63	4.32	3.09	4.05	3.71	4.16	3.13

4 Discussion

The aim of this study was to find out the students' opinion about the ongoing distance learning in comparison with face-to-face learning.

A total of 122 bachelor students from the FIM at the University of Hradec Králové, participated in the study. The ratio of men and women in this study was relatively balanced (57.4% women). Given that the study was mostly attended by first-year students (86.8%), it was possible to assume that 18–30 years (93.5%) is the age of the majority of? respondents. Respondents from full-time and combined study forms of study participated in the study, where full-time students were predominant (69.7%).

The questionnaire survey largely focused on the evaluation of online teaching and the comparison of results in terms of individual groups of respondents. Based on the results, the first research question was answered:

RQ1: How do students evaluate online teaching as compared to face-to-face? Is there a difference in the attitude of full-time and combined study students?

There is no significant difference between the evaluation of claims in combined and full-time students. Some statements are evaluated by combined students a little better than full-time students, but it is necessary to consider the relative representation of individual groups in the study.

Overall, we can say that respondents are equally satisfied with distance learning and face-to-face learning, which is in line with another study from 2020 [16].

The conducted questionnaire survey was focused on finding out which tools that support online teaching are used most often by the respondent, and how the student evaluates their contribution. The second research question was answered based on the results:

RQ2: What tools did the students use in distance learning? How do they evaluate their contribution?

Due to the fact that BlackBoard and Microsoft Teams are commonly used in distance learning at the Faculty of Informatics and Management, it was possible to expect that the majority uses these tools. Surprisingly, one respondent did not use Microsoft Teams at all. Of all the online tools, email was the least used. Due to the communication needs associated with online teaching, it could be expected that almost all respondents will use a combination of all three online tools (Microsoft Teams - BlackBoard - Email), but only 86 respondents used this combination. This can be explained by possible communication via Microsoft Teams or BlackBoard. As expected, BlackBoard was rated as the most beneficial tool since it is an environment where students have access to teaching and extension materials, as well as tests and chats, assigned tasks can be submitted, and at the same time have available feedback and evaluation of these tasks. According to a study from Australia, students have a positive attitude towards BlackBoard due to the ability of sharing knowledge and exchanging feedback, among other things [17]. As expected, email was chosen as the least beneficial tool, which compared to BlackBoard, provides students with only the possibility of mutual communication. The benefits of using Microsoft Teams and BlackBoard were expected, as the number of Teams users increased sharply during the pandemic, and BlackBoard is one of the most popular LMS [18–20]. Moreover, according to other studies, users of BlackBoard are most likely satisfied with this tool [21, 22].

5 Conclusion

During the COVID-19 pandemic, distance learning has significantly affected the education systems in all countries around the world. In response to this crisis, countries have applied various rules and methods to address changes in the various learning systems. Along with these changes, it was necessary to make changes in methodological strategies, technological readiness, introduce online learning and provide support and motivation to all stakeholders. Although we hope that the situation will return to normal soon, in the meantime, changes need to be made to the national curricula to increase flexibility, and technological readiness, which in general needs to be accelerated. Finally, education should be seen as a joint effort among the community, government, teachers, parents and schools to increase the effectiveness of teaching and learning methods that have been negatively affected.

Acknowledgements. The paper was written with the support of the specific project 2021 grant "Determinants of Cognitive Processes Impacting the Work Performance" granted by the University of Hradec Králové, Czech Republic and thanks to help of students František Hašek and Anna Borkovcová.

References

1. Ko, S., Rossen, S.: Teaching Online: A Practical Guide, 4th edn. Routledge, London (2017)
2. Ogbonna, C.G., Ibezim, N.E., Obi, C.A.: Synchronous versus asynchronous e-learning in teaching word processing: an experimental approach. South African J. Educ. **39**(2), 1–15 (2019)
3. Sturm, E., Quaynor, L.: A window, mirror, and wall: how educators use twitter for professional learning. Res. Social Sci. Technol. **5**(1), 22–44 (2020)

4. Tarman, B.: Editorial: reflecting in the shade of pandemic. Res. Soc. Sci. Technol. **5**(2), i–iv (2020)
5. Hunter, L., St Pierre, L.: Online Learning: Report to the Legislature. Washington Office of Superintendent of Public Instruction (2016)
6. Inoue, Y.: Online Education for Lifelong Learning. IGI Global (2007)
7. Richardson, J.W., Hollis, E., Pritchard, M., Novosel-Lingat, J.E.M.: Shifting teaching and learning in online learning spaces: an investigation of a faculty online teaching and learning initiative. Online Learn. **24**(1), 67–91 (2020)
8. Almaiah, M.A., Al-Khasawneh, A., Althunibat, A.: Exploring the critical challenges and factors influencing the E-learning system usage during COVID-19 pandemic. Educ. Inf. Technol. **25**(6), 5261–5280 (2020). https://doi.org/10.1007/s10639-020-10219-y
9. Khlaif, Z., Salha, S., Kouraichi, B.: Emergency remote learning during COVID-19 crisis: students' engagement. Educ. Inf. Technol. **26**(6), 7033–7055 (2021)
10. Orlov, G., et al.: Learning during the COVID-19 pandemic: it is not who you teach, but how you teach NBER Working Paper No. 28022 October 2020 (2020)
11. Mukhtar, K., Javed, K., Arooj, M., Sethi, A.: Advantages, limitations and recommendations for online learning during COVID-19 pandemic era. Pak. J. Med. Sci. **36**(COVID19-S4) (2020)
12. Utomo, M.N.Y., Sudaryanto, M., Saddhono, K.: Tools and strategy for distance learning to respond COVID-19 pandemic in Indonesia. Ingénierie des systèmes d information **25**, 383–390 (2020)
13. Sergeev, A.N.: Tools for distance learning and e-learning in communities of students and teachers: composition, usage and preferences. RUDN J. Informatization Educ. **17**, 323–336 (2020)
14. Mather, M., Sarkans, A.: Student perceptions of online and face-to-face learning. Int. J. Curriculum Instr. **10**, 61–76 (2018)
15. Wang, C., et al.: Need satisfaction and need dissatisfaction: a comparative study of online and face-to-face learning contexts. Comput. Human Behav. **95**, 114–125 (2019)
16. Radha, R., Mahalakshmi, K., Satish Kumar, V., Saravanakumar, A.R.: E-learning during lockdown of Covid-19 pandemic: a global perspective. Int. J. Control Autom. **13**(4), 1088–1099 (2020)
17. Chen, J.C., Dobinson, T., Kent, S.: Students' perspectives on the impact of blackboard collaborate on Open University Australia (OUA) online learning. J. Educ. Online **17**(1) (2020)
18. Business of Apps. https://www.businessofapps.com/data/microsoft-teams-statistics/. Accessed 29 Aug 2021
19. Alghafis, A., Alrasheed, A., Abdulghany, A.: A study on the usability of moodle and blackboard – Saudi students perspectives. iJIM **14**(10), 159–165 (2020)
20. Almekhlafy, S.S.A.: Online learning of English language courses via blackboard at Saudi universities in the era of COVID-19: perception and use. PSU Res. Rev. **5**(1), 16–32 (2021)
21. Hossain, M.M., Akhtar, S., Rahman, M.A.: A study to evaluate users' satisfaction of blackboard learn. People Int. J. Soc. Sci. **3**(1), 489–506 (2017)
22. Baig, M., Gazzaz, Z.J., Farouq, M.: Blended Learning: the impact of blackboard formative assessment on the final marks and students' perception of its effectiveness. Pakistan J. Med. Sci. **36**(3), 327–332 (2020)

Digital Technology, Creativity, and Education

Enhancing EFL Learners' English Vocabulary Acquisition in WeChat Official Account Tweet-Based Writing

Nanyan Zhang[1], Xiaobin Liu[1(✉)], and Qingsheng Liu[2]

[1] South China Normal University, Guangzhou, China
liuxiaobin@m.scnu.edu.cn
[2] The Affiliated Liwan School of Guangdong Experimental High School, Guangzhou, China

Abstract. Multimodal writing has a positive impact on students' writing competence, cooperation ability and learning motivation. Based on the theory of Multiliteracy and use of technology, this study aims to explore the effect of multimodal writing on EFL (English as a foreign language) learners' vocabulary acquisition. 70 students were recruited, including 35 in experimental group (EG) and 35 in control group (CG). After seven-week experiment, for the EG, positive improvements had been observed in vocabulary acquisition especially in vocabulary use. However, comparing traditional writing and multimodal writing, there was no significant difference. The questionnaires and interviews about learners' perceptions and attitudes towards Official Account tweet-based writing were conducted among 35 learners in EG. Most learners viewed multimodal writing as an enjoyable and effective way to improve their vocabulary acquisition.

Keywords: Multimodal writing · Multiliteracy · Vocabulary acquisition · Tweet-based writing · WeChat Official Account

1 Introduction

With the rapid development of information technology, students were no longer satisfied with paper-pen writing only with one-time text, but preferred to express their ideas or opinions through dynamic and creative multimodal text which would better display their learning results (Edwards-Groves 2011). In this way, multimodal writing is a good way to meet the needs of students. In recent years, with the development of web 2.0 technology, multimodal writing based on various social networking platforms such as blogs, microblogs, wikis, WeChat Official Account are on the rise, and these platforms mainly reflect the characteristics of expression and communication.

Wechat Official Account with information aggregation, subscription push and automatic reply functions, can achieve accurate delivery of resource content, keyword retrieval and knowledge storage (Yuan et al. 2012). As one of the most popular social platform, it often combines embedded images with supporting text, audio, etc., which provides a visual design that traditional writing cannot do.

W. Jia et al. (Eds.): SETE 2021, LNCS 13089, pp. 71–83, 2021.
https://doi.org/10.1007/978-3-030-92836-0_7

At present, Official Account tweet-based writing are prevalent, with Official Account tweets increasingly becoming an important source of people' s daily information, so many educators begin to explore how to use it in teaching (Bai and Hao 2013; Zhu and Liu 2016). The present paper will explore the effect of Official Account tweet-based writing on junior high school students' English vocabulary acquisition from the perspective of English writing.

2 Literature Review

2.1 Multiliteracy and Multimodal Writing

Multiliteracy was first proposed by the New London Group (1996), which encouraged the redefinition of the concept of multiliteracy as something fluid, pluralistic, context-dependent and perspective-dependent. Multimodal writing is a teaching practice based on the theory of multiliteracy. It refers to the combination of writing text and other modals (e.g. pictures, audio, etc.) into a multimodal whole, i.e. a system for making and conveying meaning.

Nowadays, there are many tools for multimodal writing. Researches abroad explored the application of Facebook, Twitter and Blogs in university (Tang and Hew 2017; Chawinga 2017; Tess 2013; Desselle 2017), while domestic studies focused on the application of QQ and WeChat, and often centered on the combination of social media and specific curriculum teaching (e.g. reading, listening, speaking, writing, translation) from the perspective of a teacher (Yinjian 2016; Lang 2017; Minge 2010; Biqing 2010; Jianchun 2011) or the cultivation of certain specific competence (e.g. input and debate) (Changcheng 2015; Quanyou 2014).

2.2 Vocabulary Acquisition in Traditional Writing

Lewis (1993) believed that vocabulary learning was the central task of foreign language learning, and that the learning of language competence cannot be separated from vocabulary acquisition. However, vocabulary acquisition was a key challenge for language learners, especially in the teaching context with relatively limited target language (Green and Meara 1995).

Nation (2001) has made the most comprehensive and widely agreed overview towards word knowledge that includes form, meaning, and use. He explained that a lemma consisted of a head word and some of its inflected forms and reduced forms (n't). Furthermore, knowing a word is not simply able to pronounce a word or write down the form of a word, it also means that learners should know the meaning of the word and how to use it.

Many scholars abroad believed that, like native language vocabulary acquisition, most second/foreign language vocabulary was incidentally acquired, i.e. acquire vocabulary when students completed other learning tasks (Hill and He 1999; Hill and Laufer 2003; Huckin and Coady 1999; Hulstijn, Hollander and Greidanus 1996; Hulstijn and Laufer 2001; Paribakht and Wesche 1999). Researches on reading promoted vocabulary acquisition were the most (e.g., Hulstijjn 1992; Knight 1994;

Paribakht and Wesche 1997, 1999; Hulstijn and Laufer 2001), while relatively little researches had been made on the listening, speaking or writing promoted vocabulary acquisition (Li and Tian 2005).

2.3 Multimodal Writing and Vocabulary Acquisition

With the advent of computer technology, the way we view a language as well as the way we learn a language were changing, therefore many studies began to focus on the application of technology tools to improve vocabulary acquisition.

Compared with other multimodal text applications, many scholars have studied blog-based multimodal writing (Bloch 2007; Ducate and Lomicka 2008; Wang 2007). Akdag and Özkan (2017) conducted a study in a ninth-grade classroom of a state school to find out if blogging activity would have an effect on writing skills of high school language learners. It was observed that blogging experience contributed to the students' writing skills particularly in terms of vocabulary enhancement. Teimournezhad, Sotoudehnama and Marandi's (2020) study juxtaposed the traditional paper-and-pencil mode of Journal Writing with Blog Journal Writing to explore the potential impacts on L2 learners' writing skill. The statistical findings revealed that Journal Writing in general had a positive impact on writing accuracy and that the fluency, as well as lexical complexity could be enhanced through blog-writing.

2.4 Research Questions

Throughout the literature reviewed, researches on the application of multimodal writing to English learning has attracted academic attention. Moreover, Official Account tweet has gained prominence in daily life and played an important role in individual learning, but few studies have been conducted in its effect on English vocabulary acquisition, especially on junior high school students' vocabulary acquisition. Therefore, to fill the gap, choosing students in junior high school as subjects and taking Official Account as the platform for multimodal writing, the present study aims to investigate the following three research questions:

RQ1. Is Official Account tweet-based writing effective in improving junior high school students' English vocabulary acquisition?
RQ2. What are major intervention effects of Official Account tweet-based writing on students' English vocabulary acquisition (vocabulary form, meaning and use)?
RQ3. What are students' perceptions of and attitudes toward Official Account tweet-based writing?

3 Methodology

The whole experiment lasted for seven weeks and involved two rounds of writing, one topic for each round. In order to test students' vocabulary acquisition after writing, there were vocabulary pretest, instant posttest and delayed posttest (two weeks later). Before the experiment, students were asked to complete the Vocabulary Levels Test to know if they were at the similar level of vocabulary proficiency. During the pre-instructional session, the participants signed a consent form to participate and were given the Vocabulary Test to complete. After the experiment, the author administered a questionnaire to the participants of the EG to examine their perceptions toward WeChat Official Account tweet-based writing. Then, the author interviewed the participants from the EG who volunteered to further elaborate on their perceptions of and attitudes towards tweet-based writing. The 20-min interviews for each participant were conducted during Week 7 (Table 1).

Table 1. The writing topics

Time	Topic
Week 1	None (pre-instructional session)
Week 2	A Person I Love
Week 5	Tree Planting Day

3.1 Participants

In order to ensure the reality and validity of the collected data, students from two parallel classes in a junior high school in China were chosen randomly as the participants for this study. The students signed a consent form to participate, and eventually, 70 students participated voluntarily in this study, including 35 in the EG and 35 in the CG. All the students were native speakers of Chinese and they shared very similar English learning background.

3.2 Procedures

The pedagogical procedure that the students involved in can be illustrated as follows (Fig. 1):

For the EG, after vocabulary pretest, learners were asked to write a tweet about the given topic on the WeChat Official Account. In order to accomplish the task, they were allowed to search on the Internet to collect materials and then to design the writing format. Finally, learners would have an opportunity to share their tweets to others. For the CG, to write with pen and paper about the given topic, learners were also allowed to collect some materials on the Internet, and then to write the draft. After finishing the writing task, the vocabulary instant posttest and delayed posttest after two weeks were given to all the learners (Fig. 2).

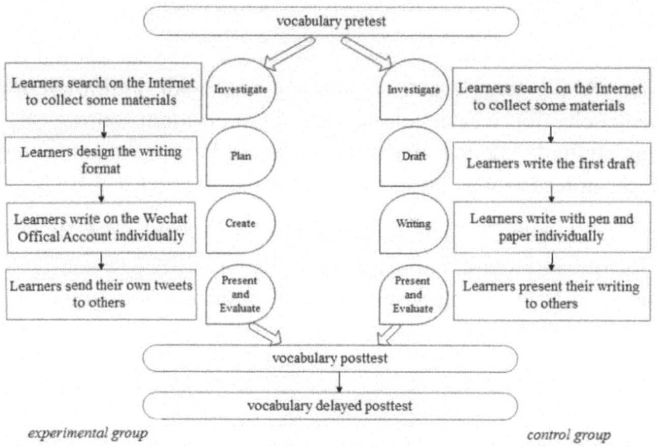

Fig. 1. Procedures of the research

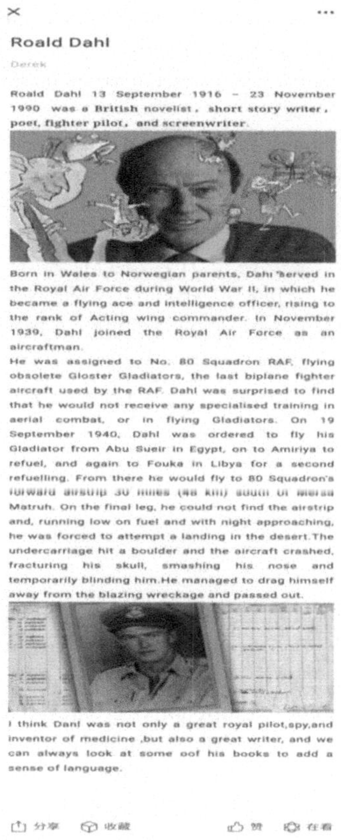

Roald Dahl

Derek

Roald Dahl 13 September 1916 – 23 November 1990 was a British novelist, short story writer, poet, fighter pilot, and screenwriter.

Born in Wales to Norwegian parents, Dahl "served in the Royal Air Force during World War II, in which he became a flying ace and intelligence officer, rising to the rank of Acting wing commander. In November 1939, Dahl joined the Royal Air Force as an aircraftman.

He was assigned to No. 80 Squadron RAF, flying obsolete Gloster Gladiators, the last biplane fighter aircraft used by the RAF. Dahl was surprised to find that he would not receive any specialised training in aerial combat, or in flying Gladiators. On 19 September 1940, Dahl was ordered to fly his Gladiator from Abu Sueir in Egypt, on to Amiriya to refuel, and again to Fouka in Libya for a second refuelling. From there he would fly to 80 Squadron's forward airstrip 30 miles (48 km) south of Mersa Matruh. On the final leg, he could not find the airstrip and, running low on fuel and with night approaching, he was forced to attempt a landing in the desert.The undercarriage hit a boulder and the aircraft crashed, fracturing his skull, smashing his nose and temporarily blinding him.He managed to drag himself away from the blazing wreckage and passed out.

I think Dahl was not only a great royal pilot,spy,and inventor of medicine ,but also a great writer, and we can always look at some oof his books to add a sense of language.

分享 收藏 赞 在看

Fig. 2. Learners' tweet

3.3 Tools

Vocabulary Test: A 30-item target vocabulary test with multiple-choice questions through purposely selection was developed and the binominal scoring of 1 (correct) and 0 (incorrect) was applied. The test items were piloted before the actual implementation and the Cronbach alpha (α) was .808, indicating that the test had high reliability.

Questionnaire: see Appendix. The Cronbach alpha of the overall scale was .884, indicating that the questionnaire had high reliability. In order to ensure the credibility of the questionnaires, these questionnaires adopted an anonymous method.

4 Results

4.1 Descriptive Statistics

Before addressing the first research question, an independent sample T-test was carried out on the pretest scores to determine differences between the English vocabulary level of these two groups before the experiment. Descriptive statistics (Table 2) showed that the initial vocabulary level of both groups of learners did not differ significantly. Therefore, it was reasonable to take these two groups as the objects of the experiment.

Table 2. The comparison of the pretest results between EG & CG

		EG		CG		t	*p*
		Mean	SD	Mean	SD		
Round 1	Score	25.229	2.510	25.171	2.738	0.910	0.928
	Form	9.143	1.192	9.029	1.071	0.422	0.674
	Meaning	9.257	0.98	9.286	1.017	−0.120	0.905
Round 2	Use	6.829	1.295	6.857	1.478	−0.086	0.932
	Score	21.971	4.322	21.686	4.726	0.264	0.793
	Form	8.400	1.519	8.371	1.61	0.076	0.939
	Meaning	7.686	1.906	7.314	1.906	0.815	0.418
	Use	5.886	1.952	6.000	2.156	−0.232	0.817

4.2 Intervention Effects

From the Table 3, we can see that the learners' vocabulary had been obviously improved. The EG improved from pretest to instant posttest in vocabulary use, and the results were significant ($t = -2.414$, $p < .05$; $t = -2.123$, $p < .05$). What' s more, the scores of delayed posttest were significantly greater than that of the pretest ($t = -7.443$, $p < .01$; $t = -4.954$, $p < .01$), especially in vocabulary use ($t = -8.300$, $p < .01$; $t = -6.000$, $p < .01$).

As shown in Table 4, the CG improved from pretest to instant posttest, but the results were insignificant. The scores of delayed posttest were significantly greater than that of the pretest ($t = -6.083$, $p < .01$; $t = -4.021$, $p < .01$), but the improvement of vocabulary meaning in Round 1 was insignificant.

Table 3. The results of the pretest and posttest of EG

		Pretest		Instant posttest		t	*p*	Delayed posttest		t	*p*
		Mean	SD	Mean	SD			Mean	SD		
Round 1	Score	25.229	2.510	26.486	2.650	−1.815	.078	28.600	1.063	−7.443	.000*
	Form	9.143	1.192	9.314	1.051	−.601	.552	9.742	0.443	−2.708	.011*
	Meaning	9.257	0.980	9.429	0.739	−.757	.454	9.829	0.453	−3.353	.002*
Round 2	Use	6.829	1.295	7.743	1.578	−2.414	.021*	9.029	0.857	−8.300	.000*
	Score	21.971	4.322	24.086	2.801	−2.136	.040*	25.914	2.914	−4.954	.000*
	Form	8.400	1.519	8.771	0.973	−1.053	.300	9.114	0.932	−2.581	.014*
	Meaning	7.686	1.906	8.429	1.243	−1.725	.094	8.514	1.147	−2.39	.023*
	Use	5.886	1.952	6.886	1.728	−2.123	.041*	8.286	1.466	−6.000	.000*

* means there is significant difference ($p < .05$).

Table 4. The results of the pretest and posttest of CG

		Pretest		Instant posttest		t	*p*	Delayed posttest		t	*p*
		Mean	SD	Mean	SD			Mean	SD		
Round 1	Score	25.171	2.738	25.971	2.955	−1.213	0.233	28.200	1.346	−6.083	.000*
	Form	9.029	1.071	9.200	0.994	−0.734	0.468	9.657	0.725	−2.75	.009*
	Meaning	9.286	1.017	9.457	0.852	−0.745	0.461	9.543	0.701	−1.358	.183
Round 2	Use	6.857	1.478	7.314	1.811	−1.207	0.236	9.000	0.686	−7.695	.000*
	Score	21.686	4.726	23.371	4.863	−1.554	0.129	25.514	3.776	−4.021	.000*
	Form	8.371	1.610	8.686	1.549	−0.828	0.414	9.057	1.162	−2.24	.032*
	Meaning	7.314	1.906	7.600	2.199	−0.654	0.518	8.400	1.519	−2.918	.006*
	Use	6.000	2.156	7.086	2.020	−2.302	.028*	8.057	1.999	−3.931	.000*

* means there is significant difference ($p < .05$).

Table 5. The comparison of the posttest results between EG & CG

			EG		CG		t	*p*
			Mean	SD	Mean	SD		
Round 1	Instant posttest	Score	26.486	2.650	25.971	2.955	0.766	0.446
		Form	9.314	1.051	9.200	0.994	0.467	0.642
		Meaning	9.429	0.739	9.457	0.852	−0.150	0.881
		Use	7.743	1.578	7.314	1.811	1.055	0.295
	Delayed posttest	Score	28.600	1.063	28.200	1.346	1.380	0.172
		Form	9.742	0.443	9.657	0.725	0.597	0.553
		Meaning	9.829	0.453	9.543	0.701	2.026	0.047
		Use	9.028	0.857	9.000	0.686	0.154	0.878
Round 2	Instant posttest	Score	24.086	2.801	23.371	4.863	0.753	0.454
		Form	8.771	0.973	8.686	1.549	0.277	0.782
		Meaning	8.429	1.243	7.600	2.199	1.940	0.056
		Use	6.886	1.728	7.086	2.02	−0.445	0.658
	Delayed posttest	Score	25.914	2.914	25.514	3.776	0.496	0.621
		Form	9.114	0.932	9.057	1.162	0.227	0.821
		Meaning	8.514	1.147	8.400	1.519	0.355	0.723
		Use	8.286	1.467	8.057	1.999	0.545	0.587

Table 5 showed that, the mean value of the instant posttest of the EG was higher than that of the CG, except for the vocabulary meaning in Round 1 and vocabulary use in Round 2. However, the mean value of the delayed posttest of the EG was higher than that of the CG in all aspects. There was not an obvious difference in the grades of instant posttest or delayed posttest between the EG and the CG.

4.3 Attitudes

Table 6. The statistical result of questionnaire

Question	Total disagree		Disagree		Not sure		Agree		Total agree		Mean
	N	P	N	P	N	P	N	P	N	P	
1	0	0%	0	0%	2	5.17%	16	45.17%	17	48.57%	4.43
2	0	0%	0	0%	4	11.43%	13	37.14%	18	51.43%	4.4
3	0	0%	0	0%	3	8.57%	12	34.29%	20	57.14%	4.49
4	0	0%	0	0%	2	5.71%	13	37.14%	20	57.14%	4.51
5	0	0%	0	0%	5	14.29%	11	31.43%	19	54.29%	4.4
6	0	0%	0	0%	5	14.29%	12	34.29%	18	51.43%	4.37
7	0	0%	1	2.86%	5	14.29%	12	34.29%	17	48.57%	4.29
8	0	0%	0	0%	7	20%	12	34.29%	16	45.17%	4.26
9	0	0%	0	0%	5	14.29%	12	34.29%	18	51.43%	4.37
10	0	0%	0	0%	3	8.57%	9	25.17%	23	65.71%	4.57
11	0	0%	0	0%	5	14.29%	13	37.14%	17	48.57%	4.34
12	0	0%	0	0%	1	2.86%	10	28.57%	24	68.57%	4.66
13	0	0%	0	0%	4	11.43%	12	34.29%	19	54.29%	4.43
14	0	0%	1	2.86%	4	11.43%	15	42.86%	15	42.86%	4.26
15	0	0%	1	2.86%	2	5.71%	8	22.86%	24	68.57%	4.57
16	0	0%	0	0%	9	25.71%	10	28.57%	16	45.71%	4.2
17	17	48.57%	12	34.29%	4	11.43%	0	0%	2	5.71%	1.8
18	15	42.86%	10	28.57%	4	11.43%	3	8.57%	3	8.57%	2.11

(N: Number P: Percentage)

Likert's five levels method was adopted to calculate the result of the questionnaires.

According to the statistics presented in Table 6, the average score of each first sixteen questions was higher than 4, and the support rates were all more than 70%. Therefore, it was believed that the WeChat Official Account tweet-based writing was basically supported by the students, as mentioned by most interviewees:

I like this way of writing, because I can learn many words from other classmates' tweets. (Student A)

I hope we can continue to write our own tweets. It is interesting. (Student G)

However, the average scores of Question 17 and Question 18 were both lower than 3, and the support rates were less than 18%. That means, most students disagreed that Official Account tweet-based writing is of little significance and a waste of time, though few students mentioned about its inconvenience in the interview.

5 Discussions

The improvement of the EG this study discerned can be attributed to the use of social networking which provides an effective learning context. Context is an important issue in second language vocabulary acquisition. Not only does it supply the necessary input; but if carefully chosen, it can also offer additional affective benefits. Yanan (2008) pointed out that applying the multimodality, such as combining images and texts, in foreign language teaching can provide learners with rich contextual information, so that they can understand and remember vocabulary effectively. WeChat Official Account tweet-based writing can combine images and texts well, so that learners can improve their literacy in multimodal environment and acquire vocabularies independently.

As for the CG, they improved their vocabulary acquisition in the delayed posttests but not the instant posttests, while the EC had improvement in vocabulary use in pretests. This may result from students' daily learning after the experiment (delayed posttests after two weeks).

Results showed that there was not an obvious difference in the grades of instant posttest or delayed posttest between the EG and the CG. One explanation for this is that some students in the EG may pay some attention to find pictures to beautify their tweets instead of focusing on writing only. Another possible explanation is that the experiment time is relatively short, so it is difficult to tell whether it would have a significant difference in the vocabulary acquisition (including vocabulary form, meaning and use) between the EG and the CG.

As a consequence, the results of questionnaire and interview further verified the positive effects of Official Account tweet-based writing. When engaging with multimodal writing, individuals chose what content to attend to, presumably leading to higher levels of motivation and allowing for individualization of the vocabulary acquired.

6 Conclusions

From the results presented above, we can see that Official Account tweet-based writing improves junior high school learners' English vocabulary acquisition. The students in the EG improves their vocabulary acquisition significantly from pretest to instant posttest in vocabulary use. Moreover, their improvements are obviously greater in delayed posttests, especially in vocabulary use.

Combining questionnaires and interviews, the current study finds that EFL learners are supportive of multimodal writing. It appears that Official Account tweet-based writing can be effective to attract junior high school learners' interest in writing and improve their vocabulary learning motivation.

Limited by some objective conditions, the study need be further improved. For example, there are only two rounds of writing. To obtain the long-term impact of the experiment on learners, more rounds of multimodal writing are needed.

Acknowledgments. This work is supported by the Center for Language Cognition and Assessment, South China Normal University. It's also the result of Guangdong "13th Five-Year" Plan Project of Philosophy & Social Science (GD20WZX01-02).

Appendix

Questionnaire

Dear all,

Hello! This questionnaire aims to investigate your views on Wechat Official Account tweet-based writing activities to promote vocabulary acquisition. This survey is conducted anonymously, and the answers you provide will be kept absolutely confidential. The data collected is used for research only and will not have any adverse effects on your academic performance and teachers' teaching.

Each number represents a different meaning, please tick√at the corresponding number.

1 = total disagree
2 = disagree
3 = not sure
4 = agree
5 = total agree

1. WeChat Official Account tweet-based writing enables me to remember the spelling of words more easily. 1 2 3 4 5

2. WeChat Official Account tweet-based writing enables me to use appropriate words for expression. 1 2 3 4 5

3. WeChat Official Account tweet-based writing enables me to learn more usage of vocabulary (such as collocation). 1 2 3 4 5

4. WeChat Official Account tweet-based writing enables me to acquire more writing words. 1 2 3 4 5

5. WeChat Official Account tweet-based writing enables me to understand and remember the meaning of words. 1 2 3 4 5

6. I can deepen my memory of vocabulary through the pictures in the WeChat Official Account tweets. 1 2 3 4 5

7. I can understand the writing words through the graphic information in the WeChat Official Account tweets. 1 2 3 4 5

8. Through the WeChat Official Account tweet-based writing, I can consciously avoid misusing the vocabulary . 1 2 3 4 5

9. Through the WeChat Official Account tweet-based writing, I was able to associate lots of related words according to a given topic. 1 2 3 4 5

10. I can find the words needed in the Official Account tweet-based writing through the Internet and use them correctly. 1 2 3 4 5

11. I can read relevant articles online to understand the authentic expression of vocabulary and apply them to tweet writing. 1 2 3 4 5

12. When I encounter a word that I do not understand in tweet writing, I will use the network resources to understand it. 1 2 3 4 5

13. Completing WeChat Official Account tweet-based writing makes me feel a sense of achievement. 1 2 3 4 5

14. WeChat Official Account tweet-based writing is more interesting than traditional paper-pen writing. 1 2 3 4 5

15. Personally, I like WeChat Official Account tweet-based writing. 1 2 3 4 5

16. WeChat Official Account tweet-based writing can be used as a routine session in English classroom teaching. 1 2 3 4 5

17. WeChat Official Account tweet-based writing is of little significance. 1 2 3 4 5

18. WeChat Official Account tweet-based writing is a waste of time. 1 2 3 4 5

References

Akdag, E., Özkan, Y.: Enhancing writing skills of EFL learners through blogging. Read. Matrix Int. Online J. **17**, 79–95 (2017)

Bingyan, Z., Shixiang, L.: Design and construction of higher vocational English teaching mode assisted by WeChat platform. China Educ. Technol. (z1), 95–98 (2016). https://doi.org/10.3969/j.issn.1006-9860.2016.z1.024

Biqing, L.: Exploration on the English writing training mode based on QQ network platform. Educ. Teach. Res. **24**(4), 102–104 (2010)
Bloch, J.: Abdullah's blogging: a generation 1.5 student enters the blogosphere. Lang. Learn. Technol. **11**(2), 128–141 (2007)
Changcheng, L.: Empirical study of using QQ platform to improve students' foreign language export ability. J. Heilongjiang Coll. Educ. **34**(3), 141–143 (2015)
Chawinga, W.D.: Taking social media to a university classroom: teaching and learning using Twitter and blogs. Int. J. Educ. Technol. High. Educ. **14**(1), 1–19 (2017). https://doi.org/10.1186/s41239-017-0041-6
Desselle, S.P.: The use of Twitter to facilitate engagement and reflection in a constructionist learning environment. Curr. Pharm. Teach. Learn. **9**, 185–194 (2017)
Ducate, L.C., Lomicka, L.L.: Adventures in the blogosphere: from blog readers to blog writers. Comput. Assist. Lang. Learn. **21**(1), 9–28 (2008)
Edwards-Groves, C.J.: The multimodal writing process: changing practices in contemporary classrooms. Lang. Educ. **25**(1), 49–64 (2011)
Dagiuklas, T., Politis, C.: Guest editorial. Telecommun. Syst. **53**(3), 263–264 (2013). https://doi.org/10.1007/s11235-013-9696-z
Hao, B., Jingjing, H.: The application of WeChat public platform in the field of college education. Chinese J. ICT Educ. **04**, 78–81 (2013)
Hill, M., Laufer, B.: Type of task, time-on-task and electronic dictionaries in incidental vocabulary acquisition. IRAL **41**(2), 87–106 (2003)
Hill, R., He, X.: The role of modified input and output in the incidental acquisition of word meanings. SSLA **21**(2), 285–301 (1999)
Hong, L., Qinxiang, T.: Study of second language vocabulary incidental acquisition. Foreign Lang. Educ. **3**, 54–58 (2005)
Huckin, T., Coady, J.: Incidental vocabulary acquisition in a second language: a review. SSLA **21**(2), 181–193 (1999)
Hulstijn, J.H.: Retention of given and inferred word meanings: experiments in incidental vocabulary learning. In: Arnaud, P.J.L., Bejoint, H. (eds.) Vocabulary and Applied Linguistics, pp. 113–125. Macmillan, London (1992)
Hulstijn, J.H., Laufer, B.: Some empirical evidence for the involvement load hypothesis in vocabulary acquisition. Lang. Learn. **51**(3), 539–558 (2001)
Hulstijn, J.H., Holander, M., Greidanus, T.: Incidental vocabulary learning by advanced foreign language students: the influence of marginal glosses, dictionary use, and reoccurrence of unknown words. Mod. Lang. J. **80**(3), 327–339 (1996)
Jianchun, D.: Construction and application of interactive extracurricular translation teaching mode based on QQ network platform. Comput.-Assist. Foreign Lang. Educ. **3**, 61–66 (2011)
Knight, S.: Dictionary use while reading: the effects on comprehension and vocabulary acquisition for students of different verbal abilities. Mod. Lang. J. **78**(3), 285–299 (1994)
Lang, S.: College English listening teaching and thinking based on social media. J. Chengdu Univ. **33**(6), 26–29 (2017)
Lewis, B.: The Lexical Approach. Language Teaching Publications, London (1993)
Minge, P.: Construction of extra-curricular spoken English context-training spoken English with a QQ group. Educ. Rev. **2**, 99–102 (2010)
Nation, I.S.P.: Learning Vocabulary in Another Language. Cambridge University Press, UK (2001)
The New London Group: A pedagogy of multiliteracies: designing social futures. Harv. Educ. Rev. **66**(1), 60–93 (1996)

Paribakht, T.S., Wesche, M.: Vocabulary enhancement activities and reading for meaning in second language vocabulary acquisition. In: Coady, J., Huckin, T. (eds.) Second Language Vocabulary Acquisition, pp. 175–199. Cambridge University Press, London (1997)
Paribakht, T.S., Wesche, M.: Reading and incidental L2 vocabulary acquisition: an introspective study of lexical inferencing. SSLA **21**(2), 195–224 (1999)
Quanyou, R.: Cultivation of students' critical thinking skills based on QQ community. Comput. Assist. Foreign Lang. Educ. **3**, 48–54 (2014)
Tang, Y., Hew, K.F.: Using Twitter for education: beneficial or simply a waste of time? Comput. Educ. **106**, 97–118 (2017)
Teimournezhad, S., Sotoudehnama, E., Marandi, S.S.: Exploring the effect of paper-and-pencil vs. Blog JW on L2 writing in terms of accuracy, fluency, lexical complexity, and syntactic complexity. J. Engl. Lang. Teach. Learn. **12**, 289–321 (2020)
Wang, H.C.: Using weblogs as peer review platform in an EFL writing class. In: Proceedings of the 24th Conference on English Teaching and Learning, pp. 400–413. Taiwan ELT Publishing Co., Ltd., Taipei (2007)
Yanan, K.: Multimodal discourse analysis and foreign language vocabulary teaching. J. Lang. Lit. Stud. **23**, 154–156 (2008)
Yinjian, J.: The experimental research of English reading teaching supported by the WeChat public platform. Comput. Assist. Foreign Lang. Educ. **3**, 58–63 (2016)

Online Statistics Teaching-Assisted Platform with Interactive Web Applications Using R Shiny

Junjie Liu, Yuhui Deng, and Xiaoling Peng(✉)

Department of Statistics, Devision of Science and Technology, BNU-HKBU United International College, Zhuhai, China
xlpeng@uic.edu.cn

Abstract. The study of uncertainty is one of the essential parts of statistics, but not easy for students to understand especially in elementary statistical classes. With the rise of new technologies and media, it is worthwhile to think about how to promote innovation in class teaching combining these new technologies with online platforms. In this article, we develop a collection of dynamic interactive web-based applications with Shiny package based on our textbook "Modern Elementary Statistics". The online and interactive teach-assisted platform seeks to facilitate conceptual understanding of the main aspects of elementary statistics, such as data description, statistical distributions, statistical inferences, and regression analysis. As the platform is affiliated with the textbook, it can ease the teaching and learning of important theorems and techniques for introductory probability and statistics.

Keywords: Statistics education · Online teaching-assisted platform · Interactive interface · Shiny app

1 Introduction

The application of statistics has become more and more extensive in our daily life, for instance, population census, marketing, risk management, ecological monitoring, psychological research, big data information mining and analysis, etc. Statistics has become a required course for many majors. However, with simply a blackboard and a slide, some statistical concepts, for example, random sampling, hypothesis testing, and spatio-temporal data mining, are commonly seen difficult for students to grasp intuitively. With the integration of computer technology, statistics courses can be more lively and interesting, computer simulations and visualizations can be illustrated basic concepts such as randomness, sampling, and variability.

This work is supported by Guangdong Natural Science Foundation No. 2018A0303130231.

W. Jia et al. (Eds.): SETE 2021, LNCS 13089, pp. 84–91, 2021.
https://doi.org/10.1007/978-3-030-92836-0_8

Multiple teaching-assisted toolkits are publicly available in GitHub and other code sharing platforms. Despite numerous existing interactive-oriented teaching tools, instructors may encounter problems in finding a suitable one as most of those tools are customized, and they are not perfectly fit to the textbook.

In this work, we develop a dynamic and interactive teaching-assisted platform using the R-based web framework, Shiny. This platform is affiliated to the textbook "Modern Elementary Statistics" (in Chinese) [3], and it can help students to better understand statistical theorem and provides convenience for instructors in teaching. We believe this approach forms a complete collection of the interactive system and establish a multidimensional practical teaching mode of introductory statistics.

2 Background and Feasibility Analysis

Many instructors start to use teaching assistant tools, for example, MS Excel and Java/JavaScript applets [6], to facilitate the technology-assisted instruction. With the Office VBA (Visual Basic for Applications), users can expand the function of Excel by writing add-ins. Gordon et al. [4] has developed multiple Excel-based applications, such as coin flipping and dice rolling, to help students understand the randomness and simulation of probability. Wu [10] takes Office 2007 and Office 2010 as examples to explain in detail the built-in statistical functions in Excel and shows some examples on how to use Excel's intuitive interface, excellent calculation function and charting tools for visual teaching.

For recent years, some instructors tried to use R and Python to develop teaching-assisted application [11]. There are many toolkits for statistics and data visualization in both R and Python, such as data.frame (R), pandas (Python), ggplot2 (R), Matplotlib (Python), etc., which are suitable for professionals to use.

Shiny, is an R-based Web framework developed by RStudio [12]. It does not require developers to be frontend and backend framework experts, but with a basic knowledge of R, which is very friendly to researchers in statistics/data science. Developers can integrate other powerful statistical toolkits in R under the Shiny framework, and Shiny can help manage the layout and data storage. The main architecture of a Shiny app includes two components: a server script (*server.R*) and a user-interface script (*ui.R*). The *server.R* is the backend of the application by providing computation components and the *ui.R* is the frontend of the application. For deploying a Shiny app, Rstudio provides a public shiny-server[1], where users can publish the Shiny app on a public server with both free and paid edition; An alternative is to deploy a Shiny app on a self-hosted shiny server. Other than the choices above, users can also pack their code into a Docker environment, which is convince for code sharing and application deploying.

More and more instructors and institutes are trying to use Shiny. The Statistics Online Computational Resource (SOCR) platform held by University of California, Los Angeles and University of Michigan has been updated from Java

[1] https://shinyapp.io/.

applet to Shiny [1,8], recently. The Statistics Department of California State Polytechnic University has also configured Shiny server and built a Shiny-based visual education platform. Lee Fawcett, from the Newcastle University London (NCL), introduced teaching innovation with the Shiny toolkit as a teaching aid in his undergraduate course MAS8306 [5].

Considered the above advantages, our textbook oriented teaching-assisted platform is also built based on the Shiny package.

3 Four Illustrative Applications

In this section, we introduce several applications in our platform. These applications are developed on those statistics topics which are not intuitive without dynamic demonstrations. For example, how data distribution changes over time and space, the impact of the different parameters on the location and shape of statistical distributions, how the confidence interval for the population mean and population proportion change with the sample, correlations between variables, and the impact of outliers on the regression model, etc.

3.1 Spatio-Temporal Data Visualization

In the past, most data description methods are built on static graphs such as bar chart, pie chart, histogram and box plot. Now with the emergence of new technologies, the dynamic display of how spatial data distribution change over time becomes feasible. As an extension of basic data description, the spatio-temporal data visualization is one of the hot topic in the field of big data analysis in recent years. Since 2020, the Covid-19 epidemic has swept almost all countries and regions in the world and consequently accelerated the changes in every aspect of our life. Under this circumstance, the spread of COVID-19 in the world in these two years becomes an attractive example for visualizing the spatio-temporal data.

Multiple packages and API has been developed in a short time providing worldwide aggregated COVID-19 data set. Most famously, Johns Hopkins University [2] provides open-source aggregated data in their GitHub repository[2]. Other researchers such as Wu and Yu [9] also developed an R package[3] on Covid-19 data aggregation.

In our platform we use the Wu's R package as our data source and generate multiple graphs to visualize the data. As it is shown in Fig. 1, users can easily do the comparison between different countries on total cases, total death, total recovered, and daily case curve. Our application also allows the user to draw the daily global heat map, so that the trend and pattern of the global epidemic development can be understood at a glance. This heat map (shown in Fig. 2) can help us to have a clear judgment and understanding of the development and control of the epidemic among different countries.

[2] GitHubrepository: https://github.com/CSSEGISandData/COVID-19.

[3] R package: nCov2019, https://cran.r-project.org/web/packages/nCov2019/index.html.

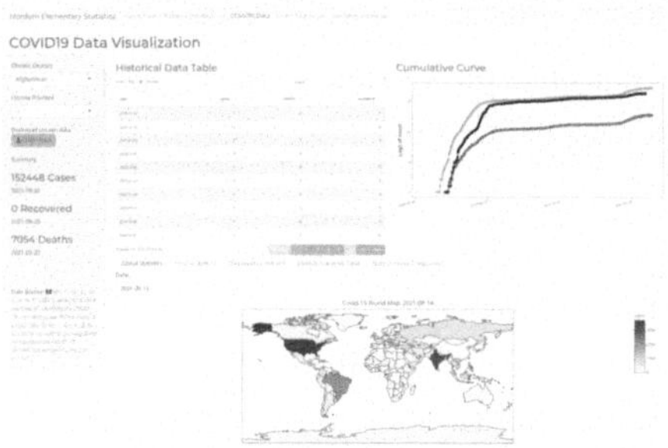

(a) COVID-19 data: basic statistics

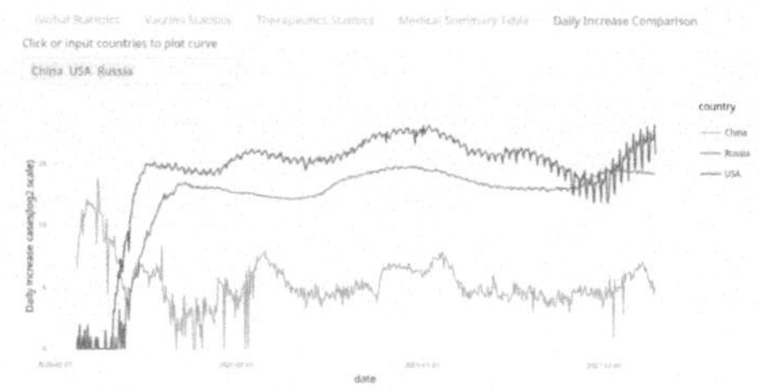

(b) Comparison of logarithmic COVID-19 daily cases

Fig. 1. Covid-19 data visualization

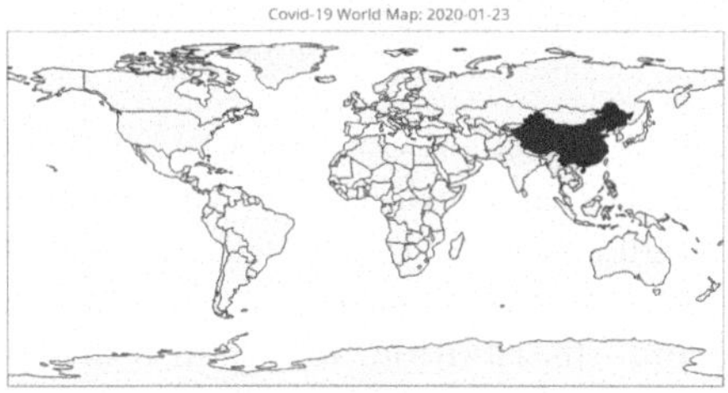

(a) 2020-01-23

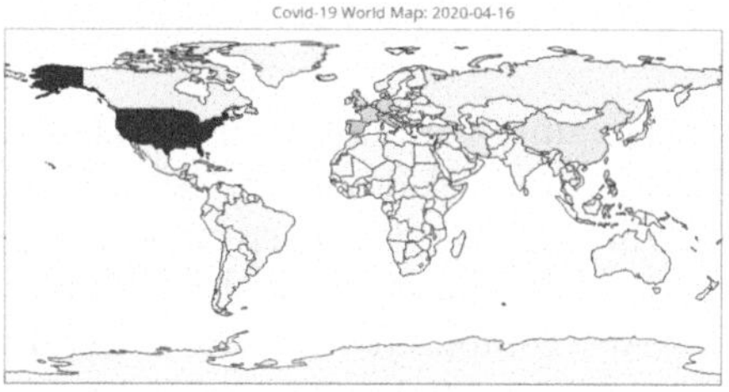

(b) 2020-04-26

(c) 2020 12 25

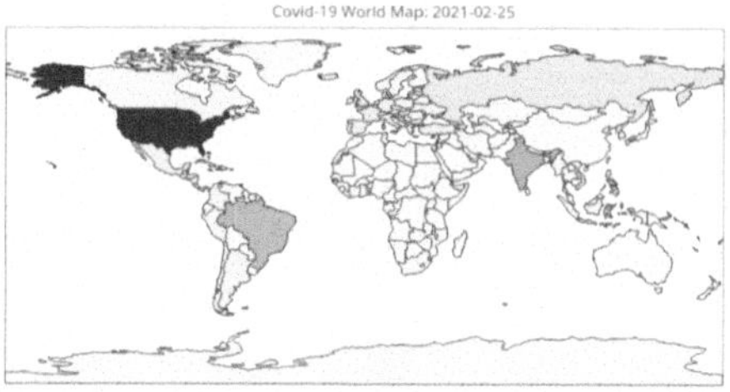

(d) 2021 02 25

Fig. 2. Spatio-temporal data visualization: the spread of Covid-19 in the world

3.2 Statistical Distributions

In statistics, random variables and their distributions were developed and used to describe and study various uncertainties. Each statistical distribution has its own characteristics, even the distributions in the same family will behave differently due to different parameters. Our application will help in teaching and learning statistical distributions when probability density curves were added and compared interactively. For now, the application has included most commonly used continuous distributions and discrete distributions (shown in Table 1).

Table 1. Commonly used statistical distributions

Continuous distribution	Normal distribution
	Student t distribution
	Beta distribution
	Gamma distribution
	Chi-squared distribution
Discrete distribution	Binomial distribution
	Geometric distribution
	Poisson distribution

An example of normal distribution is shown in Fig. 3. The user can set mean (μ) and standard deviation (σ) for the normal distribution, then the application will generate the corresponding probability density curve in real time, so that the user can capture the features of the given distribution on the location and scale, compared with the standard normal distribution, and gain a deeper understanding of the parameters' impacts.

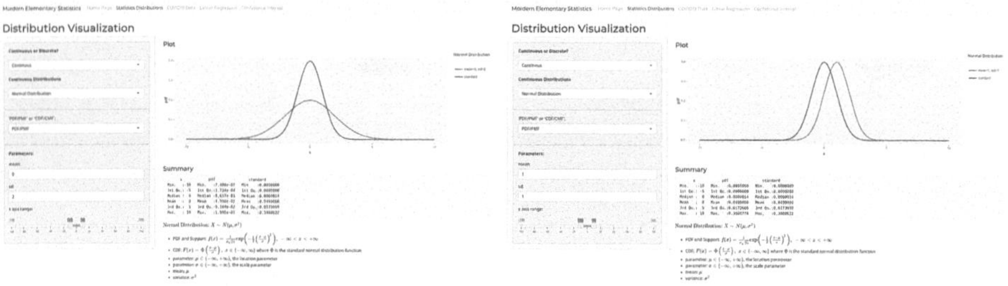

(a) $\mu = 0,\ \sigma = 2$ (b) $\mu = 1,\ \sigma = 1$

Fig. 3. Probability density function of normal distribution

3.3 Confidence Interval

Statistical inference is a method of describing sample data, inferring the unknown parameters of a population in the probabilistic form. In elementary statistics, statistical inference includes hypothesis testing and parameter estimation, where the estimation can be further divided into point estimation and interval estimation (shown in Fig. 4). In this application, we focus on the interval estimation that provide an interval (confidence interval) for the estimation of interested population parameter based on sample statistics. Due to the randomness of the sample, there is a probability (confidence level) that the computed interval will cover the true parameter.

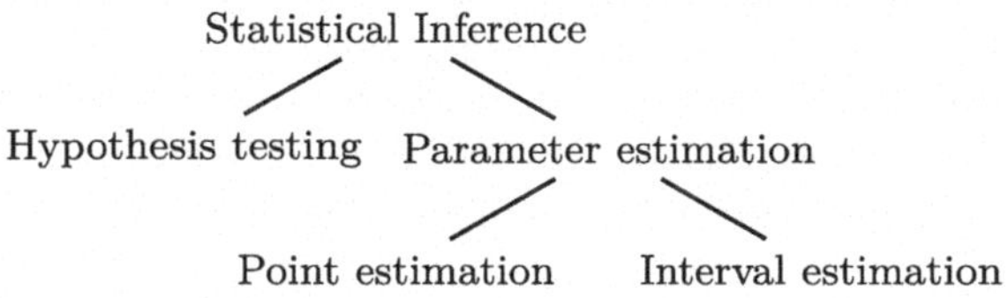

Fig. 4. Statistical inference

To help students understand these important concepts, our application computes and displays 95% confidence interval for any given sample mean under the population mean($\mu = 31.5$) and standard deviation ($\sigma = 0.8$) according to our textbook example (see Fig. 5). In case the sample mean is too small or too large, the generated confidence interval will not cover the population mean, then the estimation fail with a probability 5%.

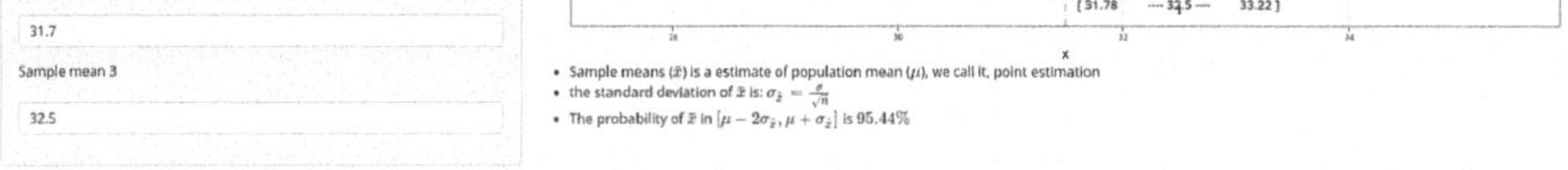

Fig. 5. Confidence interval

3.4 Linear Regression

Linear regression is a long-established statistical method, which has been widely used in variety of fields ranging from natural science, social science and business. It is a scientifically reliable method for learning and describing the correlation between the response variable and explanatory variables. In elementary statistics, we introduce some important topics related to linear regression including least square criteria and model diagnosis.

To illustrate these ideas in linear regression, the application generates multiples regression plots, such as Residuals vs Fitted plot, Residual QQ plot, Scale-

Location plot, and Residuals vs Leverage plot, which are largely used to validate the linear regression's assumptions[4] [7].

To illustrate the influence of outliers to the regression line, the application also provides an interactive widget that allows users to remove the data point and recalculate the linear model. This can help them to understand how each sample contribute to the model and what influence may be caused. Users can select the data points that they want to exclude (shown in Fig. 6b, where three data points located in the upper-left corner are removed), by clicking the "toggle out" button, the results and plots would update automatically. By comparing the results before and after removing, users can clearly see the impact of each sample point on the model and have a better understanding of least squares criteria.

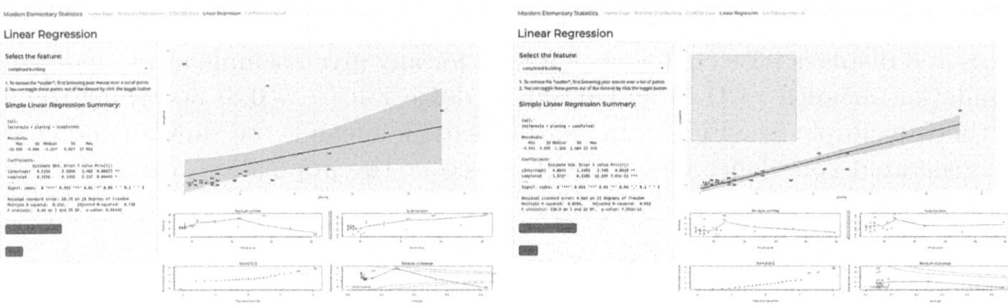

(a) Model with all data points (b) Model excludes selected data

Fig. 6. Simple linear regression

For now, our platform mainly includes 4 applications. In the future, more applications will be added into this platform, such as ANOVA, hypothesis testing and some non-parametric methods, to fulfill the instructor's requirement.

4 Discussion

We use the R web framework Shiny to develop illustrative interactive applications in our teaching-assisted platform. Based on our textbook "Modern Elementary Statistics", a complete, systematic set of probability and statistics multidimensional practice teaching mode is established, as well as an interactive teaching system. This integration of web assisted platform can help students gradually understand the essence of statistics from dynamic statistical charts, achieve a firmer grasp on the concept, and be able to interpret data and make scientific decisions based on a random sample.

[4] 1. Linearity (Residuals vs. Fitted plot) 2. Homogeneity of variance (Scale-Location plot) 3. Independence 4. Normality (Normal QQ plot).

This platform plays an important role in the multimedia teaching. Since the platform is textbook-based, lecturer can show the textbook examples dynamically via the web application during the class, or generate a GIF files[5] or static figures and embed them into the slides.

An empirical research will be conducted to evaluate the performance of using this platform in improving students' understanding in statistical concept with a well-known questionnaire "The Survey of Attitudes Toward Statistics" [13]. This questionnaires measures six aspects of student's attitudes towards statistics, includes affect, cognitive competence, value, difficulty, interest, and effort[6]. The students' test scores will also be compared to verify the effectiveness of this platform.

We will open source our codes to all the readers for their teaching and learning as soon as the platform set up is completed. Since this platform is mainly designed for Chinese college student for statistics learning, it supports two languages: Chinese and English.

References

1. Dinov, I., Sanchez, J., Christou, N.: Pedagogical utilization and assessment of the statistic online computational resource in introductory probability and statistics courses. Comput. Educ. **50**, 284–300 (2008)
2. Dong, E., Du, H., Gardner, L.: An interactive web-based dashboard to track COVID-19 in real time. Lancet Infect. Dis. **20**, 533–534 (2020)
3. Fang, K., Peng, X.: Modern Elementary Statistics. Higher Education Press, Beijing (2014)
4. Gordon, S., Gordon, F.: Visualizing and understanding probability and statistics: graphical simulations using excel. Primus **19**, 346–369 (2009)
5. Fawcett, L.: Using interactive shiny applications to facilitate research-informed learning and teaching. J. Stat. Educ. **26**, 2–16 (2018)
6. McDaniel, S., Green, L.: Using applets and video instruction to foster students' understanding of sampling variability. Technol. Innov. Stat. Educ. **6** (2012)
7. Montgomery, D., Peck, E., Vining, G.: Introduction to Linear Regression Analysis. Wiley, Hoboken (2021)
8. Potter, G., Wong, J., Alcaraz, I., Chi, P., et al.: Web application teaching tools for statistics using R and shiny. Technol. Innov. Stat. Educ. **9** (2016)
9. Wu, T., Hu, E., Ge, X., Yu, G.: nCov2019: an R package for studying the COVID-19 coronavirus pandemic. PeerJ **9**, e11421 (2021)
10. Wu, Z., Wei, W., Shui, Q., Wang, Z.: Application of excel in probability theory and mathematical statistics teaching. J. Gansu Norm. Coll. 54–58 (2020)
11. A study on the application of R in teaching probability theory and mathematical statistics. Technol. Econ. Guide 33–35+38 (2021)
12. Xie, Y., Allaire, J., Grolemund, G.: R Markdown: The Definitive Guide. CRC Press (2018)
13. Milic, N., et al.: The importance of medical students' attitudes regarding cognitive competence for teaching applied statistics: multi-site study and meta-analysis. PLoS One **11**, e0164439 (2016)

[5] GIF: Graphics Interchange Format.

[6] The full version of the survey and explanation can be founded via https://www.evaluationandstatistics.com/scoring.

Enhancing EFL Learners' English Speaking Performance Through Vlog-Based Digital Multimodal Composing Activities

Qianqian Zhang[1], Xiaobin Liu[1](✉), and Yuanyuan Chen[2]

[1] South China Normal University, Guangzhou, China
liuxiaobin@m.scnu.edu.cn
[2] Xiangjiang Yucai Experimental School, Guangzhou, China

Abstract. Both voice blogs and video blogs have been widely used in various fields, their applications in English as a foreign language (EFL) learning mostly in universities have been mainly to improve students' listening and speaking ability. Relatively few studies have explored how engaging EFL learners in making video blogs might help advance their speaking performance. This study therefore is an investigation of the effects of making voice and video blogs on EFL learners' speaking performance and of their perceptions of vlog-based digital multimodal composing (DMC). Sixty-seven middle school students from Guangdong, China were recruited in this ten-week exploratory study. Data included their pretest and posttest speaking scores, two vlog recordings, questionnaire, and semi-structured interview. The results of this study testified vlog-based DMC's positive influences on speaking performance and indicated that from their first to second vlogs, the students had performed better fluency. Also, video blog-making EFL learners outperformed its counterparts regarding accuracy, while under-performed in fluency in which they demonstrated some significant changes. Pedagogical implications and recommendations for future research are discussed.

Keywords: Vlog · EFL learners · English speaking · CAF · Multimodal composing

1 Introduction

With the surging proliferation of technology in the twenty-first century, emerging technological tools have been adopted to benefit language teaching and learning owning to its effectiveness (Alsied and Pathan 2013), authenticity (Wang 2005), and convenience (Chang et al. 2012). Among them, video blogs (hereinafter refers to as vlogs in this part) are deemed as an effective, authentic and convenient technological learning approach to exposing EFL learners to the target language with no limits of time and space (Jiang 2020). Considering its advantage and availability in EFL teaching and learning, many researchers throughout the world have investigated its effectiveness in language instruction. Aydin (2014) found that vlogs could increase opportunities for interaction between students and language, and between students and students. In addition, the production of vlogs required students to inquire about

W. Jia et al. (Eds.): SETE 2021, LNCS 13089, pp. 92–103, 2021.
https://doi.org/10.1007/978-3-030-92836-0_9

materials and also provided a cooperative learning environment, which helped to cultivate students' meta-cognitive strategies and sense of ownership (Chuang and Rosenbusch 2005; Dzekoe 2017). The production process of vlogs could truly be student-centered and provided every student with equal opportunities to participate in class (Mutmainna 2016), and transform students from passive learners to autonomous language learners (Dzekoe 2017). Also, Jiang (2020) proposed that vlog-making was a typical multimodal composing activities collection of integrated texts, pictures and videos and an effective way to cultivate students to process information, improve their multiple literacy skills and innovation abilities.

What's more, especially in the area of English as lingua franca, researches have been conducted with positive implications. Nikitina (2010) found that in order to convey ideas clearly and correctly in videos, language learners paid more attention to their own language pronunciation. Meyer and Forester (2015) believed that using video blogs as a learning medium helped students improve oral skills; in addition, it could enrich students' knowledge about vocabulary, grammar, pronunciation, accent and culture. At the same time, to present video scenes more realistically, students tended to use authentic spoken English instead of more formal English in writing for students thought that vlogs were more relevant to their daily lives and they spoke English in real life (Dukhayel Aldukhayel 2019). Among these studies which solely intended to investigate EFL students' speaking progress, more attempts should be made to investigate EFL students' vlog-making processes and their perceived advantages and disadvantages in making vlogs.

Accordingly, the present study was an exploration of vlog-based digital multimodal composing (DMC in short) activities' impact on Chinese middle school students' English-speaking performance (complexity, accuracy and fluency; CAF) and understanding of their perceptions and attitudes of vlog-based DMC.

2 Previous Studies of Vlog-Based English Teaching and Learning

Multimodal Composing (MC), refers to the design of multiple symbol resources including language and other modes (such as images, sounds, and videos) into texts for expression and communication (Kress 2003; Kress and Van Leeuwen 2001; Prior 2013; Prior and Thorne 2014). While Digital Multimodal Composing (DMC) is a new type of composing activity in the information age. It is an instruction activity designed to allow students to use digital tools to interweave text with other symbolic patterns (such as images, sounds, and motions) (Hafner 2015; Belcher 2017).

Researchers explored the effectiveness in learners' English ability by assigning different types of MC tasks, like writing practice (Barton and Lee 2012), comic creation (Kilickaya F. and Krajka J. 2012), digital narrative (Wales 2012), video production (Jiang 2017), and picture book creation (Stranger-Johannessen and Norton 2017). In addition, scholars have also analyzed the educational function of MC, such as practicing English writing and oral English (Hafner 2014), providing learners with more authentic writing opportunities (Harman ands Shin 2018), cultivating English speaking skills (Hepple and Sockhill 2014), opening up students' with writing difficulties knowledge sharing and self-expression channels (Shin and Cimasko 2008), raising learners' audience awareness (Cimasko, Shin 2017), cultivating learners' autonomous learning ability, language expression ability and genre awareness (Belcher 2017; Yi et al. 2019) and helping learners with self-reflection (Dzekoe 2017). In addition, Hafner and Ho (2020) summarized the process-based multimodal evaluation model through interviews with 7 teachers.

In terms of DMC, positive conclusions have also been drawn by researchers from different perspectives. Jiang et al. (2019) implemented a year-long case study on a college English teacher and stated that DMC teaching activities can help diversify teachers' identities, realize student-centered classrooms, and improve students class participation enthusiasm (Jiang 2017). In addition, Jiang (2017) analyzed the technical, educational and social functions of DMC through interviews and reflective diaries, and explained its positive impact on the language learning of EFL learners. Jiang and other scholars (2020) also applied DMC activities to ethnic minority students, explored and found that DMC was beneficial to provide more English oral language training opportunities, fostering students' sense of cooperation and other favorable influences.

Vlog-making is a typical MC activity in which learners experience the organization and distribution of language, audio, video, picture, animation and other multimodal resources. Its positive influence on English teaching could be seen in, including improving students' literacy skills, especially understanding of narratives (Parker 2002); benefiting the development of students' higher-order thinking skills (Swain et al. 2003); providing authentic learning environment for learners (Schuck 2004); encouraging to apply learners' background knowledge and actively establish a connection between vocabulary acquisition and their own experiences (Pritchard and Nasr 2004). At the same time, it provided students with a positive learning process, so that they had enough sense of security and confidence to talk (Cao and Philp 2006; Kang 2005). Dzekoe (2017) believed that video production activities helped students become self-directed learners because they would work hard to practice pronunciation, expand vocabulary and apply accurate language structures, and continued to participate in repeated exercises so as to produce high-quality videos.

3 Research Design

3.1 Research Questions

The present study was guided by the following research questions (RQs):

RQ1. Do vlog-based digital multimodal composing activities help improve the English speaking of Chinese EFL students?

RQ2. If yes, what intervention effects do vlog-based digital multimodal composing activities have on the speaking, in terms of complexity, accuracy and fluency?

RQ3. What are EFL students' perceptions and attitudes towards vlog-based digital multimodal composing activities?

3.2 Participants

Participants for this study were 67, including 33 in experimental class (EC for short) and 34 in control class (CC for short) EFL learners recruited in a compulsory English class at a middle school. All students, receiving the same instructional contents given by the same instructor who has 7-year teaching experience each week, around 14–16 years old were non-native speakers of English; besides, all of them didn't have studying-abroad experiences in an English as a first language context. The conversation class met once a week for 40 min that was aimed at developing students' listening and speaking skills.

3.3 Instruments

Tests. The speaking test contains three parts including one item for "reading a text aloud", two for "responding to questions", and one for "paraphrasing a story". All scores were evaluated by machine automatically. Only total score (TS for short) was retrieved in this study.

Vlog-Based Recordings. Two topics were recorded by EFL learners from a Guangdong middle school, containing 'one day' and 'Spring Festival'. CAF analysis was adopted in EFL learners' vlog-based recordings and different items were chosen to investigate learners' speaking performance. For CAF (Skehan 1996), 'C' represents complexity, 'A' for accuracy, and 'F' for fluency. For complexity, lexical complexity was chosen and measured by LCA (Lexical Complexity Analyzer) using the indice of LV (Lexical variation). For accuracy, pronunciation accuracy was chosen and measured by percentage of error-free word pronunciation. As for fluency, it was measured in terms of number of syllables per minute (or speed rate, SR in short) within each video blog or voice blog entry was measured following the formula of the syllable number divided total speaking minutes duration. Figure 1 is the screenshot of a student' s video blog about Spring Festival.

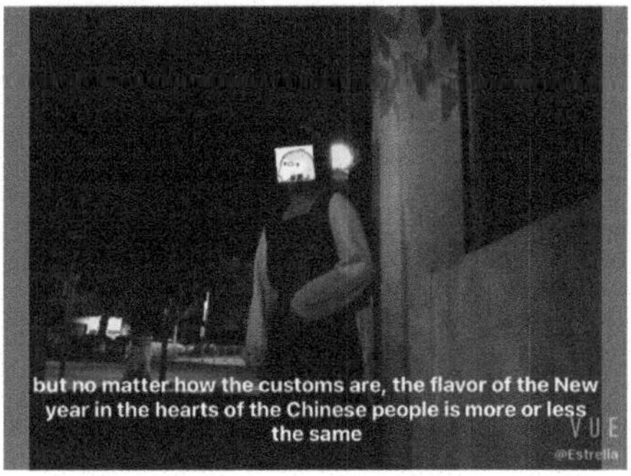

Fig. 1. Screenshot of one student' s video vlog

Questionnaire. Questionnaire designed in Likert Six Rating Scale (from 1, totally disagree to 6, totally agree) was distributed to and completed by students in EC after the experiment, containing four major sub-parts extracted from New Curriculum Standard published by China Education Ministry, namely language ability, thinking quality, learning ability and perceptions.

Semi-structured Interview. Semi-structured interview lasting for about 15 min each on average was conducted among 6 learners (2 top students, 2 average students and 2 underachievers randomly selected) from EC by one researcher under the guidance of revised interview outlines proposed by Chien et al. (2020).

3.4 Procedure

This study lasted for 10 weeks and detailed procedures can refer to Fig. 2 below. In the first week, the students took a speaking test as the pretest and the instructor gave instructions for making video blog on VUE software, a popular free video editing one, or voice blog on smart phones. From the second to fifth week, it was considered as learning period. Before the sixth week, the students made their own vlog episodes (video blog for EC and voice blog for CC) on one day by discussing, drafting, recording, and checking and uploaded them to the software or instructors directly. In the next four weeks, the students learned about Spring Festival. In the last week, two classes of students completed vlog-making about Chinese Spring Festival customs. What's more, all students took a speaking test as the posttest and those in EC accomplished questionnaire. In order to understand students' attitudes and perceptions deeply, 6 students from EC were randomly selected as targets to implement semi-structured interview to gain insights into how students prepared video blogs and their blogging experience.

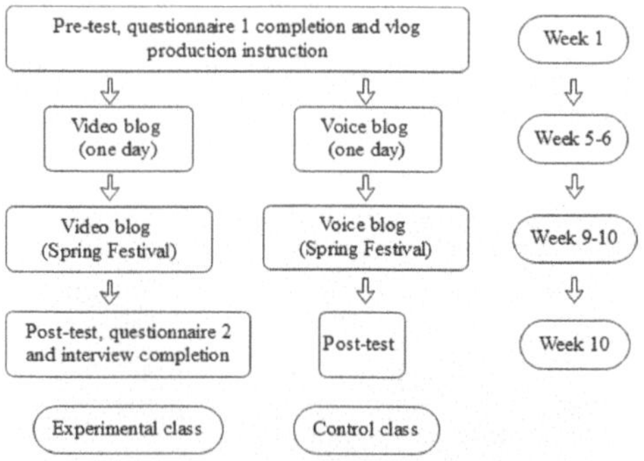

Fig. 2. Research procedures

3.5 Data Collection and Analysis

SPSS 25 software was used for analysis of variance ANOVA to ensure that there was no significant difference in the oral English level of the experimental class and the control class before the experiment and no significant differences were found. For RQ1, after experiment, independent-samples t test and paired-samples t test were also applied to test video blog and voice blog production activities' impacts on EFL learners' speaking performance based on their pretest and posttest speaking scores. As to RQ2, both video blogs and voice blogs were transcribed word by word for analysis. Due to limited human resources, just one item each under CAF is taken into consideration, including lexical complexity, pronunciation accuracy and speech rate. RQ3 was dealt with through the coding and analysis of the transcription of EC students' questionnaire results data and semi-structured interview materials.

4 Results and Discussion

4.1 Results of Effectiveness

The results of the paired sample t-test presented in Table 1 reveal a significant difference ($t = -3.02$, $p < .005$) between total scores (TA) of the speaking pretest ($M = 25.68$, $SD = 2.58$) and posttest ($M = 26.02$, $SD = 2.49$) in experimental class. For control class, a significant difference is also found from total scores in pretest to those in posttest with p value being .000, which means the students made progress in their speaking abilities with an average score gain of 1.37 in control class.

Table 1. Statistical results of the pretest and posttest speaking test for all the students

Scope (total score/TS)	Min	Max	Mean	SD	t	df	Sig. (2-tailed)
EC (N = 33)							
Pretest	17.41	28.39	25.68	2.58	−3.02	32	.005
Posttest	17.15	28.88	26.02	2.49			
CC (N = 34)							
Pretest	20.28	28.64	24.86	2.02	−4.61	33	.000
Posttest	21.64	28.76	26.23	1.85			

Independent-samples t-tests were conducted to figure out whether statistically significant differences existed between EC and CC after experiment. Unfortunately, no significant differences are captured, as is shown in Table 2. We can draw the conclusion that both two instruction tools benefited EFL learners' English performance; however, either of them exceeded the other in speaking scores.

4.2 Results of Speaking Complexity, Accuracy and Fluency

In answer to Research Question 2, paired-samples t-tests revealed a significant difference in EC between the second vlog (Weeks 9 and 10) posts and the first vlog (Weeks 5 and 6) entries being more complex than the second one in terms of accuracy ($t(33) = 2.648$, $p = .012$). Complexity and fluency, however, did not reveal a significant difference between the two video blog posts and for detailed data are listed in Table 3. Besides, for the control class, besides that a significant difference between the two voice blogs is observed in complexity ($t(34) = 2.667$, $p = .012$), in terms of accuracy with p value less than 0.01 (t(34) = 2.933, p = .006) negatively is found. And two classes improved in fluency despite not so significantly (Table 4).

Table 2. Statistical results of the post speaking test

	Mean (SD)		F value	t	Sig. (2-tailed)
	EC (N = 33)	CC (N = 34)			
Total score	26.02 (2.49)	26.23 (1.85)	.700	−.383	.703

Table 3. Difference in CAF between two video blogs

	N	Video blog1	Video blog2	t	p
		M (SD)	M (SD)		
EC					
Complexity	33	0.76 (.26)	0.66 (.29)	1.586	.123
Accuracy	33	0.97 (.04)	0.94 (.06)	2.648	.012
Fluency	33	131.71 (47.89)	143.59 (57.36)	−1.364	.182
CC					
Complexity	32	0.78 (.10)	0.73 (.10)	2.667	.012
Accuracy	34	0.91 (.05)	0.89 (.08)	2.933	.006
Fluency	34	172.76 (49.73)	179.59 (35.77)	−1.273	.212

Table 4. Statistics for the first assignment (one day)

	Mean (SD)		F	t	Sig. (2-tailed)
	EC (N = 33)	CC (N = 34)			
Complexity	0.76 (.26)	0.78 (.10)	6.493	−.433	.666
Accuracy	0.97 (.04)	0.91 (.05)	3.07	4.524	.000*
Fluency	131.71 (47.89)	172.76 (49.73)	.214	−3.441	.001*

Table 5. Statistics for the second assignment (Spring Festival)

	Mean (SD)		F	t	Sig. (2-tailed)
	EC (N = 33)	CC (N = 34)			
Complexity	0.66 (.29)	0.73 (.10)	11.61	−1.333	.187
Accuracy	0.94 (.06)	0.89 (.08)	5.08	3.185	.002*
Fluency	143.59 (57.36)	179.58 (35.77)	4.489	−3.092	.003*

In order to further explore whether significant differences occurring between the experimental class and control class, independent-samples t-tests were performed on all the CAF items (RQ2) measures between the fifth and tenth-week voice blog and video blog posts. However, Comparing CAF items in the first assignment of experimental class and those of control class, descriptive statistics presented in Table 5 point to that EC students exceeded the counterparts in terms of pronunciation accuracy (p = .000).

It's also worth mentioning that CC learners obviously gain higher scores in fluency with an average value of 172.76 than those EC learners with only 131.71 ($p = .001$). As for the second assignment, descriptive statistics illustrated in Table 6 indicate that the statistically significant differences between EC and CC with more favorable performances in terms of pronunciation accuracy ($p = .002$) and fluency ($p = .003$) separately.

4.3 Results of Questionnaire Survey and Semi-structured Interview

In answer to Research Question 3, Table 6 unveils the descriptive statistics obtained for students' attitudes towards video blog (vlog1) DMC activities, from which positive perceptions towards vlog1-making activities can be seen in many items, Although most EFL learners in EC affirm its effectiveness in English language ability, thinking ability and positive impacts on English language learning, when it comes to item 18, 56.52% of them chose not to adopt it in future English assignments.

Table 6. EC Students' attitudes towards the video blog production activities (N = 33)

Item	1	2	3	4	5	6	Mean
1. Improve language ability	2.17%	2.17%	10.87%	41.30%	21.74%	21.74%	4.43
2. Expand oral vocabulary	2.17%	4.35%	13.04%	39.13%	19.57%	21.74%	4.35
3. Care expression accuracy	2.17%	4.35%	10.87%	26.09%	32.61%	23.91%	4.54
4. Improve pronunciation	2.17%	0%	13.04%	26.09%	19.57%	39.13%	4.78
5. Care error-free grammar	2.17%	2.17%	17.39%	30%	20%	28%	4.48
6. Care expression coherence	2.17%	0%	13.04%	21.74%	36.96%	26.09%	4.7
7. Improve problem-solving ability	2.17%	2.17%	10.87%	30.43%	21.74%	32.61%	4.65
8. Improve information ability	2.17%	0%	17.39%	32.61%	21.74%	26.09%	4.5
9. Improve critical thinking	6.52%	2.17%	15.22%	23.91%	26.09%	26.09%	4.39
10. Improve meta-cognitive ability	4.35%	6.52%	13.04%	28.26%	19.57%	28.26%	4.37
11. Improve reflective ability	4.35%	0%	15.22%	34.78%	19.57%	26%	4.43
12. Increase English learning interests	6.52%	6.52%	13.04%	34.78%	17.39%	21.74%	4.15
13. Increase English learning motivation	4.35%	4.35%	19.57%	36.96%	17.39%	17.39%	4.11
14. Easy to make vlog1s	6.52%	6.52%	10.87%	26.09%	26.09%	23.91%	4.3
15. Reduce English speaking anxiety	4.35%	10.87%	15.22%	26.09%	21.74%	21.74%	4.15
16. Prefer vlog1 assignments	2.17%	10.87%	15.22%	43.48%	13.04%	15.22%	4
17. Experience English learning happiness	6.52%	8.70%	10.87%	34.78%	17.39%	21.74%	4.13
18. Prefer to adopt this learning tools	10.87%	13.04%	19.57%	24%	17.39%	15.22%	3.7

From data collected through semi-structured interviews from 6 students in EC, positive attitudes on vlog1-making production activities can also be observed. However, 2 of them stated that '*But I don't like it, because it's too time-consuming, complicated and I'm lazy. If it wasn't for homework assignment, I wouldn't do it again.*' Besides, 23% of interviewees hold that '*when recording vlog1, I will use some spoken language, and will use some simple colloquial expressions in it,*' which is similar to the research findings conducted by Dukhayel Aldukhayel (2019).

Effectiveness on Spoken English. Four admitted video blogs' positive effects on their spoken English (Nikitina 2010), and one of them said that, "*Especially in terms of pronunciation, the words cannot be read in an accurate way, I will practice repeatedly to focus on the accuracy of pronunciation*".

Clear-Cut Preparations. Most of interviewees affirmed that they would prepare for scripts before making vlogs, like "*Write the script first, then find the related materials. Practice English again and again, add subtitles at the end*".

Time-Consuming and Challenging. All complained it took plenty of time and energy to complete one and they encountered different problems during the process. One expressed, "*I didn't take pictures in the city; because of the epidemic*". Another shared that, "*I feel embarrassed to hold the camera to shoot vlog1, I don't like it.*"

Biggest Gains. Five of them thought that they gained much confidence (Cao and Philp 2006; Kang 2005), fun and sense of accomplishment through vlog-making process, saying "*Become more confident; have a sense of accomplishment*".

4.4 Discussion

The goal of the present study is to explore the potential of vlog-based digital multimodal composing (DMC) to help EFL learners improve their English speaking. As to RQ1, the above results of total score indicate that both voice blog and video blog-based DMC activities can significantly improve Chinese EFL learners' English speaking performance (Meyer and Forester 2015; Hafner 2014), but there is no significant difference existed between these two practice approaches. This may be explained by the fact that DMC enables learners to pay more attention to their English speaking and practice more in order to produce high-quality videos (Dzekoe 2017). And the two ways provide EFL learners with English speaking contexts with no time and space limits (Jiang 2020). As to RQ2, although vlog-based DMC activities cannot significantly improve English speaking complexity and fluency of EFL learners, it can help them advance their accuracy relatively. It may be explained by that they tended to use less complicated vocabularies based on accurate use consideration mentioned by students in the semi-structured interviews (Dukhayel Aldukhayel 2019). When it comes to the differences between two classes in two assignments, EFL learners in experimental class outperform significantly their counterparts in English speaking accuracy (.000) but underperform in fluency. It maybe because learners' more attention to pronunciation is paid (Nikitina 2010) and they practice many times for better viewing effects. We also concern Chinese EFL learners' perception of vlog-based DMC activities in RQ3. It is necessary to know learner's perception and acceptance of it because the potential advantages of CALL-based training cannot be in vain when learners are willing to use it (Hsu 2015). From the results of questionnaire and semi-structured interview, most learners perceive it as an effective tool to help them improve spoken English.

From above discussion, we can conclude that vlog-based DMC is conducive in helping Chinese EFL learners' fluency in English speaking performance, because vlog-based DMC provides learners with more authentic English speaking opportunities (Jiang 2020). Considering that the assignments were applied out of the class, more detailed instructions about expression complexity and accuracy need to be conducted in class.

5 Conclusion and Implications

The present study conducts a 10-week experiment with Chinese middle students by assigning vlog-based digital multimodal composing (DMC) activities to testify the specific effect of vlog-based DMC on English speaking performance. Two vlog-based DMC activities are effective in developing EFL learner' English speaking performance (same as Hepple and Sockhill 2014), which affirms its positive effects and learners accept vlog-based DMC assignment positively. Besides, most of EFL learners hold positive attitudes and a majority of students in EC believe that language ability (Belcher 2017; Yi et al. 2019), thinking quality (Dzekoe 2017), learning ability (Jiang 2020) have been enhanced. It's worth noting that 2 of interviewees considered vlog1-making as a time-consuming task and held negative attitudes towards its future adoption for English speaking improvement.

The pedagogical implications of the study point to the need for an emphasis on digital communication in both general and specific contexts to improve real-life presentations and to prepare students for the new communication way that is led by technology. Teachers should contemplate the use of video recordings and voice recordings as effective tools to prepare students for 21st-century communication, incorporating different techniques and activities that would be beneficial to them for developing skills related to digital social communication.

To conclude, it is essential to acknowledge that this study has limited itself to exploring our students' perceptions about the effectiveness of video blog-making production activities in opposition to the effectiveness of voice blog production activities for developing their English-speaking performance. Regarding future directions, it would be worthwhile to implement related studies with larger sample size and longer intervention duration to better explore their effects on EFL learners' speaking performance. With respect to the limited sub-items of CAF taken into consideration in this study, if possible, more items will be gathered to explain the intervention effects. Besides, process-based multimodal evaluation model proposed by Hafner and Ho (2020) can be adopted in future study to gain more insights. What's more, this study was conducted outside the class, future studies can be performed in class for better observance and data analysis.

Acknowledgements. This work is supported by the Center for Language Cognition and Assessment, South China Normal University. It's also the result of Guangdong "13th Five-Year" Plan Project of Philosophy & Social Science (GD20WZX01-02).

References

Alsied, S.M., Pathan, M.M.: The use of computer technology in EFL classroom: advantages and implications. Int. J. Engl. Lang. Transl. Stud. **1**(1), 44–51 (2013)

Aydin, S.: The use of blogs in learning English as a foreign language. Mevlana Int. J. Educ. **4**, 244–259 (2014)

Barton, D., Lee, C.K.M.: Redefining vernacular literacies in the age of web 2.0. Appl. Linguist. **33**(3), 282–298 (2012)

Belcher, D.: On becoming facilitators of multimodal composing and digital design. J. Second Lang. Writ. **38**, 80–85 (2017)

Cao, Y.-Q., Philp, J.: Interactional context and willingness to communicate: a comparison of behavior in whole class, group and dyadic interaction. System **34**, 480–493 (2006)

Chang, C.C., Yan, C.F., Tseng, J.S.: Perceived convenience in an extended technology acceptance model: Mobile technology and English learning for college students. Aust. J. Educ. Technol. **28**(5), 809–826 (2012)

Chien, S.Y., Hwang, G.J., Jong, M.S.Y.: Effects of peer assessment within the context of spherical video-based virtual reality on EFL students' English-Speaking performance and learning perceptions. Comput. Educ. **146**, 103751 (2020)

Cimasko, T., Shin, D.: Resemiotization and authorial agency in L2 multimodal writing. Writ. Commun. **34**(4), 387–413 (2017)

Chuang, H.H., Rosenbusch, M.H.: Use of digital video technology in an elementary school foreign language methods course. Br. J. Edu. Technol. **36**(5), 869–880 (2005)

Aldukhayel, D.: Vlogs in L2 listening: EFL learners' and teachers' perceptions. Comput. Assist. Lang. Learn. **34**(8), 1085–1104 (2019)

Dzekoe, R.: Computer-based multimodal composing activities, self-revision, and L2 acquisition through writing. Lang. Learn. Technol. **21**(2), 73–95 (2017)

Hafner, C.A., Ho, W.Y.J.: Assessing digital multimodal composing in second language writing: towards a process-based model. J. Second Lang. Writ. **47**, 100710 (2020)

Hafner, C.A.: Remix culture and English language teaching: the expression of learner voice in digital multimodal compositions. TESOL Q. **49**(3), 486–550 (2015)

Hafner, C.: Embedding digital literacies in English language teaching: students' digital video projects as multimodal ensembles. TESOL Q. **48**(4), 655–685 (2014)

Harman, R., Shin, D.: Multimodal and community-based literacies: agentive bilingual learners in elementary school. In: Onchwari, G., Keengwe, S. (eds.) Handbook of Research on Pedagogies and Cultural Considerations for Young English Language Learners, pp. 217–238. IGI Global, Hershey (2018)

Hepple, E., Sockhill, M., Tan, A., Alford, J.: Multiliteracies pedagogy: creating claymations with adolescent, post-beginning English language learners. J. Adolesc. Health. **58**(3), 219–229 (2014)

Hsu, L.: An empirical examination of EFL learners' perceptual learning styles and acceptance of ASR-based computer-assisted pronunciation training. Comput. Assist. Lang. Learn. **29**(5), 881–900 (2015)

Jiang, L., Yu, S., Zhao, Y.: Teacher engagement with digital multimodal composing in a Chinese tertiary EFL curriculum. Lang. Teach. Res. (2019)

Jiang, L.: The affordances of digital multimodal composing for EFL learning. ELT J. **71**(4), 413–422 (2017)

Kang, S.-J.: Dynamic emergence of situational willingness to communicate in a second language. System **33**, 277–292 (2005)

Kearney, M.D., Schuck, S.R.: Authentic learning through the use of digital video. In: Proceedings of the Australian Council for Computers in Education, Adelaide, Australia, pp. 1–7 (2004)

Kilickaya, F., Krajka, J.: Can the use of web-based comic strip creation tool facilitate EFL learners' grammar and sentence writing? Br. J. Edu. Technol. **43**(6), 161–165 (2012)

Kress, G.: Literacy in the New Media Age. Routledge, London (2003)

Kress, G., van Leeuwen, T.: Multimodal Discourse: The Modes and Media of Contemporary Communication. Arnold, London (2001)

Jiang, L., Yang, M., Yu, S.: Chinese ethnic minority students' investment in English learning empowered by digital multimodal composing. TESOL Q. **54**, 954–979 (2020)

Jiang, L., Yu, S., Zhao, Y.: An EFL teacher's investment in digital multimodal composing. ELT J. **76**(3), 297–306 (2020)

Meyer, E., Forester, L.: Implementing student-produced video projects in language courses: guidelines and lessons learned. Die Unterrichtspraxis/Teach. German **48**(2), 192–210 (2015)

Mutmainna, M.: Implementing blogs as a learning tool in ASIAN EFL/ESL learning context. BRAC Univ. J. **11**(01), 27–35 (2016)

Nikitina, L.: Video-making in the foreign language classroom: applying principles of constructivist pedagody. Electron. J. Foreign Lang. Teach. **7**(1), 21–31 (2010)

Parker, D.: Show us a story: an overview of recent research and resource development work at the British film institute. Engl. Educ. **36**(1), 38–44 (2002)

Prior, P.: Multimodality and ESP research. In: Paltridge, B., Starfield, S. (eds.) The Handbook of English for Specific Purposes, pp. 519–534. Blackwell-Wiley, Boston (2013)

Prior, P., Thorne, S.L.: Research paradigms: beyond product, process, and social activity. In: Jakobs, E., Perrin, D. (eds.) Handbook of Writing and Text Production (Handbooks of Applied Linguistics Series), vol. 10, pp. 31–54. Walter De Gruyte, Boston (2014)

Pritchard, R.M.O., Nasr, A.: Improving reading performance among Egyptian engineering students: principles and practice. Engl. Specif. Purp. **23**, 425–445 (2004)

Shin, D., Cimasko, T.: Multimodal composition in a college ESL class: new tools, traditional norms. Comput. Compos. **25**, 376–395 (2008)

Skehan, P.: A framework for the implementation of task-based instruction. Appl. Linguis. **17**(1), 35–62 (1996)

Stranger-Johannessen, E., Norton, B.: The African storybook and language teacher identity in digital times. Mod. Lang. J. **101**, 45–60 (2017)

Swain, C., Sharpe, R., Dawson, K.: Using digital video to study history. Soc. Educ. **67**(3), 154–157 (2003)

Wales, P.: Telling tales in and out of school: Youth performativities with digital storytelling. RiDE: J. Appl. Theatre Perform. **17**(4), 535–552 (2012)

Wang, L.: The advantages of using technology in second language education. Jouornal **32**(10), 38–42 (2005)

Yi, Y., Shin, D., Cimasko, T.: Multimodal literacies in teaching and learning English in and outside of school. In: de Oliveira, L.C. (ed.) The Handbook of TESOL in K-12, pp. 163–177 (2019)

Integrating Multimodal Courses into Mobile Learning in International Chinese Education

Shan Wang[1,2](✉) and Yuyuan Zhang[1]

[1] Department of Chinese Language and Literature, Faculty of Arts and Humanities, University of Macau, Macau, China
shanwang@um.edu.mo
[2] Zhuhai UM Science and Technology Research Institute, Guangdong, China

Abstract. Mobile learning provides a new teaching platform for international Chinese language teaching. To adapt to this new way, a variety of teaching methods is required for diversified teaching design. Multimodal courses can be integrated into this demand, which helps to create a multi-sensory teaching and learning atmosphere to enhance students' learning initiatives. It meets the designing requirements of mobile learning and can optimize learning quality. In this study, we selected the listening and speaking class "What's the date today?" (Jīntiān jǐ yuè jǐ hào?) that won the gold medal in an international Chinese teaching competition, annotated its modalities, and explored the class's features in different teaching stages. It provides a new perspective for the curriculum design for mobile learning. This paper also analyzed the shortcomings of traditional listening and speaking courses, summarized the features of a multimodal course, and suggested how to integrate multimodal courses into mobile learning in order to enhancing the student's learning experience.

Keywords: Mobile learning · Multimodal courses · Curriculum design · International Chinese language education · Listening and speaking

1 Introduction

With the advent of the new media era, mobile devices and internet technology have developed rapidly, causing technological changes in many fields. Educators combine them with teaching to produce a new learning mode – Mobile Learning, which contains many new features, such as convenience, mobility, interaction, timeliness, and so on. Its features are complementary to traditional teaching, which can effectively improve students' autonomous learning and improve teaching efficiency. It will become a crucial learning way in the future, urging teachers to optimize their professionalism and skills to meet the new demands.

The rapid development of mobile learning has placed new demands on the curriculum design of language teaching. Teachers need to design scientific, interesting and relevant teaching contents according to intended learning outcomes of different level of students. In recent years, international Chinese language education from the perspective of multimodal discourse analysis has attracted the attention of the academic community, which plays an important role in the cultivation of students' communicative

W. Jia et al. (Eds.): SETE 2021, LNCS 13089, pp. 104–121, 2021.
https://doi.org/10.1007/978-3-030-92836-0_10

competence. Integrating curriculum design of multimodal courses into curriculum design of mobile learning can contribute to provide interesting online courses, which reflects the pluralistic and open teaching concept as well. It not only helps to build an interactive teaching atmosphere, but also improve students' learning interest and autonomy.

Multimodal discourse analysis originated in the mid-1990s. Based on Halliday's systemic functional linguistics [1], the visual grammar [2] provides support for multimodal discourse analysis. Multimodal discourse refers to the discourse that communicates through various sensory systems such as speeches, actions, sounds, images, etc. It is widely used in different fields, such as skits, films, dramas, news, etc. With the development of education and information technology, the application of multimodal discourse analysis in teaching has attracted much attention, but its research in the field of international Chinese language education is not yet enough. Nowadays, Chinese is becoming more and more popular all over the world. An international Chinese listening and speaking course requires students to master the language skills of listening and speaking in order to improve communicative competence.

Based on the comprehensive theoretical framework of multimodal discourse analysis [3], this paper selects a listening and speaking lesson that won the gold medal of the 2017 *Teaching Chinese as a Foreign Language* demonstration class competition "What's the date today?" (Jīntiān jǐ yuè jǐ hào?)[1], and uses the software ELAN 5.4 to annotate various modalities and modal symbols in this lesson. It adopts both quantitative and qualitative research methods to analyze the multimodal features in this lesson. In addition, by comparing the teaching characteristics of the multimodal class with traditional classes, this study summarizes the teaching strategies conducive to improving the effectiveness of a Chinese learning class, and provides a new perspective for designing an international Chinese class for mobile learning.

2 Literature Review

2.1 Mobile Learning

In 1994, Wireless Andrew Project of Carnegie Mellon University introduced mobile learning into the world. Since the 21st century, network technology and intelligent mobile terminals have developed rapidly, and more and more mobile learning resources have been used in teaching. There is much research on mobile learning abroad, and its main research content can be divided into the following three categories: (1) Attitudes of learners and educators towards the use of mobile learning: Norazah, Ridzwan and Arif [4] showed that students have a positive attitude towards mobile learning through questionnaire survey and quantitative analysis of data results; Oz [5] investigated 144 teachers' understanding and support of mobile learning from the perspective of teachers, showing that most teachers were willing to apply mobile learning to teaching, and teachers themselves can improve their professional knowledge and skills through mobile learning; Van Vo and Thuy Vo [6] took 69 English teachers from a university

[1] https://v.qq.com/x/page/j0505270wmo.html.

in Vietnam as the experimental participants. Through the investigation and evaluation, it is found that teachers' attitude towards mobile learning is positive. (2) Factors affecting Mobile Learning: Han and Shin [7] showed that learners' own characteristics (such as age, gender, personality and learning style) affect the effect of mobile learning; Morchid [8] utilized Structural Equation Model to evaluate the four factors of behavior intention influencing mobile learning. The results show that teachers' feedback and compatibility are related to behavior intention influencing mobile learning, but performance expectation and effort expectation were not; (3) Mobile learning strategy research: Keskin and Metcalf [9] summarize the key points of mobile learning in different fields and the mobile devices and technologies adopted; Asraf and Supian [10] focused on summarizing the most common mobile learning styles in different levels of language learning (such as oral, written, word meaning, etc.) and explored the degree to which students' metacognition was improved.

The research on mobile learning in China is limited compared with studies abroad, especially for international Chinese language education. Most of the existing studies focused on English teaching, so it is still at the beginning stage of exploration. Bao [11] pointed out that integrating mobile learning into College English teaching mode can stimulate students' learning enthusiasm and improve teaching efficiency; Miao [12] explored the feasibility of applying WeChat to college English mobile learning and summarized new teaching strategies based on WeChat from different levels; Zhang [13] sed Rain class, learning link application tools to show that mobile learning can improve students' learning interest and learning effect through classroom practice and students' feedback; Zhan and Zhang [14] designed a new English vocabulary learning software for college students and proved that it improved the efficiency of College Students' English vocabulary learning.

In order to construct efficient and reasonable mobile teaching methods, some scholars conducted various experimental surveys to explore the influencing factors of learners' use of mobile learning: Liu, Liu and Zhu [15] found that learners prefer to use short, multi-level link learning resources; Xiong [16] showed that perceived interest is the biggest factor affecting college students' mobile learning through empirical analysis; Bao [17] explored the influencing factors of learners' use of mobile learning by using questionnaires, the results found that perceived interest is the strongest emotional indicator for learners to choose mobile learning and proposed that in the construction of mobile learning resources, we should improve students' learning autonomy as the starting point, and enhance the interest of teaching materials. Zhu [18] used SPSS19.0 and AMOS20.0 data analysis software to analyze the survey data and found that there was a positive correlation between the entertainment of mobile learning resources and postgraduates' attitude towards mobile learning.

In sum, the mobile learning, as a new learning mode, has a catalytic effect on improving teaching efficiency and enhancing students' motivation to learn. At the same time, learners prefer to use interesting and diversified mobile learning resources. However, there are few studies related to the application of mobile learning in international Chinese language education. Therefore, this study will explore more targeted mobile learning curriculum design by analyzing the multimodal features of international Chinese course to adapt to mobile learning.

2.2 Multimodal Discourse Analysis

Multimodal discourse is a discourse that uses multiple modes, such as auditory, visual, and tactile, to communicate through a variety of means and symbolic resources like language, images, sounds, and actions [19]. With the development of social science and technology, multimodal discourse has become a mainstream way of communication. Some modal symbols (such as images and color in visual modality) have even surpassed the language itself and occupy a dominant position [20]. Wei [21] analyzed the meaning symbols in the times in 2006, and proved that in addition to language, discourse symbols are also important elements in the construction of discourse meaning. The study of multimodal discourse can lead to more specific and accurate representation of discourse meaning.

Research on multimodal discourse analysis in the field of English teaching has received widespread attention and the scholars have explored it in depth from theoretical analysis and pedagogical research. For example, Li and Xu [22] used case studies to analyze the coordination and construction of different modal symbols in the classroom, and multimodal analysis was used to provide different perspectives for the study of English classroom discourse; Jiang and Ding [23] explored the theoretical application of multimodality in College English teaching; Zhang [24] concentrated on the different modal combinations adopted by college English teachers in constructing "three meanings" (concept representation meaning, interpersonal interaction meaning and text organization meaning) in multimodal class; Zhang [3] systematically investigated the application of multimodal discourse analysis in English teaching.

In contrast, the research of multimodal discourse analysis in international Chinese language education is in the preliminary exploration stage. Li [25] proved that multimodal teaching is conducive to improving the effectiveness of international Chinese language education; Li and Xia [26] analyzed the difficulty and challenges of multimodal teaching in international Chinese language education from the aspects of teaching mode, teaching materials, teaching methods and teachers, and pointed out that multimodal symbol system can establish a complete discourse meaning: [27–31] explored how to teaching Chinese grammar and vocabulary based on multimodal discourse analysis.

So far[2], 214 papers on the topic of "multimodality, listening and speaking" have been retrieved through CNKI. After the topic filtering, 196 papers on English listening and speaking have been found by multimodal discourse analysis, but only 5 papers on Chinese listening and speaking have been found: [32] analyzed the specific application of multimodal teaching in a Chinese listening and speaking class from two perspectives: teaching conception and teaching strategy in "Chinese Micro-Lens · Variety"; Pan [33], Pan [34] combined the multimodal theory, the multiple intelligences theory with a Chinese audiovisual speaking class to analyze the nature of an audiovisual speaking class and the redesign of textbook compilation; Li [35] based on the multimodal theory, through questionnaires and experimental tests, showed that the use of multimodal combination is conducive to the training of students' listening

[2] Search date: October 18, 2021.

comprehension ability, and different combination has different influence on students; Zheng [36] analyzed the features and teaching effect of each modal type through listening and speaking classroom teaching research and questionnaire. Based on Wanfang database, 322 papers on the topic of "multimodality, listening and speaking" were retrieved. There are 280 papers on multimodal analysis related to English listening and speaking course, but only one related to Chinese listening and speaking course. Through Hyread Taiwan full text database, Hong Kong literature database, and Hong Kong Macao journal network, we searched the topic, title and key words "multimodal, listening and speaking", but did not find any relevant literature.

Additionally, there are only 55 papers on the topic of "multimodal, mobile learning" were retrieved from CNKI. For example, Wang [37] demonstrated that in College English teaching, the combination of multimodal theory and mobile learning can make up for the shortcomings of traditional English teaching, strengthen the interaction between teachers and students, and improve the efficiency of English learning; Xu [38] used WeChat as the mobile learning platform and proved that the use of multimodal vocabulary learning can enhance students' interest in learning and improve the quality of learning through teaching experiments; Ke [39] proposed how to construct college English teaching mode based on multimodal and mobile learning and summarized the matters requiring attention in the teaching process; Shi [40] used a year of practical research and showed that the use of multimodal mobile learning can avoid the influence of time, space and environment on learning, and effectively improve students' learning autonomy.

Basing on the literature review, it is noticeable that the research about multimodal discourse analysis and mobile learning theory in international Chinese language education are rare. Besides, the research content is not deeply explored, and there is a lack of teaching design for international Chinese language teaching under the vision of mobile learning.

Therefore, this study selects the video "What's the date today?" (Jīntiān jǐ yuè jǐ hào?), the gold medal video of the 2017 Chinese as a foreign language teaching demonstration class competition, and explores the application of multimodal discourse analysis in Chinese class referring to mobile learning. The purpose of this study is to provide international Chinese teachers with more effective teaching methods, as well as to provide reference for teaching that meets the needs of mobile learning.

3 Research Design

The corpus of this study is selected from the golden award lesson "What's the date today?" (Jīntiān jǐ yuè jǐ hào?) of an international Chinese teaching competition. The total length is 9 min and 29 s the participants were 18-year-old Korean high school students. The course adopted bilingual teaching mode, with Chinese as the main language, Korean as the auxiliary language. Two teachers teach together: a Chinese teacher as the main speaker, using Chinese to explain, read and practice for students; a Korean teacher made a supplementary introduction in Korean.

The teaching process can be divided into five parts:

Stage 1 Review old lessons (00:00–1:17)
Stage 2 Vocabulary learning (1:18–5:25)
Stage 3 Cultural introduction (5:25–6:10)
Stage 4 Grammar text learning (6:11–8:35)
Phase 5 General review (8:36–9:20)

The teaching goal is to enable students to master the pronunciation and usage of Chinese "year", "month" and "day", and understand the Chinese birthday customs.

This paper aims to analyze and answer the following three questions: (1) how are the multimodalities used in this listening and speaking class? (2) What are the features of multimodality in a listening and speaking class? (3) Combined with mobile learning, what is the inspiration for teachers in international Chinese language education? This study used the video analysis software ELAN5.4 to annotate the instructional videos. This study analyze the data by combining qualitative and quantitative methods. Finally, combined with the teaching content and data results, the relationship between the modalities were summarized to analyze the cooperative use of each modality.

Based on the classification of modality types of Zhang [3] according to the modality classification of Liu and Wang [31] and combined with the teaching content, this paper divides the modality and symbol resources into the following four categories (visual modality, auditory modality, kinesthetic modality and environmental modality). The modal symbols contained in each mode are shown in Table 1.

Table 1. Modality and modal symbols

Modality	Modal symbol
Visual modalities	PPT, picture, blackboard
Auditory modalities	Teachers' discourse, students' discourse
Kinesthetic modalities	Facial expressions, body movements, gestures
Environment modalities	Social distance, personal distance

Among all kinds of modality symbols, (1) visual modalities includes PPT, pictures and blackboard as the medium for displaying teaching contents. (2) In the auditory modalities, teachers' discourse refers to the expression when explaining, guiding, correcting errors, organizing the activity; students' discourse includes the words in answering questions, following reading, reading aloud and practicing activities. (3) In kinesthetic mode, facial expression refers to the teachers' smile, frown and other expressions when facing students; body movement refers to the teachers' nodding, waving the hand, describing the actions that accompany things, etc.; gestures refers to teachers' guiding students to learn, answer questions, indicating PPT, blackboard or pictures, etc. (4) The environmental modalities is divided into two parts: social distance and personal distance. Social distance refers to the distance that teachers observe students' practice activities while they do activities, while personal distance refers to the distance when teachers participate in students' game activities.

4 Statistical Analysis of Multimodal Use in the Listening and Speaking Class

4.1 Statistics of Multimodal Annotation Results

The use of each modality after annotation is shown in Table 2. First, the PPT symbol in the visual modalities is the main symbols (62.07%), followed by teachers' discourse (47.09%), gestures (42.83%), students' discourse (23.79%), pictures (19.58%), body movements (5.16%), personal distance (4.71%), blackboard (4.26%), facial expression (1.37%) and social distance (1.01%). This paper calculated the percentage of each symbol label in the total time of all modality symbols, shown in Table 3. According to the statistical results, it can be found that the order of the percentage of each modality symbol is the same as the order of the percentage of annotation duration.

According to the modal summary of the total annotation time of each symbol (Table 4), in the whole teaching process, the visual mode is the main mode (489.62), while the auditory mode (404.04) accounts for only 85.58 s' difference from the visual mode, which belongs to the secondary mode of the teaching process, the kinesthetic modality (281.36) accounted for less time and was classified as an auxiliary modality along with the environmental modality (32.61).

Table 2. Number and duration of each modality

Modality	Layer	Annotation quantity	Total annotation time	Annotation time percentage
Visual modality	PPT	8	353.78	62.07
Auditory modality	Teachers discourse	70	268.42	47.09
Kinesthetic modality	Gestures	30	244.14	42.83
Auditory modality	Students discourse	54	135.62	23.79
Visual modality	Pictures	5	111.59	19.58
Kinesthetic modality	Body movements	6	29.39	5.16
Environment modality	Personal distance	3	26.83	4.71
Visual modality	Blackboard	4	24.25	4.26
Kinesthetic modality	Facial expressions	4	7.83	1.37
Environment modality	Social distance	1	5.78	1.01

Table 3. The percentage of each symbol in the total duration of all modality annotation time

Symbol	PPT	Personal distance	Teachers' discourse	Facial expres-sions	Social distance	Gestures	Pictures	Students' discourse	Body move-ments	Blackboard
Percentage	29.30	2.22	22.23	0.65	0.48	20.22	9.24	11.23	2.43	2.00

(Note: the percentage here refers to the percentage of each modal symbol in the total time of all modal symbols)

Table 4. Percentage of each modality

Modality	Layer	Annotation quantity	Total annotation time	Annotation time percentage
Visual modality	PPT	8	353.78	62.07
	Pictures	5	111.59	19.58
	Blackboard	4	24.25	4.26
Subtotal	/	17	489.62	/
Auditory modality	Teachers' discourse	70	268.42	47.09
	Students' discourse	54	135.62	23.79
Subtotal	/	124	404.04	/
Kinesthetic modality	Gesture	30	244.14	42.83
	Body movements	6	29.39	5.16
	Facial expressions	4	7.83	1.37
Subtotal	/	40	281.36	
Environment modality	Personal distance	3	26.83	4.71
	Social distance	1	5.78	1.01
Subtotal	/	4	32.61	/

4.2 The Use of Different Modalities

The visual, auditory, kinesthetic and environmental modalities plays a different role in the teaching process. This section analyzes it combining with the teaching content and explores how each modality is present in teaching and its role in teaching.

First, the visual modalities are foremost in the teaching. The PPT courseware ran through the whole teaching process. The Chinese teacher showed contents through PPT, pictures and blackboard, which is different from the boring and single explanation of traditional teaching, so that students can understand and learn knowledge in many aspects and make teaching more informative. For example, in the vocabulary learning part, the picture and vocabulary were combined through PPT to make the vocabulary more specific, so that students can quickly understand the target vocabulary. For example, when learning *shēngrì kuàilè* 'happy birthday', the Chinese teacher showed a birthday cake through PPT with happy pictures, so that students can easily understand the meaning of *shēngrì kuàilè* 'happy birthday' and deepen their impression. In the introduction section, the two teachers showed students the custom of eating Chinese longevity noodles through PPT, pictures, words and videos to deepen students' understanding of customs.

The auditory modalities account for almost the same proportion as the visual modality. The total annotation time of auditory modality is only 85.58 s' different from that of visual modality. It is the sub-modality of this teaching process. It reflects the discourse performance of teachers and students in the whole class, including teachers' explanation, reading, correcting students' mistakes, students' following and practice activities. The data shows that the annotation time of teachers' discourse is almost twice as long as that of students' discourse, because this teaching adopted the bilingual teaching modality of both Chinese and Korean teachers at the same time. After the Chinese teacher explained, the Korean teacher would use Korean for supplementary analysis. Bilingual teaching method can facilitate students to understand the learning content and better participate in classroom teaching.

The proportion of gestures in kinesthetic modalities is only 4.26% less than that in teachers' discourse. Gesture language mainly cooperates with teachers' discourse and guides students to follow the practice so as to make students' learning objectives clearer in the classroom. For example, in the part of reviewing the last lesson, the Chinese teacher instructed the words and sentences on the blackboard through gestures, and the students read aloud, so that the students can pay more attention. It saved the time of explanation, and made the teaching task more efficient. Body movements and facial expressions are auxiliary teaching, which made teaching more vivid.

Personal distance in the environmental modalities is mainly reflected in the activity exercises, where the two teachers participated in the students' activity. They got a more comprehensive understanding of students' learning, strengthened the interaction with them and helped to create a lively classroom atmosphere. Social distance is the two teachers' observation and recording of students' knowledge acquisition during students' presentations and activity exercises. The environmental modality has a complementary effect on the whole teaching process, making the teaching process more intimate between the students and the teachers, contributing to the construction of a good teaching atmosphere.

Although the main modality of this class is visual modalities, the proportion of auditory modality is almost the same as that of visual modality, which is the secondary modality of this teaching process. Teachers' discourse and students' discourse in auditory modality are closely related to PPT, blackboard and picture of visual modalities, while kinesthetic modalities and environmental modalities are used as auxiliary modalities of auditory modalities and visual modalities to assist teaching.

4.3 Coordination of Different Modalities

This section will analyze the coordination of multiple modalities from the perspective of the different instructional components of the listening and speaking lessons. In Stage 1 during reviewing the vocabulary of the learned lesson, the Chinese teacher used gestures to instruct the students to read the words displayed on the blackboard, and used teachers' words to correct students' pronunciation, combining kinesthetic modality, visual modality and auditory modality. When reviewing sentences, the two teachers adopted the way of dialogue, reviewed with the students through the way of questioning and answering, and combined teachers' discourse with student's discourse in the auditory modalities.

In Stage 2, during vocabulary learning, the Chinese teacher used gestures to indicate PPT and explained the target vocabulary with teachers' words, so that students can understand the meaning of the target vocabulary more easily. When teaching the pronunciation of new words, teachers' discourse is necessary to read the new words. In the process of reading, gestures and the teachers' discourse cooperate with each other, and students responded. For example, when the Chinese teacher read *jīntiān* "today", the Chinese teacher displayed the target word *jīntiān* "today" and the extended phrases (such as tomorrow, the day after tomorrow, etc.) through PPT. The Chinese teacher read it first, and then used gestures to indicate the target word, and the students followed it, reflecting the combination of PPT, gestures, teachers' discourse and students' discourse. During vocabulary practice, the two teachers organized students to play games through teachers' discourse and gestures, and participated in students' activities. After students were familiar with the game, they observed students' practice, reflecting the combination of teachers' discourse, gestures, students' discourse, personal distance, and social distance.

In Stage 3, during the cultural introduction part, the PPT was used to show the birthday cake and lead to the topic of birthday, and then the PPT was used to play a video to introduce the custom of Chinese people eating long-lived noodles on their birthday. The two teachers' discourse plays a role of explanation during this process. During the activity practice, the two teachers sang with the students through the body movement (beat), and combined with teachers' discourse, body movement and students' discourse, that is, the combination of the visual modality, the auditory modality, and the kinesthetic modality.

In Stage 4, the same combination of modal symbols was used in grammar teaching. When learning the usage of "*de*", the Chinese teacher split the sentence with "*de*" on the blackboard and explained it through the line to make the students understand the position of "*de*" in the sentence structure. This process combined blackboard, gestures and teachers' discourse. In grammar practice, the Chinese teacher directly used gestures to indicate the content of PPT, and the students answered the questions in turn. The two teachers encouraged the students by facial expression (smile) or indicated whether the students answered correctly by body movement (shaking head or nodding head), and then corrected the students' wrong pronunciation by teachers' words. During the text learning process, the two teachers used gestures to instruct the students to read the text aloud on the PPT, and then asked them to answer the questions based on the video shown on the PPT to practice their listening skills and improve their comprehension.

Finally, in Stage 5 during general review, the main task is to summarize the focus of this lesson, so that students can strengthen the practice of target knowledge. During this process, PPT was needed to show the knowledge points summarized by two teachers. Therefore, PPT and students' discourse were dominant, and teachers' discourse and gestures were used as auxiliary modal symbols to guide students to review and practice knowledge points. Each modality combines with each other to complete the final teaching task.

As can be seen, each modality cooperated with each other in different teaching stages to complete the teaching task together. According to the multimodal discourse analysis, this lesson is characterized by the main modality, the visual modalities, and sub-modality, the auditory modalities; they interpenetrated the whole teaching process.

The kinesthetic modalities and the environmental modalities complemented and strengthened the teaching according to the teaching needs.

5 Curriculum Design of Modal Teaching in International Chinese Language Education Under Mobile Learning

With the in-depth study of international Chinese language education and the continuous improvement of teaching requirements, the drawbacks of the traditional teaching mode of international Chinese listening and speaking are gradually exposed: (1) using single teaching method [41, 42]: traditional listening and speaking class mainly uses mechanical training to train students' listening and pronunciation, which is boring and makes students lose interest in learning. (2) Lack of penetration of cultural background knowledge [43]: traditional listening and speaking classes are lack of attention to the cultural nature of language, resulting in students' misuse of the target language in different contexts. (3) Lack of fostering students' comprehensive ability of listening and speaking [44]: The course of international Chinese requires students to master comprehensive language skills. The traditional listening and speaking course is not systematic, which weakens the training of language skills and makes students hard to master the language. In general, the traditional teaching mode is neither enough to comprehensively improve students' Chinese listening and speaking ability, nor does it conform to the teaching concept and application of mobile learning. Multimodal courses play an important role in cultivating students' language understanding ability and communication ability. Applying multimodal courses into mobile learning can effectively make up for the shortcomings of traditional teaching modality, increase learning interest, improve students' listening and speaking ability, and cross-cultural communication level, and promote students' interest in using mobile learning.

5.1 The Characteristic of the Multimodal Course Listening and Speaking Course

"Listening" is always the starting point of language learning. "*Listening*" can be transformed into "reading", and "listening" can be developed into "reading" and "writing" [45] listening and speaking are two complementary language abilities which are independent and interact with each other [46]. A Chinese listening and speaking course should adopt different teaching strategies, so that students can better master the language and communicate with each other. Based on the multimodal discourse analysis, this section summarizes the characteristics of the Chinese listening and speaking class by combining the statistical results of the modality annotation data of the video.

Multi-dimensional teaching methods of listening, speaking and watching. Hu [41] pointed out that teaching methods play an important role by analyzing the multi-dimensional teaching method of listening and speaking in international Chinese listening and speaking class. Qian and Wang [47] pointed out that the international Chinese listening and speaking course is characterized using multi-dimensional teaching strategies of listening, speaking, and watching. The listening and speaking course can be divided into three stages: before listening, while listening and after listening, and put forward the teaching strategy of "three-stage learning theory" (preview before listening, practice while listening and review after listening). Li [48] concluded by questionnaires that 53.4% of the teachers' classroom teaching methods are mainly listening and speaking, supplemented by teachers' explanation. This listening and speaking class is characterized by using visual modalities as main modalities, auditory modalities as secondary modalities, kinetic modalities and environmental modalities as auxiliary modalities, using a variety of modalities to cooperate with each other, increasing language input and output, and improving students' language ability. A multimodal course adopts the multi-dimensional teaching method of multi-modal cooperation, which is in line with the characteristics of multi-dimensional teaching method in an international Chinese listening and speaking class. Different from the traditional listening and speaking class, a multimodal listening and speaking class not only combines the three forms of listening, speaking and watching, but also combines all the modal symbols in the class to achieve the best teaching effect, strengthen the input and output of target knowledge, so as to enhance students' language comprehension and usage competence.

Teaching with cultural background. Culture teaching is an important part of language learning, which aims to solve the non-verbal communication barriers caused by cultural differences. Combining with the target knowledge and cultural background can assist language teaching. It can improve students' cultural perception and comprehension as well as their intercultural communication skills [49]. "One belt, one road" provides new opportunities and challenges for international Chinese education. In language education, it combines cultural background with Chinese culture to enhance China's cultural soft power and cultural exchanges with countries, promoting Chinese education internationalization [26]. In this listening and speaking class, the two teachers used PPT to show videos to disseminate traditional Chinese culture to students and conduct teacher-student Q&A interaction to deepen students' impression of the culture, paid attention to the combination of language and cultural background, spread the cultural connotation of target knowledge, and improved students' Chinese thinking ability.

Paying attention to the cultivation of students' communicative competence. The purpose of a listening and speaking course of international Chinese language education is to enhance communication ability. The content of the course is based on daily life. It cultivates and fosters students' communication competence in real daily life. In class, the two teachers used student-centered method and tried to improve the cooperation and interaction between teachers and students, and created an active classroom atmosphere. Some cliché teaching methods of traditional listening and speaking class (such as repeated mechanical listening and speaking training) are easy to cause students to lose interest in learning and produce bad learning habits; as a result, students' Chinese communicative ability can hardly be improved [50]. With the in-depth research and development of Chinese listening and speaking course, the teaching mode of a listening and speaking course is also changing. Teachers use situational teaching method to integrate listening and speaking, make students feel as if they are personally on the scene, so that they can practice their communication competence [51]. The teacher guides students to understand the text in the situation and requires the students to correctly use the learned knowledge for communication in similar situations. The teaching method of combining listening and speaking with situational training is used to improve the students' communicative competence.

In this lesson, the two teachers explained the target knowledge through PPT video, teachers' discourse, gestures and other modal symbols, so as to improve students' listening comprehension ability, and promote students' oral competence through question and answering. In general, teachers use various modalities to design a variety of situational practice, so as to improve students' communicative ability, which is in line with the characteristics of a listening and speaking class. Compared with the traditional listening and speaking class, the multimodal class is more diversified, the design situation is more vivid, the pragmatics of target knowledge is easier to understand and use, the sense of situational substitution is enhanced, and it is more effective in cultivating students' communicative ability.

5.2 Applying Multimodal Course Design to Mobile Learning

Teachers need to choose the appropriate modality to fit the teaching tasks and types of different teaching processes. Zhang [3] proposed the selection principles of teaching modality: the best effect principle (main), the effective principle, the adaptation principle and the economic principle. This part will introduce how to apply multimodal course design to mobile learning.

Teaching design of mobile learning based on multimodal characteristics. Based on the multimodal characteristics of this listening and speaking class, teachers can select materials and design tasks related to target knowledge according to students' interest as well as their ability level, so that students can complete tasks through mobile learning. Teachers should play the role of an organizer, supervisor and director, and create diversified teaching methods to make the teaching atmosphere no longer boring. Teachers can provide additional resources on a mobile learning platform based on the "i + 1" principle. The teaching modality can not only effectively foster students' listening and speaking ability, but also improve students' enthusiasm and activate the classroom atmosphere. Teachers can also get an in-depth understanding of students' acquisition in this way.

Creating an immersive mobile learning classroom. Teachers can use various multimodalities to strengthen the cultural contextualization of the target vocabulary. They can also share learning materials in a common learning platform to create an immersive online classroom in the cultural context of the target knowledge. Videos and images in the virtual classroom for students to interact with can simulate a cultural environment through real situation, which cannot be achieved in the real classroom. The different contexts created in this environment allow students to practice in real time, deepening their comprehension of the target knowledge and the cultural connotation behind it. At the same time, teachers can create a variety of activities on the learning platform, so that students can flexibly choose for cultural knowledge training. Taking the traditional Chinese birthday customs in the listening and speaking class studied in this paper as an example, the Korean teacher first introduced the traditional Chinese birthday customs through video display to attract students' interest, after that, teachers can share the materials related to birthday customs to the mobile learning platform. After students understand the cultural background, teachers should use the mobile learning platform to create a context and let students participate in the context. In this way, students can use the language correctly in similar contexts.

Using mobile learning to improve students' comprehensive language ability. Nowadays, the society has entered the era of new media. The role of mobile phones, tablet computers and other electronic devices is no longer to serve as a simple communication tool. More and more mobile learning resources are shared in these devices. Using them for teaching has become an emerging trend in education. Firstly, students don't have to listen to the teachers' explanation and reading as in the traditional teaching, they can learn more easily through the audio or video of mobile devices. In addition, students can find out the difficulty according to their own learning situation, carry out autonomous learning, and improve learning efficiency. Secondly, in traditional teaching, some language and cultural differences can hard for students to accurately understand only through explanation, while mobile learning can make up for this drawback. It can classify and summarize cultural knowledge through mobile device's functions, increase the amount of information by combining graphics, videos, audios and videos, and make students have a better understanding of the target knowledge. The use of mobile learning can create a variety of scenarios to make the language input and output complement each other to achieve the optimal learning effect. Finally, teachers can set up group training and record students' performance through mobile learning platform according to students' characteristics. For example, teachers can test students' listening and speaking situation through records and give effective guidance according to each student's specific problems. Students can also detect their speaking deficiencies and correct them according to records, which effectively improves students' listening and speaking ability. In a mobile learning platform, teachers can also create different types of communicative classes for students to choose from and use animation, sound and other technology to establish social background, which help to enhance students' communicative ability in different situations and improve their Chinese language skills.

6 Conclusion

Mobile learning is becoming prevalent in today's world. Integrating multimodal courses into mobile learning resources in international Chinese language education contributes to build a lively and interesting virtual classroom, which can better stimulate students' learning motivation and improve their comprehensive language ability. In this paper, we annotated the multimodalities of a golden prize lesson of listening and speaking and analyzed the multimodal teaching features of this class through quantitative and qualitative analysis. Compared with traditional listening and speaking classes, multimodal Chinese teaching is more conducive to improve learning efficiency. This study further discussed how to apply multimodal curriculum design to mobile learning, providing a new perspective for international Chinese language education. Taking students as the center, a multimodal course mobilizes visual, auditory and other senses to input and output knowledge, optimizes teaching effects, improves teaching quality, makes up for the teaching drawbacks of traditional classes, and promotes the reform of international Chinese teaching under the vision of mobile learning. Multimodal courses are in line with the needs of mobile learning. The two are complementary and mutually beneficial. They can build a vivid learning atmosphere to stimulate students' learning initiative. This study provides important references for building a multimodal environment for mobile learning in the information era.

Acknowledgements. This study is funded by "The 13th Five-Year" Scientific Research Grant of The State Language Commission. The project title is *Tourism and Leisure Chinese in Macau* and the project number is YB135-159.

References

1. Halliday, M.A.K.: Language as Social Semiotic: The Social Interpretation of Language and Meaning. Hodder Arnold, London (1978)
2. Kress, G.R., Van Leeuwen, T.: Reading Images: The Grammar of Visual Design. Routledge, London (1996)
3. Zhang, D.: Multimodal Discourse Analysis and Foreign Language Teaching (duōmótài huàyǔ fēnxī lǐlùn yǔ wàiyǔ jiàoxué). Higher Education Press, Beijing (2015)
4. Norazah, M., Ridzwan, C., Arif, A.A.: Relationship between the acceptance of mobile learning for AutoCAD course and learning style in polytechnic. Procedia Soc. Behav. Sci. **102**, 177–187 (2013)
5. Oz, H.: Prospective English teachers' ownership and usage of mobile devices as m-learning tools. Procedia Soc. Behav. Sci. **141**, 1031–1041 (2014)
6. Van Vo, L., Thuy Vo, L.: EFL Teachers' attitudes towards the use of mobile devices in learning English at a university in Vietnam. Arab World Engl. J. (AWEJ) **11** (2020)
7. Han, I., Shin, W.S.: The use of a mobile learning management system and academic achievement of online students. Comput. Educ. **102**, 79–89 (2016)
8. Morchid, N.: The determinants of use and acceptance of mobile assisted language learning: the case of EFL students in Morocco. Arab World Engl. J. (AWEJ) Special Issue on CALL **5**, 76–97 (2019)
9. Keskin, N.O., Metcalf, D.: The current perspectives, theories and practices of mobile learning. Turkish Online J. Educ. Technol.-TOJET **10**, 202–208 (2011)
10. Asraf, R.M., Supian, N.: Metacognition and mobile-assisted vocabulary learning. SSRN Electron. J. **8**, 16–35 (2017)
11. Bao, S.: M-learning combined teaching model of college English (rónghé yídòng xuéxí de dàxué yīngyǔ jiàoxué xīn móshì). Res. Explor. Lab. (shíyànshì yánjiū yǔ tànsuǒ) **32**, 144–147+151 (2013)
12. Miao, N.: Research on mobile learning strategies of college English based on Wechat (jīyú wēixìn de dàxué yīngyǔ yídòng xuéxí cèlüè yánjiū), 136–140 (2016)
13. Zhang, C.: Exploration and practice of the teaching mode of grouping in class based on mobile learning – take the course of spoken Mandarin as an example (jīyú yídòng xuéxí de bānnèi fēnzǔ jiàoxué móshì tànsuǒ yǔ shíjiàn—yǐ pǔtōnghuà kǒuyǔ kèchéng wéi lì). University Education (dàxué jiàoyù), 152–154 (2021)
14. Zhan, H., Zhang, L.: Design and application of lock screen mobile learning software for college English vocabulary (dàxué yīngyǔ cíhuì suǒpíng yídòng xuéxí ruǎnjiàn de shèjì yǔ yìngyòng). Distance Education in China (zhōngguó yuǎnchéng jiàoyù) 43–48 (2015)

15. Liu, A., Liu, Z., Zhu, S.: A case study of the acceptance level and influence factors of mobile learning in Nanjing (yídòng xuéxí de jiēshòu dù yǔ yǐngxiǎng yīnsù yánjiū—jīyú nánjīng de diàochá). Open Educ. Res. (kāifàng jiàoyù yánjiū) **19**, 104–111 (2013)
16. Xiong, M.: Research on influence factors of university students' acceptance of mobile learning (dàxuéshēng yídòng xuéxí jiēshòu dù de yǐngxiǎng yīnsù yánjiū). Master of Arts. Soochow University, Suzhou (2015)
17. Bao, R.: Research on influence factors for intention of learners to use mobile learning in open education (kāifàng jiàoyù xuéxí zhě yídòng xuéxí shǐyòng yìyuàn yǐngxiǎng yīnsù yánjiū). J. Dist. Educ. (yuǎnchéng jiàoyù zázhì) **35**, 102–112 (2017)
18. Zhu, J.: Based on the technology acceptance modal of graduate student the influence factors of mobile learning (jīyú TAM móxíng de yánjiūshēng yídòng xuéxí yǐngxiǎng yīnsù yánjiū). Master of Arts. Shandong Normal University, Jinan (2015)
19. Zhang, D.: On a synthetic theoretical framework for multimodal discourse analysis (duōmótài huàyǔ fēnxī zònghé lǐlùn kuàngjià tànsuǒ). Foreign Languages in China (zhōngguó wàiyǔ) **6**, 24–30 (2009)
20. Wei, Q.: On mode, medium, and modality in multimodal discourse (lùn duōmótài huàyǔ zhòng de mótài, méijiè yǔ qíngtài). Foreign Lang. Educ. (wàiyǔ jiàoxué) **30**, 54–57 (2009)
21. Wei, Q.: On the construction of the whole meaning of multimodal discourse - Discourse analysis based on a multimodal media discourse (lùn duōmótài huàyǔ de zhěngtǐ yìyì gòujiàn—jīyú yīgè duō mó tài méitǐ yǔ piān de huàyǔ fēnxī). J. Tianjin Foreign Stud. Univ. (tiānjīn wàiguóyǔ xuéyuàn xuébào), 18–23 (2008)
22. Li, D., Xu, G.: Multimodal discourse analysis of a lesson of an excellent college English teacher (yōuxiù dàxué yīngyǔ jiàoshī kètáng de duōmótài huàyǔ fēnxī). J. Lang. and Liter. (yǔwén xué kān) 98–100 (2011)
23. Jiang, X., Ding, Y.: A theoretical framework of new college English teaching model (xiàndài jiàoyù jìshù xià de xīnxíng dàxué yīngyǔ jiàoxué móshì lǐlùn kuàngjià chūtàn). Technol. Enhan. Foreign Lang. (wàiyǔ diànhuà jiàoxué) **000**, 42–46 (2012)
24. Zhang, L.: A study of multi-modal discourse based on ELAN–A case study of a teacher's classroom discourse of college English (jīyú ELAN de duōmótài huàyǔ yánjiū—yǐ dàxué yīngyǔ jiàoshī kètáng huàyǔ wéi lì). Mod. Educ. Technol. (xiàndài jiàoyù jìshù) (2012)
25. Li, L.: A study of the application of multimodal teaching mode to the teaching of chinese as a foreign language (duōmótài jiàoxué móshì zài duìwài hànyǔ jiàoxué zhōng de yìngyòng yánjiū). Master of Arts. Northwest Normal University, Lanzhou (2016)
26. Li, Y., Xia, T.: Opportunities and challenges of central Asia in Chinese international education and Chinese culture ("yīdài yīlù" bèijǐng xià zhōngyà hànyǔ guójì jiàoyù yǔ zhōnghuá wénhuà chuánbō jīyù yǔ tiǎozhàn). Contemp. Educ. Cult. (dāngdài jiàoyù yǔ wénhuà) **011**, 31–36 (2018)
27. Wang, S., Liu, J.: The application of multimodal discourse analysis in international Chinese vocabulary teaching (guójì hànyǔ cíhuì jiàoxué zhōng de duōmótài huàyǔ fēnxī). Chinese Lang. Learn. (hànyǔ xuéxí), 85–96 (2020)
28. Liu, J., Wang, S.: Multimodal coordination in international chinese grammar teaching (guójì hànyǔ yǔfǎ jiàoxué zhōng de duōmótài xiétóng guānxì). In: Wang, W., Chen, L., Xu, S. (eds.) Applied Chinese Language Studies X, pp. 135–144. Sinolingua London Ltd., London (2021)
29. Wang, S., Liu, J.: Multimodal discourse analysis of grammar teaching in teaching Chinese as an international language (guójì hànyǔ yǔfǎ jiàoxué de duōmótài huàyǔ fēnxī). In: Huang, Y. (ed.) 20 Years Since Handover: Proceedings of the Symposium on the Review and Prospects of the Sociolinguistic Situation in the Macao SAR (liánxiānghǎikuò yǔzhòngqíngshēn—àomén tèqū 20 nián shèhuì yǔyán zhuàngkuàng huígù yǔ zhǎnwàng xuéshù yántǎohuì lùnwénjí), pp. 271–281. Joint Publishing (H.K.) Co., Ltd., Hong Kong (2020)

30. Liu, J., Wang, S.: The application of multimodal discourse analysis theory in grammar teaching of teaching Chinese as a second language (duōmótài huàyǔ fēnxī lǐlùn zài guójì hànyǔ yǔfǎ jiàoxué zhōng de yīngyòng). In: Zhu, R., Wang, M. (eds.) Selected Papers of the 15th International Conference on Chinese Language Pedagogy: Interdisciplinary Development & Research in International Chinese Language Education, pp. 125–135. Foreign Language Teaching and Research Press, Beijing (2019)
31. Liu, J., Wang, S.: A multimodal discourse analysis of an elementary-level comprehensive course in international Chinese teaching (guójì hànyǔ chūjí zōnghé kè jiàoxué zhōng de duōmótài huàyǔ fēnxī). Int. J. Chin. Lang. Educ. 67–91 (2019)
32. Shen, X.: Analysis of multimodal teaching mode of Chinese audio visual oral course – taking "China micro lens · variety" as an example (hànyǔ shìtīngshuōkè duōmótài jiàoxué móshì tànxī—yǐ "zhōngguó wéi jìngtóu·zōngyì piān" wéi lì). China J. Multimed. Netw. Teach. (zhōngguó duōméitǐ yǔ wǎngluò jiàoxué xuébào (shàng xúnkān)) (2019)
33. Pan, X.: Research on international Chinese audiovisual and oral teaching from the perspective of multimodal theory (duōmótài lǐlùn shìyě xià de guójì hànyǔ shìtīngshuō jiàoxué yánjiū). In: Xu, J., Ma, J. (eds.) the 13th International Conference on Chinese Language Teaching (dì shísān jiè guójì hànyǔ jiàoxué yántǎo huì). The Commercial Press, Beijing (2018)
34. Pan, X.: Audiovisual oral teaching based on multimodal and multi-intelligence theory (jīyú duōmótài yǔ duōyuán zhìnéng lǐlùn de shìtīngshuō jiàoxué). J. Int. Chin. Teach. (guójì hànyǔ jiàoxué yánjiū) **000**, 4–8 (2019)
35. Li, L.: The effect of multimodality materials on Chinese learners' listening comprehension (duōmótài cáiliào duì hànyǔ xuéxí zhě tīnglì lǐjiě de yǐngxiǎng). Ph.D. Anhui University, Hefei (2015)
36. Zheng, Y.: Study on multimodal teaching in elementary listening and conversation courses of teaching Chinese as a foreign language (duōmótài jiàoxué zài duìwài hànyǔ chūjí tīngshuōkè de shǐyòng qíngkuàng fēnxī). Master of Arts. Jinan University, Guangzhou (2018)
37. Wang, Y.: A multimodal college English mobile learning model in the context of "Internet +" ("hùliánwǎng +" bèijǐng xià jīyú duōmótài de dàxué yīngyǔ yídòng xuéxí móshì yánjiū). J. High. Educ. (gāojiào xué kān) 18–20+23 (2019)
38. Xu, H.: The research of mobile-assisted language learning mode on WeChat-based multimodal vocabulary (jīyú wēixìn de duōmótài cíhuì yídòng yǔyán xuéxí móshì yánjiū). J. Lanzhou Jiaotong Univ. (lánzhōu jiāotōng dàxué xuébào) **34**, 80–84 (2015)
39. Ke, H.: Study of mobile teaching framework under the multimodal environment in College English (duōmótài huánjìng xià dàxué yīngyǔ yídòng jiàoxué móshì jiàngòu). J. Hainan Radio TV Univ. (hǎinán guǎngbò diànshì dàxué xuébào) **18**, 154–158 (2017)
40. Shi, T.: A research on international students in China from the perspective of intercultural communication (1950-2015) (chuánbò yǔ jiēshòu: kuà wénhuà chuánbò shìjiǎo xiàlái huá liúxuéshēng jiàoyù yánjiū (1950-2015)). Ph.D. Shanghai International Studies University, Shanghai (2017)
41. Hu, X.: Classroom teaching of listening and apeaking course of TCFL (duìwài hànyǔ tīngshuōkè de kètáng jiàoxué huánjié). Capital Norm. Univ. J. (Soc. Sci. Edn.) (shǒudū shīfàn dàxué xuébào (shèhuì kēxué bǎn)), 89–93 (2013)
42. Qiao, N.: Intermediate Chinese learning & speaking teaching design–flowers tress birds and animals (duìwài hànyǔ zhōng jí tīngshuōkè jiàoxué shèjì—yǐ "huāmù niǎo shòu" wéi lì). Ph. D. Northwest Normal University, Lanzhou (2013)
43. Xue, C.: Strategic teaching listening and speaking for Thai students – Thailand North-Chiangmai University as an example (duì tài hànyǔ tīngshuōkè jiàoxué cèlüè yánjiū). Master of Arts. Jilin University, Changchun (2013)

44. Fan, R., Jiang, Z.: Application and thinking of multimedia in Chinese listening and speaking class (duōméitǐ zài hànyǔ tīngshuōkètáng zhōng de yìngyòng hé sīkǎo). China Electr. Power Educ. (zhōngguó diànlì jiàoyù), 105–107 (2011)
45. Yang, H.: The development of listening teaching of Chinese as a foreign language in China (zhōngguó duìwài hànyǔ tīnglì jiàoxué de fāzhǎn). Chin. Teach. World (shìjiè hànyǔ jiàoxué), 53–57 (1992)
46. Wu, Q.: The teaching design and research of intermediate listening and speaking course for teaching Chinese as a second language based on situational teaching method (jīyú qíngjǐng jiàoxuéfǎ de duìwài hànyǔ zhòngjí tīngshuōkè jiàoxué shèjì yǔ yánjiū). Ph.D. Anhui University, Hefei (2015)
47. Qian, Y., Wang, H.: On the three-stage teaching method of listening and speaking course of TCFL (qiǎntán duìwài hànyǔ tīngshuōkè sānduànshì jiàoxuéfǎ). Mod. Chin. (xiàndài yǔwén (yǔyán yánjiū bǎn)), 88–89 (2014)
48. Li, P.: Constructivist learning theory under the angle of the intermediate listening and speaking teaching of Chinese design - by the case of rent (jiàngòu zhǔyì xuéxí lǐlùn shìjiǎo xià de duìwài hànyǔ zhòngjí tīngshuōkè jiàoxué shèjì). Master of Arts. Harbin Normal University, Harbin (2017)
49. Deng, X.: Study on problems and countermeasures of culture teaching in TCFL (duìwài hànyǔ wénhuà jiàoxué cúnzài de wèntí jí zhǐdǎo yánjiū). Ph.D. Chong Qing University, Chongqing (2012)
50. Zhang, X.: The exploration of task based teaching mode in intermediate-level Chinese listening and speaking course (rènwù xíng jiàoxué móshì zài zhōngjí hànyǔ tīngshuōkè zhōng de tànsuǒ). Master of Arts. Shanghai International Studies University, Shanghai (2005)
51. Yi, H.: An exploration of teaching models of Chinese for overseas students guided by constructivism (yòng jiàngòu zhǔyì tàntǎo duìwài hànyǔ tīngshuō jiàoxué móshì). J. Xinjiang Vocat. University (xīnjiāng zhíyè dàxué xuébào) **17**, 43–45 (2009)

The Syntax and Semantics of Verbs of Searching

Shan Wang[1,2(✉)] and Shuchi Chen[1]

[1] Faculty of Arts and Humanities, University of Macau, Taipa, Macau
shanwang@um.edu.mo
[2] Institute of Collaborative Innovation, University of Macau, Taipa, Macau

Abstract. This study selected five typical verbs of searching 搜索 *sōusuǒ* 'search', 搜寻 *sōuxún* 'seek', 寻找 *xúnzhǎo* 'look for', 窥探 *kuītàn* 'pry' and 探听 *tàntīng* 'snoop' to explore their syntax and semantics. With reference to the automatic tagging results of LTP, we manually checked the syntactic dependencies and semantic roles of randomly selected sentences containing the five verbs using a self-developed syntactic-semantic annotation tool. The results showed that verbs of searching take HED as the main syntactic dependency type, VOB as the secondary type, and are rarely used as SBV and ATT. 搜索 *sōusuǒ* 'search' and 窥探 *kuītàn* 'pry' can also be used as ADV. 寻找 *xúnzhǎo* 'look for', 窥探 *kuītàn* 'pry' and 探听 *tàntīng* 'snoop' can also be used as POB. When they act as HED in sentences, 搜索 *sōusuǒ* 'search', 搜寻 *sōuxún* 'seek', 寻找 *xúnzhǎo* 'look for', and 窥探 *kuītàn* 'pry' are often used in sentences with both SBV and VOB in syntax whose semantic roles are AGT and CONT respectively. The most common sentence pattern of 探听 *tàntīng* 'snoop' is the sentence with no SBV, closely followed by the sentences with both SBV and VOB. All the five verbs can collocate with the semantic roles of LOC, TIME and MANN. In addition, 搜索 *sōusuǒ* 'search' and 寻找 *xúnzhǎo* 'look for' can also collocate with TOOL, and 窥探 *kuītàn* 'pry' and 探听 *tàntīng* 'snoop' can also collocate with semantic role of CONS. This study also compared the results with existing dictionary resources, which proves the practicality and innovation of analyzing the syntax and semantics of verbs using a combination of quantitative and qualitative methods based on the annotation tool we developed.

Keywords: Dependency grammar · Syntax · Semantics · Verbs of searching

1 Introduction

Tesnière became the founder of structural grammar and valence theory because of his publication of *Eléments de Syntaxe Structurale* in 1959 [1]. His structural syntax is also known as dependency grammar. It is a linguistic theory oriented to structural analysis and understanding, as well as a semantically driven functional syntactic theory, which involves the basic components of structural syntax, such as valence, stemma and dependency. According to dependency grammar, the syntactic-semantic structure of a sentence is composed of binary asymmetric relations between words in the sentence. Tesnière held that a sentence is an organized whole. There are connections linking words together in a sentence, which establish dependencies. In a dependency relation,

W. Jia et al. (Eds.): SETE 2021, LNCS 13089, pp. 122–141, 2021.
https://doi.org/10.1007/978-3-030-92836-0_11

one word is superior over the other. The superior word is called the governor, and the inferior word is called its subordinate [2]. Thus, the study of dependency grammar is concerned with syntactic and semantic relations between words.

Currently there are rare studies on Chinese verbs of searching. In this study, we made reference to English verbs of searching in Verbnet and then refer to Chinese resources including *A Thesaurus of Modern Chinese* [3], *Lexicon of common words in contemporary Chinese* [4], and *Synonym Word Forest* [5] to find out such verbs in Chinese. Then five commonly used searching verbs 搜索 *sōusuǒ* 'search', 搜寻 *sōuxún* 'seek', 寻找 *xúnzhǎo* 'look for', 窥探 *kuītàn* 'pry' and 探听 *tàntīng* 'snoop' were selected. Sentences were extracted from large-scale corpora, and the syntactic-semantic annotation tool based on the dependency grammar developed in this project was used for manual correction of the automatic labelling results, based on which the syntactic and semantic issues of these verbs were further investigated.

2 Related Research

Dependency grammar is a structural component analysis method that reveals the internal structure of sentences, which can better explain the grammatical structure of Chinese sentences [6]. It was also proved that dependency grammar component is more inclusive and more accurate when informants choose chunks. Therefore, dependency grammar component is more suitable for predicting how informants choose to chunk sentences [7]. In the 1980s, Tesnière's dependency grammar take root in China based on the practice of developing machine translation systems [8]. And after more than 20 years of development, dependency grammar has become the mainstream analysis method in the field of natural language processing, and many language processing achievements have been produced in the field of Natural Language Processing (NLP), such as Language Technology Platform (LTP) at Harbin Institute of Technology [9].

The syntactic and semantic research of Chinese vocabulary is an important way to explore how to use these words [10–13]. There are only a few studies on verbs of searching, including analyzing the diachronic evolution of the three words 找 *zhǎo* 'seek', 寻 *xún* 'search' and 觅 *mì* 'hunt for' in the meaning of 寻找 *xúnzhǎo* 'look for' in modern Chinese [14], exploring the different expressions of "search" in different dialects from the perspective of dialectology [15], By analyzing a large number of action event clauses of "search", this paper compares the syntactic differences of similar verbs in Chinese and English [16]. Although some syntactic and semantic studies of Chinese words based on dependency grammar have emerged in recent years [8–12], there is a lack of such analysis for verbs of searching in modern Chinese based on large-scale corpora.

3 Research Methods

3.1 Syntactic and Semantic Annotation Tool Based on Dependency Grammar

This project adopts the API interface of Language Technology Platform (LTP) [17] to develop a syntactic-semantic annotation tool based on dependency grammar with the following main modules and functions: (1) sentence and lexical annotation, (2) syntactic dependency analysis, (3) semantic role analysis, (4) semantic role annotation, and (5) correction of dependency syntactic analysis and semantic role relations. In this project, Sogou Lab, BCC and CCL were used as the source corpora for model training of the annotation tool. Some research has been conducted using this tool [18, 19].

3.2 Search Verb Corpus

Using the three corpora of BCC, CCL and Sogou Lab as the source corpus, we extracted sentences containing verbs of searching according to the following steps: (1) extracted all sentences containing 搜索 *sōusuǒ* 'search', 搜寻 *sōuxún* 'seek', 寻找 *xúnzhǎo* 'look for', 窥探 *kuītàn* 'pry' and 探听 *tàntīng* 'snoop', excluding all complex sentences and single sentences that contain special symbols which do not conform to Chinese norms. The reason for choosing single sentences is that the syntax and semantics of verbs can be reflected in single sentences. In contrast, complex sentences contain complex dependencies, which lead to high error rate in automatic labeling results; if only a clause containing the target verb in a complex sentence is used, the meaning of this complex sentence is incomplete. (2) All the sentences were processed by word segmentation and POS tagging. The sentences that each of the five verbs were not divided into two parts (to ensure that each of the five verbs is the smallest unit) and were used as verbs in the sentences were selected. (3) 200 sentences were randomly selected for each verb, and the sentences with grammatical errors and overly colloquial words were excluded manually. After the above steps, a total of 967 sentences were chosen for the above five searching verbs. Specifically, we annotated 198 sentences for 搜索 *sōusuǒ* 'search', 200 sentences for 搜寻 *sōuxún* 'seek', 200 sentences for 寻找 *xúnzhǎo* 'look for', 169 sentences for 窥探 *kuītàn* 'pry' and 200 sentences for 探听 *tàntīng* 'snoop'.

3.3 Corpus Annotation and Manual Correction

Using the syntactic and semantic annotation tool developed by this project, combined with the API of LTP, the syntactic and semantic roles of each selected sentence were automatically labelled, and then all of them were manually checked and revised if there were errors. Based on the results, the statistics and discussion analysis were further carried out.

4 Syntactic and Semantic Analysis of Verbs of Searching

In this section, we analyze the syntactic and semantic roles of verbs of searching.

4.1 Syntactic and Semantic Analysis of the Verb 搜索 *Sōusuǒ* 'Search'

Using 搜索 *sōusuǒ* 'search' as the keyword, 198 sentences were automatically labelled, manually checked and statistically analyzed. The syntactic dependencies of 搜索 *sōusuǒ* 'search' are shown in Table 1. It shows that 搜索 *sōusuǒ* 'search' can act as six syntactic dependencies: HED, VOB, COO, ATT, SBV and ADV[1]. 搜索 *sōusuǒ* 'search' has 90 sentences (45.45%) as HED, 44 sentences (22.22%) as VOB, 29 sentences (14.65%) as COO, 26 sentences (13.13%) as ATT, 8 sentences (4.04%) as SBV, and only 1 sentence (0.51%) as ADV.

Table 1. Syntactic dependencies of 搜索 *sōusuǒ* 'search' and their percentage

Syntactic dependencies of搜索 *sōusuǒ* 'search'	Number of Sentences	Percentage	Example Sentences
HED	90	45.45%	他的眼睛搜索着儿子的脸。 Tā de yǎnjīng *sōusuǒ* zhe er zi de liǎn. 'His eyes searched his son's face.'
VOB	44	22.22%	这些家伙搞搜索还很有一套。 Zhèxiē jiāhuo gǎo *sōusuǒ* hái hěn yǒu yī tào. 'These guys are good at searching. '
COO	29	14.65%	它观察着、搜索着、计谋着、仇恨着。 Tā guānchá zhe, *sōusuǒ* zhe, jìmóu zhe, chóuhèn zhe. 'It is observing, searching, ploting and hating. '
ATT	26	13.13%	搜索人员立即展开行动。 *Sōusuǒ* rényuán lìjí zhǎnkāi xíngdòng. 'The searchers took immediate action. '
SBV	8	4.04%	搜索毫无进展。 *Sōusuǒ* háowú jìnzhǎn. 'There was no progress in the search. '
ADV	1	0.51%	蒋少祖冷静地、搜索地看着他。 Jiǎng Shàozǔ lěngjìngde, *sōusuǒ*de kànzhe tā. 'Shaozu Jiang is looking at him calmly and searchingly. '
Total	198	100%	-

The main syntactic dependency of 搜索 *sōusuǒ* 'search' is to act as the core verb of a single sentence. It can also act as an object, attribute and appear in a coordinate structure, but it rarely acts as a subject or adverbial. Since the proportion of 搜索 *sōusuǒ* 'search' serves as the core verb is the highest, this paper further discusses 搜索 *sōusuǒ* 'search' as a subcategory of HED in sentences, as shown in Table 2.

[1] The abbreviations of dependency relations and their meanings are listed on http://www.ltp-cloud.com/intro_en.

Table 2. Subcategories of 搜索 *sōusuǒ* 'search' as HED

Subcategories of搜索 *sōusuǒ* 'search' as HED	Number of sentences	Percentage of HED	Example Sentences
SBV+*sōusuǒ*+VOB	27	30.00%	她<u>搜索</u>着实话。 Tā <u>*sōusuǒ*</u> zhe shíhuà. 'She searched for the truth.'
SBV+(Other)+*sōusuǒ*	22	24.44%	新兵小队紧张地<u>搜索</u>着。 Xīn bīng xiǎoduì jǐnzhāng de <u>*sōusuǒ*</u> zhe. 'A team of new soldiers are searching nervously.'
SBV+*sōusuǒ*+(Other)+COO	14	15.56	你竟然还<u>搜索</u>出来转发。 Nǐ jìngrán hái <u>*sōusuǒ*</u> chūlái zhuǎnfā. 'You even searched and forwarded it.'
sōusuǒ+VOB	14	15.56%	<u>搜索</u>商品信息。 <u>*Sōusuǒ*</u> shāngpǐn xìnxī. 'Search for product information.'
(Other+) *sōusuǒ*	11	12.22%	马上<u>搜索</u>! Mǎshàng <u>*sōusuǒ*</u>! 'Search right away!'
FOB+*sōusuǒ*+Other	2	2.22%	呵呵看来韩寒这名字快<u>搜索</u>不到了! Hēhē kànlái Hán Hán zhè míngzì kuài <u>*sōusuǒ*</u> bù dào le! 'Ha-ha, it seems that the name Han Han is not going to be found soon!'
Total	90	100%	-

Among the 90 sentences with 搜索 *sōusuǒ* 'search' as HED in Table 2, there are 14 sentences in which the type of the structure is COO. Among these sentences, 搜索 *sōusuǒ* 'search' is the first event and the other verb in parallel is the second event. Among the sentences with 搜索 *sōusuǒ* 'search' as HED and non-parallel events, "SBV+*sōusuǒ*+VOB" and "SBV+(Other)+*sōusuǒ*" account for high proportions, which are 32.22% and 24.44% respectively, indicating that when 搜索 *sōusuǒ* 'search' is used as HED, in most cases, there is a subject in a sentence, and the co-occurrence of a subject and an object is common. There are relatively few cases of no subjects and the cases with fronting-object is the least. The syntactic dependencies of non SBV, VOB, COO and FOB are called "Other" in all the following tables of subcategories of key words as HED.

Since subject and object are co-occurring in most cases, we classify the semantic dependencies of 搜索 *sōusuǒ* 'search' in the subcategory "SBV+*sōusuǒ*+VOB", as shown in Tables 3 and 4. Table 4 shows the types of semantic collocations in which SBV is the subject. The statistical results in Table 3 and Table 4 show that in the semantic collocations of "SBV+*sōusuǒ*+VOB", the semantic dependencies of SBV are mainly AGT and EXP, and the semantic dependencies of VOB are mainly CONT and LOC.

Table 3. Semantic collocations of 搜索 *sōusuǒ* 'search' in "SBV+*sōusuǒ*+VOB" (SBV as AGT)

Types	Number	Percentage	Example Sentences
(Dependency marker)+*sōusuǒ* +(Dependency marker)+CONT	7	38.89%	男人们在<u>搜索</u>沙蚕留下的痕迹和气味。 Nánrénmen zài <u>*sōusuǒ*</u> shācán liúxià de hénjī hé qìwèi. 'The men are searching for traces and smells left by silkworms.'
AGT+LOC+*sōus uǒ*+CONT	4	22.22%	警方正在四处<u>搜索</u>这个危险人物。 Jǐngfāng zhèngzài sìchù <u>*sōusuǒ*</u> zhège weixiǎn rénwù. 'The police are searching everywhere for this dangerous persons.'
AGT+*sōusuǒ*+C ONT	2	11.11%	她<u>搜索</u>着实话。 Tā <u>*sōusuǒ*</u> zhe shíhuà. 'She searched for the truth.'
AGT+TOOL+*sō usuǒ*+CONT	2	11.11%	紧接着你可以百度<u>搜索</u>天蝎座B型血人的性格。 Jǐn jiēzhe nǐ kěyǐ bǎidù <u>*sōusuǒ*</u> tiānxiēzuò B xíng xuè rén dì xìnggé. 'Then you can baidu search the personality of people with Scorpio's type B blood.'
AGT+SCO+*sōus uǒ*+CONT	1	5.56%	我在无所不能的网络上<u>搜索</u>这部戏的名字。 Wǒ zài wúsuǒbùnéng de wǎngluò shàng <u>*sōusuǒ*</u> zhè bù xì de míngzi. 'I searched the omnipotent internet for the name of this play.'
AGT+TIME+ *sōusuǒ*+CONT	1	5.56%	她也不再<u>搜索</u>枯肠。 Tā yě bùzài <u>*sōusuǒ*</u> kūcháng. 'She no longer searching her brains.'
AGT+ORIG +*sō usuǒ*+CONT	1	5.56%	作者从海外馆藏资料中<u>搜索</u>到西方人描绘的中国海盗。 'Zuòzhě cóng hǎiwài guǎncáng zīliào zhōng <u>*sōusuǒ*</u> dào xīfāng rén miáohuì de Zhōngguó hǎidào.' The author searched and found Chinese Pirates depicted by westerners from overseas collections.

Table 4. Semantic collocations of 搜索 *sōusuǒ* 'search' in "SBV+*sōusuǒ*+VOB" (SBV as EXP)

Types	Number	Percentage	Example Sentences
EXP+(Dependency marker)+*sōusuǒ*+(Dependency marker)+CONT	4	44.44%	无双的眼<u>搜索</u>着营帐。 Wúshuāng de yǎn <u>*sōusuǒ*</u> zhe yíngzhàng. 'Shuang Wu's eyes are searching the tent. '
EXP+MANN+*sōusuǒ*+LOC	2	22.22%	几只手电筒交叉着来回地<u>搜索</u>海面。 Jǐ zhī shǒudiàntǒng jiāochā zhe láihuí de <u>*sōusuǒ*</u> hǎimiàn. 'Several flashlights crossed back and forth to search the sea. '
EXP+*sōusuǒ*+CONT	1	11.11%	秒拍<u>搜索</u>什么关键词？ Miǎopāi <u>*sōusuǒ*</u> shénme guānjiàn cí? 'What keywords need to search for a few seconds of shooting?'
EXP+*sōusuǒ*+LOC	1	11.11%	一双双严酷无情的眼睛<u>搜索</u>着水面。 Yī shuāngshuāng yánkù wúqíng de yǎnjīng <u>*sōusuǒ*</u> zhe shuǐmiàn. 'Pairs of ruthless eyes are searching the water. '
TIME+EXP+MANN+*sōusuǒ*+CONT	1	11.11%	这时候笔记本就会自动<u>搜索</u>出局域网上的共享打印机。 Zhè shíhòu bǐjìběn jiù huì zìdòng <u>*sōusuǒ*</u> chū júyùwǎng shàng de gòngxiǎng dǎyìnjī. 'At this time, the notebook will automatically search for the shared printers on the LAN. '

The AGT roles of 搜索 *sōusuǒ* 'search' are mainly played by human beings. The EXP roles of 搜索 *sōusuǒ* 'search' mostly consist of non-consciousness subjects, such as 眼睛 *yǎnjīng* 'eye', 手电筒 *shǒudiàntǒng* 'flashlight', and 笔记本 *bǐjìběn* 'notebook'. The objects of 搜索 *sōusuǒ* 'search' are mainly objects and persons, such as 营帐 *yíngzhàng* 'tent' and 人物 *rénwù* 'person'. In addition to the subjects and objects, the event scenarios that can be triggered by 搜索 *sōusuǒ* 'search' include LOC, TIME, SCO, TOOL, ORIG and MANN. LOC refers to where the search event takes place or the place where the object that is searched for is located, such as 水面 *shuǐmiàn* 'water surface'; TIME refers to the occurring time or the during of the search event, such as 不再 *búzài* 'no longer'; SCO refers to the scope of search event, such as 网络 *wǎngluò* 'internet'; TOOL means the tool that be used, such as 百度 *bǎidù* 'baidu'; ORIG refers to the origin of something that can be searched, such as 海外馆藏资料 *hǎiwài guǎncáng zīliào* 'Overseas collection materials'. MANN refers to the manner in which the 搜索 *sōusuǒ* 'search' is conducted, such as 交叉 *jiāochā* 'in a cross way'.

4.2 Syntactic and Semantic Analysis of the Verb 搜寻 *Sōuxún* 'Seek'

A total of 200 sentences were automatically annotated, manually checked and statistically analyzed using 搜寻 *sōuxún* 'seek' as the keyword. The number of syntactic dependencies of 搜寻 *sōuxún* 'seek' is shown in Table 5. It acts as five syntactic dependencies in sentences: HED, VOB, ATT, COO and SBV. It has 123 sentences as HED (61.50%), 35 sentences as VOB (17.50%), 19 sentences as ATT (9.50%), 17 sentences as COO (8.50%), and 6 sentences as SBV (3.00%). Unlike 搜索 *sōusuǒ* 'search', 搜寻 *sōuxún* 'seek' does not act as ADV.

Table 5. Syntactic dependencies of 搜寻 *sōuxún* 'seek' and their percentage

Syntactic dependencies of 搜寻 *sōuxún* 'seek'	Number of sentences	Percentage	Example Sentences
HED	123	61.50%	她的眼搜寻着浴室里所有的东西。 Tā de yǎn *sōuxún* zhe yùshì lǐ suǒyǒu de dōngxī. 'Her eyes are seeking for everything in the bathroom.'
VOB	35	17.50%	他知道魔眼正在搜寻着他的踪迹。 Tā zhīdào móyǎn zhèngzài *sōuxún* zhe tā de zōngjī. 'He knew that the magic eyes were seeking for his trace. '
ATT	19	9.50%	她扭头避开他搜寻的唇。 Tā niǔtóu bìkāi tā *sōuxún* de chún. 'She turned away from his seeking lips. '
COO	17	8.50%	当地的消防人员和警察目前仍在抢救伤员和搜寻幸存者。 Dāngdì de xiāofáng rényuán hé jǐngchá mùqián réng zài qiǎngjiù shāngyuán hé *sōuxún* xìngcúnzhě. 'Local firefighters and police are still rescuing the wounded and seeking for survivors. '
SBV	6	3.00%	搜寻马航失联客机仍然是首要任务。 *Sōuxún* mǎháng shīlián kèjī réngrán shì shǒuyào rènwù. 'Seeking for Malaysia Airlines' lost passenger plane remains a top priority. '
Total	200	100%	-

It can be seen that the most important syntactic dependency of 搜寻 *sōuxún* 'seek' is to act as HED in a sentence. It also often acts as a verb-object, an attribute and appears in coordinate structure, but rarely act as a subject. Because of the high proportion of 搜寻 *sōuxún* 'seek' as HED, this paper further discusses 搜寻 *sōuxún* 'seek' as HED. Table 6 shows the subcategories of the sentences with 搜寻 *sōuxún* 'seek' as

HED. Among the 123 sentences of 搜寻 *sōuxún* 'seek' as HED, there are only 2 sentences with the event structure type of COO. Among the single sentences with 搜寻 *sōuxún* 'seek' as HED and non-coordinated event type, "SBV+*sōuxún*+VOB" accounts for the highest percentage of 60.98%, indicating that in most cases, there is a subject and an object co-occurrence in a sentence. The cases of no subject are relatively rare and the cases of object preposition are also rare. Since a subject and an object co-occur in most cases, we analyze the semantic features of this type by describing semantic collocations of the subcategory "SBV+*sōuxún*+VOB".

Table 6. Subcategories of 搜寻 *sōuxún* 'seek' as HED

Subcategories of 搜寻 *sōuxún* 'seek' as HED	Number of sentences	Percentageof HED	Example Sentences
SBV+*sōuxún*+VOB	75	60.98%	警察正在搜寻肇事者。 Jǐngchá zhèngzài *sōuxún* zhàoshì zhě. 'The police are seeking for the perpetrator.'
Other+SBV+(Other)+*sōuxún*	27	21.95%	现在张总还在里面搜寻。 Xiànzài Zhāngzǒng hái zài lǐmiàn *sōuxún*. 'Now president Zhang is still seeking inside.'
sōuxún+VOB	15	12.20%	搜寻你的名字。 *Sōuxún* nǐ de míngzì. 'Seeking for your name.'
(Other+) *sōuxún* (+Other) (且无 FOB)	2	1.63%	果能切实搜寻。 Guǒnéng qièshí *sōuxún*. 'Actually we can effectively seek.'
FOB+*sōuxún*+(Other)	2	1.63%	黑无常的资料搜寻不到。 Hēi Wúcháng de zīliào *sōuxún* bùdào. 'Black impermanence's data can't be sought.'
SBV+*sōuxún*+COO+VOB	2	1.63%	当地警方搜寻发现36具遇难者遗体。 Dāngdì jǐngfāng *sōuxún* fāxiàn 36 jù yùnànzhě yítǐ. 'Local police sought and found the remains of 36 victims.'
Total	123	100%	-

Table 7 and Table 8 show the semantic collocations of 搜寻 *sōuxún* 'seek' in "SBV +*sōuxún*+VOB". In order to describe the semantic collocations more clearly, this article classifies the semantic collocational cases. Table 7 shows the type of semantic collocations in which SBV acts as AGT. Table 8 shows the type of semantic collocations in which SBV is the subject. The statistical results show that in the semantic collocations of "SBV+*sōuxún*+VOB", the semantic dependencies of SBV are mainly AGT and EXP. The semantic dependencies of VOB are mainly CONT and LOC.

Table 7. Semantic collocations of 搜寻 *sōuxún* 'seek' in "SBV+*sōuxún*+VOB" (SBV as AGT)

Types	Number	Percentage	Example Sentences
AGT+LOC+*sōuxún*+CONT	20	30.77%	她在这里搜寻什么回忆呢？ Tā zài zhèlǐ *sōuxún* shénme huíyì ne? 'What memories does she seek for here?'
AGT+MANN+*sōuxún*+CONT	17	26.15%	我努力四处搜寻妈妈的泡泡眼。 Wǒ nǔlì sìchù *sōuxún* māmā de pàopào yǎn. 'I tried to seek around for my mother's bubble eyes.'
AGT+(dependency marker)+*sōuxún*+(dependency marker)+CONT	16	24.62%	他们又搜寻着帐簿。 Tāmen yòu *sōuxún* zhàngbù. 'They are seeking the account book again.'
AGT+SCO+*sōuxún*+CONT	3	4.62%	于是我就在记忆中搜寻我认识的矮子。 Yúshì wǒ jiù zài jìyì zhōng *sōuxún* wǒ rènshí de ǎizi. 'So I sought my memory for the dwarf I knew.'
AGT+TIME+*sōuxún*+CONT	2	3.08%	自卫队和当地警方目前正在搜寻飞机残骸和机上人员。 Zìwèiduì hé dāngdì jǐngfāng mùqián zhèngzài *sōuxún* fēijī cánhái hé jīshàng rényuán. 'The self-defense forces and local police are currently seeking for the wreckage of the plane and the people on board.'
TIME+AGT+*sōuxún*+CONT	2	3.08%	目前救援人员仍在搜寻失踪者。 Mùqián jiùyuán rényuán réng zài *sōuxún* shīzōngzhě. 'Rescue workers are still seeking for the missing.'
AGT+*sōuxún*+CONT+TIME	2	3.08%	德国人搜寻了我们好几个月。 Déguó rén *sōuxún* le wǒmen hǎojǐ gè yuè. 'The Germans sought us for several months.'
AGT+*sōuxún*+LOC	2	3.08%	今晚我们还要再搜寻一遍案发现场。 Jīnwǎn wǒmen háiyào zài *sōuxún* yībiàn ànfā xiànchǎng. 'We're going to seek the crime scene again tonight.'
AGT+*sōuxún*+CONT	1	1.54%	他搜寻她清澄如镜的眼。 Tā *sōuxún* tā qīngchéng rú jìng de yǎn. 'He is seeking her glassy eyes.'

Table 8. Semantic collocations of 搜寻 *sōuxún* 'seek' in "SBV+*sōuxún*+VOB" (SBV as EXP)

Types	Number	Percentage	Example Sentences
EXP+*sōuxún*+(Dependency marker)+CONT	5	45.45%	眼睛搜寻着电脑中的歌名。 Yǎnjīng *sōuxún* zhe diànnǎo zhōng de gē míng. 'My eyes are searching for the song title in the computer.'
EXP+LOC+*sōuxún*+CONT	2	18.18%	路易斯的眼睛在地板上搜寻着泥脚。 Lùyìsī de yǎnjīng zài dìbǎn shàng *sōuxún* zhe ní jiǎo. 'Louis's eyes sought the floor for mud feet.'
EXP+*sōuxún*+CONT	1	9.09%	粗壮的手指搜寻到了那个名字。 Cūzhuàng de shǒuzhǐ *sōuxún* dào le nàgè míngzì. 'Strong fingers sought and found that name.'
EXP+*sōuxún*+CONS +CONT	1	9.09%	数字电视搜寻不到信号！ Shùzì diànshì *sōuxún* bù dào xìnhào! 'Digital TV can't seek to find the signal!'
EXP+MANN+*sōuxún*+CONT	1	9.09%	她那翠绿的眼睛无可奈何地搜寻他的目光。 Tā nà cuìlǜ de yǎnjīng wúkěnàihé de *sōuxún* tā de mùguāng. 'Her green eyes sought helplessly for his eyes.'
EXP+SCO+*sōuxún*+CONT	1	9.09%	我眼睛四下里搜寻司令夫人的尸首。 Wǒ yǎnjīng sìxià lǐ *sōuxún* sīlìng fūrén de shīshǒu. 'My eyes are searching for the body of the commander's wife everywhere.'

In the semantic collocational environment of "SBV+*sōuxún*+VOB", the most frequent is "AGT+LOC+*sōuxún*+CONT". The agents 搜寻 *sōuxún* 'seek' are mainly persons who conduct the seeking event, such as 他 *tā* 'he', 德国人 *Déguó rén* 'Germans', 救援人员 *jiùyuán rényuán* 'rescuer'. The experiencers are usually things without consciousness, such as 手指 *shǒuzhǐ* 'finger', 电视机 *diànshìjī* 'TV', etc. The objects of 搜寻 *sōuxún* 'seek' are mainly persons, concrete objects and abstract things, such as 失踪者 *shīzōngzhě* 'the missing', 眼 *yǎn* 'eye' and 回忆 *huíyì* 'memory'. In addition to AGT and EXP, the event scenarios that can be triggered by 搜寻 *sōuxún* 'seek' include CONS, MANN, LOC, TIME and SCO. CONS refers to the result of 搜寻 *sōuxún* 'seek', such as 不到 *bú dào* 'no result'; MANN refers to the way in which the 搜寻 *sōuxún* 'seek' is conducted, such as 无可奈何 *wúkěnàihé* 'feel helpless'; LOC refers to the location of 搜寻 *sōuxún* 'seek' or the location of the object of 搜寻 *sōuxún* 'seek', e.g. 地板 *dìbǎn* 'floor'; TIME refers to the time that 搜寻 *sōuxún* 'seek' event occurred or lasted, such as 今晚 *jīnwǎn* 'tonight' and 好几个月 *hǎojǐ gè yuè* 'several months; SCO refers to the scope of search event, such as 记忆 *jìyì* 'memory'.

4.3 Syntactic and Semantic Analysis of the Verb 寻找 *xúnzhǎo* 'Look for'

A total of 200 sentences with 寻找 *xúnzhǎo* 'look for' as the keyword were automatically annotated, manually checked and statistically analyzed. The results of the syntactic dependencies of 寻找 *xúnzhǎo* 'look for' are shown in Table 9. 寻找 *xúnzhǎo* 'look for' served as six syntactic dependencies: HED, VOB, COO, ATT, VOB, SBV and POB. 寻找 *xúnzhǎo* 'look for' has 100 sentences (50%) as HED, 51 sentences

Table 9. Syntactic dependencies of 寻找 *xúnzhǎo* 'look for' and their percentage

Syntactic dependencies of 寻找 *xúnzhǎo* 'look for'	Number of sentences	Percentage	Example Sentences
HED	95	47.50%	他无可奈何地寻找着乔斯。 Tā wúkěnàihé de *xúnzhǎo* zhe qiáo sī. 'He helplessly looked for Jos.'
VOB	51	25.50%	英国政府为此兴师动众进行了大规模的寻找。 Yīngguó zhèngfǔ wèi cǐ xīngshīdòngzhòng jìnxíngle dà guīmó de *xúnzhǎo*. 'The British government mobilized people to carry out a large-scale search.'
COO	30	15.00%	他们总是不经意地去探索和寻找事物之间的联系。 Tāmen zǒngshì bùjīngyì de qù tànsuǒ hé *xúnzhǎo* shìwù zhījiān de liánxì. 'They always inadvertently explore and look for the connection between things.'
ATT	14	7.00%	这是一个寻找和认识血缘的、令人惊心动魄的过程。 Zhè shì yī gè *xúnzhǎo* hé rènshí xiěyuán de, lìng rén jīngxīndòngpò de guòchéng. 'This is a thrilling process of looking for and understanding blood relationship.'
SBV	8	4.00%	寻找道路并不难。 *Xúnzhǎo* dàolù bìngbù nán. 'Looking for the way is not difficult.'
POB	2	1.00%	美帝为了寻找出路正在进行垂死的挣扎。 Měidì wèile *xúnzhǎo* chūlù zhèngzài jìnxíng chuísǐ de zhēngzhá. 'The US emperor is struggling to look for a way out.'
Total	200	100%	-

(25.50%) as VOB, 28 sentences (14.00%) as COO, 13 sentences (6.50%) as ATT, and 6 sentences (3.00%) as SBV. Unlike 搜索 *sōusuǒ* 'search' and 搜寻 *sōuxún* 'seek', 寻找 *xúnzhǎo* 'look for' also as a POB in the sentence, but there are only two sentences, accounting for very small percentage.

The result shows that the most important syntactic dependency of 寻找 *xúnzhǎo* 'look for' is as HED of a sentence. It also often acts as a verb-object and appears in the coordinate structure. It is relatively rarely as an attribute, a subject, and a prepositional object. Because of the high proportion of 寻找 *xúnzhǎo* 'look for' as HED, we further discuss 寻找 *xúnzhǎo* 'look for' as HED. Table 10 shows the subcategories of sentences with 寻找 *xúnzhǎo* 'look for' as HED. 95 sentences with 寻找 *xúnzhǎo* 'look for' as HED. "SBV+*xúnzhǎo*+VOB" accounted for 63.16% of all the sentences, indicating that when 寻找 *xúnzhǎo* 'look for' is used HED, the sentence has a subject and an object in most cases. The probability of having no subject is relatively low and the probability of having the preposition-object is the lowest. Since the subject and object are co-occurring in most cases, this section continues to analyze the semantic features of the subcategory "SBV+*xúnzhǎo*+VOB" by describing the semantic collocations of this type.

Table 10. Subcategories of 寻找 *xúnzhǎo* 'look for' as HED

Subcategories of 寻找 *xúnzhǎo* 'look for' as HED	Number of sentences	Percentage of HED	Example Sentences
SBV+*xúnzhǎo*+VOB	60	63.16%	他也在寻找一位领袖。 Tā yě zài *xúnzhǎo* yī wèi lǐngxiù. 'He is also looking for a leader.'
xúnzhǎo+(Other)+VOB	16	16.84%	寻找下一站幸福。 *Xúnzhǎo* xià yī zhàn xìngfú. 'Looking for the next happiness.'
SBV+(Other)+*xúnzhǎo*	12	12.63%	他仍在寻找着。 Tā réngrán zài *xúnzhǎo* zhe. 'He is still looking for.'
xúnzhǎo+VOB+COO	6	6.32%	寻找幸福去了嘛! *Xúnzhǎo* xìngfú qùle ma! 'Looking for happiness!'
FOB+Other+*xúnzhǎo*	1	1.05%	答案在本版面寻找。 Dá'àn zài běn bǎnmiàn *xúnzhǎo*. 'Looking for the answer in this page.'
Total	95	100%	-

Table 11 shows the types and number of semantic collocations of 寻找 *xúnzhǎo* 'look for' in "SBV+*xúnzhǎo*+VOB". The subjects of 寻找 *xúnzhǎo* 'look for' are mostly AGT, and the role of EXP appears in only one sentence. The role of AGT is mainly played by living beings, and the role of EXP is usually things without consciousness of life, such as 音乐 *yīnyuè* 'music'. The object role of 寻找 *xúnzhǎo* 'look for' is either a concrete word or an abstract word, such as 协助杀人者 *xiézhù shārénzhě* 'assistants to the murderer' and 方法 *fāngfǎ* 'method'. In addition to the event and the object, the event scenarios that can be triggered by 寻找 *xúnzhǎo* 'look for' include MANN, such as 固执 *gùzhí* 'stubbornly'; LOC, such as 官巷口 *guānxiàngkǒu* 'the entrance of the official alley'; SCO, such as 到处 *dàochù* 'everywhere'; TIME, such as 目前 *mùqián* 'at present' and 大半辈子 *dàbànbèizi* 'for most of my

Table 11. Semantic collocations of 寻找 *xúnzhǎo* 'look for' in "SBV+*xúnzhǎo*+VOB"

Types	Number	Percentage	Example Sentences
AGT+*xúnzhǎo*+CONT	32	50.79%	他去寻找吉他手。 Tā qù *xúnzhǎo* jítāshǒu. 'He went to look for a guitarist.'
AGT+LOC+*xúnzhǎo*+CONT	9	14.29%	我在官巷口寻找东平巷。 Wǒ zài guānxiàng kǒu *xúnzhǎo* dōngpíng xiàng. 'I'm looking for Dongping lane at the entrance of Guanxiang lane.'
AGT+MANN+*xúnzhǎo*+CONT	7	11.11%	有的读者刻意寻找书中虚构的贝克街旧迹。 Yǒude dúzhě kèyì *xúnzhǎo* shū zhōng xūgòu de bèikèjiē jiùjī. 'Some readers deliberately look for the fictional old traces of Baker Street in the book.'
AGT+SCO+*xúnzhǎo*+CONT	4	6.35%	他正到处寻找他们。 Tā zhèng dàochù *xúnzhǎo* tāmen. 'He is looking for them everywhere.'
TIME+AGT+*xúnzhǎo*+CONT	4	6.35%	现在两支球队都在寻找终结这轮系列赛的办法。 Xiànzài liǎng zhī qiúduì dōu zài *xúnzhǎo* zhōngjié zhè lún xìlièsài de bànfǎ. 'Now both teams are looking for ways to end the series.'
AGT+TIME+*xúnzhǎo*+CONT	3	4.76%	警方目前正在寻找可能的协助杀人者。 Jǐngfāng mùqián zhèngzài *xúnzhǎo* kěnéng de xiézhù shārénzhě. 'The police is currently looking for possible assistance to the murderer.'
EXP+MANN+*xúnzhǎo*+CONT	1	1.59%	音乐固执地在寻找一种新的调性和分离节拍。 Yīnyuè gùzhí de zài *xúnzhǎo* yī zhǒng xīn de diào xìng hé fēnlí jiépāi. 'Music is stubbornly looking for a new tonality and separated beat.'
AGT+*xúnzhǎo*+CONT+TIME	1	1.59%	我寻找了你大半辈子。 Wǒ *xúnzhǎo* le nǐ dà bàn bèizi. 'I've been looking for you for most of my life.'
AGT+REAS+*xúnzhǎo*+CONT	1	1.59%	你们为何不寻找旁人？ Nǐmen wèihé bù *xúnzhǎo* pángrén? 'Why don't you look for someone else?'
AGT+TOOL+*xúnzhǎo*+CONT	1	1.59%	乔尼和斯道麦朗通过扫描器寻找空中的敌人。 Qiáoní hé Sīdàomàilǎng tōngguò sǎomiáoqì *xúnzhǎo* kōngzhōng de dírén. 'Johnny and Steve Mai Lang look for the enemy in the air through the scanner.'

life', representing the event of occurring time or the duration of the search. Quantitatively, the semantic role of LOC appears more frequently in 寻找 *xúnzhǎo* 'look for' sentences than MANN, TIME and SCO. In addition, the semantic role of REAS also appears in the semantic collocations of 寻找 *xúnzhǎo* 'look for'; TOOL, such as 扫描器 *sǎomiáo qì* 'scanner'.

4.4 Syntactic and Semantic Analysis of the Verb 窥探 *Kuītàn* 'Pry'

A total of 169 sentences with 窥探 *kuītàn* 'pry' as the keyword were automatically annotated, manually checked and statistically analyzed. The results of the syntactic dependencies of 窥探 *kuītàn* 'pry' in sentences are shown in Table 12. 7 types of syntactic dependencies were used: HED, VOB, COO, ATT, POB, SBV and ADV. 窥探 *kuītàn* 'pry' has 64 sentences (37.87%) as HED, 42 sentences (24.85%) as VOB, 35 sentences (20.71%) as COO, 17 sentences (10.06%) as ATT, 6 sentences (3.55%) as POB. And as SBV, there are 4 sentences, accounting for 2.37%; as ADV, there is only 1 sentence, accounting for a minimum of 0.59%.

Table 12. Syntactic dependencies of 窥探 *kuītàn* ‘pry’ and their percentage

Syntactic dependencies of 窥探 *kuītàn* ‘pry’	Number of sentences	Percentage	Example Sentences
HED	64	37.87%	兰克斯在周围窥探。 Lánkèsī zài zhōuwéi *kuītàn*. ‘Ranks is prying around.’
VOB	42	24.85%	最忌的是妇女窥探。 Zuì jì de shì fùnǚ *kuītàn*. ‘The most taboo is women’s prying.’
COO	35	20.71%	它经常躲在这里窥探外部的动静。 Tā jīngcháng duǒ zài zhèlǐ *kuītàn* wàibù de dòngjìng. ‘It often hides here to pry on the outside.’
ATT	17	10.06%	你的硬盘能避开一双双窥探的眼睛吗？ Nǐ de yìngpán néng bìkāi yī shuāng shuāng *kuītàn* de yǎnjīng ma? ‘Can your hard drive avoid pairs of prying eyes?’
POB	6	3.55%	谁说看书是为了窥探自己的内心？ Shuí shuō kànshū shì wèile *kuītàn* zìjǐ de nèixīn? ‘Who says reading is to peep into your own heart?’
SBV	4	2.37%	窥探别人的家庭背景是件卑鄙的行为。 *Kuītàn* biérén de jiātíng bèijǐng shì jiàn bēibǐ de xíngwéi. ‘It’s a despicable act to pry into other people’s family background.’
ADV	1	0.59%	潜水艇窥探猎物似地同运输船并行了一会。 Qiánshuǐtǐng *kuītàn* lièwù shìde tóng yùnshū chuán bìngxíng le yīhuǐ. ‘The submarine ran side by side with the transport ship for a while like spying on its prey.’
Total	169	100%	-

The result shows that the most important syntactic dependency of 窥探 *kuītàn* ‘pry’ is to act as HED of a sentence. It also often acts as the verb-object, appears in coordination and acts as an attribute, but it relatively rarely acts as a subject, a preposition-object and adverbial. Since the proportion of 窥探 *kuītàn* ‘pry’ as HED is high, we further discuss 窥探 *kuītàn* ‘pry’ as a subcategory of HED, as shown in Table 13. There are 31 sentences have the structure “SBV+*kuītàn*+VOB’ with the highest percentage of 48.44%. It means that when 窥探 *kuītàn* ‘pry’ is used as HED, the majority of the sentences have the subject and the object co-occurrence. The probability of preposition-object and parallelism is the lowest. Since subject and object co-occur in most cases, this paper continues to analyze the semantic characteristics of this type by describing the semantic collocations of the subcategory “SBV+*kuītàn* +VOB”.

Table 13. Subcategories of 窥探 *kuītàn* 'pry' as HED

Subcategories of 窥探 *kuītàn* 'pry' as HED	Number of sentences	Percentage of HED	Example Sentences
SBV+*kuītàn*+VOB	31	48.44%	他的眼睛窥探无依无靠的人。 Tā de yǎnjīng *kuītàn* wú yī wú kào de rén. 'His eyes are prying into the helpless.'
(Other+) *kuītàn* +VOB	15	23.44%	窥探我兵虚实。 *Kuītàn* wǒ bīng xūshí. 'Pry on the reality of our soldiers.'
SBV+(Other)+*kuītàn*	12	18.75%	吃惊的哈比人纷纷从窗内往外窥探。 Chījīng de hā bǐ rén fēnfēn cóng chuāng nèi wǎngwài *kuītàn*. 'The surprised hobbits pried out of the window.'
SBV+(Other)+*kuītàn*+COO+VOB	3	4.69%	你好象窥探到、偷听到我隐秘的思想似的。 Nǐ hǎo xiàng *kuītàn* dào, tōu tīng dào wǒ yǐnmì de sīxiǎng shì de. 'You seem to have pried and overheard my secret thoughts.'
FOB+*kuītàn*+(Other)	3	4.69%	这秘密被赵巧茹窥探了个清清楚楚。 Zhè mìmì bèi Zhào Qiǎorú *kuītàn* le gè qīngqīngchǔchǔ. 'The secret was pried out by Qiaoru Zhao clearly.'
Total	64	100%	-

Table 14. Semantic collocations of 窥探 *kuītàn* 'pry' in "SBV+*kuītàn*+VOB"

Types	Number	Percentage	Example Sentences
AGT+*kuītàn*+CONT	19	61.29%	卡拉蒙边窥探着坦尼斯身后。 Kǎlāméng biān *kuītàn* zhe Tǎnnísī shēnhòu. 'Caramon is prying the back of Tanis.'
AGT+MANN+*kuītàn*+CONT	5	16.13%	我们好奇地窥探着灶膛里的奥秘。 Wǒmen hàoqí de *kuītàn* zhe zàotáng lǐ de àomì. 'We pried curiously into the mystery of the stove.'
EXP+*kuītàn*+CONT	3	9.68%	他们猫头鹰似的眼睛窥探着每一户人家。 Tāmen māotóuyīng shìde yǎnjīng *kuītàn* zhe měi yī hù rénjiā. 'Their owl-like eyes peeped at every house.'
AGT+TIME+*kuītàn*+CONT	2	6.45%	狐狸整日在窥探着佃农的鸡群。 Húlí zhěngrì zài *kuītàn* zhe diànnóng de jī qún. 'The fox pries on the tenant's chickens all day.'
AGT+LOC+*kuītàn*+CONT	1	3.23%	史东透过拱门窥探着其后的景色。 Shǐdōng tòuguò gǒngmén *kuītàn* zhe qí hòu de jǐngsè. 'Stone pried through the arch into the view behind him.'
EXP+LOC+*kuītàn*+CONS	1	3.23%	这一点在国际车企在中国的战略布局中也可窥探一二。 Zhè yīdiǎn zài guójì chēqǐ zài Zhōngguó de zhànlüè bùjú zhōng yě kě *kuītàn* yī'èr. 'This can also be pried out in the strategic layout of international auto enterprises in China.'

Table 14 shows the semantic collocations of 窥探 *kuītàn* 'pry' in "SBV+窥探 *kuītàn* 'pry'+VOB". Among the semantic collocations of SBV+*kuītàn*+VOB, "AGT +*kuītàn*+CONT" is dominant, with the largest number of 19 sentences. Among them, the dominated semantic role of the subject of 窥探 *kuītàn* 'pry' is AGT, and the frequency of EXP is relatively low. The objects of 窥探 *kuītàn* 'pry' can be either living things or entities, such as 鸡群 *jīqún* 'chicken flocks' and 景色 *jǐngsè* 'scenery'. In addition, the role MANN appears five times, the role LOC appears twice, , and the role TIME appears twice, which shows that the role MANN is more prominent in the sentence 窥探 *kuītàn* 'pry' than LOC and TIME. This feature is different from the previous three words. In addition to the subjects and objects, the event scenarios that can be triggered by 窥探 *kuītàn* 'pry' include MANN, TIME and LOC. MANN refers to the manner that the 窥探 *kuītàn* 'pry' is conducted, such as 好奇 *hàoqí* 'curiously';

TIME refers to the during of the pry event, such as 整日 *zhěng rì* 'all day'; LOC refers to where the pry event takes place, such as 拱门 *gǒngmén* 'arch'.

4.5 Syntactic and Semantic Analysis of the Verb 探听 *Tàntīng 'Snoop'*

A total of 200 sentences with 探听 *tàntīng* 'snoop' as the keyword were automatically annotated, manually checked and statistically analyzed. The results of its syntactic dependencies in sentences are shown in Table 15. The verb 探听 *tàntīng* 'snoop' is used as 7 syntactic dependencies: HED, COO, ATT, VOB, SBV and POB. There were 76 sentences (38.00%) as HED, 68 sentences (34.00%) as COO, 50 sentences (25.00%) as VOB, and only 3 sentences (1.50%) as ATT, 2 sentences (1.00%) as SBV, and 1 sentence (0.50%) as POB.

Table 15. Syntactic dependencies of 探听 *tàntīng* 'snoop' and their percentage

Syntactic dependencies of 探听 *tàntīng* 'snoop'	Number of sentences	Percentage	Example Sentences
HED	76	38.00%	探听我的隐私。 *Tàntīng* wǒ de yǐnsī. 'Snoop into my privacy.'
COO	68	34.00%	隔几天他独自去写字楼探听消息。 Gé jǐ tiān tā dúzì qù xiězìlóu *tàntīng* xiāoxī. 'Every few days he goes to the office building alone to snoop for news.'
VOB	50	25.00%	敌人想从她身上探听游击队的情况。 Dírén xiǎng cóng tā shēnshang *tàntīng* yóují duì de qíngkuàng. 'The enemy wanted to snoop on her about the guerrillas.'
ATT	3	1.50%	去探听的官吏果然瞎说！ Qù *tàntīng* de guānlì guǒrán xiāshuō! 'The officials who went to snoop were really talking nonsense!'
SBV	2	1.00%	何以忽称探听无踪？ Héyǐ hū chēng *tàntīng* wúzōng? 'Why did he suddenly say that he had snooped nothing?'
POB	1	0.50%	莫因探听而反露形迹。 Mò yīn *tàntīng* ér fǎn lù xíngjì. 'Don't reveal your signs because of snooping.'
Total	200	100%	-

The result shows that the most important syntactic dependency of 探听 *tàntīng* 'snoop' is to act as HED of a sentence. It can also often acts as an object of the verb and appears in the coordinate structure; but it only acts as a subject in a few cases. Unlike the previous four words, 探听 *tàntīng* 'snoop' is rarely used as an attribute. Because of the high proportion of 探听 *tàntīng* 'snoop' as HED, this paper further discusses 探听 *tàntīng* 'snoop' as a subcategory of HED in sentences. Table 16 shows the sentence types of 探听 *tàntīng* 'snoop' as HED. There are 30 sentences with "(other+) *tàntīng* (+other)", i.e., no subject, which accounts for the highest percentage of 39.47%. This indicates that when 探听 *tàntīng* 'snoop' is used as HED, a sentence can be formed without the subject in most cases. The co-occurrence of the subject and the object is also common, while the fronting-object and the coordinate are least likely to occur. Since in most cases there is no subject, we continue to analyze the semantic features of the subcategory "(other+) *tàntīng* (+other)" by describing the semantic collocations of this type.

Table 16. Subcategories of 探听 *tàntīng* 'snoop' as HED

Subcategories of 探听 *tàntīng* 'snoop' as HED	Number of sentences	Percentage of HED	Example Sentences
(Other+) *tàntīng* (+Other)	30	39.47%	昨日探听去了。 Zuórì *tàntīng* qù le. 'I went to snoop yesterday.'
SBV+(Other)+*tàntīng*+VOB	29	38.16%	张焘想从施官生那里探听消息。 Zhāngtào xiǎng cóng Shī Guānshēng nàlǐ *tàntīng* xiāoxī. 'Tao Zhang wanted to snoop about the news from Guansheng Shi.'
SBV+(Other)+*tàntīng*	12	15.79%	苏二伯在门外悄悄地探听。 Sū èrbó zài mén wài qiāoqiāo de *tàntīng*. 'Second Uncle Su was quietly snooping outside the door.'
(Other)+*tàntīng*+COO+VOB	4	5.26%	谁知天亮后探听得知死者是汪精卫的秘书曾仲鸣。 Shuí zhī tiānliàng hòu *tàntīng* dézhī sǐzhě shì Wāng Jīngwèi de mìshū Zéng Zhòngwū. 'However, after dawn, I snooped out that the deceased was Zhongwu Zeng, Jingwei Wang's secretary.'
FOB+Other+*tàntīng*+Other	1	1.32%	这些事你从哪里探听到的？ Zhèxiē shì nǐ cóng nǎlǐ *tàntīng* dào de? 'Where did you snoop out all this?'
Total	76	100%	-

Table 17 shows the semantic dependencies of 探听 *tàntīng* 'snoop' in the sentence types without subjects. The most frequent is "*tàntīng*+CONT". In addition, there are also Cons. The semantic dependencies involved in 探听 *tàntīng* 'snoop' can also serve as LOC, MANN and TIME without the subject.

Table 17. Semantic collocations of 探听 *tàntīng* 'snoop' in "(other+) *tàntīng* (+other)"

Types	Number	Percentage	Example sentences
tàntīng+CONT	10	33.33%	探听一切喜怒信息。 *Tàntīng* yīqiè xǐ nù xìnxī. 'Snoop for all information about happiness and anger.'
(Dependency marker)+*tàntīng*	6	20.00%	并探听孙士毅信息。 Bìng *tàntīng* Sūn Shìyì xìnxī. 'And snoop about Sun Shiyi's information.'
TIME+*tàntīng*+(Other)	5	16.67%	昨日探听去了。 Zuórì *tàntīng* qùle. 'I went to snoop yesterday.'
MANN+*tàntīng*+CONT	5	16.67%	沿途探听敌踪所在。 Yántú *tàntīng* dí zōng suǒzài. 'Snooped about the enemy's whereabouts along the way.'
tàntīng+CONS	3	10.00%	探听暹罗木料甚贱。 *Tàntīng* xiānluó mùliào shén jiàn. 'Snooped that Siam's Wood is very cheap.'
Other+LOC+*tàntīng*+CONT	1	3.33%	胆敢于宫门探听紧要公务。 Dǎngǎn yú gōng mén *tàntīng* jǐnyào gōngwù. 'Dare to snoop about important business at the palace gate.'

5 Comparison of Existing Chinese Resources for the Verbs of Searching

This paper compares the lexical information of verbs of searching in *The Contemporary Chinese Dictionary* [20], *The Modern Chinese Verb Classification Dictionary* [21], *The Modern Chinese Verb Classification dictionary*, *The Chinese Verb Usage Dictionary* [22] and *The Syntactic-Semantic Knowledge-Base of Chinese Verbs* [23]. Taking the verb 搜寻 *sōuxún* 'seek' for example, which is included in *The Contemporary Chinese Dictionary*, *The Modern Chinese Verb Classification Dictionary* and

The Chinese Verb Usage Dictionary, which contains *pinyin*, parts of speech, meaning and example sentence information, but lacks detailed syntactic-semantic descriptions. We also examined the syntactic and semantic information of 搜寻 *sōuxún* 'seek' in this Knowledge-Base, which contains semantic roles, syntactic structures and grammatical functions. First, It describes four semantic roles: the agent and patient, source (SO) and goal (GO) of 搜寻 *sōuxún* 'seek', but it does not describe the role of TIME and MANN found in this study. Second, This Knowledge-Base lists five semantic collocations. Table 18 compares semantic collocations of 搜寻 *sōuxún* 'seek' in this Knowledge-Base and this this study. (1) The semantic collocation ①in the Knowledge-Base is the same as "AGT+LOC+*sōuxún*+CONT" and "AGT+SCO+*sōuxún*+CONT" in this study. The semantic collocation ⑧ is the same as "AGT+*sōuxún*+LOC" in our study. However, according to the percentage, the semantic collocation ① is the most common, then is the semantic collocation ④, and semantic collocation ⑧ and ⑨ are not common. (2) "AGT+MANN+*sōuxún*+CONT" and "AGT+(dependency marker) +*sōuxún*+(dependency marker)+CONT" belongs to the top 3 collocation types, but the Knowledge-Base lacks the description of these common collocation types. In addition, 搜寻 *sōuxún* 'seek' can also occurs in AGT+TIME+*sōuxún*+CONT, TIME+AGT +*sōuxún*+CONT, and AGT+*sōuxún*+CONT+TIME though their frequency is not high. The Knowledge-Base lacks the description of these types. (3) The Knowledge-Base only lists semantic collocations, lacking quantity as data support. Instead, our study lists the number and frequency of each collocation type in the corpus, which provides data support for the description of syntactic and semantic features of 搜寻 *sōuxún* 'seek'. (4) The Knowledge-Base lists the use of 搜寻 *sōuxún* 'seek' in Ba and Bei sentences, but there are no such two kinds of sentences in our study, which may be not frequent in our study.

Table 18. Comparison of semantic collocations of 搜寻 *sōuxún* 'seek' between The Syntactic-Semantic Knowledge-Base of Chinese Verbs and this study

Syntactic-Semantic Knowledge - Base of Chinese Verbs		This study		
ID	semantic collocation	ID	Semantic Collocation	Percentage
①	Agent+从/在（Source）+*sōuxún*+Patient2	①	AGT+LOC+*sōuxún*+CONT	30.77%
②	/	②	AGT+MANN+*sōuxún*+CONT	26.15%
③	/	③	AGT+(dependency marker)+*sōuxún*+(dependency marker)+CONT	24.62%
④	Agent+from/at（Source）+*sōuxún*+Patient2	④	AGT+SCO+*sōuxún*+CONT	4.62%
⑤	/	⑤	AGT+TIME+*sōuxún*+CONT	3.08%
⑥	/	⑥	TIME+AGT+*sōuxún*+CONT	3.08%
⑦	/	⑦	AGT+*sōuxún*+CONT+TIME	3.08%
⑧	Agent+*sōuxún*+到(Goal）	⑧	AGT+*sōuxún*+LOC	3.08%
⑨	Agent+*sōuxún*+Patient1/Patient2	⑨	AGT+*sōuxún*+CONT	1.54%
⑩	Agent+把 Patient1/Patient2+*sōuxún*	⑩	/	/
⑪	P1/P2+被（Agent）+*sōuxún*	⑪	/	/

Third, in terms of grammatical functions, (1) the Knowledge-Base lists 9 grammatical functions of 搜寻 *sōuxún* 'seek', of which only one is the syntactic component it can be used as, that is, "6. It can be used as a predicate or predicate core (so it can generally be modified by adverbials or complements)"corresponds to HED in the syntactic type of 搜寻 *sōuxún* 'seek' summarized in this paper, but the Knowledge-Base does not give 搜寻 *sōuxún* 'seek' proportion as predicate or predicate core. This study not only lists the HED that 搜寻 *sōuxún* 'seek' can be used as a sentence, but also provides data support for the case that 搜寻 *sōuxún* 'seek' acts as a HED. It can be seen from Table 5 that the proportion of 搜寻 *sōuxún* 'seek' as a predicate or predicate core in this study is 61.5%, accounting for the highest proportion. It can be seen that 搜寻 *sōuxún* 'seek' often acts as HED in sentences. (2) Item 7 of the grammatical function in the Knowledge-Base "cannot be used as an adverbial to directly modify verb components" is consistent with the fact that ADV does not appear in the distribution of syntactic components of 搜寻 *sōuxún* 'seek' in this study. (3) The Knowledge-Base only lists the cases where 搜寻 *sōuxún* 'seek' can be used as a predicate or predicate core, which is not comprehensive. As can be seen from Table 5, 搜寻 *sōuxún* 'seek' can also be used as VOB, ATT, SBV and appear in the parallel structure. The proportions are 17.50%, 9.50% and 3.00%.

The above comparison shows that this study not only provides a more comprehensive and in-depth analysis of verbs of searching at both syntactic and semantic levels, but also provides statistical information. Therefore, this study provides rich information of the verbs than existing Chinese resources.

6 Conclusion

In this paper, we analyzed five common verbs of searching: 搜索 *sōusuǒ* 'search', 搜寻 *sōuxún* 'seek', 寻找 *xúnzhǎo* 'look for', 窥探 *kuītàn* 'pry' and 探听 *tàntīng* 'snoop' in the framework of dependency grammar. We used a self-developed syntactic-semantic annotation tool to manually check and correct the automatic annotation results of LTP. This study found that the verbs of searching exhibit a variety of syntactic dependencies, the most frequent of which is as HED in sentences, followed by VOB, and are rarely as SBV and ATT. In addition, 搜索 *sōusuǒ* 'search' and 窥探 *kuītàn* 'pry' can also be used as ADV. 寻找 *xúnzhǎo* 'look for', 窥探 *kuītàn* 'pry' and 探听 *tàntīng* 'snoop' can also be used as POB. When verbs of searching are used as HED, 搜索 *sousuo* 'search', 搜寻 *sōuxún* 'seek', 寻找 *xúnzhǎo* 'look for' and 窥探 *kuītàn* 'pry' often appear in the sentence pattern with SBV and VOB; the most common sentence structure of 探听 *tàntīng* 'snoop' is sentences with no SBV, closely followed by sentences with SBV and VOB. Under the sentence structure with SBV and VOB, the most paired semantic dependencies of 搜索 *sōusuǒ* 'search', 搜寻 *sōuxún* 'seek', 寻找 *xúnzhǎo* 'look for', 窥探 *kuītàn* 'pry' are AGT and CONT. All the five verbs can collocate with the semantic role of LOC, TIME and MANN. In addition, 搜索 *sōusuǒ* 'search' and 寻找 *xúnzhǎo* 'look for' can also collocate with semantic role of TOOL, and 窥探 *kuītàn* 'pry' and 探听 *tàntīng* 'snoop' can also collocate with semantic role of CONS. At last, by comparing with existing dictionary resources, it is clear that the analysis in this paper is more comprehensive in terms of syntactic and semantic analysis. This study contributes to an in-depth understanding of the features of Chinese verbs, helps to improve the lexical entries in dictionaries, and benefits language learning.

Acknowledgements. This research is funded by University of Macau (MYRG2019-00013-FAH). This work was performed in part at the high performance computing cluster (HPCC) which is supported by Information and Communication Technology Office (ICTO) of University of Macau.

References

1. Tesnière, L.: Eléments de Syntaxe Structurale. Klincksieek, Paris (1959)
2. Tesnière, L.: Elements of Structual Syntax. John Benjamins Publishing Company, Amsterdam (2015)
3. Su, X.: A Thesaurus of Modern Chinese (xiàndài hànyǔ fēnlèi cídiǎn). The Commercial Press (shāngwù yìnshūguǎn), Beijing (2013)
4. Research group of lexicon of common words in contemporary Chinese: Lexicon of common words in contemporary Chinese (xiàndài hànyǔ chángyòng cíbiǎo). The Commercial Press (Shāngwù yìnshūguǎn), Beijing (2008)
5. Mei, J.: Synonym Word Forest (tóngyìcí cílín). Shanghai Lexicographical Publishing House (Shànghǎi císhū chūbǎnshè), Shanghai (1996)
6. Qiu, M.: Try to compare the similarities and differences between Tesnière's dependency grammar and Bloomfield's direct component analysis (shì bǐjiào Tàiníāi'ěr yīcún yǔfǎ yǔ Bùlóngfēi'ěrdé zhíjiē chéngfèn fēnxīfǎ yìtóng). Academy (xué yuán) **07**, 129–131 (2017)
7. Niu, R., Osborne, T.: Chunks are components: a dependency grammar approach to the syntactic structure of mandarin. Lingua **224**, 60–83 (2019)
8. Feng, Z.: The history and current situation of machine translation (jīqì fānyì de lìshǐ hé xiànzhuàng). Foreign Autom. (guówài zìdònghuà) **04**, 36–40+64 (1984)
9. Liu, T., Ma, J.: Theories and methods of Chinese automatic syntactic parsing: a critical survey (hànyǔ zìdòng jùfǎ fēnxī de lǐlùn yǔ fāngfǎ). Contemporary Linguistics (dāngdài yǔyánxué) **11**, 100–112+189 (2009)
10. Wang, S.: Chinese Multiword Expressions: Theoretical and Practical Perspectives. Springer, Singapore (2020)
11. Wang, S., Luo, H.: Exploring the meanings and grammatical functions of idioms in teaching Chinese as a second language. Int. J. Appl. Linguist. **31**, 283–300 (2021)
12. Wang, S., Yin, J.: Corpus-based statistical analysis of polysemous words in legislative Chinese and general Chinese. In: Hong, J.-F., Zhang, Y., Liu, P. (eds.) CLSW 2019. LNCS (LNAI), vol. 11831, pp. 661–673. Springer, Cham (2020). https://doi.org/10.1007/978-3-030-38189-9_67
13. Wang, S., Luo, H.: A corpus-based study of the vocabulary of macao tourism Chinese. In: Tao, H., Chen, H.H.-J. (eds.) Chinese for Specific and Professional Purposes. CLLS, pp. 373–391. Springer, Singapore (2019). https://doi.org/10.1007/978-981-13-9505-5_16
14. Zhang, Q.: An investigation on the replacement of "xúnzhǎo" meaning verbs in modern Chinese (jìndài hànyǔ "xúnzhǎo" yì dòngcí gēngtì kǎo). J. Soochow Univ. (Philos. Soc. Sci. Ed.) (Sūzhōu dàxué xuébào (zhéxué shèhuì kēxué bǎn)) **03**, 91–93 (2007)
15. Xiang, M.: Verbs for "xúnzhǎo" in Chinese Dialects (hànyǔ fāngyán lǐ de "xúnzhǎo" yì dòngcí). Bull. Linguist. Stud. (yǔyán yánjiū jíkān) **02**, 482–497+663–664 (2018)
16. Lin, X.: The conceptual structure and grammatical system of search verb clauses (sōuxún lèi dòngcí xiǎojù gàiniàn jiégòu jí qí yǔfǎ tǐxì). Exam Weekly (kǎoshì zhōukān) **44**, 33–34 (2011)
17. Liu, T., Che, W., Li, Z.: Language technology platform (yǔyán jìshù píngtái). J. Chin. Inf. Process. (zhōngwén xìnxī xuébào) **25**, 53–62 (2011)

18. Wang, S., Liu, X., Zhou, J.: Research of the visual verb kànjiàn 'see' based on dependency grammar (jīyú yīcún yǔfǎ de shìjué dòngcí "*kànjiàn*" yánjiū). In: The 22nd Chinese Lexical Semantic Workshop, Nanjing Normal University, Nanjing (held online) (2021)
19. Wang, S., Tang, L.: A study of Chinese confession verbs based on dependency grammar (jīyú yīcún yǔfǎ de zhāorènlèi dòngcí yánjiū). In: The 22nd Chinese Lexical Semantic Workshop, Nanjing Normal University (held online) (2021)
20. Dictionary Editing Room, Institute of Linguistics of China Academy of Social Sciences: The Contemporary Chinese Dictionary (xiàndài hànyǔ cídiǎn) (7th ed.) The Commercial Press (shāngwù yìnshūguǎn), Beijing (2016)
21. Guo, D.: The Modern Chinese Verb Classification Dictionary (xiàndài hànyǔ dòngcí fēnlèi cídiǎn). Jilin Education Press (Jílín jiàoyù chūbǎnshè), Changchun (1994)
22. Meng, C.: The Chinese Verb Usage Dictionary (hànyǔ dòngcí yòngfǎ cídiǎn). The Commercial Press (shāngwù yìnshūguǎn), Beijiing (1999)
23. Yuan, Y.: The Syntactic-Semantic Knowledge-Base of Chinese Verbs (hànyǔ dòngcí jùfǎ yǔyì gōngnéng xìnxī cídiǎn jì jiǎnsuǒ xìtǒng). Peking University (Běijīng dàxué), Beijing (2018)

Writing Collaboratively in the Continuation Task via Shared Docs

Lining Jin[1], Xiaobin Liu[1(✉)], WeiQin Gong[2], and Guangwei Chen[3]

[1] South China Normal University, Guangzhou, Guangdong, China
liuxiaobin@m.scnu.edu.cn
[2] Nanhai No.1 Middle School, Foshan, Guangdong, China
[3] Guangdong Experimental Middle School, Guangzhou, Guangdong, China

Abstract. This study explored the effects of collaborative writing via Shared Docs on EFL (English as a foreign language) learners' writing performance in the continuation task. Participants were 53 senior high School students from an intact class in Guangdong China who were randomly divided into a collaborative writing group (n = 32) and individual writing group (n = 21). Both groups participated in a pre-test, two continuation tasks, and post-test over a 6-week period. Students in collaborative writing group worked in pairs while the others worked alone on Shared Docs. Learners' writings at pre-test and post-test were analyzed in terms of overall scores, fluency, accuracy, complexity and cohesion. Results indicated that there was no significant difference of collaborative writing using Shared Docs on learners' writing performance in all the aspects. However, data of questionnaire and interview showed that most held positive perceptions and attitudes towards collaborative writing via Shared Docs.

Keywords: Collaborative writing · Shared Docs · The continuation task

1 Introduction

Writing has long been considered as a cyclical interaction between and interplay of cognitive processes to generate, express, and refine ideas in the production of a text [10]. For English writing teaching in China, where the authentic English input is relatively rare, there is a long-standing problem, namely, the asymmetry between input and output [19]. On account of the Interactive Alignment Model (IAM) [15], Wang [20] firstly put forward the conception of continuation task. Integrating reading with writing, the continuation task requires learners to read an incomplete story and then complete the story by adding a coherent and logical ending to it [21]. Alignment in continuation task is unidirectional and static, therefore, to strengthen alignment effect, it is important to take interpersonal relationship into consideration in the continuation task [21, 22]. One possible way is to let several learners collaboratively complete the continuation task. In fact, many scholars [9, 17] once pointed out that writing wasn't an individual act and many writing activities in daily life were completed collaboratively, therefore, it is necessary to explore the effect of collaborative writing (CW) on learners' performance in the continuation task.

W. Jia et al. (Eds.): SETE 2021, LNCS 13089, pp. 142–149, 2021.
https://doi.org/10.1007/978-3-030-92836-0_12

2 Literature Review

2.1 Collaborative Writing

Collaborative writing (CW) is defined as the whole process during which the joint authors write together and share the responsibility for and the ownership of the entire text produced [17]. With the advent of Web 2.0 applications such as blogs, wikis, and Google Docs, CW becomes more popular. Many researches [3, 9, 18] have proven the positive effects of CW on L2 written outputs. The enhancement of content and accuracy have been reported in some studies [9], which revealed that wiki-mediated CW produced a positive effect on the content and accuracy of learners' written output. Multiple studies also showed that learners generally hold positive perceptions and attitudes towards CW supported by technology [2–6, 8, 11, 14, 18, 24].

It should be pointed out that there are some other researches [6, 24] indicating that CW didn't have significant difference on learners' writing performance and many learners would love to write alone if given the opportunity to choose CW or IW [5, 6]. These inconsistent findings can be caused by the experiment design, such as the number of participants [6] and self-selected versus teacher-assigned pairs [1] etc., therefore, more studies with different designs are needed.

2.2 The Continuation Task

The Interactive Alignment Model (IAM) [15] pointed out that interlocutors in a dialogue interacted and coordinated with each other dynamically so that alignment occurred at multiple levels (e.g., situational and linguistic levels), and thus the dialogue can be kept going successfully and smoothly. Based on IAM, Wang [20, 21] extended the alignment in dialogues to that between readers and the reading material, and theorized the continuation task.

A large number of empirical studies have explored the influence of different factors on the continuation task, for example, writing prompts [16] and interpersonal interaction factors [7, 25] and all have been proven to make a difference. According to Wang [21, 22], it was vital to take interpersonal interaction factor into consideration to give full play to the facilitative effects of the continuation task. Though several researches [7, 25] focused on this aspect but they all investigated face-to-face CW, few studies have been conducted to investigate the effects of CW supported by technology on learners' writing performance in the continuation task. Therefore, in present study we try to investigate the effects of CW via Shared Docs on senior high school students' overall writing performance in the continuation task. Besides, to investigate deeper into how CW via Shared Docs effect students' performance, different textual features of their writings are analyzed. After checking its effect, we take students' perceptions and attitudes into consideration to check the potential and possibility of applying this new writing form in real teaching and learning. Specifically, we seek to address the following three research questions:

1) Can collaborative writing via Shared Docs improve learners' overall writing performance in the continuation task?
2) Can collaborative writing via Shared Docs affect the textual features (fluency, accuracy and complexity) of learners' output in the continuation task?
3) What are learners' perceptions and attitudes towards collaborative writing via Shared Docs?

3 Methodology

3.1 Participants

The study was carried out within an intact class in Foshan, Guangdong, China. The participants were 53 10th-grade EFL learners. Their native language was Chinese and had at least six years of English learning experience at the time of data collection. Participants were randomly divided into collaborative or individual writing groups, finally, 32 students (16 pairs) wrote collaboratively (EG) and 21 individually (CG). Independent samples t-test revealed that EG and CG had no significant differences in their writing scores ($p = .904 > .05$) before the experiment, which ensures the reliability of the results in present study.

3.2 Writing Tasks and Instrument

To guarantee the comparability of pre-test and post-test, we adopted the continuation tasks of NMET in Zhejiang Province (NMET-ZJ)[1] last year, since NMET were held twice a year there.

The present study also adopted one of our domestic tools, Tencent Docs, as the writing tool. Tencent Docs enable multiple users to edit files simultaneously and can automatically save all the changes made. Users can also check different users' contribution by checking the history which shows all the changes made at different time.

3.3 Procedures

Before experiment all the participants were instructed on how to use Tencent Docs, and given chance to write as a trail before formal treatment. All of them demonstrated a good command of its usage. Then pre-test was conducted in paper form individually during class time (40 min) (Week 01). The two writing tasks for treatment were both done via Tencent Docs and finished during weekend, and each tasks required two weeks, one for first draft and the other for teacher's feedback and second draft (Week 02–05). Peer reviews for the first draft needed completing either synchronously or asynchronously. The instructor would provide all with some brief feedback, and they would review their first draft and revise based on feedback from both instructor and peers next week, then present their final draft. After four weeks of treatment, post-test

[1] Please browse this link (https://docs.qq.com/pdf/DRUFJZ05ZT2hQbEVB) to see detailed information of the two continuation tasks of NMET in Zhejiang Province (NMET-ZJ).

was conducted in the same way as pre-test was (Week 06). Finally, learners from EG completed a questionnaire and ten was randomly selected to conduct a semi-structured interview (Week 06).

3.4 Data Collection and Analysis

Pre-test and Post-test

1) *Scores*
   With experience in rating continuation task, two raters rated the tests according to rating criterion of NMET-ZJ. They rated respectively and their mean score was used as the final score for each writing and data analyses. For scores with discrepancy over three points, discussion and alteration would be made. The inter-rater reliability was checked using Pearson correlation coefficients. The Pearson correlation was .909 and sig. was .000, indicating that correlation of scores between two raters was significant.
2) *Textual features*
   Each writing was analyzed for fluency, accuracy, syntactic complexity and lexical complexity. Since both the pre-test and post-test were time-limited tasks, fluency can be estimated by the total number of words and of T-units. T-units was defined as one main clause plus a subordinate clause attached to or embedded in it [23]. Accuracy was measured by the ratio of error-free T-units to the total number of T-units, which was manually identified by two raters. Syntactic complexity was measured by Web-based L2 Syntactical Complexity Analyzer (L2SCA) [12, 13] through three indices, namely mean length of clause (MLC), dependent clause per clause (DC/C) and T-unit per sentence (T/S). Lexical complexity was measured by Web-based Lexical Complexity Analyzer (LCA) through five main indicators related to content words, that is, lexical word variation (LV), verb variation-II (VV2), noun variation (NV), adjective variation (AdjV) and adverb variation (AdvV). Cohesion was measured with Coh-Metrix 3.0, including all connectives incidence (CNCAll) and three indicators of Latent Semantic Analysis (LSA), namely, LSA overlap between adjacent sentences (LSASS1), LSA overlap among all sentences (LSASSP) and LSA overlap between adjacent paragraphs (LSAPP1).

Questionnaire and Interview
The 32 participants from EG completed the questionnaire with an effective rate of 100%. The questionnaire had 14 questions, which were designed with reference to previous studies [18] and some adaptations were made. Normally, questionnaire can be proven effective and reliable through Cronbach's α coefficient method with value over .80. In present study, the value of was .814, which meant the questionnaire was reliable and effective enough for further analysis. Ten learners from EG were randomly chosen for the semi-structured interview in Chinese.

4 Results and Discussion

4.1 Overall Writing Performance

Independent samples t-test of the scores at post-test between CG and EG was conducted and the results ($p = .861 > .05$) indicated that no significant difference was found, which was beyond our expectation. This suggests that CW via Shared Docs doesn't have effects on leaners' overall writing performance in the continuation task, which is inconsistent with the previous findings that CW has facilitative effects in improving learners' overall writing performance [3, 18].

Two possibilities could be listed to explain this finding: 1) type of the writing task, and 2) length of the experiment. Unlike Bikowski [3], whose study engaged the learners in CW for fifteen weeks and Suwantarathip and Wichadee [18] for fourteen weeks, the current study only engaged learners in CW for four weeks. Th continuation task was a new form of testing for Senior One students and this was the first time for the participants to practise, therefore, four weeks wasn't long enough for them to fully get familiar with the test standards. Moreover, previous studies on technology-supported CW have never adopted the continuation task as writing task before, and for those studies adopting various types of writing tasks, different findings also existed, for example, expository essay [9] as we elaborated in literature review.

4.2 Textual Features

The effects of CW via Shared Docs on textual features were analyzed from fluency, accuracy, complexity (lexical and syntactic), and cohesion. However, with all the p value greater than .05, results of independent samples t-test showed that no statistically significant difference was revealed on these four aspects, which means CW via Shared Docs doesn't affect learners' writing textual features in present study either.

Learners in EG were engaged in a writing environment where they were granted more opportunities to discuss with their partners compared with those in CG [22], according to their discussion and revision records during the treatment, most of which were concerning how the story could be developed. Just as previous studies suggested [1, 9], meaning was prioritized over form in CW. According to Limited Attentional Capacity Model [21] which posited out that humans' attentional resources were limited, with most attentions allocating to meaning, less were paid to form and grammar which was also reflected in their discussion record and interview.

Besides, since learners were instructed to write based on the requirements of NMET, in which the number of words are about 150 words, they all wrote appropriate number of words (172, EG and 176, CG on average), thus, no significant difference on fluency was no surprising. However, according to the revision history, learners indeed engaged themselves in giving each other feedback in terms of word usage and grammar. Through peer feedback, they reflected on what was written and double check for better accuracy and higher complexity.

As we can see above, learners in EG demonstrated the advantages of CW especially peer feedback and scaffolding, thus it was beyond our expectation that no significance difference was found in complexity and accuracy, which ran counter to previous studies that demonstrated positive effects of technology-supported CW on the accuracy of leaners' writing [9] and complexity. Except for the type of writing task and length of the experiment as we explained above, another possibility for the unexpected results could be the grade of the participants. They were in Senior Grade One and most of the complex grammars haven't been taught systemically, like the use of non-predicate, therefore, it wasn't easy for most to identify and revise grammar and usage errors because of knowledge and practice lacking, which probably leads to the low accuracy and complexity.

4.3 Learners' Perceptions and Attitudes

The post-test questionnaire was distributed among the 32 learners in EG in order to explore their perceptions and attitudes towards CW via Shared Docs in the continuation task. With the mean score of each question over 3.00, data from the questionnaire denoted that the participants generally had positive perceptions and attitudes. They confirmed some advantages of CW using Shared Docs. For example, in consistent with previous studies, they expressed agreement that CW via Tencent Docs was helpful to share ideas with others (Q1, 84.38%), create a friendly writing atmosphere (Q2, 56.25%), gain more confidence (Q8, 71.88%) and reduce writing anxiety (Q7, 62.50%), engage them more actively in writing (Q3, 78.13%), have more opportunity to learn from others (Q5, 90.63%), and thus improve writing skills by checking others' feedback and revision (Q6, 84.38% & Q9, 81.26%). They also expressed their willingness to receive feedback from others (Q4, 87.50%), and use tools like Tencent Docs in their future writing activities (Q10, 68.75%). Q11–14 shows that students generally believes that their pair has a good collaboration on the whole.

Semi-structured interview also proved learner's positive perceptions and attitudes, especially on content construction. The following are some examples:

a) *"I can write sentences but I don't know how to construct the whole story. My partner can figure out the content and the whole idea, and can draw out the plot as a whole, which can inspire me on how to construct the plot". (Student A)*
b) *"I'll be more serious and spend more time in writing if I write on the Internet with others, because I want to take more responsibility and perform better, but if I write alone, I will be careless and just think about completing the task". (Student B)*
c) *"I like this way of writing because my partner can help me correct some grammatical errors and give me hints of plot development, especially when I don't know how to develop the story". (Student C)*

However, some students also demonstrated negative attitudes and pointed out some problems existing in CW using Shared Docs, for example, costing too much time (Student B), inability to identify and revise errors (Student J) and inconvenience to type and revise on phones (Student D and E), which shed light on the optimization of tools and pairing with reference to learners' proficiency. Besides, one participant pointed that writing was still a totally individual act for her, because "*we have to complete the continuation task alone in test (Student E)*", which was actually a typical idea among among Chinese learners and implies that CW still got a long way to be applied widely among some learners. Anyway, though with disparate opinions, most of the participants showed their willingness to use tools like Tencent Docs for CW in the continuation task in the future, which was in accordance with previous studies and fully demonstrated the potential of Shared Docs on teaching.

5 Conclusions and Limitations

The current study explored the effects of CW via Shared Docs on learners' writing performance in continuation task, but no significant difference was found in terms of the overall writing performance or the textual features. Data from questionnaire and interview demonstrated that they generally hold a positive attitude towards CW via Shared Docs in the continuation task. Learners expressed their agreement on its helpfulness to share ideas with others, create a friendly writing atmosphere, gain more confidence and reduce writing anxiety, engage them more actively in writing etc., and thus improve writing skills by checking others' feedback and revision. All of these underlined the potential of CW via Shared Docs in English teaching and learning.

Some limitations must be acknowledged. First of all, the duration of the experiment was relatively short and more exercises should be given to get them more familiar with the continuation task. Second, continuation task of various difficulty and genres should be taken into consideration. Only narratives were used in present study.

Acknowledgements. This work is supported by the Center for Language Cognition and Assessment, South China Normal University. It's also the result of Guangdong "13th Five-Year" Plan Project of Philosophy & Social Science (GD20WZX01-02).

References

1. Abrams, Z.I.: Collaborative writing and text quality in Google Docs. Lang. Learn. Technol. **23**(2), 22–42 (2019). http://hdl.handle.net/10125/44681
2. Aydin, Z., Yildiz, S.: Using wikis to promote collaborative EFL writing. Lang. Learn. Technol. **18**(1), 160–180 (2014)
3. Bikowski, D.: Effects of web-based collaborative writing on individual L2 writing development. Lang. Learn. Technol. **20**(1), 79–99 (2016)
4. Chao, Y.-C.J., Lo, H.-C.: Students' perceptions of Wiki-based collaborative writing for learners of English as a foreign language. Interact. Learn. Environ. **19**(4), 395–411 (2011). https://doi.org/10.1080/10494820903298662
5. Ducate, L.C., Anderson, L.L., Moreno, N.: Wading through the world of wikis: an analysis of three wiki projects. Foreign Lang. Ann. **44**(3), 495–524 (2011). https://doi.org/10.1111/j.1944-9720.2011.01144.x
6. Campbell, T., Wang, S.K., Hsu, H.-Y., Duffy, A.M., Wolf, P.G.: Learning with web tools, simulations, and other technologies in science classrooms. J. Sci. Educ. Technol. **19**(5), 505–511 (2010). https://doi.org/10.1007/s10956-010-9217-8
7. Han, H.J.: A comparative study on the effects of collaborative and individual continuation task based on interactive alignment model on junior middle school students' English writing. Northwest Normal University, Lanzhou, China (2018)
8. Hidayat, F.: Exploring students' view of using Google docs in writing class. J. Engl. Educ. Teach. (JEET) **4**(2), 184–194 (2020)

9. Hsu, H.-C., Lo, Y.-F.: Using wiki-mediated collaboration to foster L2 writing performance. Lang. Learn. Technol. **22**(3), 103–123 (2018). http://hdl.handle.net/10125/44659
10. Kellogg, R.T.: Effectiveness of prewriting strategies as a function of task demands. Am. J. Psychol. **103**, 327–342 (1990)
11. Kessler, G., Bikowski, D., Boggs, J.: Collaborative writing among second language learners in academic web-based projects. Lang. Learn. Technol. **16**(1), 91–109 (2012)
12. Lu, X.: Automatic analysis of syntactic complexity in second language writing. Int. J. Corpus Linguist. **15**(4), 474–496 (2010)
13. Lu, X.: The relationship of lexical richness to the quality of ESL learners' oral narratives. Mod. Lang. J. **96**(2), 190–208 (2012)
14. Mayorga, P.O., Reinoso, A., Heredia, E.: Google docs as a collaborative writing tool towards learning English writing. Int. J. Sci.: Basic Appl. Res. (IJSBAR) **40**(1), 234–241 (2018)
15. Pickering, M.J., Garrod, S.: Toward a mechanistic psychology of dialogue. Behav. Brain Sci. **27**, 169–226 (2004)
16. Shi, B., Huang, L., Lu, X.: Effect of prompt type on test-takers' writing performance and writing strategy use in the continuation task. Lang. Test. **37**(3), 361–388 (2020). https://doi.org/10.1177/0265532220911626
17. Storch, N.: Collaborative writing. Lang. Teach. **52**(1), 40–59 (2018). https://doi.org/10.1017/s0261444818000320
18. Suwantarathip, O., Wichadee, S.: The effects of collaborative writing activity using Google docs on students' writing abilities. Turk. Online J. Educ. Technol. **13**(2), 148–156 (2014)
19. Wang, C.M., Niu, R.Y., Zheng, X.X.: Improving English through writing. Foreign Lang. Teach. Res. (Bimonthly) **32**(03), 207–212+240 (2000)
20. Wang, C.M.: Interactive alignment and foreign language teaching. Foreign Lang. Teach. Res. (Bimonthly) **42**(04), 297–299 (2010)
21. Wang, C.M.: The continuation task—an effective method in enhancing foreign language acquisition. Foreign Lang. World **5**, 2–7 (2012)
22. Wang, C.M.: Why does the continuation task facilitate L2 learning? Foreign Lang. Teach. Res. **47**(5), 753–762 (2015)
23. Wolfe-Quintero, K., Inagaki, S., Kim, H.: Second language development in writing: measures of fluency, accuracy & complexity. Second Language Teaching & Curriculum Center, Manoa (1998)
24. Woodrich, M.P., Fan, Y.: Google docs as a tool for collaborative writing in the middle school classroom. J. Inf. Technol. Educ. Res. **16**(1), 391–410 (2017)
25. Zhang, Q.: The impact of collaborative writing on the English continuation task of senior high school students. Hangzhou Normal University, Hangzhou, China (2017)

Reflections on Applying Innovative Project-Based Learning: Shadow Play in OBTL Classroom

Hoi-yung Leung(✉), Wei Jiang, Tat-keung Tam, and Doh-ming Man

Beijing Normal University-Hong Kong Baptist University United International College, Zhuhai, China
icemanleung@uic.edu.cn

Abstract. This reflective study intends to report the process of implementation and application of an iPBL model in the contexts of OBTL classroom where a student-centred pedagogy has been implemented through a PBL "Shadow Play Performance". The iPBL model consists of 7 stages: Preparation (P), Conception (C), Design (D), Implementation (I), Operation (O), Evaluation (E), and Revision (R). Thus, the iPBL proposes an innovative scaffolding that enhances the students' creativity and provides more systematic records. iPBL also includes a subjective measure under the subject-taught teachers as the only raters and assessors in the OBTL context. This implementation tries to extend the insight and reflections on how the teachers have implemented the iPBL in terms of traditional shadow play as an OBTL-facilitated context. The OBTL approach is based on the constructive alignments of how well students achieved are and assessed. There are two common questions that teachers start with in planning their teaching: 1) What would I intend my students to achieve with the expected standard? 2) How would I assess objectively my students after those learning activities? This reflective study includes face-to-face teaching of a class of 50 students, who take the class as free elective under the Division of Culture and Creativity. 10 experimental groups and 4 constructive alignments of Course Intended Learning Outcomes (CILOs) have been well defined at the beginning of the course. For assessing the OBTL classroom, the analytical rubrics are designed for peer assessments at the end of students' presentation of "Shadow Play performance". In general, this study reflects on how well the OBTL-based iPBL is implemented in a contemporary cultural content, and initiates students' intrinsic motivation and participation of the Shadow play performance.

Keywords: Outcomes-Based Teaching and Learning · Innovative Project-Based Learning · Shadow play · Creativities

1 Introduction

The Outcomes-based Teaching and Learning (OBTL) approach (Biggs 2006) has been implemented in all the universities in Hong Kong since 2006. But OBTL, indeed arguabled, demands more intensive concerns and resource from the teachers. From our

W. Jia et al. (Eds.): SETE 2021, LNCS 13089, pp. 150–157, 2021.
https://doi.org/10.1007/978-3-030-92836-0_13

empirical classroom observations, it well demonstrates that OBTL intends to have improvement and progress from a traditional teacher-centre approach:

- To assess effectively the higher-order thinking skills better than final examination, such as involving a problem-solving approach in application of innovation and creativity in practice. What would I intend my students to achieve with the expected standard?
- To assess the student-centredness in the related teaching and learning activities in a systematic manner. How would I assess objectively my students after those learning activities?

In principle, the constructive alignment of OBTL provides the teachers with reflective practices on student's engagement and enhancement in the process of teaching and learning. Although OBTL provides a framework for the teachers and fulfillment of pre-determined learning objectives, activities, and assessments, the teachers actually cannot have sufficient skills to change in order to facilitate the students to have higher order thinking. In general, OBTL contributes the mutual contribution in changing the teachers' mindset.

In this reflective study, we propose a new OBLT-Innovative Project-Based Learning (iPBL) approach by focusing on and implementing ONE free elective course. The course consists of 40 students from year 1 to year 4 with multi-disciplinary and different programs streams. A shadow-play group project as an assignment with assessment criteria is introduced to the students. The shadow play is primarily set as one of the learning outcomes. The results show that it is significant to increase students' innovation and engagement in studying cultural heritage. Besides, it also provides more systematic and objective assessment tasks by the peer students that informs the student-centered and collaborative learning.

2 Literature Review

2.1 OBTL

The basic premise of Outcomes-based Teaching and Learning (OBTL) is implemented by Teaching and Learning Activities (TLAs) and Assessment Methods (AMs). OBTL is initiated by discovering from what the learner is supposed to be able to do after teaching and learning activities and meet the standard sets of received knowledge. The common OBTL in Hong Kong higher education includes three key components, namely Intented Learning Teaching Outcomes (ILOs), TLAs & Assessment Tasks (ATs) of constructive alignment (Fig. 1).

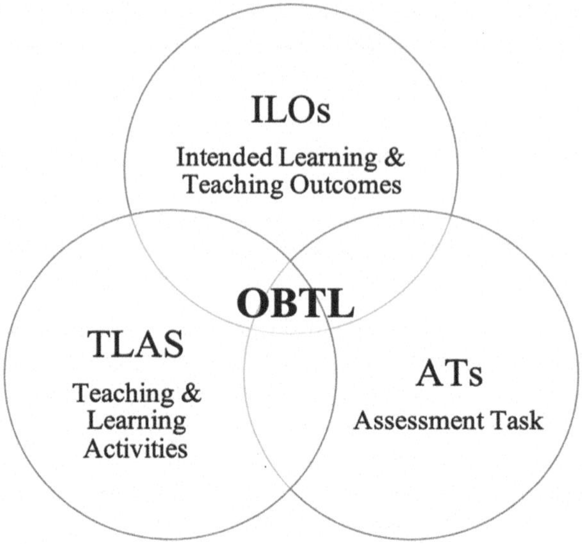

Fig. 1. Constructive alignment of OBTL

2.2 Why Use OBTL?

OBTL seems logical, effective for the both teachers and students that satisfies systematic record and long term improvement. But OBTLis arguably more resource intensive for teachers (Biggs 2003). Initially, OBTL involves more preparations from teachers, but once OBTL is established and implemented, the effectiveness and efficiency of teaching is just a little bit different when compared with traditional teacher-centred learning.

2.3 Innovative Project-Based Learning (iPBL)

iPBL model is a modified learner-centred pedagogy that includes 7 stages: Preparation, Conception, Design, Implementation, Operation, Evaluation, and Revision. The benefit of applying iPBL in teaching and learning activities is that it can enhance the creativity and design process of the learners. The 7 stages of learning activities provide a systematic cognitive process record and creativity enhancement of the knowledge (Table 1).

Table 1. 7 stages of iPBL in actions

Stage 1: Preparation	Group of students start formulating a project by defining the team members (students and the professor)
Stage 2: Conception	The project execution through discussion, target formulation, resource requirements and materials, and accumulating the prior knowledge
Stage 3: Design	Problem solving start from a systematic design or design thinking process
Stage 4: Implementation	The solution is implemented and tested on an actual platform
Stage 5: Operation	The operation involves an actual demonstration of the solution or prototype for received feedback
Stage 6: Evaluation	The projects designed, implemented, and tested are evaluated by experts
Stage 7: Revision	Based on the comments from domain and creativity experts, students are asked to revise their projects

The application and implementation of iPBL is widely used to formulate as instructional strategies and adoptable diversified creative thinking or design methods. The 7-staged iPBL integrate the pedagogies from creative learning, software engineering process, and the Conceive-Design-Implement-Operate (CDIO) framework.

2.4 Creativities in Classroom

In 2019, our empirical study highlights and illustrates the common 12 definitions of creativity (Table 2). It is obvious that researchers and educators always argue about the definitions and objective assessment of creativity related: 1) the constructs of creativity, 2) the definition of creativity, and 3) the objectivity of assessing creativity.

Table 2. The Definitions of Multiple-Unidimensional Creativity (Leung 2019)

Creativity (Classic)	… "novel and useful" …
4Ps' creativity	… "creative person, creative product, creative process & create press…"
H-creativity	Historical creativity - … "where novelty is assessed in relation to the history of humankind" …
P-creativity	Psychological creativity - … "where novelty is assessed in relation to the history of an individual" …
S-creativity	Situated creativity - … "relative to the situation that pertains during the process of designing" …
Big-C	Eminent creativity - Reserved for great
Pro-C	Professional – Level expertise that is not eminent
Little-c	Everyday creativity – college students or children as participants focus on every day and found in nearly all people
Mini-c	… "Personal and inherent in the learning process"
E-creativity	"… the application of information and communication technology to support and enhance human creativity…"
Artistic creativity	"…technical skill could be conceptualized as an enabling basis for creative artistic performance,"
Design creativity	"Novel, to be useful, to be surprise"

The above Definitions of Multiple-Unidimensional Creativity (Leung 2019) provide hypothetical constructs of creativities and help the teachers to set up related rubrics or more accurate and appropriate descriptors that become more concrete and assessable to the learning outcomes from students' perception of creativity (creative thinking or creative performance).

Therefore, this study treats the post-teaching reflection across the constructive alignments with an OBTL approach and an iPBL model, and adapts multiple constructs of creativity in the classroom contexts. A long-term benefit on students' satisfactions and learning outcomes are expected and desirable with high competency in problem-solving from a practical to cognitive knowledge dimension.

3 OBTL and iPBL in Classroom

A free-elective (FE) course, *Basic studies of cultural tourism in China*, is shortlisted and implemented in this study.

3.1 Course Description (CILOs and Rubrics for Holistic Grading)

The course aims at introducing to students the Cultural Heritage in China and its importance to the development of China tourists' industry, including key concepts and management issues of cultural heritage, and build up students' abilities to describe and evaluate tangible and intangible cultural heritage. The course will also connect the cultural heritage management with tourism business operation, so students will be able to identify and explain how to develop cultural tourism product, analyse the cultural tourists and operate cultural tourism in China.

This course offered by the BBA programme in *Culture, Creativity and Management* (CCM) (Table 3).

Table 3. The course level intended learning outcomes (CILOs) as below.

CILO	Upon successful completion of the course, students should be able to:	PILO(s) to be addressed
CILO 1	Describe the basic concepts of cultural heritage and the key issues of cultural heritage management in China	PILOs 1, 2
CILO 2	Identify the opportunities and challenges of cultural tourism in China	PILOs 2, 3
CILO 3	Analyse cultural heritage management with tourism management in China	PILOs 1, 2
CILO 4	Apply models of tourism in the context of cultural tourism management	PILOs 2, 3

Table 4. Grade of student achievement in Holistic Rubrics.

Performance level	Performance descriptors
Excellent	Strong evidence of **original thinking**; good organization, capacity to analyse and synthesize; superior grasp of subject matter; evidence of extensive knowledge base
Good	Evidence of grasp of subject, some evidence of critical capacity and analytic ability; reasonable understanding of issues; evidence of familiarity with literature
Adequate	Student who is profiting from the university experience; understanding of the subject; ability to develop solutions to simple problems in the material
Marginal	Sufficient familiarity with the subject matter to enable the student to progress without repeating the course
Failure	Little evidence of familiarity with the subject matter; weakness in critical and analytic skills; limited, or irrelevant use of literature

3.2 Student-Centered TLAs

Project theme: Chinese Shadow Puppetry (Gate Keeper/Marketer) (20%) Each group will present a live Shadow Puppetry as cultural activity in performance stage (not more than 5 min). The purpose is to promote the appreciation of this intangible heritage to Online/Offline cultural tourist.

3.3 Peer Assessments

After the Shadow play performance in the class, all groups were evaluated the video of shadow play and the ppt files by online grading system following the holistic rubrics (Table 4) in peer assessment (Fig. 2).

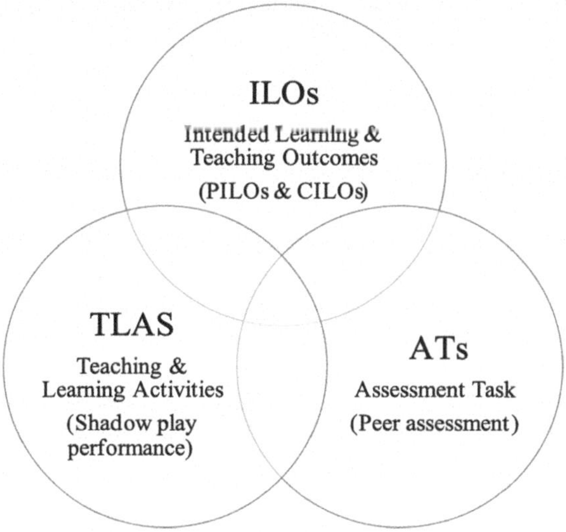

Fig. 2. Constructive alignment of OBTL in Shadow Play.

4 Discussion of Reflections

4.1 Overall Results

Contrast to the iPBL, the application of OBTL iPBL instructional strategies, mainly the from the rubrics, innovation presentation and, the teaching and learning evaluation (TLE) of students (Table 5).

Innovation of presentation

Students Feedback on TLE

Table 5. Camparasion of teaching and learning evaluations.

Students' TLE evaluation	Shadow Play (iPBL in semester 1, 2020)	Media base presentation (non iPBL in semester 2, 2020)
Average TLE (1–18 items)	4.37/5/00	4.23/5.00
*Question No. 9	4.27/5.00	4.17/5.00
**Question No. 18	4.33/5/00	4.08/5.00
Additional comments from students	Students' comment: Very Interesting, Good and Interesting Activity, Mastered rich knowledge, Meaningful and never forget experiences	Students' comment: Good experience, Clear presentation and interesting, Very useful

*Question No. 9: Overall, I think the teacher has taught the course very well.
**Question No. 18: Overall, I think I have learned a lot from this course.

4.2 Reflection of the Study

In conclusion, the constructive alignment between intended learning outcomes, teaching activities and the overall performance between ILOs, TLAs and Ats is positively enhanced creativity. Most of the students applied different form of creativities. Such as e-creativity, artistic creativity, P-creativity, S-creativity and Design Creativity. At the same time, the students' satisfaction compared to non-shadow play TLAs is also increased (TLE average, Question No. 8 and No. 18). The students' satisfaction was improved may cause from the excitement of OBEL iPBL from the shadow play performance.

5 Summary

In this reflective study, we have implemented OBTL iPBL approach for a free-elective course. The application of iPBL and non iPBL was implemented. The finding of learning outcomes and evaluation of OBTL iPBL approach demonstrated a higher positive feedback and students' engagements support by student-centered TLAs during, but the average score in both final examinations are similar. The examinations result explained the initial gaps in assessing the higher order thinking skills (create) is limted. The OBTL iPBL approach filled the gaps and developed a systematic record in assessing creativity of the students. The learning outcomes of shadow play TLAs fills the gaps of OBTL in summative assessment under the student-centered learning classroom.

This work was supported by Department of Education of Guangdong Province, China under the project grants titled "Teaching and Learning in Practice: Shadow Puppet and Cultural Innovation".

References

Attard, A., Loria, E., Geven, K., Santa, R.: Student-Centred Learning – Toolkit for Students, Staffs and Higher Education Institutions. The European Students' Union. LASERLINE, Berlin (2010)

Biggs, J.B.: Teaching for Quality Learning at University. Open University Press/McGraw Hill, Buckingham (2003)

Hwang, R.-H., Hsiung, P.-A., Chen, Y.-J., Lai, C.-F.: Innovative project-based learning. In: Huang, T.-C., Lau, R., Huang, Y.-M., Spaniol, M., Yuen, C.-H. (eds.) SETE 2017. LNCS, vol. 10676, pp. 189–194. Springer, Cham (2017). https://doi.org/10.1007/978-3-319-71084-6_21

Leung, H.Y.: Student-centered vs Teacher-centered assessment in the context of design education. In: The Pacific Rim Objective Measurement Symposium (PROMS), Fukuoka, Japan, August 2015

Leung, H.Y.: The Possibility of Measuring Creativity. Art Readers on Art • Hong Kong (I), pp. 74–92. Art Reader (Hong Kong), Brownie Publishing. (Funded by the Hong Kong Arts Development Council, ISBN 978-988-77971-4-2) (2019)

Online Collision Avoidance Algorithm for Lightweight Web3D Robot Based on M-BVH

Weiqiang Wang and Jinyuan Jia(✉)

School of Software Engineering, Tongji University, Shanghai, China
jyjia@tongji.edu.cn

Abstract. With the rapid development of robot technology, robot simulation starts from C/S to B/S. However, since online collision avoidance is a major concern, there are only a few Web3D robot simulation platforms that can operate online on the Web in the industry. In order to effectively realize fast and high precision online collision avoidance on the Web, this paper proposes a set of online collision avoidance algorithms for lightweight Web3D robots based on M-BVH. M-BVH is a binary tree which use Morton code to divide and organize all of the triangles of the robot model. In our algorithm, we constructs 2 M-BVH trees to speed up the detection process, and aids lightweight optimization methods like the inner body elimination algorithm to reduce the computational burden of high precision collision avoidance in Web3D scenes. The experimental results show that the method of this paper has accurate collision avoidance detection accuracy in the Web3D scene of complex robots, and can ensure it has a fast detection speed.

Keywords: Collision avoidance · Web3D robot · M-BVH · Robot inner body elimination

1 Introduction

In recent years, with the rapid development of robot technology, robots are entering various fields to facilitate our life [1]. At the same time, they have also become the key to the transformation and upgrading of China's manufacturing industry to intelligent manufacturing industry [2]. In the field of robot simulation platform, web browser is increasingly becoming the application platform of 3D interactive program [3]. As the key technology of robot simulation platform, the speed and accuracy of the collision avoidance's online real-time detection largely determine whether it can develop a robot simulation platform on the Web. However, lightweight Web3D robot collision avoidance still faces the challenges of

This research is partially supported by the Basic Grant of Natural Science Foundation of China (No. 6207071897) and the Key Project of Regional Joint Grant of Science Natural Foundation of China (No. U19A2063).

W. Jia et al. (Eds.): SETE 2021, LNCS 13089, pp. 158–165, 2021.
https://doi.org/10.1007/978-3-030-92836-0_14

robot lightweight bottleneck, low precision of Web3D scene collision avoidance, and slow detection speed due to a large amount of calculations in traditional collision avoidance.

In order to solve the above challenges, this paper proposes a set of lightweight Web3D robot online collision avoidance algorithms based on M-BVH, which solves the problem of online collision avoidance of complex robots on the Web.

2 Related Work

Collision avoidance refers to detecting the position relationship between objects in 3D scene, so as to correct the direction or stop the movement of the object to avoid collision. Therefore, it has high requirements for detection accuracy and speed. Especially in robot simulation platform, collision avoidance is the key for the robot to complete the task [4]. To ensure the effect and the detection speed is fast enough, the method of first bounding box detection and then triangular patch detection is usually used to reduce the number of triangular patch detection [5].

In the field of Web3D, the existing collision avoidance detection methods include "spatial decomposition method" and "hierarchical bounding box method" [6]. At present, most of the detection methods used in Web3D scenes are bounding box detection method, or static voxel division and triangular patch detection method. In 2013, Yan Fengting et al. proposed using octree and AABB bounding box for detection [7], in 2019, Jin Chengze proposed a detection method based on voxel division for WebBIM scene [8], and in 2020, Li An et al. proposed detection based on raycaster and bounding box [9]. However, these methods are either not accurate enough, or the detection time is expensive on Web3D robot, so they are not suitable for Web3D robot simulation platform.

The innovation of this paper is mainly reflected in a set of lightweight Web3D robot online collision avoidance algorithm based on M-BVH for complex robots in Web3D scene. The algorithm proposes a robot lightweight inner body elimination algorithm to screen the interior components located in the shell in the robot model. The algorithm can lighten the Web3D robot, accelerate the speed of detection and improve the efficiency of collision avoidance of Web3D robot; At the same time, ray detection and M-BVH are comprehensively used to accelerate the detection process, improve the detection accuracy from bounding box to triangular patch, and make the detection accuracy reach 100%, which provides a new optimization direction for Web3D robot collision avoidance algorithm.

3 Technology Roadmap

In order to achieve the compatibility of speed and accuracy, the technical route adopted in this paper is shown in Fig. 1.

The pretreatment part includes a lightweight inner body elimination algorithm, construct component level M-BVH and construct triangle level M-BVH. The lightweight inner body elimination algorithm is used to lightweight the

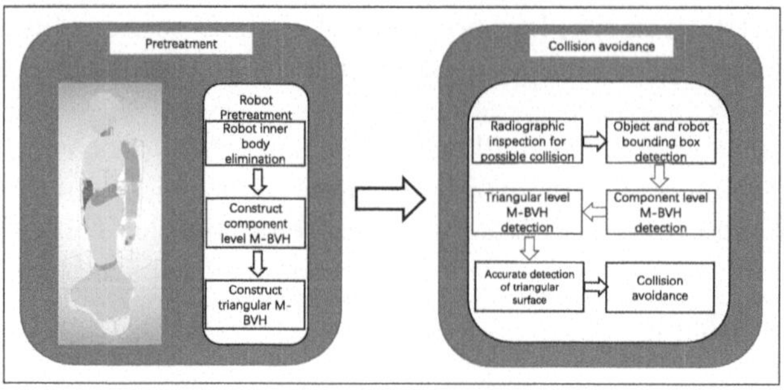

Fig. 1. Web3D robot online real-time collision avoidance technology route.

Web3D robot, which can eliminate most of the fine interior components; Component level M-BVH is a binary tree constructed from robot components according to Morton code. According to this binary tree, the detection can quickly traverse to specific robot components; Triangular M-BVH contains all the information after the secondary organization and division of all triangular patches of the robot according to Morton code. It can be used to accelerate the detection and judgment process so that Web3D robots can realize fast online real-time collision avoidance.

4 Key Technology

4.1 Lightweight Inner Body Elimination Algorithm for Web3D Robot

At present, the commonly used method is to judge whether the AABB bounding box is covered or radiographic detection. But each has its advantages and disadvantages. Radiographic detection has high accuracy, but it will take too much time, which is not suitable for Web3D scenes; The time cost of AABB bounding box coverage is low, but the accuracy is also low, and the components that do not belong to the inner body could be misjudged.

The flow chart of Web3D robot lightweight inner body elimination algorithm proposed in this paper is shown in Fig. 2. Based on the comparison between the AABB bounding box of the current component and the AABB bounding box of the component in the shell sequence, combined with the geometric characteristics and radiographic detection of the component, we can further judge whether the component belongs to the shell component. The components without coverage are added to the shell sequence. For the two components covered by AABB bounding box, the distance relationship between the center point of AABB bounding box is further judged.

Find out the center points P1 and P2 of the two bounding boxes. If the distance d between P1 and P2 on the X, Y, and Z axes is less than twice the side

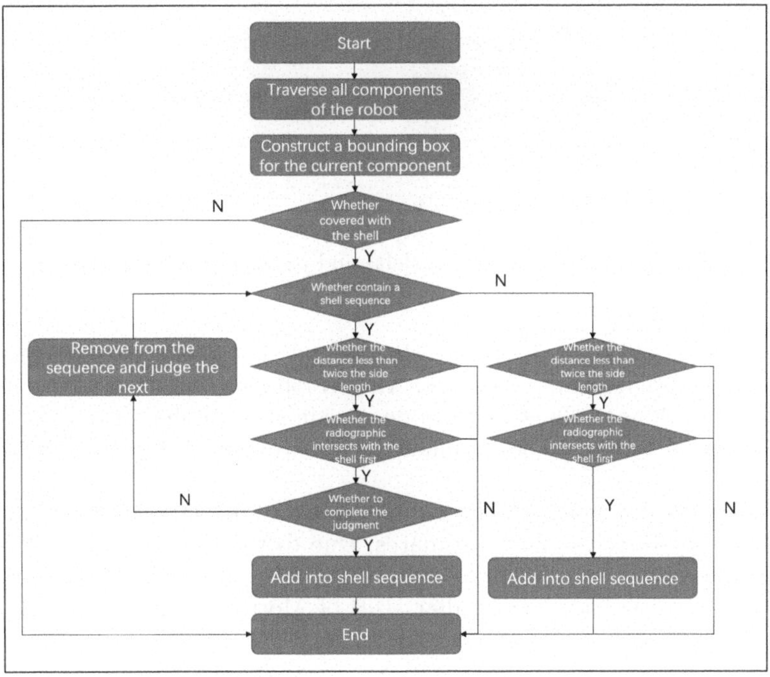

Fig. 2. Flow chart of Web3D robot lightweight inner body elimination algorithm.

length l of the smaller bounding box, it is deemed to be included, otherwise, it is judged not to be included:

$$|p1.x - p2.x| < 2lx\&\&|p1.y - p2.y| < 2ly\&\&|p1.z - p2.z| < 2lz \tag{1}$$

After completed the above judgment, the radiographic method is used to assist in judging whether the component is an inner component.

Represented by the hand with the largest number of fine components, the effect of AABB detection method is shown in the left figure of Fig. 3. The left figure shows the components judged as inner components in AABB screening, and the right figure shows the inner components judged by the method proposed in this paper. As shown in the right figure of Fig. 3, the results obtained by using the method in this paper are better than that by using the AABB bounding box method, the shell components are screened, and the correct judgment is also completed for the wrong judgment of the AABB bounding box method.

4.2 M-BVH

Morton Code. Morton code is a coding method that maps quantized multi-dimensional vectors to one-dimensional vectors [10], which can preserve the local characteristics of coordinates in space. The sequence obtained by sorting the

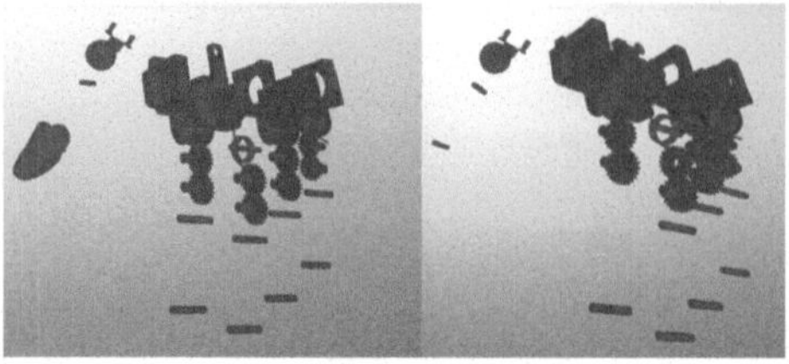

Fig. 3. AABB elimination (left) and paper method (right).

coordinate points in space based on Morton code is a Z-axis curve in space and has a certain spatial locality in space. After sorting all the triangular patches of the robot according to the Morton code coordinates obtained from the Morton code calculation formula, the obtained vertex sequence has good continuity in space.

By using Morton code, the three-dimensional coordinates in space are transformed into one-dimensional coordinates. Due to the characteristics of Morton code, the alternation of coordinate values depends on the coordinate size on X, Y, Z axis, so the points with similar sizes of Morton code must be similar in space.

Web3D Robot M-BVH. In order to realize the collision avoidance of Web3D robot, M-BVH is used to accelerate the detection process. For Web3D robot, two M-BVHs are constructed, one is component level M-BVH, which takes the robot AABB bounding box as the root node, it is divided in half by sorting according to the Morton code of the center point of all components' AABB bounding box, until the leaf node contains only one component; The other is the triangular level M-BVH, which takes a specific component as the root node, and is divided in half according to the Morton code of the center point of the group composed of all triangular patch's AABB bounding box of the component, until the leaf node contains only 100 triangular patches. In the follow-up experiment, we can see that the detection speed and accuracy are significantly improved by using our M-BVH method.

The component level M-BVH takes the whole robot as the root node, sorts the geometric centers of all components or component clusters AABB bounding boxes according to the size of Morton code, and gradually divides the M-BVH from the whole robot to each component according to the Morton sequence, and the leaf node finally stores the information of components. Ensure that the smallest unit that can be screened in the component level M-BVH screening is specific to the component.

Component level M-BVH is shown in Fig. 4(left), in which components with different colors are different nodes, and the nodes are divided according to Morton code.

As shown in Fig. 4(right), the triangular level M-BVH takes a specific component of the robot as the root node, sorts all triangular patches of the component

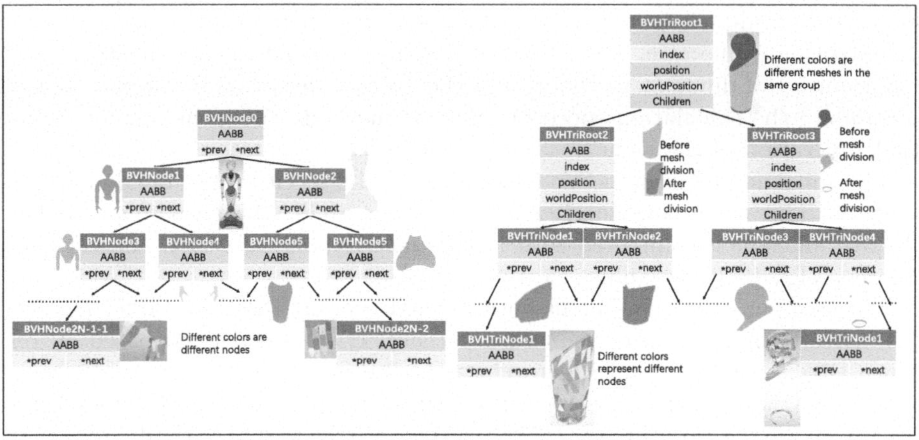

Fig. 4. Component level M-BVH (left) and triangular level M-BVH (right).

according to the Morton code size of the geometric center of the triangular patch cluster's AABB bounding box, and gradually divides the M-BVH from the component to the leaf node according to the Morton sequence.

4.3 Triangle Detection Algorithm

The triangle detection algorithm used in this paper is Guigue's algorithm, which has been proved by Xiao, L and others to have good efficiency in a large number of triangle collision detection [11].

The algorithm defines a determinant in three-dimensional space and calculates the sign size of the determinant to determine whether the two triangles intersect. Suppose a, b, c is the three vertices of a triangle and d is one of the vertex of another triangle, calculate the positive and negative values of the values of the three determinants to get their positional relationship. The determinant [a, b, c, d] is defined as follows:

$$[a\,b\,c\,d] = \begin{bmatrix} a_x & a_y & a_z & 1 \\ b_x & b_y & b_z & 1 \\ c_x & c_y & c_z & 1 \\ d_x & d_y & d_z & 1 \end{bmatrix} = \begin{bmatrix} a_x - d_x & a_y - d_y & a_z - d_z \\ b_x - d_x & b_y - d_y & b_z - d_z \\ c_x - d_x & c_y - d_y & c_z - d_z \end{bmatrix} \tag{2}$$

The detailed implementation of the algorithm can refer to [12].

5 Experimental Analysis

According to the performance evaluation method of online real-time collision avoidance algorithm for lightweight Web3D robot, two performance indexes are proposed to evaluate the experimental results: detection accuracy and the average detection frame rate. The detection accuracy is used to compare the detection accuracy of different methods, and the average detection frame rate is used to compare the calculation speed of different methods and their impact on the stable operation of the scene.

The robot model used in this test is ginger, the service robot of CloudMinds company. This robot contains 1247608 vertices and 2526076 triangular patches. The test machine is configured with 16 GB memory, 3.1 GHz CPU and NVIDIA Geforce GTX 1070Ti graphics card.

The comparative experiments are carried out on the robot model ginger with more than 2.5 million triangular patches. BVH constructed based on reference [13] is used to realize hierarchical bounding box detection, static voxel division + triangular patch detection based on reference [8] and the method in this paper. In the experiment, 1000 spherical polyhedrons are randomly generated in space to move in the direction of the robot. For the small ball about to collide, change its motion direction and make it move in the opposite direction to avoid the robot.

The comparison of the results of this experiment is shown in Table 1.

Table 1. Comparison of collision avoidance experimental results.

	Hierarchical bounding box method	Static voxel division + triangular patch detection	Paper method
Detection accuracy	18.31%	100%	100%
Running frame rate	60 FPS	9.6 FPS	59.52 FPS

In terms of detection accuracy, the hierarchical bounding box method uses AABB bounding box as the final detection method, the detection accuracy generally falls below 0.2. In three detection experiments on 1000 spherical polyhedrons, the average accuracy is 0.18207, 0.19322 and 0.17391 respectively. But paper method and static voxel division + triangular patch detection adds triangular patch accurate detection at the end, so that the detection accuracy can be 100% correct, which has a significant improvement in the accuracy.

In terms of running frame rate, the average frame rate of the hierarchical bounding box method and paper method are stable at 60 FPS. In three tests of 100 frames, the average frame rates of paper method are 59.87 FPS, 59.87 FPS and 58.81 FPS respectively, which is about 0.5 FPS lower than that of the hierarchical bounding box method, compared with the hierarchical bounding box method, there is no different in terms of vision and user experience; However, the frame rate of static voxel division decreases seriously. In three tests of 100 frames, the average frame rates are 9.87 FPS, 8.64 FPS and 10.29 FPS respectively, and the average frame rate is only 9.6 FPS, which can not achieve the expected effect.

6 Conclusion and Feature Work

The experimental results show that the method of this paper has accurate collision avoidance detection accuracy in the Web3D scene of complex robots, and can ensure it has a fast detection speed. This method uses M-BVH to accelerate the detection process, and aids inner body elimination algorithm to reduce the computational burden of high precision collision. The inner body elimination algorithm and M-BVH construction method can be applied to any model composed of triangular patches, which can help us deal with complex models in Web3D scene. The future research expansion of the subject includes the application from complex robot scene to any Web3D scene, the consideration of using GPU for parallel computing to further accelerate the detection process.

References

1. Dey, U., Jana, P.K., Kumar, C.S.: Modeling and kinematic analysis of industrial robots in WebGL interface. In: 2016 IEEE Eighth International Conference on Technology for Education (T4E), pp. 256–257. IEEE (2016)
2. Sun, L., Xu, H., Wang, Z., Chen, G.: Review on key common technologies for intelligent applications of industrial robots. J. Vib. Measur. Diagn. **41**(2), 211–219 (2021)
3. Liu, D., Fan, L., Liu, G., Wang, H.: Online kinematic simulation of COLLADA robot model based on Three.js. Manuf. Autom. **42**(2), 82–85 (2020)
4. Ghandour, M., et al.: Human robot interaction for hybrid collision avoidance system for indoor mobile robots. Adv. Sci. Technol. Eng. Syst. **2**(3), 650–657 (2017)
5. Man, R.R., Zhou, D.S., Zhang, Q.: A survey of collision detection. Appl. Mech. Mater. **3064**, 360–363 (2014)
6. Tan, Y., Jia, J., Peng, S., Huang, A., Li, G.: Survey on some key technologies of virtual tourism system based on Web3D. J. Syst. Simul. **26**(7), 1541–1548 (2014)
7. Yan, F., Liu, C., Jia, J.: Analysis and research on key technologies of mainstream Flash3D engines. J. Syst. Simul. **25**(10), 2263–2270 (2013)
8. Jin, C.: Key technologies of lightweight online interactive editing for large-scale WebBIM scenarios. Comput. Knowl. Technol. **15**(02), 234–236 (2019)
9. Li, A., Xu, H.: Research on key technologies of plug-in free virtual roaming based on WebGL. Appl. Res. Comput. **37**(S1), 227–229 (2020)
10. Thinking Parallel, Part III: Tree Construction on the GPU. https://developer.nvidia.com/blog/thinking-parallel-part-iii-tree-construction-gpu/. Accessed 15 Sept 2021
11. Xiao, L., Mei, G., Cuomo, S., et al.: Comparative investigation of GPU-accelerated triangle-triangle intersection algorithms for collision detection. Multimed. Tools Appl. (2020). https://doi.org/10.1007/s11042-020-09066-3
12. Guigue, P., Devillers, O.: Fast and robust triangle-triangle overlap test using orientation predicates. J. Graph. Tools **8**(1), 25–32 (2003)
13. Xue, J., Shi, G., Zhou, J., Qu, H., Tao, L., Pu, R.: Simplification and compression service construction of 3D model for complex products. J. Syst. Simul. **32**(4), 553–561 (2020)

Education Technology (Edtech) and ICT for Education

The Teaching Design of Sequence Limit Based on Modern Education Technology

Xueqiang Li(✉), Ming Tao, and Ning Zhang

School of Computer Science and Technology, Dongguan University of Technology, Dongguan 523808, People's Republic of China
ming.tao@mail.scut.edu.cn, zhangning@dgut.edu.cn

Abstract. Sequence limit is the most important and basic concept in advanced mathematics, and it is also the theoretical basis of continuity, derivative, differential and integral calculus. However, due to the high abstraction and rigorous logic, limit cannot be mastered by most students, and many confusions about the application and proof of limit are also bother students. Therefore, this article will analyze and design the main points based on modern education technology in the teaching of sequence limit, thus enable students to quickly grasp the content of sequence limit.

Keywords: Advanced mathematics · Sequence limit · Modern education technology

1 Introduction

The Ministry of Education issued the "Implementation Opinions on the Construction of First-Class Undergraduate Courses", which requires the comprehensive development of first-class undergraduate courses, the establishment of the elimination of "water courses", and the creation of "golden courses" that have attracted much attention [1]. Universities are also rigorously teaching curriculum and promoting curriculum reform. As a prerequisite course for multivariable calculus, probability and mathematical statistics, complex function and integral transform, as well as basic courses for many majors, advanced mathematics is a course that must be mastered by the science and engineering students, and it is also a "golden course" that must be created. A survey about advanced mathematics based on tencent questionnaire shows that more than 97% of the science and engineering students think the advanced mathematics course is important (see Fig. 1).

The content of sequence limit belongs to the first section of the first chapter of advanced mathematics [2]. Based on years of teaching experience, it will make students feel fear and even resistance to the study of advanced mathematics courses if this content is not studied well; Meanwhile, it will inevitably have a direct impact on the learning of the subsequent content, because the content of limit runs through the entire content of advanced mathematics [2], from continuity, derivative to calculus, all can be expanded by the thought of limit. The results of the questionnaire survey show that more than 95% of the science and engineering students believe that the content of limit

W. Jia et al. (Eds.): SETE 2021, LNCS 13089, pp. 169–177, 2021.
https://doi.org/10.1007/978-3-030-92836-0_15

has an impact on the learning of the follow-up content of advanced mathematics (see Fig. 2), and more than 70% of the science and engineering students believe that the advanced mathematics course is difficult (see Fig. 3).

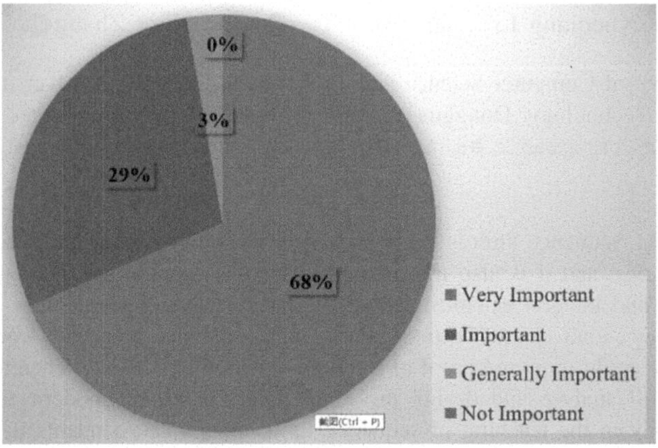

Fig. 1. Screenshot of the statistical results of the importance of the advanced mathematics.

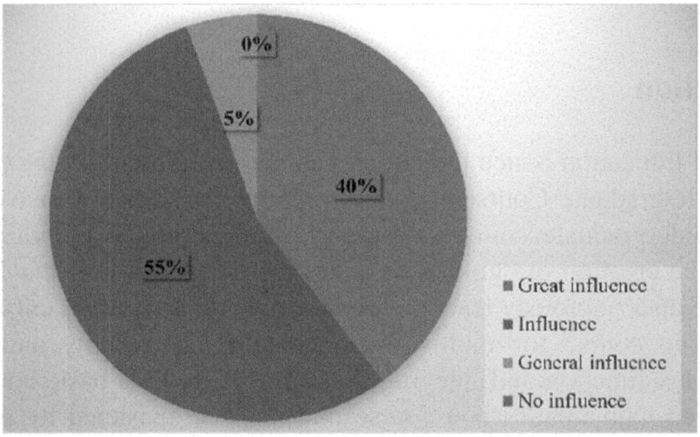

Fig. 2. The statistical results of the influence of sequence limit on contents of subsequent courses.

Due to the high abstraction and rigorous logic of the concept of limit, mastering the content of limit is a great challenge for students. Only 3% of the students think the content of limit is easy by the questionnaire survey (see Fig. 4). Therefore, teachers are particularly required to guide and explain the content effectively. However, in the syllabus of many application-oriented universities, the content of limit is only set as understanding. Therefore, many students' understanding of limit is only in a state of half-understanding. In order to improve students' mathematical foundation and literacy, it is necessary to explain the concept of limit in depth, especially applying modern educational technology to the teaching process of limit [3].

Modern education technology, in addition to emphasizing the application of computer application technology in teaching [4], also pays attention to the update of teaching methods [5]. With the advent of the digital age, modern educational technology has become an important auxiliary means for college education and teaching [3].

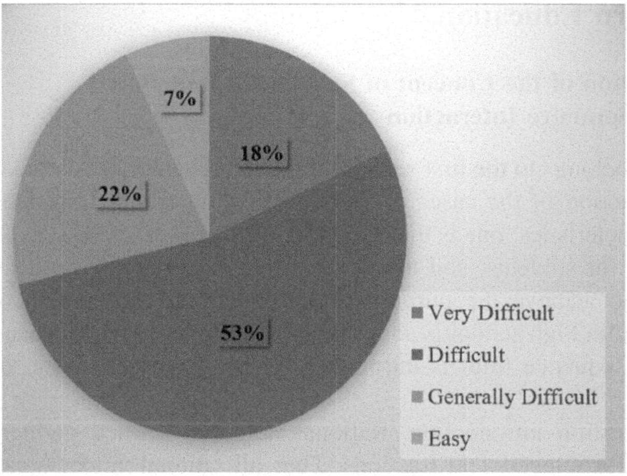

Fig. 3. The statistical results of the difficulty of the advanced mathematics.

The teaching of the content of limit has also been reasonably discussed by related teachers. Sun supplements and reforms the definition of limit [6]; Liu analyzes and transforms the definition with examples [7]; Wang explains the infinitesimal quantity through the explanation of the exercises after class [8]. Liu uses a hierarchical explanation method to explain the definition of limit [9]. These are some effective attempts to explain limit, but most of the explanations only involve a certain aspect of limit. Therefore, it is necessary to rationally design and explain the whole contents in the process of teaching limit.

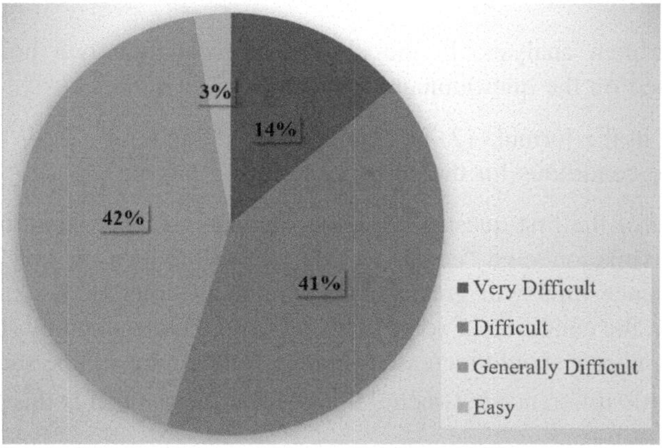

Fig. 4. The statistical results of sequence limit.

Based on the above discussion and combine with the problems encountered by students in the process of learning sequence limit, the main points in the series of teaching of the content of sequence limit are discussed by the following four sections.

2 The Teaching of the Concept of Sequence Limit Based on Modern Educational Technology

2.1 Introduction of the Concept of Sequence Limit Based on Questionnaire Interaction

Sequence limit belongs to the first section of the first chapter of advanced mathematics, thus the introduction of the cases of limit is very important. Excellent cases usually reflect two characteristics: one is that the introduced content is easy to accept, that is, it is very familiar for students, and the other is that it can arouse students' interest and enlightenment to achieve the purpose of introduction. The content of infinite loop decimals learned in high school is adopt in the introduction of sequence limit, and then the concept of sequence limit is introduced step by step according to the following steps.

Step 1: Question introduction. Rational numbers learned in high school are a collective term for integers and fractions. Thus all rational numbers can be converted into fractions. Then, the questionnaire interaction is introduced. Is the infinite recurring decimal a rational number? If so, can it be converted into a score? From this, the following examples can be imported:

$$0.\dot{1} = \frac{1}{9}, 0.\dot{2} = \frac{2}{9}, \cdots 0.\dot{8} = \frac{8}{9} \Rightarrow 0.\dot{9} = \frac{9}{9} = 1. \tag{1}$$

Through formula (1), the concept of infinity and the idea of limit are naturally understood by students. Here, whether $0.\dot{9}$ and 1 are really equal will doubt students. At this time, a simple derivation is introduced to dispel students' doubts as formula (2).

$$0.\dot{3} = \frac{3}{9} \Rightarrow 3 \times 0.\dot{3} = 0.\dot{9} = 1 \; or \; 10 \times 0.\dot{9} - 0.\dot{9} = 9 \Rightarrow 0.\dot{9} = 1. \tag{2}$$

Step 2: Problem analysis. In the above representation, two points should be emphasized based on the questionnaire interaction:

1. Should "=" in the formula (2) be changed to "≈" ?
2. What are the conditions for the above equation to be true?

The purpose of the first question is to ask students to think about the relationship between "approximation" and "equal", which is also the idea of limit. Naturally, the content of sequence limit will greatly arouse students' interest; By emphasizing the second question, the condition of sequence limit can be understood by students, that is, the sequence number n should increase infinitely. There may still be students who feel that there is a little difference between $0.\dot{9}$ and 1, but how much is this little bit, many students can't answer. Here, we can set up a suspense and leave it to explain in detail later when we talk about the concept of infinitesimals.

Step 3: Derives the mathematical form of sequence limit. After the quoted example is given, an example can be appropriately supplemented, and the mathematical representation of sequence limit can be derived from formula (3).

$$\begin{cases} 0.\overset{n}{9} : 0.9,\ 0.99,\ 0.999,\ \cdots & n \to \infty \\ \frac{1}{n} :\ 1,\ \frac{1}{2},\ \frac{1}{3},\ \cdots\ n \to \infty \\ x_n :\ x_1,\ x_2,\ x_3,\ \cdots & n \to \infty \end{cases} \Rightarrow \begin{cases} \lim\limits_{n\to\infty} 0.\overset{n}{9} = 1 \\ \lim\limits_{n\to\infty} \frac{1}{n} = 0 \\ \lim\limits_{n\to\infty} x_n = a \end{cases} \tag{3}$$

The representation of the two sequence limits is given in the form of analogy, which is naturally easy for students to accept. Here, the symbol $\lim\limits_{n\to\infty}$ should be particularly emphasized, which also contains the limit condition.

2.2 Explanation Process of the Definition of Sequence Limit Based on Animation in PPT

Through the explanation of the Subsect. 2.1, students understand the standard mathematical representation of sequence limit. The next step is to explain the definition of sequence limit. It is also the focus and difficulty of sequence limit. Similarly, it is necessary to start from the above cited examples and design the explanation process reasonably from the perspective of students. Based on this, this article designs the explanation process of sequence limit (see Fig. 5) by the segmented animation in PPT.

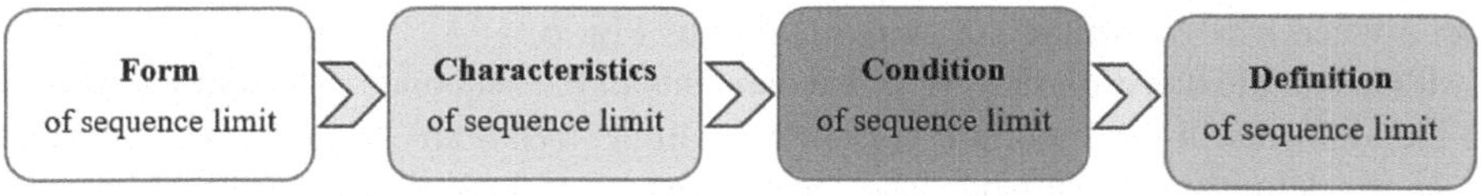

Fig. 5. Explanation process of sequence limit definition.

Animation 1: Form of sequence limit. $\lim\limits_{n\to\infty} 0.\overset{n}{9} = 1$, $\lim\limits_{n\to\infty} x_n = a$.

Animation 2: Characteristics of sequence limit. the two are infinitely close, that is, the absolute value of the left and right difference is smaller than any positive number. It is expressed in mathematical $\forall \varepsilon > 0$, $|x_n - a| < \varepsilon$.

Animation 3: Condition of sequence limit. Infinitely increase.

The concept of "infinite increase" cannot be described currently, however, based on the example of formula (1), if a very small number ε is given, it is certain when n is infinite can make the inequality $|x_n - a| < \varepsilon$ hold, but we have to ask whether n must be infinite? Or does it mean that the inequality can be satisfied as long as it reaches a certain level? Let's do a few experiments by formula (4).

It's easy to see that for a given ε, as long as n exceeds a certain number, the inequality is hold, so the conditions for sequence limit can be changed to:

$$\begin{gathered} \varepsilon = 0.01, \ \left|0.\overset{n}{9} - 1\right| < \varepsilon \Rightarrow n > 2 \\ \varepsilon = 0.0015, \ \left|0.\overset{n}{9} - 1\right| < \varepsilon \Rightarrow n > 3 \\ \vdots \\ \varepsilon = 0.00003, \ \left|0.\overset{n}{9} - 1\right| < \varepsilon \Rightarrow n > 5 \end{gathered} \tag{4}$$

Animation 3*: Condition of sequence limit. n is as large as a certain degree, that is $\exists N \in Z_+$, when $n > N$. Where the value of N is related to the value of ε, and it can be seen from the above formula (4).

Animation 4: Definition of sequence limit. Combining the three steps above, the definition of sequence limit can be defined as formula (5).

$$\forall \varepsilon > 0, \ \exists N \in Z_+, \ \text{ when } n > N, \ |x_n - a| < \varepsilon. \tag{5}$$

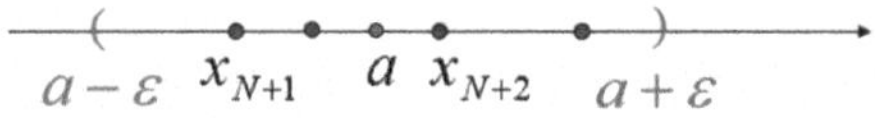

Fig. 6. The figure of geometric meaning of sequence limit.

The geometric form of sequence limit can be expressed as: the absolute value of the difference between the value of the sequence element x_n and the limit value a is smaller than ε when $n > N$, which can be expressed as Fig. 6.

Based on the convergent form of the elements in the sequence shown in Fig. 6, how do the elements in the sequence approach its limit? What are the ways to approach?

In the definition of sequence limit, there is no special requirement for it [2]. Here, a few examples of sequence limits can be given for students to think about its approach independently. For example $\frac{1}{n}$, $-\frac{1}{n}$, $\frac{(-1)^n}{n}$, $\frac{\sin(n)}{n}$, etc. These examples will greatly deepen understanding of sequence limit for students.

3 Parameter Analysis in the Definition of Sequence Limit Based on Questionnaire Interaction

After explaining the definition of sequence limit, students do not have a deep understanding of the definition. Therefore, teachers will use the definition of sequence limit to explain some proofs of sequence limit, so as to deepen the students' understanding of the definition. This is also the arrangement on the PPT of the higher education version used by most of teachers. In fact, this way is not very effective in the actual teaching process. Students will be more confused about the process of sequence limit proof. Some students even don't know what to prove at all.

Therefore, after explaining the definition of sequence limit, the sequence limit proof should not be expanded immediately. Instead, the parameters in the definition of the sequence limit should be first explained. To answer these questions, it is natural to start from the definition and analyze and explain each parameter in the definition. The following is also introduced by the way of questionnaire interaction:

Questionnaire 1: Which quantities in the definition of sequence limit are known and which are unknown?

Answer: n is the coefficient of the sequence, ε is arbitrary, x_n is given, and the corresponding limit value a of x_n can also be calculated. Only N is unknown.

According to the above analysis, the proof of sequence limit is to find the value N. The example of formula (4) shows that N is related to ε, but the value of N is not unique, because ε is arbitrarily given. For each ε, N is needed. For the value N, if there is a functional formula of N with respect to ε, then for any ε, the corresponding N can be obtained through this functional formula, so that N is always present. Therefore, the proof of sequence limit is to find N. Through the explanation, students will be able to understand what sequence limit proof is to do. Naturally, it is much easier in the explanation of sequence limit proof later.

Questionnaire 2: Can a range be set for the variable ε? And how to set?

Answer: The smaller the value of ε, the closer x_n is to a. In order to prove that x_n and a are infinitely close, ε must be able to be set to the smallest positive number. Thus the left boundary of the value range of ε is 0; If ε is set to a small value ε_1,there is a value N that makes the inequality $|x_n - a| < \varepsilon_1$ true when $n > N$, then the same value N can be set to make the inequality $|x_n - a| < \varepsilon_1 < \varepsilon_2$ true when ε is set to a large value ε_2 $(\varepsilon_1 < \varepsilon_2)$. Therefore, we can set $\varepsilon \in (0, \alpha)$, where α $(\alpha > 0)$ is arbitrary. It is easy to prove that the definition of sequence limit is satisfied at $\varepsilon \in (\alpha, +\infty)$ when the definition can be satisfied at $\varepsilon \in (0, \alpha)$.

Questionnaire 3: Can a value be set for the variable N in advance in the proof of sequence limit? And what is its meaning?

Answer: 1) It can be pre-required that $N = K, (K \in Z_+)$, which can be regarded as only studying the elements after the K-th item in the sequence x_n. Because sequence limit is to study the case of x_n when n is infinite, so naturally those elements in the sequence whose item is less than K can be ignored; 2) If the sequence x_n has a limit value a, then for a given ε, a corresponding $N = N'$ can be obtained, the inequality $|x_n - a| < \varepsilon$ holds when $n > N$. At this time, if $K > N'$, then set $N = K$, because the first K items of the sequence x_n are not considered. Otherwise, keep $N = N'$ unchanged. The two cases are unified to $N = \max\{N', K\}$.

4 The Application of Sequence Limit Through PPT

4.1 The Distinction Between the Proof and the Application of Sequence Limit

After explaining the content of the proof of sequence limit, the next section will talk about the nature of sequence limit, which is actually the application of the definition of sequence limit. The content of this part is originally very simple, but many students often confuse the proof with the application of sequence limit. Therefore, it is necessary to emphasize the difference between the proof and the application of sequence limit.

The application of sequence limit is about what useful information can be obtained when the sequence has a limit value. Otherwise the proof of sequence limit is about how to find the N to make the inequality $|x_n - a| < \varepsilon$ hold, so as to prove that the sequence has a limit value. It is a sufficient condition for a sequence has a limit value in the former, but a necessary condition in the latter.

For the application of sequence limit, if the limit value exists, it means that for any value of ε, there must be a number $N \in Z_+$ that holds the inequality $|x_n - a| < \varepsilon$. The value of ε in the inequality can be set arbitrarily, and when ε is set to a value, N always exists. There is no need to worry about the value of N, because N always exists when the limit value exists. In fact, the nature of the sequence can be obtained by setting a special value of ε for the application of sequence limit. Based on this idea, most properties of sequence limit can be understood.

For example, set $\varepsilon = \frac{b-a}{2}$ to prove sequence limit uniqueness theorem of convergent sequence in PPT, where a and b are the two assumed limit values; set $\varepsilon = \frac{a}{2}$ to prove the sign-preserving theorem of convergent sequence in PPT; set ε be an any value greater than 0 to prove the boundedness of a convergent sequence in PPT. And therefore the content of sequence limit can be more easily mastered by students through the use of the modern educational techniques.

4.2 Some Confusions in the Understanding of and Application of Sequence Limit

The content of sequence limit belongs to the first chapter of advanced mathematics. Usually, we do not ask students to preview in advance before this chapter. There are two main reasons: One is worrying that students may feel afraid of difficulties of advanced mathematics courses because they cannot understand the content of the first chapter; The second is worrying that the students' understanding of sequence limit may be biased during the preview process, and they need to be corrected continuously in subsequent studies. It also takes a certain amount of time for preview.

In addition, for the content of this section, students sometimes feel that they have understood, and sometimes feel not. At this time, they must be told to verify and consolidate their understanding by introducing examples to gradually grasp sequence limit of the content.

5 Summarize

In this paper, the content of familiar infinite decimal is reasonably introduced for the conception of sequence limit, the flow of the explanation of sequence limit definition is reasonably designed, each parameter in the definition of sequence limit is discussed for the proof of sequence limit, and the distinction between the proof and the application of sequence limit is explained emphatically, as well as the confusion encountered by the students in the process of learning sequence limit is given specific suggestions. These provides references and some guiding opinions for teachers in teaching sequence limit, which will inevitably bring a positive impact on the teaching of advanced mathematics.

References

1. MOE of China. http://www.moe.gov.cn/. Accessed 18 Aug 2021
2. Department of Mathematics of Tongji University. Advanced mathematics, 7th edn. Higher Education Press, Beijing (2014)
3. Wang, Y., Zhao, C., Zhao, R.: The impact of modern educational technology on college teaching and its application strategies. In: Sugumaran, V., Zheng, X., Shankar, P., Zhou, H. (eds.) MMIA 2019. AISC, vol. 929, pp. 999–1006. Springer, Cham (2019). https://doi.org/10.1007/978-3-030-15740-1_129
4. Hou, D., Yin, J.: Analysis on the impact of new media technology factors on college and university. Innov. Sci. Technol. (3), 39–44 (2016)
5. Zhao, J., Zhang, L.: An empirical study on college teachers' acceptance of blended teaching-based on DTPB and TTF. Mod. Educ. Technol. (10), 67–73 (2017)
6. Changxin, S.: Explanation on the definition of limit. J. Guangxi Univ. Nationalities **8**(2), 190–192 (2002)
7. Xiaoyun, L.: An explanation method of limit analysis definition. Stud. College Math. **7**(5), 14–15 (2004)
8. Chengqiang, W.: Analysis on applications of the conclusions concerning infinitesimals obtained from exercises in mathematical analysis courses. J. Jiyuan Vocat. Tech. Coll. **20**(1), 31–34 (2021)
9. Jianqiang, L.: A hierarchical teaching method about definition of sequence limit. J. Lanzhou Univ. Arts Sci. **29**(5), 99–102 (2015)

Reducing EFL Learners' Error of Sound Deletion with ASR-Based Peer Feedback

Xiaojing Wu[1], Xiaobin Liu[1(✉)], and Lu Chen[2]

[1] South China Normal University, Guangzhou, Guangdong, China
liuxiaobin@m.scnu.edu.cn
[2] Nanhai No.1 Middle School, Foshan, Guangdong, China

Abstract. As an emerging technology for Computer Assisted Pronunciation Training (CAPT), ASR (automatic speech recognition) has been used to improve language learners' pronunciation and speaking abilities. This study examined the difference in EFL (English as a foreign language) learners' sound deletion performance with peer feedback and individual practice when using an automatic speech recognition (ASR) system. During each weekend, participants used DingTalk, a software with ASR message to practice reading the passages from their textbooks. The participants marked the mistakes in the ASR by themselves (N = 30) or with feedback from partners (N = 30). The intervention spanned eight weeks. Besides the overall pronunciation performance, the frequency counts of the phoneme and syllable deletion were measured before and after the treatment. The results revealed significant differences in both groups' overall pronunciation performance, overall sound deletion performance, phoneme and syllable deletion, which showed that the peer feedback group performs better than the self-corrected group. Participants' attitudes towards the ASR-based pronunciation practice were also investigated in the present study.

Keywords: Peer feedback · ASR · Sound deletion · Reading aloud

1 Introduction

Pronunciation teaching requires teachers to give one-to-one feedback on students' pronunciation performance, which is usually more time-consuming in the context of the large-scale class [1, 2]. However, in traditional L2 pronunciation instruction, students are required to listen to the recording and then imitate the pronunciation individually which is relatively difficult for students to figure out mistakes in pronunciation without timely guidance from the teacher. ASR (Automatic Speech Recognition), a technology that can transcribe speech into texts in real time, has been increasingly used to redress the problem. Researchers have confirmed that the sentence, word and text level feedback provided by ASR system is able to make the learner aware of problems in his/her pronunciation [3] and stop learners from cultivating improper pronunciation habits [4]. As to the incorrect pronunciation habits, sound deletion is a typical one. Second language learners in China are prone to overuse the pronunciation rules in the

W. Jia et al. (Eds.): SETE 2021, LNCS 13089, pp. 178–189, 2021.
https://doi.org/10.1007/978-3-030-92836-0_16

learning process, resulting in sound deletion [5]. Therefore, Chinese EFL learners' sound deletion problem needs to be solved urgently.

As ASR-based pronunciation training is not a magic formula for learners to alter their inrooted pronunciation problems, to integrate peer feedback into the training may be a win-win way to make up for the shortfall of ASR. Thus, the present study tend to explore the effectiveness of ASR-based pronunciation instruction combined with peer feedback regarding learners' sound deletion habits in reading aloud task by exploiting the ASR message provided by DingTalk, a social networking program.

2 Literature Review

2.1 ASR-Based Pronunciation Instruction

The explicit feedback provided by ASR can help learners to detect their own high-frequency errors [6, 7]. Foreseeing the huge potential of ASR, some scholars try to explore learners' attitudes towards ASR-assisted pronunciation learning in order to explore the exact advantages of using ASR for pronunciation teaching [8]. Bashori et al. [8] found that when students use ASR for oral practice, the foreign language anxiety will be greatly reduced. A study conducted by Neri et al. [9] found that students who use the CAPT system with a simple ASR function perform the same as those who receive in-class instruction. This indicates that ASR-based programs can be used for students to conduct autonomous pronunciation training after class.

However, some mobile-based dictation ASR programs (e.g. Wechat, DingTalk) are not designed for teaching pronunciation which are unable to give scaffolding for learners to identify the errors made by themselves, provide them assessment scores or help them modify pronunciation or to correct mistakes [10, 11]. Liakin et al. [12] adopted three different feedback methods for the perception and production of the French vowel /y/: dictation ASR-based feedback, teacher's feedback and not giving any feedback to students. The results from the forty-two elementary students confirmed that the dictation ASR-based training can also significantly improve students' production of the French vowel /y/.

Nevertheless, using the speech technology alone may not suit all the L2 learners [13]. In addition to corresponding phonetic skills, it also requires a considerable amount of practice and correct feedback to improve phonetic skills [14]. Thus, some researchers tend to explore the incorporation of collaboration with ASR pronunciation instruction. With scaffolding, the effect of ASR may be more obvious [11].

2.2 Peer Feedback in Pronunciation Instruction

Peer feedback in the mobile-assisted language learning environment is more flexible, and can be carried out at anytime and anywhere [15]. Luo [16] found that the ASR-based training with peer feedback can significantly improve secondary school students' segmental and suprasegmental problems. Tasi [13] discussed the role of collaborative learning in the ASR-based pronunciation instruction. Sixty junior college students practiced pronunciation using MYET for 10 weeks with or without peer. Tasi reported that learners with peer are more aware of their pronunciation difficulties, thereby improving their pronunciation problems. Evers & Chen [17] explored the effect of using ASR software with or without peer feedback for Taiwanese working adults' pronunciation training. The results showed that peer feedback is more effective in correcting pronunciation problems than self-assessed practice, yet it does not yield much effect on the improvement of accent. Dai & Wu [10] discussed the effectiveness of feedback from peers and/or ASR by using WeChat. The results showed that peer plus ASR feedback can significantly improve students' pronunciation.

Nevertheless, the studies presented above did not focus on the improvement of the specific pronunciation problems which are urgently needed to be corrected by EFL learners. Therefore, the present study explores the effectiveness of ASR-based pronunciation training with or with peer textual feedback for pronunciation error correction.

2.3 Sound Deletion

Sound deletion is a typical one of the various phonetic errors of L2 learners. It usually refers to the variation of the phenomenon of phonology in interlanguage [5, 18].

Van Doremalen, Cucchiarini, & Strik [19] found that in the reading loud task, learners produced more substitution and deletion errors. The reasons may be accounted for interference from routinized pronunciation patterns, testing pressure or unnaturalness under the standardized environment. In addition, when the consonant deletion phenomenon occurs in the consonant cluster at the beginning would cause threaten to the intelligibility of L2 learners, especially [20–23]. Therefore, it is necessary to raise teachers and students' attention to deletion, and find suitable methods to reduce it.

2.4 Aims and Research Questions

Though previous studies started to turn their eyes to combining ASR with peer feedback in pronunciation training, they did not provide detailed analysis of what specific pronunciation problems can be solved in the training. Hence, this study focuses specifically on investigating the effectiveness of peer feedback compared with individual practice in pronunciation training through ASR in helping students at secondary high school to reduce sound deletion.

More specifically, this study aims to answer the following questions:

RQ1. To what extent does ASR pronunciation training with peer feedback reduce Chinese EFL learners' sound deletion of reading aloud?
RQ2. What types of sound deletion are specifically reflected in the reduction (phoneme deletion and syllable deletion)?
RQ3. What are students' perceptions of ASR pronunciation training with or without peer feedback?

3 Methodology

3.1 Participants

This study was conducted in a secondary school in Guangzhou China. The two groups included 60 first-year senior students from two parallel classes. One class of 30 (15 females) participants was chosen as control group (self-corrected group) while another class of 30 (14 females) participants was the experimental group (peer feedback group). Both of the two classes were taught by the same English teacher. All of the participants have learnt English for 10 to 13 years. The English proficiency of both groups is similar. The result of the pre-test shows that there is no significant difference between the two groups ($t = .143$, $P = .887 > 0.05$).

3.2 Instruments

Read Aloud. The read aloud materials practiced by the students are the passages excerpted from Students English Textbooks 2 for Senior One, published by Beijing Normal University Press.

DingTalk. DingTalk is a free communication and collaboration multi-terminal platform launched by Alibaba company. The built-in ASR is characterized by the state-of-the-art end-to-end speech recognition which can greatly guarantee the rate of recognition accuracy [24]. In this study, learners used DingTalk to send the voice message (the read aloud passages) to themselves or to their partners and take screenshots of the recognition results to mark the pronunciation errors.

Tests. Both pre-test and post-test are the same reading aloud short passage selected from the 2020 Computer-based English Listening and Speaking Tests (CELST) Guangdong version. Participants finished the tests via the ETS100.com (a platform which can be used for assigning listening and speaking tests). The full score of the read aloud tests is 20 points.

Questionnaires and Interview. Questionnaires and Interview were administered to elicit students' perceptions of ASR-based pronunciation training with and without peer feedback. The questionnaires were adapted from Luo [16], using Likert Five Rating Scale ranging from 1 ('strongly disagree') to 5 ('strongly agree'). 10 items were included in the questionnaire for the control group and 11 items were included in that of the experiment group. 20 students from each group would be selected as the interviewees to further investigate participants' willingness to use ASR-based software and their perceptions of the function of "peer".

3.3 Procedure

1. A pre-test was administered to the participants in both groups before the experiment.
2. The next eight weekends, participants would practice read aloud in Ding Talk. Participants in CG would send audio chat to themselves and mark the pronunciation

errors on the screenshot of the transcription individually. While participants in EG would send synchronous audio chat to their partners and detect each other's pronunciation errors with reference to the transcription. They would mark the errors their partners made on the screenshot and made suggestions for each other. After marking the errors in the screenshots, all the participants need to practice on their own and finally upload the final version of their read aloud recording and the screenshot with annotation in Ding Talk.

3. After 8 weeks' experiment, participants were given the post-test in three days. Participants were also required to complete the questionnaires concerning the attitudes towards the training. Twenty participants were invited to have a face-to-face interview. The figures below (Fig. 1 & Fig. 2) are the examples of both groups.

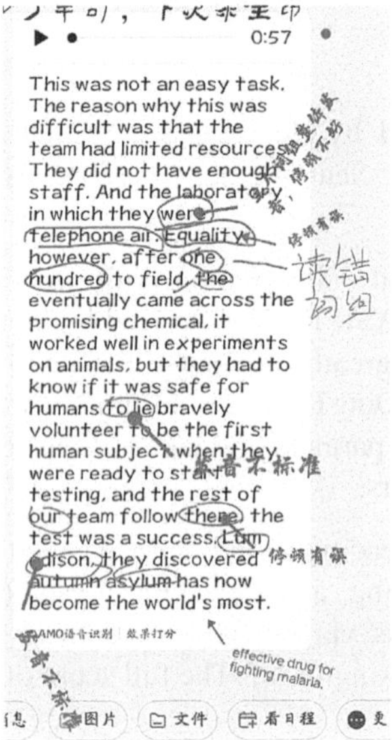

Fig. 1. Peer feedback in EG

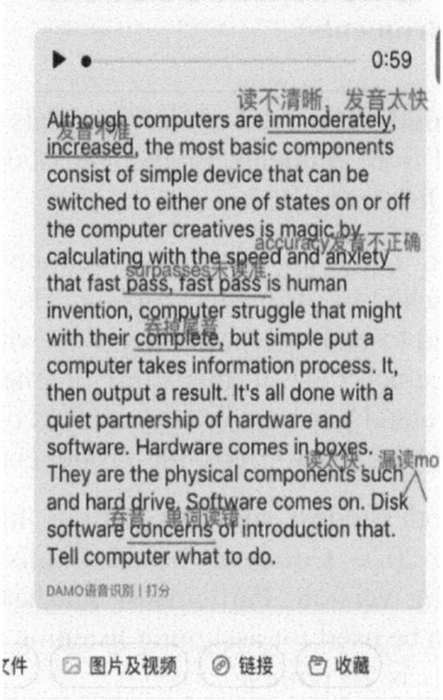

Fig. 2. Self-corrected in CG

3.4 Data Collection and Analysis

Both pre-test and post-test were scored by the two postgraduates majoring in English Teaching followed strictly the metrics of scoring standard in CELST. Then they encoded the sound deletion in all the participants' pre and post-test recordings. The coding system for sound deletion followed the outline proposed by Xu & Zeng [5].

The statistical analysis of the data was analyzed by SPSS 25.0. The data from both groups met the requirement of equal variances. Participants' overall scores, frequency counts of sound deletion adopted the pair sample t test and independent sample t-test.

Independent sample t tests of the pre-test (Table 1) were conducted to ensure the equivalence of the groups.

Table 1. Independent sample T-test of the pre-test in EG and CG

	Group	N	M	Sd	t	p
Scores	EG	30	14.17	1.724	.143	.887
	CG	30	14.10	1.882		
**FC of sound deletion*	EG	30	5.17	1.577	−1.212	.230
	CG	30	5.70	1.822		
FC of phoneme deletion	EG	30	4.10	1.447	−1.011	.316
	CG	30	4.50	1.614		
FC of syllable deletion	EG	30	1.27	.868	.301	.764
	CG	30	1.20	.155		

*FC: frequency counts

4 Results

Table 2. Independent sample T-test of the post-test in EG and CG

	Group	N	M	Sd	t	p
Scores	EG	30	16.40	1.610	.3292	.023*
	CG	30	15.40	1.714		
FC of sound deletion	EG	30	3.00	1.682	−3.333	.001**
	CG	30	4.70	2.231		
FC of phoneme deletion	EG	30	2.77	1.501	−2.139	.037*
	CG	30	3.70	1.860		
FC of syllable deletion	EG	30	.27	.583	−4.397	.000**
	CG	30	1.00	.788		

Table 3. Paired sample T-test between the pre and post-test in EG and CG

	Group	t	p
Scores	EG	−8.148	.000**
	CG	−6.196	.000**
FC of sound deletion	EG	5.782	.000**
	CG	3.218	.003**
FC of phoneme deletion	EG	4.434	.000**
	CG	2.845	.008**
FC of syllable deletion	EG	6.021	.000**
	CG	1.235	.227

The independent sample t test was conducted to compare the post-test performance of CG and EG. Table 2 presents the results of the independent sample t test for both groups in the post-tests. Within group comparison was analyzed through paired sample t test to see if there is any significant difference between pre and post-test. Table 3 shows the results of paired sample t test.

4.1 Results of the Overall Scores and the Frequency Counts of Sound Deletion in Reading Aloud

As Table 2 presented, the independent t test of the post-test between EG and CG, significant differences also found for the overall score ($t = .3292$, $p = .023 < 0.05$) and the frequency counts of sound deletion ($t = -3.333$, $p = .001 < 0.01$). Additionally, the mean score of EG was 16.40 while that of CG was 15.40.

With regard to the paired sample t test between pre and post-test in both groups found significant differences for the overall score ($t = -8.15$, $p = .000 < 0.01$ for the EG, and $t = -6.20$, $p = .000 < 0.01$ for the CG) and the frequency counts of sound deletion ($t = 5.78$, $p = .000 < 0.01$ for the EG, and $t = 3.21$, $p = .003 < 0.01$ for the CG).

These results indicate that be it the self-corrected group or peer feedback group, ASR-based pronunciation training can significantly improve learners' overall pronunciation performance and reduce their sound deletion. Notably, peer feedback group outperformed self-corrected group in overall scores and the reduction of sound deletion.

4.2 Results of the Different Types of Deletion Errors in Reading Aloud

Still, there were significant differences in the independent t test of the post-test between EG and CG for the frequency counts of phoneme deletion ($t = -2.139$, $p = .037 < 0.05$) and for the frequency counts of syllable deletion ($t = -4.397$, $p = .000 < 0.01$). The frequency counts of phoneme deletion and syllable deletion in post-test in EG was 2.77 and .27 respectively which were lower than the CG ($M = 3.70$ for phoneme deletion and $M = 1.00$ for syllable deletion).

As Table 3 showed that significant differences were detected in both groups for the frequency counts of phoneme deletion ($t = 4.43$, $p = .000 < 0.01$ for the EG, and $t = 2.85$, $p = .008 < 0.01$ for the CG). Notably, as for the frequency counts of syllable deletion ($t = 6.02$, $p = .000 < 0.01$ for the EG, and $t = 1.24$, $p = .227 > 0.05$ for the CG), the EG still showed significant improvement while CG did not. This means that participants in both groups made significant progress in phoneme deletion.

In other words, learners with peer feedback were able to correct both types of sound deletion, whereas learners who practice individually still had problems with syllable deletion. In addition, the peer feedback group perform better than the self-corrected group regardless of the phoneme deletion or syllable deletion.

4.3 Results of the Questionnaires

The Cronbach's α reliability of the questionnaire for the control group was 0.928 and 0.865 for the experimental group which are both at a highly reliable level. The results of the questionnaires are presented in Table 4.

Table 4. Results of the questionnaire survey (N = 30)

Questions	CG		EG	
	Mean	Sd	Mean	Sd
Q1. Sound deletion is a problem that I have always been difficult to correct	4.17	.747	4.27	.583
Q2. Sometimes I am not sure whether my judgment on the recognition result is correct	3.70	.877	3.53	1.008
Q3. I am satisfied with the recognition result	3.83	.834	4.17	.531
Q4. ASR is helpful to improve English pronunciation	4.10	.712	4.30	.466
Q5. ASR is helpful to reduce my English sound deletion	3.70	1.088	4.17	.531
Q6. Compared with listening to recordings, I prefer to use ASR for reading aloud training	3.67	.884	3.90	.803
Q7. Compared with traditional classroom pronunciation teaching, ASR is more helpful in improving my pronunciation	3.70	.837	3.77	.774
Q8. The use of ASR for reading aloud training improved my enthusiasm	3.53	1.008	4.03	.765
Q9. I will continue to use ASR for autonomous training	3.60	.932	3.90	.712
Q10. It would be better if I have a partner to help me correct the error (for CG)	3.87	1.042		
Q11. My feedback to my peers helps them improve their pronunciation (for EG)			4.07	.691
Q12. The feedback from my peers helps me improve my pronunciation (for EG)			4.30	.596

Q3–Q9 are about the satisfaction with the ASR-based training. The mean score for CG is 3.73 while that of for EG is 4.03. Q10 is for CG whose mean is 3.87 while Q11 and Q12 are for EG whose mean are all above 4, indicating that learners are in favor of practicing pronunciation with peer. The results show that, overall, participants in both groups are satisfied with the ASR-based pronunciation training. Yet participants were more willing to practice with peer feedback.

5 Discussion

5.1 The Reduction of Sound Deletion

Both self-corrected group and peer feedback group made significant progress in the overall pronunciation performance and sound deletion after the training. These results are consistent with the findings of Yuan & Liu [25], which shows that ASR-based pronunciation training can help students notice the deletion error and help them reduce the deletion errors. Although the self-practiced group also made stride in the post-test, the improvement was not as significant as the peer feedback group. The result is in line with the previous findings that investigate the effectiveness of collaborative ASR training [11, 17]. Despite the fact that previous studies rarely focus on the reduction of sound deletion with ASR software and peer assistance, they did explore the promotion of comprehensibility, whose important indicators include the performance of deletion [26].

The reasons of the better performance of peer feedback group may lie in that first pronunciation is characterized by ingrained and automatized which needs intensive instruction for the purpose of altering long-established habits [27]. The sound deletion is one of the most obvious pronunciation problems for Chinese EFL learners. The ASR-based program can be helpful to correct students' errors and pronunciation habits to some extent. Yet the students practice individually could not distinguish the difference between the target sound and their own, and therefore they did not understand how to correct the pronunciation errors despite they could see them [11, 28]. Whereas peer would help them detect the errors more careful and give them advice. When they made the same pronunciation errors next time, peer would remind them again which in turn raise both of the learners' awareness of avoiding making the same errors.

5.2 The Reduction of Phoneme and Syllable Deletion

In terms of the specific types of sound deletion, both groups achieved significant progress in phoneme deletion. Nevertheless, no significant difference was found in the CG's syllable deletion. Significant differences were detected between both groups in phoneme and syllable deletion. This means that compared to CG, EG performed better in both types of sound deletion while CG did not show obvious improvement in the reduction of syllable deletion.

The main type of phoneme deletion lied in the consonant deletion in both groups. The word-final consonants like the plosive sound /t/ and /d/ were easily be deleted. For example, the word light /laɪt/ was pronounced as lie /laɪ/ and back /bæk/ was pronounced as the nonsense word /bæ/. Furthermore, the fricative sound /z/ and /s/ which served as the inflectional suffix were also missed. Such kinds of phoneme deletion are quite common in Chinese EFL students. As Xu & Zeng [5] summarized that the main type of deletion error is phoneme deletion, among which the loss of consonants appears most frequent.

Regarding the syllable deletion, participants were prone to miss the ending syllable. For example, the inflectional suffix like -ed (connected), -ing (astonishing) and -es (reaches). Besides, when faced with some multi-syllable words, learners would also miss the word-medial syllable. For example, although the word imagination is quite common in learners' daily study, it contains five syllables which would be easily deleted by learners who had poor pronunciation habits. The deletion errors mentioned above were corrected by most learners effectively with the integration of ASR pronunciation training. If the learner deletes the sound, it may cause the ASR program misrecognize the word and transcribe to another word. For example, light will be recognized as lie. It is rather obvious for those ending sounds, regardless of phoneme or syllable sound, which can be detected by students effortless.

5.3 Learners' Perceptions of ASR-Based Training with or Without Peer Feedback

As stated previously, the participants in both groups hold positive attitudes towards the training. According to the questionnaire results and the individual interview, students admitted that deletion was a problem that they have long ignored in the routine training. As for the effectiveness of the ASR-based training towards the reduction of their sound deletion, compared to CG (M = 3.70), EG (M = 4.17) were more in favor of the novel training pattern. As item 10 for CG and item 11–12 for EG of the questionnaire and the interview with the participants confirm that students were more willing to practice pronunciation with partners due to the inaccurate recognition of ASR software sometimes. One of the reasons may due to the explicit corrective feedback that peer offers. The young learners tend to read the explicit textual information for self-correction. The explicit and pertinent feedback that points out students' fault may be better accepted by the learners [9, 29]. Moreover, students mentioned that they would like to appoint the time with partners who could be the role of "monitor" so that they could work together to better finish the task. Interviewees also brought up the idea that peer could help them ease their stress and provide helpful and inspiring suggestions for them. These findings echoed those from Tasi [13], whose study revealed that the collaborative pronunciation training can make the practice more interactive and enhance the awareness of cultivating the correct pronunciation habits.

6 Conclusion

The purpose of the study is to investigate whether ASR-based pronunciation training with peer feedback could help EFL learners significantly reduce sound deletion. Learners' perceptions of the training with or without peer have been also elicited and discussed.

Overall, the findings suggest that the learners could improve ingrained pronunciation habits under the ASR-based CAPT regardless of the training pattern. Peer feedback can provide more explicit corrective feedback for the learners to correct the long-established sound deletion habit. In addition, the results of the questionnaire survey and interview revealed that learners preferred to conduct the training with peer. This research adds weight to the evidence that ASR-based pronunciation training with peer feedback can break the conventional method and is conducive to the reduction of sound deletion. The incorporation of peer feedback can overcome the disadvantages of ASR [11] and improve students' peer review ability [16]. In order to cater to the increasing demands for the EFL learning, instructors should move with the times and choose the suitable CAPT for students.

Notably, some learners with relatively high English proficiency did not show any obvious improvement in the reduction of sound deletion. It is important to investigate further how students with different English proficiency's pronunciation can be promoted by the incorporation of peer feedback which would help instructors to tailor the individualized training for learners.

Acknowledgements. This work is supported by the Center for Language Cognition and Assessment, South China Normal University. It's also the result of Guangdong "13th Five-Year" Plan Project of Philosophy & Social Science (GD20WZX01-02).

References

1. Lavolette, E., Polio, C., Kahng, J.: The accuracy of computer-assisted feedback and students' responses to it. Lang. Learn. Technol. **19**(2), 50–68 (2014)
2. Paul, W., Irina, E., David, C.: Comprehensibility and prosody ratings for pronunciation software development. Lang. Learn. Technol. **13**(3), 87–102 (2009)
3. Elimat, A.K., AbuSeileek, A.F.: Automatic speech recognition technology as an effective means for teaching pronunciation. JALT CALL J. **10**(1), 21–47 (2014)
4. Eskenazi, M.: Using a computer in foreign language pronunciation training: What advantages? CALICO J. **16**(3), 447–469 (1999)
5. Xu, Y., Zeng, Y.: The impact of sounds' swallowing on examinees' reading aloud performance: a corpus-based study of computer-based English listening and speaking test (CELST) of national matriculation English test (Guangdong Version). J. PLA Univ. Foreign Lang. **39**(05), 97–105+160 (2016)
6. Chapelle, C., Jamieson, J.: Tips for Teaching with CALL: Practical Approaches to Computer-Assisted Language Learning. Pearson Education, White Plains (2008)
7. Wallace, L.: Using Google web speech as a springboard for identifying personal pronunciation problems. In: Levis, J., Le, H., Lucic, I., Simpson, E., Vo, S. (eds.) Proceedings of the 7th Pronunciation in Second Language Learning and Teaching Conference, pp. 180–186. Iowa State University, Ames (2016)
8. Bashori, M., van Hout, R., Strik, H., Cucchiarini, C.: Web-based language learning and speaking anxiety. Comput. Assisted Lang. Learn. 1–32 (2020). https://doi.org/10.1080/09588221.2020.1770293
9. Neri, A., Mich, O., Gerosa, M., Giuliani, D.: The effectiveness of computer assisted pronunciation training for foreign language learning by children. Comput. Assist. Lang. Learn. **21**(5), 393–408 (2008)
10. Dai, Y., Wu, Z.: Mobile-assisted pronunciation learning with feedback from peers and/or automatic speech recognition: a mixed-methods study. Comput. Assisted Lang. Learn. (2), 1–24 (2021). https://doi.org/10.1080/09588221.2021.1952272
11. Evers, K., Chen, S.: Effects of automatic speech recognition software on pronunciation for adults with different learning styles. J. Educ. Comput. Res. **59**(4), 669–685 (2020)
12. Liakin, D., Cardoso, W., Liakina, N.: Learning L2 pronunciation with a mobile speech recognizer: French/y/. CALICO J. **32**(1), 1–25 (2014)
13. Tsai, P.H.: Beyond self-directed computer-assisted pronunciation learning: a qualitative investigation of a collaborative approach. Comput. Assist. Lang. Learn. **32**(7), 713–744 (2019)
14. McCrocklin, S.M.: Pronunciation learner autonomy: the potential of automatic speech recognition. System **57**, 25–42 (2016)
15. Zeng, G., Wang, Y., Tan, X.: Effects of two peer feedback modes on English oral performance in a mobile assisted language learning environment. Foreign Lang. Teach. **42**(06), 109–120+150–151 (2020)
16. Luo, B.: Evaluating a computer-assisted pronunciation training (CAPT) technique for efficient classroom instruction. Comput. Assist. Lang. Learn. (2014). https://doi.org/10.1080/09588221.2014.963123

17. Evers, K., Chen, S.: Effects of an automatic speech recognition system with peer feedback on pronunciation instruction for adults. Comput. Assisted Lang. Learn. 1–21 (2020). https://doi.org/10.1080/09588221.2020.1839504
18. Feng, Y.: A survey on the swallowing of sounds of college English learners—a corpus-based study. Foreign Lang. Teach. Res. **37**(06), 55–61+83 (2005)
19. van Doremalen, J., Cucchiarini, C., Strik, H.: Phoneme errors in read and spontaneous non-native speech: relevance for CAPT system development. In: Interspeech Satellite Workshop. Second Language Studies: Acquisition, Learning, Education and Technology. Waseda University, Tokyo, Japan (2010). http://www.gavo.t.u-tokyo.ac.jp/L2WS2010/papers/L2WS2010_O3-04.pdf. Accessed 5 Aug 2021
20. Jenkins, J.: The Phonology of English as an International Language. Oxford University Press, Oxford (2000)
21. Jenkins, J.: A sociolinguistically based, empirically researched pronunciation syllabus for English as an international language. Appl. Linguist. **23**(1), 83–103 (2002)
22. Jenkins, J.: English as a Lingua Franca: Attitude and Identity. Oxford University Press, Oxford (2007)
23. O'Neal, G.: Segmental repair and interactional intelligibility: the relationship between consonant deletion, consonant insertion, and pronunciation intelligibility in English as a Lingua Franca in Japan. J. Pragmat. **85**, 122–134 (2015)
24. Gao, Z., Zhang, S., Lei, M., Mcloughlin, I.: SAN-M: memory equipped self-attention for end-to-end speech recognition (2020). https://arxiv.org/abs/2006.01713. Accessed 5 Aug 2021
25. Yuan, Y., Liu, X.: An empirical study of the effect of ASR-supported English reading aloud practices on pronunciation accuracy. In: Lee, L.-K., U, L.H., Wang, F.L., Cheung, S.K.S., Au, O., Li, K.C. (eds.) ICTE 2020. CCIS, vol. 1302, pp. 75–87. Springer, Singapore (2020). https://doi.org/10.1007/978-981-33-4594-2_7
26. Hincks, R.: Technology and learning pronunciation. In: Reed, M., Levis, J.M. (eds.) The Handbook of English Pronunciation, p. 440 (2015)
27. Pennington, M., Rogerson-Revell, P.: Phonology in language learning. In: Pennington, M. C., Rogerson-Revell, P. (eds.) English Pronunciation Teaching and Research. RPAL, pp. 57–118. Palgrave Macmillan, London (2019). https://doi.org/10.1057/978-1-137-47677-7_2
28. Garcia, C., Kolat, M., Morgan, T.A.: Self-correction of second-language pronunciation via online, real-time, visual feedback. In: Proceedings of Pronunciation in Second Language Learning and Teaching Conference, vol. 5, pp. 54–56 (2018)
29. Wang, Y.H., Young, S.C.: Effectiveness of feedback for enhancing English pronunciation in an ASR-based CALL system. J. Comput. Assist. Learn. **31**(6), 493–504 (2015)

The Digital Competence of Vocational Education Teachers and of Learners with and Without Cognitive Disabilities

Victoria Batz[1(✉)], Inga Lipowski[1], Franziska Klaba[1], Nadja Engel[2], Veronika Weiß[1], Christian Hansen[3], and Michael A. Herzog[1]

[1] Magdeburg-Stendal UAS, Breitscheidstr. 2, 30114 Magdeburg, Germany
victoria.batz@h2.de
[2] Technische Universität Braunschweig, Universitätsplatz 2, 38106 Braunschweig, Germany
[3] University of Magdeburg, Universitätsplatz 2, 39106 Magdeburg, Germany

Abstract. Nowadays, digital competence is required for participation in working life, education, and social activities. Vocational education is the key to teaching and development of digital skills. Technology enhanced learning offers enormous potential for improving equal participation and reducing access barriers. In order to meet the demands for equal access to digital technologies, to a digitized labor market and to an inclusive education system, teachers and learners need to have the necessary expertise. A survey was conducted using the Digital Competency Profiler (DCP) to explore the digital competence of teachers and learners in vocational education. The items were adapted linguistically according to requirements for people with cognitive disabilities. The aim is to identify possible gaps in the development of digital competencies in three survey groups: teachers in vocational training, trainees in food occupations, and employees with disabilities of sheltered workshops. The digital technology usage habits of the test groups are analyzed and possible differences are determined. Based on an expert assessment of the DCP items, 13 relevant competencies for vocational education are defined. Overall, the participants consider their digital competence to be good. The competencies sending text messages, making phone calls and watching videos show the highest frequency and confidence in the total sample and the competencies creating documents, writing e-mails and managing online accounts the lowest. The index value social competency is particularly high in comparison to the epistemological competency. Needs for intervention are identified, such as the systematic qualification of teachers and learners as condition for digital learning in vocational education.

Keywords: Digital competence · Digital learning · Digital readiness · Vocational education · Education for people with disabilities

W. Jia et al. (Eds.): SETE 2021, LNCS 13089, pp. 190–206, 2021.
https://doi.org/10.1007/978-3-030-92836-0_17

1 Introduction

Technologies are developing rapidly and have become an integral part of our everyday lives. They are leading to a change in activities and competence requirements in professional practice [1]. For example, processes and responsibilities in food professions are becoming increasingly digitalized (e.g. ordering goods, logistics, and service). In 2016, the German Standing Conference of the Ministers of Education and Cultural Affairs presented a strategy entitled "Education in the Digital World" for the education and vocational training sectors [2]. Pedagogical concepts, the adaptation of curricula, and the reorganization of teacher training are now to be implemented independently by schools and vocational schools. Based on this strategy, the German government adopted the DigitalPakt Schule (literally: Digital Pact School) in 2019 with the aims of improving digital equipment in schools and teaching digital skills in educational institutions [3]. Reasons for the limited use of digital media in vocational training are: outdated devices or a lack of equipment, technical problems, data privacy, and labor law [4]. Education staff need to have adequate skills for dealing with digital technologies, as well as further training [4]. The increased time needed to become qualified, the transition to digital teaching methods, and the use of appropriate media represent further challenges [5]. Data from Eurostat, the European Union's statistical office, show a lack of digital literacy in terms of computer and internet skills among older people, the unemployed, and the low educated [6]. Even the test results of so-called digital natives [7] are not particularly high in an international comparison of digital competence [8].

Digital competence is an important prerequisite for the shift from analog to digital teaching and learning methods. The European Digital Competence Framework for Citizens (DigComp) was developed as a response to questions about the meaning of digital competence and what kind of skills and acquirements are involved [8]. Ferrari et al. [8] identifies digital competence as a "set of knowledge, skills, attitudes [...] that are required when using ICT and digital media to perform tasks, solve problems, communicate, manage information, collaborate, create and share content, and build knowledge effectively, efficiently, appropriately, critically, creatively, autonomously, flexibly, ethically, reflectively for work, leisure, participation, learning, socializing, consuming, and empowerment." Digital technologies offer different modes of presentation for faster and vivid understanding; enable the active, location-, and time-independent processing of learning content; and promote collaboration and communication in teams [9]. This gives them enormous potential for improving inclusion, equal opportunities, and participation. Barriers can be reduced and opportunities for participation in work life can be increased, especially for disadvantaged groups [10]. Despite the call in Article 9 of the UN Convention on the Rights of Persons with Disabilities (CRPD) for equal access to information and communication technologies and systems, media used by people with disabilities are rarely considered in research [15]. The competent use of digital media, however, is an essential requirement for participation in social and professional life [3]. Digital inequality between social groups regarding the use of technologies contributes to significant advantages and disadvantages in private and professional contexts [11]. Learners with and without cognitive disabilities can benefit from the use of digital teaching methods and assistant technologies. In order to meet the demands for adapting the education system to the digitized labor market and for creating an inclusive education system, teachers and learners need to have the necessary expertise.

The aim of the present study is to investigate which digital competence skills are required and how these differ in the three groups of respondents: teachers, trainees, and employees of sheltered workshops. The study is based on a sample of teachers and learners in vocational education and training settings. For this purpose, digital competence is assessed using the Digital Competency Profiler (DCP). The online questionnaire is linguistically adapted to the needs of people with cognitive disabilities for a better understanding in that specific target group. In an additional survey, 12 experts evaluate the DCP items in terms of their relevance for the digital competence of teachers and learners in the vocational education field.

2 Literature Review

2.1 Test Procedures

In order to exploit the potential of digital tools in vocational education and to promote inclusion in the sense of the CRPD, it is necessary to take stock of the learners' existing digital competencies. Only by taking the status quo into account suitable learning tools can be developed. For this reason, an evaluation method was investigated to use in the present study by consulting reviews that refer to existing test procedures [8, 12, 13]. After considering their currentness, relevance and scientific characteristics, 20 test procedures were selected for the analysis. To reduce the number, all test procedures were excluded that (1) only address children under 14 years (e.g. Medien-Profis-Test) [13]; (2) address a specific target group (e.g. DigCompEdu for teachers) [14]; (3) are associated with high costs or a high preparation effort, which applies especially to certificates (e.g. ICDL Foundation). Out of the 20 test procedures, 16 were excluded: Medien-Profis-Test, DigCompEdu, IKANOS BAIT, ICDL, IC3, ACTIC, IKANOS Self-Assessment Test, CRISS System, Guagalfino self-assessment tool, Skillage, Digital Competence in the Europass CV, Pathway for employ, NAEP, MediaLitKit, iDCA, Iskills. The following procedures were selected: TILT (technological and informational literacy test) [25], DCP (Digital Competency Profiler) [17], MyDigiSkills [26], DCC (DigCompCheck) [27].

A second analysis was carried out to make a well-founded decision in favor of one of the four test procedures. For this purpose, criteria were established that were composed of the researchers' and target groups' needs, focusing on finding a test procedure with scientific standards for valid statements. Therefore, the test procedures were evaluated on the basis of the criteria *test quality (reliability, validity, objectivity)* according to Moosbrugger and Kelava [16] and *multidimensional acquisition* of digital competence. According to Ferrari [8], digital competence is composed of seven dimensions: information management; collaboration; communication; creation of content; ethics and responsibilities; evaluation and problem solving; technical operation. In addition, a *multilevel assessment* of digital competence is advantageous for the evaluation in order to enable coverage from multiple perspectives. For a valid result, the *orientation towards a framework* as well as the *empirical verification* of the test procedure are important. Another focus is the economy of the test procedure, i.e. the conservation material resources. For this purpose, the criteria of *digital availability* and the existence of an automatically *generated evaluation profile* were included. Further criteria were created considering the needs of the target group. Accordingly, the criterion consideration of the *vocational training context* was developed. With regard to people with cognitive disabilities *reasonable processing time* (about 20 min, based on experience of testing mentally disabled people) and *low barrier*s (e.g. simple wording, graphical presentation) are important. In order to adapt the test procedure precisely to the needs of the target group, the criterion *possibility of customization* of items was included.

In Table 1 the criteria mentioned serve to compare the selected test procedures in the form of a three-stage assessment. The graphical representation shows whether a test procedure fulfills, partially fulfills, or does not fulfill the respective criterion. Thus justifies the choice of the DCP for the present study. The DCP is characterized by digital availability as well as automatic generation of an individual competency profile [17]. Moreover, the DCP captures digital competence at two levels: via confidence of use and frequency of use in terms of the criterion of multilevel measurement of digital competence. The DCP has been empirically tested: Blayone et al. [1] were able to confirm the differentiation ability of the procedure. In contrast, the test quality has not yet been fully verified. Like the other test procedures, the DCP does not cover all of Ferrari's [8] seven dimensions. However, five of the criteria are considered (technical operation, communication, collaboration, informational management, evaluation and problem solving), which is rated as sufficient. In the area of participant needs, the DCP is convincing. The formulation of the items and the processing time can be classified as

Table 1. Secondary analysis for the test procedures TILT, DCP, MyDigiSkills and DCC.

		TILT	DCP	MyDigi Skills	DCC
Researcher need	Test quality (reliability, validity, objectivity)	●	◐	○	●
	Digital availability	○	●	●	●
	Multidimensional acquisition*	◐	◐	◐	◐
	Multilevel assessment **	○	●	○	●
	Generated evaluation profile	○	●	●	●
	Orientation towards a framework	●	●	●	●
	Empirical verification	●	●	○	●
Participant need	Reasonable processing time	●	◐	◐	◐
	Possibility of customization	○	●	○	○
	Low barriers	○	○	○	○
	Vocational training context	○	○	○	○
Assessment:	**criterion fulfilled ●**	**criterion partially fulfilled ◐**		**criterion not fulfilled ○**	

*Notes: *according to Ferrari's seven dimensions [8]; **refers to the methodology of the item formation*

acceptable. The DCP enables further revision due to increasing international dissemination of the DCP, which led to the customization and translation of the online questionnaire for additional application contexts. This revision is particularly necessary because neither the DCP nor any of the other test procedures is barrier-free (independently applicable for people with disabilities).

Likewise, the context of vocational training is not considered in any of the test procedures. In summary, the DCP is an economical test procedure that conserves time, financial and material resources. The presentation of the results in a personal profile allows quick evaluation and interpretation. The division into four dimensions (technical, social, informational and epistemological competency) and the comparison with relevant groups demonstrably enables a differentiated assessment of digital competence.

2.2 Digital Competence Profiler

The Digital Competency Profiler (DCP) is an online tool for the self-assessment of digital competence. It was developed at the Educational Informatics Lab (EILab) of the University of Ontario for the purpose of assessing the digital competencies of students and teachers to evaluate their readiness for fully online learning [1]. The assessment can be used to identify possible gaps in the development of digital skills to derive necessary steps for digital education and to determine whether groups of people are underrepresented in the area of digital competence [17]. The DCP is based on the General Technology Competency and Use (GTCU) Framework [18, 19]. As shown in Fig. 1, this framework draws on the IEEE definition of computer hardware "physical equipment used to process, store, or transmit computer programs or data" to define three orders of digital competency [20]. Briefly summarized, the epistemological order ("process") describes the application of computers and programs for efficient problem solving; the informational order ("store") summarizes the search for, interaction with and application of information; and the social order ("transmit") covers technology-

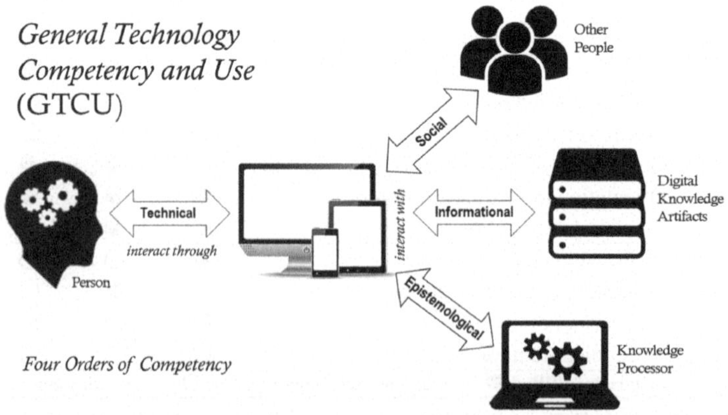

Fig. 1. "Four Orders of Competency" based on IEEE Definition of Computer Hardware [22].

based communication and collaboration [18]. Finally, a fourth dimension was added in the form of the technical order of competency, a prerequisite for successfully operating computer hardware and software [18].

In the DCP, each order of competency is surveyed with activity items (technical: 5 items, all other areas of competency: 7 items). Each item describes an activity (e.g. "To communicate with others using audio") and gives well-known application examples (e.g. Skype) to support understanding. Participants then specify how often they perform this activity (5-point Likert scale from "never" to "daily"), how confident they feel while performing it (5-point Likert scale from "do not know how to use" to "very confident, can teach others how to use"), and which device they most often use (computer, mobile device, or another device). At the end of the survey, an individual competence profile is displayed as an aster plot for the user.

3 Method

3.1 Revision

The assessment by the multi-professional expert team (psychologist, designer, pedagogue, trainer) revealed that many DCP items are not understandable for the specific target group. The aim was to adapt the questionnaire to make it understandable for people with cognitive impairments and with different levels of knowledge of the technical terms. Therefore, each of the 26 items was reviewed by the team and adapted to ensure understandable language without changing the content of the item (see Table 2).

Table 2. Overview of the 26 DCP items in the adapted version in understandable language.

Label	Adapted item
Q1: Creating documents	I create or edit electronic documents. I write texts on the computer, e.g. letters, stories, tables or slides
Q2: Creating audio recordings	I create or edit audio recordings. I record or modify voice messages e.g.
Q3: Creating photos and videos	I take photos or videos. E.g. with my smartphone or my digital camera. Partly I also edit media
Q4: Managing online accounts	I manage my accounts online. I have created an account on the internet on my own, e.g. for e-mail, Amazon, Netflix or Spotify, and I can change my settings there
Q5: Operating devices	I can operate other devices with my smartphone or computer. I can use my smartphone e.g. to turn the lights or TV on and off, raise and lower the blinds, operate the music system or adjust the heating
Q6: Sending text messages	I write text messages with my smartphone or computer. E.g. via Whatsapp, Telegram or SMS
Q7: Making phone calls	I talk on the phone with others. For this I use e.g. my mobile phone, Whatsapp or Telegram

(*continued*)

Table 2. (*continued*)

Label	Adapted item
Q8: Making video calls	I use videophony. E.g. via Skype, Zoom, Facetime or Whatsapp
Q9: Writing e-mails	I write e-mails
Q10: Using social media	I use social networks (social media). I am on Facebook, Instagram, Snapchat, TikTok or Twitter e.g.
Q11: Sharing documents	I share documents or work with others on shared documents. I upload texts for friends or colleagues, e.g. via Google Drive, Nextcloud or Dropbox
Q12: Publishing content	I share my pictures, videos or texts on the internet. I upload my photos to Facebook e.g.
Q13: Using digital maps	I use digital maps or GPS. I search for my way with my mobile phone or my navigation system e.g.
Q14: Reading articles	I search and read news or articles on the internet. E.g. about sports, movies, fashion or science
Q15: Watching videos	I search and watch videos on the internet. E.g. via YouTube, Vimeo or TikTok
Q16: Streaming movies	I search, download or stream movies on the internet. I watch movies on Netflix, Amazon, or Sky e.g.
Q17: Streaming music	I search, download or stream music on the internet. I listen to music via Spotify, iTunes or Youtube e.g.
Q18: Streaming (audio) books	I search, download, or stream books or audiobooks on the internet. I read books or listen to stories via Audible or Spotify e.g.
Q19: Managing aggregator	I use an aggregator to collect and organize digital media content (e.g. movies, music, news). An aggregator can be Twitter or an RSS feed
Q20: Managing calendar	I enter my appointments in a calendar or share them with others. I use the calendar on my phone (Google Calendar, Microsoft Outlook or iCal)
Q21: Creating graphics	I create graphical representations of relationships, processes and structures. I make an overview of my thoughts on the computer with a mind map e.g.
Q22: Creating plans	I create and use plans. E.g. on the computer with planning software for course preparation or for room and architectural planning
Q23: Sorting data sets	I create and fill tables for sorting large amounts of data. Data sets are many numbers and names that can be sorted by categories e.g.
Q24: Creating diagrams	I create diagrams. Diagrams are charts of numbers, e.g. pie charts or bar charts
Q25: Performing calculations	I make difficult calculations. I use formulas in Excel or Numbers e.g.
Q26: Programming	I program by myself. I can program devices or develop my own programs, apps or games with programming languages e.g.

Notes: The English translation of the adapted items in German has not been verified.

In the new version, an item consists of a short and concise main statement and an additional description with a common example of use. In addition to the version in understandable language, that can be completed by everyone, a test administrator offered additional help if necessary. Understandable language includes simple terms and short sentences and provides a better understanding for all without the need to follow specific rules. In contrast, "Leichte Sprache" (literally: easy language) is optimally suited for the target group of people with cognitive impairments in Germany, but also requires language rules, spelling rules, and recommendations on typography. The revision of the items was done by the multi-professional team. The first version was tested in a pre-test by two subjects with intellectual disabilities and little reading competence. Based on the analysis of the feedback, the questionnaire was adapted again and finalized by the team in close consultation with the EILab.

3.2 Data Collection

The study consists of two independent testings (see Fig. 2). The first testing took place with trainees, employees and teachers. Two separate online questionnaires were to be completed by the subjects via laptop, tablet, or mobile phone. They received a link and had to answer the demographic data questionnaire first and then the adapted DCP questionnaire. The demographic questionnaire contained questions on: survey group, gender, age, highest level of education, work experience, digital technologies in the environment (information on ownership and intended use of equipment), daily use of digital technologies, use of internet at home, and use of mobile data. The duration of the test was approximately 30 to 60 min. A test administrator was available at the testing session in the sheltered workshop and in the vocational school to explain the procedure, help with questions and problems, and read out the items and answer options when necessary. A total of 30 demographic data questionnaires were completed and only 26 DCP questionnaires. Datasets were excluded if only one of both questionnaires was completed and if there were empty datasets or test runs. After matching both questionnaires to one participant each, 25 datasets were included in the following analysis.

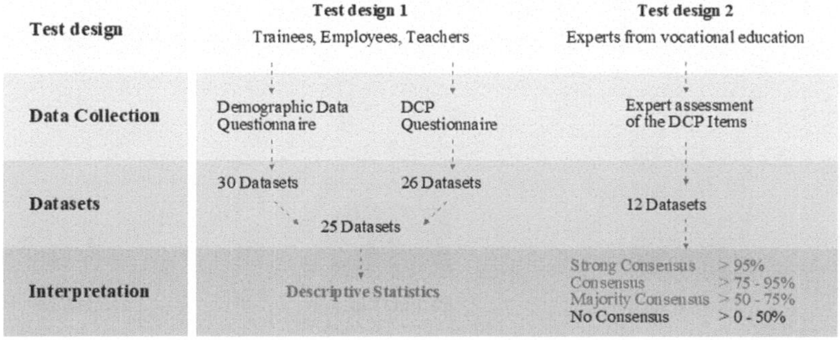

Fig. 2. Test design of the study.

The aim of the second testing was to have experts from vocational education and research rate the items of the DCP according to how relevant they considered these items to be for digital competence in the target group of teachers and learners in vocational education [21]. A total of 12 participants completed the online questionnaire. Each of the 26 DCP items could be rated as relevant or not. The items selected with more than 50% consensus are interpreted as relevant to digital competence and will be included in the further analysis. The consensus of the 12 experts was classified as follows: above 95% (12 out of 12 experts) strong consensus; above 75% to 95% (10–11 out of 12 experts) consensus; above 50% to 75% (7–9 out of 12 experts) majority consensus; 0% to 50% (0–6 out of 12 experts) no consensus. All data sets from the first and second testing were exported for further analysis using the statistics and analysis software SPSS.

4 Results

4.1 Survey Groups

A total of 25 participants (11 female and 14 male) took part in the testing with the DCP and the demographic data questionnaire. The subjects can be divided into three survey groups (see Fig. 3). The first group includes nine trainees (3 female and 6 male) who are currently undertaking vocational training in food occupations. The participants of the second group are 12 employees (6 female and 6 male) in the kitchen area of sheltered workshops. The third group includes four teachers (2 female and 2 male) in vocational education. Most of the trainees are under 20 years old (M = 18.9; SD = 1.17), while the employees have an age range from under 20 up to over 40 years (M = 25.3; SD = 11.44). All teachers are older than 40 years (M = 58.5; SD = 1.73). Eleven participants (44%) did not graduate from school or attended a special school, eight (32%) attended a secondary school, and two (8%) passed the Abitur (German school leaving certificate). Three teachers (12%) have a university degree and one teacher has a (4%) master's certificate. Ten subjects (40%) have no work experience, seven (28%) up to one year, three persons (12%) up to five years, and five (20%) over five years. All four teachers have more than five years of professional experience.

Fig. 3. Bar chart of the three survey groups of the sample with N = 25 divided by age group.

The devices that most subjects own themselves are smartphone (96%), computer (72%), game console (48%), smart TV (48%), and tablet (32%). Devices that neither the participants nor the company or school own include smart home devices (40%), voice assistants (40%), eBook readers (36%), VR or AR glasses (32%), and smartwatches (32%). On average, the subjects use digital technologies for five hours a day ($M = 4.96$; $SD = 2.99$). Trainees ($M = 5.22$; $SD = 2.11$) and employees ($M = 5.58$; $SD = 3.58$) use the technologies about three hours longer a day than teachers ($M = 2.50$; $SD = 1.73$). Almost all test persons have internet access at home (92%) and use mobile data (96%).

4.2 Expert Survey

As Table 3 indicates, the 12 experts from vocational education and research rated the following 13 items of the DCP as relevant for digital competence in the target group of teachers and learners in vocational education: *Creating documents* (Q1), *Creating photos and movies* (Q3), *Managing online accounts* (Q4), *Sending text messages* (Q6), *Making phone calls* (Q7), *Making video telephony* (Q8), *Writing e-mails* (Q9), *Using social media* (Q10), *Using digital maps* (Q13), *Reading articles* (Q14), *Watching videos* (Q15), *Streaming movies* (Q16), and *Managing calendar* (Q20).

In the expert survey four items received majority consensus (Q4, Q10, Q13, Q16), eight items consensus (Q1, Q3, Q7, Q8, Q9, Q14, Q15, Q20), and only one item strong consensus (Q6). In the dimension of epistemological competency, only the item Q20 was selected from the original seven items. In the dimension of technical competency, three out of five items were considered relevant, in the dimension of social competency five out of seven, and in the dimension of informational competency four out of seven.

Table 3. Classification of the 26 DCP items (Q1–Q26) in relation to the consensus.

Dimension	**Items**						
Technical Competency	Q1	Q2	Q3	Q4	Q5		
Social Competency	Q6	Q7	Q8	Q9	Q10	Q11	Q12
Informational Competency	Q13	Q14	Q15	Q16	Q17	Q18	Q19
Epistemological Competency	Q20	Q21	Q22	Q23	Q24	Q25	Q26

Strong Consensus	**Consensus**	**Majority Consensus**	**No Consensus**
Over 95 %	Over 75-95 %	Over 50-75 %	0-50 %

4.3 Frequency and Confidence

The frequency and confidence of the 13 items selected by the experts were analyzed (see Table 4). On average, respondents communicate most of all several times a week via text messages ($M = 3.44$; $SD = 1.16$) and telephone calls ($M = 3.08$; $SD = 0.95$). 84% use text messages and 76% make phone calls daily to weekly. Participants watch videos several times a week ($M = 3.04$; $SD = 0.98$), with 80% watching weekly to daily. Social media is used a few times a week (*M* = 2.88; *SD* = 1.56). 72% use social media daily to weekly. A few times a month, the test persons create photos and videos (*M* = 2.48; *SD* = 1.16), read articles (*M* = 2.24; *SD* = 1.62), manage online accounts (*M* = 1.84, *SD* = 1.52) as well as their calendar (*M* = 1.76; *SD* = 1.42), and make video calls (*M* = 1.72; *SD* = 1.28). Only a few times a month do the subjects stream movies (*M* = 1.56; *SD* = 1.61) and use digital cards (*M* = 1.56; *SD* = 1.33). The least often, documents are created (*M* = 1.16; *SD* = 1.55) and e-mails are written (*M* = 1.16; *SD* = 1.43), with an average use of a few times a year. 56% of the respondents never create digital documents and 48% never write e-mails.

Table 4. Descriptive statistics of the 13 relevant items for frequency and confidence with *N* = 25.

Items	M frequency	SD frequency	M confidence	SD confidence
Creating documents	**1.16**	1.55	**1.96**	1.51
Creating photos and videos	2.48	1.16	2.84	0.94
Managing online accounts	1.84	1.52	**2.12**	1.30
Sending text messages	**3.44**	1.16	**3.08**	1.15
Making phone calls	**3.08**	0.95	**3.36**	0.70
Making video calls	1.72	1.28	2.40	1.41
Writing e-mails	**1.16**	1.43	2.36	1.50
Using social media	2.88	1.56	2.64	1.25
Using digital maps	1.56	1.33	2.32	1.35
Reading articles	2.24	1.62	2.60	1.23
Watching videos	3.04	0.98	2.92	1.04
Streaming movies	1.56	1.61	2.16	1.55
Managing calendar	1.76	1.42	2.80	1.12

Notes: N = number; M = mean; SD = standard deviation; Range for frequency: 0 = never, 1 = few times a year, 2 = few times a month, 3 = few times a week, 4 = daily; Range for confidence: 0 = do not know how to use it, 1 = not confident, 2 = confident, 3 = quite confident, 4 = very confident.

The calculation of the correlation according to Bravais-Pearson showed a significant positive correlation between the frequency and the confidence for 12 of the 13 items with a medium to strong effect according to Cohen [23]. For all items except *Creating photos and videos*, it is true that the more confident a person is, the more often the action is carried out (and vice versa). The three items with the highest frequency also achieve the highest confidence. *Making phone calls* (*M* = 3.36; *SD* = 0.70), *Sending text messages* (*M* = 3.08; *SD* = 1.15), and *Watching videos* (*M* = 2.92; *SD* = 1.04) are performed quite confidently by the respondents. 48% feel very confident in *Making phone calls*, 44% in *Sending text messages*, and 32% in *Watching videos*. The subjects also feel quite confident when *Creating photos and videos* (*M* = 2.84; *SD* = 0.94), *Managing the calendar* (*M* = 2.80; *SD* = 1.12), *Using social media* (*M* = 2.64; *SD* = 1.25), and *Reading articles* (*M* = 2.60; *SD* = 1.23). The items with the lowest confidence are *Creating documents* (M = 1.96; SD = 1.51), *Managing online accounts* (M = 2.12; SD = 1.30), *Streaming movies* (M = 2.16; SD = 1.55), *Using digital maps* (M = 2.32; SD = 1.35), *Writing e-mails* (M = 2.36; SD = 1.50), and *Making video calls* (M = 2.40; SD = 1.41). 32% of the respondents do not know how to create documents and 24% how to stream movies. 20% are overwhelmed when writing e-mails, making video calls, and managing online accounts.

There are some bigger differences between the test groups (see Fig. 4). Teachers create documents more often (M = 2.25; SD = 1.26) than employees (M = 0.83; SD = 1.59) and trainees (M = 1.11; SD = 1.54). Employees (M = 1.17; SD = 1.47) manage their online accounts a few times a year, trainees (M = 2.33, SD = 1.50) a few times a month, and teachers (M = 2.75; SD = 0.96) a few times a week. Employees (M = 0.42, SD = 0.67) and trainees (M = 1.33; SD = 1.50) use e-mails less often than teachers (M = 3.00; SD = 1.41). While trainees (M = 3.33; SD = 1.32) and employees (M = 3.08; SD = 1.51) use social media a few times a week, teachers use it only a few times a year (M = 1.25; SD = 1.50). Teachers read articles much more often (M = 3.50; SD = 0.58) than trainees (M = 2.0; SD = 1.58) and employees (M = 2.0; SD = 1.76). Trainees (M = 3.33; SD = 0.50) and employees (M = 3.42; SD = 0.67) watch videos more often than teachers (M = 1.25; SD = 0.50). Teachers manage digital calendars more often (M = 3.25; SD = 0.55) than trainees (M = 1.56; SD = 1.74) and employees (M = 1.42; SD = 1.08). Employees rate their confidence in writing e-mails (M = 1.75; SD = 1.77) lower than trainees (M = 2.78; SD = 1.09) and teachers (M = 3.25; SD = 0.50). While trainees (M = 2.89; SD = 0.93) and employees (M = 2.75; SD = 1.42) feel quite confident in using social media, teachers (M = 1.75; SD = 1.26) report lower confidence. Teachers, on the other hand, feel more confident in reading articles (M = 3.25; SD = 0.50) than trainees (M = 2.78; SD = 0.97) and employees (M = 2.25; SD = 1.49).

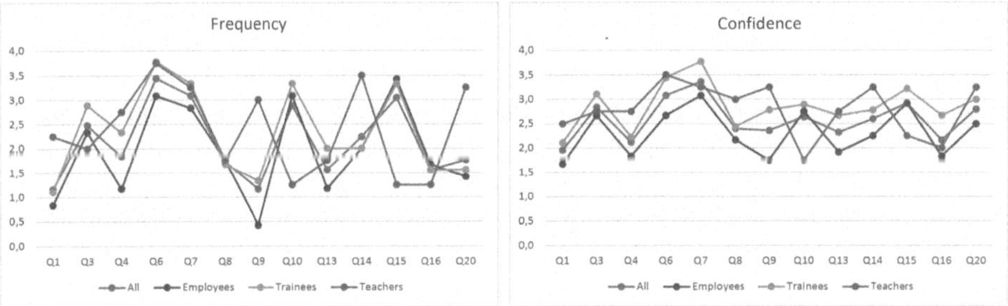

Fig. 4. Line charts of the 13 relevant items (Q1–Q20) for frequency and confidence with N = 25.

4.4 Index Values

The four DCP index values were calculated for each test person: one each for technical (TC), social (SC), informational (IC), and epistemological competency (EC). EC has the lowest mean across all test persons with M = 1.17 (SD = 1.13), followed by TC with $M = 2.73$ ($SD = 1.81$). IC achieved an average of $M = 3.43$ ($SD = 2.12$) and SC the highest value with $M = 4.54$ ($SD = 2.02$). For the index values TC, the trainees have the highest mean in comparison ($M = 3.25$; $SD = 1.70$), followed by the teachers ($M = 2.72$; $SD = 1.13$) and then the employees ($M = 2.34$; $SD = 2.08$). The same applies to the index value SC for the trainees ($M = 5.32$; $SD = 1.68$), teachers ($M = 4.53$; $SD = 0.84$), and employees ($M = 3.95$; $SD = 2.39$). The trainees have the highest IC value ($M = 4.21$; $SD = 2.36$), followed by the employees ($M = 3.20$; $SD = 2.13$), and the teachers ($M = 2.38$; $SD = 0.99$). For EC, the teachers have the highest value ($M = 1.63$; $SD = 0.55$), followed by the trainees ($M = 1.22$; $SD = 1.32$), and the employees ($M = 0.97$; $SD = 1.16$). The index value SC is highest for all test groups and lowest for EC. The t-tests for independent samples did not show any significant differences in arithmetic mean between the three survey groups of employees, trainees, and teachers. They do not differ significantly in their expression of the competence areas TC, SC, IC, and EC.

5 Discussion

5.1 Interpretation

The DCP questionnaires completed by 25 participants from the three test groups of trainees ($N = 9$), employees ($N = 12$), and teachers ($N = 4$) were analyzed and the groups were compared with each other. 12 experts from vocational education and research judged the 26 DCP items regarding their relevance for vocational education. 13 of the original 26 DCP items received over 50% agreement from the experts and were identified as relevant digital competences. The social, informational, and technical competences represent the majority with 12 items. All experts agreed on the item *Sending text messages* to be relevant. The experts rate the use of social media as more relevant than working on shared documents. Reasons could be that the usability of shared platforms and applications is perceived as too high-threshold. In contrast, social media are probably seen as new and exciting tools. Furthermore, photos, videos, and films – in contrast to music and books – are seen as essential for the target group.

Overall, the respondents rate their digital competences as good, feel quite confident to confident in performing the 13 skills, and, with the exception of *Writing e-mails* and *Creating documents*, perform them several times a month or a week. The competences with the highest frequency and confidence in the total sample are the items *Sending text messages*, *Making phone calls,* and *Watching videos*. The item *Creating documents* has the lowest frequency and confidence in the sample. The item *Writing e-mails* also shows a low frequency and *Managing online accounts* a low confidence. Since these competencies have been identified as relevant for vocational education, they should be trained. Exchanges via text messages and phone calls could be preferred to e-mail. Digital and collaborative work methods (Q3, Q4, Q20) are rarely used and have low competency. The items *Sharing Documents, Publishing Content* and *Creating plans* were classified as not relevant by the experts. Although these skills might be essential for the digitization of teaching and education in the future.

For 12 of the 13 items, there was a significant positive correlation between frequency and confidence. Repeating and teaching these skills can therefore lead to an increase in confidence. There are some differences between the survey groups. Trainees and employees show an affinity for social media and video consumption. Therefore, it can be assumed that formats such as instructional videos and tutorials are more likely to be accepted by learners than working via cooperative learning platforms. Teachers, on the other hand, show higher digital competences in creating documents, writing e-mails, reading articles, and managing calendars. The teachers' skills can be used for providing training in digital working methods. In class, emails could be sent to companies, digital shopping lists could be created, and relevant articles could be searched for and read together. Teachers, meanwhile, should be trained in the creation and use of videos and social media to support learners in their interests.

The index differences show that the social competency (SC) is particularly high in comparison to the epistemological competency (EC) in the sample. EC has the lowest and SC the highest mean across all test persons. For EC, the teachers have the highest value, followed by the trainees, and the employees. For SC, the trainees have the highest mean, followed by the teachers, and then the employees. Overall, the three test groups do not differ significantly in their expression of the competence areas. Creating graphics, plans, diagrams etc. appear to be less the focus of the professional field so far. Social skills seem to be strong in the digital context and can be used for vocational training and digital learning.

The basic prerequisites for teaching digital skills are appropriate technical equipment as well as adequate framework conditions. Teachers use digital technologies for an average of 2.5 h a day – about three hours less than trainees and employees. The use of them is presumably not yet an integral part of teachers' everyday work. The survey suggests that vocational schools are currently insufficiently equipped with technical devices. Teachers are probably not provided with work equipment and learners with digital learning materials. The aim should be to integrate the teaching and application of digital competences into the vocational education curriculum as a fixed component and to acquire the necessary equipment for this. The digital infrastructure should be further developed to increase the frequency and thus also enable learners and teachers to experience the potential of technology for all areas of life. The design of digital learning applications should be implemented according to needs, taking into account the additional workload of teachers due to the transition. The digital competences of teachers and learners and the technical equipment already available to the majority should be considered.

5.2 Limitations

Limitations result from the specific test group, the DCP test procedure, and the framework conditions of vocational education. The testing was carried out with a small number of participants. The small sample makes it possible to identify initial tendencies and put them up for discussion. For representative results a larger sample is needed. The research has shown that there is currently no ideal questionnaire available with which to assess digital competence in vocational education for people with cognitive impairments. The chosen questionnaire was therefore linguistically adapted to create a version in understandable language. In the test sessions, however, a test administrator was indispensable, particularly for reading out and explaining the items to the employees of sheltered workshops. Test participants must also be able to differentiate the general frequency with which they perform certain actions and their relative degree of confidence in performing an action on a particular type of device [1]. Making this assessment may not be equally possible for people with cognitive disabilities, and this factor may bias the overall outcome. In addition, digital competences are undergoing constant technical development and therefore need to be regularly updated or supplemented. The results of the DCP are not related to the observed performance of the participants. A combination of survey instrument and observation is costly, but can help to draw reliable conclusions from the test procedure. The adaptation of the DCP items is a first step towards improving usability, but it also does not offer a barrier-free solution.

5.3 Conclusion

This study explores the digital competence of 25 participants from vocational education with and without cognitive disabilities. It uses the linguistically modified DCP test procedure. The aims are to point out possible potential and inabilities, and to identify differences in competencies among the three survey groups of teachers, trainees, and employees of sheltered workshops. Of the original 26 DCP items, 13 were rated by experts as relevant for vocational education. Overall, the participants consider their digital competence to be good. The highest frequency and confidence in the total sample are shown by the items *Sending text messages*, *Making phone calls,* and *Watching videos*. The items *Creating documents*, *Writing e-mails,* and *Managing online accounts* have the lowest frequency and confidence. The index value EC has the lowest and SC the highest mean across all test persons. Differences between the survey groups reveal tendencies that can be observed and used for digital interventions, but the results do not show any significant mean differences between the test groups. Vocational education has the potential to create access to technology enhanced learning with regard to the relevant occupational field. If digital competencies and technologies are integrated into vocational training and the frequency of use increases as a result, confidence in action will also increase [24]. To counteract the multiple challenges, it is necessary to create an appropriate environment for educational institutions, to make digital skills an integral part of the curriculum, and to train teachers on a regular basis. A survey of digital competencies and technical equipment should be used as a baseline for designing user-centered digital interventions and lessons according to the corresponding requirements of the learners. Unfortunately, people with cognitive disabilities have received little or no attention as regards the design of survey instruments for measuring digital competence. Possible adjustments to the DCP for a barrier-free version could include a translation into "Leichte Sprache" (literally: easy language) and illustrated items. Through the systematic training of teachers and learners, the conditions can be created for inclusive learning situations with digital assistance systems and technical support.

References

1. Blayone, T.J.B., Mykhailenko, O., vanOostveen, R., Barber, W.: Ready for digital learning? A mixed-methods exploration of surveyed technology competencies and authentic performance activity. Educ. Inf. Technol. **23**(3), 1377–1402 (2017). https://doi.org/10.1007/s10639-017-9662-6
2. Kultusministerkonferenz (KMK). https://www.kmk.org. Accessed 9 Aug 2021
3. Bundesministerium für Bildung und Forschung (BMBF). https://www.bundestag.de/resource. Accessed 9 Aug 2021
4. Härtel, M., Bruggemann, M., Sander, M., Breiter, A., Howe, F., Kupfer, F.: Digitale Medien in der betrieblichen Berufsausbildung. Medienaneignung und Mediennutzung in der Alltagspraxis von betrieblichem Ausbildungspersonal. Barbara Budrich, Leverkusen (2018)
5. Hähn, K., Ratermann-Busse, M.: Digitale Medien in der Berufsbildung–eine Herausforderung für Lehrkräfte und Ausbildungspersonal? In: Wilmers, A., Anda, C., Keller, C., Rittberger, M. (eds.) Bildung im digitalen Wandel. Die Bedeutung für das pädagogische Personal und für die Aus- und Fortbildung, pp. 129–158. Waxmann, Müster (2020)
6. European Union. http://ec.europa.eu/. Accessed 10 Aug 2021
7. Prensky, M.: Digital natives, digital immigrants part 2: do they really think differently? Horizon **9**(5), 2–6 (2001)
8. Ferrari, A.: Digital competence in practice: an analysis of frameworks. In: European Commission Joint Research Centre Institute for Prospective Technological Studies, JRC IPTS, Sevilla (2012). https://doi.org/10.2791/82116
9. Ortmann-Welp, E: Digitale Lernangebote in der Pflege. Springer, Heidelberg (2020)
10. Müller-Eiselt, R., Behrens, J.: Lernen im digitalen Zeitalter Erkenntnisse aus dem Monitor Digitale Bildung. In: McElvany, N., Schwabe, F., Bos, W., Holtappels, H.G. (eds.) Digitalisierung in der schulischen Bildung: Chancen und Herausforderungen, vol. 107. Waxmann, Münster New York (2018)
11. Chen, P.D., Lambert, A.D., Guidry, K.R.: Engaging online learners: the impact of Web-based learning technology on college student engagement. Comput. Educ. **54**(4), 1222–1232 (2010)
12. Kluzer, S., Rissola, G.: Guidelines on the Adoption of DigComp. Telecenter Europe, Brussels (2015)
13. Hermida, M., Hielscher, M., Petko, D.: Medienkompetenz messen: Die Entwicklung des medienprofistests in der Schweiz. Medienpädagogik, pp. 38–60 (2017)
14. Redecker, C.: European framework for the digital competence of educators: DigCompEdu. JRC Working Papers, Luxembourg (2017)
15. Bosse, I., Haage, A.: Digitalisierung in der Behindertenhilfe. Handbuch Soziale Arbeit und Digitalisierung, pp. 529–539 (2020)
16. Moosbrugger, H., Kelava, A.: Qualitätsanforderungen an einen psychologischen Test (Testgütekriterien). In: Moosbrugger, H., Kelava, A. (eds.) Testtheorie und Fragebogenkonstruktion, pp. 7–26. Springer, Heidelberg (2012). https://doi.org/10.1007/978-3-642-20072-4_2
17. Awwadah, K., van Oostveen, R.: Exploring the Digital Competency Profiler: Operationalizing the General Technology Competency and Use (GTCU) Framework. Educational Informatics Laboratory (EILab) University of Ontario Institute of Technology (2018)
18. Desjardins, F., Lacasse, R., Bélair, L.M.: Toward a definition of four orders of competency for the use of information and communication technology (ICT) in education. In: Computersand Advanced Technology in Education, IASTED Proceedings, pp. 213–217 (2001)

19. Desjardins, F.J.: Teachers' representations of their computer related competencies profile: toward a theory of ICT in education. Can. J. Learn. Technol. **31**(1) (2005). https://doi.org/10.21432/T2F603
20. Desjardins, F.J., Davidson, A.-L., Blayone, T., van Oostveen, R., Childs, E.: General Technological Competency and Use Foundations. https://eilab.ca/general-technology-competency-use/. Accessed 12 Aug 2021
21. Blayone, T.J., Mykhailenko, O., vanOostveen, R., Grebeshkov, O., Hrebeshkova, O., Vostryakov, O.: Surveying digital competencies of university students and professors in Ukraine for fully online collaborative learning. Technol. Pedagog. Educ. **27**(3), 279–296 (2018)
22. EILab (n.y.) General Technology Competency and Use (GTCU) Framework. https://ei-lab.ca/general-technology-competency-use/. Accessed 30 July 2021
23. Cohen, J.: The statistical power of abnormal-social psychological research: a review. J. Abnorm. Soc. Psychol. **65**, 145–153 (1962)
24. Akaslan, D., Law, E.L.-C.: Analysing the relationship between ICT experience and attitude toward e-learning. In: Ravenscroft, A., Lindstaedt, S., Kloos, C.D., Hernández-Leo, D. (eds.) EC-TEL 2012. LNCS, vol. 7563, pp. 365–370. Springer, Heidelberg (2012). https://doi.org/10.1007/978-3-642-33263-0_28
25. Senkbeil, M., Ihme, J.M., Wittwer, J.: The test of technological and information literacy (TILT) in the national educational panel study: development, empirical testing, and evidence for validity. J. Educ. Res. Online **5**(2), 139–161 (2013)
26. MyDigiSkills. https://mydigiskills.eu/. Accessed 18 Aug 2021
27. DigCompCheck. https://www.gepedu.de/digitale-kompetenz/messen. Accessed 18 Aug 2021

An Action Research of Using SAMR to Guide Blended Learning Adoption During Covid-19

Jonas Kelsch[1(✉)] and Tianchong Wang[2]

[1] English Language Centre, Beijing Normal University Hong Kong Baptist University United International College, 2000 Jintong Road, Zhuhai 519087, Guangdong Province, China
jkelsch@uic.edu.cn

[2] Department of Curriculum and Instruction, The Education University of Hong Kong, Tai Po, Hong Kong S.A.R., China
twang@eduhk.hk

Abstract. SAMR (Substitution, Augmentation, Modification and Redefinition) model is a framework that offers educators direction in advancing technology integration in their teaching practice. It has been praised for its elegance and capacity to help teachers design and implement learning activities where technology can play a role, although it has been criticised for its lack of academic rigour and emphasis on product over process. During the global Covid-19 pandemic, the question of whether and how the SAMR model can support quality instruction in an online/blended environment warrants investigation. The teacher-researcher, a higher education EFL teacher based in Zhuhai, China, has assessed the SAMR model with an action research. The study spanned a challenging transition–from a period of fully online instruction in Spring semester 2019–20, to a blended learning (BL) format during Autumn and Spring 2020–21. The findings of this paper illustrate that SAMR can be useful as a compass to help teachers navigate towards effective technology-based education, despite the fact that using the model may not always lead towards promising practice. The findings also challenge the general conception of the SAMR model as a ladder that must be climbed. This study contributes to a critical discussion of SAMR, with examples of how the model was utilised to cope with rapid change in educational mode. The study also provides BL practitioners with some lessons learned from utilising SAMR as a guide for high-impact technology integration.

Keywords: Online learning · Blended learning · SAMR · Covid-19 · Higher education

1 Introduction

Sometimes uncontrollable circumstances force educators to radically alter the way they do things, and Covid-19 has been one such event. During the pandemic, as physical access to classrooms of higher education institutions (HEIs) was restricted, university teaching staff had to quickly adopt online methods to facilitate continued learning.

W. Jia et al. (Eds.): SETE 2021, LNCS 13089, pp. 207–218, 2021.
https://doi.org/10.1007/978-3-030-92836-0_18

While many teaching staff welcomed the idea of using web-based technology to confront this challenging situation, others found that online teaching paled in comparison to classroom-based teaching, or that it was rather difficult to implement. But as the world gradually recovers from the Covid-19 pandemic, and schools gradually reopen their doors, it appears that web-based instruction will continue to form an indispensable part of the learning experience; and many project that blended learning (BL)—the combination of face-to-face and online learning experiences—will become the "new normal" [1].

This begs the question of how teachers can leverage the "danger-opportunity" posed by a shift to BL—not only to settle into this new normal but also to take a more inventive approach to teaching practices. One way to facilitate this shift could be SAMR, a four-level taxonomy that describes the impact technology has on teaching and learning. Since its inception, the model has served as a guide to help teachers around the world navigate through their technology-based instructional practices. This action research reports a journey of a Zhuhai, China-based higher education EFL teacher-researcher's adoption of BL examined through the guiding lens of SAMR. The purpose of this ongoing study was twofold: 1) to critically examine the teacher-researcher's own BL practices within a liberal arts college setting during the Covid-19 pandemic, and 2) to examine how the teacher-researcher used the SAMR model to plot their BL implementations.

2 Literature Review

2.1 BL

BL refers to the practice that generally involves a combination of face-to-face and online learning [2]. BL has been responsive to new developments in higher education and has evolved over time [3]. Research studies suggest that optimal BL implementation may afford positive impacts on student learning engagement and outcomes [4–9]. Studies also show that good facilitation of BL affords active learning through engaging students in online discussion and reflective journals, along with more active participation in face-to-face lessons [8, 10–13]. BL may also stimulate student deep learning through the community of inquiry that is characteristic of this approach [8, 14, 15]. BL affords a high degree of personalisation and learner autonomy, as it provides students greater control over the learning process [16]. It may also afford agency to students through interactivity and collaboration [17].

2.2 SAMR Model

SAMR [18] stands for *Substitution*, *Augmentation*, *Modification*, and *Redefinition* and is represented as a four-level taxonomy (See Fig. 1). It is a model that describes how technology impacts teaching and learning. According to its originator, the SAMR model was designed as a tool to plan, implement, and evaluate technology use in education settings [18].

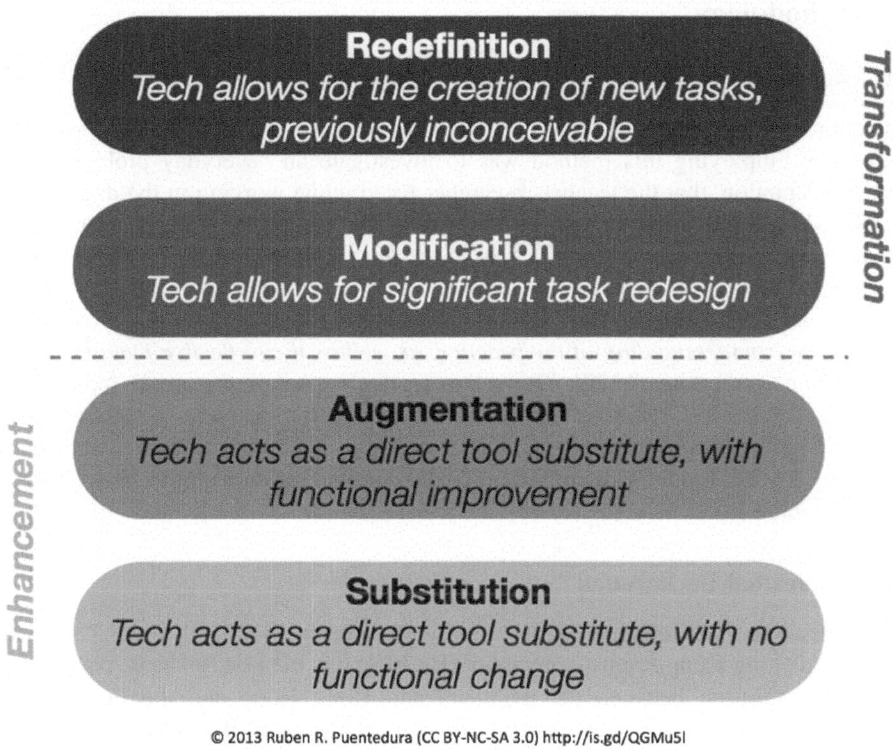

Fig. 1. The SAMR model

At the *Substitution* level, technology is substituted for a traditional method, but the *Substitution* generates no functional change. At the *Augmentation* level, technology use exceeds substitution to improve functionality in some way, whereas *Modification* uses technology for task redesign. The *Redefinition* level is achieved when technology is used to create novel tasks that were not previously feasible in a classroom-based setting. Learning activities that fall within the *Substitution* and *Augmentation* classifications are said to enhance learning, while activities falling within the *Modification* and *Redefinition* categories are considered as transformative.

The SAMR model has been praised for being clear and simple to use as a practical guide [19]. Puentedura [18] encourages teachers to move up from lower to higher levels of technology-aided teaching by following the successive stages towards transformative teaching and learning. Meanwhile, the model has been criticised for its absence of context, lack of rigid structure, and emphasis on product over process [20].

3 Methodology

3.1 Research Design

An action research method [21] was employed to answer the research questions. The purpose of employing this method was to investigate an "everyday problem" [21], namely adaptation, that the teacher-researcher faced while working in the dramatically altered educational environment of the Covid-19 pandemic. The problem raised questions of: "*How could the teacher-researcher best pursue the most promising affordances of BL, so as to ensure optimal learning experiences for their EFL students?*" and "*How would this pursuit ensure the teacher-researcher's improved practice, their understanding of the practice, as well as their effective management of the teaching environment*" [22]. The action research spiral in this study required the teacher-researcher to form an initial plan, which they then implemented, reflected upon, evaluated and revised before repeating the cycle [23]. To answer the research questions, the SAMR model was applied as a BL implementation guide as well as an analytical lens.

3.2 Contextual Background

United International College (UIC) is jointly founded by Beijing Normal University (BNU) and Hong Kong Baptist University (HKBU). It is the first full-scale cooperation in higher education between the mainland and Hong Kong and the first Chinese mainland college that upholds a liberal arts education model. It is situated in Zhuhai city in the Greater Bay Area. At UIC, English is the medium of instruction (EMI). And *English I* and *II* are freshman-year courses set up by UIC's English Language Centre (ELC). These courses aim to help students reach an acceptable English standard roughly on a par with their counterparts from HEIs in Hong Kong, through developing the four language skills of reading, listening, speaking and writing. Both courses rely considerably on continuous assessment, with the final exam making up 30% of the final grade.

The teacher-researcher is a course lecturer of *English I* & *II*. They had previously been a sceptic of digital-based learning despite having colleagues who enthusiastically integrated such technology. But the Covid-19 situation forced the teacher-researcher to adopt a fully online teaching method in their *English II* course during the Spring Semester 2019–20. After a period of experimenting with *Moodle*-based chat and online discussion forums early in the semester, the ELC management directed their teaching staff to use *Zoom* as the primary teaching medium. As China's Covid-19 situation eased, the teacher-researcher resumed their face-to-face teaching in the Autumn semester 2020–21, while retaining and exploring several online teaching activities in conjunction with their classroom instruction. This is to say, after the first semester of teaching during the pandemic, BL became a usual practice for the teacher-researcher.

3.3 Data Collection

The teacher-researcher served as the data-collection instrument. The naturalistic setting described above offered necessary support for the present study and provided the teacher-researcher a great deal of logistical convenience to collect data and take appropriate actions. The teacher-researcher gathered data from several sources, including their own reflective journals; observations of student participation in class and in *Moodle*-based discussion activities; the end-of-semester Teaching and Learning Evaluation (TLE); student progress in continuous assessment; and *ad hoc* feedback gained from students.

3.4 Data Analysis

Inductive thematic analysis [24] was conducted for analysing the data. Data analysis was undertaken alongside the teacher-researcher's data collection and data processing. This strategy helped the research team check biases and address errors along the way, as well as fine-tune the research process. The teacher-researcher organised notes extracted from their reflective journal and searched for significant events and patterns. This was supplemented by analysis of classroom artefacts (e.g., student discussion posts on *Moodle*) and other sources of data (such as student feedback in the TLE). The teacher-researcher categorised the data into core themes, and the research team met on several occasions to discuss these themes. This helped mitigate misinterpretation and bias, thus contributing to the validity of the findings. Such a dialogue-based approach also helped the researchers achieve consensus on key lessons learned and potential strategies for future implementations.

4 Findings and Discussion

During the three-semester period, the teacher-researcher engaged in several forms of BL, including greater use of ICT-enabled educational modes in the classroom. They also experimented with flipped classrooms, an emerging BL approach. Continual reflection on these implementations gradually made the teacher-researcher's engagement with BL more focused and their implementations more deliberate. Below is a brief account of some implementations that demonstrate the teacher-researcher's approach to BL. The implementations are organised according to the four language skills assessed in *English I & II*, and their significance is evaluated from the SAMR perspective.

4.1 BL Implementations

Listening. According to the SAMR model, the teacher-researcher's BL implementations in listening activities can be considered a combination of *Substitution* and *Augmentation*. The primary goal of implementation for the fully online Spring 2019–20 semester was to substitute previously classroom-bound skill-development exercises with fully online versions. But in the subsequent semesters of on-campus teaching, the goal of blending shifted more to *Augmentation.* This was done by moving certain lower-order thinking activities online, which freed up classroom time for activities that encouraged higher-order-thinking.

Up until Spring 2019–20, the teacher-researcher mostly delivered listening exercises during class. These exercises centred on authentic listening texts such as TED Talks and National Public Radio news stories. In response to the high learning expectations of *English I & II*, the teacher-researcher made their listening exercises especially challenging, and lower-level students in particular struggled. This learning strategy was often found to be time consuming, as the teacher-researcher struggled to elicit answers from students who toiled with the difficult material.

In the Spring 2020–21 semester, the teacher-researcher began to make more significant changes in their listening instruction methods. For example, they adopted a flipped classroom activity in two sections of *English II.* The students were tasked with completing video learning material for homework and returning to class to present the content in small groups, while the remaining *English II* sections conducted the activity during a single class session. The students in the flipped classroom sections gave more accurate and detailed representations of the video content than those in the traditional classrooms. The success of blending this activity encouraged the teacher-researcher to maintain the practice of *Augmenting* listening activities, so that receptive tasks like listening and note-taking were transferred to the homework sphere, allowing more class time for students to demonstrate their listening skills.

Speaking. The teacher-researcher's BL implementations for speaking instruction can be characterised as *Redefinition* in the SAMR model, as they opened up new possibilities to enhance teacher feedback quality while also empowering students to take responsibility for self-assessment and independent learning.

In the Autumn 2020–21 semester, when the teacher-researcher taught *English I*, they attempted few technology-enabled interventions to enhance their speaking instruction. But with their *English II* students in Spring 2020–21, the teacher-researcher attempted two successive BL implementations—the first being a pilot activity to encourage student peer feedback via *Moodle* discussion forum, and the second being mostly a self-assessment based on videos of their practice group discussions.

The Pilot: Impromptu Speech Feedback. For the pilot activity, the teacher-researcher attempted to Modify an in-class peer feedback activity by giving four of six *English II* sections a task to engage in constructive peer feedback via *Moodle* discussion forum. The teacher-researcher facilitated this by uploading videos of several student speeches to *Moodle* and creating a discussion forum for each section. Students were instructed to make at least three posts in the forum.

Student engagement in the activity was regrettably low. Two of the four sections involved had around 50% and 20% participation in their forums respectively. Perhaps unsurprisingly, the group with higher participation rate also had the highest proportion of quality feedback comments (about 75% of posts). In the other two sections, most students gave feedback, but hardly any students who received feedback gave a reply or developed the discussion thread further. Only a minority of the feedback in these sections (around 20% of posts) included advice detailed enough for the recipient to make meaningful speaking improvements. The student comment below represents that minority of feedback that indicated more astute observation on the part of the student reviewer:

> *"I think you can be more confident and make more eye contact with the audience...but remember not to put your hands in your pockets, it seems that you are a little disdainful, and it will make people feel that you are not a good speaker. However, I must say you have strong adaptability, even you were asked not to watch your phone, you could still say something in your own words."*

Whereas the following student comment cites no specific examples; it is representative of the majority of student posts in the forum discussion:

> *"The speaker has a good start and finish. He did good in body language and eye contact part as well. Also, his topic ideal was clear. The speaker still needs to improve his pausing frequency though."*

The teacher-researcher compared the low participation in this forum discussion with a course they had previously taught called *Project Presentation*. In that course, forum discussions made up 15% of the grade, and each student's thread routinely had three or more posts. However, creating such a grade incentive was not possible under the *English II* syllabus, so the teacher-researcher decided to focus their second BL implementation on student self-assessment in preparation for a graded Group Discussion.

The Second Attempt: Preparing the Group Discussion. In the week preceding the second *English II* speaking assessment, the Group Discussion, the teacher-researcher again employed a flipped teaching approach. With all six *English II* sections, 40 to 90 min of class time was replaced with a self-assessment homework activity. After each group delivered their practice discussion in class, the teacher-researcher gave each student a self-checklist, along with typed feedback for each student delivered via *WeChat*. Students were instructed to view a video of their practice discussion on *Moodle* and use the teacher feedback and self-checklist to assess their performance.

The assessed Group Discussions the following week saw significantly improved speaking performance, with exceptional improvement among one low-level section (average improvement of about 18%). And across all sections, most students (78%) received better grades than in the Impromptu Speech assessment, 10% had no change, and 10% dropped in score. The most surprising improvement was in the fluency of three students in a low-level section. Their speech during the practice discussion was dominated by stuttering and hesitation, but in the assessed discussion they mastered significant portions of their spoken content while maintaining eye contact with their group members and showing few visible signs of recitation.

The teacher-researcher believes that the relative success of this assessment was in part due to the fresh BL implementation derived through critical reflection on the previous, unremarkable pilot activity. The experience could suggest a promising way to scaffold students working in small groups to improve their speaking ability—that is, a combination of teacher feedback and self-evaluation of their speaking performance. Lastly, the implementation suggests that an ICT-enabled flipped classroom approach can possibly *Redefine* both teacher practice and the student-teacher dynamic by shifting more feedback responsibility to students.

Reading and Writing
Within the SAMR framework, the teacher-researcher's BL implementations impacted their reading and writing instruction mainly through *Substitution*. This is because the online-based activities to train reading and writing and the LMS-based feedback for assessments had little functional change; but adopting online quick marks for writing assessments did appear to increase feedback efficiency while maintaining quality.

4.2 Reflections: "The Journey Matters as Much as the Destination"

These accounts may portray a relatively smooth transition in the teacher-researcher's BL adoption, but their actual implementation path from Spring 2019–20 to the present can be understood mostly as wandering towards better practice. Beginning with the teacher-researcher's struggle to conduct a fully online classroom in Spring 2019–20, this section discusses student reactions to the teacher-researcher's BL implementations.

Student Dissatisfaction with Fully Online Learning, Spring 2019–20. Student resistance to *Zoom*-based lessons emerged early in the semester as UIC teaching resumed during the height of China's Covid-19 epidemic. A persistent issue was student reluctance to turn on their cameras. The teacher-researcher opted to made cameras optional. Since all but a few students ended up keeping their cameras off during lessons, the teacher-researcher attempted to make up for a lack of visual interaction by trying to call on each student at least once each class. Compared with the proceeding two classroom-based semesters, the teacher-researcher believes this approach in their *Zoom* lessons may have catered to differences in extroversion between students—i.e., all students were required to contribute during class, but they also had control over their anonymity via the camera button. The TLE results for that *Zoom*-based semester suggested that the approach may have been appropriate, because the students tended to respond that the instructor was open to their input in class. But the teacher-researcher's personal observations revealed a general disparity in participation between the few students who regularly had their cameras on versus the ones who tended to display a black screen.

Despite the teacher-researcher's attempt to create an open classroom atmosphere during *Zoom* classes, their average TLE ratings in Spring 2019–20 tended to be lower than the course and college averages. This feedback—combined with a lack of proactive student engagement in *Zoom* lessons—showed that students had mixed feelings about the teacher-researcher's online classroom. Further discussion with colleagues suggested that students still missed the classroom environment and were unsatisfied with the quality of online learning. This was understandable, since the Covid-19 epidemic had forced many freshman students to relinquish the college campus lifestyle to which they had become accustomed in the Autumn semester.

While this may explain a general dissatisfaction among UIC students with *Zoom* lessons, a pressing issue for the teacher-researcher was the relative student discontent in their own online classes. Further examination of student open-ended feedback in the Spring 2019–20 TLE suggested that students expected the teacher-researcher's online classes to be better organised. This sentiment is echoed in the proceeding account.

Return to Zoom (Autumn 2020–21). In September 2020, the teacher-researcher was asked to teach a section of special intake students who would study on *Zoom* for the first month of the semester and then finish the semester with on campus teaching. Teaching this group was not as constructive an experience as the teacher-researcher had expected. This can be attributed to the teacher-researcher's failure to deliver the same course content at the same quality in BL and traditional formats. The *Zoom* sessions, which again relied primarily on *Substitution*, proved problematic, and rapport with the special intake students was lower than with the other *English I* sections. Some students even openly expressed that they would rather receive the course in person. By the time the teacher-researcher did finally meet the students on campus, the crucial window to establish strong rapport had closed, and the teacher-researcher continued to struggle teaching the class. This was reflected in the students' TLE responses, as this section rated their experience lowest among the teacher-researcher's five *English I* sections that semester. Taken together, these events convinced the teacher-researcher that simply using a *Substitution* mentality to guide *Zoom*-based lessons would not suffice when it came to forming a meaningful BL integration.

4.3 Lessons Learned

The teacher-researcher's most successful BL implementations have helped to transform their teaching practice, mostly via *Substitution*, but with some effective *Augmentation* and one instance of *Redefinition*. Excessive *Substitution* for some previously classroom-based activities in this case seems to have done little to enhance student learning experience. And TLE feedback from Spring 2020–21 has convinced the teacher-researcher that they must further *Augment* and *Transform* their teaching style in general.

Student Engagement, Independent Learning and Collaborative Learning. One promising direction of *Augmentation* could be to move some classroom discussions and group work online, for example, in the form of purposefully designed LMS forum discussions that include grade incentives. But as the Group Discussion case shows, blended activities do not necessarily have to be graded to be effective. Potentially *Redefining* practices such as giving students a structured means to self-evaluate their language performance could be a means of utilising technology for independent learning and improved learning outcome achievement. To improve student collaboration, the teacher-researcher could further experiment with flipped classroom group work. For instance, students in small groups can make use of time outside of class to discuss the meaning of a listening or reading text before they are asked to demonstrate their knowledge in the classroom. This may help students feel more confident to contribute during class, while time-intensive tasks such as note-taking can be moved to the homework sphere.

Achievement of Learning Outcomes. In-class observations, and in particular the substantial improvement observed in the Group Discussion assessment scores of several *English II* sections, show that novel implementations refined through teacher self-reflection could help close the gap between students of disparate English levels. The present study shows how this could be the case for encouraging student progress in speaking assessment, although the researchers cannot make similar claims about learning outcome attainment in the other three language skill domains.

Revisiting Instructional Style, with BL as a "New Normal". Spring 2020–21 presented the teacher-researcher with opportunities and challenges to implement fresh and effective BL approaches. *Substitutions* like replacing handwritten feedback on writing assessments with a bank of bespoke "quick marks" proved useful, but excessive use of *Substitution* across the teacher-researcher's practice has hindered the adoption of more innovative practices that could potentially *Redefine* what can be achieved with BL in their college-level EFL course. On top of this, the teacher-researcher has had considerable difficulty getting students to engage in attempted *Modifications* aimed at student-led collaborative learning. Viewed from the SAMR perspective, such setbacks have convinced the teacher-researcher that they must reduce their overreliance on particular strategies and platforms if they are to harness BL for consistent student engagement and effective teaching across activities. Meanwhile, the question of how to best promote collaborative learning through BL remains unclear.

SAMR: Product over Process? Although SAMR has been criticised for its emphasis on product over process [20], the teacher-researcher's experience in the Covid-19 classroom presents an example showing that SAMR does not have to be so utilitarian as some critics argue. In this study at least, SAMR has offered a systematic yet highly adaptable means for one educator to elevate their pedagogy through regular critical reflection. While it could be tempting to think of SAMR as a single peak to summit, teachers who utilise it as a compass may actually climb towards different peaks of best practice—whether they seek to *Augment* as a means to perfect existing effective methods or *Redefine* what it means to achieve a successful educational outcome. In other words, using SAMR does not mean following a linear path from *Substitution* to *Redefinition* in every case. The way teachers use the model should depend on their classroom context and expected learning outcomes. This is not to say that teachers using SAMR need to be isolated in their individual journeys towards transformative practice; they may take shared paths if their visions are aligned. In the case of this action research experiment, the broad scope of SAMR has proven useful for the teacher-researcher to explore the multi-faceted affordances of BL during a period of intense disruption.

The Broadness of BL: Boon or Bane? While the research community accepts the *status quo* of BL as being without a universally agreed upon definition [25], this study argues that the diverse pedagogical opportunities afforded by BL gave the teacher-researcher space to experiment with a range of implementations to suit their current technical capacity and unique cultural and educational context during the pandemic. The most successful implementations resulted in meaningful, uncomplicated learning experiences that were the result of reflection-based adaptation. Those successes suggest that the complex answers to pressing questions like what, how and why to blend can be mediated through SAMR to discover useful practices customised to an instructor's teaching style and educational context.

5 Concluding Remarks

This paper reports on an action research that investigates how an EFL teacher-researcher at a liberal arts HEI in China used the SAMR framework to guide and develop their BL implementation during Covid-19. The study reveals that a quick pick up of BL can present numerous challenges in the short term, although implementations can be adapted and refined over the longer term so that students receive higher quality teaching. With such findings, it is argued that BL must be carefully planned, reflected upon and adjusted, and that SAMR does not need to be employed in a linear fashion. Teachers can pursue *Substitutions*, *Augmentations* and *Modifications* that enhance the teaching and learning experience while discovering new ways to *Redefine* the way they deliver content and create opportunities for student and teacher self-learning.

References

1. Cahapay, M.B.: Rethinking education in the new normal post-COVID-19 era: a curriculum studies perspective. Aquademia **4**(2), 1–5 (2020)
2. Garrison, D.R., Vaughan, N.D.: Blended Learning in Higher Education: Framework, Principles, and Guidelines. Wiley, New York (2008)
3. Dziuban, C., Graham, C.R., Moskal, P.D., Norberg, A., Sicilia, N.: Blended learning: the new normal and emerging technologies. Int. J. Educ. Technol. High. Educ. **15**(1), 1–16 (2018). https://doi.org/10.1186/s41239-017-0087-5
4. Al-Qahtani, A.A., Higgins, S.E.: Effects of traditional, blended and e-learning on students' achievement in higher education. J. Comput. Assist. Learn. **29**(3), 220–234 (2013)
5. Kiviniemi, M.T.: Effects of a blended learning approach on student outcomes in a graduate-level public health course. BMC Med. Educ. **14**(1), 1–7 (2014)
6. Lim, D.H., Morris, M.L.: Learner and instructional factors influencing learning outcomes within a blended learning environment. Educ. Technol. Soc. **12**(4), 282–293 (2009)
7. López-Pérez, M.V., Pérez-López, M.C., Rodríguez-Ariza, L.: Blended learning in higher education: students' perceptions and their relation to outcomes. Comput. Educ. **56**(3), 818–826 (2011)
8. McKenzie, W.A., Perini, E., Rohlf, V., Toukhsati, S., Conduit, R., Sanson, G.: A blended learning lecture delivery model for large and diverse undergraduate cohorts. Comput. Educ. **64**, 116–126 (2013)
9. Vo, H.M., Zhu, C., Diep, N.A.: The effect of blended learning on student performance at course-level in higher education: a meta-analysis. Stud. Educ. Eval. **53**, 17–28 (2017)
10. Aspden, L., Helm, P.: Making the connection in a blended learning environment. Educ. Media Int. **41**(3), 245–252 (2004)
11. Bower, M., Dalgarno, B., Kennedy, G.E., Lee, M.J., Kenney, J.: Design and implementation factors in blended synchronous learning environments: outcomes from a cross-case analysis. Comput. Educ. **86**, 1–17 (2015)
12. Snodin, N.S.: The effects of blended learning with a CMS on the development of autonomous learning: a case study of different degrees of autonomy achieved by individual learners. Comput. Educ. **61**, 209–216 (2013)
13. So, H.J., Brush, T.A.: Student perceptions of collaborative learning, social presence and satisfaction in a blended learning environment: relationships and critical factors. Comput. Educ. **51**(1), 318–336 (2008)

14. Ginns, P., Ellis, R.: Quality in blended learning: exploring the relationships between online and face-to-face teaching and learning. Internet High. Educ. **10**(1), 53–64 (2007)
15. Owston, R., York, D., Murtha, S.: Student perceptions and achievement in a university blended learning strategic initiative. Internet High. Educ. **18**, 38–46 (2013)
16. Yoon, S.Y.: Exploring learner perspectives on learner autonomy for blended learning in EFL conversation classes. STEM J. **17**(1), 197–220 (2016)
17. Spring, K.J., Graham, C.R., Ikahihifo, T.B.: Learner engagement in blended learning. In: Encyclopedia of Information Science and Technology, 4th edn, pp. 1487–1498. IGI Global (2018)
18. Puentedura, R.R.: SAMR: a brief introduction (2013). http://www.hippasus.com/rrpweblog/archives/2013/10/02/SAMR_ABriefIntroduction.pdf
19. Lacruz, N.: SAMR model. Technology and the Curriculum: Summer 2018 (2018). https://techandcurriculum.pressbooks.com/chapter/samr/. Accessed 2 May 21
20. Hamilton, E.R., Rosenberg, J.M., Akcaoglu, M.: The substitution augmentation modification redefinition (SAMR) model: a critical review and suggestions for its use. TechTrends **60**(5), 433–441 (2016)
21. Elliot, J.: Action Research for Educational Change. Open University Press, Milton Keynes (1991)
22. Carr, W., Kemmis, S.: Becoming Critical: Education, Knowledge, and Action Research. Routledge, Oxon (1986)
23. Williamson, K.: Action research: theory and practice. In: Johanson, G., Williamson, K. (eds.) Research Methods: Information, Systems, and Contexts. Chandos, Cambridge (2018)
24. Creswell, J.W.: Research Design: Qualitative, Quantitative, and Mixed Methods Approaches, 4th edn. Sage Publications, Thousand Oaks (2014)
25. Moskal, P., Dziuban, C., Hartman, J.: Blended learning: a dangerous idea? Internet High. Educ. **18**, 15–23 (2013)

Education + AI

A Parsing Scheme of Mind-Map Images

Bo Wang[1(✉)], Ju Zhou[1(✉)], and Bailing Zhang[1,2(✉)]

[1] Suzhou Aunbox Software Co., Ltd, Suzhou, China
[2] School of Computer and Data Engineering, NingboTech University, Ningbo, China

Abstract. At present, there are a large number of mind-map images generated by different software on the Internet. These images contain rich knowledge that has been summarized by people for learning or teaching. In order to exploit knowledge and reconstruct the mind-map, we propose a scheme to parse the image of mind-maps. Firstly, we apply text detection and deep learning-based OCR models to extract the text content and the corresponding position information, and then use the line segment detection model to detect the line segments which represent the structural relationships between text blocks. The detected line segments will be matched with the text blocks with the image features of the mind map. The results are utilized to analyze the parent-child relationship between the text blocks. Experiments have been conducted to illustrate the reconstruction of mind-map with the parsing of the corresponding images.

Keywords: Text detection · Line segment detection · Parent-child relationship

1 Introduction

Mind-map uses graphics and text to display the relationship between themes at different levels with hierarchical diagrams of mutual subordination and correlation. By turning a long list of monotonous information into a colorful, impressive and highly organized chart, mind-map is helpful for divergent thinking and mastering knowledge, and is generally welcomed by students and professionals. In recent years, there are a large number of mind-map images generated by different software on the Internet, and these images contain rich information and valuable knowledge that has been summarized by people. Sometimes, one may need to extract the text information in these images or re-edit the mind-map with updated knowledge or different styles. However, there does not exist any tools to help people.

In order to facilitate the re-editing of mind-map and the extraction of information in the image, we propose a parsing scheme based on the deep learning to analyze the mind map. To simplify the discussion, we focus on the type of the mind-map which use line segments or curves to connect different parent-child nodes in the mind-map image, as shown in Fig. 1.

In recent years, deep learning technologies have developed rapidly, with extensive applications in computer vision. The research results on text detection and recognition, line detection and image segmentation algorithms provide the necessary tools to

W. Jia et al. (Eds.): SETE 2021, LNCS 13089, pp. 221–231, 2021.
https://doi.org/10.1007/978-3-030-92836-0_19

analyze the mind-map images. For general documents, a range of optical character recognition (OCR) tools are available to detect and recognize text efficiently, for example, CPTN [1], EAST [2], TextSnake [3], DBNet [4], CRNN [5], GTC [6], and TextScanner [7]. However, all of these models have strict restriction on the image resolution for both of the training and inference stages, and scale normalization is the necessary step. Beyond a pre-defined range, it will not only increase the computation cost and memory requirement, but also reduce the accuracy of OCR. Scale variation remains a challenging problem for most of the deep learning models. Different from other document images, mind-map images not only have big variation in resolution, but also have more irregular layouts and text font styles. Therefore, it is not feasible to directly apply OCR or other deep learning models with normalization stage to mind-map image. To solve this problem, we adopt an adaptive image division method to automatically split an image into multiple blocks with the equal size to make it consistent with the requirements of the text detection and recognition models.

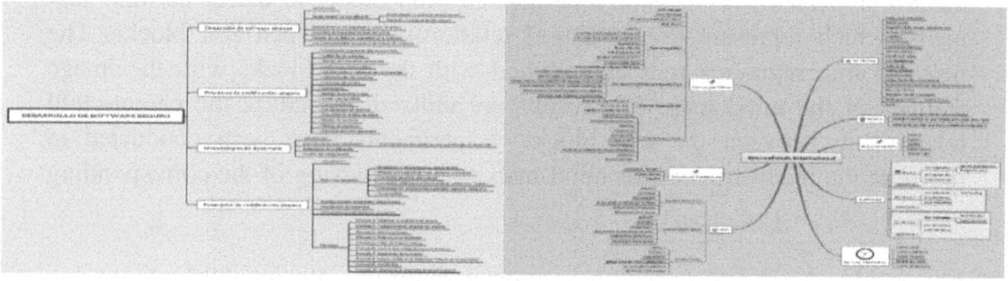

Fig. 1. Linear mind-map image samples

Line segment is an important cue in a mind-map for the relationship of text blocks or nodes. Line segment detection is the first step to analyze the parent-child connections. There are many algorithms for detecting straight lines or line segments, such as the traditional Hough line detection method, LSD [8] line detection method, L-CNN [9], HAWP [10], ULSD [11], F-Clip [12] and LETR [13] based on deep learning line-segment or wire-frame detection algorithm. The traditional straight line detection methods usually have poor robustness, which will become fragile to be interfered by background elements. In addition to that, classical straight line detection methods do not provide mathematical parameters of the line segment. By contrast, line segment or wire-frame detection model based on deep learning can not only detect the line segment more accurately, but also give accurate end point of the line segment. Figure 2 illustrates the line segment detection effect from two models, namely, HAWP [10] and ULSD [11]. In order to detect line segments as accurately as possible when performing line segment detection, we also adopt image division method similar to the practice for text detection.

After completing text detection and recognition, and line segment detection, the detected line segments will be matched with the text blocks with the help of image characteristics of the mind-map. The example mind-map image is shown in Fig. 3, which has the following features: (1) one horizontal line segment matches one text node; (2) one meaningful vertical line segment intersects at least three horizontal line segments, and the vertical line segment does not match the text node; (3) The horizontal line segments that intersect with both sides of the vertical line segment usually fit in a one-to-many relationship, corresponding to the parent-child node connection. Then, according to the structural characteristics of line segments, we can transform the relationship between line segments and text nodes into the connection between text nodes, so as to complete the analysis of text and its node parent-child relationship in mind map.

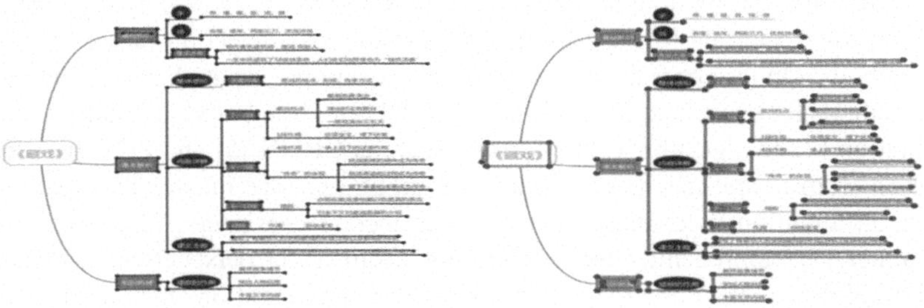

Fig. 2. HAWP (left, blue line), ULSD (right, yellow line) line segment detection test sample (Color figure online)

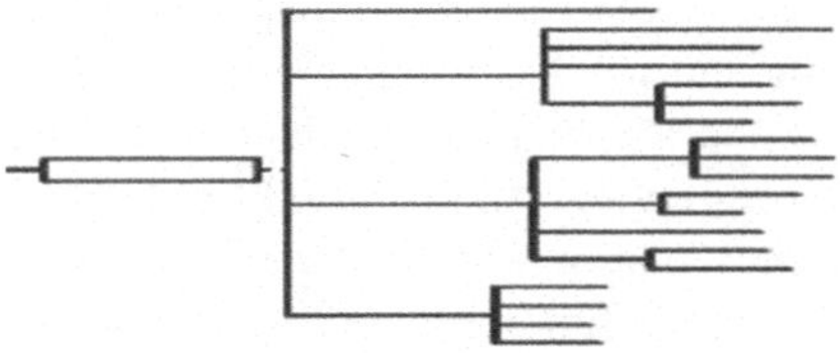

Fig. 3. The typical line segment structure of mind-map

In summary, our main contributions are:

1. Utilizing adaptive image division to improve the accuracy of text detection and line segment detection in scale variant mind-map images;
2. Combining text detection and line segment detection methods based on deep learning to analyze the parent-child relationship of text nodes in mind-map images;
3. Improving the efficiency of automatically extracting and editing text information in mind-map image.

2 Related Works

Text Detection and Recognition. Text detection and recognition is the core technology in an OCR system. Though some papers have published for end-to-end text detection and recognition, general OCR practice still treats text detection and recognition as separate modules. Text detection includes regression-based methods and segmentation-based methods. The former directly regresses the bounding boxes of the text instances. CPTN model [1] improves the anchor regression mechanism in Faster-RCNN [14] to detect small text boxes and then merge them instead of directly detecting large text boxes. EAST [2] are anchor-free methods, which applies pixel-level regression for multi-oriented text instances. Segmentation-based methods usually combine pixel-level prediction and post-processing algorithms to get the bounding boxes. TextSnake [3] is a text detector based on the fully convolutional network to solve the detection problem of arbitrary shape text. DBNet [4] is widely used because it further improves the real-time performance of scene text detection based on segmentation methods. On the other hand, there are also two popular paradigms in the state-of-the-art methods for scene text recognition: 1) RNN-attention based method, 2) semantic segmentation-based algorithms. The former, such as CRNN [5] and GTC [6], drawing inspiration from neural machine translation (NMT), encodes images into features and employs an attention mechanism to align and decode characters. The latter, such as TextScanner [7], approaching text recognition from a 2D perspective, first adopts a fully convolutional network to perform semantic segmentation, then finds the connected components in the segmentation maps, and finally infers the class of each connected component.

Line Segment Detection. The traditional line segment detection methods such as LSD algorithm [8] generate vectorized lines based on the edge map, which will make it prone to mistakenly detect the edge of the mind map as a line segment. Deep learning-based line segment detection and wireframe parsing have different performance though they all generate vectorized line segment representations. L-CNN [9], HAWP [10], and ULSD [11] are wireframe parsing algorithms based on deep learning. Compared with traditional line segment representation, wireframe parsing leverages the constraint of endpoint junctions, thus the output line segments are of higher quality in terms of line completeness and robustness to noise. F-Clip [12] is a real-time single-stage fully convolutional network model for line segment detection, which detects line segments in an end-to-end fashion by predicting them with each line's center position, length, and angle. LETR [13] is a general-purpose approach for line segment detection without heuristics-driven intermediate stages for edge and junction proposal generation.

3 Method

In this section, we introduce the whole process and corresponding methods in detail. The flowchart of mind map image parsing is shown in Fig. 4.

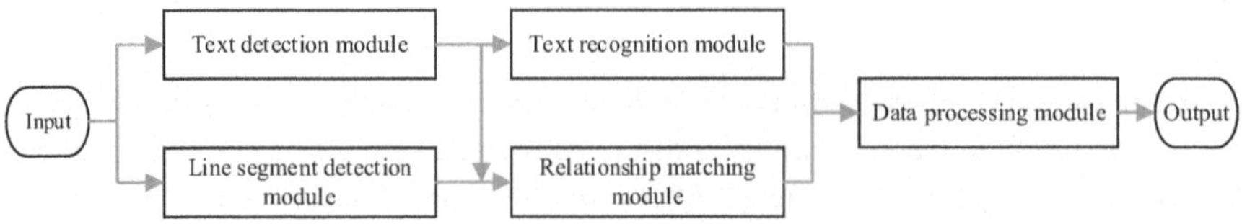

Fig. 4. The linear mind-map image parsing flow chart

3.1 Text Detection Module

When a text detection model is directly applied, the input image should be normalized to a uniform scale. In general scenarios, this practice is acceptable for the compromise between detection accuracy and real-time performance. But for scale variant mind-map images, this will increase the false and missed detection rate of text detection to an unacceptable level. The side length of the mind-map image ranges from a few hundred to tens of thousands of pixels, and the character size and font styles also change dramatically. To make it worse, it is common to find mind-map images with large resolution but tiny font size. If the mind-map images are scaled to a uniform scale, the textual information will be easy to be lost. In order to solve the problem, we adopt an adaptive image division method, which splits an image into multiple blocks with the equal size. It should be noted that there is a pixel overlap area between each block and the edge of adjacent blocks. When merging blocks later, we only take the mask of non-overlapping area for merging. This largely solves the problem of text detection accuracy decline in the edge area of image blocks after image division.

After the image is split, text detection is performed on each image block separately, and a masking block of the text area is generated. From the implementation perspective, we have not redesigned and trained the text detection model, but adopted the text detection model CPTN [1] for text line detection. Then, the generated text-area masking blocks are recombined into a complete mask of original image size. After merging the text area masks, some morphological operations are performed to adjust the connectivity of the text area mask. Finally, we obtain the coordinate of the text area by searching the outline of the text area mask. The process is shown in Fig. 5, where M represents the number of split blocks in each row of the image, N the number of split blocks in each column of the image, and [p_tl, p_tr, p_br, p_bl] represents the four vertices of the text box from left to right and from top to bottom.

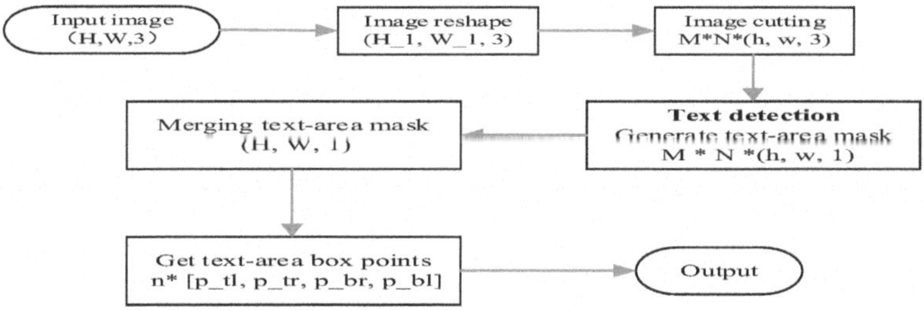

Fig. 5. Flowchart of the text detection process

3.2 Text Recognition Module

The text recognition module first extracts the corresponding text-area in the fine-tuned image according to the coordinate information obtained from the text detection, and then performs text recognition on the text area, and outputs the corresponding text information after some corrections to the recognized text. The text recognition algorithm adopts the widely used CRNN model, with pre-trained parameters. CRNN model is composed of convolution layer for extracting image features, Recurrent layer composed of bidirectional LSTM network and transcription layer for aligning output text through CTC. The model can recognize Chinese and English text with high accuracy. Since CRNN is used to recognize Chinese and English characters at the same time, the model is easy to misidentify similar punctuation marks in Chinese and English, so special characters such as punctuation marks need to be corrected.

3.3 Line Segment Detection Module

Line segment detection is a very critical step in parsing the mind-map. There is currently no line detection method specifically designed for mind-map images. We compared a number of line detection algorithms, confirming that line segment detection models based on deep learning has advantages for the mind map image. Taking the accuracy and computational cost into consideration, we choose the HAWP [10] model as the line segment detection. The HAWP model architecture is shown in Fig. 6.

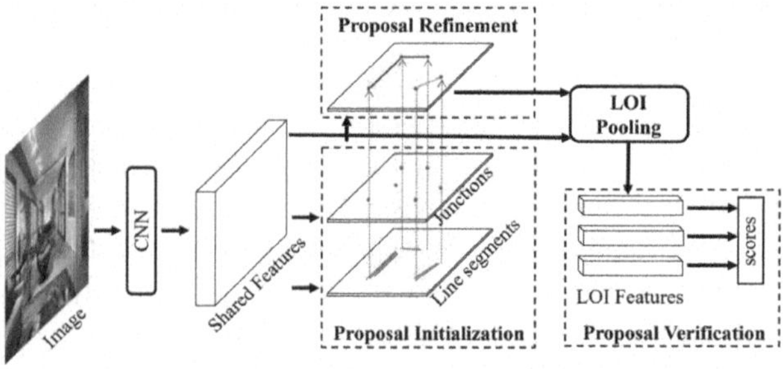

Fig. 6. Flowchart of the text detection process

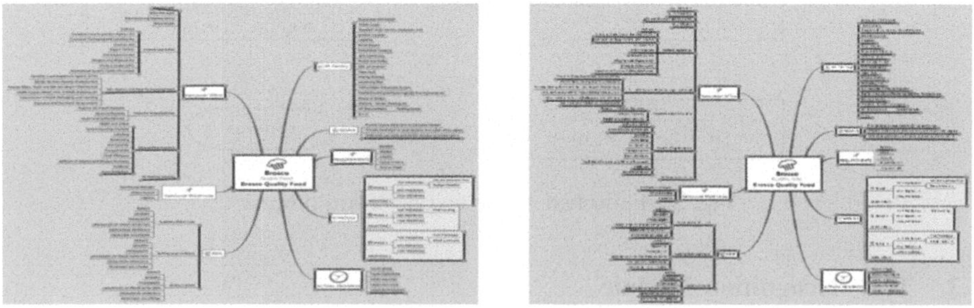

Fig. 7. Flowchart of the text detection process

The detection of line segments in mind-map images encounter the same scale problems with text detection. If a unified normalization strategy is adopted, it will cause serious problem of information loss and dramatically reduce the final detection accuracy. As shown in Fig. 7, after increasing the zoom size of the same image from 512 * 512 to 768 * 768, it can be found that the missed detection rate of line segment detection is significantly reduced. However, increasing the scale of the input image also significantly increases the amount of calculation of the model. To solve this problem, we adopt the same image division process, as shown in Fig. 8. Following the adaptive division on the input image, line segment detection is performed together with other operations. Based on the detection results, we generate three different masks: horizontal line, vertical line and oblique line. This is due to the fact that there exist intersecting line segments in the image, which need to be processed separately to correctly distinguish different line segments when merging mask images. In addition, the output result uses two endpoints to define a vectorized line segment, which is more conducive to post-processing.

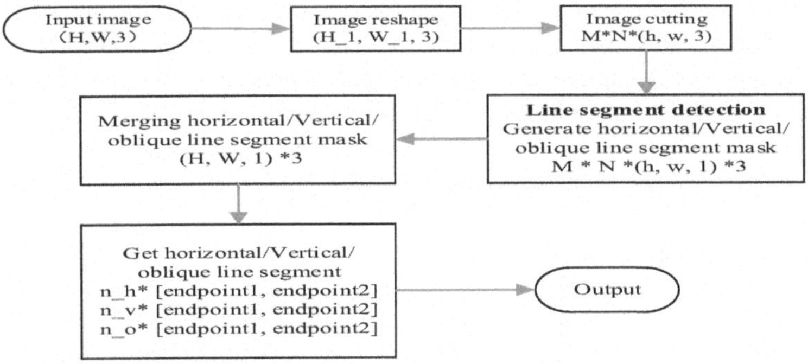

Fig. 8. The line segment detection module flow chart

3.4 Relationship Matching Module

The relationship matching rules are mainly designed based on the characteristics of mind map, and the simple process is shown in Fig. 9. After completing the text detection and line segment detection, we can get the parameters of the text-area boxes and line segments. The relationship matching module first matches the text-box/node with the line segment. The basic rule is that each text-box/node matches a horizontal line closest to it. Then, the horizontal lines on both sides of each vertical line intersecting with the vertical line are matched according to the distribution characteristics of the intersecting line segments of the mind map. The basic rule is that the side with fewer intersecting horizontal lines selects an optimal line segment as the parent node, and the intersecting horizontal line on the other side as the child node. Finally, according to the matching relationship between text-box and line segment, the matching relationship between line segments is transformed into the parent-child node connection relationship between different text-boxes.

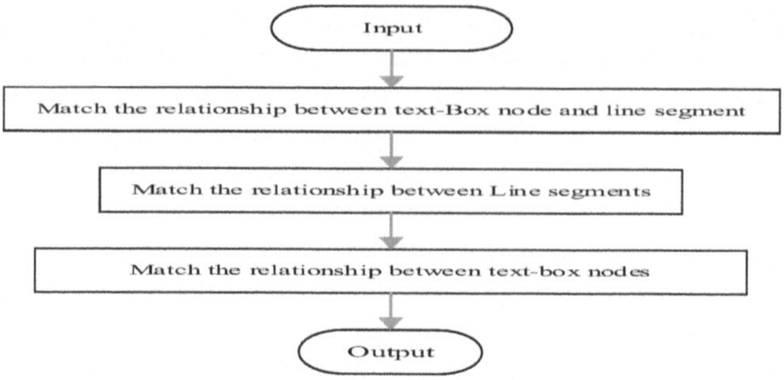

Fig. 9. Relationship matching module flow chart

4 Experimental Evaluation

4.1 Implementation Details

In this section, we first provide implementation details. The experiments are conducted with the PyTorch-1.4 framework, and the models are trained on a TITAN-RTX GPU with 24 GB memory. It should be noted that during text detection, the maximum long side length of the split image block is 1280 by default, and the short side length is the value calculated with the length-width ratio of the input image. In line segment detection, the size of the split image block is 512 * 512 by default.

4.2 Experimental Results

In the experiment, we did not completely retrain model parameters such as text detection and line segment detection. Instead, we used official or third-party model parameters that were pre-trained on the original model. Our focus is to combine these different models or algorithms to parse the mind-map image. We collected 50 mind-map images from the Internet for testing. Some of the samples is shown in Fig. 10. The left image is the original image, and the right image is the visual parsing result. It should be noted that line segments with arrows are used to represent the parent-child relationship of different text nodes, and the arrows point to the child nodes.

Since many images contain a small number of undetectable curves, we do not count the number of missed detections but focus on the false connection rate of the connected line segments in the evaluation. Incorrect connection rate mainly refers to the proportion of connections with incorrect connection nodes or wrong parent-child node relationship in all connections. We count the number of false detections and the number of all connected segments of 50 mind map images respectively. Finally, we calculate that the average false connection rate of mind-map image analysis is 7.37%, and the number of node false connections of general mind-map is less than 13. The number of missed inspections is also under reasonable control, which can reduce the workload of manual connection. It should be noted that although curves are not specifically detected, some curves or parts of curves may be detected as straight lines, affecting the accuracy of subsequent analysis. Preferably, background of mind-map images should be texture-free, and the structure should be clear, mainly with thin straight line or only a small number of curve connections.

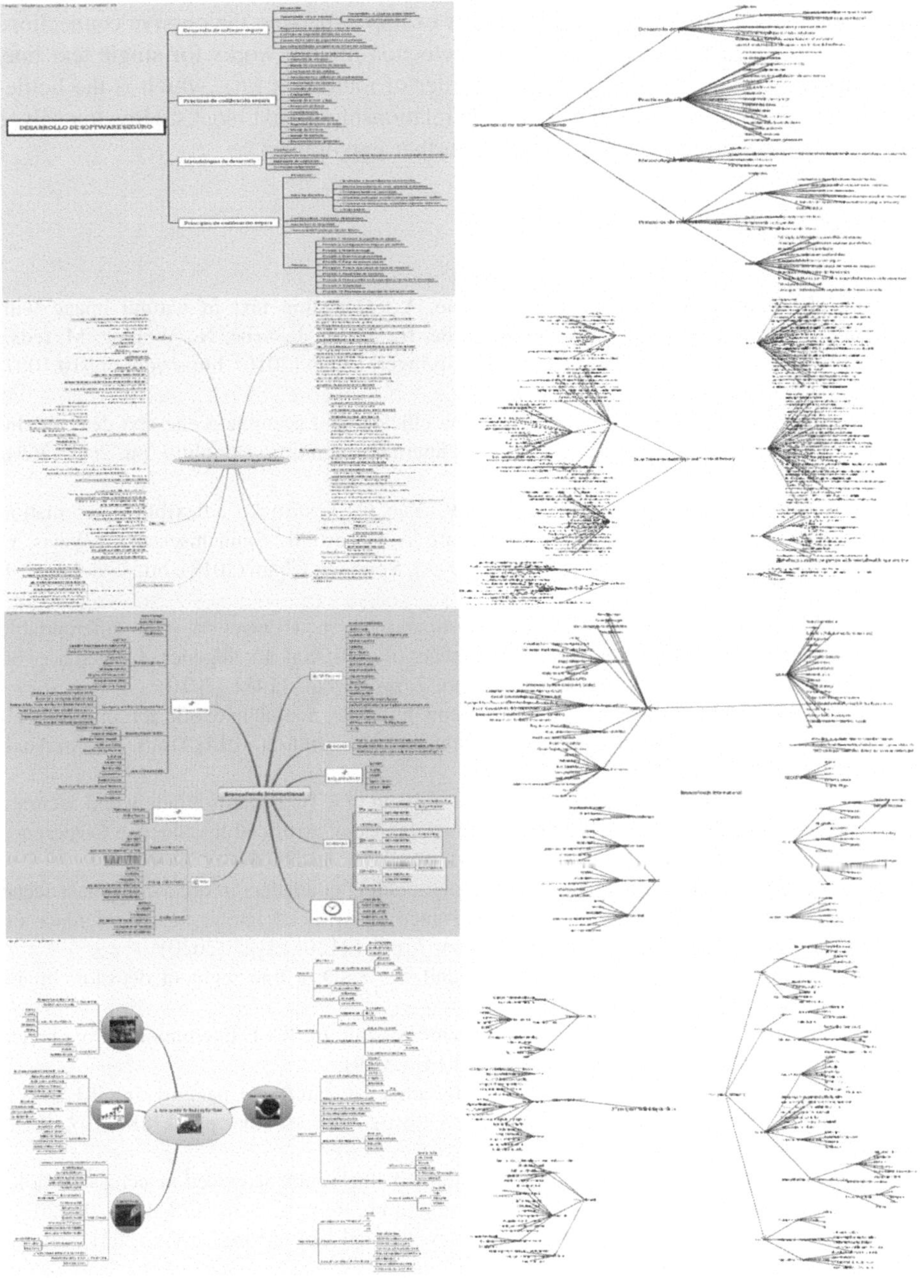

Fig. 10. Some of the mind-map image samples

5 Conclusion

In this paper, we propose a practical method to parse mind-map images with text detection and line segment detection. We propose an adaptive image division approach to solve the scale variance problem, with preliminary success. However, there are still some limitations to be further dealt with, for example, parsing the cursive connections of the text blocks. At the same time, text detection mainly works for single text line, which cannot correctly identify the text border of multi text line, which is the bottleneck to the identification of the parent-child relationship of text blocks. How to analyze more general mind-map image still needs further exploration.

References

1. Tian, Z., Huang, W., He, T., He, P., Qiao, Y.: Detecting text in natural image with connectionist text proposal network. In: Leibe, B., Matas, J., Sebe, N., Welling, M. (eds.) ECCV 2016. LNCS, vol. 9912, pp. 56–72. Springer, Cham (2016). https://doi.org/10.1007/978-3-319-46484-8_4
2. Zhou, X., Yao, C., Wen, H., et al.: EAST: an efficient and accurate scene text detector. In: IEEE Conference on Computer Vision and Pattern Recognition, Honolulu, pp. 2642–2651. IEEE (2017)
3. Long, S., Ruan, J., Zhang, W., He, X., Wu, W., Yao, C.: TextSnake: a flexible representation for detecting text of arbitrary shapes. In: Ferrari, V., Hebert, M., Sminchisescu, C., Weiss, Y. (eds.) ECCV 2018. LNCS, vol. 11206, pp. 19–35. Springer, Cham (2018). https://doi.org/10.1007/978-3-030-01216-8_2
4. Liao, M., Wan, Z., Yao, C., et al.: Real-time scene text detection with differentiable binarization. In: Association for the Advance of Artificial Intelligence Conference on Artificial Intelligence, New York, vol. 34, no. 7, pp. 11474–11481 (2020)
5. Shi, B., Xiang, B., Cong, Y.: An end-to-end trainable neural network for image-based sequence recognition and its application to scene text recognition. IEEE Trans. Pattern Anal. Mach. Intell. **39**(11), 2298–2304 (2016)
6. Hu, W., Cai, X., Hou, J., et al.: GTC: guided training of CTC towards efficient and accurate scene text recognition. In: Association for the Advance of Artificial Intelligence Conference on Artificial Intelligence, New York, vol. 34, no. 7, pp. 11005–11012 (2020)
7. Wan, Z., He, M., Chen, H., et al.: TextScanner: reading characters in order for robust scene text recognition. In: Association for the Advance of Artificial Intelligence Conference on Artificial Intelligence, New York, vol. 34, no. 7, pp. 12120–12127 (2020)
8. Gioi, R., Jakubowicz, J., Morel, J.M., Randall, G.: LSD: a line segment detector. Image Process. Online **2**(4), 35–55 (2012)
9. Zhou, Y., Qi, H., Ma, Y.: End-to-end wireframe parsing. In: IEEE International Conference on Computer Vision, Seoul, pp. 962–971. IEEE (2019)
10. Xue, N., Wu, T., Bai, S., et al.: Holistically-attracted wireframe parsing. In: IEEE/CVF Conference on Computer Vision and Pattern Recognition, Seattle, pp. 2788–2797. IEEE (2020)
11. Li, H., Yu, H., Yang, W., et al.: ULSD: unified line segment detection across pinhole, fisheye, and spherical cameras. ISPRS J. Photogramm. Remote. Sens. **178**, 187–202 (2021)
12. Dai, X., Yuan, X., Gong, H., et al.: Fully convolutional line parsing. arXiv (2021). https://arxiv.org/abs/2104.11207v1

13. Xu, Y., Xu, W., Cheung, D., et al.: Line segment detection using transformers without edges. In: IEEE/CVF Conference on Computer Vision and Pattern Recognition (2021)
14. Ren, S., He, K., Girshick, R., et al.: Faster R-CNN: towards real-time object detection with region proposal networks. IEEE Trans. Pattern Anal. Mach. Intell. **39**(6), 1137–1149 (2017)

Research on OBE Online Teaching Mode Combined with Expression Recognition—Taking Digital Image Processing Course as an Example

Yingying Tai, Dapeng Qu(✉), and Yan Wang

College of Information, Liaoning University, Shenyang 110036, China
dapengqu@lnu.edu.cn

Abstract. Although the engineering education has been widely developed in China, the training for engineers cannot completely satisfy the requirements from the society. The output-based education (OBE) designs education process according to the results of education so that students can have a certain level of ability when they graduate. However, influenced by the COVID-19 pandemic, plenty of offline practical activities have changed to online ones. Thus, the digital image processing course is taken as an example, and the online class video is taken as the test data for students to do practical experiments. Moreover, an algorithm extracting harr-like features to detect face and recognize expression is applied. The eyes are further extracted from the detected face images to calculate the ratio of width and height, and then the students' studying state can be determined. The experimental results demonstrate that the algorithm can help teachers understand the students' state and improve the teaching efficiency. Moreover, the OBE online teaching mode can improve the students' practical ability.

Keywords: OBE (outcome-based education) · Harr-like feature · Cascade classifier · Video tracking

1 Introduction

The epidemic that began in 2020 has made online teaching popular. The universities in the world have begun to study how to conduct online lectures, online seminars, and how to complete online training well. Moreover, Chinese technological power is so strong that not only make the teachers use the Internet and various platforms to complete teaching and scientific research, but also make the teachers rethink the current teaching model in the new technological environment. For many years, the training method of college education has taken the teacher as the only leader, emphasizing knowledge over abilities, and taking examinations as the key or even the only indicator. This method originated in the era of mechanized mass production. It used to efficiently cultivate talents for that era. However, it has been unable to adapt to the new

W. Jia et al. (Eds.): SETE 2021, LNCS 13089, pp. 232–241, 2021.
https://doi.org/10.1007/978-3-030-92836-0_20

requirements for talents in the Internet age, and it is necessary to have a radical transformation from concept to form. The colleges and universities are called ivories due to their cultivating talents and fostering morality. So graduates from colleges and universities should adapt to the times and meet the needs of society well. This is also the value of OBE (Outcome based education).

2 Outcome Based Education

The concept of OBE originated in the United States. With the continuous deepening and development of its concept, the OBE model has gradually become the basis for the training of engineering talents [1–3]. Its essence is to take the main performance of students during this semester as an important indicator of education quality assessment. It focuses on the learning results of students in the process of talent training. And all these would be used as important factors for feedback on the quality of teaching activities.

The “Report on the Quality of Engineering Education in China” [4] pointed out that the number of enrolments and graduates of engineering majors in our colleges and universities ranked first in the world. This data was three to five times higher than those of Russia and the United States. The source of engineering students is stable, and the one-time employment rate of graduates remained above 95%. However, the report also believed the facts that the current structural surplus and shortage of engineering graduates in our country have happened. The number of engineering graduates at the junior and postgraduate could not fully follow the requirements of enterprises and industries. We should take the measures to strengthen to connect training chain with the national innovation and industrial development. Similarly, the “World Competitiveness Yearbook” [5] showed that the qualification level of our engineers was at the bottom of the world. This was mainly because there was a disconnection between our country’s engineering education and the development of emerging industries and the new economy. In June 2016, China was accepted as a full member by the “Washington Accord” organization and became the 18th full member. Then the professional certification of engineering education in our country has achieved international substantive equivalence, which provided a good opportunity for deepening the reform of engineering education. At present, the country has promoted innovation-driven development, implemented major strategies such as “One Belt One Road initiatives” “Made in China 2025”, and “Internet+” [6]. Moreover the new economy represented by new technologies, new formats, new models, and new industries has been booming. Higher requirements are put forward, and there is an urgent requirement to accelerate the reform and innovation of engineering education. So the “OBE” model is outcome-based education. It is necessary for the educators to have a clear idea of the ability and level that students should achieve when they graduate, and then try to design an appropriate educational activities to ensure that students could reach these expected goals.

3 Digital Image Processing Course Based on AI

3.1 Artificial Intelligence

Artificial Intelligence (AI) is an interactive computer system that simulates human thinking and behavior patterns. It is a combination of multiple applications, such as speech recognition, image recognition, text understanding, and content generation. These technologies can be effectively adapted and combined. That means application of artificial intelligence. Education must proactively adapt to the new requirements of the intelligent era, promote the reform of education and teaching models with deepened applications, and fully realize the potential value of the integration and innovation of artificial intelligence and education. The prospect of the combination of education and AI is very broad, and the boundaries of the education industry may be continuously widened due to the use of AI technology [7, 8].

3.2 Algorithm Description

We use cascade classifier to finish face detection based on harr-like features. Haar features include three types as shown in Fig. 1. Each classifier extracts corresponding features from the image. The cascade classifier will carry out in stages according to the harr-like features. For example, there are one feature in the first stage, 10 features in the second stage, and 25 features in the third stage, and so on. And every stage will detect 10 features in average. If the first feature cannot be detected in the first stage, this area will be rejected and not come into the next stage. If they can pass through all the stages, they must be a face area.

We capture the videos of students online, then have face detection and facial expression recognition. After that, we will further carry on expression classification and statistics. Last, if most of students showed the emotions of sleepy and boring, then that is the better time to transfer teaching mode. We could change our teaching mode from lecture to discussion, from one topic to another, and finish our teaching task well. We would carry on face identification by the method of cascading weak classifiers into strong classifiers and extract the field of human face. After that, we would begin to fatigue testing. Extract 68 key points to represent parts of the face. Detect 68 key points of the human face, obtain the indexes of the left and right eye facial signs respectively, and perform gray-scale processing on the video stream through openCV to detect the position information of the human eye. There was a fatigue qualification, that was the ratio of width and height of the eyes.

We further use harr-like features for feature detection and make the sum of integration graph to accelerate in face identification. Then we continue to train the weak classifiers and cascaded them to a stronger one. This kind of cascade classifier is obtained through machine learning through a large number of pictures with and without faces. At the beginning of training, all pictures in the training set have the same weight. For pictures that are classified incorrectly, the weight is increased, and a new error rate and new weight are recalculated until the error rate or the number of iterations meets the requirements. This method is called Adaboost.

The detailed whole process can be denoted as follows.

Firstly, we extract the harr-like features.

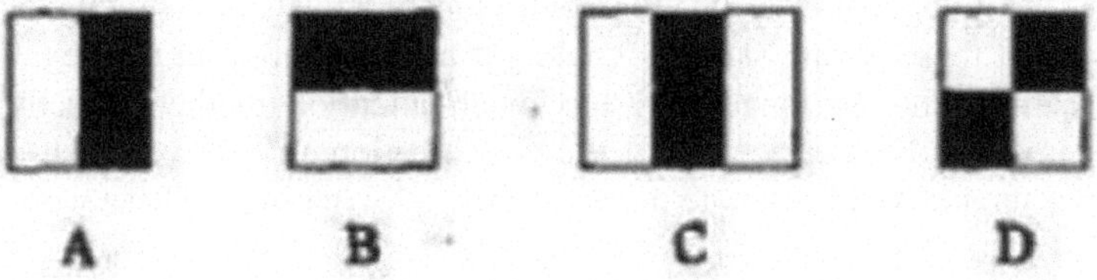

Fig. 1. Model of Harr-like feature

Secondly, in the process of feature extraction, the entire image is traversed through the sliding of the rectangular window, and the process of solving the feature value is to subtract the sum of the pixel values in the white area from the sum of the pixel values in the black area every time the rectangular box slide a window, so as to get a characteristic dimension. We use integration graph to accelerate the extraction process, which is shown in Eq. (1):

$$SAT(x, y) = \sum I(x_i, y_i) \tag{1}$$

where $I(x_i, y_i)$ is the grey value of the left bottom image and can be shown in Fig. 2.

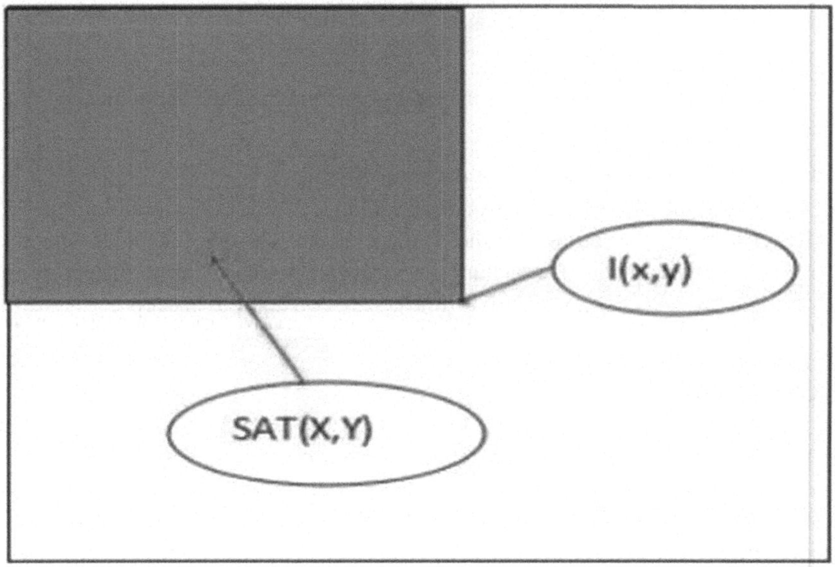

Fig. 2. The principles of integration

Thirdly, the Adaboost classification continuously adjusts the weights of the wrong samples, so that these wrong samples could get more attention in the next iteration of the classification, and no longer pay too much attention to the correctly classified samples to improve the correctness of the classification. When we finish training the first classifier then it could generate more classifiers by iteration. These weak classifiers are cascaded to a strong one.

The method of splitting images accelerates the process of solving, and finally uses the classification algorithm to identify the process of the face area. The second part is expression identification. The function of fatigue is calculated as Eq. (2):

$$EAR = \frac{||p_2 - p_6|| + ||p_3 - p_5||}{2||p_1 - p_4||} \tag{2}$$

where p1, p2, p3, p4, p5, and p6 are feature points, and shown in Fig. 3.

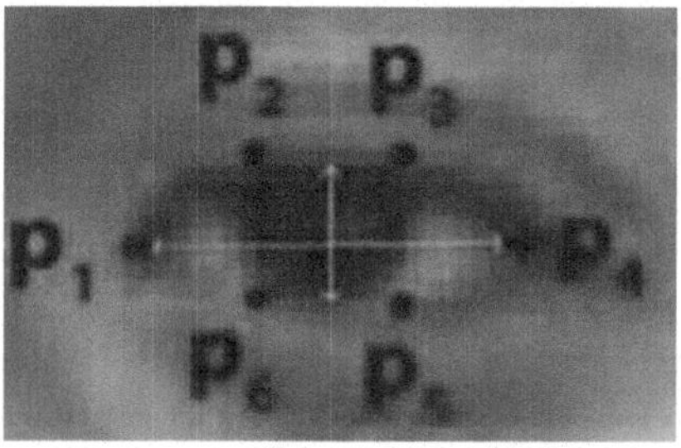

Fig. 3. Schematic diagram for the ratio of the width and height of an eye

If the absolute value (EAR) of the difference between the two pairs of eyes in the current frame and the previous frame is greater than 0.2, it is considered fatigue. When the EAR is lower than a certain threshold, the eyes are closed. Calculate whether the value of eye length/width is greater than the threshold for each frame of picture in the video, and if it exceeds 50 consecutive times, it is considered "asleep".

4 Experiments

We pick a few frames of video in our online class and then extract their faces and made expression identification. Our experiments have been completed in a computer with 3.20-GHz CPU, 8 GB memory, and 64-bit OS. The experimental results can be shown as follows (Figs. 4, 5 and 6).

Fig. 4. The face detection result for one frame

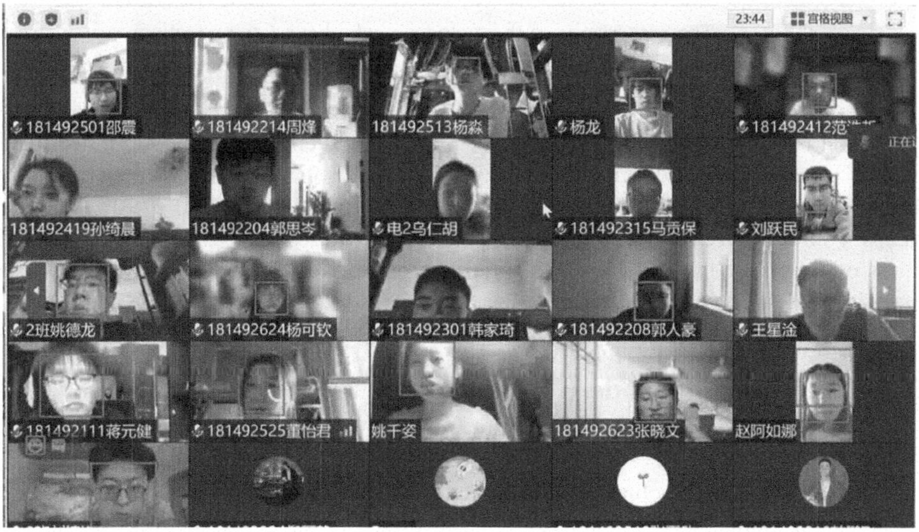

Fig. 5. The face detection result for another frame

Fig. 6. The expressions of three students who have fatigue feelings

This video is about 10 min. The amount of data is about 18 MB. The video resolution is not very high. Considering of the factors such as the bandwidth occupied by the transmission and processing speed in real application, our video has only 480 dpi with 30 fps. The face detection rate of each frame is about 60%–90%, and the sleepy expression recognition rate is about 80% in those of faces by computing the ratios of weight and height for eyes. When the number of facial sleepy expressions is over 30% in one frame, and that has last 2 min, we will transfer the teaching mode.

5 OBE Teaching Mode Combined with AI for Digital Image Processing Course

In order to solve the teaching problems, such as poor pertinence, backward teaching organization mode, for the course of "Digital Image Processing", this paper proposes that we can adopt the teaching mode based on OBE to reform it. In the pandemics, due to the transfer of courses from offline to online, it is necessary to remake the original OBE-based teaching model. Many teaching contents are needed to be adjusted appropriately to adapt to the online teaching. It is well known that the biggest problem with online teaching is that students should stare at the screen for a long time, which is easy to have psychological and visual fatigue. Therefore, teachers should adjust their teaching methods or modes at appropriate time to keep students in a state of excitement. All these could be realized by AI.

5.1 Teaching in Class

For online OBE-oriented teaching, the entire curriculum planning and teaching should be for students. Teachers could use demonstrations and guidance in the class, at the same time, they could analyze, evaluate, and diagnose students' learning through students' class performance with AI. The teachers could drive and promote ability and knowledge of students. First of all, we must choose a suitable teaching platform, which had simple operation and good stability. Secondly, the teachers should actively use modern multimedia, try to use pictures for teaching, make the lecture vivid, and use heuristic and discussion to fully drive students' enthusiasm and initiative, and inspire students to think actively. The teacher can introduce many algorithm in class, for example, There are many methods for face recognition, from the local features to machine learning, the researchers study very deeply. Nowadays, with the developments of AI technologies, harr-like feature and adaboost algorithm are used for the video of the students listening to the class to form a cascaded classifier, and get a better detection; then for every collected face, the AI algorithm would compute the fatigue function of the eyes. The teacher could decide whether transfer the teaching way or not by the last statistic of classification results. In addition to the teaching tasks and goals, the teacher could popularize the progress of some digital image processing in certain application fields, track the frontiers of international and domestic research, and send these reports to students in advance, so that students could think, ask questions and communicate with each other.

5.2 Practical Teaching

Various typical algorithms of image processing technology are assigned to students as homework, and then they will be inspected, discussed and evaluated in class. The teacher will take the students to the enterprises, production bases, and establish experimental training and internship center with enterprises offline. However, these tasks must be completed in other ways. Due to the epidemic, we must try to avoid going out and collecting. So we can give a task which is made research in a company to our students. We give some description of the company's background, production process and related products, so that students could have a full understanding of their difficulties, then they could offer their talents, apply their creativity and knowledge to solve the problems, integrate theory with practice, moreover improve engineering capabilities. Moreover, we could use the videos or images that we had to the students and inspire them to finish some researches. A vivid example is the teacher can pass the video images of each lesson to the students, ask the students to extract faces according to the knowledge they have learned, and then classify the expressions, analyze the class status as mentioned before. Construct a knowledge education system, technical skills training system, experimental training and internship environment according to the requirements of the combination of work and learning. While the students proposed solutions according to the actual background of the enterprise, an optimized plan also would be proposed.

Moreover, some image data come from the projects can be taken to the students, so they can make some analysis and operation, such as denoise, enhancement, match, then make some statistics or identification. What algorithms would be adopted to process these images are decided by the students. Whether these methods are good or not depend on the students' knowledge, creativity and flexibility. This is the application of teaching mode on the course of digital image processing based on OBE.

5.3 Improving the Evaluation System of Theory Courses

Outcome-oriented education believed that every student is different, and the evaluation of each student must be different, and there is no fixed and unified standards. Evaluation is not only an important key to check the quality of teaching, but also the continuation of teaching content. The theoretical evaluation method of digital image processing courses is mainly composed of major assignments, topic discussions, personal expressions and the performance of intra-class interaction. The evaluation of each student is to master the student's learning status by formulating a personalized evaluation level, and to provide guidance for further revision of teaching strategies. The evaluation of practice consists of practical effects, operational skill level, the quality of the "Case Analysis" homework, and the performance of cooperative tasks. Innovation abilities are evaluated through innovation achievements, scientific research papers, summary reports, and so on.

6 Conclusion

Teaching Online based on OBE is no longer restricted to form and location, and mobilized students' learning enthusiasm to a greater extent, but it also tests students' learning consciousness. The digital image processing course focus on the student in teaching, shortens the time for teachers to lecture, increases the time for discussion and communication, and distributes the courseware and materials of this course to students at the beginning of the semester, so that students could understand and master the teaching content. In the class, in addition to teaching, discussing homework and subject frontiers, it is also necessary to guide students to use the current technology platform to acquire professional frontier technology, expand students' understanding of the latest developments in the field, from theory to experiment, from basics to frontiers, Students could deeply understand the basic principles and some methods of digital image processing. All above have created favorable conditions for cultivating high-quality innovative top-notch talents. It strives to promote teaching reform and practice through the update of the examination model, so that students can smoothly integrate with society. The results showed there were 43 students picking this course. All of them passed the written test, of which the excellent rate reached 78%, 43 assignments were submitted, 11 discussion have been held. The students gave the feedback that this mode aroused their enthusiasm and interests, learning efficiency was generally improved.

Acknowledgements. This paper is supported by the project of National key research and development program (2019YFB1405804), Natural Science Basic Research Fund of Liaoning Provincial Education Department (LJC202002), and Project of Undergraduate Teaching Reform Research of Liaoning University (JG2020KCSZ016, JG2020KCSZ023).

References

1. Zhao, J., Gao, H., Li, P.: The application and research of the case-based evoked hybrid teaching model based on the OBE in application-oriented universities. In: IEEE International Conference on Computer Science and Educational Informatization (CSEI), Kunming, pp. 282–285. IEEE (2019)
2. Xu, H., Cheng, M.: Exploration of teaching reform of "Integrated Circuit CAD" based on OBE concept. J. Shangrao Normal Univ. **38**(3), 41–45 (2018). (in Chinese with English Abstract)
3. Li, Z., Chu, P., Zhang, Y.: The evaluation of the objectives achievement degree for "principles and application of single-chip microcomputer" course based on OBE model. In: International Conference on Information Science and Education (ICISE-IE), Sanya, pp. 109–112. IEEE (2020)
4. Report on the Quality of Engineering Education in China, Ministry of Education of the People's Republic of China, Higher Education Press (2020). (in Chinese)
5. Cui, Q., Liu, S.: A summary of the research on the construction and development of new engineering in China. World Educ. Inf. **31**(04), 19–26 (2018). (in Chinese with English Abstract)
6. Qu, D., Wu, S.: A competition-oriented student team building method. In: ACM TURC, Chengdu, pp. 1–2. ACM (2019)
7. Qiu, X.: Research on the teaching of "Internet plus continuing education" from the perspective of AI. In: International Conference on Artificial Intelligence and Education (ICAIE), Tianjin, pp. 112–115. IEEE (2020)
8. Zhu, A.: Application of AI identification technology in foreign language education. In: International Conference on Artificial Intelligence and Education (ICAIE), Tianjin, pp. 71–75. IEEE (2020)

A Fitness Education and Scoring System Based on 3D Human Body Reconstruction

Haiyi Tong, Chenyang Li, and Hui Zhang(✉)

Beijing Normal University-Hong Kong Baptist University United International College, Zhuhai, China
amyzhang@uic.edu.cn

Abstract. Affected by the Covid-19 epidemic, online fitness education has attracted a large number of users. However, when there are a large number of students in a same online classroom, it is difficult to get the coach's advice and scores in time. To overcome this problem, we propose an AI fitness education system that uses 3D reconstruction technology to restore the shape of the human body and its bones. The skeleton is used for posture scoring. The 3D human body model is reconstructed by our improved VIBE network, with the accurate posture, shape and movement of the coach and students. By adding the loss function of the end limbs to the 3D human body model, compared with the performance of the original VIBE, we reduce the jitter noise in continuous motion. The training results show the accuracy of our improved VIBE. In addition, we have also established a scoring system, which can score the posture of the trainees based on the coach's posture, and provide feedback through visual tag points. The experimental results show that our method is feasible and worthy of further exploration.

Keywords: Fitness education scoring system · Improved-VIBE · 3D human body reconstruction

1 Introduction

As the pace of modern life continues to accelerate, life pressure seems to have been increasing. Health has become a common concern for people who want to keep in shape, strengthen the immune system, and relieve fatigue caused by excessive nervousness. These requirements are increasingly resonating with the public. In addition to more and more standard fitness education videos, there are emerging online services designed to bring fitness home (such as Keep, Wake, or FitTime, etc.). However, whether at home or in the gym, fitness enthusiasts will face a prominent challenge: how to ensure that they exercise properly without a personal trainer. In order to overcome this problem, this paper proposes a posture scoring system based on a improved VIBE for 3D reconstruction model of the human body. Human body estimation is one of the most important research issues in the field of computer vision, and it has a wide range of applications in the fields of behavior recognition [1], human-computer interaction [2] and so on. Human body pose estimation can be divided into two-dimensional and three-dimensional human body estimation. In terms of two-dimensional human pose

W. Jia et al. (Eds.): SETE 2021, LNCS 13089, pp. 242–253, 2021.
https://doi.org/10.1007/978-3-030-92836-0_21

data sets, LSP [3], FLIC [4], MPII [5], MSCOCO [6] have appeared in recent years; in terms of algorithm framework, it is divided into single-person pose estimation [7, 8] and multi-person pose estimation [9, 10]. The goal of 2D human pose estimation is to locate and identify the key points of the human body, and connect these key points in the order of joints to form a projection on the two-dimensional plane of the image, thereby obtaining the skeleton on the two-dimensional image of the human body. We can see that the disadvantages of the two-dimensional reconstruction of the human posture are obvious. It discards the depth information in the video (image) and cannot accurately describe the posture of the human body. For this reason, 3D human body estimation is urgently needed.

The main task of 3D human pose estimation is to predict the three-dimensional coordinate positions and angles of human body joint points. In the current research, three-dimensional human body estimation methods can be divided into two categories: traditional methods and deep learning methods. Many traditional methods are based on the human body model to describe and infer the human body posture. These methods need to extract the features in the image, so there are higher requirements on the spatial position relationship between the feature representation and the key joint points. In addition to low-level features such as borders and colors, high-level features such as Scale Invariant Feature Transforms (SIFT) [11], Histogram of Oriented Gradients (HOG) [12] have stronger expressive capabilities and effectively compress feature space dimensions. Although they have advantages in time efficiency, they are still manually designed and have many shortcomings. For example, video (image) data needs to avoid the effects of occlusion, lighting, etc., so the cost of data collection is relatively high. In contrast, deep learning methods have obvious advantages in feature extraction compared with traditional feature methods. Deep learning-based methods are gradually being widely used in in the task of 3D human body estimation, while deep networks are used to obtain higher-precision feature extraction, without the need for prior knowledge as in traditional methods. In addition, deep learning with transfer learning can well apply models trained on large data sets to small data sets, which is more flexible than the tradition methods.

We need to reconstruct or restore the 3D model of the human body from pictures or videos. At present, researchers mainly use two methods based on SMPL model [13] and voxel regression network model [14] to estimate the 3D human body dense model. Based on these two methods, DensePose [15] is a typical method using SMLP model to estimate 3D human pose dense model. BodyNet [16] uses voxel construction methods to directly infer the shape of the human body from a single image. Although the above methods have achieved good results, there is still a lack of labeled 3D human pose and shape data sets, and the predicted shape is not realistic enough, and the limb kinematics is not reasonable enough. VIBE [17], based on Generative Adversarial Networks (GAN) [18], uses large-scale motion capture datasets (AMASS [19]) and unpaired in-the-wild 2D annotations. Although VIBE can generate accurate models, it is not reasonable enough in the kinematics of human limbs. For example, the end limbs of a 3D human body will jitter slightly during continuous movement.

In order to solve these problems, we propose an improved VIBE network to add constraints on the human limbs of the 3D model. We also built a posture scoring algorithm to compare the similarity of postures between students and coaches. According to the degree of similarity, students' postures can be scored.

We summarize our contributions as follows:

- We propose an improved VIBE network for 3D human body reconstruction from a monocular camera.
- By adding end limb constraints to the loss function of the 3D human body model, the jitter noise in continuous motion is reduced.
- According to the coach's posture, we have implemented a scoring system to score students' actions.

The paper is organized as follows. Section 2 introduces preliminary works, including generative adversarial networks and skinned multi-person linear model. Section 3 presents the fundamentals of 3D human body reconstruction and posture scoring. Section 4 describes in detail how the improved VIBE network adapts to our case. Section 5 demonstrates the experimental results, and Sect. 6 gives the conclusions.

2 Preliminaries

2.1 Generative Adversarial Networks

Supervised learning relies on labeled data. However, in the data generation task of our 3D reconstruction human body model, it is not even feasible to obtain labeled data. Therefore, unsupervised learning methods such as GAN will be the way to solve this problem. The idea of GAN comes from the zero-sum game in game theory. The generator and the discriminator can be regarded as two players in the game. In the process of model training, the generator and the discriminator will update their own parameters to minimize the loss. Through continuous iterative optimization, a Nash equilibrium state is finally reached, and the model reaches the optimal state. The objective function of GAN is defined as [18]

$$\min_{G}, \max_{D} V(D,G) = \mathbb{E}_{x \sim p_{\text{data}}(\mathrm{x})}[\log D(x)] + \mathbb{E}_{z \sim p_z(z)}[\log(1 - D(G(z)))] \quad (1)$$

Where the function means the generative model G and the discriminative model D play two-player minimax game with value function $V(D, G)$. We train the two networks together. It is worthy to notice that generative adversarial networks (GANs) have had a significant impact on image modeling and synthesis. Based on the advantage of GANs, our system aims to estimate 3D human body model parameters for each frame in a video sequence using a temporal generation network, which is trained together with a motion discriminator. The discriminator has access to a large corpus of human motions in SMPL format.

2.2 Skinned Multi-person Linear Model

Skinned multi-person linear model (SMPL) refers to the parametric three-dimensional model of the human body constructed in an article by Max Planck in 2015 [20]. SMPL can be understood as the sum of a basic human body model and the transformation based on the model. After pose normalization, principal component analysis (PCA) is run on the shape registrations from the multi-shape database. At the same time, the kinematic tree is used to represent the posture of the human body, that is, we need to analysis the rotation relationship between each joint point and its parent joint. This relationship can be expressed as a three-dimensional vector. The local rotation vector of each joint constitutes the pose parameter of the SMPL model. The biggest difference between SMPL and traditional linear blend skinning (LBS) is that SMPL proposed a surface mesh for human body posture. SMPL can simulate the bulges of human muscles during limb movement. Therefore, the deformation of the human body surface during exercise can be avoided, and the appearance of human muscles stretched and contracted can be accurately simulated.

3 Methods

3.1 3D Body Reconstruction

The human body model generated by the existing video-based human body shape and pose estimation methods usually lacks the rationality of the actions. The main reason is that in-the-wild pictures or videos lack real 3D annotation. Most of the work still use data collected with 2D annotations in indoor or laboratory environment, but these data are often limited in the number of individuals, the range of motion, and the complexity of the picture background. More importantly, the amount of 2D labeled data is not enough to train a deep neural network. Inspired by the HMR (Human Mesh Recovery) method, we use 2D joint points and unpaired static 3D human body shape and pose data sets to predict the pose of the human body from a single picture by training in a fully weakly-supervised manner without using any paired 2D-to-3D supervision. We use the large-scale human 3D motion capture data set AMASS, which is rich enough to learn models that characterize and simulate human motion. The goal of improved VIBE is to use labeled 2D joint points (and 3D joint points, if any) to predict the 3D pose of the human body from the video, so that the discriminator cannot distinguish between the predicted 3D motion and the motion in the AMASS data set. Specifically, we trained a Sequence-based Generative Adversarial Networks (GANs). Given a human body video, we first train a timing model to predict the SMPL human model parameters for each frame in the video. There is an action discriminator that attempts to distinguish between predicted and real human pose sequences. In this case, the regressor tends to generate a reasonable human posture by minimizing the counter loss, while the discriminator learns the static, physical and dynamic characteristics of human motion through real motion capture data.

Loss Function. We follow the same 2D to 3D process in the video as [20]. The 2D pose of each frame is obtained by the existing 2D pose detector, and then the continuous 2D pose sequence is input into the neural network to estimate the final 3D pose.

At present, compared with previous work, a novel loss function was used. And then the accuracy of the evaluation on the data set has been improved. According to the result of the existing supervised method [20], in terms of accuracy, there will be obvious jitters at the end of the limbs (arms and calves) and the problem that the predicted motion cannot fit the video material. In terms of smoothness, the numerical analysis of the spatial coordinates for joint points found that the jitter noise in the data is very large, which will cause obvious jumps in the movement. In the continuous movement, the limbs also have a slight jitter. Adding too many constraint loss functions cannot effectively solve the jitter problem of the generated data. Therefore, in terms of accuracy, we proposed a method of constraining only the bones of the limbs, which is adding a loss function, Cosine similarity, to the limbs. The loss function is shown as following:

$$\cos\theta = \frac{\overrightarrow{l_{pre}} \cdot \overrightarrow{l_{data}}}{\|\overrightarrow{l_{pre}}\|_1 \cdot \|\overrightarrow{l_{data}}\|_1} \tag{2}$$

Where the $\overrightarrow{l_{pre}}$ represents the 2D limb end vector of the prediction human body model, and the $\overrightarrow{l_{data}}$ represents the 2D limb end vector of the data set human body model. We iterate the loss function for getting the minimum value of the function. The reason why adding the control and constraints of the limbs in the generator, the human body movement with the data set merges the smooth data in the data set with the motion generated in the generator to form smoother motion data. In other words, we want the limb movement of prediction human body could be more seasonable.

3.2 Posture Scoring

While we got a series of continuous 3D human body models from a video, which can accurately simulate the real human body. We can then refer to the coach's model and give scores to the postures of these students. In this part, we implemented a posture scoring system that compares student videos with coaches. Our scoring system extracts the joint points and angles on the 3D human body model. These joints will be connected in the three-dimensional space and evolved into a skeleton, as shown in Fig. 1:

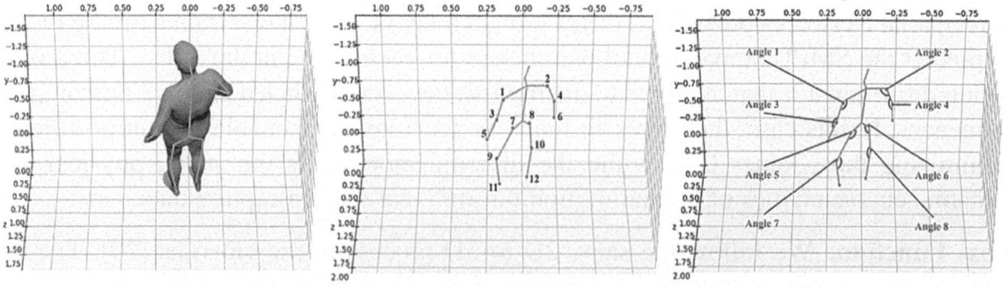

Fig. 1. Body joint points and angles in 3D human body model.

Next, we need to rate the posture of the students in the video based on the pose of the skeleton. More specifically, we obtain a three-dimensional human body model through the improved network of VIBE, extract joint points from the model, and connect the associated joint points. We score based on 12 joint points and 8 angles. The purpose of normalization is to connect the joint points into a vector for calculating the angle between different vectors. At the same time, normalization can speed up the calculation, unify the value range of each attribute, and make different attributes get the same weight in the calculation:

$$\overline{x}_k = \frac{x_k - x_0}{\sqrt{\sum_{i=1}^{N} (x_i - x_0)^2}} \tag{3}$$

After inputting the coach (standard postures) video and the student video separately, we can get the three-dimensional coordinate position of the joint point of the coach and the student under each frame of the image, and normalized the total 12 joints coordinate based on the Eq. 2.

While we got the 12 joints' coordinate, the corresponding 8 angles need to be calculated. After connecting two associated joint points, and using cosine similarity to calculate the corresponding 8 angles, which is shown as following:

$$\theta = \cos^{-1} \frac{\vec{V}_1 \cdot \vec{V}_2}{\|\vec{v}\|_1 \cdot \|\vec{v}\|_1} \tag{4}$$

Here we have the two basic parameters, distance_error and angle_error, which represent the level of the similarity between coach and student. The distance_error is to detect the three-dimensional coordinate position of the joint point of the coach and the student in each frame of the video, and then use the Euclidean Distance to calculate the error of each corresponding joint and mean it. Besides, the angle_error is the coach's angle minus the student's corresponding angle, and the absolute value is taken.

After we get these two errors, we have a criterion algorithm for scoring. For this we set two different scoring methods, as shown below:

$$S_{angle} = 100 * \left(\frac{angle_{error}}{angle_{error} + distance_{error}}\right) \tag{5}$$

In other words, it is to reassign the weights so that the scoring system will not fluctuate sharply within a certain deviation, but will remain at weight 1 or decrease exponentially. As shown below:

$$weight = \begin{cases} 1, & x \in [0, \alpha] \\ \exp(-k(x - \alpha)) - \beta, & x \in [\alpha, \infty] \end{cases} \tag{6}$$

In Eq. 6, there are two group parameters for distance error and angle error. First, the distance parameter: α is for error redundancy, it is maybe in [0,1], k controls speed of decent of curve, initialization value could assign 1, and by testing, assign other suitable value. β is to punish the relatively large error value. Second, the angle parameters: this error is in [0, π], therefore you should assign the relatively small parameters for initialization.

4 Algorithms and Implementations

4.1 Training Datasets

MPI-INF-3DHP is a multi-view data set collected by the markerless motion capture system, most of which are in indoor environments. Its training set contains 8 categories, and each category has 16 videos. The author uses this data set for training and evaluation.

3DPW is an in-the-wild 3D data set collected with the help of IMU sensors and handheld cameras, including 60 segments of outdoor and outdoor activities. The author uses this data set for training and evaluation.

We evaluate our model on a commonly used 3D HPE dataset 3DPW. The 3DPW dataset is collected by a handheld camera with an IMU in a natural scene to capture daily activities, for example, shopping in the city, going upstairs, doing exercise, drinking coffee, and then taking the bus. There are 60 video sequences in this dataset (over 51,000 frames) and the corresponding 3D pose is calculated by the wearable IMU. The test set contains 9,600 frames from 9 HD cameras. In the follow-up work, more data set evaluations will be added to get the best generalization results. There are better results on more data sets, indicating that the generative model can adapt to a variety of environments and can get better prediction results in different environments.

4.2 Evaluation

We compared the results of improved-VIBE with previous single-frame and video-based methods on multiple data sets. Evaluation criterions include:

- Procrustes Aligned Mean Per Joint Position Error (PA-MPJPE): The average error of joint points aligned by rotation, translation, and scaling operations
- Mean Per Joint Position Error (MPJPE): Mean Per Joint Position Error after the root joint is aligned
- Per Vertex Error (PVE): Average vertex error of mesh
- Acceleration Error (Accel): The mean difference between ground-truth and predicted 3D acceleration for every joint

4.3 Training Procedure

In the human pose and shape estimation task for a single frame, we use the ResNet-50 convolution neural network, using the official pre-trained image data set. We will pre-calculate the image features of each frame, and will not update the parameters of ResNet-50 with the training of the model. We use T = 16 as the sequence length, the minimum batch size is 32, and the model is trained on a single NVIDIA RTX3090 GPU.

In order to solve the problem of insufficient accuracy of hands and feet in previous work, the ground truth results of the data set are analyzed and exported to obtain 3D joint points and 2D joint points, and the data is input into the neural network to obtain the predicted camera parameters. Under the predicted camera parameters, the 3D joint points are projected onto the 2D picture, and then the corresponding limb joint points are separated, and the end is connected with the elbow (knee) joint point to construct a vector in the outward direction of the human body. We call such a vector as end limb vector. We calculate the cosine similarity between the predicted end limb vector and the end limb vector in the data set, and use the sum of the results as the supervised training loss value. If the difference between the predicted end limb vector and the real data set is too large, the final cosine similarity sum of the limbs will become larger, and the training process is to minimize the sum of the cosine similarity components.

5 Experimental Results

5.1 3D Human Body Reconstruction

Our evaluation on the 3DPW data set is in Procrustes Aligned Mean Per Joint Position Error, Mean Per Joint Position Error, Percentage of Correct Keypoints, Per Vertex Error indicators are better than the existing results of VIBE. In comparison with the prediction method based on frame sequence, a relatively excellent final index was also obtained. As shown in Table 1, we compare our results with the original VIBE and the latest frame-based prediction methods. In the test of the MPI-INF-3DHP data set, our results are also improved compared to the VIBE test results. Compared with the original VIBE, the training result with the limb constraint loss function has been improved in training accuracy.

Table 1. Evaluation of the latest model on the 3DPW data set. Our results are better than the state-of-the-art method.

	3DPW				MPI-INF-3DHP			
	PA-MPJPE	MPJPE	PVE	Accel	PA-MPJPE	MPJPE	PVE	Accel
Kanazawa *et al.* [21]	59.2	96.9	116.4	29.8	-	-	-	-
VIBE (direct comp.)	56.5	93.5	113.4	27.1	99.15	64.85	912.4	31.49
Our method	56.1	89.1	105.8	23.8	97.05	64.92	899.8	28.00

In the process of training the network, the generator will calculate the output value of the loss function of each cycle and improve the method of calculating the loss. Existing work only considers the 3D and 2D coincidence degree of the bone points when calculating the loss value. Their results showed that the accuracy loss of reconstruction mainly lies in the limbs. When calculating the loss value. Their results showed that the accuracy loss of reconstruction mainly lies in the limbs. And the positions of the second joint and the end joint of the arms and legs are not sufficiently coincident. Increasing the loss calculation of the end limb will improve the training under supervised learning to a certain extent.

We decided to use the MPJPE and PVE criterions because the loss function model we designed encourages the consistency of the shape. However, in the existing results, we found that some extreme movements cannot be well predicted, even if corresponding constraints are added to the limbs. For example, extreme actions such as raising the hands above the head, the angle of the bifurcation of the legs are very large, and the data set that is not produced, labeled, and the actions involved are not able to make a good fit between the human body action and the shooting video. The performance of our network is shown as follows (Figs. 2 and 3):

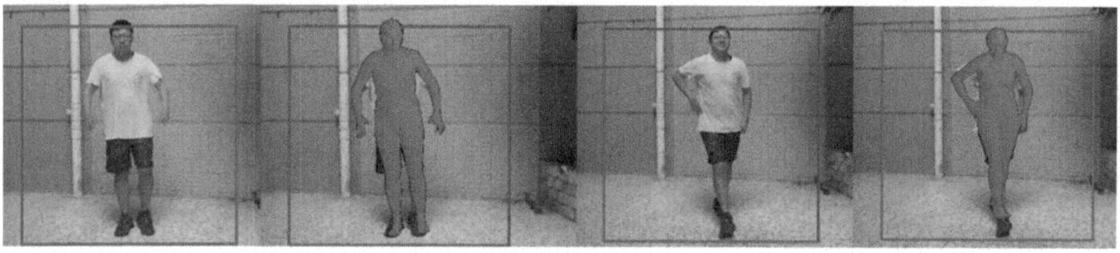

Fig. 2. The 3D model can better fit the edges of the characters, the limbs and body movements of the characters are better constrained, and the characters' movements in each frame can be reconstructed.

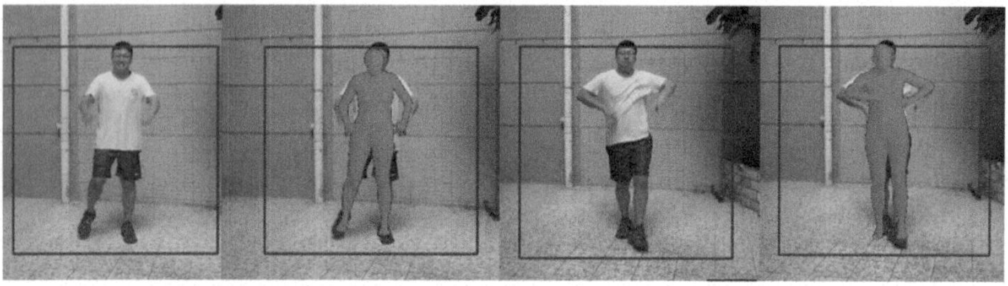

Fig. 3. When encountering some movements that are not included in the data set, extreme stretched human movements cannot fit well.

5.2 Posture Scoring System

Using the scoring algorithm mentioned earlier, we selected an instructional video as the standard action, and the 3D human body model in the previous chapter was used as the scoring object. We extract the joint points and angles on the 3D human body model, these joints would correspondingly connect in the three-dimensional space and evolve into a skeleton. The result is shown as follows (Figs. 4 and 5):

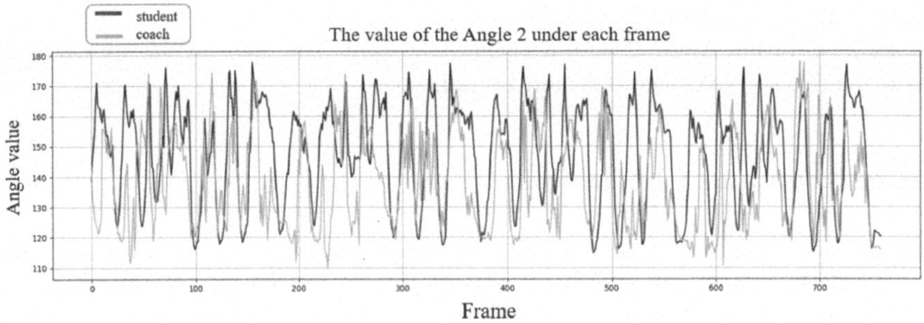

Fig. 4. The posture scoring system, we calculated the value of Angle 2 under each frame in the student and coach video.

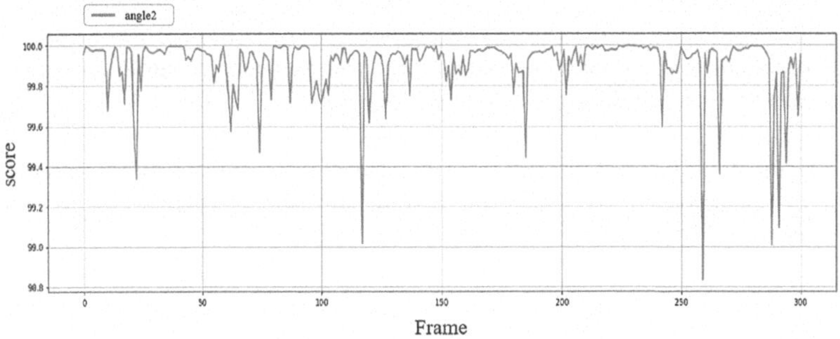

Fig. 5. The value of S_{angle} which represent the student's score of the Angle 2.

In order to make the users to directly get feedback, we use the visual label which represent the accuracy level of the student's actions. The feedback result is shown as follows:

The scoring system would score the trainee posture in each frames of the video. As shown in Fig. 6, we use the red bounding box to locate the trainee, then generating the

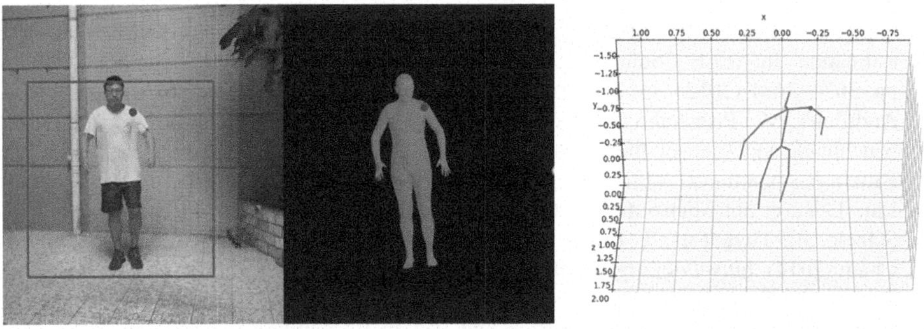

Fig. 6. The feedback information of the scoring system. Where the visual label point means the student's accuracy level of the Angle 2. If the $S_{angle} \geq 90$, the color of visual point would change to green; else, it would be red.

corresponding 3D model and extracting the joint points from the model. We score the accuracy level of the Angle 2 with a visual label spot. The color of the spot would be green if the $S_{angle} \geq 90$, else, it would be red.

6 Discussion and Conclusion

In this article, we demonstrate a fitness education and scoring system based on the improved VIBE, which can reconstruct 3D body posture and movement more coherently, and estimate the difference between the standard model learned from the coach and the trainee model. We propose an improved VIBE network for 3D human body reconstruction from a monocular camera. And by adding end limb constraints to the loss function of the 3D human body model, the jitter noise in continuous motion is reduced. Our method has achieved good performance results and successfully applied it to online fitness education. In addition, the research of 3D human pose estimation has important practical significance for other applications such as intelligent monitoring, medical rehabilitation, autonomous driving, and game animation.

Acknowledgements. The work described in this paper was supported by the Natural Science Foundation of Guangdong (Project no. 2017A030313362) and an internal funding (Project no. R202012) from United International College.

References

1. Yang, C., Xu, Y., Shi, J., Dai, B., Zhou, B.: Temporal pyramid network for action recognition. In: IEEE Conference on Computer Vision and Pattern Recognition (CVPR), pp. 588–597 (2020)
2. Mencarini, E., Rapp, A., Tirabeni, L., Zancanaro, M.: Designing wearable systems for sports: a review of trends and opportunities in human-computer interaction. IEEE Trans. Hum. Mach. Syst. **49**(4), 314–325 (2019)
3. Johnson, S., Everingham, M.: Clustered pose and nonlinear appearance models for human pose estimation. In: Proceedings of the British Machine Vision Conference (BMVC), pp. 12.1–12.11 (2010)
4. Sapp, B., Taskar, B.: MODEC: multimodal decomposable models for human pose estimation. In: IEEE Conference on Computer Vision and Pattern Recognition (CVPR), pp. 3674–3681 (2013)
5. Andriluka, M., Pishchulin, L., Gehler, P., Schiele, B.: 2D human pose estimation: new benchmark and state of the art analysis. In: IEEE Conference on Computer Vision and Pattern Recognition (CVPR), pp. 3686–3693 (2014)
6. Lin, T.-Y., et al.: Microsoft COCO: common objects in context. In: Fleet, D., Pajdla, T., Schiele, B., Tuytelaars, T. (eds.) ECCV 2014. LNCS, vol. 8693, pp. 740–755. Springer, Cham (2014). https://doi.org/10.1007/978-3-319-10602-1_48
7. Toshev, A., Szegedy, C.: DeepPose: human pose estimation via deep neural networks. In: IEEE Conference on Computer Vision and Pattern Recognition (CVPR), pp. 1653–1660 (2014)
8. Wei, S., Ramakrishna, V., Kanade, T., Sheikh, Y.: Convolutional pose machines. In: IEEE Conference on Computer Vision and Pattern Recognition (CVPR), pp. 4724–4732 (2016)

9. Chen, Y., Wang, Z., Peng, Y., Zhang, Z., Yu, G., Sun, J.: Cascaded pyramid network for multi-person pose estimation. In: IEEE Conference on Computer Vision and Pattern Recognition (CVPR), pp. 7103–7112 (2018)
10. Insafutdinov, E., Pishchulin, L., Andres, B., Andriluka, M., Schiele, B.: DeeperCut: a deeper, stronger, and faster multi-person pose estimation model. In: Leibe, B., Matas, J., Sebe, N., Welling, M. (eds.) ECCV 2016. LNCS, vol. 9910, pp. 34–50. Springer, Cham (2016). https://doi.org/10.1007/978-3-319-46466-4_3
11. Lowe, D.G.: Distinctive image features from scale-invariant keypoints. Int. J. Comput. Vision **60**(2), 91–110 (2004)
12. Dalal, N., Triggs, B.: Histograms of oriented gradients for human detection. In: IEEE Conference on Computer Vision and Pattern Recognition (CVPR), pp. 886–893 (2005)
13. Bogo, F., Kanazawa, A., Lassner, C., Gehler, P., Romero, J., Black, M.J.: Keep it SMPL: automatic estimation of 3D human pose and shape from a single image. In: Leibe, B., Matas, J., Sebe, N., Welling, M. (eds.) ECCV 2016. LNCS, vol. 9909, pp. 561–578. Springer, Cham (2016). https://doi.org/10.1007/978-3-319-46454-1_34
14. Moon, G., Chang, J.Y., Lee, K.M.: V2V-PoseNet: voxel-to-voxel prediction network for accurate 3D hand and human pose estimation from a single depth map. In: IEEE Conference on Computer Vision and Pattern Recognition (CVPR), pp. 5079–5088 (2018)
15. Güler, R.A., Neverova, N., Kokkinos, I.: DensePose: dense human pose estimation in the wild. In: IEEE Conference on Computer Vision and Pattern Recognition (CVPR), pp. 7297–7306 (2018)
16. Varol, G., et al.: BodyNet: volumetric inference of 3D human body shapes. In: Ferrari, V., Hebert, M., Sminchisescu, C., Weiss, Y. (eds.) ECCV 2018. LNCS, vol. 11211, pp. 20–38. Springer, Cham (2018). https://doi.org/10.1007/978-3-030-01234-2_2
17. Kocabas, M., Athanasiou, N., Black, M.J.: VIBE: video inference for human body pose and shape estimation. In: IEEE Conference on Computer Vision and Pattern Recognition (CVPR), pp. 5252–5262 (2020)
18. Goodfellow, I., et al.: Generative adversarial nets. In: Advances in Neural Information Processing Systems (NeurIPS), pp. 2672–2680 (2014)
19. Mahmood, N., Ghorbani, N., Troje, N., Pons-Moll, G., Black, M.J.: AMASS: archive of motion capture as surface shapes. In: IEEE/CVF International Conference on Computer Vision (ICCV), pp. 5441–5450 (2019)
20. Loper, M., Mahmood, N., Romero, J., Pons-Moll, G., Black, M.J.: SMPL: a skinned multi-person linear model. ACM Trans. Graph. **34**(6), 248 (2015)
21. Kanazawa, A., Zhang, J.Y., Felsen, P., Malik, J.: Learning 3D human dynamics from video. In: IEEE Conference on Computer Vision and Pattern Recognition (CVPR), pp. 5607–5616 (2019)

Threat Analysis of IoT Security Knowledge Graph Based on Confidence

Shuqin Zhang[1], Minzhi Zhang[1(✉)], Hong Li[2], and Guangyao Bai[1]

[1] College of Computer, Zhongyuan University of Technology, Zhengzhou, China
2019107117@zut.edu.cn

[2] Institute of Information Engineering, Chinese Academy of Sciences, Beijing, China

Abstract. The identification, analysis and application of vulnerabilities and weaknesses exposed after attacks on devices in the IoT security field are imminent. It is very important to combine the concepts of IoT security and knowledge graph to build the IoT security knowledge base and apply it to the defense and attack of IoT devices. From this we propose an ontology to build an IoT security knowledge graph. And it carries on the method of knowledge extraction and threat analysis. IoT security knowledge graph is extracted from several widely used knowledge databases and stored in the graph database. First, build the ontology of the IoT security field based on the five-tuple model. Secondly, natural language processing technique is used to process and analyze IoT security events. The extracted entity will be linked to the IoT security knowledge graph and added as new knowledge. Finally, based on the confidence, conduct horizontal reasoning and analysis on the IoT security knowledge graph. And present sample cases to demonstrate the practical usage of the method. Realize the gradual intelligence of threat analysis in the field of IoT security.

Keywords: IoT security · Ontology · Knowledge graph · Knowledge extraction · Threat analysis

1 Introduction

In recent years, with the rapid development of attacks on Internet of Things (IoT) equipment, the IoT security [1] is facing challenges. It is of great research value to obtain and manage a large number of high-quality IoT security data, which can enhance the security of IoT equipment.

IoT security field has many widely used knowledge bases [2], which are stored in structured and semi-structured forms. National Vulnerability Database (NVD), NVD is a high-quality vulnerability management database that provides information related to IoT security about software defects, product configuration and impact measurement. NVD links a series of vulnerability-related databases, including Common Vulnerabilities & Exposures (CVE), Common Weakness Enumeration (CWE), Common Platform Enumeration (CPE), Common Vulnerability Scoring System (CVSS), etc.

W. Jia et al. (Eds.): SETE 2021, LNCS 13089, pp. 254–264, 2021.
https://doi.org/10.1007/978-3-030-92836-0_22

NVD is a vulnerability database built on the CVE list and fully synchronized with CVE so that any updates to CVE can appear immediately in NVD. NVD links to other data sets such as CWE through CVE, for example, CWE links to databases such as Common Attack Pattern Enumeration and Classification (CAPEC). In addition, there are many unstructured data sources [3], such as IoT security-related blogs, hacking forums, security bulletins and security news. These information need to use Natural Language Processing (NLP) technology to obtain the key classes.

In order to manage network security data in a more intelligent way, we use knowledge graph [4] and try to store the data as knowledge. Knowledge graph can link the data from different sources together, which is what NVD does to other network security-related databases. Knowledge graph stores vulnerability objects, weakness objects, attack patterns, and product objects, which are linked by relationships defined in the ontology [5]. Threat analysis based on knowledge graph can be inferred and analyzed according to the stored knowledge. This function can help to mine some hidden rules in knowledge graph, which is difficult to do in traditional databases.

To achieve real-time information extraction and threat analysis. We propose a new model for threat analysis of ISKG, which mainly includes IoT security knowledge graph (ISKG), NLP part and threat analysis part. The combination of these parts forms a threat analysis of ISKG, which can be used as a knowledge base for many complex queries and correlation analysis. Our contributions are as follows:

- We propose a new model for integrating and analyzing databases in the IoT security domain.
- Extract information from the latest IoT security event descriptions for knowledge graph knowledge updates.
- Based on confidence, we propose a new perspective for lateral inference and threat analysis of IoT security knowledge graph.

2 Construction of IoT Security Knowledge Base

Based on the ontology modeling method of network security knowledge graph proposed by Li [6], we proposes a new model for constructing the IoT security knowledge base, as shown in Fig. 1.

Figure 1 shows the specific process of building the IoT security knowledge base. This process includes four parts. The first of which is to identify knowledge in the field of IoT security. Through the IoT security field experts to analyze the requirements for constructing ISKG, and research the data in the knowledge bases such as NVD, CVE and CWE. The second part is to build the IoT security ontology model. It includes defining entities, attributes and relationships. The third part is knowledge extraction [7]. Extract key classes from the latest IoT security reports. The fourth part is the threat analysis, and gradually build the IoT security knowledge base.

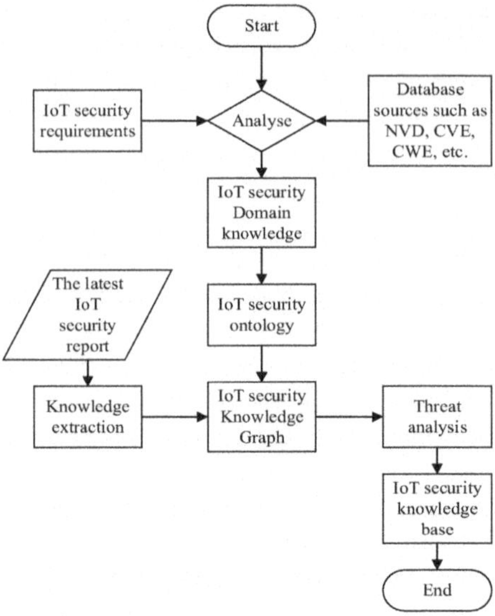

Fig. 1. Construction framework of IoT security knowledge base

2.1 IoT Security Ontology Model

We constructs the IoT security ontology based on the five-tuple model [8] proposed by Jia et al. Five-tuple model includes concepts, entities, entity attributes, relationships between entities and reasoning rules. Based on this, we construct the ISKG ontology from five dimensions of IoT devices, vulnerabilities, weaknesses, attackers, and attack patterns. Ontology construction uses the development tool protégé. The specific structure of ISKG ontology is shown in Fig. 2.

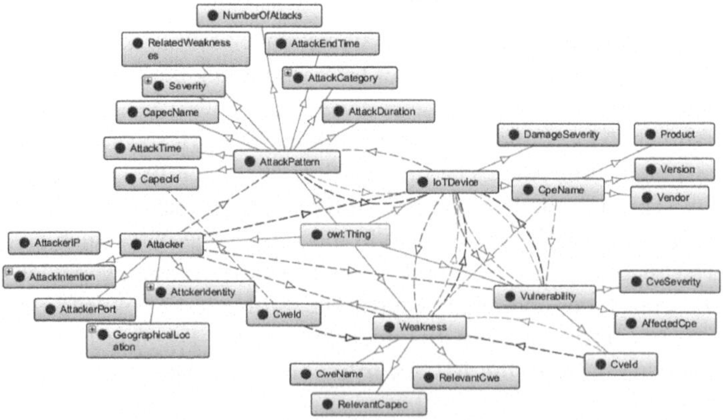

Fig. 2. The specific diagram of equipment safety ontology of the IoT.

In the IoT constructed security ontology, the main types of inter-class relationships are HasVulnerability, Affect, HasWeakness, Attack, RelatedCwe, RelatedCapec, etc. Figure 3 describes the main relationships of classes.

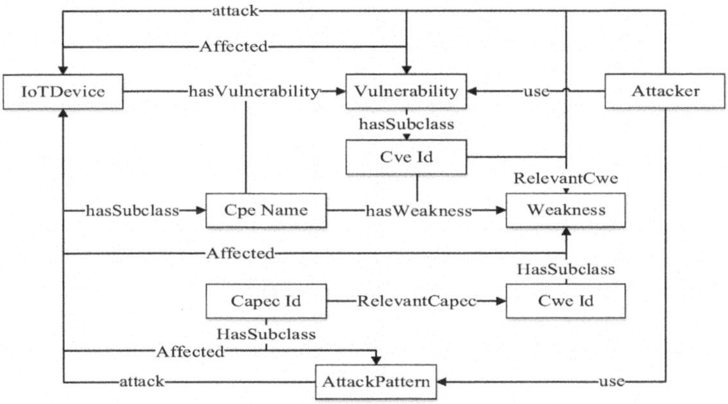

Fig. 3. Relationship between classes

Among them, IoTDevice uses CPE to describe its attacked product and version. Vulnerability is mainly described by CVE and CVSS, Weakness is mainly described by CWE. Attack pattern is mainly described by CAPEC. And NVD links CPE, CVE, CWE, and CVSS. CVE and CWE are related to each other. CAPEC is related to some CWE.

2.2 Extract Entities from the Latest Security Incidents

The source websites of IoT security include Vulhub and FreeBuf, which described in natural language text, and can only be applied to knowledge updating and threat analysis after learning and understanding, with low efficiency. Therefore, we use the model BiLSTM CRF in Named Entity Recognition (NER) [9] to achieve the function of extracting entities from real-time updated security events, which is one of the most advanced methods for performing NER tasks in the network security field.

The complete identification process is shown in Fig. 4. First, preprocess the input text, and input it into the BiLSTM-CRF model for training. Then, when the model is trained, the test prediction is used for testing. Finally, we output the annotation result of the text sequence that is the ontology corresponding entity we extracted. We will show a security event description on the left side of Fig. 5, and the corresponding identification results as shown on the right side of Fig. 5.

NER can automatically analyze and process the latest security incident descriptions. We use the NER results for entity alignment and updating of ISKG. We believe that NER may identify new entity instances. If we identify new entity instances, we can create a new entity object instance update to ISKG. We identify entities through IoT

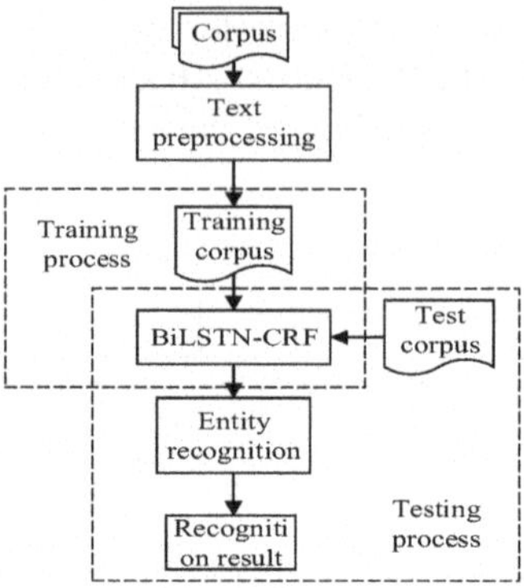

Fig. 4. The framework of the named entity recognition model for IoT security

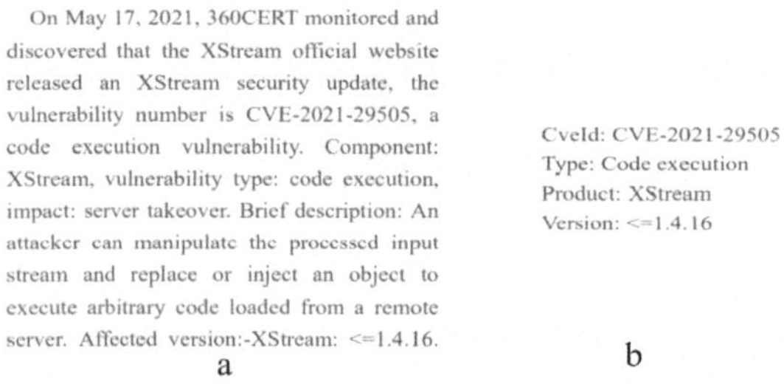

Fig. 5. Example of the security event description. (a); Sample of recognition results. (b)

security events to obtain new data, entities and instances of ISKG. Continuously update and perfect ISKG knowledge.

3 ISKG Threat Analysis Based on Confidence

3.1 Generation and Aggregation of CVE Chains

The threat analysis of ISKG is based on confidence [10]. ISKG is stored through Neo4j, which is a widely used graph database. ISKG integrates NVD, CVE, CWE, CVSS, CAPEC and other knowledge bases through Neo4j, stores hundreds of thousands of data updated to December 2020. In this section, we mainly explore the relationship between vulnerabilities, and thus define the ISKG threat analysis problem and give the evaluation method.

Based on ISKG, we define the threat analysis task: mining and analyzing the hidden vulnerability chain, namely CVE Chain. And Aggregate product-related vulnerability chains. Vulnerability chains are two or more independent sequences that are closely related to the product in ISKG. A vulnerability can create conditions for another vulnerability to occur or when two vulnerabilities are highly correlated, the two vulnerabilities have hidden chain relationships.

The definition satisfying the generation and aggregation of *CVEChain* concept [11] is: *CVEChain* represents the object type that can be operated by the operator defined below, which contains *st* and *num*, *st* representing the active state that can generate *CVEChain*; *num* represents the number of vulnerabilities in *CVEChain* that are linked to Product by CVE. *ChainSet* represents the aggregation of *CVEChain*.

Definition of relations: The combination of relations can be EXIST and INTERSECT, we use operators $\exists$ and $\wedge$ respectively. Calculation flow conditions for *CVEChain* and *ChainSet*: We mark $A = CVEa \exists Product$, $B = \mathrm{CVEb} \exists Product$, $C = CVEa \wedge CVEb$. Marker $D = CVEChain \exists ChainSet$, $E = CVEChain_i \wedge CVEChain_j$. Here, we represent *CVEa*, *CVEb*, *Product*, $CVEChain_i$, $ChainSet_j$, *CVEChain* and *ChainSet* as *Va*, *Vb*, *Pr*, Cv_i, Cv_j, *Cv* and *CS* respectively. We can define the calculation process of *CVEChain* and *ChainSet* as follows:

$$
\begin{aligned}
&Va.st = \begin{cases} True\ if\ Va.st\&\&Vb.st \\ False\ otherwise \end{cases} \\
&Va.num = \begin{cases} Va.num\ if\ Va.st\&\&(Va\&\&Pr) \\ +\infty\ otherwise \end{cases} \\
&Vb.st - \begin{cases} True\ if\ Va.st\&\&Vb.st \\ False\ otherwise \end{cases} \\
&Va.num = \begin{cases} Vb.num\ if\ Vb.st\&\&(Vb\&\&Pr) \\ +\infty\ otherwise \end{cases} \\
&c.st = \begin{cases} Ture\ if\ Va.st\&\&Vb.st\&\&[(Va\&\&\mathrm{Vb})\&\&Pr] \\ False\ otherwise \end{cases} \\
&c.num = \begin{cases} num(Va, Vb)\ if\ Va.st\&\&Vb.st\&\&[(Va\&\&\mathrm{Vb})\&\&Pr] \\ +\infty\ otherwise \end{cases} \\
&A = \{Va\}, B = \{Vb\}, C = \{Va\} \cap \{Vb\} = \{Vc\} \\
&D = \bigcup_{\substack{Va \in Cv \\ Vb \in Cv}} Va \cup Vb = (Va\ Vb), E = \bigcup_{\substack{Cv_i \in CS \\ Cv_j \in CS}} Cv_i \cup Cv_j
\end{aligned} \tag{1}
$$

In the process of ISKG threat analysis under the above conditions, the key of chain mining is CVE chain confidence (*Ccve*). The chain confidence calculates the conditional probability of a pair of vulnerabilities in the same product, which is used to identify the sequence results of *Cv*. We identify the relevant indicators in *Ccve* by setting thresholds. CVE Chain confidence is formally defined as:

$$C_{cve} = \left(\frac{P_{Vab}}{P_{Va}} + \frac{P_{Vab}}{P_{Vb}}\right)/2 \tag{2}$$

Where P_{Va} is the number of *Product* with specific vulnerabilities as *CVEa*. P_{Vb} is the number of *Product* with specific vulnerabilities as *CVEb*. And P_{Vab} is the number of products with specific vulnerabilities as *CVEa* and *CVEb*. *Ccve* represents the confidence value of *Cv*.

Table 1. Correlation of CVE chain under different thresholds

P_{Va}	P_{Vb}	P_{Vab}	Ccve	(CVEa CVEb) correlation
50	50	50	0.1	Low
100	100	100	0.2	Middle
150	150	150	0.3	High
200	200	200	0.4	Higher

Ccve represents the hidden correlation between vulnerabilities and products. We calculate Ccve based on the data in ISKG, and set thresholds for PVa, PVb, PVab and Ccve. When analyzing and exploring the CVE chain, the correlation frequency between vulnerabilities and products should be high enough, and our chain confidence Ccve reflects the strength of this correlation from a statistical point of view. We set different thresholds for the number of vulnerabilities and products in the ISKG threat analysis function, as shown in Table 1.

After repeated experiments, we obtained the appropriate threshold. We finally set the threshold of ISKG threat analysis as PVa (100), PVb (100), PVab (100) and Ccve (0.2). If the index exceeds the threshold, the chain candidate is determined as the mining result. Identifying the sequence results of the CVE chain through the threshold can help security experts to detect the set of vulnerabilities and related vulnerabilities involved in the products in the Internet of Things security, and provide new ideas for malicious software in the Internet of Things security to use vulnerabilities to attack the threat event analysis of products.

3.2 Case Study of CVE Chain Exploration and Aggregation

In this section, we demonstrate the identification process of the sample vulnerability chain: (CVE-2020-0543 CVE-2020-0548), which is a result sequence of *Cv*. Product and vulnerability threat analysis based on ISKG. The first step to identify the CVE chain is to determine the strong correlation of the unidentified sample CVE chain according to the threshold. The second step is to query in ISKG to calculate *Ccve*. Finally, to show the vulnerability description query in ISKG to verify the correctness of the results identified in example *Cv*.

We first query CVE and CPE that exceed the preset thresholds of these three parameters. The Cypher query is shown in Fig. 6.

```
MATCH (a:Cve)-[:REL_SOFT]->(p:Cpe)<-[:REL_SOFT]-(b:Cve)
where id(a)<id(b) with a,b,collect(p) as numcpe where size(numcpe)>100
return a.id as cveId_a, b.id as cveId_b,size(numcpe) as num_cpe
```

Fig. 6. Cypher query with threshold 100 in ISKG

A total of 23817 records are queried in Fig. 7, and only part is displayed here. We can find that the vulnerabilities between the CVE chains in the graph have a high coincidence. We can get a vulnerability set of certain products from the same vulnerability. A vulnerability (CVE-2020-0543 CVE-2020-0548 CVE-2020-0549 CVE-2020-0550 CVE-2020-0551 CVE-2020-0529 CVE-2020-0528) involved in aggregating a product or a type of product.

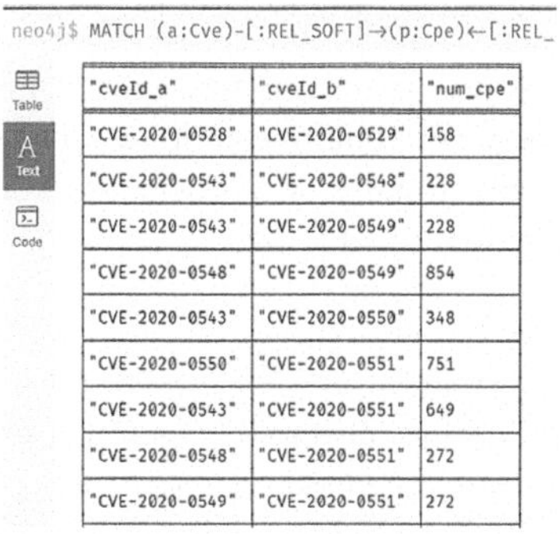
neo4j$ MATCH (a:Cve)-[:REL_SOFT]→(p:Cpe)←[:REL_

"cveId_a"	"cveId_b"	"num_cpe"
"CVE-2020-0528"	"CVE-2020-0529"	158
"CVE-2020-0543"	"CVE-2020-0548"	228
"CVE-2020-0543"	"CVE-2020-0549"	228
"CVE-2020-0548"	"CVE-2020-0549"	854
"CVE-2020-0543"	"CVE-2020-0550"	348
"CVE-2020-0550"	"CVE-2020-0551"	751
"CVE-2020-0543"	"CVE-2020-0551"	649
"CVE-2020-0548"	"CVE-2020-0551"	272
"CVE-2020-0549"	"CVE-2020-0551"	272

Fig. 7. Visualization of Cypher query results

Then query the P_{Vab} of sample Cv. According to the definition, the P_{Vab} of the sample chain is the number of products with vulnerabilities CVE-2020-0543 and CVE-2020-0548 at the same time. The Cypher query of P_{Vab} is shown in Fig. 8.

```
MATCH (a:Cve{id:"CVE-2020-0543"})--(b:Cpe)--(c:Cve{id:"CVE-2020-0548"}) return a,b,c
```

Fig. 8. Cypher query to calculate the number of P_{Vab} in ISKG

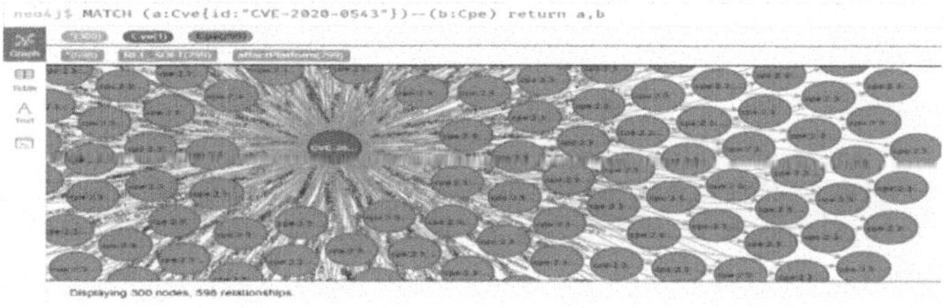

Fig. 9. Visualization of Cypher query results

The query shows 230 nodes, 912 relationships, and the results in Fig. 9 are shown only. From the query results visualization, we count the number of CPE objects linked to two CVE nodes as PVab of the sample chain. Next, we use the query results to calculate Ccve. After obtaining the indicators of chain reasoning. We compare them with the preset threshold. The statistical results with threshold are shown in Table 2.

Table 2. Statistical results of CVE sample chain with threshold

	CVEa	P_{Va}	*CVEb*	P_{Vb}	P_{Vab}	*Ccve*
Sample chain	CVE-2020-0543	674	CVE-2020-0548	854	228	0.302628
Threshold		150		150	150	0.3

As shown in Table 2, the reasoning indexes exceed the threshold. Therefore, the sample chain is mined as a CWE chain candidate. Try to determine whether the candidate is a real CWE chain. Finally, we verify the candidate of CVE chain and query the sample chain, as shown in Fig. 10.

```
MATCH (a:Cve)-[:REL_SOFT]->(p:Cpe)<-[:REL_SOFT]-(b:Cve) where id(a)<id(b) with a,b,collect(p) as numcpe
where size(numcpe)>100 return a.id as cveld_a, a.description as description_a,
b.id as cveld_b, b.description as description_b, size(numcpe) as num_cpe
```

Fig. 10. Cypher query of CVE chain and related sample chain set in ISKG

The vulnerability description of CVE-2020-0543 and CVE-2020-0548 is shown in Fig. 11. A total of 67200 records are queried, and only part is displayed here. We can find from the query that the correlation between vulnerability descriptions in our vulnerability chain is very high, so the logic behind the sample candidate chain is reasonable.

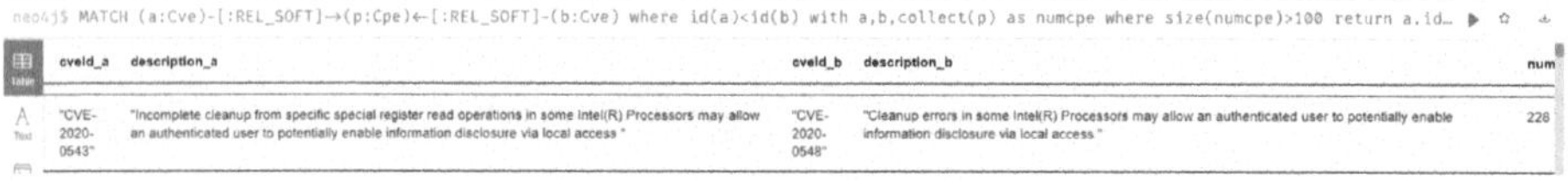

Fig. 11. Visualization of Cypher query results.

Table 3 compares ISKG with other network security domain ontology, knowledge graph threat analysis content of different focuses. ISKG focuses on the threat analysis on the entity class corresponding to the devices and vulnerabilities of the IoT and expands the association on a series of related information between the threatened devices and vulnerabilities, namely, the association of weaknesses, attackers, and attack modes through the integrated knowledge graph. ISKG associates knowledge bases such as NVD, CVE, CWE, and CPE through the contents in Table 3. Through the vertical correlation between these existing knowledge bases, horizontal reasoning and analysis are carried out based on confidence, which enhances the relevance and integrity of the IoT security field.

Table 3. Comparison of the focus of the threat analysis work between the ontology and the knowledge graph

Heading level	(IoT) Device	Vulnerability	Weakness	Attacker	AttackPattern
VulKG [10]	√		√		
[4]	√	√			√
CSKG [11]	√	√			√
CSKB [12]	√				√
ISKG	√	√	√	√	√

4 Summary

The IoT security ontology and knowledge graph are constructed based on the IoT equipment security in the paper, and are updated and improved through knowledge extraction and other technologies. Then, we propose a knowledge graph threat analysis method based on confidence, which expands the correlation between knowledge bases such as NVD, CVE, CWE and CPE, supplements the new chain of hidden relations in the IoT security. The future work we will continue to dig deeper into the threat information related to the IoT security. We will try to use deep learning and other methods for more complex information mining and reasoning analysis.

References

1. Mozzaquatro, B., Agostinho, C., Goncalves, D.: An ontology-based cybersecurity framework for the internet of things. Sensors **18**(9), 3053 (2018)
2. Hemberg, E., Kelly, J., Shlapentokh-Rothman, M.: BRON – linking attack tactics, techniques, and patterns with defensive weaknesses, vulnerabilities and affected platform configurations (2020)
3. Tao, L., Yuanbo, G., Ankang, J.: Triple extraction of network security knowledge based on fusion against active learning. J. Commun. **41**(10), 80–91 (2020)
4. Yan, J., Yulu, Q., Huaijun, S.: A practical approach to constructing a knowledge graph for cybersecurity. Engineering **4**(1), 53–60 (2018)
5. Zhu, L., Zhang, Z., Xia, G.: Research on vulnerability ontology model. In: ITAIC 2019, Chongqing, China, pp. 657–661 (2019)
6. Zhengjun, L., Zhi, S., Jianfeng, C.: STIX-based network security knowledge graph ontology modeling method, pp. 152–157 (2020)
7. Jiayi, P., Yong, F., Cheng, H.: Research on named entity recognition in the information security field based on deep active learning. J. Sichuan Univ. **56**(03), 457–462 (2019)
8. Yan, J., Yulu, Q., Huaijun, S.: A practical approach to constructing a knowledge graph for cybersecurity. J. Eng. **4**(1), 53–60 (2018)
9. Jiang, Y., Zhao, T., Chai, Y., Gao, P.: Bidirectional LSTM-CRF models for keyword extraction in Chinese sport news, vol. 11430, pp. 114300H–114300H-7 (2020)
10. Qin, S., Chow, K.P.: Automatic analysis and reasoning based on vulnerability knowledge graph. In: Ning, H. (ed.) CyberDI/CyberLife -2019. CCIS, vol. 1137, pp. 3–19. Springer, Singapore (2019). https://doi.org/10.1007/978-981-15-1922-2_1

11. Yulu, Q., Rong, J., Yan, J.: Attack analysis framework for cyber-attack and defense test platform. Electronics **9**(9), 1413 (2020)
12. Li, K., Zhou, H., Tu, Z., Feng, B.: CSKB: a cyber security knowledge base based on knowledge graph. In: Yu, S., Mueller, P., Qian, J. (eds.) SPDE 2020. CCIS, vol. 1268, pp. 100–113. Springer, Singapore (2020). https://doi.org/10.1007/978-981-15-9129-7_8

Adaptive Learning, Emotion and Behaviour Recognition and Understanding in Education

Adversarial Training Leaded Robust MRC Method

Bo Sun[1,2], Hang Li[2(✉)], Rong Zhong[1], Mengqi Zhao[1], Hao Liang[1], Xiaoqi Jiang[1], Yongkang Xiao[2(✉)], Rong Xiao[2], Yinghui Zhang[1], Jun He[1,2], and Peidi Gu[1]

[1] College of Education for the Future, Beijing Normal University at Zhuhai, No. 18, Jinfeng Road, Tangjiawan, Zhuhai 519087, Guangdong Province, People's Republic of China

[2] School of Artificial Intelligence, Beijing Normal University, No. 19, Xinjiekouwai St., Haidian District 100875, Beijing, People's Republic of China

202021210041@mail.bnu.edu.cn, xiaoyk@bnu.edu.cn

Abstract. Machine Reading Comprehension (MRC) is one of the basic tasks in Natural Language Processing, which can be used to test the ability of natural language comprehension of a model. Several models and methods have succeeded in MRC, but they are seldom robust enough, which makes them work ill in the real-world question and answering tasks filled up with noises and confusions. To tackle with that, we propose a model based on pretrained Chinese-MacBERT-Large. In order to get enough robustness, we apply two adversarial methods, i.e. FGM & VAT in training process. The experiments on DuReader_robust show that our model outperforms the baseline based on Chinese-MacBERT-Base without adversarial methods, which means our model is more stable to noises and confusions.

Keywords: Machine reading comprehension · Robustness · Adversarial training

1 Introduction

MRC is one of the most basic NLP tasks, which aims at mining processors' ability to automatically answer questions based on specific natural language contexts. According to the form of the answers, MRC tasks can be classified into four clusters: Cloze, Multiple Choice, Span Extraction and Free Answering [1]. For flexible and easy understanding, we choose Span Extraction, whose definition is shown as Definition 1. It may contain more noises and confusions than Cloze and Multiple Choice, but less distracting than Free Answering, since it doesn't need the model to re-construct the answer sentences. Note that, although many datasets and real-world tasks are all answerable, the unanswerable option is still available in the definition for general.

Supported by the National Natural Science Foundation of China (Grant No. 62077009, 62177006).

W. Jia et al. (Eds.): SETE 2021, LNCS 13089, pp. 267–277, 2021.
https://doi.org/10.1007/978-3-030-92836-0_23

Definition 1. *Span Extraction Task: Given a natural language text pair (C, Q), in which C refers to context and Q refers to question. Take a substring of C as the answer if Q is answerable according to C, or classify Q as unanswerable.*

Span Extraction MRC is a traditional task, and several datasets, models and methods have been proposed for its study [1]. Since most of them only focus on the ideal natural language comprehension, ignoring the noises (typing mistakes, informal abbreviations e.g.) and confusions (similar but irrelevant sentences e.g.), which are inevitable in the real-world question and answering scene. In this paper, we mainly focus on improving the model's ability under the real-world MRC datasets.

Generally, most researches take Span Extraction as three classification tasks, which are answerable prediction, start position prediction and end position prediction. Answerable prediction gives the probability of whether a question is answerable under a specific context. Start position prediction works out the probability of each token in the context whether it is the span start position. End position prediction is similar to start position prediction. Based on that framework, we use Chinese-MacBERT-Large [2] with some additional layers to generate the three probability distributions for more general ability of natural language comprehension. To make the model more robustness, we use two adversarial training methods, i.e. FGM and VAT in training process.

In Summary, the main contributions of our work are concluded as follows:

- We take Chinese-MacBERT-Large as our backbone to get sufficient capacity to tackle with the noises and confusions in the real-world MRC tasks.
- We use both FGM and VAT method to make the model more robust, and alleviate the overfitting problem.

2 Related Work

2.1 Machine Reading Comprehension

As one of the basic tasks, MRC has been widely researched even before the emergence of neural networks. The earliest MRC research is QUALM QA system developed by Lehnert et al. in 1970s. However, limited by the low technical level of that time, the system cannot work well.

After the generation of deep learning, researchers have tried many models based on recurrent layers (LSTM, GRU e.g.) and attention layers (self-attention e.g.). Huang et al. proposed a model called FlowQA [3], which used attention method to fuse the information in the contexts and the questions, and used the BiLSTM layers to process the matrix along both row and column directions. Xiong et al. proposed DCN+ [4], which included BiLSTM and CoAttention modules.

BERT, released in 2018, has made a qualitative leap in natural language processing model [5]. Nowadays, most of the newest NLP models has tried to take BERT-like models as their backbone, adding some task specific layers and outer knowledge, and some of them have reached considerable performances.

Zhang et al. proposed SG-Net [6], using BERT as the backbone and taking grammatical dependency relationship into the model by masking the attentions according to the grammatical dependency tree. Ding et al. used BERT to guide a "multi hop" system to provide open domain QA based on Wiki database [7].

2.2 Pretrained Models

To take the advantage of large corpus and the capability of large models, experts have constructed many pre-trained models. Having been trained on general corpuses with auxiliary tasks, they can be fine-tuned on different task-specific datasets.

BERT, proposed by Google in 2018, is the most successful pre-trained model so far. Based on the encoder of transformer [8], it is pre-trained with MLM (Masked Language Model) task and NSP (Next Sentence Prediction) task. The former aims at predicting the correct token by masking the input sequence, and the latter aims at figuring out whether two sentences are in the correct order [5]. Even so, BERT still has some weakness. RoBERTa uses dynamic masking technology to introduce more randomness into the training set to get a promotion in performance [9]. MacBERT uses correction task instead of the original MLM task to shorten the difference between training and fine-tuning [2]. Transformer-XL and XLNet remove the limitation of max length in BERT by using recurrent connections [10,11].

2.3 Adversarial Training

Adversarial training (AT) is a group of training methods based on adversarial samples, which are created by adding non-random perturbation on the original samples. They can indicate the model performance degradation much [12]. It is because the model is not robust enough. The main thought of AT is to train a model with adversarial samples so that a small input perturbation should not change the result of its output. According to that, researchers have proposed a lot of AT algorithms.

Goodfellow et al. proposed FGM, which was based on the loss gradient on the input samples [13]. The perturbation is in the direction of loss gradient, which makes the model's performance drop most significantly. Thus, the model will be trained with those created samples. FGSM uses Max normalization instead of L2 normalization [14]. For unsupervised learning, or samples without ground truth, Virtual Adversarial Training firstly adds random perturbation on the original samples to train two models with original samples and perturbed ones respectively, between whom the KL divergence can be calculated, and then the derivative of the KL divergence is taken to form the gradient on the embedding, finally the embedding is disturbed [15].

Note that, because the natural language token sequences are always sparse high-dimensional, which makes direct perturbations to the input is inappropriate, Miyato et al. suggested making such perturbations to the embedding layers rather than the original inputs [13]. Our work follows that suggestion.

3 Proposed Method

3.1 Whole Training Algorithm

Our work is a Span Extraction MRC model based on Chinese-MacBERT-Large. To optimize the model for the noise and confusion in the real scene, we apply the original gradient-based optimization algorithm and two adversarial training algorithms (FGM and VAT). Those three optimization algorithms are processed one after another.

3.2 Model Structure

Our model takes pretrained Chinese-MacBERT-Large as the backbone, using single linear layer as the classifier. The structure of the model is shown in Fig. 1.

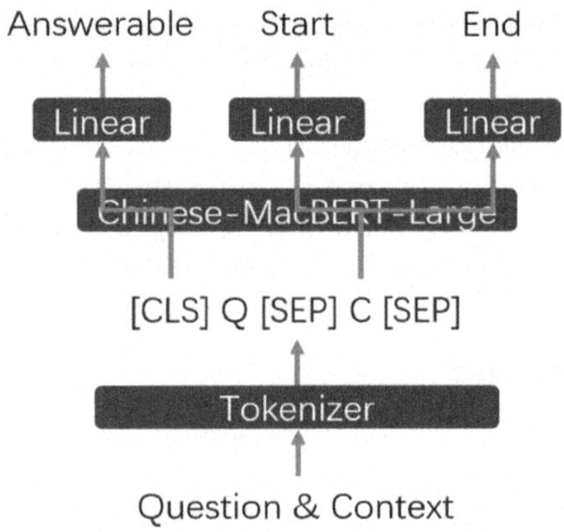

Fig. 1. Model structure

Here we take one sample as an example. Firstly, we use the tokenizer of Chinese-MacBERT-Large to get the token sequences of context (C) and question (Q), and concatenate them into the form of "[CLS] Q [SEP] C [SEP]", in which "[CLS]" and "[SEP]" are both special tokens required by BERT-like models. Those sequences are the input of the Chinese-MacBERT-Large model. Assume that the length of C is m, the length of Q is n and the dimension of the hidden state is d, the last hidden state should be a real matrix in the shape of $(3+m+n) \times d$, as is shown in Eq. (1).

$$Output = MacBERT([CLS]Q[SEP]C[SEP]) \in R^{(3+m+n)\times d} \quad (1)$$

Secondly, this matrix is separated into two parts: the hidden state of "[CLS]" and the hidden state of C.

$$ClassHiddenState = Output[0] \in R^{d} \quad (2)$$

$$ContextHiddenState = Output[2+n:2+n+m] \in R^{(m \times d)} \tag{3}$$

Thirdly, the $ClassHiddenState$ will be fed into a classifier to predict whether the question is answerable ($IsAnswerable$), while the $ContextHiddenState$ will be fed into two classifiers to get the probability distribution of the start position ($SpanStartPosition$) and the end position ($SpanEndPosition$) of the answer span. The formula is shown below. In which, $Linear$ refers to linear layer, which can transform a matrix into a vector, and $Softmax$ refers to softmax function, which transform a real vector into a probability distribution.

$$IsAnswerable = Softmax(Linear(ClassHiddenState)) \in R^2 \tag{4}$$

$$SpanStartPosition = Softmax(Linear(ContextHiddenState)) \in R^m \tag{5}$$

$$SpanEndPosition = Softmax(Linear(ContextHiddenState)) \in R^m \tag{6}$$

3.3 FGM Algorithm

FGM is one of the supervised adversarial training methods. It assumes that any small perturbation should not change the ground truth of the input. As is discussed before, the perturbation is not added directly on the input tokens but on the embedding layer.

To make it more efficient, FGM do not make completely random perturbation. The perturbation is a small step in the direction of the gradient of the embedding layer, which is produced in backward process. The loss function here is the cross-entropy between the model output and the ground truth.

In practice, we firstly get the model output with a sample, and then compute the cross-entropy loss between the output and its ground truth, as shown below. Where $Model$ refers to the model in our work, and the subscript of $Model$ refers to the embedding layer it uses. $CrossEntropyLoss$ refers to the cross-entropy loss function.

$$\hat{y} = Model_E(x) \tag{7}$$

$$Loss = CrossEntropyLoss(y, \hat{y}) \tag{8}$$

Secondly, we do backward to compute the embedding layer's gradient. Where ∇_E refers to computing the gradient of the embedding layer.

$$GE = \nabla_E Loss \tag{9}$$

Thirdly, we add a perturbation to the original embedding layer based on its gradient. In which ε is a hyperparameter which controls the strength of FGM. $\|GE\|_2$ is the level-2 normalization of GE.

$$E' = E + \varepsilon \times \frac{GE}{\|GE\|_2} \tag{10}$$

Fourthly, we re-compute the model's loss.

$$\hat{y}' = Model_{E'}(x) \tag{11}$$

$$Loss' = CrossEntropyLoss(y, \hat{y}') \tag{12}$$

Finally, optimize the model parameters to get a lower loss. In which *Optim* refers to the optimizer used in the experiments. Note that, the embedding layer is not optimized in FGM process.

$$Optim(Model_E, Loss') \tag{13}$$

The pseudo-code is shown as Fig. 2.

input : Sample: (x, y)
$\hat{y} = Model\,(x)$;
$loss = CrossEntropyLoss\,(\hat{y}, y)$;
$loss.backward()$;
$GE = Model.embedding.gradient$;
$OE = Model.embedding.data$;
$Model.embedding.data+ = \varepsilon \times \frac{GE}{\|GE\|_2}$;
$zero\_gradient()$;
$\hat{y}' = Model\,(x)$;
$loss' = CrossEntropyLoss\,(\hat{y}', y)$;
$loss'.backward()$;
$Optim(Model)$;
$Model.embedding.data = OE$;
$zero\_gradient()$;

Fig. 2. FGM algorithm

3.4 VAT Algorithm

VAT can be used in both supervised and unsupervised situations. The basic assumption is that any perturbations should not change the output of the model. Unlike FGM, it does not assume that there is ground truth.

In practice, we firstly get two outputs of a sample, one of which is from the original model while the other is from a perturbed model. The perturbation here is just adding a random matrix to the embedding layer. Where $u = \mathcal{N}(0, 1)$ means that u is a normal random matrix who has the same shape with E.

$$\hat{y} = Model_E(x) \tag{14}$$

$$u = \mathcal{N}(0, 1) \tag{15}$$

$$E' = E + u \tag{16}$$

$$\hat{y}' = Model_{E'}(x) \tag{17}$$

Secondly, we compute the KL-divergence between the two outputs. Where $KL-Divergence$ refers to the function of KL-divergence, which measures the distance between two probability distributions.

$$KL_1 = KL - Divergence(\hat{y}, \hat{y}') \tag{18}$$

We thirdly compute the gradient of the perturbed embedding layer, and add a new gradient-based perturbation to the embedding layer to create a perturbed embedding layer. The purpose is to make the KL-divergence higher. Here μ is a hyperparameter controlling the strength of VAT, which is different from ε.

$$E'' = E' + \mu \times \frac{\nabla_{E'} KL_1}{\|\nabla'_E KL_1\|_2} \tag{19}$$

Finally, we re-compute the KL-divergence between the output of the original model and the model with perturbed embedding layer, so that apply an optimizer to lower the KL-divergence.

$$\hat{y}'' = Model_{E''}(x) \tag{20}$$

$$KL_2 = KL - Divergence(\hat{y}, \hat{y}'') \tag{21}$$

$$Optim(Model_E, KL_2) \tag{22}$$

Note that, the gradients of all outputs of the original model are not computed. They are seen as constants in the process.

The pseudo-code of the algorithm is shown as Fig. 3.

4 Experiment

4.1 Dataset

We use DuReader_robust [16] provided by Baidu as the experiment dataset. This dataset is mainly aimed at testing the robustness of MRC model, so it is filled up with noises and confusions.

There are three data files in DuReader_robust, and only "train" and "dev" contains ground truth, so the experiments are all conducted on the "train" subset and the "dev" subset. To be precise, the models are all trained on "train" subset, and the data shown in the tables below are the test results on "dev" subset.

Note that, there are no unanswerable questions in the original DuReader_robust dataset. To maintain the flexibility of the model, we still retain the "unanswerable" option in the model. Since there is a max length setting in BERT, an input should be cut if it is too long. If the cut point is inside the answer span, we simply set the specific input as unanswerable, which is reasonable.

input : Sample: x
$\hat{y} = Model\,(x)$;
$OE = Model.embedding.data$;
$Model.embedding.data+ = \mathcal{N}\,(0, 1)$;
$\hat{y}' = Model(x)$;
$KL_1 = KL - Divergence\,(\hat{y}, \hat{y}')$;
$KL_1.backward()$;
$GE = Model.embedding.gradient$;
$Model.embedding.data+ = \mu \times \frac{GE}{\|GE\|_2}$;
$zero\_gradient()$;
$\hat{y}'' = Model\,(x)$;
$KL_2 = KL - Divergence\,(\hat{y}, \hat{y}'')$;
$KL_2.backward()$;
$Optim(Model)$;
$Model.embedding.data = OE$;
$zero\_gradient()$;

Fig. 3. VAT algorithm

4.2 Settings

In this experiment, we use a Tesla V100. The code are in Python and the main framework is PyTorch. We choice 16 as the batch size. The pre-trained model is Chinese-MacBERT-Large provided by HuggingFace [2]. The max input length is set to 256 and the max answer length is set to 128. The learning rate for linear classifier layer is 1e−4, and the fine-tune learning rate for pre-trained model is 1e−5. We take AdamW as the optimizer, whose weight decay is set as 1e-3. We set early stop epoch to 5, which means when the model cannot get better result in 5 epochs, the training process will stop automatically. The strengths of FGM and VAT are different in the experiments, therefor, they are specified in the next subsection. We set a threshold to 0.7, which means that the model will give "no answer" as the output if the confidence of answerable is lower than 0.7.

4.3 Results

The best results of our method and the baseline method is shown as Table 1. The baseline method is based on Chinese-MacBERT-Base and trained without any adversarial strategy. In this part, the strengths of FGM and VAT in our work are both 6.0.

In Table 1, F1 refers to F1-Score and EM refers to Exact Match, which are both common evaluating indicators in MRC tasks. The Epoch column shows the epochs when the specific methods reach the convergency. The experiment results suggest that our method can not only get a better score, but also converge much more faster than the baseline.

Table 1. The best results

Method	F1	EM	Epoch
Baseline	79.01	57.73	14
Ours	**82.79**	**63.73**	**2**

Secondly, we conduct ablation experiments to explore the impact of the larger pretrained model and training algorithms. The results comparation is shown in Table 2. In this part, the strengths of FGM and VAT are both 6.0.

Table 2. The ablation experiments results

Method	F1	EM	Epoch
Baseline	79.01	57.73	14
Large	81.05	60.69	5
Large+FGM	80.28	60.13	4
Large+VAT	80.88	60.90	3
Ours(Large+FGM+VAT)	**82.79**	**63.73**	**2**

In Table 2, Large refers to using Chinese-MacBERT-Large model instead of Chinese-MacBERT-Base model. It shows that using a larger pretrained model is very helpful in promoting the performance. Also, there is an interesting phenomenon: although using either FGM or VAT can cause performance degradation, using both FGM and VAT together can cause a promotion. That maybe because the targets of FGM and VAT is different and complemental. When facing a perturbation, FGM tries to predict correctly, while VAT tries to predict similarly.

To evaluate the robustness of our method more clearly, we also conduct another experiment only using 10% of the training set. The results in Table 3 shows that our work can still get a very high score and a very fast convergency speed when the training dataset is as small as the testing dataset. In this part, the strengths of VAT and FGM are set to 2.0.

Table 3. The results on sampled data

Method	F1	EM	Epoch
Baseline	73.19	51.52	13
Ours	**79.06**	**56.18**	**2**

Table 4 shows that the best strengths of FGM and VAT maybe different according to datasets, that is why we choose different strengths in different experiments. In which Whole refers to using the whole training set, and Sampled refers to using just 10% of the training set.

Table 4. The results of different datasets and strength

	FGM = 2.0, VAT=2.0	FGM = 6.0, VAT = 6.0
Whole	81.62	**82.79**
Sampled	**79.06**	76.68

5 Conclusion

In the real world, question and answering tasks always contain noises and confusions. In this paper, we use Chinese-MacBERT-Large model and use FGM and VAT to train the model. The experiments show that these strategies is helpful to make the model more robust and get a higher F1-Score and EM on DuReader_robust dataset. Our work does not include outer knowledge to guide the model, which maybe a way to get an extra improvement.

Acknowledgment. We use the PyTorch version Baidu MRC competition baseline made by zhoujx4 on Github [17], add VAT to it and fix some bugs for it. DuReader_robust is an open dataset provided by Baidu, which can be easily downloaded from Github [18]. We also use some simple data pre-processing methods such as deleting some duplicate punctuations.

This work is supported by the National Natural Science Foundation of China (Grant No. 62077009, 62177006)

References

1. Liu, S., Zhang, X., Zhang, S., Wang, H., Zhang, W.: Neural machine reading comprehension: methods and trends. Appl. Sci. **9**(18), 3698 (2019)
2. Cui, Y., Che, W., Liu, T., Qin, B., Wang, S., Hu, G.: Revisiting pre-trained models for Chinese natural language processing. In: Proceedings of the 2020 Conference on Empirical Methods in Natural Language Processing: Findings, pp. 657–668. Association for Computational Linguistics (2020)
3. Huang, H.-Y., Choi, E., Yih, W.-T.: FlowQA: grasping flow in history for conversational machine comprehension. In: 7th International Conference on Learning Representations. Elsevier, Amsterdam (2019)
4. Xiong, C., Zhong V., Socher R.: DCN+: mixed objective and deep residual coattention for question answering. In: 6th International Conference on Learning Representations. Elsevier, Amsterdam (2018)
5. Devlin, J., Chang, M.-W., Lee, K., Toutanova K.: BERT: pre-training of deep bidirectional transformers for language understanding. In: Proceedings of the 2019 Conference of the North American Chapter of the Association for Computational Linguistics: Human Language Technologies, pp. 4171–4186. Association for Computational Linguistics, Minneapolis, Minnesota (2019)
6. Zhang, Z., Wu, Y., Zhou, J., Duan, S., Zhao, H., Wang, R.: SG-Net: syntax-guided machine reading comprehension. In: Proceedings of the AAAI Conference on Artificial Intelligence, pp. 9636–9643. AAAI Press, California (2020)

7. Ding, M., Zhou, C., Chen, Q., Yang, H., Tang, J.: Cognitive graph for multi-hop reading comprehension at scale. In: Proceedings of the 57th Annual Meeting of the Association for Computational Linguistics, pp. 2694–2703. Association for Computational Linguistics, Florence (2019)
8. Vaswani, A., et al.: Attention is all you need. In: Proceedings of the 31st International Conference on Neural Information Processing Systems, pp. 6000–6010. Curran Associates Inc., California (2017)
9. Liu, Y., et al.: RoBERTa: A Robustly Optimized BERT Pretraining Approach, arXiv preprint arXiv:1907.11692
10. Dai, Z., Yang, Z., Yang, Y., Carbonell, J., Le, Q., Salakhutdinov, R.: Transformer-XL: attentive language models beyond a fixed-length context. In: Proceedings of the 57th Annual Meeting of the Association for Computational Linguistics, pp. 2978–2988. Association for Computational Linguistics, Florence (2019)
11. Yang, Z., Dai, Z., Yang, Y., Carbonell, J., Salakhutdinov, R.-R., Le, Q.-V.: XLNet: generalized autoregressive pretraining for language understanding. In: Advances in Neural Information Processing Systems. Curran Associates Inc., New York (2019)
12. Szegedy, C., et al.: Intriguing properties of neural networks. In: 2nd International Conference on Learning Representations. Elsevier, Amsterdam (2014)
13. Miyato, T., Dai, A.-M., Goodfellow, I.: Adversarial training methods for semi-supervised text classification. In: 5th International Conference on Learning Representations. Elsevier, Amsterdam (2017)
14. Goodfellow, I.-J., Shlens, J., Szegedy, C.: Explaining and Harnessing Adversarial Examples, arXiv preprint arXiv:1412.6572v3
15. Miyato, T., Maeda, S.-I., Koyama, M., Ishii, S.: Virtual adversarial training: a regularization method for supervised and semi-supervised learning. IEEE Trans. Pattern Anal. Mach. Intell. **41**(8), 1979–1993 (2019)
16. Tang, H., Li, H., Liu, J., Hong, Y., Wu, H., Wang, H.: DuReader_robust: a Chinese dataset towards evaluating robustness and generalization of machine reading comprehension in real-world applications. In: Proceedings of the 59th Annual Meeting of the Association for Computational Linguistics and the 11th International Joint Conference on Natural Language Processing, pp. 955–963. Association for Computational Linguistics (2021)
17. zhoujx4/DuReader-Checklist-BASELINE. https://github.com/zhoujx4/DuReader-Checklist-BASELINE. Accessed 28 Aug 2021
18. PaddlePaddle/Research. https://github.com/PaddlePaddle/Research/tree/master/NLP/DuReader-Checklist-BASELINE. Accessed 28 Aug 2021

Deep Knowledge Tracking Based on Exercise Semantic Information

Rong Xiao, Ruili Zheng(✉), Yongkang Xiao, Yinghui Zhang, Bo Sun, and Jun He

School of Artificial Intelligence, Beijing Normal University, Beijing 100875, China
{xiaorong, xiaoyk, zhangyinghui, tosunbo, hejun}@bnu.edu.cn, 201921210049@mail.bnu.edu.cn

Abstract. In order to provide students with personalized practice recommendation in computer-aided intelligent education, a basic task is to predict students' performance in future exercises, in which it is essential to track the changes of knowledge acquired by each student in practice activities. But the existing methods can only use students' exercise records. Therefore, the rich information in the exercise is not fully utilized, so that it is impossible to achieve a more accurate prediction of student performance and a more explanatory analysis of knowledge acquisition. In this paper, we propose an overall study of student achievement prediction. In order to achieve the primary target of performance prediction, we use a variety of methods to fuse the exercise semantic information, and propose a deep knowledge tracking model that takes into account both knowledge concepts and exercise semantic information. In addition, in order to verify the portability of semantic extraction methods, we integrate semantic information into different deep knowledge tracing model. Through the experiment on the real online education data set, compared with the existing knowledge tracking model, the model proposed in this paper has better prediction performance.

Keywords: Deep learning · Knowledge tracking · Exercise semantic information

1 Introduction

Computer-aided education systems are widespread, it provides students millions of online courses or exercises based on their level of knowledge mastery [1]. This improves the mastery of knowledge by repeating exercises that are difficult for students and improving learning efficiency by skipping exercises that students have already mastered [2]. Figure 1 shows an example of a students' exercising process. The education system posts an exercise (e2), then the student will read exercise content and apply the relevant knowledge to answer the question. As shown in the figure, student has done four exercises, and he answers exercise e1,e3 and e4 right, which indicates that he has mastered "Function" and "Inequality" except the "Probability". The basic task in education systems is to predict whether students will answer the questions

W. Jia et al. (Eds.): SETE 2021, LNCS 13089, pp. 278–289, 2021.
https://doi.org/10.1007/978-3-030-92836-0_24

correctly. Therefore, it prompts us to track the change of students' knowledge mastery in exercising process. In real life, the success of accurate prediction is good for both student and systems: (1) Students can be aware of their weak knowledge concepts in time and prepare specific exercises; (2) System can help different students provide better proactive services [3].

For knowledge tracing, many efforts have been made in predicting student performance from both educational psychology and data mining. However, the existing methods mainly exploits students' exercising process, the exercise is regarded as the corresponding knowledge concepts. All in all, existing models only simulate the student's knowledge state based on the knowledge concepts. Two exercises labeled with the same knowledge concept are simply identified as the same. However, even if two exercises examine the same knowledge concept, their degree of difficulty may be different. Only modeling the knowledge concept will result in the loss of information. Therefore, these approaches cannot distinguish the knowledge acquisition of students precisely. As a result of the above problems, it is beneficial to combine both exercising records and exercise sematic information to improving student performance. There are many challenges in modeling exercise semantic information. First of all, there are various forms of expression of exercises, which needs a unified way to represent the characteristics of exercises from the perspective of semantics. Secondly, students' future performance largely depends on their long-term historical exercise, especially on important knowledge states. Thus, the way to track the historically information is important and crucial. Last but not least, The existing methods of embedding exercise semantic information in DKT models are simple, and the effect of other feasible methods has not been verified and explored.

To directly achieve the primary goal of predicting student performance, according to the students' practice records and the text content of the corresponding exercises, we propose a variety of methods to integrate the text information of the topic on the basis of the deep knowledge tracking method, and proposes a deep knowledge tracking model that takes into account both learning and exercise semantic information. Through experiments on real online education data sets, compared with the current knowledge tracking model, the model in this paper can better track the status of students' knowledge mastery, and has better predictive performance.

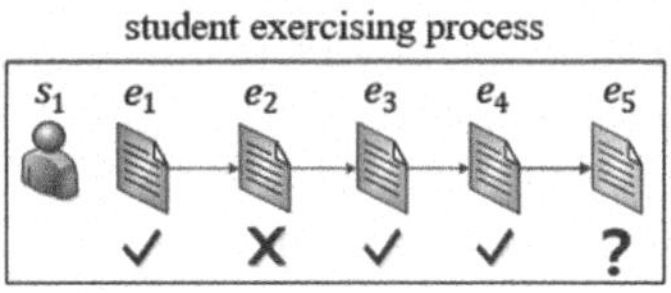

Exercise	Exercise Content	Knowledge Concept
e_1	If function $f(x) = x^2 - 2x + 2$ and $x \in [0,3]$, What is the range of $f(x)$?	Function
e_2	If four numbers are randomly selected without replacement from set $\{1, 2, 3, 4\}$, what is the probability that the four numbers are selected in ascending order?	Probability
e_3	What is the y-intercept of the graph of equation $y = 2 \times \|4 \times x - 4\| - 10$?	Function
e_4	What is the value of x If the inequality $\frac{2x-1}{x+2} \leq 3$?	Inequality
e_5	If function $f(x) = 2x - 2$ and $\frac{2x-1}{3x+2} \leq 4$, what is the range of $f(x)$?	Function, Inequality

Fig. 1. A student's practice process

2 Related Work

2.1 Knowledge Tracing

Knowledge tracking is a basic task, which is used to track each student's knowledge state, thus we can predict performance in future exercises. Bayesian knowledge tracking (BKT) [4] is one of the most popular models. This model assumes that each student's knowledge state is a set of binary variables, in which each variable represents her "Mastery" or "non Mastery" of a specific concept. Generally speaking, BKT uses hidden Markov model to update each student's knowledge state, and then update practice results. On the basis of BKT, many extensions are proposed, such as practice difficulty, multi knowledge concept and individual students.

2.2 Deep Knowledge Tracing

Inspired by the excellent performance of deep learning technology in many applications, some researchers try to establish a deep model for students' performance prediction. Deep knowledge tracking (DKT) [5] is the first attempt, recursive neural networks are used to model students' exercise process to predict performance. In addition, Zhang et al. Proposed a dynamic key value memory network model by connecting the relationship between practice and knowledge concepts to improve the interpretability of prediction results. Chen et al. Used knowledge structure information to deal with data sparsity in knowledge tracking. The experimental results show that the deep model has achieved great success.

Our work differs from previous studies as follows. First of all, the existing methods mainly focus on using students' historical exercise records, while ignoring the important of exercise semantic information. We explore students' knowledge concepts and exercise semantic information, as far as we know, this work is the first attempt to explore the impact of different text extraction methods on deep knowledge tracking model. Secondly, in order to find the most effective combination of text information, we use a variety of methods to integrate the practice semantic information. Last but not least, our work can achieve good prediction results and interpretability.

2.3 Text Feature Extraction

Traditional text feature extraction methods require manual design of effective features, which is time-consuming and labor-intensive. With the development of deep learning, people can quickly obtain text features from a large amount of data. RNN/LSTM, textCNN, and transformer are common methods for extracting text features.

TextCNN

Yoon et al. proposed the TextCNN [6] model. Convolutional Neural Network (CNN) can be used to capture local features. For text, similar to N-gram, a sliding window composed of multiple words can be compared to this local feature. CNN can combine these N-gram features to obtain semantic information at different levels of abstraction. Figure 3 shows the TextCNN model. The following briefly introduces the structure of each layer of the model (Fig. 2):

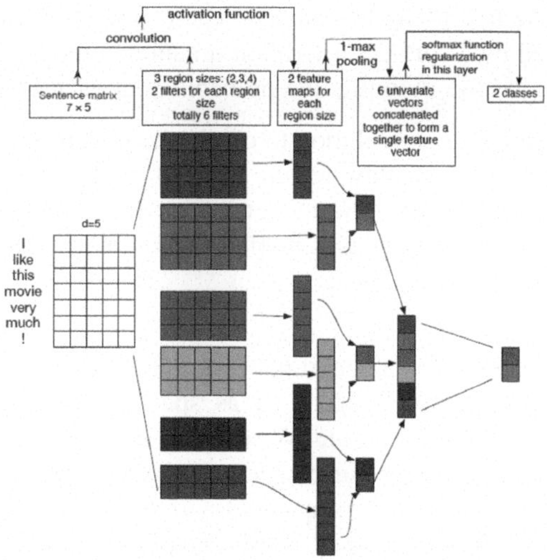

Fig. 2. TextCNN model

1) The first layer is the input layer. The input of the model is a sentence matrix of n × d, n is the number of words in the sentence, and d is the fixed dimension of the word, that is, each row represents a word vector. If the number of words in the input sentence is greater than or less than n, the padding operation is used to make the sentence always a fixed length. For each d-dimensional word vector, it can be trained in the network, or it can be directly used pre-trained in other large corpora. The advantage of the former is that the characteristics of the trained word vector may be more in line with the current task, and the advantage of the latter is that the pre-trained word vector can obtain more prior knowledge and has good versatility.
2) The second layer is a convolutional layer. In the NLP field, the width of the convolution kernel is equal to the dimension d of the word vector, that is, the place where the convolution kernel moves each time is a number of complete word vectors. The TextCNN model uses multiple convolution kernels of different sizes to extract the differentiated information brought by different ranges of words in a sentence, so as to better capture the local relevance of the sentence, extract important features more efficiently, and also Multiple convolution kernels of the same size are used to learn different information about a certain focus in a sentence.
3) The third layer is the pooling layer. Use the maximum pooling operation, that is, select the largest value in the feature vector and join these features together. You can also choose average pooling, that is, select the average value of each dimension in the feature vector and join these features together. At this point, the TextCNN model converts a sentence matrix into a fixed-length vector that can represent the sentence, and the vector can represent the semantic features of the sentence.

4) After obtaining the fixed-length sentence vector, through a fully connected layer, and then processed by a softmax activation function, a model for text classification can be obtained, and the output is the probability of each text category.

The TextCNN model uses convolution to obtain the feature vector of the text. It has a strong ability to extract the shallow feature level of the text and is suitable for short text classification scenarios. Since the model mainly relies on convolution to extract features, its ability to model long texts is limited and is not suitable for the field of long texts.

RNN

Recurrent Neural Network [7] is a neural network that processes sequence data, which is widely used in NLP related fields such as speech recognition [8, 9], machine translation [10], and knowledge tracking. We can use the time series $\{x_1, x_2, x_3, \cdots, x_n\}$ of length n as the input of the recurrent neural network, and then we will get the corresponding n hidden layer state sequences $\{h_1, h_2, h_3, \cdots, h_n\}$, Then the output sequence $\{o_1, o_2, o_3, \cdots, o_n\}$ is obtained. As shown in Fig. 5, at time t, the hidden layer state h_t is obtained by the joint action of the input x_t of the model at time t and the hidden layer state h_{t-1} at the previous time, as shown in formula (1) Shown.

$$h_t = f(W_x x_t + W_h h_{t-1} + b_h) \tag{1}$$

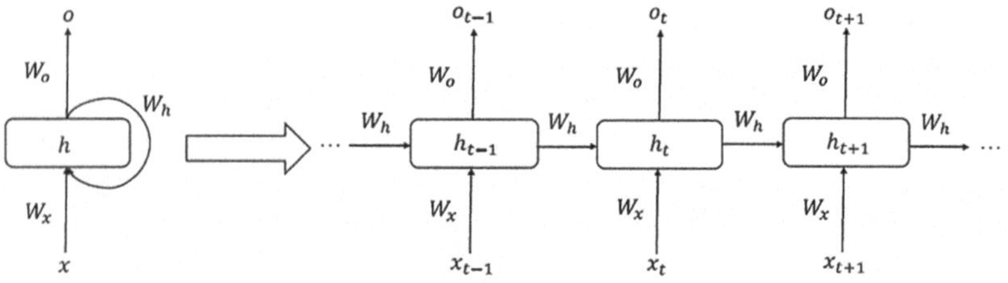

Fig. 3. RNN model

Transformer

Google proposed a Transformer model for Seq2Seq tasks in the article "Attention Is All You Need" [11]. It does not have the convolution structure of CNN or the loop structure of RNN, and is widely used in natural language processing related tasks. The encoder part of Transformer can be used to extract text features. It is composed of multiple encoder layers stacked. Each encoder layer contains Multi-Head Attention and Feed Forward Networks. There are two sub-layers, and each sub-layer has a residual connection and layer standardization operation. The residual connection helps to avoid the vanishing gradient problem in the deep network. Since the model does not contain any convolution or recursion, position coding is added to the input to provide the model with information about the relative position of words in the sentence (Fig. 4).

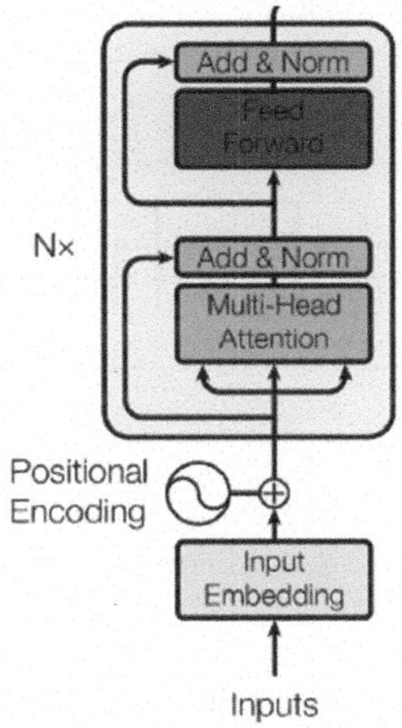

Fig. 4. The encoder part of transformer

In terms of text feature extraction models, the TextCNN model based on the CNN network is more suitable for short text fields due to the characteristics of convolutional extraction features; the RNN model adopts a linear sequence structure to collect input information from the front to the back, but this linear sequence structure is reversed There is an optimization problem when propagating backward. The back propagation path is too long, which can easily lead to severe gradient disappearance or gradient explosion. In addition, the RNN sequence structure is quite unfriendly for large-scale parallel computing; sentences in Transformer are processed as a whole, rather than one by one. Word processing, so it is not troubled by long-term dependence problems. The multi-head attention sublayer divides the model into multiple heads to form multiple subspaces, allowing the model to focus on different aspects of the sentence.

3 Methods

In order to verify the effectiveness of the text semantic extraction method, we conduct experiments on different deep knowledge tracking models. The following takes EKTA [12] model as an example:

3.1 EKT-M

We propose a deep knowledge tracking model EKT-T based on Transformer feature extractor, as shown in the figure below.

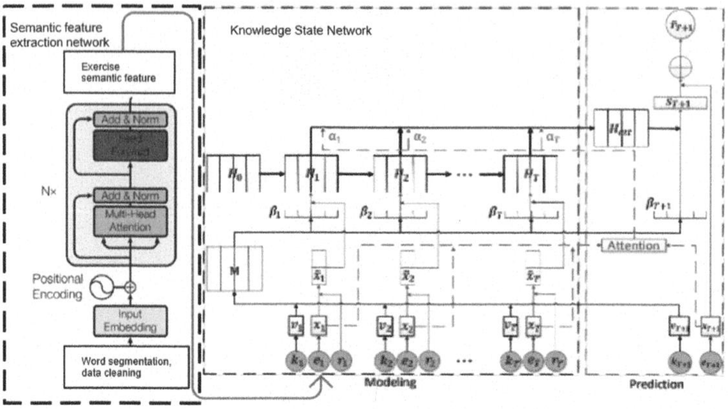

Fig. 5. The architectures of EKT-T

The EKT-T model is divided into practice embedding layer, student embedding layer, and prediction layer.

Exercise Embedding Layer

The function of the embedding layer is to obtain the semantic characteristics of the exercise questions. Transformer feature extractor extracts topic text features $\boldsymbol{et}_t$. The construction process of $\boldsymbol{et}_t$ is shown in the left part of the figure. Since the title text in the data set used in this article is Chinese text, for the Chinese title, first use the jieba word segmentation tool to segment the title, and then the special symbols and stop words Wait for cleaning, and finally get the word segmentation feature. After the above processing, the topic text can be described as a sentence containing m words. In order to better handle topic texts of different lengths, we set m to a fixed size. The topic text longer than m words will be truncated from the back. Title text shorter than m words will be filled in at the end. After all the title texts are represented as component word features, count all the words that have appeared to form a vocabulary. The size of the vocabulary is the number of all words that make up the data set. In order to obtain the vector representation of the word, first convert each word into a corresponding one-hot vector, so that the word vector obtained does not describe the relationship between words, so Word2vec [13] technology must be used to convert each word into d_0 dimension Word vector. Then, for the title text $\boldsymbol{E}_i$, it can be expressed as an $m \times d_0$ dimensional sentence matrix, which can be represented by $\boldsymbol{E}_i = \{\boldsymbol{w}_1, \boldsymbol{w}_2, \boldsymbol{w}_3, \cdots, \boldsymbol{w}_m\}$, where $\boldsymbol{w}_m$ represents the word vector of the mth word. Since the Transformer structure cannot learn the sequence information of the sequence, it is necessary to construct a d_0 dimensional position vector for each word to form an $m \times d_0$ dimensional position matrix. After the sentence matrix and the position matrix are added, they are linearly projected to three A different space is used as the Key, Value, and Query input model, and then through the multi-head attention layer and the feedforward neural network, the text feature $\boldsymbol{e}_t$ of the topic is obtained.

Student Embedding Layer

Based on the EKT framework, the text feature $\boldsymbol{e}_t$ of the topic, the knowledge concept feature $\boldsymbol{k}_t$, and the student's answer $\boldsymbol{r}_t$ are spliced together to form the input of the model. The goal of the knowledge concept vector $s = \{(e_1, k_1, r_1), \cdots, (e_T, e_T, r_T),\}$ is to explore the influence of each exercise on improving the students' state from the knowledge concept $\boldsymbol{k}_t$ of this exercise, and the weight of this influence is represented by $\boldsymbol{\beta}_t$. If the exercise is only related to the i-th knowledge concept, we can only consider the impact of this specific concept, without considering other knowledge concepts. Some researches show that knowledge concepts are not isolated in a specific discipline but are interrelated. Therefore, we assume that for a student, learning a concept will also affect the mastery of other concepts. Therefore, it is necessary to quantify the relative weights between all K concepts in the knowledge space.

Through the softmax operation of the inner product between the given knowledge concept vector $\boldsymbol{k}_t$ and each knowledge concept vector in the memory module $\boldsymbol{M}_i$, the influence weight $\boldsymbol{\beta}_t$ of the knowledge concept $\boldsymbol{k}_t$ of the exercise $\boldsymbol{e}_t$ on the i-th concept is further calculated as:

$$\beta_t^i = Softmax\left(v_t^T M_i\right) = \frac{\exp\left(v_t^T M_i\right)}{\sum_{i=1}^{K}\left(\exp\left(v_t^T M_i\right)\right)} \tag{2}$$

Then, update the hidden layer student state $\boldsymbol{H}_t$ with the student's practice sequence:

$$\boldsymbol{H}_t = RNN\left(s_t, H_{t-1;}\theta_t\right) \tag{3}$$

The calculation formula is:

$$i_t = \sigma(W_{xi}x_t + W_{hi}h_{t-1} + b_i). \tag{4}$$

$$f_t = \sigma\left(W_{xf}x_t + W_{hf}h_{t-1} + b_f\right) \tag{5}$$

$$o_t = \sigma(W_{xo}x_t + W_{ho}h_{t-1} + b_o) \tag{6}$$

$$c_t = f_t \circ c_{t-1} + i_t \circ tanh(W_{xc}x_t + W_{hc}h_{t-1} + b_c) \tag{7}$$

$$h_t = o_t \circ tanh(c_t) \tag{8}$$

Then calculate the students' understanding of the topic knowledge:

$$s_{T+1} = \sum_{i=1}^{K} \beta_{T+1}^i H_T^i \tag{9}$$

A students' current knowledge state is related to all previous knowledge states. The attention mechanism is added to comprehensively consider all knowledge states, and finally $\boldsymbol{h}_{att}$ is obtained, and then according to $\boldsymbol{h}_{att}$ and the new exercise vector $\boldsymbol{e}_{t+1}$, the probability of students doing the right question is predicted:

$$H_{att}^{i} = \sum_{i=1}^{T} H_{j}^{i} a_{j}, a_{j} = \cos(x_{T+1}, x_{j}) \tag{10}$$

By calculating the similarity between the exercises, the corresponding weights are obtained. If a student faces a problem similar to the one they have done before, then the state of knowledge at that time will become more important.

Prediction Layer
Predict the student's answer to question *t + 1*:

$$y_{T+1} = ReLU(W_3 \cdot [s_{T+1} \oplus x_{T+1}] + b_3) \tag{11}$$

$$\widetilde{r_{T+1}} = \sigma(W_4 \cdot y_{T+1} + b_4). \tag{12}$$

All parameters in the model are updated through the cross-entropy loss function between the student's actual problem-solving situation and the probability predicted by the model. The loss function is:

$$L = -\sum_{t=1}^{T} (r_t \log \widetilde{r_t} + (1 - r_t) \log(1 - \widetilde{r_t})) \tag{13}$$

4 Experiments

In this section, we conduct extensive experiments to demonstrate the effectiveness of our proposed frameworks and their implementations.

4.1 Dataset

In order to evaluate the performance of the integrated text semantic model, we conduct experiments on the BnuAi dataset. BnuAi dataset comes from the advanced and sophisticated center of future education and contains unit test answer data in the information and intelligent teaching system. Students practice on the teaching system to generate answer data. Each piece of answer data contains six fields: student number, question number, knowledge concept number, question text, answer time, and timestamp. 30,456 answer records of 2987 students on 417 questions are recorded, of which there are 159 knowledge points. In this article, the experiment on this data set uses the knowledge point number as the input of the model (Table 1).

Table 1. Dataset

Dataset	Students	Skills	Questions	Interactions	Sequence length
BnuAi	2987	159	417	30456	10.19

4.2 Experimental Setup

We implement all methods with TensorFlow. In this paper, the dataset is randomly divided into training set, verification set and test set according to the number of students, accounting for 56%, 14% and 30% respectively. We used the Adam [14] optimizer and set the initial learning rate to 0.1. All models were implemented by ourselves by Tensorflow [15] using Python on a Linux server with Tesla K20c GPU.

4.3 Evaluation Index

In fact, the knowledge tracking model can be regarded as a classification problem. For the classification model, we selected AUC [16] as our evaluation index. Generally, The larger the value, the better the effect.

4.4 Baselines

In order to evaluate the effectiveness of our model, we use the following models as our baselines:

1. DKT is the first method that uses deep learning to model knowledge tracing task. It uses recurrent neural network to model knowledge state of students.
2. EKT uses LSTM/RNN obtains question sematic information, which makes use of both knowledge concepts and text information.
3. DKVMN [17] uses memory network to store knowledge state of different concepts respectively instead of using a single hidden state.

4.5 Overall Performance

Table 2 reports the AUC results of all the compared methods. From the results we observe that our model achieves the highest performance, which verifies the effectiveness of our model. Besides, we also integrate exercise sematic information into EKTM, DKT and DKVMN, the experimental results show that the method of integrating exercise semantic information has good mobility. To be specific, adding the sematic feature to the model can greatly improve the AUC, indicating that only relying on the number of knowledge concepts can not well represent the semantics of the exercises, and a lot of useful information will be lost. In transformer, sentences are processed as a whole rather than word by word, so they are not troubled by long-term dependence. The multi-head attention sub-layer divides the model into multiple heads to form multiple subspaces, which can let the model pay attention to different aspects of sentence information. Therefore, among the three methods of extracting topic text features, transformer is significantly better than CNN or LSTM.

Table 2. Ablation experiment

Model	AUC	Model	AUC
DKT(baseline)	77.53%	DKT+lstm	79.44%
DKT+cnn	79.56%	DKT+transformer	79.76%
EKTM+lstm(baseline)	78.35%	EKTM+cnn	78.41%
EKTM+transformer	79.02%	EKTA+lstm(baseline)	78.79%
EKTA+cnn	78.92%	EKTA+transformer	79.68%
DKVMN	77.66%	DKVMN+lstm	79.68%
DKVMN+cnn	79.73%	DKVMN+transformer	79.97%

5 Conclusion

In this paper, we propose a deep knowledge tracking model based on exercise semantic information. We first proposed a text feature extraction method, in order to verify the effectiveness of different extraction methods, we use a variety of methods to fuse the exercise semantic information. Then, we propose a deep knowledge tracking model that takes into account the knowledge concept and exercise semantic information. At the same time, in order to verify the mobility of our method, we have incorporated text information into different models. Finally, we conducted extensive experiments on a large-scale real-world dataset, the experimental results show that our model achieve better performance and has good mobility.

Acknowledgements. This work was supported by the National Nature Science Foundation of China (Grant No. 62077009 and 62177006) and the State Key Laboratory of Cognitive Intelligence under Grant iED2019-Z04, Deep knowledge tracking model with multiple features.

References

1. Pardos, Z.A., et al.: Ensembling predictions of student post-test scores for an intelligent tutoring system. In: EDM, pp. 189–198 (2011)
2. Corbett, A.T., Anderson, J.R.: Knowledge tracing: modeling the acquisition of procedural knowledge. User Model. User-Adap. Inter. **4**(4), 253–278 (1994)
3. Brusilovsky, P., Millán, E.: User models for adaptive hypermedia and adaptive educational systems. In: Brusilovsky, P., Kobsa, A., Nejdl, W. (eds.) The Adaptive Web. LNCS, vol. 4321, pp. 3–53. Springer, Berlin, Heidelberg (2007). https://doi.org/10.1007/978-3-540-72079-9_1
4. Yudelson, M.V., Koedinger, K.R., Gordon, G.J.: Individualized Bayesian knowledge tracing models. In: Lane, H.C., Yacef, K., Mostow, J., Pavlik, P. (eds.) Artificial Intelligence in Education. AIED 2013. LNCS, vol. 7926, pp. 171–180. Springer, Berlin, Heidelberg (2013). https://doi.org/10.1007/978-3-642-39112-5_18
5. Piech, C., et al.: Deep knowledge tracing. In: Proceedings of the 28th International Conference on Neural Information Processing Systems-Volume 1, pp. 505–513 (2015)
6. Kim, Y.: Convolutional neural networks for sentence classification. arXiv preprint arXiv: 1408.5882 (2014)

7. Pascanu, R., Mikolov, T., Bengio, Y.: On the difficulty of training recurrent neural networks, pp. 1310–1318. In: International Conference on Machine Learning. PMLR (2013)
8. Graves, A., Mohamed, A., Hinton, G.: Speech recognition with deep recurrent neural networks. In: 2013 IEEE international conference on acoustics, speech and signal processing, pp. 6645–6649. IEEE (2013)
9. Hannun, A., et al.: Deep speech: Scaling up end-to-end speech recognition. arXiv preprint arXiv:1412.5567 (2014)
10. Bahdanau, D., Cho, K., Bengio, Y.: Neural machine translation by jointly learning to align and translate. arXiv preprint arXiv:1409.0473 (2014)
11. Vaswani, A., et al.: Attention is all you need. arXiv preprint arXiv:1706.03762 (2017)
12. Liu, Q., Huang, Z., Yin, Y., et al.: EKT: exercise-aware knowledge tracing for student performance prediction. IEEE Trans. Knowl. Data Eng. **33**(1), 100–115 (2019)
13. Mikolov, T., et al.: Efficient estimation of word representations in vector space. arXiv preprint arXiv:1301.3781 (2013)
14. Kingma, D.P., Ba, J.: Adam: A method for stochastic optimization. arXiv preprint arXiv: 1412.6980 (2014)
15. Abadi, M., et al.: Tensorflow: a system for large-scale machine learning. In: 12th {USENIX} Symposium on Operating Systems Design and Implementation ({OSDI} 16), pp. 265–283 (2016)
16. Wu, R., Xu, G., Chen, E., Liu, Q., Ng, W.: Knowledge or gaming? Cognitive modelling based on multiple-attempt response. In: Proceedings of the 26th International Conference on World Wide Web Companion, pp. 321–329. International World Wide Web Conferences Steering Committee (2017)
17. Zhang, J., et al.: Dynamic key-value memory networks for knowledge tracing. In: Proceedings of the 26th International Conference on World Wide Web 2017, pp. 765–774 (2017)

Automated Analysis of Student Verbalizations in Online Learning Environments

Nazik A. Almazova[1], Jason O. Hallstrom[1](✉), Megan Fowler[2], Joseph Hollingsworth[3], Eileen Kraemer[2], Murali Sitaraman[2], and Gloria Washington[4]

[1] Florida Atlantic University, Boca Raton, FL 33433, USA
jhallstrom@fau.edu
[2] Clemson University, Clemson, SC 29634, USA
[3] Rose-Hulman Institute of Technology, Terre Haute, IN 47803, USA
[4] Howard University, Washington, DC 20059, USA

1 Introduction

Online learning has become desirable for many students. In the U.S., more than one-third of all enrolled students participate in at least one online course [13]. The most effective online learning environments allow students to work at their own pace, from any location, at any time, and to receive automated feedback. In light of these benefits and the likely protracted impact of the current public health crisis, the trend toward online learning is likely to increase.

In traditional face-to-face learning environments, instructors adjust instruction based on student questions, specific misunderstandings, and attitudes (e.g., uncertainty, frustration). The limitation of many online learning environments is that they rely exclusively on objective student response data (e.g., a specific technical answer to a coding question) to base their feedback. This could result in less effective learning and students' giving preference to in-person instruction [19]. This research is about using more "noisy" data, student verbalizations, as a basis for personalized feedback.

While the ideas and results in this paper are broadly applicable to any online learning system, we have chosen to focus on an extension to an online environment for teaching code reasoning skills that our research team has developed over the past decade. In prior research, we have investigated how students perceive the tool, how well they understand the concepts taught, and the specific difficulties they encounter during various exercises. Achieving this understanding while students are using the tool (i.e., not just *post hoc*) is essential to being able to design *automated* interventions that help students overcome difficulties when they arise—not just for the reasoning tool, but for any online tool.

Objective assessments and attitudinal surveys are readily introduced in online environments, and these instruments help to reveal technical and attitudinal difficulties. However, these instruments are insufficient by themselves;

W. Jia et al. (Eds.): SETE 2021, LNCS 13089, pp. 290–302, 2021.
https://doi.org/10.1007/978-3-030-92836-0_25

they often fail to provide a high-fidelity view of the subtle technical and attitudinal difficulties students face when engaging in online problem-solving activities. Achieving this level of fidelity requires a view into students' internal cognitive processes.

A "think-aloud" protocol, which asks students to verbalize their thought processes during a problem-solving activity, offers a glimpse into student thinking. It can be powerful in illuminating technical and attitudinal problems that would otherwise be missed, but scalability is a problem. The protocol requires individual student sessions, manual transcription of audio data, and skilled interpretation of results. The process is labor-intensive, and with typical resource shortages, cannot be applied across large student populations.

To overcome these scalability limitations, we present an automated approach to collecting and analyzing think-aloud data in online learning environments. The approach relies on an extension to web-based environments, which provides automated screen and audio recording, transcription, and labeling of specific characteristics of student attitudes (e.g., uncertainty), behaviors (e.g., guessing), and difficulties (e.g., logic misunderstandings). The implementation uses natural language processing and machine learning. The long-term goal of this labeling is to support automated interventions that are tailored to the specific misunderstandings student face, as well as their evolving emotional and attitudinal states, which have been shown to have a significant impact on learning. We evaluated the approach in two online sections of a required, junior-level algorithms course during the Spring of 2020 ($n = 18$, $n = 13$, respectively).

We expect the approach will improve online learning for a variety of learners, across subjects and topics. Here we focus on understanding the difficulties learners face when reasoning about code. Concretely, we focus on the following questions: ***ERQ 1:*** How accurate are existing transcription tools in transcribing domain-specific language, specifically, language associated with code reasoning? ***ERQ 2:*** How suitable are existing natural language processing and machine learning models to identify points of interest in student attitudes, behaviors, and cognitive processes for purposes of automating interventions?

2 Background and Related Work

Think-aloud Analysis. Analysis of think-alouds has found a variety of uses. In Nielson [29], think-alouds are considered among the set of usability inspection methods for evaluating user interfaces. Fan et al. [12] discuss the high value of using a think-aloud protocol for identifying and pinpointing users' problems and the cost of manual processing of think-aloud data. In [21], a real-time, in-class note-taking system for hearing-impaired CS students is discussed. Accuracy rates for real-time transcription range from 75% for an untrained system, to 94% for a trained system using a customized dictionary and customized pronunciations for 10 domain-specific words. The idea of detecting morphological forms of software-specific terms found in informal writing has also received attention. In [5], an automatic natural language processing approach is used for creating a thesaurus [7] from question and answer posts on forums such as Stack Overflow.

Role of Emotions and Guessing in Learning. The labels used in our verbalization analyzer are informed by the literature. Emotions, in particular, play an important role in learning [22,31,32,41]. A number of groups have focused on identifying the links between learning and emotions [4,10,20,23,36], with application to improving the effectiveness of intelligent learning systems and providing personalized feedback [11,15,37]. Various emotions and affects have been considered (e.g., boredom, confusion, delight, surprise, frustration).

Bosch et al. consider the emotions experienced during the first programming experience and their correlation with performance [4], with a goal of automating detection and adaptation in intelligent learning environments. Affective states most commonly observed in the study include *confusion/uncertainty*, *frustration*, *boredom*, and *neutral*. Not surprisingly, confusion/uncertainty at an early stage is associated with a significant decline in performance. In a related study, frustration (usually associated with a negative outcome) is found to be positively correlated with learning [30].

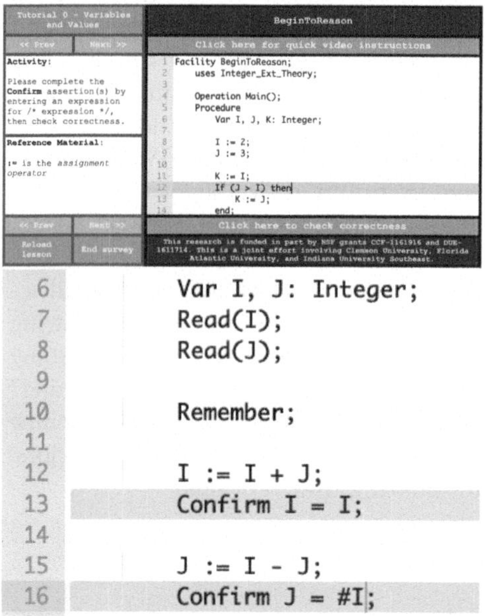

Fig. 1. BTR tracing activity

Girard et al. identify a similar set of labels for an affective learning companion in a meta-tutor project [15]. The *gaming* label identifies students who try multiple answers in a short period of time without allocating enough time to think about the problem (i.e., guessing). In [2], Baker et al. associate students "gaming the system" (i.e., guessing) with reductions in learning. The authors emphasize the importance of detecting and addressing guessing behaviors in intelligent learning environments.

Existing Tool Background. The experience reported here applies to a variety of online learning systems. The present experimentation has involved an extension to an online tool we have used to teach analytical reasoning that we use in our classrooms.

The online reasoning tool, BTR [35], aims to facilitate abstract code reasoning. Tracing and gaining code understanding based on *arbitrary* inputs (i.e., symbolic reasoning), instead of using one or two concrete inputs, is essential to becoming a strong programmer. Exposure to code reasoning basics, particularly through symbolic input values, provides further benefits since a variety of other concepts and skills become easier to grasp (e.g., in algorithms and data structures).

BTR includes a variety of activities, from code tracing on specific, concrete inputs; to symbolic reasoning over arbitrary inputs; to reasoning about objects, contracts, and invariants. The tool has been tested by over a thousand students over multiple years and courses. Results show that it is possible to help students learn the basics of abstract reasoning with minimal instruction [14], and it is possible to pinpoint key technical challenges students encounter based on directed activity paths and assessment of student response data [9].

BTR's student interface, shown in Fig. 1, consists of *Activity*, *Reference Material*, and *Exercise* sections. The Activity section describes the current exercise, with instructions on how to complete it. The Reference Material section provides definitions for any mathematical symbols and/or operators used in the exercise. The Exercise section displays the current exercise, instructing students to trace through a small fragment of Pascal-like code and to complete a logical `Confirm` assertion on the program variables, which tests their understanding.

After an answer is entered, *Check Correctness* is clicked to validate the student's answer. Importantly, the system relies on a verifying compiler [45] to validate the student's answer using mathematical verification; it does not rely on code execution or a prescribed list of student responses. The interface then provides immediate visual feedback [1], reducing cognitive load [27].

The example shown in Fig. 1 asks students to assert the relationships between variables `I` and `J` at the two points marked `Confirm`, using `#I` and `#J` to refer to the values of these variables at the point marked `Remember`. Feedback is shown as red and green highlights, denoting incorrect and correct responses.

3 Online Think-Aloud Extension

As a first step towards building a verbalization analyzer and to pilot the think-aloud extensions, the tool was configured with 14 reasoning activities. The activities included tracing a concrete value assigned to a variable, swapping symbolic values of variables, finding the smallest and largest symbolic values given, finding the absolute value of a symbolic variable, and other similar exercises.

The think-aloud extension to BTR provides automated recording of screen and audio data, real-time transcription and logging, and automated tagging of transcribed speech with inferred characteristics of technical and attitudinal challenges expressed. When the tool is first loaded, students are presented with instructions on how to think out loud.

Before proceeding to the reasoning activities, the think-aloud extension requests access to the student's microphone and screen, and then runs a five-second recording test. The test may have to be repeated if there are problems, though for most users, one round of testing is sufficient. Once testing is complete and quality is ensured, the system enters the think-aloud state. When in the think-aloud state, the tool records audio and screen content, performing real-time transcription as the student works through the exercises.

The extension is built as a conventional web application, with an Amazon Web Services (AWS) back-end designed to support a large number of simultaneous think-aloud sessions. Media content is stored in an AWS S3 bucket, with transcribed speech stored in an AWS RDS instance to facilitate downstream analysis. Browser-based recording of screen and audio content relies on the *MediaStream Recording* API [44]. Recordings are captured in 30-second fragments and uploaded to AWS incrementally, limiting load.

While speech-to-text services have advanced significantly in recent years, high accuracy is only possible in perfect conditions. There are limitations in typical environments, stemming from background noise, recording equipment quality, muffled and/or quiet speech, and domain-specific technical terms—a key focus of this paper. We explored multiple transcription options, including Google's SpeechRecognition [17] interface and the DeepSpeech [28] library.

Google's SpeechRecognition interface is part of the Web Speech API, a W3C Community Specification [16], currently implemented only in Chromium-based browsers (i.e., Chrome, Edge, Opera). The current implementation relies on the Google Cloud Speech-to-Text API. Benchmarking results show that the API achieves an error rate of 12.23% on LibriSpeech's test-clean dataset [34,38]. While these results are impressive, it is important to note that they reflect performance on typical, conversational speech. Understanding whether they translate to domain-specific speech is a key goal of the work presented here.

DeepSpeech [28] is an open-source speech-to-text engine developed by Mozilla, which uses a TensorFlow-based deep learning algorithm. Benchmarking results show that the implementation achieves a 6.5% error rate on LibriSpeech's test-clean dataset [26]. These results are comparable to human performance [24] – but again reflect performance on conversational speech. Of note, DeepSpeech makes it difficult to achieve real-time transcription. In the current implementation of the verbalization analyzer, transcription via SpeechRecognition occurs in real-time, whereas transcription via DeepSpeech occurs post hoc.

4 Experimental Set Up

The experiments were conducted in a required third-year algorithms course at a Hispanic-Serving Institution. They were conducted in synchronous online settings via WebEx. Two sections of students were involved (n = 18, n = 13).

Each pilot began with a brief introduction to the goals of the study and the structure of the experiment. Students were introduced to the BTR tool and the think-aloud extension. The instructor demonstrated how to use the tool, how to complete a reasoning exercise, and how to think out loud. Students were encouraged to describe the steps in their thinking process while solving the exercises. The introduction was followed by the individual think-aloud sessions. Students were instructed to disconnect from the WebEx conference, and to use the web link to begin their think-aloud sessions. Each student completed a think-aloud session individually, from home, at their own computer.

5 ERQ 1: Transcription Accuracy

In the first pilot, students completed an average of 11 exercises out of a possible 14, with 9 students completing all exercises. Audio and video were captured per student, per session. The average recording length was 41.1 min per session, with a minimum length of 13 min, and a maximum length of 110 min. In the second pilot, students completed an average of 10 exercises, with 4 students completing all exercises. The average recording length was 29 min per session, with a minimum length of 9 min, and a maximum length of 46 min. Video content was used to study how students engaged with the tool, to support transcription correction, and to select the label set.

Audio recordings were processed using the Speech-Recognition and Deep-Speech implementations, generating per student, per session transcripts. All recordings were also manually transcribed to enable accuracy evaluation. The first pilot generated 18 transcripts, with an average word count of 1,562, a minimum word count of 288, and a maximum word count of 3,161. The second pilot generated 13 total transcripts, with an average word count of 1,269, a minimum word count of 192, and a maximum word count of 2,605. In total, 31 per-session transcripts were collected across the two pilots.

Table 1. Error rate per transcript, across pilots

WC	SR WER	DS WER	WC	SR WER	DS WER
288	0.51	0.59	1755	0.42	0.53
714	0.47	0.48	1756	0.53	0.57
718	0.12	0.21	1835	0.21	0.29
747	0.43	0.57	1889	0.36	0.49
810	0.35	0.48	1996	0.63	0.55
1114	0.33	0.44	2618	0.29	0.43
1423	0.59	0.63	2688	0.37	0.45
1487	0.34	0.49	3161	0.18	0.40
192	0.14	0.22	1257	0.23	0.32
397	0.34	0.39	1800	0.34	0.39
662	0.37	0.40	1837	0.39	0.49
716	0.37	0.44	1898	0.34	0.52
830	0.41	0.42	2446	0.43	0.58
861	0.43	0.56	2605	0.36	0.49
1005	0.23	0.33			

Table 1 details the per-transcript word error rates (WER) for the two pilots, respectively (top-half = pilot 1, bottom-half = pilot 2). Overall, DeepSpeech exhibited an error rate of 45% (DS WER), and SpeechRecognition exhibited an error rate of 36% (SR WER). From these results, we conclude that at this time, neither state-of-the-art tool offers sufficient accuracy of transcription in the context of code reasoning.

Given the significantly better performance of SpeechRecognition and DeepSpeech in prior benchmarking studies, the relatively poor performance of these systems may be surprising. Comparisons between the manually collected and automatically collected transcripts show that a significant portion of the errors are due to limitations in handling references to the code text. Both systems were trained using conversational speech, presenting a context mismatch during transcription. Note that this limitation might be overcome using DeepSpeech, which supports training on a custom corpus. With training on a robust corpus collected in the context of code reasoning, performance is likely to improve.

6 ERQ 2: Identification Accuracy

We now turn our attention to identifying points of interest in student behaviors, attitudes, and difficulties. Given the error rates in the automatically generated transcripts, manually generated and validated transcripts are used hereafter.

Dataset Labeling. Labels corresponding to points of interest likely to be relevant in the design of automated interventions were identified through a careful literature review and manual analysis of audio, video, and transcript content. They are summarized in Table 2. Each of the 435 transcripts were manually labeled with the appropriate tags for testing purposes.

One important threat to validity is the subjective nature of the labeling process. Labels such as `uncertain` and `guessing`, for instance, are subject to interpretation, varying from one observer to another. To mitigate subjectivity, the label set was established iteratively through independent consideration of a subset of transcripts by two independent labelers. After multiple iterations of independent labeling and comparison, the intent of each label was carefully described and documented, along with heuristics and examples. Subsequently, the transcript set was shuffled, and labels were independently assigned to all 435 transcripts. Inter-rater reliability was assessed using Cohen's kappa [8]. The agreement rate was high, with individual label agreement ranging between 0.84 and 1.0, with an overall agreement rate of 0.91. The final dataset used for analysis was created by merging the two independent datasets, with conflicting labels argued between the raters until consensus was reached.

Preprocessing and Vectorization. The input data for each student attempt includes a think-aloud transcript and BTR state (e.g., exercise number, attempt count, whether the exercise was solved correctly). Each response (i.e., answer) is encoded as a vector of tokens, including a boolean indicating correctness (i.e., 0 or 1). The vectors are padded, if necessary, to ensure consistency.

Table 2. Attitude/behavior/misunderstanding labels

Label	Definition
`read_instructions`	The student read the exercise instructions out loud
`traced_code`	The student traced the code out loud
`uncertain`	The student was not confident in her reasoning
`guessing`	The student was guessing, using brute-force
`btr_confusion`	The student misunderstood a core BTR concept
`logic_confusion`	The student misunderstood a core logic (programming) concept
`intermediates_conf.`	The student misunderstood how to differentiate and/or carry-through intermediate states across multiple, dependent statements

Transcript data is preprocessed to remove low-value content. This includes removal of punctuation, symbols, single-letter words, numbers, and stop-words. We use NLKT's [3] default set of stop-words (e.g., "it", "its"). Lemmatization is also performed: Multiple forms of the same word are often used—for instance, multiple verb forms, such as *thinks* and *thinking*. It is often beneficial to reduce inflectional forms of a word to its root [18,43]. Lemmatization is performed using NLTK's part-of-speech tagger and WordNet [42].

Most natural language labeling algorithms operate on *vectorized* text, collapsing each transcript to a vector of real numbers, or a set of such vectors, representing *features* of the text. We explore a range of vectorization techniques.

TF-IDF [40] computes a vector of weights for each transcript, where the length of each vector is equal to the number of words contained in the corpus (i.e., all preprocessed transcripts). The weight for each word in the vector for a specific transcript is calculated as the word's frequency in the transcript, divided by its frequency in the corpus. (Words that are rare in the corpus, but appear frequently in a transcript, receive larger weights in that transcript's vector.) Note that the approach ignores information about word position. A phrase like, "I don't understand" is treated as a collection of three words, not a single concept. To overcome this limitation, we consider TF-IDF using phrase lengths of one to three words (i.e., *n-gram* lengths of one to three).

Word2Vec [25] is a *word embedding* algorithm that relies on a neural network model to generate a vector of real numbers for each word in the corpus. The vectors are intended to capture relationships among words, so that, for instance,"don't understand" - "don't" = "understand". The mechanics of the neural network are omitted here, but they rely on the relative context of words within phrases across the corpus. A Word2Vec model was trained on the think-aloud corpus, using a specified vector dimension of 100. This resulted in a set of vectors for each transcript, containing one vector for each word in the transcript.

GloVe [33] is another embedding algorithm intended to capture the relationships among words. The mechanics, again omitted, rely on word-word co-occurrence statistics. While a custom GloVe model can be trained, we use the pre-trained model, which benefits from a large corpus. Whereas our domain-specific corpus includes 10,898 tokens (total words), and a vocabulary of 772 distinct words, the GloVe corpus includes 840B tokens and a vocabulary of 2.2M words. Encoding using the pre-trained model generated a vector of dimension 300 for each word in the corpus and corresponding sets of vectors for each transcript. While all three methods were evaluated in the context of the labeling algorithms described next, only GloVe performed significantly better than 50% labeling accuracy. It remains the focus hereafter.

7 Data Analysis and Results

The binary relevance method [46] is one of the most common techniques for approaching multi-label classification. The problem is decomposed into seven sub-problems, one for each label (i.e. positive or negative). As detailed next, a variety of models were explored to automate label assignment. A key factor in achieving high accuracy when training these classifiers is the size of the training set (a portion of our transcript set) and the distribution of labels across the set. Labels that are underrepresented or overrepresented can bias the classifier's performance. Even at 435 per-attempt transcripts, our training sets are relatively small. More importantly, as illustrated in Fig. 2, the label distributions are not balanced. The `guessing` label, for instance, is assigned to only 47 transcripts, whereas the `traced_code` label is assigned to 265 transcripts.

To achieve balance across labels, weight adjustments were applied during training. While the exploratory results are omitted here, the balancing approach improved the accuracy of label assignment by as much as 30% for some labels. The labeled, vectorized dataset was shuffled and split, with 70% of the transcripts used for training, 10% withheld for validation and 20% withheld for testing. The split was stratified across labels to ensure balanced representation.

7.1 Classifier Architecture and Model Training

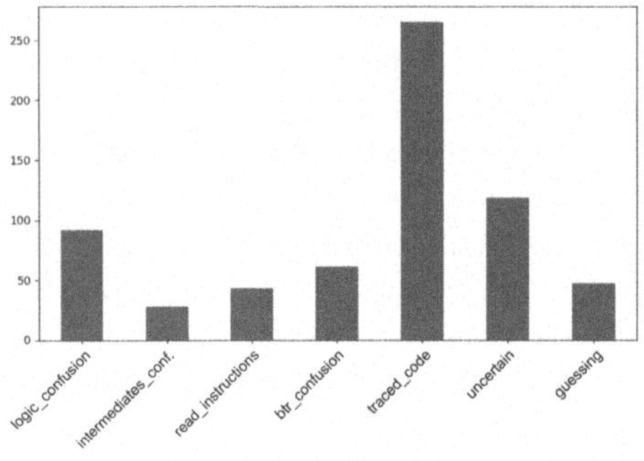

Fig. 2. Dataset label distribution

Several neural network architectures were evaluated, all with previously demonstrated success in text classification problems, including fully connected neural networks, convolutional neural networks, recurrent neural networks (RNN) with gated recurrent units, and long short-term memory (LSTM) networks [39]. The open-source Keras library [6] was used for network implementation and evaluation. The best performing architecture is structured as follows.

The first input layer accepts a tokenized transcript (i.e., a set of integers corresponding to the corpus vocabulary), which is passed to a pre-trained embedding layer. The embedding layer transforms the integer set into a GloVe-based embedding representation (i.e., a set of embedding vectors of dimension 300). The embedding layer is followed by two LSTM networks [39], recurrent structures designed for problems involving order-dependence. An interspersed dropout layer limits network over-fitting, enhancing generalizability. The second input layer (dimension = 3) accepts exercise number, attempt count, and attempt outcome. The third input layer (dimension = 66) accepts the tokenized solution entered by the student. A concatenation layer combines the three inputs into a single tensor. A fully connected layer of 32 units with rectified linear activation (ReLU) trains on all data combined. Finally, a fully-connected output layer with one sigmoid activation function outputs a likelihood score (0.0–1.0) corresponding to the label result. A score at or above 0.5 corresponds to *true*, and lower values correspond to *false*. This architecture was trained to generate seven different models, corresponding to each of the labels, respectively. (Details concerning hyper-parameter tuning for each model are omitted.) All models required fewer than 1,000 epochs to converge. The best performing models, with minimal loss scores across both the training and validation sets were used.

Table 3. Automated labeling accuracy (per label)

Label	Acc	n	Label	Acc	n	Label	Acc	n
`uncertain`	88.5%	26	`btr_confusion`	87.8%	15	`traced_code`	87.0%	56
`logic_conf.`	80.2%	20	`read_inst.`	92.4%	12	`inter._conf.`	96.2%	10
`guessing`	94.7%	10						

Table 3 summarizes labeling accuracy over the withheld test set (n = 87), as well as the number of transcripts with each label. There were 20 transcripts corresponding to the `logic_confusion` label, for instance, and these were identified correctly 80.2% of the time – the lowest across the labels. There were 10 transcripts corresponding to students who had `intermediates_confusion`, and these were correctly identified 96.2% of the time – the highest accuracy across the labels. Of course, the significance of the results varies from one label to another due to variation in representation within the test set – but overall, the classifier performed well, with an average accuracy of 89.5%

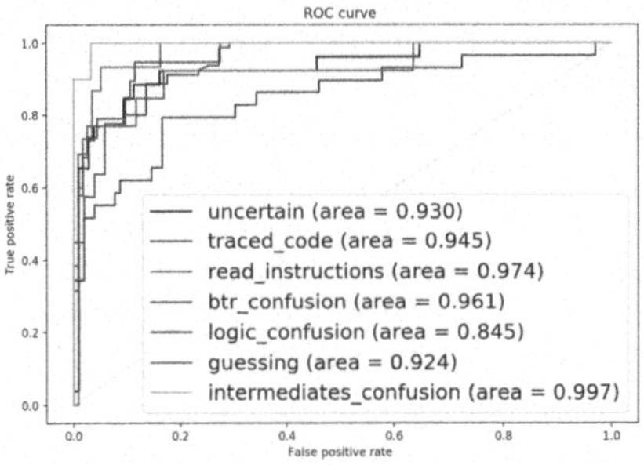

Fig. 3. ROC curves for all models

Recall that each of the seven trained networks outputs a likelihood score (0.0–1.0) for each transcript, with a discrimination threshold of 0.5. The *receiver operating characteristic* (ROC) plot shown in Fig. 3 is generated by varying this threshold to explore the trade-off between the true positive rate and the false positive rate. Increasing the discrimination threshold to 1.0, for instance, guarantees a 100% true positive rate, but at the cost of false positives. The area beneath each curve, shown parenthetically in the legend, is a measure of the network's discriminatory power – the likelihood the classifier will rank positive cases above negative cases. The discriminatory performance is strong, with an average area-under-curve of 0.94.

8 Conclusion

This paper presented results in automating the analysis of student verbalizations in online learning environments, using an existing code reasoning tutor as the study context. A new extension automatically transcribes student verbalizations and uses machine learning to identify specific student attitudes, behaviors, and difficulties. We presented an analysis of transcription accuracy and utility in identifying seven learner characteristics of interest. The results were based on experimentation in two online sections of a required, junior-level algorithms course, resulting in 435 think-aloud transcripts.

Unfortunately, the accuracy offered by current transcription tools appears to be insufficient to enable reliable transcription in the context of domain-specific verbalizations (e.g., code reasoning), hindering a fully automated implementation. However, this is only a temporary problem, almost certainly due to the absence of sufficient training on an appropriately robust, domain-specific verbalization corpus. Developing such a corpus is only a matter of time – and looking to the future, there is reason to invest in that effort. When transcription accuracy is high, our results provide evidence that a broad set of interesting characteristics concerning student attitudes, behaviors, and difficulties can be identified automatically, with high accuracy, in real-time. Enabling automatic identification of student difficulties would have a profound impact on the design and efficacy of online tutoring systems, in computer science education and beyond.

References

1. Azevedo, R., Bernard, R.M.: A meta-analysis of the effects of feedback in computer-based instruction. J. Educ. Comput. Res. **13**(2), 111–127 (1995)
2. Baker, R.S., Corbett, A.T., Koedinger, K.R., Wagner, A.Z.: Off-task behavior in the cognitive tutor classroom: when students game the system. In: Proceedings of SIGCHI, pp. 383–390 (2004)
3. Bird, S., Klein, E., Loper, E.: Natural Language Processing with Python: Analyzing text with the Natural Language Toolkit. O'Reilly Media, Inc., Sebastopol (2009)
4. Bosch, N., D'Mello, S., Mills, C.: What emotions do novices experience during their first computer programming learning session? In: Lane, H.C., Yacef, K., Mostow, J., Pavlik, P. (eds.) AIED 2013. LNCS (LNAI), vol. 7926, pp. 11–20. Springer, Heidelberg (2013). https://doi.org/10.1007/978-3-642-39112-5_2
5. Chen, C., Xing, Z., Wang, X.: Unsupervised software-specific morphological forms inference from informal discussions. In: The 39th International Conference on Software Engineering, Buenos Aires, Argentina. IEEE (2017)
6. Chollet, F., et al.: Keras (2015)
7. Chunyang, C.: Sethesaurus: synonyms and abbreviations for software-related terms
8. Cohen, J.: A coefficient of agreement for nominal scales. Educ. Psychol. Measur. **20**(1), 37–46 (1960)
9. Cook, M., et al.: Where exactly are the difficulties in reasoning logically about code? Experimentation with an online system. In: Proceedings of the 23rd Annual ACM Conference on Innovation and Technology in Computer Science Education, pp. 39–44 (2018)
10. Craig, S., Graesser, A., Sullins, J., Gholson, B.: Affect and learning: an exploratory look into the role of affect in learning with autotutor. J. Educ. Media **29**(3), 241–250 (2004)
11. Doddannara, L.S., Gowda, S.M., Baker, R.S.J., Gowda, S.M., de Carvalho, A.M.J.B.: Exploring the relationships between design, students' affective states, and disengaged behaviors within an ITS. In: Lane, H.C., Yacef, K., Mostow, J., Pavlik, P. (eds.) AIED 2013. LNCS (LNAI), vol. 7926, pp. 31–40. Springer, Heidelberg (2013). https://doi.org/10.1007/978-3-642-39112-5_4
12. Fan, M., Lin, J., Chung, C., Truong, K.N.: Concurrent think-aloud verbalizations and usability problems. ACM Trans. Comput.-Hum. Interact. **26**(5) (2019)
13. N.C. for Education Statistics: Trend generator (student enrollment)

14. Fowler, M., et al.: Impact of steps, instruction, and motivation on learning symbolic reasoning using an online tool. In: Proceedings of the 50th ACM Technical Symposium on Computer Science Education, pp. 1039–1045 (2019)
15. Girard, S., et al.: Defining the behavior of an affective learning companion in the affective meta-tutor project. In: Lane, H.C., Yacef, K., Mostow, J., Pavlik, P. (eds.) AIED 2013. LNCS (LNAI), vol. 7926, pp. 21–30. Springer, Heidelberg (2013). https://doi.org/10.1007/978-3-642-39112-5_3
16. W.C. Group: Web speech API
17. W.C. Group: Web speech API the speechrecognition interface
18. Han, P., Shen, S., Wang, D., Liu, Y.: The influence of word normalization in English document clustering. In: 2012 IEEE International Conference on Computer Science and Automation Engineering (csae), vol. 2, pp. 116–120. IEEE (2012)
19. Kemp, N., Grieve, R.: Face-to-face or face-to-screen? Undergraduates' opinions and test performance. Front. Psychol. **5**, 1278 (2014)
20. Khan, I.A., Hierons, R.M., Brinkman, W.P.: Mood independent programming. In: Proceedings of the 14th European Conference on Cognitive Ergonomics: invent! explore!, pp. 269–272 (2007)
21. Kheir, R., Way, T.: Inclusion of deaf students in computer science classes using real-time speech transcription. SIGCSE Bull. **39**(3), 261–265 (2007)
22. Knörzer, L., et al.: Facilitators or suppressors: effects of experimentally induced emotions on multimedia learning. Learn. Instr. **44**, 97–107 (2016)
23. Kort, B., Reilly, R., Picard, R.W.: An affective model of interplay between emotions and learning: reengineering educational pedagogy-building a learning companion. In: Proceedings IEEE International Conference on Advanced Learning Technologies, pp. 43–46. IEEE (2001)
24. Lippmann, R.P.: Speech recognition by machines and humans. Speech Commun. **22**(1), 1–15 (1997)
25. Mikolov, T., Chen, K., Corrado, G., Dean, J.: Efficient estimation of word representations in vector space. arXiv preprint arXiv:1301.3781 (2013)
26. Morais, R.: A journey to <10% word error rate
27. Moreno, R.: Decreasing cognitive load for novice students: Effects of explanatory versus corrective feedback in discovery-based multimedia. Instr. Sci. **32**(1–2), 99–113 (2004)
28. Mozilla: Project DeepSpeech
29. Nielsen, J.: Usability Engineering. Morgan Kaufmann Publishers Inc., San Francisco, CA, USA (1993)
30. Pardos, Z.A., Baker, R.S., San Pedro, M.O., Gowda, S.M., Gowda, S.M.: Affective states and state tests: investigating how affect throughout the school year predicts end of year learning outcomes. In: Proceedings of the Third International Conference on Learning Analytics and Knowledge, pp. 117–124 (2013)
31. Park, B., Plass, J.L., Brünken, R.: Cognitive and affective processes in multimedia learning (2014)
32. Pekrun, R., Linnenbrink-Garcia, L.: International Handbook of Emotions in Education. Routledge, London (2014)
33. Pennington, J., et al.: Glove: global vectors for word representation. In: Empirical Methods in Natural Language Processing (EMNLP), pp. 1532–1543 (2014)
34. Picovoice: Speech-to-text benchmark
35. RESOLVE: Software Research Group at Clemson University. BeginToReason
36. Rodrigo, M.M.T., Baker, R.S.: Coarse-grained detection of student frustration in an introductory programming course. In: Proceedings of the Fifth International Workshop on Computing Education Research Workshop, pp. 75–80 (2009)

37. Sidney, K.D., Craig, S.D., Gholson, B., Franklin, S., Picard, R., Graesser, A.C.: Integrating affect sensors in an intelligent tutoring system. In: Affective Interactions: The Computer in the Affective Loop Workshop at, pp. 7–13 (2005)
38. O. Speech and L. Resources: LibriSpeech ASR corpus
39. Staudemeyer, R., Morris, E.: Understanding lstm-a tutorial into long short-term memory recurrent neural networks. arXiv preprint arXiv:1909.09586 (2019)
40. tfidf.com. TF-IDF: A single-page tutorial - information retrieval and text mining
41. Um, E., Plass, J.L., Hayward, E.O., Homer, B.D., et al.: Emotional design in multimedia learning. J. Educ. Psychol. **104**(2), 485 (2012)
42. P. University: About wordnet
43. Uysal, A.K., Gunal, S.: The impact of preprocessing on text classification. Inf. Process. Manag. **50**(1), 104–112 (2014)
44. W3C: Mediastream recording
45. Welch, D., Cook, C., Sun, Y.S., Sitaraman, M.: A web-integrated verifying compiler for RESOLVE: a research perspective. In: Janakiram, D., Sen, K., Kulkarni, V. (eds.) 7th India Software Engineering Conference, Chennai, ISEC 2014, Chennai, India, 19–21 February 2014, pp. 12:1–12:6. ACM (2014)
46. Zhang, M.-L., Li, Y.-K., Liu, X.-Y., Geng, X.: Binary relevance for multi-label learning: an overview. Front. Comp. Sci. **12**(2), 191–202 (2018). https://doi.org/10.1007/s11704-017-7031-7

A Model of Teachers' Excellent Teaching Behaviors Based on Natural Language Processing

Xiumeng Liu[1], Yuyao Li[2(✉)], and Yang Huang[1]

[1] Faculty of English Language and Culture, Guangdong University of Foreign Studies, Guangzhou 510420, Guangdong, China
[2] School of Information Science and Technology/School of Cyber Security, Guangdong University of Foreign Studies, Guangzhou 510420, Guangdong, China

Abstract. Student Evaluations of Teaching (SET) plays a vital role in the improvement of teachers' teaching. The accumulated large amount of SET data has motivated many pieces of research. However, the Chinese SET texts still lack practical mining and application. With the TF-IDF and sentiment dictionary in Natural Language Processing (NLP), this study proposes a model of teachers' excellent teaching behaviors, including a quantitative model and a word cloud of keywords in different aspects. The proposed model is practical than existing work for its quantification and specific aspects. The model is tested on a dataset of more than 8,000 students' comments in different languages, proving that the model is valid.

Keywords: Student evaluations of teaching · TF-IDF · Aspect classification

1 Introduction

Student Evaluations of Teaching (SET) in Higher Education has over 100 years, and its development in China has a history of about 40 years [1]. The form of SET includes qualitative and quantitative ones. In terms of effectiveness, the quantitative approach, represented by the mentor behavior scale (MBS) [2], is more studied than the qualitative one. However, the latter provides possible information because of its form and content flexibility, and complexity. The study and analysis of these textual contents give information about students' sentiment polarity [3], students' reactions to different aspects of teaching [4], and students' preference to teachers of different genders [5]. Natural language processing (NLP) is an effective tool to deal with texts. Many pieces of research are done with SET texts, but these researches tend to focus on a particular language and specific aspects. For example, Nikolić et al. [4] apply aspect-based sentiment analysis to reviews in the Serbian language. The research results of SET texts have not been fully utilized yet.

Our study proposes a model of teachers' excellent teaching behaviors of different aspects, with the TF-IDF values and sentiment dictionary being the measurement. The model is built with qualitative data and is used as a quantitative measurement to

W. Jia et al. (Eds.): SETE 2021, LNCS 13089, pp. 303–311, 2021.
https://doi.org/10.1007/978-3-030-92836-0_26

evaluate teachers' behaviors. It rates the teachers' teaching behavior from attitude, students' emotions, teaching methods, and course contents. Moreover, each aspect has both positive and negative evaluations. By generating a Word Cloud of keywords in different aspects, specific qualities of excellent teaching behaviors can be seen.

The remainder of this paper is divided into four parts. First is an overview of the research background and current studies—secondly, our work methodology. Thirdly, the experiment and its results. Finally, discussion of the results and future work.

2 Related Work

At present, natural language processing is used in various domains to deal with comments and textual data. Some studies deal with the student evaluation texts using NLP, and the focus is mainly sentiment analysis.

2.1 Natural Language Processing in Student Evaluations of Teaching

SET texts are mostly short texts, and this makes NLP applicable. NLP is used to analyze texts in SET, and many pieces of research are done with this topic.

The Machine-Learning-Based Approach. Machine-learning is a widely-used tool to deal with texts. Altrabsheh et al. [6] manually annotate different emotions of comments to check the accuracy of machine learning classification techniques, including Naïve Bayes, Complement Naïve Bayes, Maximum Entropy, and Support Vector Machine (SVM). Tan et al. [7] adopt Latent Semantic Analysis (LSA) to reduce the dimensionality of Chinese SET text and used SVM to make the classification. After comparing the effect of different factors on the result, they propose a sound classification model.

Bert is a deep neural network that contains twelve layers and 110 million parameters in its base version proposed by Devlin et al. 2018 [8]. Rybinski et al. [9] train Bert models from over 1.6 million SET texts to prove their efficiency. The data in Rybinski et al.'s study is previously tagged with ratings from 1–5. Furthermore, the length of the chosen dataset provides enough preceding and following contexts for the pretraining of the Bert model. However, data used to pre-train the Bert model needs to be large, have clear labels, and have preceding and following contexts. These requirements of data limit its application.

Aspect-Based Sentiment Analysis. Studies focusing on the polarity of emotions in texts may not be adequate. Nikolić et al. [4] try Aspect-Based Sentiment Analysis (ABSA) on student reviews collected from official surveys and social media and review websites. Their study is enabled by using NLP techniques, machine learning models, rules, and dictionaries. Though comments in this study are in the Serbian language, it helps conduct ABSA on Chinese texts. Chauhan G S et al. [10] conduct ABSA of students' feedback using both machine-learning-based and lexicon-based approaches.

Using a machine-learning algorithm, they extract aspect terms from students' comments using a part-of-speech (POS) tagger and use them for sentiment classification. Their approach performs well in discovering different aspects of different categories, including teaching evaluation positive, teaching evaluation negative, course evaluation positive, and course evaluation negative. However, their experiment in this study is only conducted in English comments, and their data merely contains 1000 students' comments, which makes it less convincing.

2.2 Applications of the Results from Student Evaluation of Teaching

The purpose of conducting SET is to help improve the teaching. Therefore, the application of the study results of SET texts should be practical. Chen Yuchan and Liu Wei [11] extract core views of each comment and classify similar views using a clustering algorithm. They visualize the statistical analysis results in the form of word cloud as their study's application. Okoye K et al. [5] propose an Educational Process Data Mining Model (EPDM) to understand the relations or correlation of words and sentiments of students by considering the gender differences. The EPDM model is convincing and objective in that it leverages the opinions or perspectives of students quantitatively. Their study focuses on Spanish and English comments. Though applying a quantitative approach, the model focuses on the emotional polarity instead of specific aspects, making the model less practical in improving teachers' teaching behaviors.

3 Methodology

This section describes the construction and application of the proposed model of teachers' excellent teaching behaviors. Figure 1 is the flowchart of our approach.

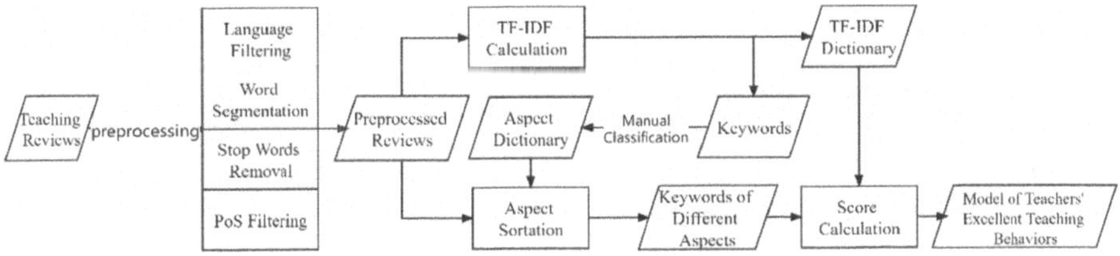

Fig. 1. Flowchart of the model of teachers' excellent teaching behaviors

3.1 Data Preprocessing

The review data in this study contains multiple languages, such as Chinese, English, Japanese, Bosnian, and Greek. However, most are in Chinese. Thus, we use the module *fasttext* to identify languages and translate non-Chinese texts into Chinese with Google Translation in the module *translators*. Then, we manually proofed the translation result to ensure that the only non-Chinese words left are teachers' names and course names.

We use *jieba* to make word segmentation with our customized stop words and user dictionary. The PoS tagging is also done with *jieba*. Suppose there are no non-stop words or only "无," the comment would be deleted. Only adjectives and idioms are left in the corpus for the accurate description of teachers' excellent teaching behaviors.

3.2 TF-IDF Calculation

We use *TfidfTransformer* in *sklearn* to calculate the TF-IDF of the whole dataset. According to different teacher numbers, school numbers, and class numbers, there are different groups of TF-IDF values.

TF-IDF values of the whole dataset are the sum of TF-IDF in each review. We use a min-max scaler to normalize the total TF-IDF value, used as the TF-IDF dictionary. Words left in the TF-IDF dictionary are keywords of the dataset. These keywords are manually classified into eight aspects and are used as the aspect dictionary.

3.3 Aspect Sortation and Score Calculation

Preprocessed reviews are classified into different aspects according to the aspect dictionary. The TF-IDF value of each keyword in the normalized TF-IDF dictionary is used as the weight. Keywords of different aspects are grouped. By summing up each aspect's word weights, the score of each aspect is calculated. The score of the whole dataset is the model of teachers' excellent teaching behaviors. Each teacher, school, or course also has its scores. Thus, we can make the quantitative analysis and visualized comparison. Word Clouds of keywords in different aspects are generated.

4 Experiment and Results

Following the procedure mentioned in the last section, we conducted the experiment. The data source, results, and comparison will be discussed in this section.

4.1 Data Description

The data used in this study is one semester's students' reviews of a high school in mainland China. It has 8366 pieces reviews. After preprocessing, 4386 pieces of reviews are left. The user dictionary contains words used to describe teachers' teaching behaviors, buzzwords, and proper names. Examples of these words are in Table 1.

Table 1. Examples of the user dictionary

Word	Part-of-speech Tag
认真负责 (careful)	Adjective
教学相长 (teaching benefits teachers as well as students)	Adjective
详略得当 (proper distribution of contents)	Adjective
人美心善 (beautiful and kind)	Adjective
…	…

4.2 TF-IDF Dictionary

We used the preprocessed data to generate a TF-IDF dictionary. There are 497 keywords. Figure 2 shows the top 45 keywords and their normalized TF-IDF values.

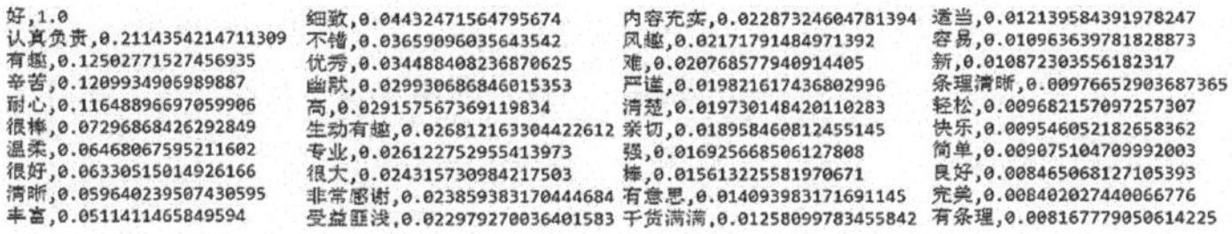

Fig. 2. Top 45 keywords and their normalized TF-IDF values

4.3 Aspect Sortation

Keywords are divided into eight categories: positive attitude, negative attitude, positive emotions, negative emotions, positive teaching methods, negative teaching methods, positive course contents, and negative course contents. Table 2 shows their content.

Table 2. Content of aspect dictionaries

positive attitude	认真负责，耐心，温柔，幽默，专业，风趣，严谨，亲切，要求严格，友善，善良，友好，博学，严格要求，严肃，善解人意，人美心善，专业性，学识渊博，激情，温和，尽职尽责，漂亮，人格魅力，谈笑风生，十分关心，一丝不苟，热爱生活，活泼可爱，德高望重，尊重学生，严苛，尽责任，干练，很酷，不辞辛苦，治学严谨，稳重，甜美，亲切友好，帅，恪尽职守，打成一片，直爽
negative attitude	苛刻
positive emotions	好，很棒，很好，不错，优秀，受益匪浅，棒，良好，完美，厉害，强烈推荐，挺好，真不错，获益匪浅，挺不错，无可挑剔，很感兴趣，挺好玩，极佳，如沐春风，惊喜，好极了，稳步前进，博闻强识，大开眼界，非常感激，大大提高，豁然开朗，恍然大悟，叹为观止
negative emotions	凶
positive teaching methods	清晰，细致，清楚，条理清晰，有条理，深入浅出，启发性，循循善诱，舒服，通俗易懂，形式多样，生动形象，针对性，循序渐进，流畅，接地气，详尽，引人入胜，详略得当，寓教于乐，贴切，不厌其烦，精确，简明扼要，恰到好处，突出重点，有条不紊，浅显易懂，简洁明了，明晰，条理清楚，讲清楚，一通百通，学以致用，简明，灵动，别出心裁，平实，由浅入深，一字一句，严密，口齿伶俐，活泼生动，旁征博引，生动活泼，教学相长，细致入微，一针见血，不快不慢，细，举一反三，声情并茂，活灵活现，化繁为简，与时俱进，深入分析，舒心
negative teaching methods	枯燥，咄咄逼人，枯燥无味，不耐烦
positive course contents	有趣，丰富，生动有趣，内容充实，有意思，干货满满，新，容易，轻松，快乐，简单，充足，积极性，互动性，有效，紧凑，活泼，非常丰富，趣味性，组织有序，具体，准确，灵活，广，丰富多彩，深，多样化，新颖，实践性，批判性，逻辑思维，积极思考，结合实际，灵活多样，广阔，逻辑性，舒适，容易接受，宽泛，开阔视野，参与性，覆盖面广，各抒己见，学术性，实用价值，精美，相关性，井井有序，别具一格，代表性，引人深思，打基础，花样繁多，各式各样
positive course contents	有趣，丰富，生动有趣，内容充实，有意思，干货满满，新，容易，轻松，快乐，简单，充足，积极性，互动性，有效，紧凑，活泼，非常丰富，趣味性，组织有序，具体，准确，灵活，广，丰富多彩，深，多样化，新颖，实践性，批判性，逻辑思维，积极思考，结合实际，灵活多样，广阔，逻辑性，舒适，容易接受，宽泛，开阔视野，参与性，覆盖面广，各抒己见，学术性，实用价值，精美，相关性，井井有序，别具一格，代表性，引人深思，打基础，花样繁多，各式各样
negative course contents	难，无聊，繁琐，肤浅，较难，沉闷，旧，干瘪

4.4 The Model and Application

The score of each aspect is calculated by adding up each keyword's weight in the TF-IDF dictionary. Figure 3 shows the model of teachers' excellent teaching behaviors.

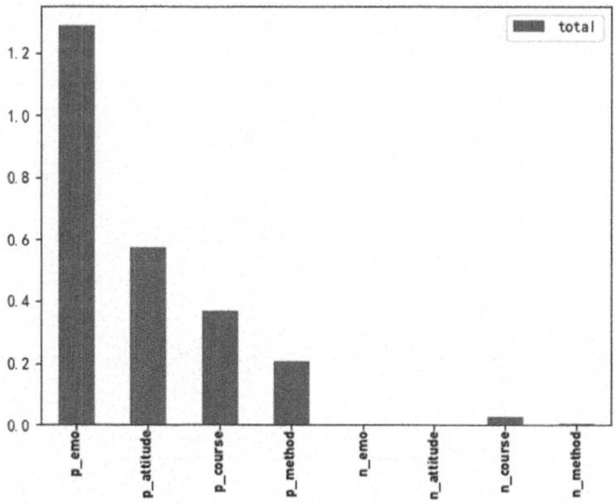

Fig. 3. Model of teachers' excellent teaching behaviors

By putting the score of teachers and the total data in the same chart, we could make a visible contrast. If the teacher's score in a specific aspect is higher than that in the total dataset, this teacher's unique keywords may help advise teachers to improve their teaching. Moreover, if the teacher's score in one aspect is relatively low, they may need to pay attention to this aspect. Figure 4 shows some teachers' samples of comparisons.

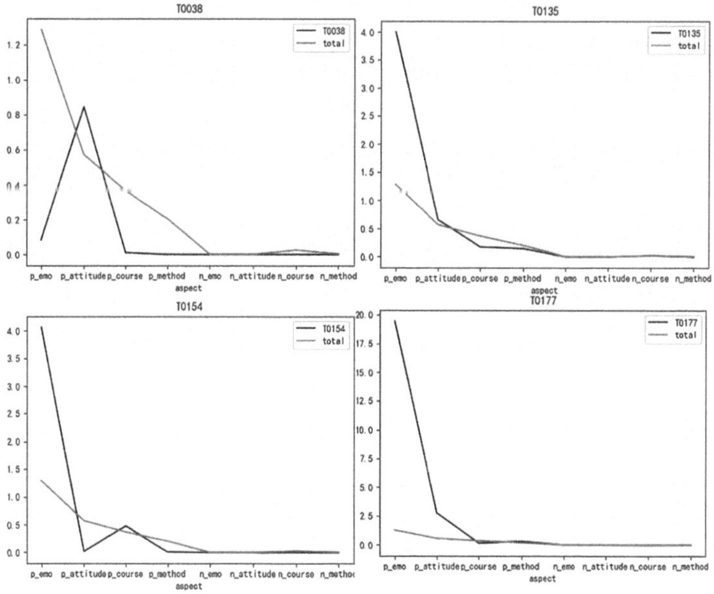

Fig. 4. Teachers' samples of comparisons

Word Cloud is used to present the keywords in describing teachers' excellent teaching behaviors. Figure 5 shows keywords of different aspects.

Fig. 5. Keywords of different aspects

5 Conclusion and Future Work

This paper proposes a model of teachers' excellent teaching behaviors based on natural language processing. Our study uses TF-IDF both for keyword extraction and quantitative evaluation. The division of aspects in the proposed model provides more credibility and application for teachers to improve their teaching. The experimental results are directly shown in charts and Word Cloud.

There are still limitations. Our dataset is composed mainly of positive comments. Thus, the scoring of negative aspects needs more tests. A dataset with a bigger size may provide more aspects than the current four. Further division of aspects can provide much more detailed information.

Acknowledgement. This work was supported by Guangdong University of Foreign Studies under X202111846058.

References

1. Mei, P., Jia, Y.: Research on the validity of student evaluation of teaching in China's HEIs during the past 10 years: a literature review. Mod. Univ. Educ. **04**, 29–34+111 (2013)
2. Brodeur, P., Larose, S., Tarabulsy, G., Feng, B., Forget-Dubois, N.: Development and construct validation of the mentor behavior scale. Mentor. Tutor. Partnersh. Learn. **23**, 54–75 (2015)

3. Newman, H., Joyner, D.: Sentiment analysis of student evaluations of teaching. In: Penstein Rosé, C. et al. (eds.) Artificial Intelligence in Education. AIED 2018. LNCS, vol. 10948, pp. 246–250. Springer, Cham (2018). https://doi.org/10.1007/978-3-319-93846-2_45
4. Nikolić, N., Grljević, O., Kovačević, A.: Aspect-based sentiment analysis of reviews in the domain of higher education. The Electronic Library (2020)
5. Okoye, K., et al.: Impact of students evaluation of teaching: a text analysis of the teachers qualities by gender. Int. J. Educ. Technol. High. Educ. **17**(1), 1–27 (2020). https://doi.org/10.1186/s41239-020-00224-z
6. Altrabsheh, N., Cocea, M., Fallahkhair, S.: Learning sentiment from students' feedback for real-time interventions in classrooms. In: Bouchachia, A. (eds.) Adaptive and Intelligent Systems. ICAIS 2014. Lecture Notes in Computer Science, vol. 8779, pp. 40–49. Springer, Cham (2014). https://doi.org/10.1007/978-3-319-11298-5_5
7. Zheng, T., Hongxia, S., Lihong, W., Qingxian, P.: Research of classification model for Chinese evaluation text of teaching. J. Yantai Univ. (Nat. Sci. Eng. Edit.) **25**, 122–126 (2012)
8. Devlin, J., Chang, M.-W., Lee, K., Toutanova, K.: Bert: Pre-training of deep bidirectional transformers for language understanding. arXiv preprint arXiv:1810.04805 (2018)
9. Rybinski, K., Kopciuszewska, E.: Will artificial intelligence revolutionise the student evaluation of teaching? A big data study of 1.6 million student reviews. Assess. Eval. High. Educ. **46**, 1127–1139 (2021)
10. Chauhan, G.S., Agrawal, P., Meena, Y.K.: Aspect-based sentiment analysis of students' feedback to improve teaching–learning process. In: Satapathy, S., Joshi, A. (eds.) Information and Communication Technology for Intelligent Systems. Smart Innovation, Systems and Technologies, vol. 107. Springer, Singapore (2019). https://doi.org/10.1007/978-981-13-1747-7_25
11. Yuchan, C., Wei, L.: Opinion extraction and clustering of students' teaching evaluation text based on sentiment analysis. J. Comput. Appl. **40**(S1), 113–117 (2020)

International Symposium on User Modeling and Language Learning (UMLL2021)

Examining the Efficacy of Video-Based Multimodal Three-Dimension Input on the Acquisition of English Phrases

Zina Zhang[1], Jia Yu[1], Yuanlin Huang[1], Yuhong Huang[2], and Xiaobin Liu[1](✉)

[1] South China Normal University, Guangzhou, China
liuxiaobin@m.scnu.edu.cn
[2] Xincheng Middle School, Shanwei, China

Abstract. Most researches have suggested that multimodal input may have an advantageous impact on second language (L2) phrase learning; however, how to ensure that it is effective rather than leading to cognitive overload for L2 learners remains unexplored. Drawing from Larsen-Freeman's Three-Dimensional Grammar Theory and Nation's taxonomy of knowledge of vocabulary, English phrase learning materials for EFL (English as a foreign language) learners were developed in the form of instructional short video clips, offering multimodal representations integrated with the form, meaning and use of every target phrase. The participants (N = 66) of the study were randomly divided into two groups, learning L2 lexical phrases with video- or paper-based materials. A pre-, middle- and post-test were conducted to examine learners' gains in L2 lexical phrase learning. The results showed that with the assistance of the video-based materials, students achieved higher substantial gains. Furthermore, students also held a positive attitude towards the use of the multimodal learning resources. This study confirmed the benefits of multimodal input, incorporated with the three dimensions of target phrase, for L2 phrase acquisition, and showed that phrases can be learned efficaciously with exposure to such input.

Keywords: Multimodal input · Three dimensions · English phrase · Instructional video

1 Introduction

Lexical phrases, or lexical chunks, are defined as conventionalized and recurring word combinations [23]. Researchers have suggested that the knowledge of the whole chunks is crucial for learners to attain high levels of language proficiency and fluency in second/ foreign language [9, 22, 28], as they tend to store and retrieve whole chunks of language rather than isolated words [32]. However, it appears that mastery of lexical phrases is a demanding challenge to L2 learners [9, 12, 30]. Several studies have suggested that L2 learners' knowledge of multi-word items is far less than single-word one [2, 25], and their mistakes made with collocations occupy a large proportion of learner errors, even for advanced L2 learners [12, 24]. With a sizeable repertoire of lexical phrases, L2 learners could express idiomatic expressions instead of

W. Jia et al. (Eds.): SETE 2021, LNCS 13089, pp. 315–324, 2021.
https://doi.org/10.1007/978-3-030-92836-0_27

unconventional phrasal expressions that may ruin smooth communication [6]. By this token, research that suggests a way to achieve L2 lexical phrase acquisition efficaciously may have practical implications for pedagogy.

Although previous studies have identified the overall positive effects of multimodal input on L2 lexis learning, there are still conflicting results on its exact effects [42]. As Nation [21] suggested, word knowledge includes three dimensions (form, meaning and use). This actually provides a new perspective for how to ensure multimodal input's efficacy. In other words, by incorporating these aspects of phrase knowledge into learning materials, it is quite possible to guarantee the effectiveness of multimodal learning materials on L2 lexical phrases. The instructional materials developed in this study are exactly in line with this requirement, i.e., three-dimensional presentations of target phrases, in an attempt to effectively promote L2 phrase acquisition.

In this study, learners will be exposed to multimodal presentations of L2 lexical phrase in three dimensions and their achievement will be tested to examine whether students benefit from the proposed educational materials. The key pedagogical implication of this study is that with the integration of the three knowledge dimensions (form, meaning and use) of L2 phrase, the benefits of multimodal input to boost L2 phrase knowledge may be promised.

2 Literature Review

2.1 Multimodal Input and Phrase Learning

Mayer [18] proposed Cognitive Theory of Multimedia Learning (CTML), arguing that the human brain processes information using two discrete channels, auditory and visual. The former is responsible for processing auditory information and the latter processes visual information [17]. CTML states that the brain employs the two systems to encode and store information to produce mental constructs. Thus, it is desirable to provide learners with multimodal environment allowing for stronger mental representations of information; hence, facilitating learning outcomes [19]. For instance, Webb and Chang [41] explored incidental learning of L2 collocations by comparing three input modes: reading, listening, and reading-while-listening. The results suggested that the last condition made the most contribution to learning collocations. Findings from Puimège and Peters [30] also confirmed the incidental learning of formulaic sequences from multimodal input, a one-hour English-language documentary without subtitles. Taken together, these studies showed that exposure to multimodal input could make contribution to L2 lexical phrase acquisition.

Though the majority of investigations have demonstrated the advantages of multimodal input [7, 29], some researchers have reported that multimodal input did not lead to more efficacious L2 lexicon acquisition, and even had adverse impact on L2 vocabulary acquisition [14, 15], which was theoretically consistent with the Cognitive Load Theory (CLT) [33]. CLT posits that the amount of information able to be processed at one time in working memory is limited. In a multimodal L2 learning environment, learners have to hold and process information from multiple modalities presented to them simultaneously, which may involve a higher cognitive demand, leading to a detrimental effect on learning. In Taylor's [36] study, for example, full captions were considered to be distracting for L2 learners, because processing video content was already a high-load activity, and having to deal with additional input (captions) imposed cognitive overload on L2 learners. Hence, it is important to ensure multimodal information provided to learners is not overwhelming, in order to avoid cognitive overload. In sum, research into the potential of a good balance of various modes, which would not impose cognitive overload upon learners, on L2 phrase learning is warranted.

2.2 Three-Dimensional Model and Phrase Learning

Celce-Murcia and Larsen-Freeman [3] proposed a conceptual framework for teaching grammar, namely Three Dimensions of Grammar. They recommended adopting a three-prong approach, including three interconnected dimensions of grammar, i.e., the form themselves, their meaning, and the pragmatic conditions governing their use. Similarly, Nation and Webb [22] listed three aspects of knowledge of a word, each of which is applicable to multiword units. According to them, what is involved in knowing a phrase comprises form, meaning and use. However, few research has specifically addressed lexicon learning from a perspective of this three-dimensional model. Elgort et al.'s research [5] affirmed the value of additional form-focused engagement with L2 words, in addition to learning its meaning from context. Each target item was presented in contextual learning (i.e., presented in three informative sentence contexts), with either form-focused elaboration or meaning-focused elaboration. The form-focused group outperformed the meaning-focused one on vocabulary acquisition. The results showed that form-focused treatment in conjunction with contextual word learning facilitated form-meaning mapping, thus significantly boosted quality of lexical knowledge. This research actually had implications for the benefit of incorporating the three dimensions when teaching vocabulary. Yet, in previous studies, the three-dimensional model has mainly been used as a theoretical foundation for vocabulary knowledge test [13, 16, 37], rather than as input enhancement. No research or program explored the efficacy of multimodal material, which is designed on the basis of three-dimensional model, allowing for enrichment of the L2 phrase items.

To sum up, while the benefits of multimodal input are generally recognized in existing studies, the boundary conditions on whether multimodal input facilitates or damages the learning of a given phrase are less clear cut, because excessively heavy information processing tasks are likely to result in high cognitive load. And taking the three dimensions into consideration when presenting multimodal input to learners may shed light on solving this problem, thus ensuring efficacious L2 phrase learning. In this light, it would appear a welcome trend for phrase learning materials designed for L2 learners to include multimodality and three-dimensional model at the same time. The current study aimed to bridge these gaps by investigating the effects of multimodal three-dimension input on senior high school students' phrase learning.

3 Methodology

3.1 The Present Research

RQ1: What's the effect of video-based multimodal three-dimension input on the acquisition of English L2 phrases?
RQ2: What are the students' attitudes towards the use of the video materials?
RQ3: Whether adding pictures and movie clips in phrasal learning material results in cognitive load for EFL learners?

3.2 Participants

The implementation of this study occurred in two classes in a senior high school in China. Both classes had the same teacher to teach the English course. 68 participants whose native language was Chinese were included, 44 females and 24 males ranging from 17 to 18 years of age. However, only 66 had finished all the tests throughout the research process, each class having 33 students.

3.3 Materials

Pre-/middle-/post-phrase Tests. Pre- and post-test contained 35 separate sentences. Each sentence contained a target phrase which was left out and required participants to fill in according to the hint in their first language. Non-significant difficulty differences were found between the two tests ($F = 1.241$, $p = .270$). The middle-test included 30 sentences. Phrases in pre- and post-test were randomly selected from 360 EFL phrases, while phrases in middle-test were selected from those learned in Week 2.

Questionnaire. To address RQ2, a questionnaire was adapted with reference to Sydorenko's [35]. The questions involved participants' perception on phrase learning and acquisition (6 items), their evaluation of the effectiveness of multimodal videos (11 items), and their satisfaction of the multimodal videos (4 items). Each item was measured in the form of a five-point Likert scale. A question which required participants to list 5 impressive phrases and write down the corresponding sentences used in the video was added, which was to examine participants' phrase retention. The Cronbach's alpha reliability was .942.

Interview. A semi-structured interview was designed to answer RQ3 and explore how students think about the multimodal material.

Learning Materials. The learning materials in this study were 360 English phrases selected from the frequently-used phrases in National College Entrance Examination (NCEE) in China. They are presented to participants either with video or with paper. Each video-based material included (a) an EFL phrase, (b) corresponding Chinese meaning, (c) an audio of the phrase, (d) a picture illustrating the meaning of the phrase, (e) a movie-clip using the phrase. For paper-based materials, they only included (a) EFL phrases, (b) corresponding Chinese meanings and (c) sample sentences using the phrases. Sentences used in paper-based materials were the same as those in movie clip in video-based materials.

3.4 Procedures

Two classes were randomly assigned to two groups: the control group (CG) was presented with paper-based materials and the experimental group (EG) with video-based one. Before the experiment, all participants completed the written informed consent forms and finished a pre-test. During the experiment, EG was presented with video-based EFL phrase learning materials while CG was given paper-based materials. Participants were required to learn 90 EFL phrases in a week, and 360 phrases in four weeks in total. On Saturday morning in Week 2, both groups finished a middle-test. After the experiment, participants finished a post-test. A questionnaire was given to EG and 10 students in EG were randomly selected for an interview.

3.5 Scoring and Analyses

In three tests, participants received 1 point for each correct phrase and 0 point for a wrong phrase or a misspelling. All scores were transformed into the hundred-mark system, so the possible highest score was 100.

4 Results

4.1 Results of Participants' Phrase Acquisition

The analysis was conducted using a two-way repeated measures ANOVA with Group as the between-subject factor and Time as the within-subjects factor. The result of Mauchly's Test of Sphericity was not statistically significant ($p = .814 > .05$), which indicated that sphericity has not been violated. The results of normal distribution test indicated that the data were not normally distributed ($p_{pre} = .015$, $p_{middle} = .000$, $p_{post} = .004$).

Results of tests of within-subjects and between-subjects effects showed that there was a significant large main effect for time [F (2,128) = 514.99, $p < .001$, $\eta_p^2 = .89$] and group [F (1,64) = 18.64, $p < .001$, $\eta_p^2 = .23$]. Besides, time and group interaction was also significant [F (2,128) = 15.24, $p < .001$, $\eta_p^2 = .19$].

The results of pairwise comparisons for three tests in both groups were presented in Table 1. It indicated that the scores of middle-test were significantly higher than that of pre-test and post-test in both (*MD* middle-pre = 66.53, $p < .001$; *MD* middle-post = 12.45, $p < .001$) and CG (*MD* middle-pre = 53.27, $p < .001$; *MD* middle-post = 20.26, $p < .001$), and the scores of post-test were significantly higher than that of pre-test in EG (*MD* post-pre = 54.08, $p < .001$) and CG (*MD* post-pre = 33.01, $p < .001$).

Table 1. Results of pairwise comparisons for three tests in both groups.

Group	(I) Time	(J) Time	*MD (I-J)*	Sig.
EG	Middle-test	Pre-test	66.53	.000***
		Post-test	12.45	.000***
	Post-test	Pre-test	54.08	.000***
CG	Middle-test	Pre-test	53.27	.000***
		Post-test	20.26	.000***
	Post-test	Pre-test	33.01	.000***

According to the results of pairwise comparisons for two groups in three tests, no significant difference was found between EG and CG in pre-test scores ($MD_{EG-CG} = .841$, $p = .775 < .05$). However, a significant difference was found between two groups in middle-test ($MD_{EG-CG} = 14.14$, $p < .001$) and post-test scores ($MD_{EG-CG} = 21.95$, $p < .001$), with EG scoring higher than CG in middle-test and much higher in post-test.

4.2 Results of the Questionnaire

Each item of the questionnaire was measured in the form of a five-point Likert scale, so the possible full score for each item was 5.

The results indicated that participants generally appreciated the importance of phrase leaning and most of them reported a good command of the form, meaning and use of phrases ($M = 4.02$, $SD = .815$). An overall positive perception of multimodal resources mentioned above was also reported ($M = 4.50$, $SD = .675$). Besides, most participants strongly agreed that the videos had helped them a lot in their learning process ($M = 4.51$, $SD = .648$).

In the end of the questionnaire, participants were asked to write down five impressive phrases and their corresponding sentences presented in the video. The results suggested that participants in experimental group can either recall most of the sentences ($M = 3.88$, $SD = 1.495$) or create correct sentences by themselves ($M = 4.00$, $SD = 1.069$).

4.3 Results of the Interview

10 students from EG were randomly selected to attend the interview (S1-S10).

Firstly, regarding the commonly-used methods adopted by students to learn new phrases, most students just look for the Chinese meaning. As S3 replied, "*I used to check the Chinese meaning when I come across a new phrase.*" But some students learn phrases differently. S1 reported that "*I used to learn a new phrase by looking it up on the Internet for its Chinese meaning and relevant pictures to get a deeper impression.*" These suggested the potential benefits of multimodal videos in phrase learning.

Secondly, as to students' opinions towards multimodal phrase learning material, all students held a positive view. For example, S4 commented that "*I think this method is good and effective. I can learn a lot of phrases within a small amount of time, because these resources impressed me a lot.*"

Thirdly, 9 out of 10 showed preference towards multimodal material rather than monomodal material. But S2 held a neutral view between these two methods, replying that "*It depends. If I have enough time to learn, I prefer the second(multimodal) method. But if I don't have enough time, for example, when I am doing a reading comprehension, I think the first method is also good for me.*"

Fourthly, as to RQ3, most students showed favorable attitudes on the addition of pictures and clips. S1 held a positive view on pictures, saying that "*Pictures helped me because they were colorful and vivid, which made me better understand the meaning of the phrases.*" There were also a few challenges for the chosen clips. S1 commented that "*Sometimes, the meaning provided by the clips did not match with the Chinese meaning, which made me confused.*"

Lastly, as for students' evaluation of the effectiveness of multimodal material, all students thought that it was effective for their phrase learning. S5, for instance, reported that "*I did not expect to remember English phrases for a long time, but the videos helped me to recall the phrases when doing tests.*"

5 Discussion and Conclusion

This study aimed to examine the efficacy of unimodal paper-based or multimodal video-based phrases learning method on the L2 phrases acquisition. Multimodal video-based phrases learning method addressed lexicon learning from a perspective of Nation and Webb's [40] three-dimensional model, i.e., through input which integrated form, meaning and use. The written form of the phrases is presented with words, meaning with L1 translation and images and use with video (intercepted from cartoon, movie and TV series).

RQ1 addressed the effect of paper-based or video-based learning material on the phrases acquisition of EFL learners in middle school. Based on the test results of the pre-test and immediate post-test, the results showed first, that both methods resulted in significant gains in phrase acquisition. However, when comparing the gains made by the two groups, the results indicate an advantage in immediate gains following video-based phrases learning method. As for the advantage of multimodal video-based phrases, it's generally aligned with previous studies [1, 4, 11, 31]. Video clips employed in the multimodal method provide context of the phrases which facilitate learners to learn the meaning and use of the phrases in context. In this study phrases were presented in a variety of contexts and in a variety of forms: spoken, written and pictorial.

Moreover, empirical studies showed that L1 translation was the most effective method for vocabulary learning [20, 38]. Clear, short, and familiar definitions of L1 translations were found to speed up the process of vocabulary acquisition [39]. Meanwhile, it's found that correspondence between text and imagery contributed to the acquisition of formulaic sequence [30]. Videos and images selected in this study have high correspondence to the target phrases, and this might be one of the possible reasons of the significant learning gains found in this study. The finding suggests that multimodal method has positive effect in the teaching and learning of L2 phrases. The cooperation of different modes enables learners to learn phrases effectively.

As for the RQ2 regarding the students' attitudes, students generally held positive attitudes towards the employment of multimodal video for its effectiveness in learning phrase, relieving learning stress, motivating interest and building confidence. Movies and TV series enjoy high popularity among learners which could simultaneously arouse learners' interest [10, 26] and alleviate learners' anxiety [16] which could lead to better acquisition of phrases. In this study, pictures and movies arouse students' interests in phrases acquisition and provide appropriate context, in which learners could learn the use and meaning of the phrases more effectively, and therefore contributes to better acquisition of phrases.

With regard to RQ3, whether adding pictures and movie clips in phrasal learning material results in cognitive load for EFL learners. Cognitive load theory focuses on the effects of information processing load on the construction of long-term memory [34]. In the interview conducted a month later, many participants reported that they could still recall the meanings of target phrases clearly, which indicates that video-based multimodal three-dimension input contributes to learners' long-term memory construction. Therefore, adding pictures and movie clips in phrasal learning material does not result in cognitive load for EFL learners but "*help me gain the meaning of the phrases as a tool*" as reported by S10. Furthermore, research showed that simultaneous processing of two different types of information that are not automatized can lead to inadequate processing of either or both types of information [8]. In this study, in video-based learning materials, form (spelling, pronunciation), meaning (L1 translation, image), use (video) were presented in a sequence. And learners concentrate on the form and then on the meaning of the phrase, thus avoiding the influence of "trade off" effect. However, in paper-based materials, form, meaning and use of the phrase are presented to the learners at the same time, and learners might not adequately process all three types of information.

There are several limitations on this study. First, we did not compare the gains with different types of multimodal methods, for example learning material with text and picture, learning material with words and video and that with words, picture and video. Future study could also address the effects of the combination of modes in different order on phrase learning. Secondly, learners might not distribute equal attention to all the three modes (text, picture and video). To investigate the extent to which each of three modes receives attention from learners, further investigation by means of eye-tracking techniques and its relation with phrase acquisition is needed. Third, a delayed post-test should be carried to examine the long-term retention. Moreover, since cognitive load is researched by subjective interview, future research could adopt subjective measurement technique [27] or other objective measurement techniques.

References

1. Alzahrani, S., Roberts, L.: The effect of visuospatial designing elements of zoomable user interfaces on second language vocabulary acquisition. System **96**, 102–396 (2021)
2. Bahns, J., Eldaw, M.: Should we teach EFL students collocations? System **21**(1), 101–114 (1993)

3. Celce-Murcia, M., Larsen-Freeman, D.: The Grammar Book: An ESL/EFL Teacher's Course, 2nd edn. Heinle/Cengage, Boston, MA (1999)
4. Chun, D.M., Plass, J.L.: Effects of multimedia annotations on vocabulary acquisition. Mod. Lang. J. **80**(2), 183–198 (1996)
5. Elgort, I., Candry, S., Boutorwick, T.J., Eyckmans, J., Brysbaert, M.: Contextual word learning with form-focused and meaning-focused elaboration. Appl. Linguis. **39**(5), 646–667 (2018)
6. Eyckmans, J., Boers, F., Lindstromberg, S.: The impact of imposing processing strategies on L2 learners' deliberate study of lexical phrases. System **56**, 127–139 (2016)
7. Hagiwara, A.: Effect of visual support on the processing of multiclausal sentences. Lang. Teach. Res. **19**(4), 455–472 (2015)
8. Han, Z., Peverly, S.T.: Input processing: a study of ab initio learners with multilingual backgrounds. Int. J. Multiling. **4**(1), 17–37 (2007)
9. Hou, J., Loerts, H., Verspoor, M.H.: Chunk use and development in advanced Chinese L2 learners of English. Lang. Teach. Res. **22**(2), 148–168 (2018)
10. Hussein, I.A., Parilah, M.S.: Motivation and attitudes towards learning English among undergraduates in national university of Malaysia (UKM). Int. J. Engl. Educ. **3**, 209–227 (2014)
11. Khezrlou, S., Ellis, R., Sadeghi, K.: Effects of computer-assisted glosses on EFL learners' vocabulary acquisition and reading comprehension in three learning conditions. System **65**, 104–116 (2017)
12. Laufer, B., Waldman, T.: Verb-noun collocations in second language writing: a corpus analysis of learners' English. Lang. Learn. **61**(2), 647–672 (2011)
13. Lee, P., Lin, H.: The effect of the inductive and deductive data-driven learning (DDL) on vocabulary acquisition and retention. System **81**, 14–25 (2019)
14. Liu, Y., Jang, B.G., Roy-Campbell, Z.: Optimum input mode in the modality and redundancy principles for university ESL students' multimedia-enhanced learning. Comput. Educ. **127**, 190–200 (2018)
15. Lwo, L., Lin, M.C.T.: The effects of captions in teenagers' multimedia L2 learning. ReCALL **24**(2), 188–208 (2012)
16. Lu, H.W., Lee, J.-Y., Lin, M.H.: Effects of authentic English-language videos on EFL students' speaking anxiety. Int. J. Inf. Educ. Technol. **9**(6), 423–428 (2019)
17. Mayer, R.E., Moreno, R.: A split-attention effect in multimedia learning: evidence for dual processing systems in working memory. J. Educ. Psychol. **90**(2), 312–320 (1998)
18. Mayer, R.E.: Multimedia Learning. Cambridge University Press, New York (2001)
19. Mayer, R.E.: Multimedia Learning, 2nd edn. Cambridge University Press, Cambridge, UK (2009)
20. Moskovsky, C., Jiang, G., Libert, A., Fagan, S.: Bottom-up or top-down: English as a foreign language vocabulary instruction for Chinese university students. Tesol Q. **49**, 256–277 (2015)
21. Nation, I.S.P.: Learning Vocabulary in Another Language. Cambridge University Press, Cambridge, UK (2001)
22. Nation, I.S.P., Webb, S.: Researching and Analyzing Vocabulary. Heinle, Boston, MA (2011)
23. Nattinger, J.R., De Carrico, J.S.: Lexical Phrases and Language Teaching. Oxford University Press, Oxford, UK (1992)
24. Nesselhauf, N.: The use of collocations by advanced learners of English and some implications for teaching. Appl. Linguis. **24**(2), 223–242 (2003)
25. Nguyen, T.M.H., Webb, S.: Examining second language receptive knowledge of collocation and factors that affect learning. Lang. Teach. Res. **21**(3), 298–320 (2017)

26. Nooreiny, M., Indira Malani, M.: Learner's learning experiences & difficulties towards (ESL) among UKM undergraduates. Adv. Lang. Lit. Stud. **6**, 83–87 (2015)
27. Paas, F.: Training strategies for attaining transfer of problem-solving skill in statistics: a cognitive-load approach. J. Educ. Psychol. **84**, 429–434 (1992)
28. Perera, N.S.: The role of prefabricated language in young children's second language acquisition. Biling. Res. J. **25**(3), 327 (2001)
29. Peters, E.: The effect of imagery and on-screen text on foreign language vocabulary learning from audiovisual input. TESOL Q. **53**(4), 1008–1032 (2019)
30. Puimège, E., Peters, E.: Learning formulaic sequences through viewing L2 television and factors that affect learning. Stud. Second. Lang. Acquis. **42**(3), 525–549 (2020)
31. Ramezanali, N., Faez, F.: Vocabulary learning and retention through multimedia glossing. Lang. Learn. Technol. **23**(2), 105–124 (2019)
32. Shabani, G., Rahimy, R.: An investigation of the effectiveness of enhancing input through glossing and skewing techniques on knowledge of lexical collocation. J. Psycholinguist. Res. **49**(6), 1011–1025 (2020). https://doi.org/10.1007/s10936-020-09729-0
33. Sweller, J.: Implications of cognitive load theory for multimedia learning. In: Mayer, R. (ed.) Cambridge Handbook of Multimedia Learning. Cambridge University Press, New York, NY (2005)
34. Sweller, J., van Merrienboer, J.J.G., Paas, F.: Cognitive architecture and instructional design: 20Years later. Educ. Psychol. Rev. **31**(2), 261–292 (2019)
35. Sydorenko, T.: Modality of input and vocabulary acquisition. Lang. Learn. Technol. **14**(2), 50–73 (2010)
36. Taylor, G.: Perceived processing strategies of students watching captioned video. Foreign Lang. Ann. **38**(3), 422–427 (2005)
37. Teng, M.F.: Vocabulary learning through videos: captions, advance-organizer strategy, and their combination. Comput. Assist. Lang. Learn. 1–33 (2020)
38. Tian, L., Hennebry, M.: Chinese learners' perceptions towards teachers' language use in lexical explanations: a comparison between Chinese-only and English-only instructions. System **63**, 77–88 (2016)
39. Wang, K.H.I.: The use of dialogic strategy clusters for vocabulary learning by Chinese students in the UK. System **51**, 51–64 (2015)
40. Webb, S., Kagimoto, E.: Learning collocation: do the number of collocates, position of the node word, and synonymy affect learning? Appl. Linguis. **32**(3), 259–276 (2011)
41. Webb, S., Chang, A.: How does mode of input affect the incidental learning of collocations? Stud. Second Lang. Acquis. 1–22 (2020)
42. Zhang, R., Zou, D.: A state-of-the-art review of the modes and effectiveness of multimedia input for second and foreign language learning. Comput. Assist. Lang. Learn. 1–27 (2021)

Synchronous Computer Mediated Communication in English Language Classes During the Pandemic: A Case Study of Wuhan

Zilin Wang and Di Zou(✉)

The Education University of Hong Kong, 10 Lo Ping Road, TaiPo, New Territories, Hong Kong SAR
wzilin@friends.eduhk.hk, dzou@eduhk.hk

Abstract. This research reports on a case study applying synchronous computer-mediated communication (SCMC) in a Wuhan university's English language classes during the COVID-19 pandemic. The aim was to identify the advantages and disadvantages of using synchronous technology applications in online English language courses. The dataset consisted of ethnographic observations and in-depth interviews with the teacher and students. The thematic analysis revealed that the advantages of the SCMC include the availability of abundant learning resources, the affordance of instant information exchange, and a comparatively relaxed learning environment. Two major disadvantages were that the non-face-to-face communication tended to lead to the teacher's "one-person" show, and the limited screen size reduced eye contact between the teacher and students. The present research indicates that SCMC can be applied during and after the pandemic to foster student discussion and collaboration. We also suggest that when language teachers deliver courses using SCMC tools or platforms, students should be given abundant opportunities to express their opinions.

Keywords: Synchronous learning · Computer-mediated communication · English

1 Introduction

COVID-19 has influenced educational practices over a wide range of aspects. On Jan. 30, 2020, the World Health Organization (WHO) declared a Public Health Emergency of International Concern (PHEIC), and Wuhan became the focus of world attention due to it being the place of the initial outbreak and heavy suffering. Subsequent school closures reduced influenza outbreaks by reducing social contact among students (Jackson et al. 2016). Hence, distant teaching and learning became a main-stream pedagogical practice. Synchronous computer-based communication (SCMC) tools, such as ZOOM (Bailey et al. 2021; Cheung 2021), Moodle (Brandl 2012), Skype (Develotte and Vincent 2010; Knight et al. 2017; Martin and Valdivia 2017) and QQ (Xu 2008; Zhang et al. 2013), with multiple supporting functions including video conferencing, real-time communication, and document sharing, are now widely applied in language education. Although SCMC in distant learning is not an emerging

W. Jia et al. (Eds.): SETE 2021, LNCS 13089, pp. 325–333, 2021.
https://doi.org/10.1007/978-3-030-92836-0_28

technology, the synchronous teaching mode has dramatically increased under the present pandemic and has become common in language teaching (Cheung 2021). However, teachers have also noted several shortcomings of SCMC, such as unstable network connections, high literacy requirements, and student distraction. The present study aims to identify the effectiveness of the SCMC tool in a QQ group used in university English literature classes, where SCMC was a compulsory and unique teaching mode due to the severe pandemic situation in Wuhan. The findings and pedagogical implications of this research may be helpful for designing synchronous tasks and promoting online language teaching quality.

2 Literature Review

Synchronous learning refers to using any learning tool in real-time, such as instant messaging, allowing students and teachers to ask and answer questions immediately ("Synchronous vs. Asynchronous", n.d.). The instant chat feature of synchronous tools enables spontaneous online language learning experiences similar to face-to-face learning (Okuyama 2005). Even though physical interactions are lacking in the online mode, the text chat facility can be used for quick queries and comments, thus compensating for the lack of visual cues such as gestures and facial expressions (Hampel 2006). However, some research has also revealed the differences between SCMC language learning and offline language learning. Abrams (2003) argues that students can produce more oral output by SCMC platforms than in traditional offline classes, and the SCMC platform offers both simultaneous text and audio exchanges to students promoting individual practices (Bailey and Hatcher 2021).

The research on the advantages of SCMC mainly rests on its convenience and flexibility. SCMC is convenient for communicative exchange where users can quickly upload texts, images, audio, and video (Brandl 2012; Sato et al. 2017; Zeng and Takatsuka 2009). Similarly, Bailey et al. (2021) claim that the merits of SCMC are its practical synthesis combining oral and other modalities, such as text-chat, pictures, and videos. Further, flexibility is highly appreciated by re-searchers because the saving of time and space leads to cost reductions (Sato et al. 2017). In addition, without the need for face-to-face interaction, students perform in a more confident way (Mellati et al. 2018) and concentrate better (Ko and Chen 2011; Takatsuka 2009).

SCMC's disadvantages are primarily related to the excessive freedom it affords and the high requirements for other skills. Mellati et al. (2018) state that the online environment leads to student distraction. This mode might not fit every type of language learner because it requires a high degree of conscientiousness (Arispe and Blake 2012; Moorhouse et al. 2021; Stickler and Shi 2013). Grant (2016) also notes that students must have mastered time management and group coordination skills when using SCMC tools. Palladin and Guardado (2018) found that SCMC is a challenge not only for the students but also for teachers.

The present study contributes to discussions about the effectiveness of SCMC tools when it is the solitary teaching mode. The pedagogical implications proposed here may be helpful for language trainers to design their online class activities and promote synchronous teaching quality. Accordingly, the research questions are:

1) What are the advantages and disadvantages of a QQ group (the SCMC tool used in this case)?
2) How do these advantages and disadvantages influence online teaching and learning during the COVID-19 pandemic?

3 Method

This qualitative research is a case study of English literature classes in a university. The teacher's and students' behavior were observed and recorded to understand the classroom interactions. In addition, in-depth interviews with the teacher and one student were conducted to investigate their individual experience in synchronous learning and teaching.

The class participants were 27 sophomore English major students (1 male and 26 female), whose ages ranged from 18–20 years old, and their instructor who was teaching an English Literature course in a Wuhan university. Students chose this major intending to become English teachers.

The research data was comprised of observations and interviews. Class observations were conducted from March to May 2020. The SCMC tool applied in teaching was a QQ group (a platform created by Tencent, a Chinese company). Within the QQ group, the teacher created a conference for delivering synchronous classes. Students have the option to open or close their microphones and camera. In the class, students could communicate with others or propose their questions using a chatbox (Fig. 1). Figure 2 shows a picture of the QQ group conference interface. With permission from the teacher to participate in the class as students, the authors developed a deeper understanding of what happened during class. The interview questions for the two interviewees (one teacher and one student) had subtle differences, mainly related to their experience and reflections on online teaching and learning. The interviews, ranging from about 40 to 90 min in Chinese, were audiotaped, transcribed, and translated.

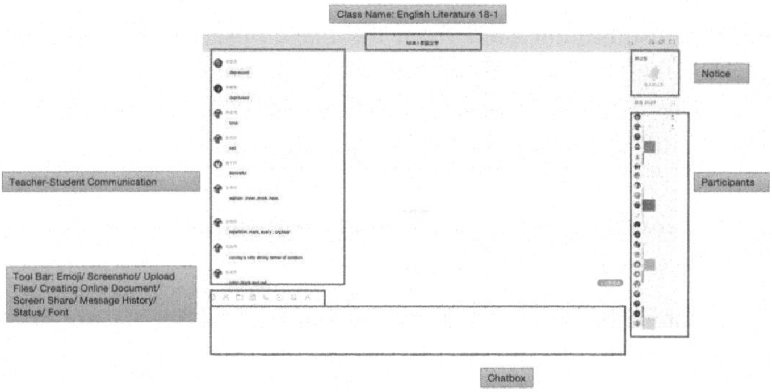

Fig. 1. The QQ group

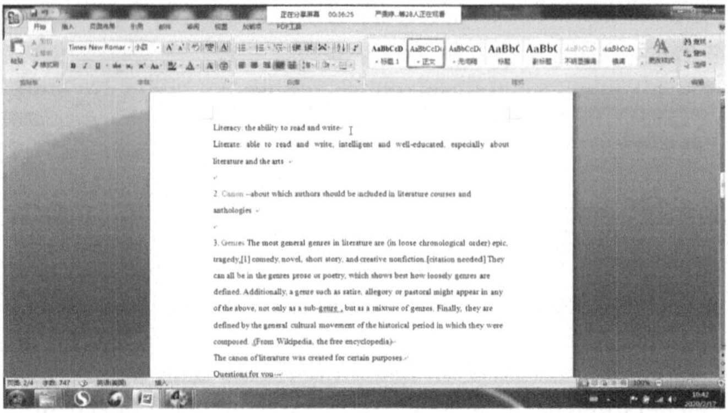

Fig. 2. The teacher's screen sharing

Thematic analyses were used to analyze the data. The latest research on thematic analysis by Clarke and Braun (2019) proposes six phases: familiarizing with the data; generating codes; generating themes; reviewing potential themes; defining and naming themes: and producing the report. We rigorously followed these six steps to code the manuscripts and integrate the analysis. The audio recordings of the observations and interviews were first transcribed and read twice. After becoming familiar with the dataset, the initial coding phase was conducted, aiming to "remain open to all possible interpretations" (Douglas et al. 2009) via a re-reading and recoding process. Instead of superficially abstracting the high-frequency words in interviews to establish themes, DeSantis and Ugarriza (2000) proposed combining the interview content analysis and labeling words or phrases, which can create essential categories. Therefore, in the next phase of identifying themes, similar codes were clustered together, and these also were related to our research aims. When potential themes were identified, a visual thematic map was created (Fig. 3).

4 Results and Discussion

In this section, the results generated from the class observations, and in-depth interviews are explained thematically. As shown in Fig. 3, five themes were identified, three of which carry more detailed information. Hence, this paper focuses on these three themes, with authentic recordings analysis supporting each theme.

4.1 Theme #1: Low-Effective Communication Resulted from Non-face-to-Face Interaction

Non-face-to-face interactions, a distinctive feature of SCMC, were identified as a weakness compared with the offline classrooms by both the teacher and students. Students worried they could not understand the complicated terms and concepts that were normally explained by the teacher several times in face-to-face contexts. The teacher was concerned that the limited screen interface could not show students' facial

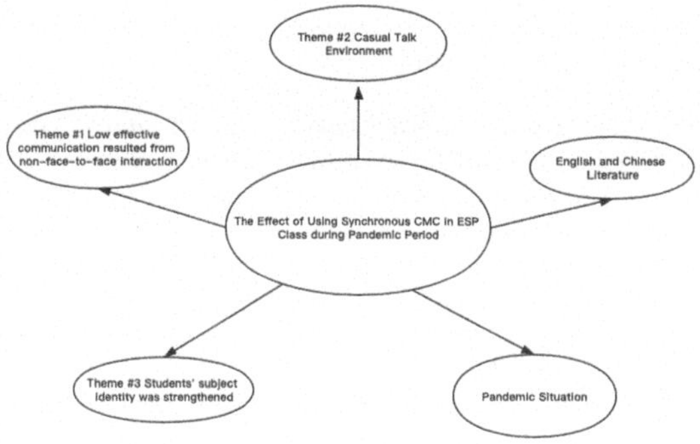

Fig. 3. The thematic map

expressions, which she claimed was important for judging students' feelings and understanding.

From the students' perspective, it was not easy to propose timely questions on SCMC. Serving as a class monitor, Lee, on behalf of the student body, commented that the most significant challenge was using the chatbox in SCMC:

My classmates and I don't think we understand what the teacher delivered. In online communication mode, typing is different from face-to-face talking because when we type [in the chatbox], we need to express our ideas in a written manner, and it takes a lot of time. We believe this is a not an effective way. (Excerpt 1)

Here, Lee describes the communication difficulties in the QQ group:

In my opinion, although the teacher tried to make complex knowledge as explicit as possible, I still felt it hard to communicate with the teacher using chatbox. For example, when I was confused about the rhythm of English poems, I attempted to type my questions on the screen. But on the one hand, I found I couldn't express my confusion in writing; therefore, I would like to study difficult ideas by myself. On the other hand, after I sent the message in chatbox, other messages immediately overwhelmed my questions. Sometimes, the teacher allowed us to open the microphones and to communicate or propose a question to her. However, it did not always work since the communication heavily relied on the internet connection. (Excerpt 2)

Lee's account reveals the limitations of SCMC in three ways. First, typing the message required students to pose their questions or ideas in writing which was a challenge for most students. Even though Lee's grade was excellent, he still thought that writing his feedback was difficult and wasted time. Secondly, sending a message in chatbox was so convenient that many instant messages overwhelmed the teacher. Thirdly, the unstable internet connection sometimes interrupted communication. These three factors impacted students' willingness to ask complex academic questions. As Lee said, instead of asking the teacher, he preferred to study by himself. These impediments led the teacher to perform as a "knowledge holder" (Manoliu 2015) resulting in delivering a "one-person" show.

From the teacher's perspective, the limited screen size could not provide enough visual feedback from the students. Her previous teaching experience emphasized using visual cues from students to assess whether they had understood her explanations.

However, through SCMC learning, students had the right to turn off the camera which made the teacher feel anxious. She said:

> *In a traditional offline class, I really enjoyed talking with my students in class. Through eye contact, I could know whether they had understood what I said. But now, I always feel anxious that I cannot receive eye contact with my students. I know some complex terminologies they must take time to comprehend, but students might pretend to understand them due to low-effective communication on academic affairs by SCMC. Unexpectedly, the course progress is faster than my initial plan. I regard this as a dangerous signal. (Excerpt 3)*

The lack of instant eye contact made this experienced teacher lose control of her class progress. During SCMC classes, students could turn off their cameras anytime, and in our observations, most students closed their cameras and microphones. They preferred to communicate via typing rather than speaking. These features of SCMC negatively impacted the teachers' teaching skills to some extent.

This result is consistent with Moorhouse et al.'s finding (2021) that non-face-to-face interaction brings about more "teacher talking time". In their research, the teachers were reported to complain about the difficulties associated with students turning their cameras off and limitations on the number of students visible on the screen, making it difficult for the teacher to create a positive classroom atmosphere. Clearly, these impediments influenced the students' desire to communicate when the teacher played a dominant role in the class.

4.2 Theme #2: Casual Talk Environment

Unlike teacher-student communication, the online communication in the chatting room had a relaxed and casual environment facilitating communication. In the interview with Lee, he mentioned a change of language register.

> *We tend to communicate in the chatbox in online classes, even using Internet slang since we used to regard online chat as a daily conversation. For example, we use "JINGLEI," a recently popular word when the internet broke down. Besides that, we also like to use the anonymous name to chat, which is a funny function on QQ. When we chose "talk in anonymous," QQ would distribute us a name at random. This makes online communication very interesting. By the way, some classmates like use images or emojis to express their mood as well. (Excerpt 4)*

Students showed a common interest in using the internet chatting style of QQ in the class. Bloor and Bloor (2007, p. 9) indicate that close interactions on internet communities contribute to common interests. The style of the online language is flexible and easily creates a relaxing atmosphere. In contrast to traditional teacher-student communication, online peer communication in the chatting room created a comparatively relaxed atmosphere among the teacher and students. The students and the teacher communicated as "netizens" in a friendly teacher-student relationship. Certain internet slang appeared frequently, such as in excerpt 4, the internet pop word JINGLEI, meaning feeling shocked by an emergency, which is non-academic. Other evidence of using internet language, such as communicating anonymously and using emojis, also congested the online communication, although this kind of interaction facilitated students' willingness to communicate in classroom discussions.

Other researchers have also found that SCMC promoted students' peer discussion. Bailey et al. (2021) showed that students enjoy the opportunity to develop relationships with their classmates when participating in ZOOM speaking activities. Zeng and Takastsuka (2009) found that interactions amplify learners' mutual attention using the Moodle platform, and they also found that SCMC fostered peer discussions and collaboration.

4.3 Theme #3: Students' Subjective Identity Was Strengthened

In the dataset, both the teacher and student commented on the teacher-student relationship constructed by QQ, and these comments developed the third theme. In the online teacher-student relationship, the students' subject identity was constructed by increasing self-study time, and students even became a decisive factor for class progress.

When asked questions about the differences between the online and offline classes, both the teacher and the student emphasized the increasing importance of self-learning ability:

> *Lee: I have to say online learning offers me many opportunities and much time to self-study and reflect. If I propose a question on the chatbox, it might be overwhelmed by other fast messages. Fortunately, the teacher provided us with more materials as well. In the online group file, we could find not only the PowerPoint slides and the textbook, but also some videos and references related to our study content. At the same time, I like to search new terms on the internet, which I think is the most effective way for me to understand them. I could feel that students now had totally become the class center since some teachers had no idea how to deliver classes by QQ group and only assigned silent tasks. When all students finished the tasks, the class could go on. (Excerpt 5)*
>
> *The teacher: I agree that students work harder when they have classes in the QQ group since at least I uploaded more learning material than before due to convenient file and link sharing functions. I feel proud of my students. They tolerate the limitations of online classes and study harder than before. Everyone submitted assignments on time. Sometimes they performed quite actively, not shyly; I think it might be because they didn't need to talk face to face. (Excerpt 6)*

Students strengthened subject identities were constructed via learner-centered online learning, and their willingness became the decisive factor in determining whether the class was successful. Simultaneously, students were learning content and conducted more self-study than they would normally do in offline situations. Excerpts 5 and 6 reveal two factors leading to students spending more time on self-study. The first was because the information exchanges on SCMC were rapid, which led to the chatbox being overwhelmed with questions and comments. Instead of proposing questions on chat-box without feedback, students were willing to learn the content by themselves. The second reason was that the sharing functions available in SCMC provided students with abundant resources from both the teacher and the internet. Thus, students could achieve effective self-study through versatile support.

Compared with offline learning, one distinct advantage of SCMC was the way it stimulated learner autonomy. Mellati et al. (2018) also found that instant resource availability addresses learners' needs for interaction and expressing their opinions more confidently. Chen et al. (2021) claim the increased expressive performance of learners can be attributed to valuable peer support since SCMC immediately transfers feedback among learners. Obtaining the study resources from both the teacher and the internet, students have opportunities to explore the content by themselves deeply; meanwhile, the instant peer exchange is conducive to students' self-reflection (Sato et al. 2017). Zeng and Takastsuka (2009) believe that the fast information exchanges in SCMC enhance learners' common study goals and promote their collaborative efforts to resolve language learning problems in language acquisition classes. In sum, the ample study resources and instant peer talk on the SCMC platform enhance learner autonomy.

5 Conclusion

This study investigated the advantages and disadvantages of the SCMC tool, QQ group, applied as a unique teaching mode in a series of English literature classes dur-ing the COVID-19 outbreak. With interview and observation data from an online English Literature class in a Wuhan university, the approaches and frameworks of thematic analysis were applied to analyze the results. The primary disadvantage of SCMC was the low effectiveness of teacher-student communication caused by the non-face-to-face environment. When teaching complex content, the students' chatbox questions easily overwhelmed the system. Further, the limited size of the computer screen could not present students' facial expressions providing visual feedback to the teacher. These drawbacks compromised teacher-student interaction. However, the advantages of SCMC somewhat compensated for the shortcomings to some extent. The environment in the chatbox promoted casual and friendly interactions including internet slang, emojis, and anonymous communication allowing students to learn with less stress and more expressiveness. SCMC also motivated students to study autonomously.

The findings of the present study, which involved interviews of only one class teacher and one student, clearly cannot be generalized to larger contexts; therefore, our results are indicative only. However, we believe the findings may have significant pedagogical implications for online education during the pandemic. Online language teaching should focus on making adjustments to address the noted shortcomings to non-face-to-face communication.

References

Arispe, K., Blake, R.J.: Individual factors and successful learning in a hybrid course. System **40**(4), 449–465 (2012)

Abram, Z.I.: The effect of synchronous and asynchronous CMC on oral performance in German. Mod. Lang. J. **87**(2), 157–167 (2003)

Bailey, D., Almusharraf, N., Hatcher, R.: Finding satisfaction: intrinsic motivation for synchronous and asynchronous communication in the online language learning context. Educ. Inf. Technol. **26**(3), 2563–2583 (2021). https://doi.org/10.1007/s10639-020-10369-z

Bloor, M., Bloor, T.: The Practice of Critical Discourse Analysis: An Introduction. W.B. Saunders, Philadelphia (2007)

Brandl, K.: Effects of required and optional exchange tasks in online language learning environments. ReCALL J. EUROCALL **24**(1), 85 (2012)

Cheung, A.: Language teaching during a pandemic: a case study of zoom use by a secondary ESL teacher in Hong Kong. RELC (2021)

Chen, L., Wang, Y., Rodway, C.: Social strategy use in online Chinese learning. Comput. Assist. Lang. Learn. 1–28 (2021)

Clarke, V., Braun, V., Terry, G., Hayfield, N.: Thematic analysis. In: Liamputtong, P. (ed.) Handbook of Research Methods in Health and Social Sciences, pp. 843–860. Springer, Singapore (2019). https://doi.org/10.1007/978-981-10-5251-4_103

DeSantis, L., Ugarriza, D.N.: The concept of theme as used in qualitative nursing research. West. J. Nurs. Res. **22**(3), 351–372 (2000)

Develotte, C., Guichon, N., Vincent, C.: The use of the webcam for teaching a foreign language in a desktop videoconferencing environment. ReCALL **22**(3), 293–312 (2010)

Douglas, H., Hamilton, R., Grubs, R.: The effect of BRCA gene testing on family relationships: a thematic analysis of qualitative interviews. J. Genet. Couns. **18**(5), 418–435 (2009)

Grant, S.: Peer review process completion rates and subsequent student perceptions within completely online versus blended modes of study. System **62**, 93–101 (2016)

Hampel, R.: Rethinking task design for the digital age: a framework for language teaching and learning in a synchronous online environment. ReCALL **18**(2), 105–121 (2006)

Jackson, C., Vynnyckc, E., Mangtani, P.: The relationship between school holidays and transmission of influenza in England and Wales. Am. J. Epidemiol. **184**(9), 644–651 (2016)

Knight, J., Barbera, E., Appel, C.: A framework for learner agency in online spoken interaction tasks. ReCALL: J. EUROCALL **29**(3), 276 (2017)

Ko, L., Chen, N.S.: Online-interpreting in synchronous cyber classrooms. Babel **57**(2), 123–143 (2011)

Manoliu, M.: Educational discourse analysis. Int. J. Commun. Res. **5**(3), 222–230 (2015)

Martin, S., Alvarez Valdivia, I.M.: Students' feedback beliefs and anxiety in online foreign language oral tasks. Int. J. Educ. Technol. High. Educ. **14**(1), 1–15 (2017). https://doi.org/10.1186/s41239-017-0056-z

Mellati, M., Khademi, M., Abolhassani, M.: Creative interaction in social networks: multi-synchronous language learning environments. Educ. Inf. Technol. **23**(5), 2053–2071 (2018). https://doi.org/10.1007/s10639-018-9703-9

Moorhouse, B.L., Li, Y., Walsh, S.: E-classroom interactional competencies: meidating and assisting language learning during synchronous online lessons. RELC J. (2021). https://doi.org/10.1177/0033688220985274

Okuyama, Y.: Distance language learning via synchronous computer-mediated communication (SCMC): eight factors affecting NS-NNS chat interaction. JALT CALL J. **1**(2), 3–20 (2005)

Palladino, V., Guardado, M.: Extending the heritage language classroom: experiences of digital technology use in two community schools in Alberta, Canada. Lang. Cult. Curric. **31**(2), 150–167 (2018)

Sato, E., Chen, J.C., Jourdain, S.: Integrating digital technology in an intensive, fully online college course for Japanese beginning learners: a standards-based performance-driven approach. Mod. Lang. J. **101**(4), 765–775 (2017)

Stickler, U., Shi, L.: Supporting Chinese speaking skills online. System **41**(1), 50–69 (2013)

Synchronous vs asynchronous eLearning tools and technologies. https://www.talentlms.com/elearning/synchronous-vs-asynchronous-elearning. Accessed 10 Aug 2021

Xu, X.: Learning with a QQ-based collaborative e-learning system. In: 2008 Seventh International Conference on Web-based Learning, pp. 47–49. IEEE (2008)

Zhang, G., Li, J., Bi, L., Pang, L.: An analysis on information exchange characteristic about tourism synchronous virtual community: a case study of QQ group. Tour. Tribune **28**(2), 119–126 (2013)

Zeng, G., Takatsukla, S.: Text-based peer-peer collaborative dialogue in a computer-mediated learning environment in the EFL context. System **37**(3), 434–446 (2009)

Systematic Evaluation of Research Progress on Technology-Enhanced Language Learning: Content Analysis and Knowledge Mapping

Xieling Chen[1], Di Zou[2](✉), Haoran Xie[3], and Gary Cheng[1]

[1] Department of Mathematics and Information Technology, The Education University of Hong Kong, Hong Kong, Hong Kong SAR, China
chengks@eduhk.hk

[2] Department of English Language Education, The Education University of Hong Kong, Hong Kong, Hong Kong SAR, China

[3] Department of Computing and Decision Sciences, Lingnan University, Hong Kong, Hong Kong SAR

Abstract. Owing to the recent advances in information and communications technologies, technology-enhanced language learning (TELL) research has resulted in diverse theories and empirical evidence, showing the complex and dynamic nature of TELL. The retrospective amount of TELL research literature is ever-growing, making it difficult to produce a comprehensive overview. However, knowledge mapping and clustering technologies are capable of visualizing and structuring research literature on a large scale. Therefore, based on 1,295 SCI/SSCI peer-reviewed TELL research articles from 1995 to 2019, we aim to systematically investigate and map the TELL literature to generate implications and insights into future research. Results identify recent major TELL research issues like technology-assisted vocabulary/word learning, computer-facilitated communication, language learning driven by applying computers, virtual reality, mobiles, and digital games, as well as a focus on learners and the use of experimental design. Additionally, scholars are advised to pay attention to issues like robots-assisted language learning, multimodal strategies for language learning, synchronous technologies for language learning, anxiety towards TELL, and artificial intelligence in TELL.

Keywords: Technology-enhanced language learning · Content analysis · Knowledge mapping · Bibliometric analysis

1 Introduction

Digital technologies have facilitated learning in diverse subjects like mathematics, nursing, art, music, and English. Language learning is promising to gain benefits [1] through exposing to diverse language learning contexts and lowering affective barriers like anxiety to language learning. Ubiquitous personal computers with interactive nature and internet access and advanced smartphones and diverse internet-accessible applications allow researchers to expand their interest in the professional research issues on technology-enhanced language learning (TELL).

W. Jia et al. (Eds.): SETE 2021, LNCS 13089, pp. 334–343, 2021.
https://doi.org/10.1007/978-3-030-92836-0_29

With TELL publications in large volume, many researchers have systematically reviewed them. These reviews described the enhancement of learners' language learning and disclosed the future possible research topics of TELL. For example, Acquah and Katz [2] systematically reviewed 26 studies regarding computer-assisted language learning (CALL) from 2014 to 2018, analyzing the positive impacts and outcomes of digital game-based language learning on students in primary/high schools, and the influence of game characteristics and context on learning outcomes. Reinhardt [3] synthesized 87 CALL articles from 2009 to 2018. The extant reviews were conducted mainly using manual coding approaches like systematic reviews and study synthesis, suffering from a limited number of reviewed articles (i.e., from 19 to 350). Second, manual literature analysis may be error-prone because it involves a tedious and laborious coding process. Also, the results of a small sample of TELL studies cannot be generalized to the whole community. Therefore, there is a lack of a comprehensive overview of TELL's trends and issues in empirically scientific studies.

This study employs advanced knowledge mapping and clustering technologies to visualize literature data to reveal frequently-used keywords and their connections using co-word analysis. Such analysis provides important implications about the trends and topics focused on by TELL research. Particularly, results obtained uncover major trends in keyword networks via keyword co-occurrence degree computation, allowing an overview of TELL knowledge structure and a detailed understanding of keyword relations and thus the interactions between TELL's diverse research issues.

This bibliometric study analyzed 1,295 English-language TELL articles published in professional journals indexed by the Science Citation Index Expanded (SCIE) and the Social Science Citation Index (SSCI) databases during 1996–2019 in terms of research trends and issues, documents, and future research directions.

1.1 Data and Methods

TELL ("technology-enhanced language learning") and its relevant terms (e.g., "computer-assisted language learning," "mobile-assisted language learning," and "game-based language learning") were used. The Web of Sciences (WoS), with a widespread use in bibliometric studies, was selected as the data retrieval database.

Publication data (e.g., titles, year of publication, citation counts, and abstracts) of all the retrieved articles are collected on literature. Then manual screening was conducted to exclude irrelevant ones if an article: a) did not target on TELL; b) was not published during 1995–2019; c) was not published in peer-reviewed SCIE/SSCI-indexed journals; or d) was not written in English.

The manual screening resulted in 1,296 eligible TELL research articles. We then conducted data processing in the following aspects. First, keywords were extracted from titles and abstracts using the natural language toolkit[1]. Second, keyword processing was conducted to ensure data quality. Particularly, keywords with similar meanings were unified, and corresponding full names replaced abbreviations.

[1] www.nltk.org.

Two types of data analyses were conducted, including keyword co-occurrence analysis and co-citation analysis of references. We adopt VOSviewer[2] to produce knowledge maps based on keyword co-occurrence frequencies indicated by node sizes to identify predominant topics and emergent trends.

2 Results

2.1 Co-occurrence Analysis of Keywords Analysis

During the period 1995–1999, Fig. 1 (a) indicates four major clusters labeled as "multimedia technology," "vocabulary learning," "hypermedia technology," and "speech learning" with colors blue, yellow, red, and green, respectively. Given the top TELL research articles, scholars mainly focus on vocabulary learning, particularly with the use of multimedia annotations and hypermedia technologies. Listening and speech are also key issues, particularly about language-learning impaired children, for example, improving speech discrimination and language comprehension abilities of language-learning impaired children using a speech processing algorithm. Besides, scholars are interested in improving listening comprehension using multimedia. Chung [4] examined "the effects of applying video texts supported with advance organizers and captions on Chinese college students' listening comprehension (p. 295)." Additionally, scholars work on applying computers in language learning, for example, computer-assisted interactive glosses to improve reading comprehension.

During period 2000–2004, Fig. 1 (b) indicates four major clusters labeled as "Internet use," "language learning," "computer-assisted language learning," and "interactive learning," respectively, indicated by the colors green, yellow, blue, and red. Within the top-cited TELL research articles, multimedia is a major technology adopted, particularly for reading and vocabulary learning. Specifically, in vocabulary learning, influential research is related to computer-animated vocabulary and grammar tutoring for autistic children and child-friendly computer software programs for enhancing kindergarteners' early literacy skills. Second, scholars seek the potential of bringing chat into language classrooms. One influential article is related to distance language learning of negotiations using a web-based chat program [5]. Another influential research explored how people navigated across contexts of socialization in a bilingual chat room. Additionally, videoconferencing is adopted for basic English course teaching and to support synchronous distance language learning. Kötter [6] analyzed meaning negotiation and discourse code-switching during online exchanges. Compared to face-to-face (F2F) discourse, there was an obvious difference between conversational repair in spoken interactions and online exchanges. Besides, the telecollaborative learning environment starts to be introduced into language classes for developing second language (L2) pragmatic competence.

During the period 2005–2009, Fig. 1 (c) indicates five major clusters labeled as "online learning," "experimental design," "computer-assisted communication," "mobile technology," and "computer-assisted language learning" in colors blue, yellow,

[2] https://www.vosviewer.com/.

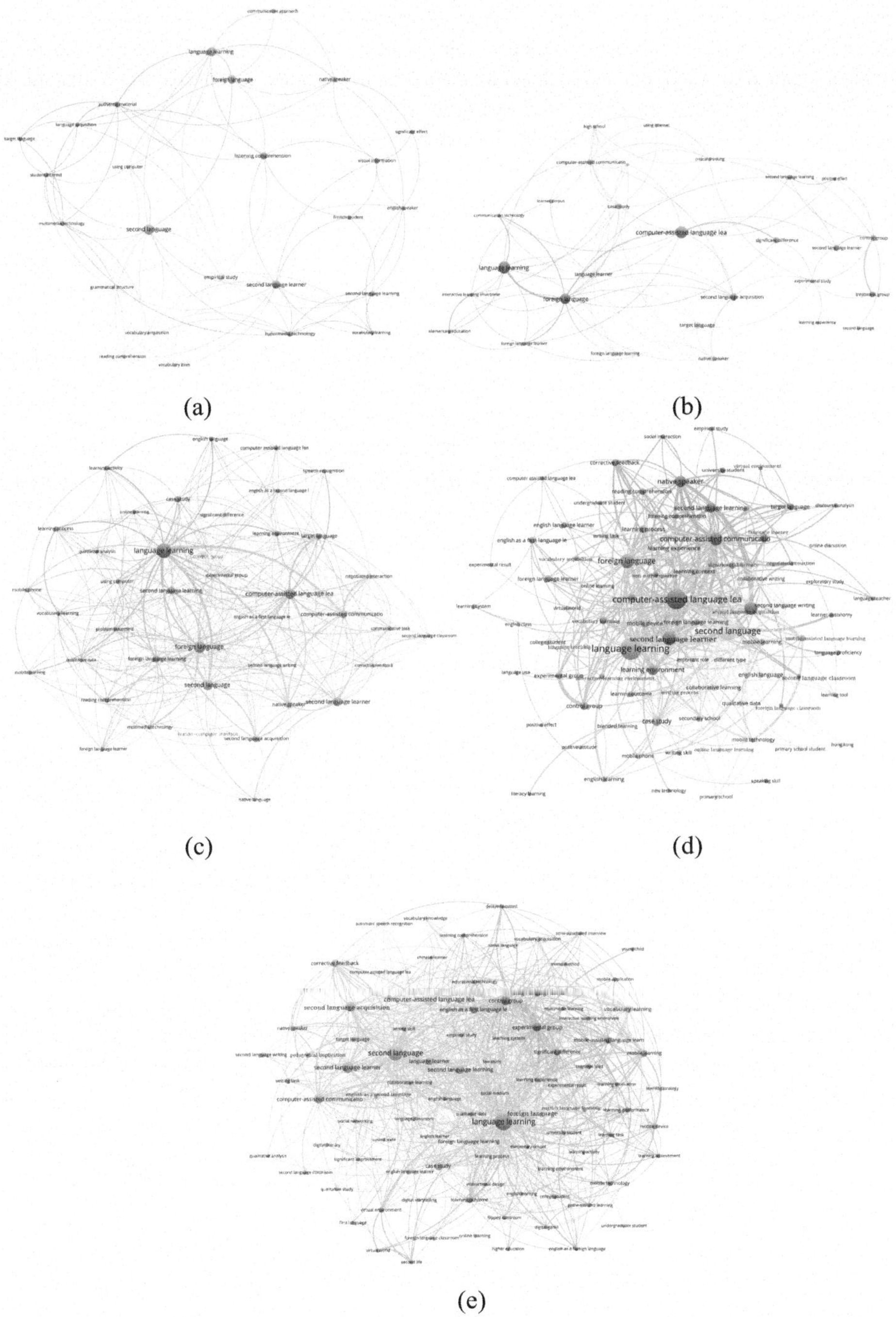

Fig. 1. Bibliographic map for TELL articles

green, red, and pink, respectively. Given the top-cited TELL research articles, with the gradual prevalence of learning strategies like ubiquitous learning and mobile learning, technologies like web and mobiles are adopted in language classrooms with more specific issues being considered, for example, learners' perception towards technology use, quality of interaction brought by technology, and short message service in vocabulary learning. Second, blogs are popular in L2 writing and enhancing critical reflection and community of practice. Third, another wide concern lies in promoting researchers in collecting language history information online using a web-based interface. Moreover, research regarding the test of hypothesis with technology use is also available, for example, an online reading test for the testing hypothesis that non-native comprehends underuse syntactic information in L2 processing. Besides, augmented reality (AR) started to be used to support context-aware ubiquitous listening and speaking learning. Additionally, there is a trend in combining technologies with practical tools like multimedia storytelling for language learning.

During the period 2010–2014, Fig. 1 (d) indicates four major clusters labeled as "computer-assisted communication," "collaborative learning," "vocabulary learning and experimental design," and "mobile-assisted language learning," respectively. Research foci become diverse with learning strategies like personalized learning, collaborative learning, and ubiquitous learning, and technologies like personal digital assistants, wiki, social media, games, and robot in addition to mobiles. First, mobile is still popular with extended applications to language learning of primary school students and serves specifically for personalized recommendations. Second, vocabulary learning is closely connected to contingent interactions and personalized context-aware ubiquitous learning using personal digital assistants. Additionally, several emerging research tendencies are highlighted, for example, collaborative writing using wikis, social networks like Facebook for facilitating language learning, ubiquitous games for promoting motivation, and iPad for literacy learning.

During 2015–2019, Fig. 1 (e) indicates six major clusters labeled as "learner-centered education and experimental design," "computer-assisted language learning," "computer-assisted communication," "mobile and game learning," "virtual learning environment" and "vocabulary learning," respectively. The blue cluster appears to be concerned about experimental design in comparing the differences between TELL and traditional learning, particularly regarding learner-centered perspective. The rise of learner-centered approaches in language classrooms enables learners to play a central role during language learning, where not only what they can achieve via learning but also how they behave during learning are essential issues. Experimental design in TELL research has become significant owing to the emergence of innovative technologies where educators and researchers need to test and examine the feasibility and effectiveness of newly developed technologies like mobiles and multimedia via experimental design before they are introduced into classrooms.

The green cluster mainly concerns computer-mediated communication (CMC), particularly by using "qualitative analysis" and content analysis methods to analyze qualitative data such as dialogues and communications of both "non-native speaker" and "native speaker." Dialogue is an important data source in qualitative studies due to its ability to offer interaction opportunities with other speakers, particularly for meaning negotiation and feedback provision, making learners aware of the gap between their production and targeted structures. The prevalent social software (e.g., wikis) in L2 collaborative writing are effective for understanding L2 learners' interactional patterns and perceived experiences. Scholars are working on collaborative writing quantity and quality in networked online and social networking contexts like Facebook. Besides, digital storytelling is proven effective in facilitating learner autonomy during language learning. It has been popularly adopted to assist communications and interactions, especially in collaborative language learning.

The red cluster mainly encompasses research exploring the application of mobile devices and digital games to assist language learning. Emergent mobile technologies are regarded as novel forms of social and cultural artifacts mediating people's language learning. Video/digital games have developed into mainstream language-assisted activities attracting millions of L2 learners across the world. In the previous period, interest in using mobile devices and games to enhance students' learning in language classrooms runs high; however, relatively little empirical research about their effects has been conducted. In this period, various empirical studies concerning mobile- and game-assisted language learning, including vocabulary learning, pronunciation training, writing, and reading, are available. Mobile-based learning has expanded and evolved with diverse forms of mobile-based applications available, for example, mobile instant messaging, mobile social networking, and mobile AR. Additionally, research has shown a positive effect of flipped instruction in language classrooms for self-regulation learning and on L2 learners' cognitive processing.

The yellow cluster focuses mainly on CALL. First, CALL systems provide significant chances to practice speaking assisted by automatic speech recognition (ASR). However, ASR is challenging with non-native speech. Relevant studies are closely linked with corrective feedback for enhancing pronunciation, oral and spoken grammar practice, and enhancing partial and synchronized caption to promote listening. Besides, ASR is also popularly adopted to facilitate human-machine and human-robot interactions. Second, alongside Internet prevalence, online learning has been an important way of instruction in higher education. Additionally, online reading exercises are prevalent in various L2 learning systems. Nevertheless, researchers are still concerned about how online learning can be adopted more effectively using techniques like sentiment-enhanced learning models and task-based instruction.

The pink cluster mainly concerns language learning in virtual environments. Particularly, three-dimensional virtual worlds like second life are considered promising for immersive language learning. Studies on foreign language oral interactions and communications in virtual worlds indicated a positive perception of the social and physical presences, the potential for aiding in delivering L2 speaking assessments through live voice communication among individuals, and improvements in various context-specific communicative competency acquisition and collaborative communication. Moreover, the virtual world is effective in facilitating active learning, providing visual and linguistic support, accommodating students' cultural and world knowledge, simulating real-life scenarios, and enabling learners' language and communication in bilingual contexts. Additionally, since chatbots and time machines are capable of increasing learners' sense of immersion and presence, researchers are suggested to integrate them into virtual worlds to facilitate L2 learning.

The cluster in light blue mainly indicates a growing interest in vocabulary/word learning and acquisition, particularly among primary school students. Learning new vocabulary is always a major challenge in L2 acquisition since learners commonly come across vocabularies difficult to remember, and thus effective vocabulary learning strategies are valuable. Innovative technologies such as mobiles, online games, tablets, digital storybooks, and multimedia have been applied to facilitate vocabulary learning. Although e-learning systems are popularly in L2 learning, most vocabulary learning systems fail to capture learners' prior vocabulary knowledge. Thus, powerful learner profile models capable of representing learners' prior knowledge are essential to more effectively support personalized vocabulary learning.

2.2 Co-citation Analysis and References

Figure 2 (a) and (b) specifically top references cited in TELL articles during 1995–2009 and 2010–2019, respectively. Among the 7,164 unique references cited in 237 TELL articles published during 1995–2009, the top 64 each has a citation count of at least seven. There are four clusters. Among the 32,703 references in 1,058 articles published during 2010–2019, the top 64 displayed were cited at least 20 times.

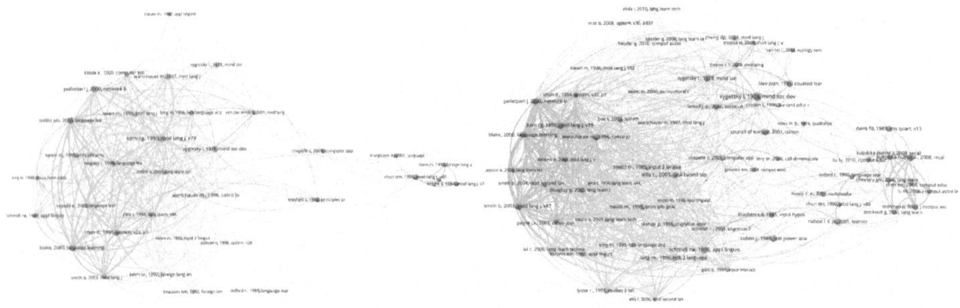

(a) (b)

Fig. 2. Network map of the most-cited references 1995–2009 (a) and 2010–2019 (b)

There are differences between the two network maps. First, looking at the cluster (communication/interaction) in the green color of the 1995–2009 map, key references in this cluster concerned about communication and interaction issues like chatting for developing grammatical competence and facilitating communicative language use via synchronous and written classroom interaction [7]. In the 2008–2018 network map, computers [8], particularly synchronous and asynchronous computer-mediated communication (SCMC), became significant in facilitating L2 communication and interaction. However, despite the evolution, two studies concerning negotiation in cyberspace and classroom interaction with networked computers [7] remained an important foundation in communication and interaction research.

Second, key references in the red cluster (focus on form) of the 1995–2009 map are about the application of focus on form. Similar to communication/interaction, most references are related to communication and interaction. However, the difference lies in technologies, particularly computers. During 2008–2018, although communication is a key focus, major concerns have expanded, with more issues related to cognition and consciousness being considered. Besides, negotiation as a form of communication has emerged to be a research of interest. Additionally, task-based learning has become increasingly important. However, despite the evolution, the role of focus on form in L2 acquisition became more significant.

Third, anchored on the yellow cluster (computer-assisted learning) of the 1995–2009 map, key references concerned about the adoption of computers in assisting language learning. Additionally, scholars focused more on comparing computer-assisted classrooms and traditional classrooms in language learning to examine the effectiveness and usefulness of computer use. Such comparisons are understandable and necessary to prove that computer outperforms traditional way of language instruction and learning before it is widely adopted in classrooms. In the second period, scholars gradually combined collaborative learning into a computer environment. Particularly, issues concerning collaborative writing become essentially focused on the adoption of innovative technologies like wikis. Additionally, interaction in collaborative language learning is also a concern.

Key references in the blue cluster of the 1995–2009 map are about technologies in L2 classrooms. Additionally, two widely cited references indicate concerns about language learning in virtual environments and multimedia annotations on vocabulary acquisition. In the second period, this cluster has expanded with various advanced technologies like mobiles, online games, and the Internet. Collaborative language learning using mobile devices is also a research focus. Additionally, as for Vygotskian sociocultural approaches, in the first period, it related closely to communication/interaction in language learning. Subsequently, its role becomes more significant to be linked with more aspects of language learning.

3 Discussion and Conclusion

This study uses bibliometric mapping and co-occurrence analysis to study trends and changes in TELL research during 1995–2019. Based on 1,295 research articles collected from the WoS, analyses on references, and research topics, were conducted. Increasingly, scholars from diverse institutions across the world have participated in TELL studies, a promising and active area of research, in the forms of either inter-regional or cross-regional collaborations. Technologically speaking, there is a shift from multimedia and communication technologies use for interactive learning to the use of mobiles, online technologies, virtual and digital technologies for learner-centered L2 education. These diverse technologies are popular to facilitate the learning of varied L2 skills like vocabulary learning, speech and pronunciation, and collaborations and communications. Based on results and findings, we suggest future directions for TELL research, including robot use, multimodality, and synchronous technologies, psychology and cognitive issues, and AI and learning analytics.

First, social robots are machines socially interacting and communicating intelligently with humans and are nowadays increasingly used as educational tools to facilitate early language and literacy skill development among young children, particularly through authentic communicative practices in a foreign language. Currently, empirical studies and experimental designs are limited, and robots have not yet been put into wide practice. More empirical evidence is needed to prove robots' effectiveness in enhancing speaking accuracy, fluency, and pronunciation, reducing learning anxiety, and promoting learning motivation.

Second, while DMC for multiliteracy development is well documented, exploration of how it facilitates English learning remains limited. Besides, digital animation is powerful for multimodal literacy learning where impassioned multimodal communication is enhanced with knowledge and understanding of different facial expressions, body movements, and physiological changes.

Third, video-SCMC tools like Skype software are showing great promise and effectiveness to provide L2 learners with opportunities to interact, particularly with native speakers SCMC. Comparing to text-based SCMC, video-based SCMC is effective for fluency development and pronunciation improvement. However, it remains unclear why some learners get more improvement than others. Furthermore, comparing to F2F, L2 learners use articles more correctly and raise advanced questions more often in text-based SCMC.

Fourth, anxiety about L2 speaking can negatively affect L2 learners' learning autonomy, learning performance, and fluency development since they are less willing and confident to produce output. One way to minimize L2 learning anxiety impact is to stimulate learners to speak, ideally without being restricted by physical language classrooms. Besides, L2 learners often find it difficult to comprehend while listening to others talking in L2, leading to anxiety during communication. This can be relieved by CMC to increase access to native speakers and frequencies to listen. Furthermore, little is known about anxiety levels' effects on learning performance, gaming performance, and learning processes during game-based language learning and mobile systems' impacts on learners' learning motivation and anxiety.

Fifth, it is only in the recent years that artificial intelligence gradually came into use in personalized and adaptive language learning. For example, ASR is widely adopted for feedback provision, and it credibly simulates native speakers' understanding, enables learners to narrow the intelligibility gap and learn meaningful interpersonal communications, and provides immediate corrective feedback about learner errors. Besides, ASR-integrated CALL systems are promising for oral grammar practice, with corrective feedback concerning oral production being offered without negative affective responses. Second, neural networks simulate and evaluate learners' individualized cognitive abilities during L2 acquisition. Additionally, sentiment computing and eye-tracking are integrated into e-learning systems for affect detection.

Additionally, there is an increase in applying learning analytics and data-driven learning in TELL studies. Methodologically, learning analytics is promising to alleviate drop-out and promote retention, and understand online learning behaviors and improve pedagogies based on learning activity data. However, learning analytics in language learning only received attention in the last two years, with the affordances of providing instructors and materials designers with valuable insights into task design and learners with suitable learning strategies to learn in a personalized way. Data-driven learning facilitates L2 learning because of its inductive nature and authentic language samples, providing learners with numerous opportunities to achieve deep and discovery learning. However, this may induce a cognitive load that has received increasing attention.

Acknowledgements. This work was supported by General Research Fund (No. 18601118) of Research Grants Council of Hong Kong SAR, China, One-off Special Fund from Central and Faculty Fund in Support of Research from 2019/20 to 2021/22 (MIT02/19-20) of The Education University of Hong Kong, Research Cluster Fund (RG 78/2019-2020R) of The Education University of Hong Kong, and Dean's Research Fund 2019/20 (IDS-2 2020) of The Education University of Hong Kong.

References

1. Young, S.S.-C., Wang, Y.-H.: The game embedded CALL system to facilitate English vocabulary acquisition and pronunciation. J. Educ. Technol. Soc. **17**, 239–251 (2014)
2. Acquah, E.O., Katz, H.T.: Digital game-based L2 learning outcomes for primary through high-school students: a systematic literature review. Comput. Educ. **143**, 103667 (2020)
3. Reinhardt, J.: Social media in second and foreign language teaching and learning: Blogs, wikis, and social networking. Lang. Teach. **52**, 1–39 (2019)
4. Chung, J.: The effects of using video texts supported with advance organizers and captions on Chinese college students' listening comprehension: An empirical study. Foreign Lang. Ann. **32**, 295–308 (1999)
5. Tudini, V.: Using native speakers in chat. Lang. Learn. Technol. **7**, 141–159 (2003)
6. Kötter, M.: Negotiation of meaning and codeswitching in online tandems. Lang. Learn. Technol. **7**, 145–172 (2003)
7. Kern, R.G.: Restructuring classroom interaction with networked computers: effects on quantity and characteristics of language production. Mod. Lang. J. **79**, 457–476 (1995)
8. Smith, B.: Computer–mediated negotiated interaction: an expanded model. Mod. Lang. J. **87**, 38–57 (2003)

The Effect of Oral Practice via Chatbot on Students' Oral English Accuracy

Yiwen Ye, Jiaxuan Deng, and Xiaobin Liu(✉)

South China Normal University, Guangzhou, Guangdong, China
liuxiaobin@m.scnu.edu.cn

Abstract. Traditional EFL (English as a foreign language) learners could find it difficult to practice speaking after class and obtain effective feedback. With the development of technology, chatbot could be one solution to tackle this dilemma. Employing the chatbot Microsoft Xiaoying as the main tool in a teaching experiment, this study aimed at figuring out whether using chatbot in oral English practice would exert a positive effect on learners' oral English performance in grammar and pronunciation aspects. By analyzing the collected data, the results showed that: daily practice with chatbot could be suggested as part of oral English practice as it was proved to be effective on promoting learners' oral English accuracy.

Keyword: Chatbot · Oral English practice · Oral accuracy · Grammar error · Pronunciation error

1 Introduction

The key to master languages is that one needs to master only 50%–90% of its grammar, 1% of its vocabulary and 100% of its knowledge on pronunciation (Liu et al. 2018, p.333). Thereby, it is reasonable to note that grammar and pronunciation are the foundation of English. However, large-class language teaching not only reduces students' opportunities to speak, but also makes it impossible for teachers to evaluate and correct each student's oral performance (Cao 2011; Liu 2002). One remedial measure is to engage students into oral training after school. However, students find it hard to pair up with an effective partner around to practice. The emergence of chatbot offers a solution. Brennan (2006) defined chatbot as an artificial construct designed to chat with human beings by the means of using natural language to input and output. Some of usefulness of chatbots for learners proposed by Fryer and Carpenter (2006) includes less anxiety and more patience, more effective feedbacks in speaking, etc.

Microsoft Xiaoying (hereafter called Xiaoying), a chatbot launched by Microsoft on WeChat, is designed as a learning partner for young learners. This study intended to apply chatbot Xiaoying as a language learning tool in after-class oral practice, with the aim to lessen students' errors in dialogues and investigate the effect of this tool on improving learners' oral English accuracy, mainly in grammar and pronunciation.

W. Jia et al. (Eds.): SETE 2021, LNCS 13089, pp. 344–354, 2021.
https://doi.org/10.1007/978-3-030-92836-0_30

2 Literature Review

2.1 Related Research on Chatbot as a Language Learning Tool

In the past decades, researchers have been maintaining great interest in applying chatbot to language learning. For instance, Jia (2004) explored the application of a web-based human-computer dialogue system and found that participants are interested in chatbot functioning as a chatting partner and that they are more confident talking with the chatbot. Goda et al. (2014) explored the effects of a preceding talk with a chatbot on EFL learners' later discussion, and found that a conversation with a chatbot is likely to increase students' contribution to discussions. Similarly, Jia and Chen (2008) displayed pedagogical functions of a chatbot called CSIEC in English learning, and confirmed that CSIEC can motivate learners to study and practice English. Wang et al. (2013) employed their self-created chatbots (i.e., tangible learning robots) into experiment, and found that such chatbots showed positive effects on learners' language learning motivation, engagement, and oral proficiency, especially for lower-level achievers. Haristiani (2019) reviewed the data in previous chatbot studies and observed the results from a chatbot-based language learning medium, and proved that chatbot could have a high possibility to be functioned as a language learning medium, both as an independent learning medium and as a tutor in language practice.

2.2 Using Chatbot to Improve Oral Accuracy

Since chatbots have been verified as an appealing tool for language practice, some researchers tend to center on exploring the linguistic accuracy of chatbots. To specifically promote learners' grammar accuracy in oral tasks, Cucchiarini and Strik (2018) developed a virtual chatbot system called DISCO which could automatically present the conversation content in the form of text and identify learners' grammatical errors in conversation practice, leading to possible enhancements of such a chatbot system in language learning. Kim et al. (2019) compared the use of two AI chatbots (Google assistant and Alexa) in secondary schools' English curriculum, which revealed that both chatbots share a high rate of more than 86% success in responding to participants.

Above all, it can be concluded that chatbots are proved to be a welcoming language learning tool as there are many merits of them, but the related evidences remain limited. As Li and Min (2010) stated that there is still a large gap to be bridged in terms of in-depth research and enlarging research aspects on oral English expression, including researches on empirical studies employing chatbots in after-class oral training aiming to enhance learners' grammar and pronunciation accuracy in oral English.

3 Research Design

3.1 Research Questions

This study utilized chatbot Xiaoying to support after-class oral training, targeting at exploring the effect of chatbot on lessening students' grammar and pronunciation errors in oral English tasks and monitor the related accuracy improvement in oral English. The study tended to answer the following three questions:

RQ1: Can oral English practice via chatbot Xiaoying improve learners' grammar and pronunciation accuracy in dialogues?
RQ2: If yes, what grammar and pronunciation errors can oral English practice via chatbot Xiaoying help to correct? If not, why is that?
RQ3: What are learners' perceptions of oral English practice via chatbot Xiaoying?

3.2 Participants

The participants were from two parallel classes in a senior high school, with one class of 28 students being an experiment group (EG) while the other 28 students a control group (CG), aging from 15 to 16 years old. There was no significant difference regarding English proficiency (Sig. (2-tailed) = 0.746($p > 0.05$)), while the mean scores of both groups were almost the same (i.e., 107.2679 and 107.8036), which indicates that these two groups shared a similar level of English proficiency before the experiment.

3.3 Instrumentation

This research collected data through six instruments, namely training instrument, training materials, four tests, evaluation instrument, scoring rubric, a questionnaire.

Training Instrument. Microsoft Xiaoying (Xiaoying), an intelligent human-machine interaction service, integrates artificial intelligence technologies such as speech recognition, oral evaluation, natural language processing and speech synthesis.

Training Materials. The same training materials for both groups are dialogues in chatbot Xiaoying including 27 simulated scenes with 217 dialogues in total. EG conducted dialogues with chatbot Xiaoying, while CG practiced with human partners.

Tests. Four oral dialogue tests were launched to check whether participants' oral performance could be enhanced after two-month practice via chatbot Xiaoying. The two pretests and post-tests just namely simulate the role play task in CELST (Computer-based English Listening and Speaking Test). Before the tests, students were firstly required to watch a video, from which participants would know the task requirements.

Evaluation Instrument. The English teacher of both groups worked together to transcribe participants' recordings in four tests and mark their grammar and pronunciation errors, using the same marking system. Grammar errors for marking include the following types: 1. Agreement errors (AE, Yuan and Ellis 2003) 2. Other verb errors (VE, Yuan and Ellis 2003) 3. Case errors (CE, Rowland 2007) 4. Preposition errors (PrepE, Ting et al. 2010) 5. Plural errors (PE, Ting et al. 2010) Similarly, the error types to qualify participants' pronunciation mainly refer to Xu and Zeng's classification in 2015, including the following types: 1. Deletion errors (DE) 2. Addition errors (AE2) 3. Phonemic errors (PE2) 4. Word errors (WE) 5. Stress errors (SE).

Scoring Rubric. The rubric to score grammar is referenced to the grammar accuracy standard of Lee et al. (2011), and role play task in CELST, while the pronunciation part is based on the pronunciation criteria of Lee et al. and Shi as well as imitation reading-aloud task in CELST. The scoring rubric for pronunciation contains four levels: 1. Hardly make any pronunciation mistakes. (score 4–5) 2. Make a few pronunciation mistakes, like phonemic errors, deletion errors, addition errors, etc.; The expressed information can still be recognized and understood. (score 2–3) 3. Make lots of pronunciation mistakes, like phonetic errors, deletion errors, etc.; The expressed information can be hardly recognized and understood. (score 1) 4. No responses (score 0). The scoring rubric for grammar is designed in the similar format.

Questionnaire. This questionnaire consists of 15 items, one was about what has hindered their oral English proficiency, while the other 14 surveying participants' attitudes towards the effect of chatbot Xiaoying on promoting oral proficiency. Each question was evaluated on 5-point Likert scale. The reliability and validity of it were qualified, as the Cronbach α coefficient was 0.844 (> 0.7) while Kaiser-Meyer-Olkin Measure of Sampling Adequacy was 0.784 (> 0.7).

3.4 Procedure

The present study lasted approximately for two months. Figure 1 demonstrates the main procedures of this research, consisting of pretests, training guide for both groups to proceed oral practice as suggested, training experiment, post-tests, questionnaire.

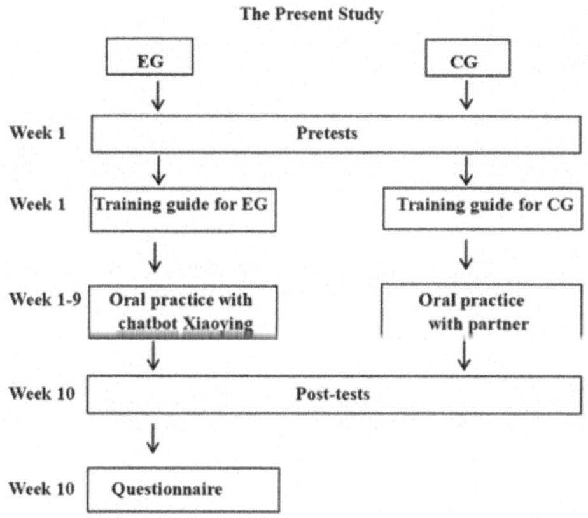

Fig. 1. The main procedures of the present study

Before the oral training, both groups of students finished two role-play tests as pretests. And then, CG will be instructed to conduct dialogue practice with partners while EG will be guided to use chatbot Xiaoying. The operation steps are as follows:

Step 1: Students choose "scenario simulation" in the menu bar "daily per exercise".
Step 2: There are 27 main topics for scenario simulation dialogue practice. Students choose a "scenario simulation" (e.g., At the airport) and then choose a specific scenario (e.g., At Customs 2). There would be introduction and vocabulary learning of the scene.
Step 3: After reading the scene introduction, students enter the formal scene simulation exercise. Xiaoying initiates the dialogue and gives the Chinese meaning and English keyword prompt of the answer, with which students respond orally. The response will be recorded and assessed, and participants will get the feedback of it (Fig. 1).
Step 4: At the end of the simulation conversation, the students get an overall score of each practice. Students can compare their pronunciation and the audio clip sample given by Xiaoying, and imitate and read repeatedly, correct their wrong oral expressions and strengthen the correct expressions multiple times after dialogue practice (Fig. 3).

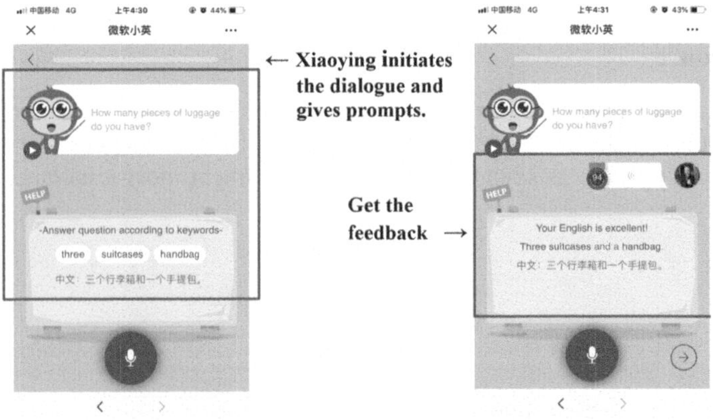

Fig. 2. Step 3 of using Xiaoying to conduct human-machine dialogue practice

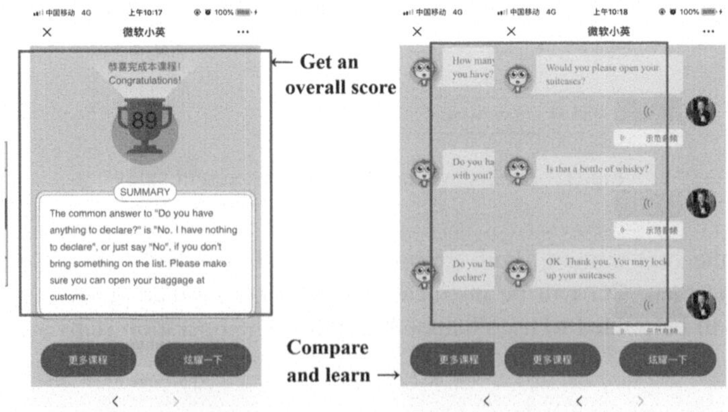

Fig. 3. Step 4 of using Xiaoying to conduct human-machine dialogue practice

Just right after the whole period of oral training, both groups of students completed another two role-play tests. And EG needed to finish a questionnaire on the website Wenjuanxing.

4 Data Analysis and Discussion

4.1 Analysis on Pretest

The results showed that there were no significant differences between two groups on total oral English accuracy, grammar accuracy and pronunciation accuracy ($p = 0.913$, $p = 0.515$, $p = 0.493$, > 0.05).

After two English teachers marked the grammar errors during transcribing both groups' recordings of pretests, the frequency of each grammar error and the error to per sentence in two pretests were calculated. EG made 399 instances of grammar errors, while 402 instances were found in CG, conforming to the fact that EG averagely scored a little bit higher (1.4 points) than CG on grammar accuracy and that both groups showed no significant differences in grammar accuracy ($p = 0.515$, > 0.05) before the training experiment.

Table 1. Statistics of grammar and pronunciation errors(percentage) at pretest.

Grammar error			Pronunciation error		
Type	EG	CG	Type	EG	CG
AE	13.39%	14.29%	PE2	33.48%	32.81%
PE	4.24%	8.04%	WE	8.93%	16.07%
VE	11.61%	9.82%	AE2	10.71%	4.69%
PrepE	7.37%	5.13%	SE	1.34%	1.34%
CE	1.56%	2.23%	DE	18.30%	15.63%
MW2	1.56%	0.89%	Total	72.77%	70.54%
MW	37.05%	37.05%			
/	12.28%	12.28%			
Total	89.06%	89.73%			

According to Table 1, the four top errors for both groups included AE, PE, VE, and PrepE, with the error ratio around 36%–37%, while the remaining error ratio of MW and "/" for both groups was the same, at about 49%, indicating that both groups shared similar difficulty in choosing accurate grammar pattern and word choice, and responding in dialogues. CE and MW2 are the least frequent grammar errors as their ratios together accounted for just about 3%.

Similar to statistics of grammar errors, both groups had almost the same ratio of pronunciation errors, accounting for 72.77% and 70.54% respectively, which conforms to the fact that CG scored a bit higher (1 point on average) than EG on pronunciation accuracy and that there were no significant differences in grammar accuracy in both groups (p = 0.493, > 0.05) at pretest. The results also showed that the top specific pronunciation errors were PE2, WE, AE2, and DE, occupying a total percentage of 71% in EF and 69% in CG Particularly, PE2 was the most frequent pronunciation errors in both groups, as their error ratio reached to about 33%.

4.2 Analysis on Post-test

The scores for both groups at post-test revealed that the difference of improvements on overall accuracy between both groups was significantly evident, with EG exceeding CG significantly (p = 0.001, < 0.05). The grammar scores showed that there was significant difference in grammar accuracy between both groups (Sig.(2-tailed) = 0.000 (p < 0.05)), indicating that EG outran CG largely. It suggests that compared with the traditional oral practice, oral practice via chatbot Xiaoying could better develop students' grammar accuracy.

As for grammar errors, Table 2 showed that both groups made less errors, as the number of grammar errors made by EG dropping by about 38%, while CG's decreasing by about 14%, indicating EG made greater improvements on grammar accuracy.

To summarize, both ways of oral practice were proved to be effective in lessening grammar errors, with chatbot Xiaoying to practice speaking outperforming the other way, as it could reduce almost each mentioned type of grammar errors in EG, while the errors including predicate errors, preposition errors, case errors and misuse of words in CG using traditional way were not solved but intensified.

Table 2. Statistics of grammar and pronunciation errors(percentage) at post-test.

Grammar error			Pronunciation error		
Type	EG	CG	Type	EG	CG
AE	2.46%	4.46%	PE2	10.49%	27.46%
PE	4.69%	4.91%	WE	13.17%	10.04%
VE	3.13%	11.16%	AE2	4.69%	4.02%
PrepE	6.25%	7.81%	SE	2.01%	4.91%
CE	2.68%	4.46%	DE	9.15%	12.95%
MW2	1.34%	1.34%	Total	39.51%	59.38%
MW	25.45%	30.36%			
/	5.13%	11.38%			
Total	51.12%	75.89%			

In Table 2, both groups' pronunciation accuracy was also strengthened at the end of their oral practice period. EG increased by over 6 points on average at post-tests, while CG just gained less than 2 points averagely. Also, there was a significant difference between pretests and post-tests in CG after traditional oral practice with partners (Sig. (2-tailed) = 0.039(p < 0.05))while EG reflected a much more remarkably significant difference between pretests and post-tests (p = 0.000, <0.05).

Both groups made fewer errors, with the total number of pronunciation errors made by EG dropping by about 33%, while CG decreased decreasing by about 11%, implying EG made a greater progress on pronunciation accuracy, which proved that EG scored considerately higher (i.e., 4.5 points on average) than CG on pronunciation accuracy.

To sum up, both two ways of oral practice were effective in reducing the pronunciation errors. However, the way of using chatbot Xiaoying to conduct oral practice outperformed the other way to a greater extent, especially on coping with phonemic errors, deletion errors as well as addition errors, while the other way of oral practice with human partners might be more beneficial to tackle word errors. Both groups seemed to still have the difficulty in coping with stress errors.

4.3 Analysis on Questionnaire

28 effective questionnaires were collected. In general, the results of questionnaire showed that most subjects' attitude towards chatbot Xiaoying was positive. As they admitted their two major problems hindering oral proficiency were the correct use of grammar and pronunciation, reducing errors of grammar and pronunciation would be highly needed for participants. After two-month oral English practice with chatbot Xiaoying, about 80% of participants in EG agreed that chatbot Xiaoying was the preferred partner for oral practice. Furthermore, the majority of participants acknowledged the advantages of chatbot Xiaoying on oral practice, namely increasing opportunities to speak English, realizing what to chat in possible situations in daily life, etc., conforming to the merits of chatbots concluded by Fryer and Carpenter (2006).

Besides, about 88% of them confirmed that the feedback in chatbot Xiaoying was beneficial to enhance grammar and pronunciation accuracy, and that they could practice at least one more time to correct their errors on these two aspects and gain higher marks, while just over 70% of them believed their accuracy in grammar and pronunciation improved, suggesting that a small number of them might doubt their improvements. Interestingly, 86% of them stated that their oral proficiency was promoted, hinting that not just grammar and pronunciation of oral proficiency but other aspects of it might be also enhanced. That is to say, chatbot Xiaoying might have other potential effects on facilitating learners' oral performance. Although the data proved the effect of chatbot Xiaoying and most participants confirmed its effect, chatbot Xiaoying was not a total solution for oral accuracy. Teachers would be also needed in the training as over 96% of the participants agreed that specific instructions on related accuracy problems offered by teachers should also get involved.

5 Conclusion

5.1 Major Findings

To start with, compared with traditional oral practice with human partners, employing chatbot Xiaoying was proved to be a more effective way to enhance learners' grammar and pronunciation accuracy. Due to the fact that Xiaoying also share similar advantages of chatbots such as scaffolding learners with introduction of new vocabulary, model expressions and the related consistent understandable repetition (Fryer et al. 2019), and providing synthesized speeches and effective feedback (Fryer and Carpenter 2006).

Secondly, daily oral practice with chatbot Xiaoying was able to considerately reduce the grammar errors such as AE, VE, MW and no responses (/), and PE2, AE2 as well as DE, outperforming CG in these two aspects. These specific improvements were also triggered by the above-mentioned advantages of chatbot Xiaoying, proving that chatbot Xiaoying did earn some certain credits on increasing oral accuracy by decreasing the main grammar and pronunciation errors mentioned above. However, this way of oral English practice could not obviously help lessen other grammar errors like PrepE, MW2, PE, and CE as well as other pronunciation errors such as SE and WE.

Last but not least, regarding participants' perception of chatbot Xiaoying, the results of questionnaire showed that most subjects' attitude towards the use of this chatbot to improve oral accuracy remained positive as they admired the functions of this chatbot in language practice, such as promoting oral performance (Jia and Ruan 2008; Zako and Capper 2008), and increasing interest in interacting with people in English (Jia 2004), and providing learners with detailed and instant feedback (Fryer and Carpenter 2006) and a consistent conversational partner (Shawar 2017), which is consistent with the previous findings (Bii et al. 2013, Colace et al. 2018).

5.2 Limitation and Implication

Some limitations appeared to be inevitable because of some restrictions of objective and subjective reasons.

Firstly, the findings might be more solid if the duration expanded to a whole semester. Also, the volume of samples might not be sufficient. These two aspects probably would influence the reliability and validity of the study. Therefore, further studies should be centered on longer experiment time and larger samples.

Secondly, daily involvement in oral practice for both groups would also affect their oral performance. Although their English teacher would walk around in case students got distracted to other things, such as playing games with phone or doing homework, it is still not guaranteed that she could make each student 100% get engaged in oral practice. The further research could observe participants' degrees of involvement on oral practice, then sort them into certain groups, which might contribute to the investigation of the effect of degrees of engagement on oral performance.

The study theoretically enriched the investigations on computer-assisted pronunciation training (CAPT). Furthermore, the empirical evidences showed the potentials of chatbot on facilitating learners' oral accuracy, such as reducing grammar and pronunciation errors. This would enrich CAPT studies and offer some insights for further researches in the use of chatbot on oral accuracy. Besides, this research might contribute to more studies on chatbots facilitating learners' oral performance in other aspects except for grammar and pronunciation accuracy.

Acknowledgements. This work is supported by the Center for Language Cognition and Assessment, South China Normal University. It's also the result of Guangdong "13th Five-Year" Plan Project of Philosophy & Social Science (GD20WZX01-02).

References

Bii, P., Too, J., Langat, R.: An investigation of student's attitude towards use of chatbot technology in instruction: the case of Knowie in a selected high school. Educ. Res. **4**(10), 710–716 (2013)

Brennan, K.: The managed teacher: Emotional labour, education, and technology. Educ. Insights **10**(2), 55–65 (2006)

Colace, F., De Santo, M., Lombardi, M., Pascale, F., Pietrosanto, A., Lemma, S.: Chatbot for e-learning: a case of study. Int. J. Mech. Eng. Robot. Res. **7**(5), 528–533 (2018)

Cucchiarini, C., Strik, H.: Second language learners' spoken discourse: practice and corrective feedback through automatic speech recognition. In: Khosrow-Pour, M. (eds.) Smart Technologies: Breakthroughs in Research and Practice, pp. 367–389 (2018)

Fryer, L., Carpenter, R.: Bots as language learning tools. Lang. Learn. Technol. **10**(3), 8–14 (2006)

Fryer, L.K., Nakao, K., Thompson, A.: Chatbot learning partners: connecting learning experiences, interest and competence. Comput. Hum. Behav. **93**, 279–289 (2019)

Haristiani, N.: Artificial intelligence (AI) chatbot as language learning medium: an inquiry. J. Phys.: Conf. Ser. **1387**, 012020 (2019)

Jia, J.: The study of the application of a web-based chatbot system on the teaching of foreign languages. In: Society for Information Technology & Teacher Education International Conference, pp. 1201–1207 (2004)

Jia, J., Chen, W.: Motivate the learners to practice English through playing with Chatbot CSIEC. In: Pan, Z., Zhang, X., El Rhalibi, A., Woo, W., Li, Y. (eds.) Edutainment 2008. LNCS, vol. 5093, pp. 180–191. Springer, Heidelberg (2008). https://doi.org/10.1007/978-3-540-69736-7_20

Jia, J., Ruan, M.: Use chatbot CSIEC to facilitate the individual learning in English instruction: a case study. In: Woolf, B.P., Aïmeur, E., Nkambou, R., Lajoie, S. (eds.) ITS 2008. LNCS, vol. 5091, pp. 706–708. Springer, Heidelberg (2008). https://doi.org/10.1007/978-3-540-69132-7_84

Liu, X., Zhu, C., Jiao, J., Xu, M.: Promoting English pronunciation via mobile devices-based automatic speech evaluation (ASE) technology. In: Cheung, S.K.S., Kwok, L., Kubota, K., Lee, L.-K., Tokito, J. (eds.) ICBL 2018. LNCS, vol. 10949, pp. 333–343. Springer, Cham (2018). https://doi.org/10.1007/978-3-319-94505-7_27

Li, Y., Ming, S.: Reflections on EFL speaking researches in china during the past decade. Zhongguo Waiyu, pp. 85–91 (2010)

Lee, S., et al.: On the effectiveness of robot-assisted language learning. ReCALL **23**(1), 25–58 (2011)

Kim, H., Shin, D.K., Yang, H., Lee, J.H.: A study of AI chatbot as an assistant tool for school English curriculum. J. Learn.-Centered Curric. Instr. **19**(1), 89–110 (2019)

Shawar, B.A.: Integrating CALL systems with chatbots as conversational partners. Computacióny Sistemas **21**(4), 615–626 (2017)

Wang, Y.H., Young, S., Jang, J.: Using tangible companions for enhancing learning English conversation. J. Educ. Technol. Soc. **16**, 296–309 (2013)

Liu, J.J.: The talk-to-machine method used in teaching speaking English in college. Comput.-Assist. Foreign Lang. Educ. China **2002**(1), 15–17 (2002)
Yuan, F., Ellis, R.: The effects of pre-task planning and online planning on fluency, complexity and accuracy in L2 monologic oral production. Appl. Linguis. **24**(1), 1–27 (2003)
Zakos, J., Capper, L.: CLIVE–an artificially intelligent chat robot for conversational language practice. In: Darzentas, J., Vouros, G.A., Vosinakis, S., Arnellos, A. (eds.) Artificial Intelligence: Theories, Models and Applications. LNCS, vol. 5138, pp. 437–442. Springer, Berlin (2008). https://doi.org/10.1007/978-3-540-87881-0_46
Ting, S.H., Mahanita, M., Chang, S.L.: Grammatical errors in spoken English of university students in oral communication course. GEMA: Online J. Lang. Stud. **10**(1), 53–70 (2010)
Rowland, C.F.: Explaining errors in children's questions. Cognition **104**(1), 106–134 (2007)
Xu, Y., Zeng, Y.: How to deal with students' pronunciation errors—a study based on the corpus of test-takers' performance in the computer-based English listening and speaking test (CELST) of Gaokao (Guangdong Version). Curric. Teach. Mater. Method **35**(9), 90–96 (2015)

Investigating the Impact of Teacher Feedback on Content Revisions in EFL Students' Writing by the Automated Tracking Approach

Gary Cheng[1(✉)], Mike Hin Leung Chui[1], and Bernie Chun Nam Mak[2]

[1] The Education University of Hong Kong, Tai Po, New Territories, Hong Kong
{chengks,mikechui}@eduhk.hk
[2] Hong Kong Baptist University, Shatin, New Territories, Hong Kong
bcnmak@hkbu.edu.hk

Abstract. Teacher feedback plays an important role in motivating students who learn English as a Foreign Language (EFL) to revise and improve their writing. Investigating how EFL students revise their writing in response to various types of teacher feedback has long received research attention. However, such investigation is human dependent, which requires considerable time and effort, limiting its application to a wide range of EFL writing classes in practice. To address this issue, this study was designed to adopt a systematic and automated approach to investigate the impact of different types of teacher feedback on the content revisions of EFL students at a larger scale. A total of 114 EFL undergraduate students and 3 experienced English teachers from three universities participated in this study. The writing draft and final writing of students and the written feedback from teachers were collected as data and were entered into an automated tracking system for analysis. The analytical results indicate that constructive criticism and imperative appeared to be most effective in triggering content revisions, advice could have a comparable effect, and that question was least effective. The automated analysis would be helpful to teachers in making informed adjustments to their feedback and instructional strategies to better support student revisions.

Keywords: Teacher feedback · Content revision · Second language writing · Automated tracking

1 Introduction

Effective feedback can not only help students to note the discrepancies between what they know and what they need to know [1], but also encourage them to expend efforts to their own learning [2]. In the context of English as a Foreign Language (EFL), written feedback from the teacher is particularly important for student writing [3, 4] because it can help students enhance their texts at different writing stages such as drafting, reviewing, and revising [5, 6].

However, it is not guaranteed that teacher feedback can always be effective to bridge the gap between the actual and desired writing performances of students. There

W. Jia et al. (Eds.): SETE 2021, LNCS 13089, pp. 355–363, 2021.
https://doi.org/10.1007/978-3-030-92836-0_31

has been a long debate over the effectiveness of written corrective feedback (also known as error/grammar correction) in developing EFL students' writing skills. Truscott [7, 8] argued that written corrective feedback could lead students to present their ideas in simple sentences vis-à-vis the complex ones and thus it should be abandoned. Against this view, Ferris [9] argued that written corrective feedback could take different forms, among which the indirect form of indicating errors only would help EFL students be committed to the long-term improvement of their own writing.

A large body of studies have been conducted to demonstrate the roles of teacher feedback in student writing, especially in grammar correction (e.g. [7, 8, 10, 11]), but their data were often drawn from a small number of students and therefore may not be generalised to the wider population. It is still necessary to collect and analyse more empirical data to investigate how EFL students, especially those who live and study in their home countries, respond to different types of teacher feedback in other writing aspects such as content development [12]. To this end, this study aimed to apply an automated tracking method for analysing the effectiveness of different types of teacher feedback in triggering revisions of students from three universities in Asia. In particular, it was framed by the following research question: how do different types of teacher feedback relate to student revisions to the content of EFL writing? The findings of this study would provide new insights into the impact of teacher feedback on student revisions at a larger scale.

2 Method

2.1 Context

This study is part of a wider project investigating automated tracking of student responses to teacher feedback in draft revision. The project has developed an online automated tracking system to identify various types of teacher feedback and student revisions. Furthermore, it can track whether the revisions made respond to the feedback given. A detailed discussion on the design and functionality of the online system is outside the scope of this paper and can be found elsewhere [13, 14].

This study was designed to use the abovementioned online system to generate automated analysis of teacher feedback and student revisions as well as their interconnections. It was conducted at two Hong Kong universities (HKU-1 and HKU-2) and one Taiwan university (TWU) between 2017 and 2018. The participants of this study were undergraduate students from the three universities. They enrolled in one of the following three EFL courses, namely 'Advanced English for University Studies' (offered by HKU-1), 'Academic English for Science Students' (offered by HKU-2) and 'English Reading and Discussion' (offered by TWU).

2.2 Participants

A total of 114 Chinese undergraduate students (61 males and 53 females) from the three universities participated in this study. Prior to the outset of the study, all participants gave their informed written consent to grant permissions to analyse their writing assignments and the written teacher feedback. They came from three different academic disciplines including Actuarial Science, Applied English, and Engineering. Their ages ranged from 17 to 22 years, with a mean age of 19.3 years. Alongside student participants, three experienced EFL teachers were involved in this study to offer written feedback on student writing. They are referred to as T1, T2 and T3 for the rest of the paper.

2.3 Classification of Feedback and Content Revisions

Drawing on the classification frameworks for teacher feedback [15, 16] and student revisions [17, 18], the categories of feedback and content revision used by the automated tracking system are illustrated in Tables 1 and 2, respectively [14].

Table 1. Categories of feedback.

Code	Category	Description
F1	Praise	Positive and non-controlling comments
F2	Criticism	Negative comments or evaluation
F3	Imperative	Comments informing the student writer to do something, often starting with a verb in the non-finite base form
F4	Advice	Suggestive comments in a non-authoritative tone
F5	Closed question	Questions expecting an answer of 'yes' or 'no' or otherwise a single word
F6	Open question	Questions expecting more than a 'yes' or 'no' answer, often starting with 'what', 'where', 'why', 'who, 'when' and 'how'

Table 2. Categories of content revision.

Code	Category	Description
R1	Claim	An assertion that something is or is not true
R2	Evidence and details	Facts and information
R3	Reasoning	The use of reasons to support a belief or proposition
R4	Analysis	A logical connection between the claim and evidence/reasoning

2.4 Data Collection and Analysis

Two pieces of writing were collected from each participant in this study. The first was the draft of a written assignment and the second was the polished final product upon the teacher feedback. In the 'Advanced English for University Studies' course offered by HKU-1, students were required to write a draft position argument essay on their proposed topic in about 600 words and then a final essay of 1200 words built on the draft. In the 'Advanced English for Science Students' course offered by HKU-2, students were asked to produce a draft and a final article regarding Popular Science in about 700 and 1400 words, respectively. In the 'English Reading and Discussion' course offered by TWU, students needed to draft a book review with a personal reflection on "Chinese

Cinderella" first and then revise it for final submission. Both submissions were 3 pages long at maximum. Teacher feedback was given on the writing drafts to help students enhance their final products. The two pieces of student writing and teacher feedback were entered into the automated tracking system to generate cross-tabulated frequencies and percentages in order to explore the relationship between teacher feedback and student revisions to the content in each EFL course.

2.5 Procedure

Participants from the same university enrolled in the same EFL course. By the midterm of their courses, students were required to submit a writing draft to their class teacher for feedback. In two to three week's time, the teacher would send back his or her written feedback to the students concerned. Upon consideration of the feedback received, students revised their drafts and finalized the assignments by the second last week of their courses. The first draft with feedback and final writing product of each participant were collected and subsequently analysed by the automated tracking system to evaluate the effectiveness of different types of teacher feedback to encourage the content revisions of students.

3 Results and Discussion

3.1 Praise

All praises given by the teachers T1 to T3 are found to result in no changes to student writing. This finding indicates that praise has no or little immediate effect on triggering content revisions. After receiving praises from the teacher (e.g. "the paragraph is well-developed with logical arguments"), students might think that their writing performance exceeds the teacher's expectations and that it is not necessary to revise their drafts. Notwithstanding, praising comments are still considered important because they can help EFL students develop a positive attitude towards writing and increase their confidence in written English [19].

3.2 Criticism

Figure 1 shows the content revisions made by students in response to the criticisms given by teachers. More specifically, each bar denotes the percentage of criticism on content that can actually trigger content revisions in each class. Criticism on content was likely to lead to content revisions (T1: 47.7%, T2: 84.5% and T3: 55.3%), especially in the areas of claim (T1: 23.4%) as well as evidence and details (T2: 47.1% and T3: 37.7%).

Criticism is recognised as one of the most controlling feedback types [16]. This feedback type can point out what needs to be done and is phrased without a hedging device. Figure 1 suggests that students could generally make changes to the aspects criticised by the teacher due to the evaluative and corrective nature of criticism. Nevertheless, it is noted that students were occasionally not able to respond to the criticisms in the absence of specific guidance (e.g. "poor expression", "improper citation", and so on).

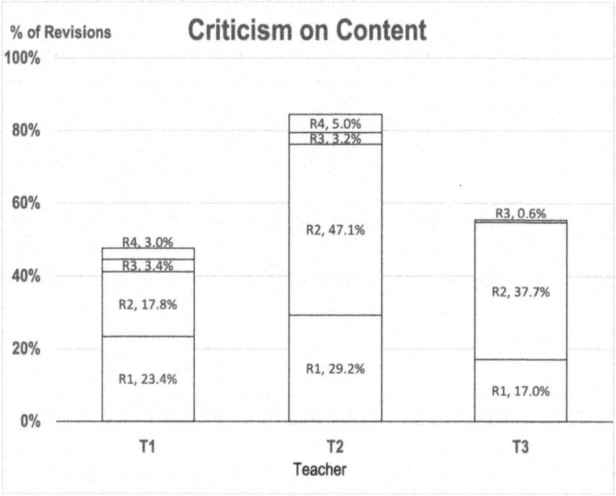

Fig. 1. Relationship between criticism and content revision.

3.3 Imperative

Figure 2 illustrates the relationship between imperative and content revision. Imperatives on content could likely lead to content revisions (T1: 41.1%, T2: 47.5% and T3: 60.7%), especially in relation to evidence and details (T1: 25.3%, T2: 27.5% and T3: 38.0%).

Imperative is identified as one of the most controlling feedback types [16]. It often requests a change by order of the teacher. In some cases, the imperative is action-oriented and gives a step-by-step instruction on improvement (e.g. "do not repeat the same ideas over and over again"). Given these characteristics, imperatives can potentially push students to make revisions to what the teacher is concerned about.

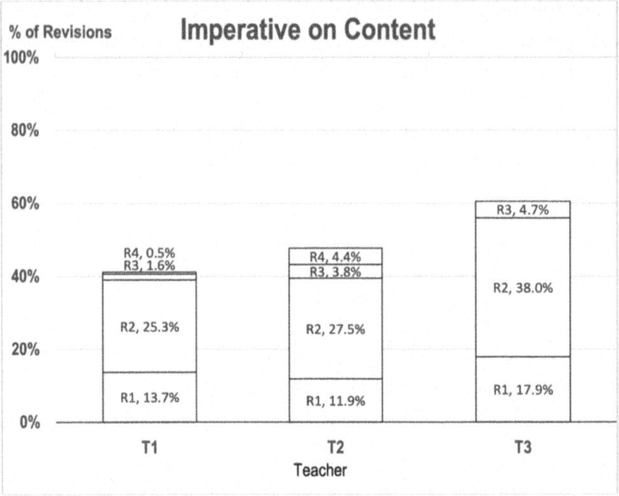

Fig. 2. Relationship between imperative and content revision.

3.4 Advice

Figure 3 presents the relationship between advice and content revision. Advice on content was likely to lead to changes to content (T1: 47.1% and T2: 80.6%), mainly in areas of evidence and details (T1: 41.2% and T2: 47.2%) as well as claim (T2: 33.3%). It is worthy to note that the teacher T3 did not offer advice on student writing, so content revisions triggered by advice cannot be found in her class.

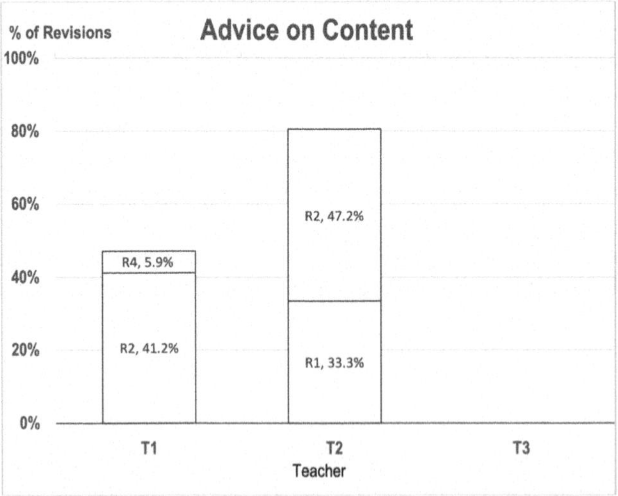

Fig. 3. Relationship between advice and content revision.

Advice is known to be less controlling than criticism and imperative. It enables the teacher to give students a choice of how and whether to make revisions. Advice often contains practical recommendations for improvement [20], so students tend to prefer and accept this type of teacher feedback [19]. This is possibly why the percentage of content revisions triggered by advice was comparable to that by criticism and imperative.

3.5 Question

Figure 4 and Fig. 5 show the types of content revision made by students in response to the closed and open questions from their teachers, respectively. Closed questions on content are found to lead to content revisions (T1: 35.6% and T2: 30.8%) where most of them are related to evidence and details (T1: 28.9% and T2: 30.8%). Open questions on content could likely lead to content revisions (T1: 40.9% and T2: 28.6%), including changes to claim (T1: 21.9%) as well as evidence and details (T1: 16.8% and T2: 14.3%). Again, the teacher T3 did not give feedback in form of question, so content revisions triggered by question cannot be found in her class.

Closed and open questions are less controlling than criticism and imperative, which can direct students' attention to the unclear parts of their drafts. Unlike advice, however, both types of question neither explicitly indicate the problems nor suggest how to fix them [16]. Most EFL students tend to dislike feedback in form of question because they would prefer direct written corrective feedback [3]. Perhaps this is a reason for the lower percentages of content revisions triggered by question than by other feedback types.

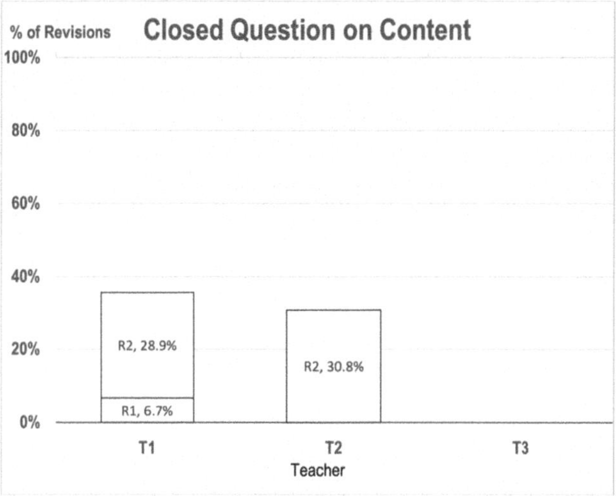

Fig. 4. Relationship between closed question and content revision.

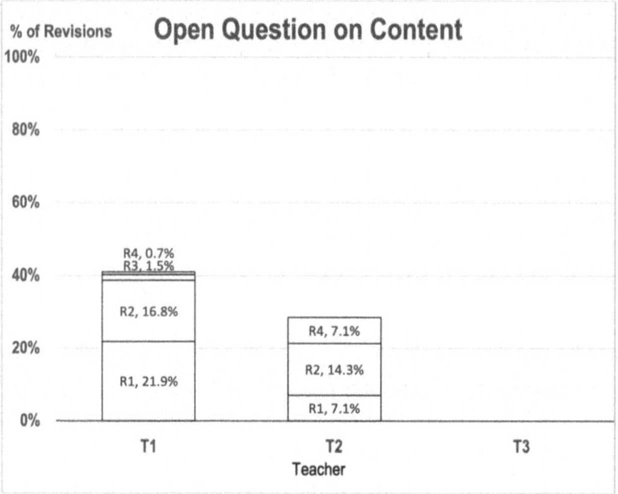

Fig. 5. Relationship between open question and content revision.

4 Concluding Remarks

This study was designed to take the automated tracking approach to explore the impact of teacher feedback on content revisions of EFL students' writing. The results from the automated analysis indicate that the most controlling feedback types, namely imperative and criticism, are particularly effective in encouraging student revisions to content. Advice is also effective for content revisions, and its effect is comparable to that of imperative and criticism. Closed and open questions was least effective for content revisions. In addition, it is found that EFL students were more able to make revisions to evidence and details, but less able to revise the areas related to reasoning and analysis. Considering the findings, teachers are recommended to make informed adjustments to their feedback and instructional strategies so as to better encourage EFL students to improve their writing. In the future, more research can be carried out to adopt or develop a similar approach to investigate the impact of teacher feedback on other writing aspects, such as the organisation and cohesion of ideas in student writing, at a larger scale.

Acknowledgments. This research was supported by the Research Cluster Fund (RG 78/2019-2020R), and the Interdisciplinary Research Scheme of the Dean's Research Fund 2019–20 (FLASS/DRF/IDS-2) of The Education University of Hong Kong, Hong Kong.

References

1. Hattie, J., Timperly, H.: The power of feedback. Rev. Educ. Res. **77**(1), 81–112 (2007)
2. Hattie, J.: Visible Learning for Teachers: Maximizing Impact on Learning. Routledge, New York (2012)

3. Hyland, K.: Second Language Writing, 2nd edn. Cambridge University Press, Cambridge (2019)
4. Hyland, K., Hyland, F.: Feedback on second language students' writing. Lang. Teach. **39**(2), 83–101 (2006)
5. Badger, R., White, G.: A process genre approach to teaching writing. Engl. Lang. Teach. J. **54**(2), 153–160 (2000)
6. Graham, S., Sandmel, K.: The process writing approach: a meta-analysis. J. Educ. Res. **104**(6), 396–407 (2011)
7. Truscott, J.: The case against grammar correction in L2 writing classes. Lang. Learn. **46**, 327–369 (1996)
8. Truscott, J.: The effect of error correction on learners' ability to write accurately. J. Second Lang. Writ. **16**, 255–272 (2007)
9. Ferris, D.R.: Does error feedback help student writers? New evidence on the short- and long-term effects of written error correction. In: Hyland, K., Hyland, F. (eds.) Feedback in Second Language Writing: Contexts and Issues, pp. 81–104. Cambridge University Press, Cambridge (2006)
10. Elwood, J.A., Bode, J.: Student preferences vis-à-vis teacher feedback in university EFL writing class in Japan. System **42**, 333–343 (2014)
11. Tian, L., Zhou, Y.: Learner engagement with automated feedback, peer feedback and teacher feedback in an online EFL writing context. System **91**, 1–14 (2020)
12. Chong, I.: Interplay among technical, socio-emotional and personal factors in written feedback research. Assess. Eval. High. Educ. **43**(2), 185–196 (2018)
13. Cheng, G., Chen, J., Foung, D., Lam, V., Tom, M.: Towards automatic classification of teacher feedback on student writing. Int. J. Inf. Educ. Technol. **8**(5), 342–346 (2018)
14. Cheng, G.: Exploring the effects of automated tracking of student responses to teacher feedback in draft revision: evidence from an undergraduate EFL writing course. Interact. Learn. Environ. (2019).https://doi.org/10.1080/10494820.2019.1655769
15. Hamp-Lyons, L., Chen, J.: An investigation into the effectiveness of teacher feedback on student writing. Engl. Lang. Teach. Learn. **3**, 207–219 (1999)
16. Straub, R.: Students' reactions to teacher comments: an exploratory study. Res. Teach. Engl. **31**(1), 91–119 (1997)
17. Conrad, S.M., Goldstein, L.M.: ESL student revision after teacher-written comments: text, contexts, and individuals. J. Second Lang. Writ. **8**(2), 147–179 (1999)
18. Faigley, L., Witte, S.: Analyzing revision. Coll. Compos. Commun. **32**(4), 400–414 (1981)
19. Mahfoodh, O.H.A.: "I feel disappointed": EFL university students' emotional responses towards teacher written feedback. Assess. Writ. **31**, 53–72 (2017)
20. Hyland, F., Hyland, K.: Sugaring the pill: Praise and criticism in written feedback. J. Second Lang. Writ. **10**(3), 185–212 (2001)

Exploring the Potential, Features, and Functions of Small Talk in Digital Distance Teaching on *Zoom*: A Mixed-Method Study by Quasi-experiment and Conversation Analysis

Mike Hin Leung Chui[1](✉), Bernie Chun Nam Mak[2], and Gary Cheng[1]

[1] The Education University of Hong Kong, Tai Po, New Territories, Hong Kong, China
{mikechui, chengks}@eduhk.hk
[2] Hong Kong Baptist University, Shatin, New Territories, Hong Kong, China
bcnmak@hkbu.edu.hk

Abstract. Small talk has existed across different face-to-face settings in human communication, but it remains unclear what subtle impact it can have on digital distance teaching. This study employed a mixed method to explore the potential, features, and functions of small talk in distance teaching on *Zoom*. The first phase, quantitative in nature, conducted a quasi-experiment to test whether the in-class small talk of a teacher, Tom, would have a significant impact on his students' perceived level of satisfaction in learning experience on *Zoom*. The second phase, qualitative in nature, analyzed Tom's recordings of teaching on *Zoom* to elucidate any recurring procedures or sequences of in-class small talk using conversation analysis. The first phase showed that students in a *Zoom* lesson with Tom's small talk were associated with a statistically significantly larger mean level of satisfaction in learning experience than those in the same mode but without his small talk. The second phase, though, indicated that Tom's students only occasionally responded to his small talk. Even when they did so, they tended to delay and chose to respond in the chatbox. The study concludes that teacher small talk will have a positive but invisible impact on student learning experience online. It is suggested that developers of online teaching software should consider designing commands to create multimodal effects to aid teacher users to perform small talk in an easy way and in a friendly manner.

Keywords: Small talk · Distance teaching · Online learning · Computer-assisted language learning · Computer-mediated communication · Conversation analysis

1 Introduction

The speech event small talk originates from Malinowski's [1] concept phatic communion, which refers to the most ritualistic and least informative exchange to start a conversation (e.g., How're you doing? I'm doing alright.) or fill a moment of awkward

W. Jia et al. (Eds.): SETE 2021, LNCS 13089, pp. 364–372, 2021.
https://doi.org/10.1007/978-3-030-92836-0_32

silence (e.g., What's your plan for this weekend? I'm hanging out with my kids.) during a conversation. However, societal development has made exchanges of this kind more extended and complicated across different institutional settings [2]. In the workplace, small talk can refer to non-mandatory talk which is primarily intended to convey friendliness and keep affiliate engagement [3]. While the umbrella term can still denote a restrictive phatic exchange (as taught in textbooks for learners of a foreign language), it also covers more specific and informative talk for common interpersonal goals in contrast to core-business talk for transactional purposes [4]. In this regard, small talk can occur in the form of phatic exchange, social talk, chitchat, etc. [5]. Each of them can occur as a single speech event (e.g., in the pantry), but they can also take place within a larger goal-directed speech event from a broader perspective of talk at work (e.g., in an internal meeting; in a medical consultation).

Research has explicitly addressed the essential functions of doing small talk, namely warming up an upcoming discussion [6], passing on partially relevant information [7], and providing a relaxed work environment [8]. Among all conversational contexts, the classroom is an interesting one. Although it is a space for formal teaching, small talk is often utilized to explore or mention a co-topic to stimulate a further discussion about the key topic [9]. It is commonly used by the teacher to maintain easy rapport with students [10]. In teaching English as a foreign language (EFL), it is even employed as a strategy for raising students' awareness of talk(ing) as a social skill [11]. But still, these findings have grown out of studies which investigated small talk in the face-to-face classroom. The global pandemic of *coronavirus disease 2019* (COVID-19) has led to a shift from face-to-face teaching to distance teaching via a video-conferencing device, such as *Zoom* and *Cisco Webex*. Such a new mode of teaching has not only caused different technical problems of teaching and learning, but also increased the perceived distance between the teacher and students, which casts doubt on the nature and roles of small talk between or during teaching activities [12]. After all, in-class small talk is not compulsory, so in some people's eyes it can be omitted whenever necessary. This is particularly the case in Asian countries where local teachers are unfamiliar with digital pedagogy and often expected to disseminate information about the assignment and/or examination only.

In view of the need for more research on small talk in digital distance teaching, this small-scale study aims to address two questions:

- Will teacher small talk in the digital classroom have an impact on student learning experience?
- Supposing the answer to the first question is yes, what is the overall pattern of teacher small talk in digital distance teaching?

2 Research Site and Participants

2.1 Context

The research site was an educational unit (the college hereafter) of a government-funded tertiary institution in Hong Kong. The college consisted of over 6000 full-time students and about 400 full-time staff members. Owing to the COVID-19 pandemic, all classes have shifted from the physical classroom to *Zoom* since January 2020 (i.e. the second semester of the academic year 2019–2020). Except for courses on Chinese and communication, teachers were supposed to use English as the primary medium of instruction in class.

2.2 Participants

This study focused on a local male teacher with approximately 10 years of experience in teaching English as a second language. The teacher, with the pseudonym Tom, taught both common core and concentration-based courses in each semester. One of the former was on English academic writing (EAW hereafter), and one of the latter was on computer-mediated communication (CMC hereafter). The two courses contributed quantitative and qualitative data respectively to the current study, which was carried out in two phases.

3 Phase 1 – Quasi-experiment on Teacher Small Talk on *Zoom*

3.1 Procedure

In the first phase, a quasi-experiment was conducted to address the first research question. Three sections of Tom's EAW were invited to participate. In the third teaching week of EAW, Sect. 1 (N = 25) was the control group where students were given a *Zoom* lecture on English and arguments without any teacher small talk. Section 2 (N = 22) was experimental group A where students were given the same *Zoom* lecture with teacher small talk between any two teaching activities. Section 3 (N = 25) was experimental group B where students were given the same *Zoom* lecture with teacher small talk during each teaching activity. For all the three sections, the breakout room was temporarily disabled. To minimize the effect of external variables on the result, Tom was required to strictly adhere to the lesson plan for week 3 and pre-set small talk topics, together with the following explicit guidelines:

- In Sect. 1, the control group, he should not initiate any small talk once he was on *Zoom*;
- In Sect. 2, experimental group A, he should initiate small talk with the pre-set topics when he moved i) from formal lecturing to video watching, and then ii) from video watching to the in-class exercises; and
- In Sect. 3, experimental group B, he should initiate small talk with the same pre-set topics as Sect. 2, but i) during his formal lecturing, ii) at the video time, and iii) within the in-class exercise period.

After the *Zoom* lecture, students of each section were asked to complete the same questionnaire on their learning experience. Given the exploratory nature, it collected personal information and their answers to one question only: To what extent have you been satisfied with your learning experience in today's lesson? This question required them to answer on a five-point Likert scale: Very satisfied (5), Satisfied (4), Neither satisfied nor unsatisfied (3), Unsatisfied (2), Very unsatisfied (1). To avoid any loading effect, the question did not mention the keyword small talk and other relevant concepts.

The quasi-experiment aimed to examine whether teacher small talk would have a statistically significant impact on students' perceived level of satisfaction in learning experience on *Zoom*. It follows that:

- H_0 = The three sections perceive the same level of satisfaction in learning experience.
- H_a = The three sections perceive different levels of satisfaction in learning experience.

3.2 Results and Discussion

The descriptive statistics associated with student satisfaction levels across the three sections are reported in Table 1. The control group (i.e., Sect. 1) without teacher small talk was associated with the numerically smallest mean level of satisfaction in learning experience (M = 3.00). Experimental group B (i.e., Sect. 3) with teacher small talk during a teaching activity was associated with the numerically highest mean level of satisfaction in learning experience (M = 3.88). To test the hypothesis that teacher small talk had an effect on students' learning experience on *Zoom*, a between-groups ANOVA was conducted. Because the sample size was small, prior to conducting the test, the assumption of normality was evaluated and determined to be satisfied as the three groups' distributions were associated with skewness and kurtosis less than |1.96| respectively. The assumption of homogeneity of variances was tested and satisfied based on Levene's *F* test, $F(2, 69) = .988$, $p = .378$.

Table 1. Descriptive statistics for students' satisfaction level across the three sections.

	N	Mean	Std. Deviation	Std. Error	95% Confidence Interval for Mean		Minimum	Maximum
					Lower Bound	Upper Bound		
Control group	25	3.00	.707	.141	2.71	3.29	2	4
Experimental group A	22	3.68	.839	.179	3.31	4.05	2	5
Experimental group B	25	3.88	.927	.185	3.50	4.26	2	5
Total	72	3.51	.904	.107	3.30	3.73	2	5

The between-groups ANOVA yielded a statistically significant effect, $F(2, 69) = 7.694$, $p = .001$. The null hypothesis of no differences among the means was rejected. To evaluate the nature of the differences between the three means further, the statistically significant ANOVA was followed up with three Fisher's LSD post-hoc tests. The difference between the control group and experimental group A was statistically significant, $t(69) = -.682$, $p = .006$, $d = -.877$. The difference between the control group and experimental group B was statistically significant, $t(69) = -.880$, $p < .001$, $d = -1.067$. The effect sizes associated with the statistically significant effects are considered large based on Cohen's [13] guidelines. However, the difference between the two experimental groups was statistically insignificant, $t(69) = -.198$, $p = .416$, $d = .226$.

The analysis demonstrates that students who learned in a *Zoom* lesson with teacher small talk were associated with a statistically significantly larger mean level of satisfaction in learning experience than those who learned in the same mode but without teacher small talk. It also shows that teacher small talk during a teaching activity was associated with a slightly higher mean. For ethical reasons, all student participants in this phase received a report written in layperson's terms to explain what had been investigated and found in the EAW lesson of week 3.

4 Phase 2 – Conversation Analysis of Teacher Small Talk on *Zoom*

4.1 Procedure

In the second phase, a qualitative design was used to address the second research question. As phase 1 had confirmed the impact of Tom's small talk on his students' perceived levels of satisfaction in learning experience, one of his CMC sections (N = 29) in the subsequent semester was invited to participate in this study. Upon the students' informed written consent to grant permission to analyze their communicative behavior on *Zoom*, recordings of the CMC lectures and chat logs were collected from weeks 3 to 10. They were coded according to i) who initiated small talk, ii) who responded to small talk, iii) when small talk was initiated, iv) when small talk was responded to, v) how small talk was initiated, and vi) how small talk was responded to. Afterwards, the data were analyzed using the conversation analysis (CA) method, focusing on structure and the pattern of conversational development. A follow-up interview with Tom was conducted to collect basic contextual information about the representative excerpts for more in-depth analysis.

The analysis centered on the similar procedures or sequences of teacher small talk, through which the general norms of interaction could be revealed and applied by other people in a similar setting or context in the future. Thus, it concerned recurring patterns only. Minor findings were not reported or discussed.

4.2 Results and Discussion

Data from CMC constituted eight *Zoom* recordings of 24 teaching hours (i.e., 8 three-hour lectures) and eight chat logs of 3100 English words in total. Upon coding and analysis, 39 excerpts of small talk were documented, including short phatic exchanges (N = 19), extended social talk which was clearly related to the teaching topic (N = 10), loose chitchat which was largely unrelated to the teaching topic (N = 6), and narratives with plots and characters (N = 4). Included below are the main patterns found in the 39 representative small talk instances:

The Launch of and Response to Small Talk. Small talk was often initiated by Tom orally, but it only occasionally elicited responses from students. They tended to delay and give their responses in the chatbox.

Example. At 00:42:15, Tom orally asked whether it is rough for students to have an early lecture, but students only responded in the chatbox after 20 s. All student names are pseudonyms.

00:42:38	Aaron	I woke up at 7:30 = =
00:42:47	Brenda	6:30 ar sir
00:42:49	Calvin	could we start late, eg, at 8:40??
00:42:53	David	research says teenagers need to sleep more
00:43:05	Edmund	lol

On the other hand, small talk was seldom initiated by students. When there was student small talk, it was usually initiated in the chatbox but yielded oral responses from Tom. This pattern may originate from the imbalance in the rights to talk in the traditional classroom. In face-to-face class, the teacher has the exclusive rights to hold the conversational floor and speak to the whole class, unless he or she has asked a question or selected a student to respond to a question. Otherwise, students are expected to mute themselves during class time. Therefore, when it comes to small talk on *Zoom*, it is still the teacher who dominates orally. When the teacher invites a response from students, every student has the right to speak after handing up. If there is a selected student, he or she automatically gains the right to speak immediately. Yet, partly because the hands-up function on *Zoom* is limited, and partly because verbal participation of students looks more marked on *Zoom*, students still choose to respond in the chatbox, especially when they want to avoid accidental overlaps and are more fluent in typing than in speaking. Meanwhile, when the teacher focuses on teaching on Zoom, the hands-up signs from students may not really catch his attention. This also explains why student responses, if any, are usually found delayed in the chatbox.

Teacher Small Talk During a Teaching Activity. Small talk initiated by Tom during a teaching activity was often short phatic exchange but did not yield any student responses. Even delayed responses in the chatbox were rare.

Example. Tom mentioned the start of rain when he orally described the background of blogging, but no students responded to the phatic talk about rain, whether orally or in the chatbox. The transcription conventions can be found in the appendix.

Tom: so blogging on the Internet develops from dairy writing on paper. but the latter was seldom published (.) unless you were <u>Anne Frank</u> (0.5) do you know her? I mean the (Jewish) girl in World War II when she hid from the Nazi and – oh start to rain. the rain drops echo her life (.) which was sad. hh anyway, in normal situations, traditional diaries were read by the writers themselves only, but your sharing on blogs (.) will be read by <u>everyone</u> with Internet access. hah actually bloggers <u>expect</u> their blogs to be read by the public.

This pattern may originate from the intended use of small talk during core teaching. Teacher small talk of this kind usually runs very short and may not aim at relationship building, but rather at attention-drawing. Hence, no pause is given for any possible student input. The preferred response is not a verbal one but their attention, which is not easily seen on *Zoom*. Thus, the phatic exchange which comes as an adjacency pair [14] misses the second part, but without any negative consequences. This phenomenon somewhat violates the existing understanding that small talk requires mutual participation or awkward silence will result [15].

Teacher Small Talk between Two Teaching Activities. Small talk initiated by Tom between two teaching activities was often extended social talk but did not evoke any student responses. Even delayed responses in the chatbox were rare.

Example. Tom touched on Cantonese when he orally summarized a point about the linguistic situation of English online and moved onto a discussion exercise, but no students responded to the social talk about Cantonese, whether orally or in the chatbox.

`Tom: okay (.) now you know (0.5) the Internet has made more non-native:: English speakers. this is why most digital natives know some English (.) no matter what the mother tongue is. speaking of our mother tongue, it seems (.) Cantonese is less preferable than English hh it's strange isn't it Hong Kong people (.) many of us like the second language more than our first language hah actually this attitude originates from political (.) historical reasons. okay now, let's have a look at an excerpt of how non-native hh non-standard English:: is used on the Internet.`

This pattern may be attributed to the use of small talk as a transitional device between moves in classroom teaching. In institutional meetings, small talk is often used to oil the wheels between two activities or conversational topics which are different in nature [15]. Teacher social talk with co-topical information [9] serves a similar function. However, on *Zoom* where it takes extra time to undertake activities, a smooth flow to the next move is more preferred than a student interruptive response. Consequently, not responding to social talk of this kind is acceptable (or even expected) from both teacher and student perspectives.

5 Conclusion

The present study has employed a mixed method (i.e., quantitative and qualitative) to explore the potential, features, and functions of teacher small talk in distance teaching via the video-conferencing device *Zoom*. In the quantitative part, it was found that the means of the two experimental groups with teacher small talk were significantly different from, and higher than, the mean of the control group without teacher small talk. This has indicated that teacher small talk would have a positive effect on students' perceptions of satisfaction in learning experience on *Zoom*. The first phase also showed that the second experiment group was associated with a higher mean level of satisfaction. This has suggested that integrating small talk into teaching would bring more satisfactory learning experience than using small talk as a transitional device only. In the second phase, namely the qualitative part, it was revealed that teacher small talk occurred far more frequently than student small talk did. Such small talk from the teacher could be primarily used to seek attention from students and smooth transitions between in-class activities. As small talk of this kind might not be relationship-oriented, it did not necessarily occur as a two-way process, so student responses could be missing, delayed, or only given in written form, but without negative consequences in the conversation.

To put together the findings from the two phases, this study concludes that teacher small talk will have a positive but invisible impact on digital distance teaching. It can be considered a discursive strategy for enhancing teaching performance and enriching learning experience in the online classroom. Unlike its counterparts in other everyday or institutional settings, teacher small talk during teaching in the online classroom does not always expect an immediate verbal response, so it can tolerate few or even zero responses from students. These findings have implications for pedagogy, classroom management, and development of online teaching software. During the online mode of teaching, teachers can lead in (or bring up) interesting topics which are correlated to the key learning content if time permits, so as to catch students' attention, motivating them to know more, smooth the transition between classroom activities, and create a lightening classroom atmosphere. For example, teachers may start an online lesson with chitchat which is supported by a picture on the shared screen. In doing so in the long run, teachers can develop a professional culture in which e-learning can occur in a reasonably pleasant digital classroom, through which they can manage the classroom (and engage their students) in a subtle but effective way.

Since distance teaching online relies on the use of e-tools, software engineers or program developers should consider designing instructions to create multimodal effects to aid teacher users to do in-class small talk in an easy way and in a friendly manner. For example, the interface may afford small tasks in which teachers can do phatic talk with sound effects when introducing the task to students. It may also afford pop-up emoticons on the screen by a click during small-talking time, which can assist teachers in empowering their small talk and help students to visualize their minimal responses. Last but not least, as mentioned in the introduction section, small talk occurs in different forms, and its topics vary across cultures. Academics should conduct other experiments to replicate the findings in consideration of variables such as the teacher's work experience and students' proficiency in English. They should also conceive other studies using qualitative methods to illustrate how teacher-student small talk exactly takes place in different synchronous or asynchronous online teaching settings.

Appendix: Transcription Conventions [16]

`(.)`	A dot within parentheses indicates a very short pause.
<u>`Anne Frank`</u>	Stressed parts of an utterance is underlined.
`(0.5)`	A number in parentheses indicates the length of pause in second.
`(Jewish)`	Doubtful item in spoken speech is shown in parentheses.
–	A dash indicates an abrupt cut-off the prior sound.
`hh`	Aspiration is indicated by one or more "h"s.
`hah`	Laughter is indicated by one or more "hah"s.

: : A colon indicates lengthening of the prior sound; the number of colon increases with the degree of lengthening.

References

1. Malinowski, B.: The problem of meaning in primitives. In: Ogden, C.K., Richards, I.A. (eds.) The Meaning of Meaning: A Study of the Influence of Language upon thought and of the Science of Symbolism (4th ed.), pp. 296–336. Routledge & K. Paul, London (1923)
2. Săftoiu, R.: Small talk - a work of frame. In: Măda, S., Săftoiu, R. (eds.) Professional Communication Across Languages and Cultures, pp. 213–235. John Benjamins, Philadelphia (2012)
3. Holmes, J.: Doing collegiality and keeping control at work: small talk in government departments. In: Coupland, J. (ed.) Small Talk, pp. 32–61. Longman, Harlow (2000)
4. Koester, A.: Workplace Discourse. Continuum, New York (2012)
5. Mak, B.C.N.: Doing business and constructing identities through small talk in workplace instant messaging. Pragmat. Soc. **10**(4), 559–583 (2020). https://doi.org/10.1075/ps.16064.mak
6. Holmes, J.: When small talk is a big deal: sociolinguistic challenges in the workplace. In: Long, M.H. (ed.) Second Language Needs Analysis, pp. 344–372. Cambridge University Press, Cambridge (2005)
7. Drew, P., Chilton, K.: Calling just to keep in touch: regular and habitualised telephone calls as an environment for small talk. In: Coupland, J. (ed.) Small talk, pp. 137–162. Longman, Harlow (2000)
8. Jin, Y.: Small talk in medical conversations: data from China. J. Pragmat. **134**, 31–44 (2018). https://doi.org/10.1016/j.pragma.2018.06.011
9. Dooly, M., Tudini, V.: Now we are teachers: the role of small talk in student language teachers' telecollaborative task development. J. Pragmat. **102**, 38–53 (2016). https://doi.org/10.1016/j.pragma.2016.06.008
10. Aslan, E.: 'Oiling the social wheels' in an undergraduate chemistry lab: an ITA's participation in small talk. Classr. Discourse **11**, 252–271 (2020). https://doi.org/10.1080/19463014.2019.1585891
11. Kuznetsova, I.: Creating high-frequency, naturalistic opportunities to develop small talk skills in EFL classrooms. J. Lang. Educ. **3**(2), 55–62 (2017). https://doi.org/10.17323/2411-7390-2017-3-2-55-62
12. Maíz-Arévalo, C.: Small talk is not cheap: phatic computer-mediated communication in intercultural classes. Comput. Assist. Lang. Learn. **30**(5), 432–446 (2017). https://doi.org/10.1080/09588221.2017.1304423
13. Cohen, J.: A power primer. Psychol. Bull. **112**, 155–159 (1992)
14. Schegloff, E.A., Sacks, H.: Opening up closings. Semiotica **8**(4), 289–327 (1973). https://doi.org/10.1515/semi.1973.8.4.289
15. Holmes, J., Stubbe, M.: Power and Politeness in the Workplace: A Sociolinguistic Analysis of Talk at Work, 2nd edn. Routledge, New York (2015)
16. Atkinson, M.J., Heritage, J. (eds.): Structures of Social Action: Studies in Conversation Analysis. Cambridge University Press, Cambridge (1984)

Chatbots for Learning: A Facebook Messenger 'Bot'

Lucas Kohnke(✉)

Education University, Hong Kong SAR, China
lmakohnke@eduhk.hk

Abstract. The last two years have changed how students access formal and informal education. Due to the COVID-19 pandemic, language learners have had limited opportunities to interact actively with teachers and fellow students.

However, chatbots can help to fill this gap. This paper describes an educational chatbot employed on Facebook Messenger as a supplement to direct teacher input. It was developed using Google's Dialogflow, which allows teachers to build omnichannel chatbots using natural language understanding models.

Specific branching (question and answer) was employed to limit the chatbot's scope to specific language areas. Chatbots, if employed successfully, could have widespread applications in higher education institutions and shape language teaching in the future.

Keywords: Chatbot · Facebook · Language learning · COVID-19

1 Introduction

In many regions, the COVID-19 pandemic necessitated the suspension of face-to-face classes. Higher education institutions turned to online, blended, and hybrid learning to provide instruction and a sense of normality during this unprecedented time [1]. Language teachers have had to rapidly adapt existing pedagogies and platforms to serve the new educational landscape [2]. Chatbots present unique opportunities for interactive learning without face-to-face contact. Students can have text or chat exchanges with chatbots anytime and anywhere, using their mobile phones, laptops, tablets or desktops. Through national language processing, chatbots can provide linguistics input [3], stimulate interest in language learning [4] and motivate students [5], contributing to learners' linguistic growth [6]. Today, chatbots are frequently employed by businesses on their websites and social media channels but remain rare in the educational sector [7]. Chatbots employed on social networks such as Facebook can support language acquisition by encouraging interaction and active participation in learning. This short paper provides a brief overview of a pedagogical chatbot developed to supplement direct teacher input.

W. Jia et al. (Eds.): SETE 2021, LNCS 13089, pp. 373–377, 2021.
https://doi.org/10.1007/978-3-030-92836-0_33

2 Related Work

Although there are numerous technological tools available to language learners (apps and websites, for example), few allow learners to communicate and converse in the target language. Language learning occurs through comprehensible input, feedback on output and the opportunity to modify output [8]. Chatbots provide interaction and communication on demand and allow language users to personalize their input and output through natural language interfaces [9]. They have been employed in education since the 1970s [10] and can be divided into text or voice-based models [7]. A.L.I.C.E., one of the largest and most well-known text-based chatbots, is built around categories that speed the process of finding the most appropriate response to user input. A.L.I.C.E. can consider the context and apply additional branching to produce more precise responses. In contrast, the Jabberwacky chatbot stores everything said to it and learns from these conversations to produce the most appropriate response [11]. Today, Jabberwacky has evolved into Cleverbot using AI to learn from user interactions [12].

Fryer and Carpenter [3] proposed five functions of chatbots in language learning: immediate grammar and spelling feedback, review of words and expressions, listening practice, and providing a supportive learning environment. Chatbots enhance students' enjoyment in learning [13], improve their interactions and language negotiation skills [14] and increase learning satisfaction [15].

In the last decade, the instant messaging functions, portability and flexibility of mobile devices have motivated educators to integrate them into teaching and learning. Social media platforms such as Facebook and its Messenger platform have made it possible to employ chatbots easily to provide informal and formal learning opportunities. Specifically, Facebook can be used to support learning because it offers.

- Familiarity: little technical knowledge is required;
- Availability: 24/7;
- Usefulness: student information sharing and collaboration;
- Peer feedback: communication among students;
- Cooperation: the exchange of ideas by students;
- Knowledge sharing: exchange of resources (documents, videos, images) by students.

By incorporating Facebook as a learning platform, teachers can offer students increased avenues of learning. Chatbot developers can exploit Facebook's infrastructure, which allows the use of any programming language, or employ a third-party no-code platform.

3 Chatbot System

The chatbot presented here is built and powered by Google's artificial intelligence software Dialogflow and deployed on Facebook Messenger. The chatbot supports rich, intuitive conversations and can handle both linear and non-linear conversations with users. Moreover, because it is employed on Facebook, it can use Facebook's application programming interface to handle user authentication. This chatbot acts as a conversational agent and responds to users' questions following a set of rules. This limits its overall scope, which facilitates effective interaction and avoids disappointment with its limitations. The following figure offers snapshots of the branching of the chatbot. One example shows how it answers a student question and the other how it directs the student towards further language learning resources (Fig. 1).

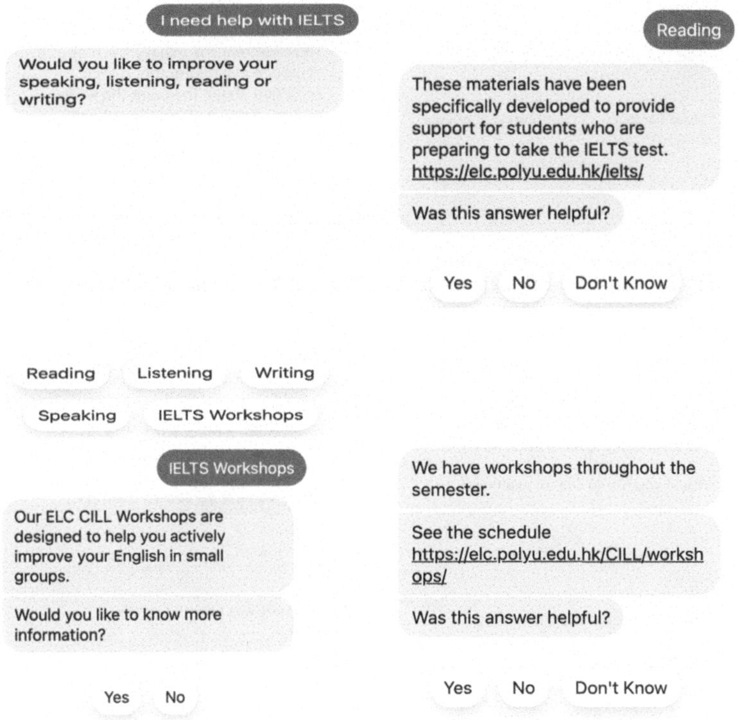

Fig. 1. Example of question and answer about IELTS

As can be seen from the above example, a student who writes the word 'IELTS' is provided with learning options for all four skills covered on the test as well as information about workshops. Figure 2 shows how the chatbot would guide a student who entered the word 'paragraph'.

As shown in Fig. 2, students can choose how much knowledge they require on a topic. The chatbot can pre-empt the need for follow-up questions by suggesting further information. It can also provide more detailed answers to student questions. For example, Fig. 3 illustrates lessons on the active and passive voice.

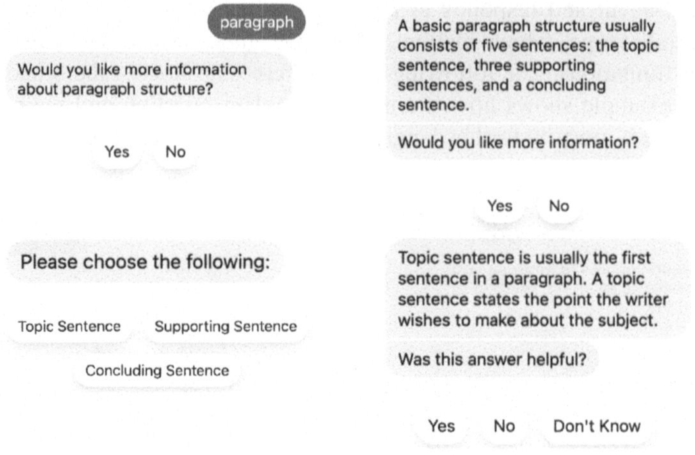

Fig. 2. Example of question and answer relating to paragraph structure

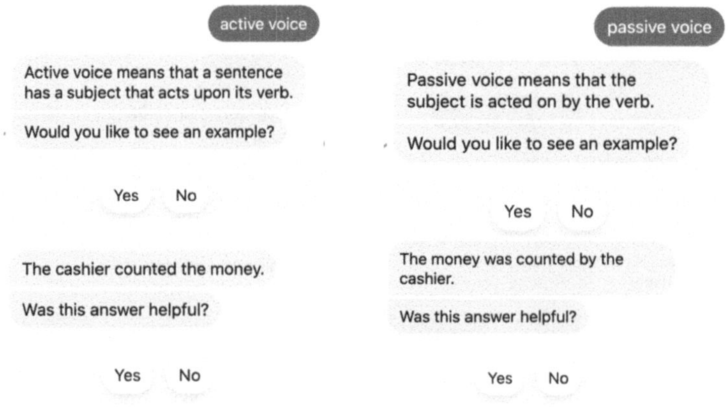

Fig. 3. Example of question and answer about active and passive voice

4 Conclusion

In the past year, chatbots have gained attention for their ability to provide language learning input during the suspension of face-to-face classes [16]. Chatbots can promote active learning, supplement face-to-face instruction, and allow learning to continue anytime and anywhere. Students can find answers to language-learning questions and have rapid access to rich content tailored to their needs. Accordingly, higher education institutions need to explore how the opportunities offered by Facebook and chatbots can be integrated into the formal education system.

References

1. Kohnke, L., Moorhouse, B.L.: Adopting HyFlex in higher education in response to COVID-19: students' perspectives. Open Learn.: J. Open Dist. e-Learn. (2021). https://doi.org/10.1080/02680513.2021.1906641
2. Moorhouse, B.L., Kohnke, L.: Thriving or surviving emergency remote teaching necessitated by COVID-19: university teachers' perspectives. Asia Pac. Educ. Res. **30**(3), 279–287 (2021). https://doi.org/10.1007/s40299-021-00567-9
3. Fryer, L.K., Carpenter, R.: Emerging technologies – Bots as language learning tools. Lang. Learn. Technol. **10**(3), 8–14 (2006)
4. Fryer, L.K., Ainley, M., Thompson, A., Gibson, A., Sherlock, Z.: Stimulating and sustaining interest in a language course: an experimental comparison of chatbot and human task partners. Comput. Hum. Behav. **75**, 461–468 (2017)
5. Kohnke, L.: A qualitative exploration of student perspectives of chatbot use during emergency remote teaching. Int. J. Mob. Organ. (in-press, a)
6. Kim, H., Shin, D., Yang, H., Lee, J.H.: A study of AI chatbot as an assistant tool for school English curriculum. J. Learn.-Cent. Curric. Instruct. **9**(1), 9–110 (2019)
7. Lee, J.H., Yang, H., Shin, D., Kim, H.: Chatbots – technology for the language teacher. ELT J. **74**(3), 338–344 (2020)
8. Mackey, A.: Input, Interaction, and Corrective Feedback in L2 Learning. Oxford University Press, Oxford (2012)
9. Shawar, B.A.: Integrating CALL systems with chatbots as conversational partners. Comput. Sist. **21**(4), 615–626 (2017)
10. Laurillard, D.: Rethinking University Teaching: A Conversational Framework for the Effective Use of Learning Technologies. Routledge, London (2013)
11. Shawar, B.A., Atwell, E.: Fostering language learner autonomy through adaptive conversation tutors. Paper Presented at the Proceedings of the Fourth Corpus Linguistics Conference (2017)
12. Gilbert, R.L., Forney, A.: Can avatars pass the turing test? Intelligent agent perception in a 3D virtual environment. Int. J. Hum.-Comput. Stud. **73**, 30–36 (2015)
13. You, Z., Shen, C., Chang, C., Liu, B., Chen G.: A robot as a teaching assistant in an English class. IEEE Explore (2006). https://ieeexplore.ieee.org/document/1652373. Accessed 20 Aug 2021
14. Lee, S., Min, D., Shim, G.: Effects of using an educational robot on interactional aspects in group based communicative activities. J. Korea Engl. Educ. Soc. **12**(2), 61–80 (2013)
15. Ban, J.-C., Jin, K.-A., Han, J.-H., Kim, S., Lee, S.-E., Ryu, Y.-S.: Effectiveness of applying telepresence type robots in English class. Engl. Lang. Teach. **22**(2), 255–277 (2010)
16. Kohnke, L.: L2 learners' perception of a chatbot as a potential independent language learning tool. Int. J. Mob. Organ. (in-press, b)

International Workshop on Educational Technology for Language Learning (ETLL 2021)

Self-assessment Activities of Translation: A Case Study of Undergraduate, Master and Doctoral Students

Tiantian Wang[1] and Shili Ge[2](✉)

[1] Center for Linguistics and Applied Linguistics, Guangdong University of Foreign Studies, Guangzhou 510420, China
[2] Laboratory of Language and Artificial Intelligence, Guangdong University of Foreign Studies, Guangzhou 510420, China
geshili@gdufs.edu.cn

Abstract. Self-assessment (SA), an important metacognitive strategy and a main type of classroom assessment, plays a crucial role in promoting EFL learning. However, the current SA research in EFL teaching is mostly classroom-based, focusing on speaking, reading and writing skills, so it is impossible for them to reveal how SA interacts with learners. To this end, this study used the method of case study to profile the SA activities of learners at varied proficiency levels. Three undergraduates, one MA student and one doctoral student are enrolled to find out whether their performance and perceptions differ on such SA activities. Semi-structured interviews are main source of data. The results show that there are significant differences in performance and perceptions on self-assessment across grades, mainly reflecting on the degree of clarity in describing their own translation strengths and weaknesses, and the relevance and feasibility of the obtained feedback. These findings point out that SA ability and translation ability are synergistic, and the improvement of the former requires systematic training and continuous practices. It is suggested that SA training should be carried out under the guidance of metacognitive theory, so as to improve learners' translation performance and cultivate their metacognitive awareness.

Keywords: Self-assessment · Translation · EFL learners · Case study

1 Introduction

Limited feedback from large-scale exams for learning [1] has generated the demand for classroom-based assessment (CBA) that is able to offer timely feedback since the end of the last century. Besides, the growing interest in learner autonomy and the conceptual shift from teacher-centered instruction to learner-centered instruction [2] have also generated great enthusiasm in employing self-assessment (SA), a main type of CBA, as an alternative method for evaluating language performance [3, 4].

Self-assessment studies in EFL teaching mostly focuses on the four language skills of listening, speaking, reading, and writing [5], self-assessment of translation remains under-researched [6]. In addition, previous translation SA studies [7–12] were all

W. Jia et al. (Eds.): SETE 2021, LNCS 13089, pp. 381–389, 2021.
https://doi.org/10.1007/978-3-030-92836-0_34

classroom-based. Thus, participants in those studies are highly homogeneous with undergraduates takes a big portion, which makes it difficult to understand the development of learners' SA ability in a dynamic manner. Furthermore, studies on translation SA mostly adopted a mixed research method, focusing not only on the quantitative indicators of the accuracy of students' SA, but also on students' experience and opinions. This seemly comprehensive method in fact determines the incapability of existing studies to unravel such a complex metacognition activity.

By reason of the foregoing, the current study adopts a case study method to describe in detail the translation SA of three English-majored undergraduates, one MA students, and one doctoral student, with an aim to reveal the difficulties encountered by learners of different stages in SA activities, and provide feasible suggestions for translation teaching and learning.

2 Theoretical Framework

This research is conducted under the validity framework of classroom-based assessment (CBA) [13] and the metacognitive theory [14].

Based on Cronbach's validity framework [15], Kane & Wools established a validity framework for CBA, which is comprised of measurement validity and functional validity. The measurement perspective focuses on the accuracy and precision of scores as measures of some construct, and the functional perspective focuses on how well the assessment serves its intended purposes. According to them, for classroom assessment, the functional validity is of central concern, and the measurement perspective plays a supporting role. The current study is built on that statement by emphasizing the feedback obtained from translation SA rather than the accuracy of SA scores.

In order to maximize the effect of translation SA, we put SA under the framework of metacognitive theory, with the purpose of exploring the possibility of improving learners' metacognitive ability through translation SA. Metacognition refers to "one's knowledge about one's own cognitive processes or anything related to them" [16]. It comprises two components: knowledge about cognition and regulation about cognition. Self-assessment, belonging to latter part, is defined as "appraising the products and regulatory processes of one's learning," and includes revisiting and revising one's goals [14] (Fig. 1).

To sum up, SA in this study is recognized as an important form of CBA and an integral part of metacognition. Therefore, students' SA activities are investigated from the aforementioned two aspects. In other words, the quality of translation SA lies in the degree to which students correctly reflect on their own strengths and weaknesses [17] and further learning [14] after the SA activity.

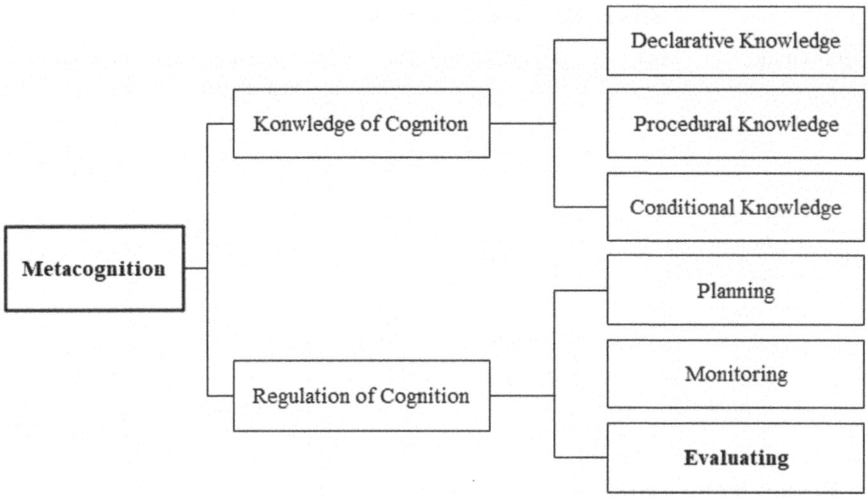

Fig. 1. Theoretical framework of metacognition [14]

3 Research Design

This research observes the translation SA activities of three undergraduates, one MA student and one doctoral candidate in a key foreign language university, and designed semi-structured interviews based on the observation results. The translation SA activity is a two-phase one: 1) complete a language background information questionnaire and a Chinese-to-English translation task; 2) self-assess translation scripts with the translation rubric and reference translation provided. Specifically, the language background information questionnaire includes grade, major, gender, date of birth, college entrance examination English scores, time for formal English learning and that for taking translation courses. In order to emphasize the learning effect of SA, the translation task must be of moderate difficulty and ensure that all participants have not been exposed to it. Therefore, it was decided to select the translation task from the CATTI (China Accreditation Test for Translators and Interpreters) 3 in the early years. The SA rubric used is an overall one (see Appendix) adapted from the existing analytical rubric [7].

3.1 Participants

All participants are recruited on a voluntary basis, and specific background information is shown in Table 1. It is found that gender is not related to the metacognitive ability of translation learners [18], and that there are often more female English majors than males, we have reason to believe that participants are all girls will not affect the results of the study.

Table 1. Background information of participants

Student	Grade	Major	Gender	Age	English scores in NCEE	Formal English learning time (Year)	Time for taking translation courses (Term)
A1	Freshman	BE	Female	20	140	13	1
A2	Sophomore	BTI	Female	20	130	16	4
A3	Senior	BE	Female	21	125	9	2
B1	2nd year	MA	Female	25	119	12	6
C1	2nd year	Linguistics	Female	27	125	17	6

Note: A represents undergraduates, B for master degree and C for doctoral degree. BE = Business English. BTI = Bachelor degree of Translation and Interpreting. MA = Master of Arts.

3.2 Research Questions

The study intended to answer the following research questions:

1) What are the differences on perceptions of translation SA between undergraduates and graduate students?
2) What are the differences on learning effects of translation SA between undergraduates and graduate students?
3) What are the suggestions for future SA practices?

3.3 Data Collection

We use one-on-one semi-structured interviews to collect data. Based on the literature review, we designed the interview outline, including students' overall perceptions on this SA activity, their recognition on their own strengths during the whole translation process, challenges encountered in the translation process and their future learning goals, and specific difficulties in translation SA. All recording materials were transcribed into words verbatim, and then handed over to the participants for verification to confirm the authenticity of the transcribed contents. Based on the qualitative case study method, we carried out in-depth analysis on students' SA performance through thematic analysis.

4 Results and Discussion

In order to unravel the reasons behind the above SA behaviors of all participants, we conducted one-on-one interviews with the them as soon as the SA activities ended. See Table 2 for details on semi-structured interviews.

Table 2. Overview of semi-structured interviews

Student	Conducted	Date	Time (min)
A1	Face to face	June 30, 2021	45
A2	Face to face	June 29, 2021	25
A3	Online	June 26, 2021	31
B1	Face to face	June 29, 2021	40
C1	Face to face	June 29, 2021	28

Based on CBA's validity theory and metacognitive theory, our study judges the learning effects of translation SA from general perceptions on SA, strengths and weaknesses of translation process and scripts, future learning goals, and difficulties in translation SA.

4.1 Perceptions on the Self-assessment Activity

Participants views on translation SA can be divided into general perceptions and perceptions on translation task, rubric and reference translation. Generally, all participants have a positive view on translation SA, and A1 said in connection with his own experience:

"My writing teacher attaches great importance to SA and has practiced SA of our essays in the classroom. The writing SA is based on a table that is comprised of five questions, and our task is to judge our level of completion in each dimension. However, due to the standard of each round of SA remains unchanged, and the teacher will not provide targeted feedback after each round, no matter how many rounds of SA are carried out, the essay quality can only be improved in grammar, vocabulary, syntax, etc. Moreover, I don't want to read my composition after reading it twice, nor do I assess it seriously".

It is easy to find that although SA has entered language teaching, its effects is greatly weakened due to the lack of timely feedback from teachers.

When talking about the translation task, all participants said positively "although the translation task is not difficult, I can still learn a lot from it".

When asked whether the rubric is helpful for SA, participants give opinion about its descriptors, degree of distinction, and the degree of fit with translation teaching. In general, all students expressed a positive attitude towards the role of rubric in SA:

"The rubric can help me evaluate my translation scripts, and it is highly consistent with the knowledge repeatedly highlighted by my translation teacher".

However, A1 puts forward her own views on one of the descriptors:

"As far as this translation task is concerned, the first descriptor in the rubric is not very useful. Because the original text is easy to understand, and the difficulty lies in the expression".

Undergraduates and graduate students have different views on the value of the reference translation. All undergraduates (A1, A2, A3) believe that the reference translation is more valuable than the rubric:

"No matter in terms of promoting learning or assisting SA, the value of the reference translation is greater than that of the translation rubric, because the reference translation can let me clearly know where I am and where I am going".

On this basis, A1 further pointed out:

"The rubric is abstract, and there is basically no way to directly know how to improve my script through the rubric. Even if such standard is not provided, I basically evaluate my script from these dimensions after taking the translation course. But by comparing my script with the reference translation, I can immediately know where need to be improved and how to improve".

Unlike undergraduates, graduate students believe that the rubric and the reference translation are equally important, and B1 said that:

"Translation is different from other language skills as there is no standard answer or even an optimal solution. So the reference translation can only provide one of a variety of options, while the translation rubric is a set of criteria that needs to be internalized".

In the same token, C1 gave a more profound answer in connection with his own theoretical knowledge:

"Each rubric has gone through a series of scientific steps, such as the collection and classification of descriptors and validation. It is a highly condensed scientific achievement. The reference translation can provide more detailed translation knowledge. What I mean is that it is more important for us to use both to achieve better SA instead of simply comparing the two".

4.2 Description of Their Own Strengths

Through data analysis, we found that undergraduates and graduate students clearly diverged on the necessity of clearly describing their strengths. Specifically, three undergraduates thought it was difficult to describe their own advantages. Not only that, A3 also questioned the necessity of describing her own translation advantages:

"The advantage of my own translation is what I do well. Since I can do it well, it is difficult for me to perceive it consciously. Moreover, my teacher only emphasizes where I can improve, so I find this question difficult to answer. I also feel that this has little effect for my learning".

In contrast, two graduate students believe that it is necessary to clarify their own advantages, and C1 further summarizes two reasons accounting for why it is necessary to clearly describing one's own strengths:

"First, in the context of teachers focusing on students' weaknesses, students usually focus on their weaknesses. If one can clearly recognize one's strengths, it will enhance one's learning motivation that has a positive impact on learning. Second, students may do well in the translation task by chance. They may not be able to do it well next time. But by clarifying their own advantages, this understanding can be strengthened".

In addition to disparities in viewpoints, undergraduates and graduate students talked their translation strengths differently, that is, graduate students' narratives are more abstract and general, while undergraduates tend to pay attention to language details. This finding further validate the claim that learning effects of SA can be judged by the level of abstraction of reflection[8]. For example, C1 said when summarizing her strengths:

"I think my advantage lies in proper diction, because I will consciously use words in context and avoid word overuse. Reasons behind my behavior is that context is the essence of word selection, and vocabulary richness is also an important indicator of translation quality".

In comparison, A1 can only reflects that she "translate fast", and A2 believes that her advantage lies in "consciously using a variety of sentence patterns".

4.3 Challenges in Translation and Future Learning Goals

Descriptions of translation difficulties between the two groups are relatively consistent. The main translation difficulties are: inaccurate translation of proper nouns, missed detailed information, insufficient vocabulary, grammatical errors, unconcise sentence structures, and misunderstanding of the original text.

When it comes to the issue of future learning goals, there are obvious differences between undergraduates and graduate students. For instance, A1 thinks that in future translation learning, "she will pay attention to the accumulation and use of different sentence patterns" and "translate more decisively"; A2 will "read more and practice more" and "consolidate grammatical foundation"; A3 says "I will learn more about authentic expressions in foreign journals". In contrast, B1 set a specific goal of "studying synonyms", and C1 said that "she will carry out sentence-division practices and strengthen the study of invisible cohesive structures".

In a nutshell, undergraduates' descriptions of learning objectives are so abstract and vague that they do not need to be derived from translation SA, which reduced the learning effects of translation SA. By contrast, postgraduates' explanations for further learning are closely revolved around this SA activity and are very specific, reflecting that they've gotten constructive suggestions from SA. This phenomenon fully demonstrates that undergraduates are not getting effective feedback from translation SA.

4.4 Difficulties in Self-assessment

The consensus is basically reached on the problems encountered in translation SA between undergraduates and graduate students, but ways of expressing obstacles are quite different between the two groups. For example, A1 and A2 said that "I do not know how to conduct SA when my vocabulary and sentence structures are different from the reference translation". B1 and C1 point out that "I do not know how to make decisions when my version is obviously different from the reference one". In other words, for both undergraduate and graduate students, the difficulty of translation SA lies in the discrepancy between one's own translation and the reference translation, which make decision-making difficult.

5 Conclusion

This research is an in-depth case study on the translation SA of three undergraduates, one MA student, and one doctoral student. The results can be summarized as: 1) Undergraduates' understanding of translation SA is not as deep as that of graduate students, resulting in the fact that learning effects of SA is more obvious at the graduate level; 2) The quality of translation SA can be determined by the combination of the abstraction of the description of its own translation performance, the relevance and operability of future learning goals, which is a useful complement to relevant research [8]; 3) All participants faced difficulties in SA, all of which were due to limited language or translation ability. That reinforces the importance of teacher intervention in such learning-oriented assessment (LOA) practices [19].

The findings of this research provide the following enlightenment for translation teaching: 1) SA ability is positively correlated with translation ability, so translation ability can be improved by improving students' SA ability [20, 21], thus promoting the integration of metacognitive skills and translation teaching to make students better prepared for future career; 2) as SA is the most challenging part of the metacognitive theory, it is easy to accept that effects of student SA is not ideal without systemic and proper training. Thus, it is appropriate to organize and conduct such training under the framework of metacognition. That is, SA training, as a component of cognitive regulation, should be based on the acquisition of cognitive knowledge; 3) teachers should pay attention to the strengths of students while discovering students' deficiencies in translation teaching, which contributes to the cultivation of SA ability and learning motivation.

Acknowledgments. This work is financially supported by the scientific research and innovation project for postgraduates titled "Developing, Validating and Applying a Self-Assessment Tool of Translation Process Under the Framework of China's Standards of English Language Ability (CSE)" (NO. 21GWCXXM-063) of Guangdong University of Foreign Studies.

References

1. Gebril, A., Eid, M.: Test preparation beliefs and practices in a high-stakes context: a teacher's perspective. Lang. Assess. Q. **14**(4), 360–379 (2017)
2. Cheng, H., Ding, Q.: Examining the behavioral features of Chinese teachers and students in the learner-centered instruction. Eur. J. Psychol. Educ. **36**(1), 169–186 (2021)
3. Butler, Y.G., Lee, J.: The effects of self-assessment among young learners of English. Lang. Test. **27**(1), 5–31 (2010)
4. Dann, R.: Promoting Assessment as Learning: Improving the Learning Process. Routledge, London (2012)
5. Li, M., Zhang, X.: A meta-analysis of self-assessment and language performance in language testing and assessment. Lang. Test. **38**(2), 189–218 (2021)
6. Li, X.: Self-assessment as 'assessment as learning' in translator and interpreter education: validity and washback. Interpret. Transl. Train. **12**(1), 48–67 (2018)
7. Robinson, B.J., López Rodríguez, C.I., Tercedor Sánchez, M.I.: Self-assessment in translator training. Perspectives **14**(2), 115–138 (2006)
8. Fernández, F., Zabalbeascoa, P.: Correlating trainees' translating performance with the quality of their metacognitive self-evaluation. Perspectives **20**(4), 463–478 (2012)
9. Campbell, S.: Translation into the Second Language. Routledge, New York (2014)
10. Anabel, G.M.: Learning portfolio in translator training: the tool of choice for competence development and assessment. Interpret. Transl. Train. **10**(2), 161–182 (2016)

11. Mellinger, C.D.: Metacognition and self-assessment in specialized translation education: task awareness and metacognitive bundling. Perspectives **27**(4), 604–621 (2019)
12. Han, C., Fan, Q.: Using self-assessment as a formative assessment tool in an English-Chinese interpreting course: student views and perceptions of its utility. Perspectives **28**(1), 109–125 (2020)
13. Kane, M.T., Wools, S.: Perspectives on the validity of classroom assessments. In: Brookhart, S.M., McMillan, J.H. (eds.) Classroom Assessment and Educational Measurement, pp. 11–26. Routledge, New York (2019)
14. Schraw, G., Crippen, K.J., Hartley, K.: Promoting self-regulation in science education: metacognition as part of a broader perspective on learning. Res. Sci. Educ. **36**(1), 111–139 (2006)
15. Cronbach, L.J.: Five perspectives on validity argument. In: Wainer, H., Braun, H. (eds.) Test validity, pp. 3–17. Erlbaum, Hillsdale (1988)
16. Flavell, J.H.: Metacognition and cognitive monitoring: a new area of cognitive-developmental inquiry. Am. Psychol. **34**(10), 906 (1979)
17. Dochy, F., Segers, M., Sluijsmans, D.: The use of self-, peer- and co-assessment in higher education. A review. Stud. High. Educ. **24**(3), 331–350 (1999)
18. Hashempour, M., Ghonsooly, B., Ghanizadeh, A.: A study of translation students' self-regulation and metacognitive awareness in association with their gender and educational level. Int. J. Comp. Lit. Transl. Stud. **3**(3), 60–69 (2015)
19. Banerjee, H.L.: Approaches to researching learning-oriented assessment in second and foreign language classrooms. In: Learning-Oriented Language Assessment, pp. 49–68. Routledge, New York (2021)
20. Pietrzak, P.: The effects of students' self-regulation on translation quality. Babel **64**(5–6), 819–839 (2018)
21. Hu, Z., Zheng, B., Wang, X.: The impact of a metacognitive self-regulation inventory in translator self-training: a pre-post study with English-Chinese translation students. Interpret. Transl. Train. **15**(4), 1–20 (2020)

Research on Construction of Translation Self-assessment Activity for Self-regulated Learning in Chinese EFL Context

Shili Ge[1] and Xiaojun Pi[2(✉)]

[1] Laboratory of Language and Artificial Intelligence, Guangdong University of Foreign Studies, Guangzhou 510420, China
[2] School of Interpreting and Translation Studies, Guangdong University of Foreign Studies, Guangzhou 510420, China

Abstract. In response to students' lack of self-regulated learning ability and method in translation learning, as well as ignoring the value of translation products, this paper puts forward a translation self-assessment activity based on research on self-assessment, translation self-assessment criteria and social constructionism in Translation Teaching. The translation self-assessment activity is a specific method of student-centered translation self-assessment which aims at improving the initiative of self-regulated learning in translation learning. It consists of five parts: translation evaluation, feedback collection, translation revision, translation comparison, and self-reflection throughout the self-assessment activity. By this self- assessment activity, students can not only be more aware of reflecting on the translation process, but also make full use of their translation products, resulting in higher initiative of self-regulated learning in their translation learning from the metacognitive level.

Keywords: Self-assessment · Translation self-assessment activity · Self-regulated learning

1 Introduction

As the learner-centered educational philosophy has been developed and applied in the field of teaching and learning, student-centered assessment has also attracted the attention of teachers and researchers [20, 37, 50]. One of the most common forms of student-centered assessment in higher education is self-assessment [16, 23, 47], in which students make judgments about their own learning, referring in particular to evaluative judgments about their achievement and outcomes [10]. In EFL teaching, many teachers and researchers have been practicing models and methods of student self-assessment for teaching and learning in their teaching [6, 8, 19, 28, 40]. However, the research on the application of self-assessment in Translation Teaching is still relatively small and has not receive expected focuses, especially in terms of lacking clear, systematic operational processes for translation self-assessment activity (TSAA). Therefore, this paper tries to promote students' translation learning by constructing TSAA with a solid theoretical basis.

W. Jia et al. (Eds.): SETE 2021, LNCS 13089, pp. 390–402, 2021.
https://doi.org/10.1007/978-3-030-92836-0_35

2 Necessity for Constructing TSAA

First of all, *The Teaching Guidelines for Undergraduate Foreign Language and Literature Majors in General Higher Education Institutions* [49] (hereinafter referred to as *the Teaching Guidelines*) released by Foreign Language Teaching and Research Press in April 2020 puts forward clear educational objectives and specifications for translation teaching, requiring students to possess the ability not only to translate but also to learn for lifelong time. In other words, translation majored students should develop their translation competence, as well as cultivating self-regulated learning skills and ability in order to better deal with the requirements of higher-level jobs as independent learners out of campus. As the work environment is different from the campus where students are accustomed to waiting for teachers' evaluation of their performance, students in working will be required to assume the responsibility of self-assessment [27]. Therefore, school education should provide opportunities for students to develop self-regulated learning and lifelong learning skills and habits that will prepare them for the changing market demands and higher intensity jobs.

Secondly, the traditional translation teaching mainly focuses on translation products (all Translation Teaching referred to in this paper is limited to written translation for translation majored undergraduates), in which teachers assign translation tasks; students complete them independently after class and submit them to teachers, who review their homework and then evaluate them in the next class against reference translations or teachers' versions [61]. This kind of translation teaching has indeed played a certain role and been valuable to students learning [30, 38, 51]. However, with the introduction of the concept of "student-centered" education into Translation Teaching, translation teachers have begun to focus on the translation process of students and promote their translation competence by guiding them to pay attention to the translation process [13]. Guided by this philosophy, teachers and researchers have engaged in innovative exploration into translation teaching modes, and translation teaching is realizing a critical shift from teacher-centered classrooms to student-centered classrooms to improve the main role of students in the classroom. Therefore, the teaching mode and method oriented to the translation process have effectively promoted teachers' translation teaching and students' translation learning. However, any rigid teaching modes and methods is not conducive to the both teachers and students. Teachers and students over-emphasize the attention to translation processes, which leads them to neglect the value of translation products or under-utilize the translation products. Both translation products and translation process are important components of translation activities. The attention to translation process helps students produce higher-quality translation products. In other words, focusing on translation processes can help students produce high-quality translation products, and fully utilizing translation products can help students work more effectively in the next translation.

At last, students are at the center of self-assessment that is a formative assessment tool, by which students can be trained to obtain the ability of learning autonomy, self-regulation, and lifelong learning [22]. Participating in self-assessment, students will assume more responsibilities and power, and pay more attention to quality of their translation products; they will engage in self-reflection, develop translation skills and ultimately become qualified professionals [14, 40, 45]. It is self-evident that self-assessment has a great significance in promoting students' translation learning. However, in domestic EFL teaching, research on self-assessment has mainly focus on writing, whose topics include the accuracy and consistency of self-assessment [31–33, 48], the development, validation, and application of self-assessment scales [18, 37, 59, 60], and the relationship between self-assessment and autonomy learning [34]. Research on self-assessment is very scarce in Translation Teaching in China, and there is still a gap in research on how students practice self-assessment in translation learning.

Based on the discussion of the above three reasons, this study theoretically constructs a specific translation self-assessment method in order to help students improve their initiative in self-regulated learning, thus promoting their translation learning.

3 Theoretical Basis for Constructing TSAA

3.1 Social Constructionism in Translation Teaching

Translation teaching under social constructionism requires students to actively participate in a dynamic, cooperative learning process, where students no longer passively are poured with rigid translation knowledge and translation skills, but taking responsibility for their own learning and steps to achieve their goals [26]. This educational approach incorporates two important concepts: reflective action [26] and communities of knowledge builders [26]. Reflective action occurs in all aspects of tasks, including planning, implementation, and revision. With a virtual mental platform, students consciously reflect and revise their learning methods, goals and actions, and then incorporate the results into their existing knowledge system, thus improving the academic performance and professional competence [26]. In the community of knowledge builders both beginners and experts in translation are learners and they co-construct knowledge in the group through constant exchanges and cooperation [26].

3.2 Self-assessment

Learning process is about students exploring their own observations and thoughts, seeking to maximize self-discovery and self-awareness [26]. Students evaluate their own work, i.e., self-assessment, as a way to promote self-discovery and self-awareness and to help students acquire self-monitoring. Empowering students with methods and tools for self-discovery, self-awareness, and self-monitoring is what makes students capable of self-regulating their learning and becoming lifelong learners [56].

Self-assessment involves evaluation on competencies, processes and products [4]. Self-assessment of competencies usually means an individual conduct an overall assessment of his or her competence and self-awareness, which is an isolated reflection; self-assessment of processes can be seen as synonymous with self-regulated learning, of which self-assessment is a central component; self-assessment of products is usually based on explicit, relevant, evaluative criteria and subsequent opportunities for relearning and/or revision [3]. In the pedagogical perspective, self-assessment of competencies is a self-judgmental or self-scoring assessment that was initially used to reduce teachers' work burden [17]; self-assessment of processes and products is a learning strategy that promotes improved student performance and learning abilities [4]. In this paper, self-assessment means that students reflect on the quality of their assignments, determine whether they meet the set goals or standards, and make changes to their assignments based on the evaluation results [5]. Self-assessment activities are not simply self-grading, but are formative processes that consist of a series of sequential activities. In this process, students firstly need clear evaluation criteria to measure their performance or product, and secondly students take active measures to obtain different feedback and reflect on the learning process and product quality based on the feedback information to identify their strengths and weaknesses in order to adjust the learning process and improve the quality of outcomes. After a series of activities, a final judgment is arrived at, and the judgment is continuously calibrated based on continuous feedback, resulting in a more accurate or authentic self-assessment [57].

Self-assessment is a key element of self-regulated learning and a concrete means of developing students' self-regulated learning skills [43]. Besides, developing students' self-regulated learning skills helps to improve the quality of students' translations [46].

3.3 Translation Self-assessment Criteria

Student translation self-assessment includes the evaluation of the translation process as well as the translation product, in which students need clear evaluation criteria to guide the evaluation of the translation product. Translation evaluation criteria can be divided into analytical and holistic scoring criteria [19]. Students are expected to fully reflect on their translation products, learn and understand translation scoring criteria, so the analytical scoring criteria provide students with clear descriptors that help them score their own products more objectively. In terms of the characteristics and rules of translation, the core elements of translation quality evaluation are "faithfulness" and "fluency" [54]. This paper adopts the scoring criteria designed by Fan and Ji [19], including three dimensions which are fidelity, language expression and translation style. Among them, fidelity is mainly reflected in the accuracy of the translator's understanding of the content of the original text and the integrity of the translation in the target language. Language expression includes five aspects: accuracy of wording, richness of vocabulary, accuracy of grammar, richness of syntax and writing. Translation style refers to the consistency of the overall translation with the stylistic features of the original work. And a 4-point Likert scale (1 - very poor; 2 - poor; 3 - good; 4 - excellent) is used for all scoring dimensions [19] (see Appendix).

4 Constructing TSAA

4.1 Operationalized Definition

In this paper, self-assessment activity is operationally defined as a process in which students evaluate their translation products against translation criteria and reference translation, collect feedback for improvement and revise them accordingly, then compare the first and revised translation draft to find the strengthens and weaknesses, during which students go through self-reflection on each part of translation evaluation, feedback collection, translation revision and comparison.

At first, for translation evaluation, well-designed, specific and effective scoring criteria for self-assessment help to make more realistic and objective judgments and avoid the shortcomings caused by subjective feelings and experience [28, 41, 42]. This paper uses the translation criteria designed by Fan and Ji [19], which includes fidelity, language expression and translation style, and a 4-point Likert scale (1-very poor; 2-poor; 3-good; 4-excellent) (see Appendix). The self-assessment criteria are adopted for two reasons: (1) Among the existing criteria used for translation self-assessment in China, the self-assessment criteria designed by Fan and Ji [19] emphasis the quality of translation products in great detail, with students' English language ability as the core. English language proficiency as the foundation and core of translation competence should receive extra attention and is the key to enhancing and strengthening translation competence [24]. The basic courses for translation majors in *the Teaching Guide* [50], which cover comprehensive English, listening, speaking, reading, writing, and translation, requiring high bilingual competence of students. Translation majors are expected to have solid language proficiency and know how to apply it. Whether students do literary translation or applied translation, bilingual competence is still an important factor in determining the quality of translation products. (2) Self-assessment is a student-centered assessment [23]. Translation self-assessment activities empower students to evaluate their own translation products in a standardized way, which helps give full play to students' learning initiative and responsibility for learning. The criteria can both guide students in evaluating their translations and help them reflect on the translation process and translation problems in order to contribute to translation revision.

In addition, reference translations are used as supplementary materials to help students evaluate their translations. Reference translations are usually accurate, informative, and linguistically authentic. Based on the preliminary exploration data, it is known that without the reference translation, students are more likely to be influenced by subjective assumptions, over- or under-assessing the translation. in this way, students may be reduced to lower learning motivation or contributing to students' complacency in learning. Therefore, the co-usage of translation self-assessment criteria and reference translations can enable students to assess their own translations more objectively and increase their motivation to participate in the self-assessment activity.

It should be noted that students' evaluation of their own translation products does not effectively and credibly reflect students' translation competence. But, accompanied by appropriate guidance and students' positive attitudes, self-assessment can serve as a very effective motivational tool that prompts students to improve their awareness of their abilities in translation practice [1].

Second, students collect feedback based on the assessment results. Self-assessment emphasizes student learning autonomy, instead of being subject to external pressure or against their will; at the same time, self-assessment is not an isolated process and requires external participation [9, 11]. Feedback can help students construct and reinforce their understanding of domain knowledge and promote effective learning [2, 7].

Feedback is classified into external and internal feedback [57]. In translation learning, translators need to interact in and receive resources from a community of knowledge builders [25].

In translation practice, students actively add explanations or remove repetitive or useless information from the original text, depending on the function of the text or the requirements of the translation task. Thus, omissions, additions, or other translation phenomena in a translation may be limited by the student's source language proficiency or misunderstanding of the original text, or by the translation strategies and techniques employed by the student [21]. The teacher, as an outsider, cannot judge students' consideration based on the translation product. In addition, some eternal factors (e.g., lack of time and technical resources) may lead to students' misunderstanding of the original text, inaccurate expressions in the translation, incorrect spelling and use of grammar, etc. At this point, students need internal feedback to self-monitor translation mistakes and errors. When reviewing their own translations, on the one hand, students may get caught up in their own thinking and fail to identify the problems; on the other hand, students tend to include their own workload in assessing the quality of their translations, assuming that the translation task they have carefully completed is satisfactory. Translation activities are not a head-in-the-sand exercise [26]. Students need to use external feedback to help reflect on their translation products in order to develop a comprehensive perception of the translation and acquire multiple solutions to their translation problems [26]. Among other things, external feedback provided by peers helps students to maintain an equal communication attitude and learn different translation ideas; however, the quality of peer feedback cannot be guaranteed and difficult problems still remain unsolved [44]. Feedback from teachers, experts, etc. has certain quality assurance, but clear and detailed feedback can lead to students' dependence and lacking deep thinking [53]. Both internal and external feedback require students' cognitive thinking and understanding to utilize the conscious reflection on translation learning process to help unconscious translation practice [25].

Therefore, in this translation self-assessment activity, feedback refers to the information that students obtain throughout the self-assessment activity and is used to help improve the quality of the translation, including both internal and external feedback. External feedback is, on the one hand, translation-related resources obtained by students using various technologies or tools, such as terminology checking and background information of the original text; or reflective reports obtained from previous translation exercises or self-assessment exercises. On the other hand, there are suggestions or opinions from classmates, teachers or people related to translation. Students can likewise use the Internet to exchange thoughts about translation learning with people who can hard to get connected in real life. Internal feedback occurs when students monitor their cognitive, motivational and emotional state during the translation process, as well as self-reviewing the translation product. Internal feedback tends to be more unconscious or intuitive. Moreover, students are easily influenced by internal feedback rather than mentally and physically demanding external feedback [57]. In this paper, internal feedback is simplified to student self-reflection. When collecting feedback on their own, students should pay attention to combining internal and external feedback to critically understand and internalize the feedback into their own knowledge system in order to improve translation quality.

The third step is to revise the translation based on feedback. Self-assessment without adjustment and revision is meaningless for student-centered teaching, learning, and assessment [3]. With the research and development of cognitive models, revision is seen as extremely complex behavior [39]. The translation process and the revision process are different cognitive behaviors. The translator usually acts unconsciously during the translation process [25], but the revision process requires the translator to consciously review his or her translation and replace the content of the original translation based on the feedback [55]. When translators find translation problems, they will consciously adopt translation strategies which they are familiar with to solve the problem and come to the best solution within their limitation. However, it is no doubt that too much conscious translation process means that translators encounter more translation problems, which is not helpful to produce high-quality translations [25]. The revision process is to enable students to internalize the conscious comprehension into their own translation system for better unconscious translation. According to the translation self-assessment criteria in this paper, students can analyze translation problems in three dimensions: fidelity, language expression and translation style, making the necessary revisions.

Finally, students are required to compare the first draft with the revised draft. After the above steps, with the revised draft and the first draft of the translation at hand, students now reflect on the problems in the translation process, the strengths and weaknesses of the translation products in comparison, and then complete a reflection report. Whether the self-assessment activity is conducted after class or in class, students can actively share their reflection reports with their classmates or teachers to obtain more guaranteed and authoritative comments, thus strengthening their learning and reflection. In addition, teachers can use students' reflections to provide feedback to promote teaching, so that teachers will have clearer and more focused plans for subsequent instruction.

Data for language learning studies usually come from students' self-reports, such as retrospective interviews, stimulated recall interviews, questionnaires, written diaries and journals, and think aloud thinking. Despite the drawbacks, these methods are the only viable methods for exploring students' thinking processes [12]. In this paper, students present their views on the translation process and the translation product in the form of a reflective report. The reflective reports are adapted from critical translations, learning journals, problem reports, and reflection journals [13, 29, 52, 58]. In this reflective report, students are expected to reflect on translation problems and solutions, as well as on the strengths and weaknesses of their products by answering the following questions: (1) What do you think are the strengths and weaknesses of your translations? (2) What translation problems did you encounter in the translation process? (3) How did you solve these translation problems? What was the method and basis of the solution?

4.2 Operationalized Processes

The translation self-assessment activity is illustrated as Fig. 1:

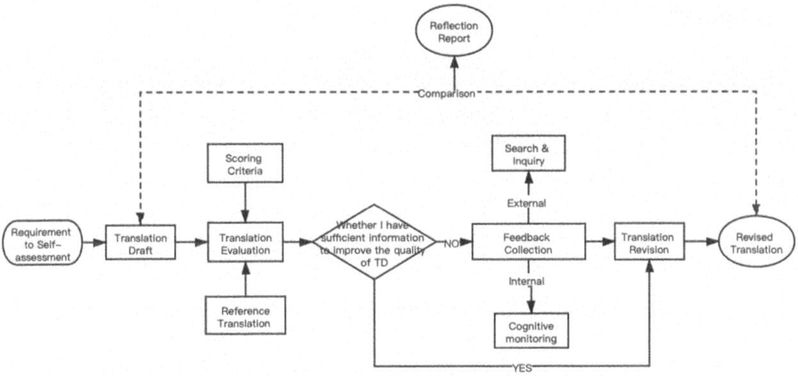

Fig. 1. Translation self-assessment activity

At first, students have the requirement to self-assess when they obtain their translation products after finishing homework assigned by teachers or doing exercise by themselves. With the scoring criteria of translation in this paper and the corresponding reference translation, students then assess the translation work according to the criteria.

Secondly, with the assessment result, students need to make a judgment on whether they have enough information to improve the translation quality. If the first draft is regarded satisfactory by students, they can skip the part of feedback collection and come to revision. If not, students have to take the initiative to collect more feedback information for translation revision. Internal feedback comes from students' reflection on their own cognitive, motivational and emotional states during the translation, and self-reviewing the translation product by identifying possible translation errors or mistakes from a virtual third-party perspective. To gain external feedback, students actively use various technologies and tools to search for relevant information of this translation task, as well as to seek help from peers, teachers or experts. With the help of Internet, students have access to professionals in the translation field through social media platforms, all of which can be used as sources of external feedback to help students' translation learning.

In the third step, students should take a critical eye on the feedback, and then revise the first draft.

Finally, students should discover the strengths and weaknesses of the translation by reflecting on and comparing the first and revised drafts of the translation. Strengths help boost students' self-confidence, and weaknesses help students aware of the problems, thus contributing to their translation skills and competence. The self-assessment report can be served as written evidence for students to strengthen the merits and avoid unnecessary translation errors or mistakes in future translation learning. Besides, it can also be submitted to their teachers in order to get more reliable evaluation and feedback, calibrating the self-assessment results.

5 Conclusion

In response to students' lack of self-regulated learning ability and method in translation learning, this paper put forward a translation self-assessment activity based on research on self-assessment, translation self-assessment criteria and social constructionism in Translation Teaching. By this self-assessment activity, students not only are more aware of reflecting on the translation process, but also make full use of their translation products, resulting in higher initiative of self-regulated learning in their translation learning from the metacognitive level. Students' self-assessing their own work realize the transfer of evaluation right to the students from teachers and empowers them to treat their translation learning with more responsibilities. In addition, the translation self-assessment activity proposed in this paper can not only be used for students' translation practice after class, but can also be used by teachers in the translation classroom, help construct and strengthen student-centered translation teaching in combination with the teacher's scaffolding role [23]. The effectiveness of this self-assessment activity should be further verified through implementation in real translation situations. The steps of the self-assessment activity can be modified and improved as well so that students can implement the translation self-assessment activity more smoothly.

Appendix

(See Table 1)

Table 1. Translation self-assessment criteria.

Scoring dimensions	Description	Scoring (1–4)
Fidelity	Accuracy in understanding the content of the original	
	Completeness of expression of the translation	
Language expression	Accuracy of word choice	
	Richness of vocabulary	
	Accuracy of grammar	
	Richness of sentence	
	Writing	
Style of translation	Consistency of the translation as a whole with the stylistic features of the original	

References

1. Al-Emara, F.S.M.: Is self-assessment a credible indicator of translation competence? Arab World Engl. J. (AWEJ) Spec. Issue Transl. (5), 232–248 (2016). https://doi.org/10.2139/ssrn.2795882
2. Alfayyadh, H.M.: The feedback culture in translator education: a comparative exploration of two distinct university translation programs. Doctoral dissertation, Kent State University (2016)
3. Andrade, H.: Students as the definitive source of formative assessment: academic self-assessment and the self-regulation of learning. In: Andrade, H., Cizek, G. (eds.) Handbook of Formative Assessment, pp. 90–105. Routledge, New York (2010)
4. Andrade, H.: A critical review of research on student self-assessment. Front. Educ. **4**(87), 1–13 (2019). https://doi.org/10.3389/feduc.2019.00087
5. Andrade, H., Du, Y., Mycek, K.: Rubric-referenced self-assessment and middle school students' writing. Assess. Educ.: Principles Policy Pract. **17**(2), 199–214 (2010). https://doi.org/10.1080/09695941003696172
6. Blanche, P., Merino, B.: Self-assessment of foreign-language skills: implications for teachers and researchers. Lang. Learn. **39**(3), 313–340 (1989). https://doi.org/10.1111/j.1467-1770.1989.tb00595.x
7. Black, P., William, D.: Assessment and classroom learning. Assess. Educ. (5), 7–74 (1998)
8. Birjandi, P., Hadidi Tamjid, N.: The role of self-, peer and teacher assessment in promoting Iranian EFL learners' writing performance. Assess. Eval. High. Educ. **37**(5), 513–533 (2012). https://doi.org/10.1080/02602938.2010.549204
9. Boud, D.: Enhancing Learning Through Self-Assessment. Kogan Page, London (1995)
10. Boud, D., Falchikov, N.: Quantitative studies of student self-assessment in higher education: a critical analysis of findings. High. Educ. **18**(5), 529–549 (1989)
11. Bourke, R.: Self-assessment to incite learning in higher education: developing ontological awareness. Assess. Eval. High. Educ. **43**(5), 827–839 (2018). https://doi.org/10.1007/bf00138746
12. Chamot, A.U.: The role of learning strategies in second language acquisition. In: Breen, M. P. (ed.) Learner Contributions to Language Learning, pp. 25–43. Longman, Harlow (2001)
13. Cheng, S., Wu, Q.: Analyzing the dynamics of translation competence development in learning logs from a problem-solving perspective (in Chinese). Chin. Transl. J. **1**, 51–57 (2016)
14. Choi, J.Y.: Metacognitive evaluation method in consecutive interpretation for novice learners. Meta J. Traducteurs **51**(2), 273–283 (2006). https://doi.org/10.7202/013256ar
15. Dai, W.D., Liu, C.Y.: New developments in learning theory and the transmutation of foreign language teaching models (in Chinese). Foreign Lang. **4**, 10–17 (2004)
16. Earl, L.M.: Rethinking classroom assessment with purpose in mind. Government of Manitoba, Manitoba (2006)
17. Falchikov, N., Boud, D.J.: Student self-assessment in higher education: a meta-analysis. Rev. Educ. Res. **59**(4), 395–430 (1989). https://doi.org/10.3102/00346543059004395
18. Fan, J.S.: Exploring the validity of self-assessment scales by Rasch (in Chinese). Contemp. Foreign Lang. Stud. **2**, 34–40+57 (2017)
19. Fan, J.S., Ji, P.Y.: A study of teacher assessment, self-assessment and mutual assessment in translation teaching - a multi-level Rasch model-based approach (in Chinese). Foreign Lang. World **4**, 61–70 (2017)

20. Fanghanel, J., Voela, A.: Using self-assessment to bridge the gap between academic and professional translation. In: Tennent, M. (ed.) Training translators and interpreters in the new millennium, pp. 45–65. University of Portsmouth, Portsmouth (2001)
21. Gile, D.: Integrated problem and decision reporting as a translator training tool. J. Spec. Transl. **2**, 2–20 (2004)
22. Han, C., Fan, Q.: Using self-assessment as a formative assessment tool in an English-Chinese interpreting course: student views and perceptions of its utility. Perspectives **28**(1), 109–125 (2020). https://doi.org/10.1080/0907676x.2019.1615516
23. Huba, M.E., Freed, J.E.: Learner-Centered Assessment on College Campuses: Shifting. The Focus from Teaching to Learning. Allyn & Bacon, Boston (2000)
24. Huang, Y.Y.: See more and less foreign languages and translation after the outbreak (in Chinese). Foreign Lang. China **17**(6), 1+11–12 (2020)
25. Kiraly, D.: Pathways to Translation: Pedagogy and Process Translation Studies. Kent State University Press (1995)
26. Kiraly, D.: A Social Constructivist Approach to Translator Education. St. Jerome, Manchester (2000)
27. Kiraly, D.: Beyond social constructivism: complexity theory and translator education. Transl. Interpret. Stud. **1**(1), 68–86 (2006)
28. Kostons, D., van Gog, T., Paas, F.: Training self-assessment and task-selection skills: a cognitive approach to improving self-regulated learning. Learn. Instr. **22**(2), 121–132 (2012). https://doi.org/10.1016/j.learninstruc.2011.08.004
29. Li, X.S., Ke, P.: The application of process-oriented teaching in translation teaching - an example of peer-to-peer assessment and commentary translation. Foreign Lang. Teach. **34** (5), 106–109 (2013)
30. Lian, S.N.: Exploring the teaching methodology of translation classes - tips on teaching methodology of English to Chinese course (in Chinese). Foreign Lang. Their Teach. **4**, 29–34 (2007)
31. Liu, J.D.: Self-assessment of students' English writing competence (in Chinese). Mod. Foreign Lang. **3**, 241–249 (2002)
32. Liu, J.D.: Test of English language proficiency of Chinese students. Foreign Lang. Their Teach. **4**, 259–265+319 (2006)
33. Liu, X.L., Yang, Z.Q.: A study on the effectiveness of self-assessment in EFL classroom teaching. Foreign Lang. Teach. **3**, 56–59 (2006)
34. Lou: The relationship between self- and peer assessment and the autonomy learning. Foreign Language Teaching (4), 60–63 (2005)
35. Min, S.C., He, L.Z., Luo, L.: Validation of the descriptive language validity of listening ability scale of china standards of English - analysis of a multilevel scoring IRT model based on students' self-evaluation. Foreign Lang. China **15**(2), 72–81 (2018)
36. Mou, J.Z., Shi, Q.M.: Translation practice classes. Should be process-oriented. Shandong Foreign Lang. Teach. J. **5**, 61–62+66 (2002)
37. Martínez, M.N., Albir, A.H.: Assessment in translation studies: research needs. Meta **46**(2), 272–287 (2001). https://doi.org/10.7202/003624ar
38. Oscarson, M.: Approaches to self-assessment in foreign language learning. Council of Europe (1980)
39. Oscarson, A.: Self-Assessment of Writing in Learning English as a Foreign Language: A Study at the Upper Secondary School Level. Geson Hylte Tryck, Göteborg (2009)
40. Robinson, B., Rodrígueza C.L., Sáncheza M.T.: Self-assessment in Translator Training. Perspect.: Stud. Translatol. (14), 115–138 (2006)

41. Panadero, E., Alonso-Tapia, J., Reche, E.: Rubrics vs. self-assessment scripts effect on self-regulation, performance and self-efficacy in pre-service teachers. Stud. Educ. Eval. **39**(3), 125–132 (2013). https://doi.org/10.1016/j.stueduc.2013.04.001
42. Panadero, E., Romero, M.: To rubric or not to rubric? The effects of self-assessment on self-regulation, performance and self-efficacy. Assess. Educ.: Principles Policy Pract. **21**(2), 133–148 (2014). https://doi.org/10.1080/0969594x.2013.877872
43. Panadero, E., Jonsson, A., Botella, J.: Effects of self-assessment on self-regulated learning and self-efficacy: four meta-analyses. Educ. Res. Rev. **22**, 74–98 (2017). https://doi.org/10.1016/j.edurev.2017.08.004
44. Panadero, E., Jonsson, A., Strijbos, J.W.: Scaffolding self-regulated learning through self-assessment and peer assessment: guidelines for classroom implementation. In: Laveault, D., Allal, L. (eds.) Assessment for Learning: Meeting the Challenge of Implementation, vol. 4, pp. 311–326. Springer, Boston (2016). https://doi.org/10.1007/978-3-319-39211-0_18
45. Pietrzak, P.: Students' engagement in metacognitive activities as a source of feedback for the translation teacher. J. Transl. Educ. Transl. Stud. **1**(1), 45–67 (2016)
46. Pietrzak, P.: The effects of students' self-regulation on translation quality. Babel: Int. J. Transl. **64**(5/6), 819–839 (2018). https://doi.org/10.1075/babel.00064.pie
47. Saltourides, E.: Discovering Language Strategies through Self-assessment: students Becoming Independent Learners. In: Arizona Working Papers in SLAT, no. 13, pp. 55–76 (2006)
48. Sun, X., Li, Q.J.: A comparative study of self-, peer-, and teacher-assessment in basic English writing instruction (in Chinese). Foreign Lang. China **12**(1), 75–81 (2015)
49. The Teaching Guidelines for Undergraduate Foreign Language and Literature Majors in General Higher Education Institutions (in Chinese). Foreign Language Teaching and Studies Press (2020)
50. Waddington, C.: Different methods of evaluating student translations: the question of validity. Meta **46**(2), 311–325 (2001). https://doi.org/10.7202/004583ar
51. Wang, S.H.: Western translation teaching research: characteristics, paradigms and implications (in Chinese). Shanghai J. Transl. **3**, 43–49 (2009)
52. Wang, W.: Exploring process-oriented translation teaching (in Chinese). J. Xi'an Foreign Lang. Univ. (4), 102–105 (2019)
53. Wang, L.N., Zhang, F., Wu, Y.Y.: An empirical study on the effectiveness of teaching translation with different feedback methods (in Chinese). Shanghai Transl. (1), 82–87+95 (2020)
54. Wang, J.Q., Wan, X., Dong, Z.Y.: Methods of translation quality assessment and their application in computerized translation evaluation systems (in Chinses). China Transl. **39**(4), 73–78 (2018)
55. Willis, M.S.: Deep revision: a guide for teachers, students, and other writers. Teachers & Writers Collaborative, 5 Union Square West, New York (1993)
56. Witter-Merithew, A., Taylor, M., Johnson, L.: Guided self-assessment and professional development planning: a model applied to interpreters in educational settings. In: Nettles, C. (ed.) Proceedings of the 17th National Conference of the Registry of Interpreters for the Deaf, pp. 153–226. RID Publications, Alexandria (2001)
57. Yan, Z., Brown, G.T.L.: A cyclical self-assessment process: towards a model of how students engage in self-assessment. Assess. Eval. High. Educ. **42**(8), 1247–1262 (2017). https://doi.org/10.1080/02602938.2016.1260091
58. Ye, M.: A study on the interactivity model of translation teaching (in Chinese). Foreign Lang. World (3), 51–56+91(2007)
59. Zhou, Y.Q.: Validation of self-assessment scales validity of china standards of English (in Chinese). Mod. Foreign Lang. 1–12 (2020)

60. Zhu, L.H.: A self-assessment of english reading competence of higher education students based on China standards of English (in Chinese). Foreign Lang. Test. Teach. **4**, 43–50 (2020)
61. Zhu, Y.B., Xu, J.: Process-oreiented: a natural turn in modern translation teaching - a theoretical discussion of process-oriented translation teaching and its pedagogical implications (in Chinese). Foreign Lang. Theory Pract. (1), 84–88 (2010)

Constructing a DELC-Based Blended Learning Model in the Interpreting Course

Jing Ning[1] and Aiping Mo[2(✉)]

[1] School of Foreign Studies, Southern Medical University, Guangzhou 510515, China
[2] Guangdong University of Foreign Studies, Guangzhou 510420, China
moaiping@gdufs.edu.cn

Abstract. In the IT era, Internet social media, online resources, and technological tools have greatly contributed to the improvement of instructional modes. Meanwhile, the issue of whether or how the technology-enabled method such as blended learning can trigger deeper learning capabilities, and how can deep learning incorporate more diversified IT tools need further investigation. This paper, by analyzing the pedagogical foundations of the Deeper Learning Cycle (DELC) and blended learning (BL), attempts to construct the DELC-Based Blended Learning Model. Besides, an illustration of the Traditional Chinese Medicine (TCM) Interpreting class is expounded to explain the practice of this model in training deep learners in interpreting. It is expected this model can help foster students' deeper learning capabilities in interpreting, providing some implication and reference value to the E-learning of interpreting education.

Keywords: DELC · Blended learning · TCM interpreting · Autonomous learning · Collaborative learning

1 Introduction

The way professional interpreting is taught and learned today has been continuously revolutionized. However, problems still exist in the current interpreting teaching: fast pace and dense content in the class; limited access to learning resources; inflexible training method and the single subject and means of evaluation. Conventional interpreting teaching is in urgent need of reform to promote students' deep learning capabilities. Blended learning, as an integral part of educational reform in China, underlines the mixture of face-to-face (F2F) class and virtual class; digital learning resources and traditional printed textbooks; the teachers' guidance and students' autonomy; independent inquiry and collaborative learning. Despite a much-discussed topic in pedagogy, study on BL mainly focuses on its technological aspect, and the learning aspect remains under-investigated. In addition, the interaction between DELC and BL is worthy of further discussion. Specifically, how BL, an IT-enabled learning method can bring about deeper learning, and how the concepts and theories of deeper learning can be incorporated with the BL process. Therefore, this study attempts to construct the DELC-Based Blended Learning Model based on the pedagogical foundations of DELC and BL. An illustration is given on the practice of the model by the

W. Jia et al. (Eds.): SETE 2021, LNCS 13089, pp. 403–414, 2021.
https://doi.org/10.1007/978-3-030-92836-0_36

Medical Interpreting Course. It is expected this model can help enhance the deep learning capabilities of interpreting students and provide some reference for E-Learning interpreting education in the future.

2 Pedagogical Foundations

2.1 Deeper Learning Cycle (DELC)

The Concept of Deep Learning is Derived from Cognitive Psychology and Education Science. According to Bloom's taxonomy of the cognitive domain, the cognitive domain comprises six levels, i.e. Knowledge, Comprehension, Application, Analysis, Synthesis, and Evaluation [1]. They are arranged according to hierarchy and complexity, which means the simple cognitive skills are mastered before the higher-order ones. Simple learners' cognition level is limited to memorization and understanding, while deep learners can accomplish higher-order cognitive objectives, i.e. application, analysis, synthesis, and evaluation. Deep learning, centered on higher-order thinking, highlights learners' autonomous and active learning state; the ability to activate, connect, and deep process knowledge; the effective transfer and application of knowledge in solving problems; and the ability to critically evaluate learning outcomes.

The Deeper Learning Cycle (DELC) is an Effective Pedagogical Strategy to Realize the Concept of Deep Learning. DELC was proposed by Eric Jensen and LeAnn Nickelsen in Deeper Learning: 7 Powerful Strategies for In-Depth and Longer-Lasting Learning [2]. Accordingly, DELC consists of seven steps: planning standards and curriculum; pre-assessing; building a positive learning culture; priming and activating prior knowledge; acquiring new knowledge; processing the learning deeper; and evaluating student learning. In contrast to conventional teaching, DELC underlines designing meaningful content tailored to the students' levels; pre-assessing learners' learning levels and personal characteristics; creating a safe and stimulating learning environment; focusing on the effective activation, connection, deep processing, and application of knowledge; appreciating individualized learning styles and adopting formative, multi-subject, and intelligent evaluation.

2.2 Blended Learning (BL)

BL shares much in common with DELC in pedagogical philosophy yet complements DELC in pedagogical tools. For both DELC and BL, it is believed the teacher plays the guiding role in organizing, inspiring, and monitoring while students play the center role of autonomous, collaborative, and reflective learning [3, 4]. More importantly, both deem contextualization necessary, such as event-based activities, live E-learning, and self-paced learning [5]. BL's supplementary significance to DELC lies in the adoption of IT tools. The key advantages of BL are the combined utilization of web-based courses, virtual simulations, multimodal resources, and teaching technologies such as micro-videos, question banks, and corpora [6–10]. Furthermore, technologies make the integration between online teaching and F2F teaching possible. BL, by integrating the advantages of online learning and F2F activities, diversifies the tools and enriches the content of teaching and learning, thus better fulfilling the teaching objectives [11, 12]. This suggests that DELC and BL are complementary and mutually reinforcing. Through IT technologies advocated by BL, DELC is achieved by multiple means of information activation for self-paced and collaborative learning. BL also requires a shift from emphasizing the form and means of teaching to enhancing the depth of knowledge in learning. Therefore, it is of great value to establish a DELC-Based Blended Learning Model (see Fig. 1).

3 DELC-Based Blended Learning Model

In Fig. 1, the DELC-Based Blended Learning Model can be divided into four stages: preparation stage; knowledge construction stage; knowledge transfer and application stage; and evaluation and reflection stage. The following is a detailed explanation of the elements and working of this model.

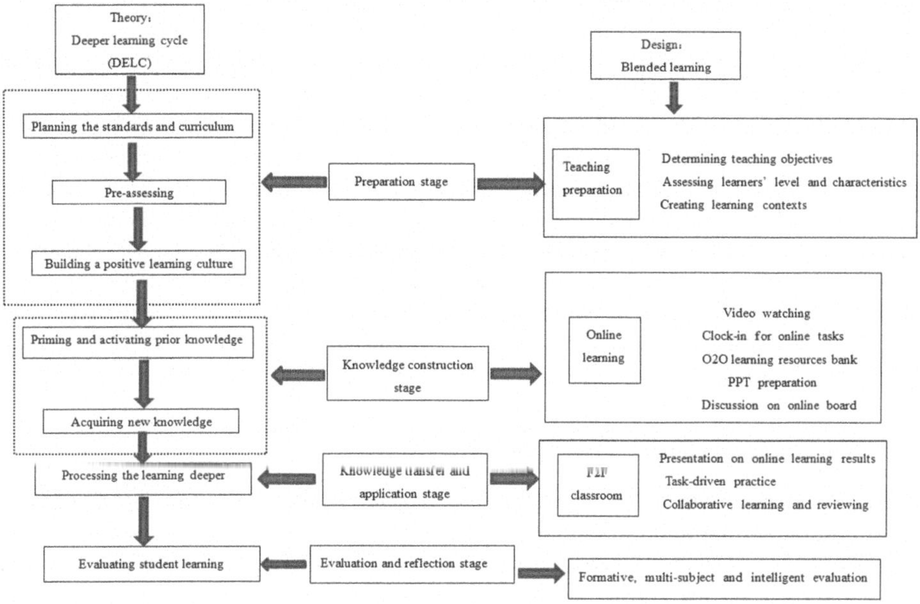

Fig. 1. The DELC-based blended learning model

3.1 Preparation Stage

In the preparation stage, both DELC and BL involve determining the teaching objectives and contents, pre-assessing the learners' level and characteristics, and building a positive learning atmosphere. The rationale behind this is the relevance between different learning elements including knowledge features, students' characteristics, learning objectives, and the learning context. Only by depending on the comprehensive consideration on such relevance can the meaningful teaching objectives and content be designed. Therefore, pre-assessment is the prerequisite to set sensible teaching objectives, which could be an oral, or written test, combined with a questionnaire, either online or F2F, for acquiring the information on students' capability level, learning styles, motivation, and interest, thus making the proper decision on the instructional method, time arrangement, and teaching material. Apart from this, creating a positive learning atmosphere is essential to ensure that students' brains developed in a positive mode is the key to deep learning. This is because in extremely stressful and tense contexts, the brain's short-term and long-term memory is suppressed and neuronal dendrites are fewer and shorter. Only in a positive and open learning environment will the students feel psychologically secured. Their cognitive processing will run smoothly, and they will be able to keep deep learning at its best.

3.2 Knowledge Construction Stage

In the knowledge construction stage, priming and activating prior schema is a bridge to connect students' existing background knowledge to the new knowledge. Studies have shown that the brain cannot process too much information at the same time, or in a single form. The best way for the brain to receive information is in small chunks, fragments, or groups of similar unit information. Accordingly, BL has many advantages in diversifying the learning patterns and learning activities. On the one hand, BL extends the time and space for learning by moving the knowledge construction section online, so that teachers have more time to interact with students for deeper processing. On the other hand, online teaching makes various activities possible, such as autonomous learning including video watching, online practice clock-in, and O2O learning resources searching; and collaborative learning such as PPT preparation and discussion. A variety of learning activities and learning manners will be extremely conducive to the activation and development of efficient and meaningful linkages between prior schema and new knowledge.

3.3 Knowledge Transfer and Application Stage

In the knowledge transfer and application stage, processing the learning deeper constitutes the most important step in the DELC. Deep processing must be purposeful in that learners process raw information into complete, meaningful knowledge through consolidation, transformation, and internalization. Deep processing consists of the domain of awareness; the domain of analysis and synthesis; the domain of application and the domain of assimilation. Despite being interrelated, these four domains have different functions in the development of students' thinking. Teachers need to use appropriate and effective strategies to guide students to apply what they have learned to solve real-world problems in different contexts, based on the characteristics of each domain. To be more specific, the domain of awareness is for guiding students into deeper learning, mainly through a series of activities that stimulate their interest, laying the foundation for learning in other domains. In the F2F classroom, the presentation not only serves as a recollection of the knowledge that was learned online but also a prelude to the knowledge to be deeper processed in the F2F classroom. The Analysis and Synthesis domain focuses on how to help students acquire new knowledge, which can be achieved by training students' ability to integrate knowledge in their cognitive schema through F2F classroom's task-driven practice, case analysis, or group discussion. The application and assimilation domain can be realized through collaborative learning and reviewing therein learners internalize new knowledge reflectively, form their unique cognitive structures, and then transfer it to new situations to solve problems.

3.4 Evaluation and Reflection Stage

In the DELC-Based Blended Learning Model, feedback generally runs through every stage of teaching. Feedback is preferably conducted through a multi-subject evaluation system in which teachers evaluate students' mastery of teaching goals, and students as learners evaluate themselves and their peers. Based on the theories of DELC, if students can see, hear, and experience the results of what they have done, they're more prone to accept fair feedback and adjust themselves. This indicates that teachers should pay attention to the types of activities and the types of feedback that students get. Teachers not only need to give feedback on the learning content of students but also their learning process. Commentary, self-reflection report, examinations and quizzes, the portfolio is an integral part of formative evaluation. Formative evaluation of the DELC-Based Blended Learning Model generally includes online evaluation and classroom evaluation. Through the combination of online and offline feedback, qualitative data such as students' learning attitude, amount of effort, and progress can be visualized and examined comprehensively, so teachers can at once understand the students' current problems, which can not only provide the reference for individual learning guidance but make the adjustment of teaching design for each stage possible. In addition, intelligent evaluation in which deep learning data can be recorded and visualized is gaining more and more attention nowadays.

4 Implementing a DELC-Based Blended Learning Model in the Medical Interpreting Course

The following is an example of Traditional Chinese Medicine (TCM) interpreting class by practicing the DELC-Based Blended Learning Model. An elaboration of the class is displayed in four stages: Pre-Class Stage: Objective Design and Learners' Analysis; Knowledge Construction Stage: Online Activation; Knowledge Transfer and Reflection Stage: In-Class Deep Processing; and Evaluation and Reflection Stage: Formative, Multi-subject, and Intelligent Evaluation.

4.1 The Medical Interpreting Course

Medical Interpreting is a compulsory course for English majors at some medical universities. It aims to improve students' overall medical bidirectional interpreting ability of Chinese and English, to enable students to interpret basic medical phrases and sentences between English and Chinese without preparation; and to enable students to interpret general medical content between English and Chinese after some preparation. The course is designed to promote the integration and application of students' medical knowledge and interpreting skills. The course is 2 periods per week, for a total of 32 periods in a whole semester.

4.2 Pre-class Stage: Objective Design and Learners' Analysis

The course objective of Medical Interpreting is to enable the students to interpret short medical sentences and to perform brief medical consecutive interpreting with preparation, so there should be a balance between interpreting skills and subject-matter knowledge. Besides, it is necessary to prior-assess learners' levels and characteristics. The level assessment reflects students' current interpreting ability and the assessment of characteristics examines the student's motivation and interest in learning interpreting. Medical Interpreting is a course open to English majors with medical direction in the first semester of their junior year. So by the time they take this course, they've already taken the Liaison Interpreting in the second semester of their sophomore year, which means they've already mastered basic interpreting skills and can interpret short conversations without too much subject-matter knowledge. In terms of assessment data collection, at the beginning of the course students are required to fill out a Personal Learning Style Assessment Form distributed on the Rain Classroom platform, which includes 40 questions on their interpreting level, medical knowledge, motivation to learn medical interpreting, expectations for the course, etc., together with medical interpreting test to position their current level. What's more, encouraging students to study in groups is crucial to creating favorable learning contexts. Medical interpreting is a combination of terminology, complex sentences, interpreting skills, and subject-matter knowledge. Given that, it is easy to get depressed if learners study alone. Learning in groups helps to build on each other's strengths and creates a safe, positive, and open learning environment. Besides, the teacher can provide some technical support, such as familiarizing students with the operation of the online teaching platform, such as the functions available in Rain Classroom, the MOOC course schedule, the use of WeChat learning groups, and so on.

4.3 Knowledge Construction Stage: Online Activation

The course interface mainly includes courseware, discussion board, learning progress, interpreting learning websites, WeChat subscription accounts, course calendar, and two reference textbooks.

The online task starts with video watching. The video of each unit is about 45 min long, divided into 3 parts, each part is 15 min. Video creation software is both easily available and convenient to operate, including Camtasia Studio, Focusky, BBflashback, etc. Furthermore, functions including sound effects, subtitles, and images could be utilized if needed. What's worth noting is that a single video is preferably no more than 20 min, since students' concentration may gradually decrease after 20 min. Teachers should also remind students of taking notes or doing the corresponding tasks as instructed by the video, instead of merely watching for nothing.

After self-studying the videos, students clock in for the practice of interpreting skills which will be lectured in the F2F classroom. For instance, sight interpreting, a comprehensive method of testing interpreting skills, reaction, and TCM knowledge, can serve as a desirable online clock-in task. Choice of sentences can either be made by adjusting the difficulty of some sentences on printed textbooks to be more colloquial in style or designed by referring to other O2O resources.

Students can build an O2O learning resources bank through information searching by themselves or the resources uploaded by the teachers. Given that there are no medical interpreting textbooks for undergraduate English majors on the market, teachers should actively explore online teaching platforms such as MOOC and other online resources generated by websites such as Putclub English, TED talk, and WeChat subscription accounts, all of which can be uploaded to the Rain Classroom platform for students' self-study. The rich online resources can improve learning efficiency, enhance learning interest, and maximize the learning experience.

Building a small parallel English-Chinese corpus of TCM by teams is an ideal way to acquire subject-matter knowledge and linguistic knowledge. For example, The *White Paper on Chinese Medicine in China (Chinese-English version)* is an official report with a total of about 15,000 words in Chinese and English, including five sections on the history of TCM; policy measures for TCM in China; the heritage, and development of TCM; international exchanges and cooperation in TCM; Concluding remarks. TCM interpreting involves a large number of Chinese medical concepts, terms, and fixed sentence structures, so students can build their corpus of the document to familiarize themselves with the terminology and sentence structures; and understand the principles, history, status quo, and future of TCM.

Collaborative learning online could also be carried out through PPT preparation in a problem-driven manner. The activation of new knowledge is closely related to the mastery of prior knowledge, and questions are effective to connect new knowledge with prior knowledge In TCM Interpreting. For example, teachers can ask the following questions: ① What is the philosophical basis of TCM? ② What are the characteristics of TCM? ③ What are the differences between TCM and western medicine? ④ Could you briefly describe China's current principles and measures envisioned to develop TCM? ⑤ What do you think about the prospect of TCM? For the answers to these questions, students can work in groups and later present them in the F2F classroom if necessary. Through thinking, learning, summarizing, and reporting, students' ability to construct knowledge, autonomous learning, and teamwork can be effectively trained.

Finally, the online discussion board is a platform for students to summarize their difficulties and doubts during self-inquiry. On the online discussion board, some questions could be either figured out by classmates, or answered by the teacher, or simply brought to the classroom. Deep learning, as reflected in the online learning preparatory activation stage, is the overall improvement of students' capability through autonomous learning, technology use, and online discussion.

4.4 Knowledge Transfer and Reflection Stage: In-Class Deep Processing

The F2F classroom is the main venue for the deep processing of knowledge. At the beginning of the class, students give a 10-min presentation on their self-study online by groups (not necessarily by every group because of the time constraints). Accordingly, the teacher sorts out the key or difficult points for teaching. Afterward, the interpreting practice unfolds in the forms of task-driven, problem-driven, and collaborative learning. The practice material starts with single sentence interpreting or sight interpreting, followed by dialogue interpreting (see Fig. 2).

单句口译/视译	对话口译（1）——中医原理	对话口译（2）——拔火罐
① 针灸可能有点痛，而且也会使你感到有点麻木和发胀。 ② 你的病应该采用中西医结合治疗方法。 ③中医有五千年的历史。它对疾病的发生、发展和治疗都有着完整的理论体系。 ④第一，重视整体。中医认为人与自然、人与社会是一个相互联系、不可分割的统一体，人体内部也是一个有机的整体。重视自然环境和社会环境对健康与疾病的影响，认为精神与形体密不可分，强调生理和心理的协同关系，重视生理与心理在健康与疾病中的相互影响。 ⑤ 第二，注重"平"与"和"。中医强调和谐对健康具有重要作用，认为人的健康在于各脏腑功能和谐协调，情志表达适度中和，并能顺应不同环境的变化，其根本在于阴阳的动态平衡。 ⑥ 第三，强调个体化。中医诊疗强调因人、因时、因地制宜，体现为"辨证论治"。"辨证"，就是将四诊（望、闻、问、切）所采集的症状、体征等个体信息，通过分析、综合，判断为某种证候。 ⑦ 第四，突出"治未病"。中医强调生活方式和健康有着密切关系，主张以养生为要务，认为可通过劳逸适度、膳食合理、起居有常等，也可根据不同体质或状态给予适当干预，以养神健体，提高抗邪能力，从而达到保健和防病作用。	D：你好，史密斯先生。今天感觉如何？ P: Much better, thank you! I can sit straight today. The acupuncture is really great. D：不错。中医有五千年的历史。它对疾病的发生、发展和治疗都有着完整的理论体系。针灸只不过是治疗像你的椎骨侧突疾病的一种最有效方式。 P: All the same, many of my colleagues feel much puzzled about TCM. Would you please tell me more about it? D：没问题。根据中医理论，疾病的发生是阴阳失调所致。而疾病的治疗就是阴阳的平衡。 P: Oh, what's Yin and Yang? D：它们是中国古代哲学的两个概念并代表一切事物的两个对立面。中医学运用阴阳理论来解释人体的生理和病理现象。同时，阴阳也是诊断和治疗疾病的法则。 P: Then how do you Chinese doctors treat your patients by using this theory? D：大体说来，中医有两种治疗方式：药物治疗和非药物治疗。	D：非药物治疗包括针灸、按摩、拔火罐等。 P: I know a little about acupuncture and massage. What's cupping? D：拔火罐就是把一个真空的杯子放在皮肤上引起局部充血的一种治疗方法。通常，医生把一个点燃的酒精棉球放在杯子里一会儿以排出里面的空气使它成为一个真空杯，接着快速地把空杯子放在选定的皮肤上。 P: Is it effective? D：就像我们治疗你的病用的针灸一样有效。但是拔火罐特别适合痛症。 P: That's really fantastic. D：实话告诉你，据资料统计，与西医相比，中医更擅长于病毒感染性疾病、免疫系统疾病、心脑血管疾病和神经系统疾病的治疗，而且无任何副作用。 P: Thank you very much, Doctor! I've got a better understanding of TCM now.

Fig. 2. Medical interpreting practice material in the F2F classroom

According to Ausubel's Meaningful Reception Learning Theory, knowledge transfer and reception, independent learning and collaborative inquiry should be properly combined. For example, in medical interpreting, students can work in groups of four, playing the roles of doctor, patient, interpreter for the Chinese side, and interpreter for the English side, and performance is noted down and reviewed by other groups. Later, the teacher guides students to identify problems, facilitates deep thinking about interpreting strategies and knowledge through interactive activities. In this way, by constructing contexts in interpreting training, a networked knowledge structure is established, not only conducive to the in-depth processing, transfer, and application of knowledge, but also deepens students' sense of experience and participation, and mobilizes their enthusiasm, interest, and motivation for learning. This will be specifically discussed below through an interaction between the teacher and students.

***Example:* 风寒外感, 给你开两贴麻黄汤吧.**
Literal interpretation: You've got wind-cold sensation, and I'll prescribe two packs of Mahuang soup.
Proper interpretation: You've caught a cold, and I'll prescribe two packs of Mahuang Decoction.
Lucy's interpretation: You've caught a cold, and I'll prescribe two packs of Mahuang soup.

Teacher's Review: The difficulty of the sentence is "风寒感冒" and "麻黄汤". Lucy interpreted them into 'catch a cold' and 'Mahuang soup', what do you think?

Intergroup's Review: The transliteration of 'Mahuang soup' does not achieve the communicative effect, so maybe further explanation is needed. All the others are very good.

Teacher's Comment: The interpretation 'catch a cold' reflects his full understanding of the meaning behind the lines which is pretty good. In addition, there is an implied logical relationship between 'Ephedra Soup' and 'catch a cold' in the text, so it is acceptable to apply transliteration in interpreting "麻黄汤", and both 'ephedra' and 'Mahuang' are fine. But, is 'soup' accurate?

Lucy's Self-review: I know that this refers to a kind of TCM drug, not the soup we usually drink, but I don't know the exact interpretation.

Collaborative Learning: Now let's look up the English explanation of soup.

Experiential Learning: It is 'liquid food especially of meat or fish or vegetable stock often containing pieces of solid food', which is not appropriate here.

Teacher's Summary: So, never take it for granted when we interpret, since there is always a more accurate interpretation. Here a more precise one would be 'Mahuang Decoction' or 'Ephedra Decoction'.

Scaffolding (Raising Questions of the Same Kind as the Contextual Question): Think about what interpreting strategy you would use if you had to translate the names of acupoints.

Situation Constructing: For example, if a patient went to the doctor with pain in the shoulder and neck and the doctor said that he could press the Fengchi acupoint to relieve the pain.

Independent Inquiry + Collaborative Learning: Pressing Fengchi acupoint can relieve the pain in your shoulder and neck?

Problem Extension: Is just the transliteration enough? Can the patient know where the acupoint is located? Is the communicative achieved to help the patient with his discomfort?

Collaborative Learning: Oh, yes! It is probably best to adopt the strategy of transliteration plus action, where the interpreter illustrates the action of pressing the Fengchi acupoint to make the interpretation clearer thus communicative effect is achieved.

In this case, the teacher acts as an expounder, observer, and guide throughout, rather than the dominant holder in a traditional classroom. This helps to reduce students' psychological stress, increase their interest and participation in the classroom, and allow them to feel that they are the main body of knowledge construction. The teacher takes notes, makes comments after the dialogue interpretation is completed, and guides students to self-review and peer-review. After dispelling doubts, the teacher drew up similar questions to trigger further deeper thinking. In the above-mentioned example, the teacher guides students to understand key points, develop reflective thinking, draw universal rules and solve practical problems by heuristic and scaffolding approaches, which is quite the essence of DELC. Classroom interaction for DELC does not stop at superficial answers to 'what', but focuses on the higher-order questions such as 'why' and 'how', and the general method of solving the problem should be summarized by solving the sub-problems. Students also enhance their deep learning such as metacognition, critical reflection, transfer and application of knowledge, evaluation, and feedback through multi-parties. After the class, a reflective report is written. Homework contains interpreting practice related to the lesson objectives, and recording for students' homework assignments is needed, combined with an analysis of their classroom performance, forms a reflective report to be uploaded to the platform as part of their usual performance.

4.5 Evaluation and Reflection Stage: Formative, Multi-subject, and Intelligent Evaluation

From the perspective of process, teachers should adopt the formative evaluation that covers the whole process of learning, on account of the individualization and diversification of knowledge acquisition. Interpreting is a bilingual transcoding activity that requires high bilingual ability, encyclopedia knowledge, interpreting skills, psychological quality, and cognitive resources. If students' final score is determined solely by a single test, they are prone to negative emotions such as anxiety and depression, frustrating their motivation and interest in interpreting learning. Therefore, quantitative data generated from interpreting products is needed, but DELC-based evaluation calls for more qualitative data, which are all important indicators for formative evaluation. In terms of evaluators, it is rational to combine teacher evaluation, self-evaluation, and peer evaluation. This not only enables students to analyze their problems from multiple perspectives, but also promotes reflective learning and critical thinking while evaluating others. As for the tools for evaluation, intelligent evaluation tools for interpreting are gaining more and more attention. A technology-enabled and data-based evaluation approach can help better decipher the qualitative data through visualization, such as online learning video viewing, material reading frequency, interpreting task clock-in, reflective report, etc. With the help of computational models and visualized outcomes, the results of learning can become detectable.

5 Conclusion

This paper attempts to construct the DELC-Based Blended Learning Model based on the pedagogical foundations of the Deeper Learning Cycle (DELC) and blended learning (BL). As an illustration of the model, the Medical Interpreting course is explained during pre-class, in-class, and post-class teaching links. It is found that the DELC-Based Blended Learning Model provides a scientific basis for the implementation of the interpreting course based on the theoretical basis of cognitive psychology, brain science, and education science. Under the guidance of this model, students can effectively carry out an independent inquiry, collaborative learning, and critical reflection to achieve the purpose of deep learning. It is also hoped that this model can be of reference value to interpreting E-learning education, and application value to other language learning courses.

Acknowledgments. The work was supported by the Fund of Key Research Projects of Humanities and Social Sciences in Colleges and Universities of Guangdong Province (grant number 2018WZDXM010); Guangdong Young Innovative Talent Project for Universities (grant number 2020WQNCX008); and Guangdong Higher Education Teaching Research Project by Southern Medical University (grant number JG2020032).

References

1. Anderson, L.W., et al. (eds.): A Taxonomy for Learning, Teaching, and Assessing: A Revision of Bloom's Taxonomy of Educational Objectives. Pearson Education Group, Boston (2001)
2. Glasscock, S.: Deeper Learning - 7 Powerful Strategies for In-Depth and Longer-Lasting Learning. Education Libraries (2008)
3. He, K.K.: New development of educational technology theory on blending learning. Educational Technology Research (2004)
4. Lin, X.Y., Pan, J.S.: Design and implementation of a hybrid teaching model based on flipped classrooms. China Vocat. Tech. Educ. (002), 15–20 (2016)
5. Graham, C.R.: Blended learning systems: definition, current trends, and future directions. In: Bonk, C.J., Graham, C.R. (eds.) Handbook of Blended Learning, pp. 3–21. Pfeiffer, San Francisco (2006)
6. Osguthotpe, R.T., Graham, C.R.: Blending learning environments: definitions and directions. Q. Rev. Dist. Learn. **4**(3), 227–233 (2003)
7. Finn, A., Bucceri, M.: A case study approach to blended learning. Centra Software, Los Angeles (2004)
8. Mortera-Gutierrez, F.: Faculty best practices using blended learning and face-to-face instruction. Int. J. E-Learn. **5**, 313–337 (2006)
9. Sharma, P., Barrett, B.: Blended Learning. Macmillan, Oxford (2007)
10. Tomlinson, B., Whittaker, C.: Blended learning in English language teaching: course design and implementation. British Council, London (2013)
11. Garrison, D.R., Kanuka, H.: Blended learning: uncovering its transformative potential in higher education. Internet High. Educ. **7**, 95–105 (2004)
12. Garrison, D.R., Vaughan, N.D.: Blended Learning in Higher Education: Framework, Principles, and Guidelines. Josey-Bass, San Francisco (2007)

13. Zhao, C.Y., Feng, Q.H.: Translation ability in the 'undergraduate teaching guide for translation majors': connotation, elements and cultivation suggestions. Foreign Lang. World **3**, 12–19 (2020)
14. Wang, H.S., Li, Z.: Status quo, problems and prospects of interpretation technology research (1988–2019)-a quantitative analysis based on literature. Shanghai J. Transl. **3**, 50–55+95–96 (2020)
15. Fantinuoli, C.: Computer-assisted preparation in conference interpreting. Transl. Interpret.: Int. J. Transl. Interpret. Res. **2**, 24–37 (2017)

Integrating Blended Learning in Computer-Assisted Translation Course in Light of the New Liberal Arts Initiative

Wenchao Su(✉)

School of Interpreting and Translation Studies, Guangdong University of Foreign Studies, Guangzhou 510420, China

Abstract. The Construction of New Liberal Arts in China advocates innovative approaches to translation and interpreting training, e.g., the integration of information technology such as online learning into translation and interpreting education. Using the theoretical framework of constructive alignment, this paper aimed to identify key intended learning outcomes (ILOs) of a computer-assisted translation (CAT) course via a survey on students' expectations and on this basis design a series of teaching and learning activities in a blended learning mode. The online activities in the blended learning mode include mini-lectures and screenshot videos concerning the key concepts and operations of translation technology, as well as discussions about the love letters and hate letters to the CAT tools. These online activities aimed at preparing students to have basic understandings of the concepts and operations of the CAT tools as well as their attitudes towards the tools before face-to-face classes.

Keywords: Blended learning · Computer-assisted translation · New liberal arts

1 Introduction

As technology is integrated into different aspects of translation and interpreting processes, real-world translation and interpreting tasks have become mostly assisted by computing technology. Therefore, translation training programs have attached great importance to computer-assisted translation and interpreting courses. Scholars have discussed different approaches to the design of computer-assisted translation courses, such as project-based teaching, the maximalist and minimalist approaches, and authentic experiential learning (e.g., Mitchell-Schuitevoerder 2020; Austermuehl 2013; Massey 2019). The concept of New Liberal Arts in the context of Chinese education calls for more "international, interdisciplinary, cutting-edge and theoretical" translation training programs (Wang 2021: 75). To be more specific, trainers should effectively integrate information technology into translation training programs and design courses that are aligned with the pre-stated learning outcomes. The theory of Constructive Alignment stresses the importance of learning outcomes and linking course design and assessment with the learning outcomes (Biggs and Tang 2011). In other words, implementing constructive alignment in translation technology training is to "plan learning activities with a view to producing significant learning outcomes" (Rico 2017:

W. Jia et al. (Eds.): SETE 2021, LNCS 13089, pp. 415–424, 2021.
https://doi.org/10.1007/978-3-030-92836-0_37

83). This indicates that Constructive Alignment is a useful framework for designing computer-assisted translation courses from the perspective of New Liberal Arts Initiative.

In this study, we focus on how to make full use of blended learning to design teaching and learning activities for a computer-assisted translation course that can effectively achieve the learning outcomes of the course.

2 Why Blended Learning in Computer-Assisted Translation Course

One of the major problems facing translation technology training is the lack of learning effectiveness due to the insufficient use of online resources. For instance, in the Chinese context, five specific problems in translation technology training were identified: the dominance of teacher-centered lecturing, inadequate hands-on experience with translation tools, lack of qualified instructors, few opportunities for real-world translation practices using technological tools and little formative assessment (see Wang and Li 2021). Many translation technology courses are teacher-centered. Instructors spent lots of time explaining the functions and operations of different tools and students barely had chances in class to practice with the tools in actual translation tasks. After the course, students might simply remember the operational steps of each tool instead of knowing how to use it to help with their translation work. Given that not many university teachers are qualified to teach translation technology, universities have to invite experts in language service providers to help with the teaching. The cost is usually higher to invite such experts to the actual classrooms than to guide students' learning online. Students had few chances to participate in real-world translation projects or translation contests using technological tools. Lastly, the assessment of translation technology training did not pay enough attention to students' interactive processes with the course.

Overall, we believed the inclusion of online teaching in face-to-face teaching might be one of the effective solutions to address these problems in translation technology training. The two major rationales of adopting blended learning in translation technology courses were that more in-class time could be reserved for students to develop in-depth understanding of concepts and theories and practice with the tools if the knowledge and concepts concerning translation technology and computer-assisted translation were studied online, and the teaching of computer-assisted translation naturally involved the use of a large number of online resources (see Xu 2010). Therefore, we decided to make full use of blended learning to make translation technology training more productive. In this article, blended learning is understood as the inclusion of online resources in face-to-face learning, and the online resources can be used either in or outside the classroom (Seljan et al. 2006). In order to enhance the effectiveness of translation technology training, we aimed to incorporate blended learning in a computer-assisted translation course for Year 2 undergraduate students of translation and interpreting major in accordance to Constructive Alignment. To determine the intended learning outcomes of the CAT course, the researcher conducted a survey which I will briefly detail in the following sections. This study refers to the following two questions as the guide:

(1) What are students' needs and expectations of the CAT course?
(2) How might the intended learning outcomes of the CAT course be specified to ensure students achieve the learning outcomes?

3 The Present Study

According to Constructive Alignment, the first step for trainers to design the CAT course was to write the intended learning outcomes (ILOs). ILOs could be written based on trainers' personal experience or students' perceived needs and expectations. We decided to prioritize students' needs and expectations by conducting a survey to identify what they expected to learn by attending the computer-assisted translation course. The ILOs of the CAT course would then be formulated based on students' expectations and the instructor's understanding of the course. After identifying the ILOs, we shall also illustrate how blended learning could be used in the CAT course to achieve the ILOs.

3.1 The CAT Course

'Computer-assisted Translation' was a core optional course offered for the second-year undergraduate students of translation and interpreting majors. The CAT course lasted for one semester and the students were required to complete in-class training of 80 min each week. The students also needed to complete the tasks and practices assigned by the instructor outside the classroom. Usual enrollments were around 30 students. The course aims were to familiarize students with the key concepts concerning computer-assisted translation and equip students with skills of applying mainstream CAT tools to translation work. Machine translation post-editing and translation quality assurance, which in some universities and institutions were listed as part of the teaching content of a CAT course, were designed as separate courses in the degree program of the researchers' university.

Considering the lack of effectiveness of translation technology training as mentioned in Sect. 2, the author decided to integrate online learning into the CAT course. The students who were about to choose the CAT course showed great interest in translation technology and they were keen to learn CAT tools to help with their translation work. The author, who would teach the CAT course, decided to prepare the teaching and learning activities in consultation with the students. Specifically, blended learning would be incorporated into the CAT course based on the theoretical framework of Constructive Alignment. The intended learning outcomes of the CAT course were written with students' needs, expectations and preferences taken into account.

3.2 Participants

The participants were 30 undergraduate students who just completed their studies in Year 1. They were translation and interpreting majors who were about to choose the course of computer-assisted translation in the first semester of Year 2. They had finished courses that aimed at improving competence of critical reading, listening and writing and basic computer skills during Year 1. None of them had received formal training on translation and interpreting technology before the survey.

3.3 Research Instrument and Data Analysis

To gather information on what students expected to learn in the CAT course, we conducted a questionnaire survey with 6 questions in total. Using a five-point Likert scale, Question 1 asked the students to rate how much they knew about translation technology (5 = very much, 3 = neutral, 1 = very little). Question 2 to 6 were open-ended questions. Question 2 asked what aspects of translation technology the students were familiar with; Question 3 and 4 asked the students how they understood the concept of computer-assisted translation and the relationship between computer-assisted translation and machine translation. Question 5 and 6 were the most relevant questions for the present study, which surveyed the students' expectation of their learning outcomes after completing the CAT course and the way they would like the instructor to teach computer-assisted translation. Students were encouraged to write down their expected learning outcomes from the CAT course that they deemed workable and important.

The answers to Question 5 would serve as the most important references for writing the intended learning outcomes of the CAT course (the first research question). The answers to Question 6 would be referred to when we designed the CAT course with blended learning (the second research question). The answers to the rest survey questions would be taken into account in writing the learning outcomes of the CAT course. 30 students were invited to complete the questionnaire survey two months before they started to take part in the CAT course. 30 students completed and returned, with a return rate of 100%.

Following Li (2002), the researcher examined all the answers to the open-ended questions repeatedly and carefully and identified recurrent themes on the students' expectations of their learning outcomes from the CAT course. After that, the researcher summarized the total mentions of each theme and categorized the themes into six intended learning outcomes of the CAT course.

4 ILOs Based on Students' Expectations for the CAT Course

Overall, the students reported that they were unfamiliar with translation technology (mean = 2.3, SD = 0.92). 16 out of the 30 students (53.3%) felt they barely knew anything about technologies concerning translation and interpreting practices, 12 students chose neutral and only 2 students believed they somehow understood translation technology. The results from Question 5 on students' perceptions on what they expected to learn from the CAT course are reported as per the six intended learning outcomes of the CAT course.

The majority of the students (22 out of 30 students, 73.3%) hoped that they were able to apply one or two major CAT tools to their translation work after completion of the course. One typical comment was:

- After learning this course, I want to be skillful at using CAT tools to help with my translation. (Q5: Daniel)

14 out of 30 students (46.7%) expressed their need for understanding the important concepts concerning translation technology:

- I heard of many concepts about translation technology, such as CAT tools, translation memory, term bases, and machine translation. I want to figure out what they mean and how they relate to each other. (Q5: Jane).

This need was further evidenced by students' confusion about computer-assisted translation and machine translation as shown in their responses for Question 3 and 4. Apart from learning to apply CAT tools to translation tasks, half of the respondents (15 out of 30, 50%) stressed the importance of making use of CAT tools to improve their translation speed and quality. Several students mentioned that they wanted to have a rational understanding of translation technology and know clearly what things CAT tools were able to help translators to do and what aspects CAT tools were not able to help translators to do at the moment. 2 students wrote that they wanted to learn how to efficiently post-edit machine translated texts.

After a careful examination of students' comments on their expected learning outcomes of the CAT course, the researcher decided to focus on six intended learning outcomes of the course, bearing in mind that the ILOs should be manageable and fit for students' cognitive level and the aims of the CAT course (Biggs and Tang 2011). Since the course aims did not include machine translation post-editing as stated in Sect. 3.1, the topic of post-editing was excluded in the CAT course. As a result, the six ILOs of the course Computer-assisted Translation were summarized as follows:

After completing the course Computer-assisted Translation, students should be able to

- ILO1: Explain, compare and contrast the key concepts of translation technology
- ILO2: Apply two mainstream CAT tools (e.g., YiCAT and SDL Trados Studio) to translation tasks
- ILO3: Analyze what CAT tools can do and what CAT tools cannot do for translators
- ILO4: Critique the functions of the CAT tools and suggest how they can be improved
- ILO5: Reflect on how CAL tools can help translators improve efficiency and translation quality
- ILO6: Reflect on what role translators play in computer-assisted translation tasks

After describing the intended learning outcomes of the CAT course, the researcher designed the associated teaching and learning activities in the form of blended learning in order to improve the effectiveness of translation technology training.

5 Linking the ILOs with Blended Learning in the CAT Course

Teaching computer-assisted translation in a blended mode was considered to be one of the effective teaching methods to improve learning effectiveness in translation technology training. When designing teaching and learning activities in a CAT course in a blended mode, it is important to consider to what extent a teaching and learning activity is feasible and in what way such an activity can help students to learn computer-assisted translation. Therefore, trainers need to firstly design what students are expected to learn from a CAT course. This is how the theoretical framework of Constructive Alignment was understood and implemented in the present study.

To successfully implement blended learning in the CAT course, two major teaching instruments were prepared for the students, namely, the teaching and learning management platform called *Duifene* and the computer-assisted translation lab for in-class training.

- *Duifene* is a free, cloud-based teaching and learning management platform which students and teachers can access online from their computers or mobile phones. It has several functions that are particularly useful for teaching and learning computer-assisted translation in a blended mode. Teachers can upload online learning resources in different formats such as text files, PowerPoint slides, audios, videos, and websites. Students can study these resources online in preparation for the upcoming face-to-face teaching. Teachers can check who read the resources and when they read them, which is convenient for teachers to monitor students' learning process. Students are also encouraged to raise their own questions or answer peers' questions in the online discussion forum, which indicates how much students contribute to the course topics, the degree of interaction among students, and individual learner's engagement in the course. Students' questions and doubts posted in the online forum become the important issues to be addressed during in-class training. Teachers can design exercises on the platform and receive instant feedback on students' performance. Competitive Q&A games and bullet screens can also be used by teachers to enhance interaction and communication during face-to-face training.
- The computer-assisted translation lab is designed for students who participate in the CAT course. The computers are distributed in nine circles with six computers in each circle. Students are seated in circles to facilitate group discussion and collaboration. Each computer is installed with SDL Trados Studio and other relevant translation tools. Instructors use the multimedia teaching system to broadcast course contents, monitor students' learning progress and give instant feedback on students' performance.

To summarize, *Duifene* is mainly used for the online part in the blended learning mode of the CAT course, whereas the computer-assisted translation lab is for the face-to-face teaching. With the teaching instruments at hand, the researcher designed the teaching and learning activities of the CAT course in order to optimize the six intended learning outcomes as listed in Sect. 4.

5.1 Addressing the Basics: Pre-class Online Mini-lectures and In-Class Interactive Lectures

As discussed in Sect. 4, the first intended learning outcome of the CAT course is to explain, compare and contrast the key concepts of translation technology, such as translation technology, computer-assisted translation (CAT), computer-assisted interpreting (CAI), CAT tools, CAI tools, machine translation, translation memory, termbases, terminology management and machine translation post-editing. The related teaching and learning activities should center on effective ways of addressing such declarative knowledge. Pre-class online mini-lectures and in-class interactive lectures could be two of the optimal activities to achieve ILO1.

The materials for pre-class online learning consist of mini-lecture videos and PowerPoint presentations with voice recordings about the key concepts of translation technology (see Lee 2018). In order to ensure more efficient pre-class online study so that students can be more or less well-prepared for higher levels of learning activities such as relating, comparing and contrasting in class, the online input in preparation for the in-class training should be contextualized (Wang et al. 2021). Contextualized online input in blended learning means the online input should resonate with learners and remind them of real-world situations. The voiced PowerPoint presentations on the concept and classification of translation technology are supposed to provide lots of real-life examples that are highly relevant to students' actual translation and interpreting work. For instance, when introducing Pietrzak and Kornacki (2021)'s understanding of translation technology and automatic interpreting technology in particular, the instructor of the CAT course provides additional screenshots of how the mainstream automatic interpreting tools function. Some mini-lectures are made by external speakers who are industry experts in order to provide students with fresh ideas different from those taught by the academic staff and pack students with a sense of agility to deal with constant changes in translation markets.

The pre-class online learning paves the way for the in-class interactive lectures, because teachers now have more time to implement interesting and interactive activities in class rather than boring students with monotonous talks on translation technology. Work-along exercises and real-time quizzes can be employed as two practical means of interactive lectures in the CAT course (see Biggs and Tang 2011), which could be implemented via *Duifene* inside the classroom. The design of these in-class exercises and quizzes should enable students to develop more complex cognitive skills such as comparing and contrasting, justification and inferencing. Also, the instructor can see students' real-time performances on the exercises via *Duifene* and give instant feedback in class.

5.2 Moving from Declarative to Functioning Knowledge: Online Screenshots with Step-by-Step Guidance and In-Class Hands-On Workshops

The second, third and fourth intended learning outcomes as discussed in Sect. 4 are mainly concerned with the functioning knowledge of computer-assisted translation, which means the corresponding teaching and learning activities should focus on hands-on practices with CAT tools. In traditional face-to-face classroom, the instructor spends most of the time talking about the operations of the tools, and students are usually passive knowledge receivers. What's worse, more often than not, students forget about how to use the CAT tools quickly after class, let alone using the CAT tools to complete a new translation task. The reason is they did not really involve themselves into learning these tools. They were just told by the teacher to operate the translation tools.

To address this problem, students are provided with and encouraged to learn a series of online screenshots about how to use the CAT tools in *Duifene* before the class, so that more time could be allocated to in-class applications of the CAT tools. Some CAT tools have offered free online demonstration videos, but these videos may not be directly used and need to be adapted for students to learn because each course has its specific course aims, intended learning outcomes and content layout. The researcher decided to redesign and record by herself the tutorial screenshots with step-by-step guidance of how to use the CAT tools, namely, YiCAT and Trados.

Following the segmenting principle in multimedia learning (Mayer 2009), the functioning knowledge of computer-assisted translation in relation to ILO2, ILO3 and ILO4 is broken into several segments of online screenshot videos, including:

- Carry out single-file translation with machine translation (e.g., install a third-party plug-in of machine translation)
- Create, use and manage terminology bases (e.g., term extraction and translation of monolingual terms in the preparation phase of translation and checking terminology consistency after translating the text)
- Create, use and manage translation memories (e.g., use concordance search in translation memories to speed up translation)
- Carry out single-file translation with translation memories, termbases and machine translation applied (e.g., prioritize the suggestions of a particular translation memory with multiple translation memories applied)
- Implement project package translation with machine translation
- Implement project package translation with translation memories, termbases and machine translation applied

The logic behind the segmentation is to start with single file translation completed by individuals and gradually move to project translation completed with the collaboration of several students. Another logic is to begin with computer-assisted translation with the use of machine translation only and gradually move to computer-assisted translation with the use of machine translation, translation memories and termbases. Apart from the segmenting principle, the screenshot videos are made with conversational styles and a friendly voice in order to enhance students' learning on the CAT tools (Mayer 2009).

Students come to the classroom with a basic understanding of how the CAT tools function. The instructor conducts a series of in-class hands-on workshops to develop students' skills and competencies of applying the CAT tools to real-world translation tasks. These workshops are structured around the concepts of work-integrated learning and project-based learning (see Li et al. 2015; Cooper et al. 2010), where students are trained to be equipped with professional skills that meet the demands of translation markets.

So far, students have the essential declarative and functioning knowledge of computer-assisted translation before commencing to reflect on their use of translation technologies.

5.3 Reflection at the Spotlight: Posting Love Letters or Break-Up Letters Online and Solving Problems in Class

The fifth and sixth intended learning outcomes are concerned with developing students' abilities to reflect on the influence of technologies on translation practices and the role of translators in computer-assisted translation tasks. In place of formal presentations and reports, the researcher asks the students to write love letters or break-up letters to the CAT tools that they learn in the course (Koskinen and Ruokonen 2017), and share their letters with their classmates by posting them to the online discussion forum in *Duifene*. Writing love or break-up letters is considered to be a fresh teaching and learning activity that allows students to make free and spontaneous reflections on their interactions with translation technology. Students are encouraged to comment on their peers' letters in the following aspects, such as whether the author use evidence and examples to back up their reflections on the CAT tool, how well the examples support their ideas, and whether the letter shows bias towards the CAT tool.

Since the love and hate letters could reflect the usability of translation technology (Koskinen and Ruokonen 2017) and some students might complain about the CAT tools, students have chances to think about how to solve the problems that occurred when translators use the CAT tools. The merit of blending learning in this scenario is that students do not need to spend time understanding the letters in class, but rather they can get directly involved in finding solutions to enhance the learning effectiveness of the translation tools.

6 Summary and Conclusion

In light of the Construction of New Liberal Arts, this article presents a curricular design for the undergraduate-level course Computer-assisted Translation, focusing on the integration of blended learning in the CAT course in order to improve learning effectiveness on translation technology. Applying the framework of Constructive Alignment, this study identified six intended learning outcomes with reference to the surveyed students' perceptions of what they expected to learn in the CAT course, and then relevant teaching and learning activities in a blended mode. Future research can put the blended learning activities to empirical tests and assess the effectiveness of these activities.

Acknowledgements. This work was supported by the Research Projects of Humanities and Social Sciences Foundation of Ministry of Education of China (21YJC740046) [教育部人文社会科学研究青年基金项目 "计算机辅助口译技术下的同声传译过程与效果研究", 项目批准号: 21YJC740046] and University-Industry Collaborative Education Program of Ministry of Education of China (202002242004). This work is also supported by Center for Translation Studies of Guangdong University of Foreign Studies (Grant No. CTSHQ202101).

References

Austermuehl, F.: Future (and not-so-future) trends in the teaching of translation technology. Rev. Tradumàtica: Tecnol. Traducció **11**, 326–337 (2013)

Biggs, J., Tang, C.: Teaching for Quality Learning at University: What the Student Does. McGraw-Hill Education, Berkshire (2011)

Cooper, L., Orrell, J., Bowden, M.: Work Integrated Learning: A Guide to Effective Practice. Routledge, London and New York (2010)

Koskinen, K., Ruokonen, M.: Love letters or hate mail? Translators' technology acceptance in the light of their emotional narratives. In: Kenny, D. (ed.) Human Issues in Translation Technology, pp. 8–24. Routledge, London and New York (2017)

Lee, J., Huh, J.: Why not go online? A case study of blended mode business interpreting and translation certificate program. Interpret. Transl. Train. **12**(4), 444–466 (2018)

Li, D.: Translator training: what translation students have to say. Meta **47**(4), 513–531 (2002)

Li, D., Zhang, C., He, Y.: Project-based learning in teaching translation: students' perceptions. Interpret. Transl. Train. **9**(1), 1–19 (2015)

Massey, G.: Learning to learn, teach and develop: co-emergent perspectives on translator and language-mediator education. InTRAlinea: Online Translation Journal. inTRAlinea Special Issue: New Insights into Translator Training (2019). http://www.intralinea.org/specials/article/learning_to_learn_teach_and_develop. Accessed 29 Aug 2021

Mayer, R.E.: Multimedia Learning, 2nd edn. Cambridge University Press, Cambridge (2009)

Mitchell-Schuitevoerder, R.: A Project-Based Approach to Translation Technology. Routledge, London and New York (2020)

Pietrzak, P., Kornacki, M.: Using CAT Tools in Freelance Translation: Insights from a Case Study. Routledge, London and New York (2021)

Rico, C.: The ePortfolio: constructing learning in translation technology. Interpret. Transl. Train. **11**(1), 79–95 (2017)

Seljan, S., Banek, M., Špiranec, S., Lasić-Lazić, J.: CALL (computer-assisted language learning) and distance learning. In: Biljanović, P., Skala, K. (eds.) Proceedings of the 29th International convention MIPRO 2006, pp. 145–150. Croatian Society for Information and Communication Technology, Electronics and Microelectronics, Rijeka (2006)

Wang, H., Li, Y.: Translation technology teaching in the new era: problems and countermeasures. Foreign Lang.World **3**, 13–21 (2021)

Wang, N.: Translation studies from the perspective of new liberal arts. J. Foreign Lang. **44**(2), 75–79 (2021)

Wang, N., Chen, J., Tai, M., Zhang, J.: Blended learning for Chinese university EFL learners: learning environment and learner perceptions. Comput. Assist. Lang. Learn. **34**(3), 297–323 (2021)

Xu, Y.S.: When translation technology meets educational technology: the way forward for teaching computer-aided translation. J. Transl. Stud. **13**(1 & 2), 283–304 (2010)

Translation of Long English Sentences Based on Clause Complex Theory

Jingyi Li[1] and Xiaoxiao Chen[2](✉)

[1] Center for Linguistics and Applied Linguistics, Guangdong University of Foreign Studies, Guangzhou 510420, China
[2] School of English for International Business, Guangdong University of Foreign Studies, Guangzhou 510420, China
201410043@oamail.gdufs.edu.cn

Abstract. The translation of long sentences in English is hard to handle for translators in the English-Chinese translation. The first and very key factor contributing to this problem is the high complexity of sentence structures and constitute relationships in long English sentences. Additionally, since English and Chinese are two unrelated languages with huge differences, translators' understanding and handling of these differences, to a large extent, affects their performance in translation practice. Taking above-mentioned factors into consideration, numerous methods were proposed by scholars previously in the practice of translating long English sentences. However, there is no decent standard and sufficient sample analyses provided for translators to judge from. More importantly, analyzing sentences in traditional linguistic ways is not always practical in translation practice. Therefore, Clause Complex Theory is proposed to provide framework for clause-based analysis of clause complex structures in both English and Chinese. Following the Clause Complex Theory, this paper introduces an English-Chinese clause alignment annotation system, including English clause tagging and Chinese translation generation and combination. Furthermore, selected research samples together with concrete analysis are anticipated to be presented. To conclude, this study has described an effective Component Sharing based method for the proper treatment of long sentences in English-Chinese translation.

Keywords: Long English sentences · Component sharing · Clause complex theory · English-Chinese translation

1 The Complexity of Translating Long Sentences in English

The translation of long sentences in English has been a critical problem in English-Chinese translation because of its high complexity. Reasons contributing to such a high complexity are varied, while there are two key factors that are widely accepted: the differences between English and Chinese and the characteristics of long sentences in English [1–3].

W. Jia et al. (Eds.): SETE 2021, LNCS 13089, pp. 425–435, 2021.
https://doi.org/10.1007/978-3-030-92836-0_38

1.1 The Differences in English and Chinese

English and Chinese are from two different language families with huge differences [4]. This section is an attempt to illustrate the representative differences in English and Chinese that may prevent translators from translating long English sentences into Chinese faithfully and smoothly. Xu [5] advocates the intercultural awareness is in favor of avoiding the misunderstanding or improper rendering of expression in translation practice.

Bell [6] regarded the contrast between hypotaxis and parataxis as one of most significant studies in relation to translation, especially in English and Chinese. The term parataxis is used to refers to the phenomenon "conjunctions to be dropped", meant for contrasting it with hypotaxis in English in relation to the use of conjunctions in linking clauses [7]. Besides, Qin and Wang [4] agreed that English sentences are tightly combined as a tree structure, but Chinese sentences are loose in structure and deliberately ignore unnecessary devices in form.

Additionally, Li and Thompson [8] came up with the view that English is the subject-prominent language and Chinese is the topic-prominent language. The consensus view seems to be that English sentences are limited to following grammar rules such as Subject-Predicate Agreement; On the other hand, Chinese sentences consist of only two elements, the Topic and the Comment interpreting it, with the focus primarily on the identification of the topic and aboutness of the comment to the topic [10]. When English-Chinese translation is carried out, these differences call for transformation of syntactic patterns.

1.2 The Characteristics of Long Sentences in English

As the name implies, long sentences in English are with a long length. Undoubtedly, as a sentence becomes longer, the syntactic structure of this sentence becomes more ambiguous. According to Halliday and Matthiessen [9], a sentence, which is always interpreted as a clause complex, is a grammatical and semantic unit formed with two or more clauses. In English, there are two main types of sentences with grammatical constructions consisting of multiple clauses: sentences including coordinate clauses, and sentences including a matrix clause and a subordinate clause [11].

Situations are varied when it comes to these two types of sentences. On the one hand, the coordinating conjunctions connect one coordinate clause or more together so as to make them joined to the main clause. The coordinating conjunctions are indispensable linkers, hence the syntactic structure of this kind of sentence can be easily analyzed by cutting the original sentence into several simple sentences [1]. On the other hand, the subordinate clauses tend to follow the matrix clause adherently [11].

With the exception of complicated syntactic structures, the complexity of long English sentences may also be presented by lengthy and confusing modifiers within clauses. Specifically, the order and amounts of modifiers have a great impact on whether translators get command of the major structure and main information without ambiguity, which is further evidence on whether they know the views or contents in the original logically correctly [5].

Dealing with long English sentences from English to Chinese is a tough task for a translator but every translator creates his or her own ways to handle the problems from language and meaning in different ways. If taken each situation into consideration, then, it is a major undertaking. Consequently, a well-organized system is anticipated to be proposed especially on the basis of established rules with little impact of subject factors, such as syntactic structures.

2 Related Work of Translating Long English Sentences

Previously, Zhang [2], Xu [5] and Zhong [12] claimed that correct comprehension of the original is always the first and foremost step, which may lie in the understanding of the main idea, the logic sequence and grammatical relations in the lone sentence to be translated. With the exception of correct comprehension, they emphasized another prerequisite, the capacity for adequate representation of the original thought in the target language. In order to meet above-mentioned standards, accordingly, numerous methods or approaches have been devised by domestic scholars to tackle the translation of long English sentences. To recapitulate briefly, there are three main methods summarized from previous researches.

Most noteworthy is the highly emphasis on following or reversing the original order. If the English sentence shares the same logic sequence and grammatical relations with the Chinese sentence, translators are recommended to follow the original syntactic order. On the contrary, the translation version should be in reverse order, accord with expression of Chinese habits. Commonly, the latter method is applied in the situation where the position of lengthy attributive clauses or adverbial clauses in English should be reversed to make the Chinese version compact and coherent, for example, from the beginning of the sentence to the end.

1. Following the original order
   But even on the federal bench, specialization is creeping in, and it has become a subject of sharp controversy on the newest federal appeals court.
   但即使是在联邦法院，专业化也正在悄悄蔓延，而且这在最新的联邦上诉法院中已经成为一个有尖锐争议的话题。
2. Reversing the original order
   USI FAR EAST will hold a 60% stake in Luzon Petrochemical, according to papers signed with the Philippine government's Board of Investment.
   与菲律宾政府投资委员会签署的文件显示，环旭电子远东子公司将持有吕宋岛石化60%的股份。

Sometimes, nonetheless, translators need to analyze certain elements separately within the clause level and translate them by division. By means of dividing, sense groups divided by connectives are expected to be viewed as new clauses with punctuation marks, so as to make the Chinese version both clear and smooth. "Dividing" here also refers to splitting or embedding. To be more concise, certain elements can be separated from the main clause to act as parenthesis; Or certain phrases, especially modifiers, are suggested to be embedded before the object to be modified. In most cases, one single method alone cannot guarantee faithful and smooth rendition. As a result, translators can flexibly choose several kinds of method together for the proper treatment, the method of which is known as synthesis or recasting.

3. Dividing the original sentence
   It's the line-item veto, a procedure that would allow the president to kill individual items in a big spending bill passed by Congress without vetoing the entire bill.
   它是一个采用单项否决权的程序。这个程序将允许总统取消国会通过的一个巨额开支法案中的个别条款, 但是不用否决整个法案。
4. Synthesis
   "The ramifications are enormous," says Rep. Don Edward, a California Democrat who is a senior member of the House Judiciary Committee.
   加州民主党人众议员–也是众议院司法委员会的资深成员–唐·爱德华说道, "影响巨大。

3 Clause Complex Theory and Component Sharing

Given that English is a subject-prominent language, while Chinese topic-prominent, it is not such convenient to analyze the English-Chinese translation just on the basis of English syntactics. Consequently, from the viewpoint of characteristics of Chinese sentences, the topic-related discussions have endured throughout the ages, such as topic-chain [13], the omissions of the subject [14] and the progression of topic [15]. Importantly, Ge and Song [16] transformed the application of Clause Complex Theory from Chinese to English, which is a naming-centered syntactical structure.

3.1 Overview

Clause Complex Theory, first named as Generalized Topic Structure in 2013, was finally defined by Song in 2017, to illustrate the syntactical structure in Chinese sentences. The basic unit for analyzing is the punctuation clause, which is a string of words separated by comma, colon, period, exclamation mark, question mark or colon preceding a direct quotation. According to regulations of Clause Complex Theory, whether in English or Chinese, a punctuation clause is a text segmentation and several punctuation clauses form a clause complex which, in other words, is a traditional sentence in most occasions. With the progress of research on this theory, it is found that a component-sharing relationship is widespread among punctuation clauses. If a component in a punctuation clause is discussed by other punctuation clauses, that component is a generalized topic and the latter is the explanation of the topic.

Later, the Generalized topic was redefined as Naming in 2015. To be more precisely, Naming, which is defined as the 'topic' used together with a few adverbial and predicative components, conveys information at the starting point of the utterance [16]. And the element around the naming is defined as Telling, aimed at predicting or explaining the naming. To conclude, a naming and a telling comprise an NT clause, whereas it should be emphasized here that a clause complex is basically composed by one or more than one NT clause consisting of a naming and a telling. In another word, the NT clause is the basic unit of the clause complex in the Clause Complex theory [17].

3.2 Component Sharing Patterns

Besides, the flexible relationship between the naming and telling reflects on the structure as well. The telling may sometimes appear in the front of the naming which is followed by either one or more than one telling simultaneously. Most of the time, the naming is the first appearing element and shared by the 'telling' part with indefinite amount of the telling. What described above is exactly the naming-centered syntactical structure.

There are three representative patterns constructing the English NT clause: the Stack Pattern, the Back Position Pattern, and the New Branch Pattern [17]. In example 5, the sentence is segmented into several parts, illustrated by forms of five lines. Exactly, Line 2 is treated as the stack bottom and Line 3 and 4 at the right end is the stack top, which is a process of top and push of a stack, so this kind of pattern is termed as the Stack pattern. Apparently, the Naming "the low margin" is shared in common. However, working as the telling, Line 5 is lack of a naming which actually is "a lot of small investors", not "the low margin" anymore; hence, "a lot of small investors" as a whole looks like a new branch growing on a tree trunk, which is exactly the New Branch Pattern.

5. Mr. Cheng says the low margin required for trading futures attracted a lot of small investors before the 1987 crash who didn't realize that their risk was virtually unlimited.

Line 1: Mr. Cheng says
Line 2: {the low margin
Line 3: required for trading futures
Line 4: attracted a lot of small investors … crash
Line 5: | who … un-
limited.}

Lastly, in the following example, Line 1 appears at the beginning of the sentence but functions as the new information to complete the characteristics that "the Norwegian unit" possesses. In other words, "the Norwegian unit" is found as the naming of "18% stake in the Veslefrikk offshore field" in this case. Apparently, this kind of situation conforms the Back Position Pattern, which means that the interpretation of the "topic" appears ahead of this "topic".

6. In addition to an 18% stake in the Veslefrikk offshore **field**, the Norwegian unit has interests ranging from 10% to 25% in three other Norwegian oil and gas production licenses.

Line 1: D|In addition to an 18% stake…**field**,
Line 2: The Norwegian unit has interests ranging from 10% ... gas production licenses.

3.3 English-Chinese Clause Alignment Annotation

The English-Chinese clause alignment annotation system is guided by Parsing-Translating-Assembling (PTA) Model with three stages: English Naming-Telling Clause tagging, Chinese translation generation and Chinese translation combination [17]. Last section witnessed how the Clause Complex Theory works in English Naming-Telling Clause tagging. Then, this section continues to interpretate the remaining two steps.

Following the manual parse with strict rules, the sentence has been cut down into multiple chunks with different tags referring to the logical-grammatical and naming-telling relationship respectively at the end of every line, such as SV standing for simple sentence with a clear subject-predicate relationship and corresponding a Naming-Telling Clause (Step 1: Naming-telling clause tagging). Then, Chinese translations are provided separately (Step 2: Chinese translation generation). Lastly, operators need to put these chunks together in a logical and fluent manner (Step 3: Chinese translation combination).

[1] Raw materials
Mr. Cheng says the low margin required for trading futures attracted a lot of small investors before the 1987 crash who didn't realize that their risk was virtually unlimited.

[2] Procedures of clause alignment annotation

Step 1: Naming-telling clause tagging
Line 1: Mr. Cheng says//SV-
Line 2: {the low margin//NNM
Line 3: required for trading futures//ED
Line 4: attracted a lot of small investors … crash//PRD
Line 5: | who … unlimited.//WS}

Step 2: Chinese translation generation
Line1: 郑先生表示
Line2: 【低保证金
Line3: 交易期货所需
Line4: 在1987年股灾之前吸引了许多小投资者
Line5: | WHO没有意识到它们的风险实际上是无限的。】

Step 3: Chinese translation combination
Line 1: 郑先生表示，
Line 2: 【交易期货所需的低保证金在1987年股灾之前吸引了许多小投资者，
Line 3: 这些投资者没有意识到期货的风险实际上是无限的。】

In this regard, Professor Song launched his research team to work on the establishment of English-Chinese Clause Alignment Corpus with the long-term goal to help improve the quality and readability of machine translation. Raw language materials used for tagging on PTA Model are chosen from Wall Street Journal in the corpus of The Penn Treebank Project. Previous studies based on the data collected from this tagging system also reveal that the Clause Complex Theory and PTA Model contribute to solve translation problems in English-Chinese translation practice: Chinese translation of adpositional structure, "what" object clause and "which clause" and so on.

4 Sample Analysis

Under the guidance of the Clause Complex Theory and PTA Model, more than 5,000 sentences from the Wall Street Journal have been annotated. This section is expected to present some sentences as example to illustrate how the Clause Complex Theory work in long English sentence translation. Here is one sentence from the Wall Street Journal:

7. Morishita, whose art gallery last month became a major shareholder in Christies International PLC, the London auction house, is one man who doesn't fit the mold.

In this sentence, "Morishita" is a noun as the naming part, while the remaining parts are defined as the telling to interpretate "Morishita". The relative pronoun, whose, refers to the fact that the art gallery belongs to Morishita. However, "the London auction house" here modifies the specific company "Christies International PLC". Lastly, the subject of the clause "is one man who doesn't fit the mold" is far away from the predicate. Literally, there are two naming-telling clauses: Morishita is one man; The man doesn't fit the mold. Therefore, both assertive and negative attitude exist in the last clause. It is hard for language learners to figure out the logical relationship at once and translate various clauses in one sentence smoothly. At the same time, the PTA Model can help Chinese translation assembling.

Step 1: Naming-telling clause tagging
Line 1: Morishita,//NNM
Line 2: whose in Christies International PLC,//WSA
Line 3: | the London auction house,//EXPL
Line 4: is one man//PRD
Line 5: | who doesn't fit the mold.//WS

Step 2: Chinese translation generation
Line 1: 森下康一，
Line 2: WHOSE画廊上个月成为克里斯蒂国际公司的大股东，
Line 3: | 伦敦拍卖行，
Line 4: 是一个人
Line 5: | WHO不合标准。

Step 3: Chinese translation combination
Line 1: 森下康一的画廊上个月成为伦敦拍卖行克里斯蒂国际公司的大股东，
Line 2: 这个人不合标准。

At the third step, the original English sentence is divided into two clauses in Chinese translation, because Chinese sentences are always with multiple pauses but no relative pronoun to use as reference. The phrase "one man" refers to the antecedent, a specific person named "Morishita". Therefore, "一个人" in this case being used broadly as a deixis word should be transformed into the specific term "这个人" as the subject of Line 5, by which the formal marker "WHO" is deleted to avoid redundant.

It can be found on above sentence that the parenthesis content consists of an appositive nominal phrase and an attributive clause, together on a lengthy description. Except for this kind of situation, the PTA Model helps to deal with complexing adpositional structures as well. Here is an example in exibit:

8. The wounds from the 1987 crash haven't yet healed, and not all claims against the exchange clearinghouse – by those who bet the Hang Seng index would fall – have been settled.

Clearly, in this example, the most confusing part appears following the simple sentence at the beginning of the sentence. Adpositional structures, such as "against the exchange clearinghouse" and "by those who bet the Hang Seng index would fall", are without doute the modifiers of the antecedent "claims". Next on, the translation process of this sentence is listed as follows.

Step 1: Naming-telling clause tagging
Line 1: The wounds from the 1987 crash haven't yet healed,//SV
Line 2: and not all claims//NNM
Line 3: | against the exchange clearinghouse//PP
Line 4: | -- by those//PP
Line 5: | who bet the Hang Seng index would fall -- //WS
Line 6: have been settled.//PRD

Step 2: Chinese translation generation
Line 1: 1987年崩盘造成的创伤还未愈合，
Line 2: 而且不是所有索赔都
Line 3: | 对交易清算所
Line 4: | -- 那些人
Line 5: | WHO押注恒生指数会下跌--
Line 6: 得以解决。

Step 3: Chinese translation combination
Line 1: 1987年崩盘造成的创伤还未愈合，
Line 2: 而且不是所有对交易清算所的索赔,
Line 3: | -- 由押注恒生指数会下跌的那些人提出的--，
Line 4: 都得以解决。

More precisely, the tag PP means prepositional phrases as the telling and WS is used in the situation where the antecedent plays the "subject" role in the dependent clause. If the naming part and the corresponding telling part are combined together, the naming-telling clauses are presented.

NT 1: The wounds from the 1987 crash haven't yet healed.
NT 2: All claims are against the exchange clearinghouse.
NT 3: All claims are (laid) by those (people).
NT 4: Those (people) bet the Hang Seng index would fall.
NT 5: And not all claims have been settled.

In this case, the result of parsing indicates the inner-relationship between constitutes. Traditional translation methods tend to suggest translators to put post-modifiers in front of the noun phrase in most occasions in E-C translation. Besides, when the attributive constitute is too long to comprehend, double dash or round brackets can be kept or added manually. Thus, at the assembling stage, topic sufficient sentences are assembled by taking these techniques into consideration. As seen in two previous examples, several clauses tend to share one nominal naming in one sentence; while in the New Brach Pattern, one naming may be contained in another naming, taking the following sentence as an example.

9. Oji Paper's sales strength was evident in overall paper products sales, including newsprints, printing and wrapping papers, which rose to 221.61 billion yen in the first half from 200.70 billion yen a year earlier.

In the source text, "paper products" consist of newsprints, printing and wrapping papers. On the other hand, "which" here does not refer to "paper products" but a new naming – "overall paper products sales". In order to present the logical-grammatical relationship clearly in form, the Parsing-Translating-Assembling process will be listed below.

Step 1: Naming-telling clause tagging

Line 1: Oji Paper's … overall paper products sales,//SV
Line 2: < > including … papers,//ING
Line 3: | which rose to … a year earlier.//WS

Step 2: Chinese translation generation

Line 1: 王子纸质有限公司的销售优势在整体纸制品销售中显而易见,
Line 2: < > 包括新闻纸、印刷纸和包装纸在内,
Line 3: | WHICH从去年上半年的2007亿日元上升到今年同期的2216.1亿日元。

Step 3: Chinese translation combination

Line 1: 王子制纸有限公司的销售优势在包括新闻纸、印刷纸和包装纸在内的整体纸制品销售中显而易见,
Line 2: 销售额从去年上半年的2007亿日元上升到今年同期的2216.1亿日元。

What is worth mentioning is that, at the Chinese translation combination stage, "sales" can be translated into either the act of selling money in Line 1 or quantity of the products that has been sold in Line 2. Nevertheless, in Chinese, these two kinds of expressions are "销售" and "销售额". To conclude, in Step 3, it is of equal important to figure out the correct expression and make necessary changes, according to the naming-telling relationship in step 2.

5 Conclusion

In the practice of English-Chinese translation, as a sentence gets longer, translators may encounter many problems. The first and very key factor contributing to this problem is the high complexity of sentence structures and constitute relationships in long English sentences. Furthermore, translators' understanding and handling of these differences, to a large extent, affects their performance in translation practice. Traditional sentence translation methods to tack these issues have limits in their performance.

Till now, the English-Chinese clause alignment corpus has been still under establishment. More than 5,000 English sentences from the Wall Street Journal have been annotated based on the Clause Complex Theory. Using the naming-telling clause as the basic translation unit, the Parsing-Translation-Assembling Model requires English sentences to be translated in three stages. Firstly, the original language material is expected to be parsed under the guidance of naming-telling clause model. Then, the Chinese translation will be given respectively line by line with the same order as English presents. Lastly, the separated Chinese translation will be combined to one or more than one complete sentences in accordance with Chinese syntax and semantics.

Although the PTA Model governs a fairly large number of language materials, new problems arise as the work continues. For future work, adequate expanding number of language resources should be taken into investigation. Shang (2014) conducted empirical studies and prove the 99% coverage of the use of Clause Complex Theory in Chinese sentences. The PTA Model provides a branding new perspective for translation studies, which is ease-to-translate for translators and broad-to-adapt for language materials. With the aid of the Clause Complex Theory, the translation of some grammatical units are perfected, especially adpositional structures, attributive clauses, substantive clauses and so on. To conclude, this study has described an effective Component Sharing based method for the proper treatment of long sentences in English-Chinese translation.

References

1. Roh, Y.H., Seo, Y.A., Lee, K.Y., et al.: Long sentence partitioning using structure analysis for machine translation. In: NLPRS, pp. 646–652 (2001)
2. Zhang, P.: A Course in English-Chinese Translation. Shanghai Foreign Language Education Press, Shanghai (2008)
3. Xiong, B.: Comparison of English and Chinese and Translation: An Introduction. Huazhong Normal University Press, Wuhan (2012)

4. Qin, H., Wang, K.: Comparison and Translation Between English and Chinese. Foreign Language Teaching and Research Press, Beijing (2010)
5. Xu, J.P.: A Practical Course of English-Chinese and Chinese-English Translation. Tsinghua University Press, Beijing (2013)
6. Bell, R.T.: Translation and Translating. Longman, London (1991)
7. Tse, Y.K.: Parataxis and hypotaxis in the Chinese language. Int. J. Arts Sci. **3**, 351–359 (2010)
8. Li, C., Thompson, S.: Subject and Topic: A New Typology of Language. Ed. by Li. Academic Press, New York (1976)
9. Halliday, M.A.K., Matthiessen, C.M.I.M., Halliday, M., et al.: An Introduction to Functional Grammar. Routledge, Abingdon (2014)
10. Lina, X.: The topic-prominence of Chinese sentences and its implications for EC translation. Chin. Transl. J. **31**(03), 63–69+96 (2010)
11. Diessel, H.: The Acquisition of Complex Sentences. Cambridge University Press, London (2004)
12. Zhong, S.: A Coursebook for English-Chinese Translation Skills. University of International Business and Economics Press, Beijing (2017)
13. Cao, F.: Sentence and Clause Structure in Chinese: A Functional Perspective. Beijing Language and Culture University Press, Beijing (2005)
14. Song, R.: The delesion of the fronts of clauses in Chinese narratives. J. Chin. Inf. Process. **6**(3), 62–68 (1992)
15. Chen, P.: Studies in Modern Linguistics: Theory, Methodology and Fact. Chongqing Publishing House, Chongqing (1991)
16. Ge, S., Song, R.: The naming sharing structure and its cognitive meaning in Chinese and English. In: Proceedings of the 2nd Workshop on Semantics-Driven Machine Translation (SedMT 2016), pp.13–21 (2016)
17. Ge, S., Song, R.: English-Chinese clause alignment corpus tagging system based on corpus annotation. J. Chin. Inf. Process. **34**(6), 27–35 (2020)

The Development of Artificial Intelligence Education in Primary and Secondary Schools in China

Qiqi Xu[1], Jinlin Li[1], Hai Liu[1,2](✉), and Tianyong Hao[3]

[1] School of Computer Science, South China Normal University, Guangzhou, China
{xuqiqi,lijinlin,liuhai}@m.scnu.edu.cn
[2] Guangzhou Key Laboratory of Big Data Intelligent in Education, Guangzhou, China
[3] Institute for Advanced Study of Educational Development in Guangdong-Hong Kong-Macao Greater Bay Area, South China Normal University, Guangzhou, China
haoty@m.scnu.edu.cn

Abstract. Textbooks are essential materials for students to acquire subject knowledge and carry out subject learning, as well as an important basis for teachers to carry out classroom teaching. This paper conducts a comparative analysis of the main popular artificial intelligence textbooks in primary and secondary schools in mainland China based on "General High School Information Technology Curriculum Standards", and carries out comparative analysis in four aspects, including teaching content, textbook style, teaching activity arrangement, and teaching evaluation design. It is found that the preparation of AI teaching materials is showing a fast development, but at the same time there are problems such as the lack of unified curriculum standards.

Keywords: Artificial intelligence · Education · Primary and secondary schools

1 Introduction

Since the 21st century, artificial intelligence has been popular after experiencing a period of development trough and has become a key technology which leading the intelligent era. The development level of artificial intelligence technology has also become the main indicator of the comprehensive scientific and technological strength of a country. To develop artificial intelligence technology, on the condition that it is fundamental to cultivate talents in the field of artificial intelligence, mainland China has attached great importance to promoting the development of artificial intelligence education in recent years. In 2017, the "New Generation Artificial Intelligence Development Plan" issued by the State Council clearly pointed out that artificial intelligence-related courses should be set up in primary and secondary schools, and the education of artificial intelligence in primary and secondary schools should be raised to the level of national development strategy [1]. In the just-concluded 2021 China Artificial Intelligence Education Conference, Sun [2], the former director of the

W. Jia et al. (Eds.): SETE 2021, LNCS 13089, pp. 436–447, 2021.
https://doi.org/10.1007/978-3-030-92836-0_39

Ministry of Education, emphasized: "Artificial intelligence education must be started from primary and secondary schools to lay the foundation, and must incorporate artificial intelligence education into the classroom, into learning plans and arrangements". The compulsory education stage's development in artificial intelligence teaching is the trend of the times. As an essential carrier of classroom teaching, textbooks are key materials to carry out subject learning, and are also the main basis for teachers to conduct classroom teaching [3]. Since that many major scientific research societies, universities, and individual scholars have joined the team that compiles artificial intelligence textbooks, artificial intelligence education is showing a new situation of good development.

To that end, this paper investigates existing artificial intelligence textbooks in primary and secondary schools in mainland China. A comparative analysis based on "General High School Information Technology Curriculum Standards" is carries out in various perspectives including teaching content, textbook style, teaching activity arrangement, and teaching evaluation design. Findings are presented and discussed to assist the understanding and development of artificial intelligence teaching materials.

2 Current Teaching Materials

To orient to the primary and secondary school sections, this research is mainly based on local news reports related to artificial intelligence education, supplemented by online bookstores and search engine data results to conduct research to understand the main popular artificial intelligence teaching materials for primary and secondary schools in mainland China. According to the survey results, the following 9 sets of textbooks are selected, which contain 33 books in total. The following is a brief introduction of the selected textbooks (Table 1).

3 Mainstream Textbook Analysis

Curriculum standards, as programmatic guidance documents for various disciplines, play the role of "organizers" of teaching work [3], based on which writing textbooks can ensure the continuity of teaching and the consistency of goals since that textbooks are the concretization of curriculum standards. In the "General High School Information Technology Curriculum Standards (2020 Revised Edition)" (hereinafter referred to as the "New Curriculum Standard"), "Artificial Intelligence" is included as an optional compulsory module into the teaching plan. The "New Curriculum Standard" gives suggestions on the four aspects of artificial intelligence, which are teaching content, teaching materials style, teaching activity arrangement, and teaching evaluation design. This article will study the mainstream artificial intelligence teaching materials in primary and secondary schools from these four aspects.

Table 1. Introduction to selected textbooks.

Abbreviation	Textbook name	Breif introduction	Publisher and date	School-oriented
Textbook A (1–6 Volumes)	Fantastic animals on AI (AI上神奇动物)	This set of books which consists of six volumes, covers three school levels: elementary school, junior high school and high school. Each book contains thematic course content and activity course content, with content selected around a topic. The thematic courses introduce students to the basics of artificial intelligence with the help of programmable building block kits, and the activity courses are the expansion and extension of the thematic courses	East China Normal University Press Nov. 2018	Elementary school
	Smart life on AI (AI上智慧生活)			
	AI in the deformation workshop (AI在变形工坊)			
	AI cute pet "E" (AI萌宠小E)			Junior high school
	AI super engineer (AI超级工程师)			
	Python on AI (AI上Python)			High school
Textbook B (1–2 Volumes)	Elementary School Artificial Intelligence Foundation (Volume 1) (小学人工智能基础(上册))	This set of books use teaching tools such as graphical programming and open source hardware, and design familiar life situations for students to integrate into learning more quickly. The textbook reasonably select knowledge in the field of artificial intelligence such as knowledge representation, machine perception, big data, etc., so that students can understand the basics of artificial intelligence after learning	Science and technology of China press Aug. 2019	Elementary school
	Elementary School Artificial Intelligence Foundation (Volume 2) (小学人工智能基础(下册))			

(*continued*)

Table 1. (*continued*)

Abbreviation	Textbook name	Breif introduction	Publisher and date	School-oriented
Textbook C	Artificial Intelligence (Elementary School Edition) (人工智能(小学版))	With the carrier of graphical programming and open source hardware, this textbook adopts a project-based learning method to understand the history and the principles behind artificial intelligence in the process of hands-on programming	Tsinghua University Press Aug. 2020	Elementary school
Textbook D (1–8 Volumes)	The infinite challenges of artificial intelligence (人工智能的无限挑战)	Each book is organized around a topic, which consists of five parts: learning map, introduction to scenarios, creative production, career exploration, and extracurricular expansion. The topic chosen for the materials are closely related to students' lives, so that students can apply Artificial intelligence into live after understanding the basics of Artificial intelligence	Soochow University Press May 2018	Elementary school
	VR is more realistic than reality (比真实更逼真的VR)			
	Sniping natural disasters (狙击自然灾害)			
	The first step towards the universe-launch vehicle (迈向宇宙的第一步—运载火箭)			
	Faster and more accurate-smart medical (更加快速、更加准确——智能医疗)			
	The Internet of Things that Changed Life (改变生活的物联网)			Junior high school
	Learn about game engines from A to Z (从A到Z了解游戏引擎)			
	The third generation gene scissors CRISPR (第三代基因剪刀CRISPR)			

(*continued*)

Table 1. *(continued)*

Abbreviation	Textbook name	Breif introduction	Publisher and date	School-oriented
Textbook E	Artificial Intelligence Elementary School Edition (人工智能 小学版)	The textbook focuses on the "initial perception" of artificial intelligence. Through course learning, students can understand the meaning and application of artificial intelligence, master the way of communicating and dialogue with machines, and cultivate a positive attitude towards the arrival of the artificial intelligence era	Shanghai Educational Publishing House Aug. 2019	Elementary school
Textbook F	Artificial intelligence (1–8 volumes) (人工智能(1-8册))	This set of textbooks covers the third to eighth grades of compulsory education. Each volume is composed of three parts: general knowledge, application, and programming of artificial intelligence, in which students can master artificial intelligence related knowledge and form an understanding of artificial intelligence	Guangzhou Institute of Educational Research March 2020	Elementary school
	Artificial intelligence (9–12 volumes) (人工智能 (9-12册))			Junior high school
Textbook G	Artificial Intelligence High School Edition (人工智能 高中版)	The textbooks are based on the concept of project-based learning. Through each project, students are guided to understand several important sections of artificial intelligence, such as path planning, image recognition, speech recognition, video analysis, natural language, etc.	Shanghai Educational Publishing House Feb. 2020	High school

(continued)

Table 1. (*continued*)

Abbreviation	Textbook name	Breif introduction	Publisher and date	School-oriented
Textbook H	Initial AI (人工智能初步)	This book bases on task-based learning, arranging four units of learning content including the basic knowledge and application of artificial intelligence, knowledge representation, expert systems and artificial intelligence algorithms	Sinomaps Publishing Press June 2005	High school
Textbook I	Artificial Intelligence Fundamentals (人工智能基础)	This book is composed of three parts: theoretical foundation, programming language foundation, and application practice, which introduces the basic theoretical knowledge of artificial intelligence and the Python language, and conducts specific practice of artificial intelligence based on theoretical knowledge	China Machine Press Jan. 2021	Junior high school and high school

3.1 Textbook Content Analysis

The "New Curriculum Standard" puts forward four core literacy requirements in the course of subject teaching, namely, information awareness, computational thinking, digital learning and innovation, and information society responsibility [4]. In the "Artificial Intelligence" module, suggestions are made on core teaching content based on the core literacy of the subject: the foundation of artificial intelligence, the technology of artificial intelligence, the future and prospects of artificial intelligence, the construction of artificial intelligence application modules, artificial intelligence application systems and the ethical and safety challenges of artificial intelligence. According to the above suggestions, the following results can be obtained by researching and analyzing the textbook A-I.

Table 2. Teaching material content classification

Core literacy	Involved content	Involving teaching materials
Computational thinking	Construction of artificial intelligence application modules	Textbook A, B, C, D, F, I
	Artificial intelligence application system	Textbook H
Digital learning and innovation	Artificial intelligence technology	Textbook A, B, C, D, E, F, G, H, I
	The future and prospects of artificial intelligence	Textbook A, C, D, E, F, G
Information awareness and information society responsibility	The foundation of artificial intelligence	Textbook A, B, C, D, E, F, G, H, I
	Ethics and security challenges of artificial intelligence	Textbook C, E, F, G

From Table 2, it can be found that the teaching material A-I can be guided by the core content suggested by the new curriculum standard, integrate the core literacy of the subject into the curriculum teaching, and write around the relevant knowledge in the field of artificial intelligence:

(1) Introduce the concept, development history and application of artificial intelligence to students, put forward the ethical and moral issues involved in the development of artificial intelligence, such as technology abuse, responsibility attribution, job substitution, etc., and cultivate students' information awareness and information society responsibility literacy in the process of introducing general knowledge of artificial intelligence.
(2) Enable students to understand the core technologies in the field of artificial intelligence: algorithms (such as heuristic search, etc.), text recognition, face recognition, speech recognition, speech synthesis, natural language processing, etc. Make students understand the technical principles behind artificial intelligence products in life and their implementation process by taking life cases as the entry point. Cultivate students' digital and innovative thinking to make students more available to apply artificial intelligence to their lives, which can benefit the construction of artificial intelligence in a new era.
(3) With the help of graphical programming tools, open source hardware and other teaching tools, students can experience the construction of artificial intelligence modules, establish simple intelligent systems, and exercise their computational thinking in the process of hands-on practice.

Among them, in addition to the core content recommended in the "New Curriculum Standard", some textbooks also incorporate the characteristics and teaching requirements for students of the school period, and add other teaching content to enrich the content of the textbook. For example, in each volume of textbook D, a "career exploration" module is added to combine career education with subject education. While demonstrating the charm of the subject, it also provides a scientific reference direction for students' future employment [5].

3.2 Analysis of Textbook Style

The textbook style refers to the presentation form of the chapter content of the textbook [6]. In this report, it specifically refers to the chapter headings, contextual introduction materials and knowledge expansion [7]. In the textbook A-I, about 79% of the textbooks have chapter headlines, which mostly use general language to introduce the chapter learning content, or set up questions about life cases to make students start learning by thinking about questions. Among them, the textbooks B, F, and G are also set up with the section headings to propose the learning objectives of this section of the course to the students, and to clarify the learning points. The textbooks containing situational introduction materials accounted for 94% of the total. Based on the knowledge points in this section, through the description of common situations in life or starting from actual cases in life, students are more likely to start course learning in familiar situations. About 70% of the textbooks will set up a knowledge expansion module after the end of each course, most of which is the popularization of the technology and development of the frontier field of artificial intelligence. Some textbooks also add scientific knowledge to broaden the knowledge of students.

In addition, the research also found that: Textbooks B and D are equipped with "learning maps", which present the knowledge framework of chapters in the form of mind maps to help students sort out the chapter knowledge and make it convenient for students.

3.3 Analysis of Teaching Activities

In subject teaching, if students are properly organized, their learning will lead their development [8]. In other words, the teaching materials should not only teach subject knowledge, but also design various teaching activities to enable students understand and master the process of knowledge formation, from learning knowledge to cultivating ability, and training students to learn to analyze and solve problems. Summarizing the teaching activities of the textbook A-I, it can be found that most of the textbooks for each school stage are set up with teaching activities, accounting for about 97% of the total.

In the setting of teaching activities, the differences between the various stages are mainly reflected in the presentation form. According to the three major areas of teaching activity goals, this report divides the types of teaching activities into cognitive, skill and affective types [9]. The teaching activities of the textbook A-I are classified, and the results are shown in Table 3.

Table 3. Classification of teaching activities

Textbook	Cognitive	Skill	Affection
Textbook A (primary school)	Wonderful world (奇妙世界), Youxue U Music (优学U乐), Different "views" (knowledge expansion) (不同"视"界 (知识拓展))	Creation factory (造物工厂), Different "views" (knowledge expansion) (不同"视"界 (实践创新))	N/A
Textbook B (primary school)	Xiaozhi set sail (小智起航)	Experimental experience (实验体验), Expand application (拓展应用)	N/A
Textbook C (primary school)	Thinking (思考), expanding reading (拓展阅读)	Outreach activities (拓展活动)	N/A
Textbook D (primary school)	N/A	Extracurricular development (课外拓展), activities (活动)	N/A
Textbook E (primary school)	Spotlight (热点聚焦), Happy Rubik's Cube (快乐魔方), Life face to face (生活面对面), hyperlink (超级链接), Fangcao reading place (芳草阅读地)	N/A	Social Surfing (Teamwork) (社会大冲浪 (团队合作))
Textbook F (secondary school)	Take a look (看一看), Think about it (想一想), Talk about it (说一说), Do it (做一做), Further reading (拓展阅读), have a show (秀一秀)	N/A	Give it a try (debates, team practice) (试一试 (辩论会、团队实践))
Textbook G (secondary school)	Situational introduction (情境导入), Expanding issues (拓展性议题)	Practical experience (实践体验)	N/A
Textbook H (secondary school)	Practice and thinking (实践与思考)	N/A	N/A

It can be found from the table:

(1) Only textbooks E and F have sentimental activities. It can be seen that artificial intelligence textbooks for primary and secondary schools in China only use artificial intelligence as knowledge content to explain, and rarely carry out sentimental activities.
(2) The type of teaching activities is closely related to the school-oriented. The textbooks at the elementary level set up a variety of cognitive teaching activities and interesting and easy-to-operate skills activities, allowing students to stimulate

interest in artificial intelligence subjects and understand the basics of artificial intelligence in the process of interacting with agents. The teaching materials of the middle school stage are mainly based on cognitive teaching activities, guiding students to carry out exploratory learning that is supposed to clarify each problem.

3.4 Teaching Evaluation Design

The main purpose of teaching evaluation is to promote students' learning, improve teachers' teaching, and perfect the design of teaching programs [4]. After reading and analyzing the textbook A-I, the teaching evaluation in it is summarized and statistics, and the results are shown in Table 4.

Table 4. Teaching evaluation statistics table

School-oriented	Primary school	Junior high school	High school	Total
Number of textbooks with teaching evaluation	10	4	1	25
Total number of teaching materials	20	9	4	33
Percentage	50%	44%	25%	76%

It can be seen from the statistical data that: (1) About half of the textbooks at the elementary and junior high school stages have teaching evaluations, accounting for 50% and 44% respectively; (2) Most high school textbooks do not have a clear teaching evaluation system, and can only rely on teachers to set evaluation standards for each course based on the teaching content and teaching experience according to the situation.

Among the 25 textbooks with teaching activities, Textbook F gives an evaluation form which clearly provide a summary of all the knowledge points that needs to be mastered at the end of each course, and the students are supposed to evaluate them according to their grades. Textbook C and Textbook E set up a scoring table after each unit, but the evaluation methods are different: Through the design of "yes or not" judgment questions, textbook C allows students to understand the interrelationships in the process of human-computer interaction and master basic value judgments. Textbook E designs a unit evaluation form, combining self-evaluation and group evaluation to carry out teaching evaluation. The teaching material G revolves around the project, sets multiple tasks in each project, and closely integrates the link of teaching evaluation. In the project, through the design of the practice evaluation table, students are supposed to carry out self-evaluation on the mastery of the knowledge points with the project evaluation table every after each project, combining the three parts of self-evaluation, other evaluation, and teacher evaluation to complete diversified evaluation.

4 Discussions

Textbooks are essential materials for students to acquire subject knowledge and carry out subject learning, as well as an important basis for teachers to carry out classroom teaching [3]. This report conducts a comparative analysis of the main popular artificial intelligence textbooks in primary and secondary schools in China from the four aspects of teaching content, textbook style, teaching activity arrangement, and teaching evaluation design and discusses the analysis results from four aspects: the development of teaching activities, the preparation of unified curriculum standards, the construction of the teaching staff, and the establishment of a teaching evaluation system.

Based on the research of 33 mainstream artificial intelligence textbooks for primary and secondary schools, this report puts forward the following five suggestions:

(1) Most of the textbooks lack of attention to affective activities by only focusing on the development of cognitive and skill activities, and do not give full play to the moral education function of artificial intelligence education. It is necessary to take advantage of the moral education resources contained in the teaching process, carry out more affective activities such as teamwork, debate and competition, and actively create a healthy classroom learning atmosphere.

(2) Some textbooks only focus on the teaching of artificial intelligence subject knowledge, and seldom carry out practical innovation activities. The requirement of training talents in the new era is not only to cultivate talents who master subject knowledge, but more importantly, to cultivate students' learning ability. It is necessary to pay attention to the cultivation of students' information technology literacy, problem-solving ability and innovation ability.

(3) At present, the teaching of artificial intelligence subjects does not have a clear curriculum standard for all stages of compulsory education, which is reflected in the teaching materials is that different teaching materials have different emphasis on the selection of teaching content. Some textbooks attach importance to programming education and popularize the subject knowledge of artificial intelligence in programming; some textbooks attach importance to explaining the principles and implementation process of artificial intelligence technology; some textbooks combine artificial intelligence with life scenarios, focusing on enabling students learn how to Apply cutting-edge technology to life. The lack of guidance from programmatic documents not only makes it difficult to achieve consistency and continuity in teaching in different regions, but it is also more likely to be confused with other disciplines in the selection of core content, and mistakenly regard the part of artificial intelligence as a whole picture for teaching.

(4) A matching teaching team should be established so that the teaching materials can play a real role. Starting from the top-level design, a comprehensive and three-dimensional policy guarantee system should be established to cover all aspects of macro guidance, curriculum standards, teacher training, financial support, and social resource mobilization.

(5) A complete teaching evaluation system should be established. Combining multiple evaluation methods such as self-evaluation, other evaluation, group evaluation, and fusion of diagnostic evaluation, process evaluation, and summative evaluation [10] to build a complete teaching evaluation system with pre-class diagnosis, real-time supervision, and effectiveness testing.

5 Summary

The investigation of existing artificial intelligence textbooks in primary and secondary schools in mainland China is reported. A comparative analysis is carries out from the perspectives of teaching content, textbook style, teaching activity arrangement, and teaching evaluation design. Findings are presented and discussed to assist the development of artificial intelligence teaching materials for the artificial intelligence education in primary and secondary schools.

Acknowledgements. This work was supported by National Social Science Fund of China (AGA200016).

References

1. The State Council of the People's Republic of China: 2017-07-08. The State Council's notice on the issuance of a new generation of artificial intelligence development plans [EB/OL]. http://www.gov.cn/zhengce/content/2017-07/20/content_5211996.htm
2. Xinhuanet: 2021 Artificial Intelligence Education Conference for Primary and Secondary Schools [EB/OL] (2021) [2021-7-28]. https://news.ruc.edu.cn/archives/338452
3. Jointly compiled by twelve key normal universities across the country: Fundamentals of Education. Educational Science Press (2013)
4. Ministry of Education of the People's Republic of China: Standards for General High School Technical Curriculum (2017 Edition 2020 Revision). People's Education Press, Beijing (2020)
5. Ling, P.: Thoughts and explorations on the setting of vocational career education content in geography textbooks for middle schools. Curric. Textb. Teach. Method **36**(11), 85–90 (2016)
6. Chen, C.Y.: Comparative research on several comprehensive science textbooks of secondary vocational education in my country. Shanghai Normal University (2008)
7. Wang, D.L., Zhou, D.Q., Wang, Y.R., Yang, X.M.: A review of artificial intelligence textbooks in primary and secondary schools - based on an analysis of 45 published textbooks. Mod. Educ. Technol. **31**(02), 19–25 (2021)
8. Zhong, Q.Q.: An investigation of the theory of teaching activities. Educ. Res. (05), 36–42 +49 (2005)
9. Li, S.L.: The theoretical framework of teaching activity design - an analysis perspective of activity theory. Educ. Theory Pract. **31**(01), 54–57 (2011)
10. Liu, Y., Lu, Y.L.: Research on the blended teaching evaluation system based on learning communication. Ind. Technol. Forum **20**(11), 205–207 (2021)

Scholar-Course Knowledge Graph Construction Based on Graph Database Storage

Dongyang Zheng, Yongxu Long, Zekai Zhou, Wande Chen, Jianguo Li, and Yong Tang(✉)

School of Computer Science, South China Normal University, Guangzhou, China
{flash,longyongxu,2020022974,chenwande,
jianguoli,ytang}@m.scnu.edu.cn

Abstract. Knowledge graph is an effective way to model and represent complex linked data, which have attracted broad research in recent years and have been applied in different fields. Considering the data characteristics and development needs of course platform in SCHOLAT, Scholar-Course Knowledge Graph (SCKG) is built with scholars and courses as the core concept and integrated it into the next version of our course platform. The ontology structure of SCKG is constructed first and then extracted knowledge from different data sources by employing D2R technology, web crawlers, etc. so as to add them to SCKG. There are 110,856 entities and 1,674,961 pairs of relationships in total after the construction of SCKG. 13 b-tree indexes and 3 full-text indexes are created on some key properties to speed up the query and we also defined some constraints on SCKG to ensure data consistency.

Keywords: Knowledge graph construction · Knowledge acquisition · Knowledge storage · Neo4j

1 Introduction

Knowledge Graph (KG) is a technical method for describing knowledge and modeling the relationships between everything in the world using graphical models [1–3]. With the help of knowledge graph, it is possible to create links between concepts on top of entities, thus organizing information into the more structured knowledge [1,4]. The value of the knowledge graph is that it can change the existing information retrieval methods, which enables concept retrieval through inference as opposed to fuzzy string matching [2], and presents linked structured data graphically, making researchers to better understand information and the relationships between information. Since Google applied knowledge graph to search engine services in 2012 [3], KG has attracted widespread attention from

This work was supported in part by the National Natural Science Foundation of China under Grant U1811263 and Grant 61772211.

W. Jia et al. (Eds.): SETE 2021, LNCS 13089, pp. 448–459, 2021.
https://doi.org/10.1007/978-3-030-92836-0_40

academia to industry, and with the dive into knowledge graph research, KG has played an increasingly significant role in semantic search, intelligent Q&A, recommendation systems, aided big data analysis, and enhanced the interpretability of machine learning [1,4,11,14,30]. Various generic knowledge graphs and domain knowledge graphs are emerging rapidly such as Wikidata [5], Yago [6], GeneOnto [7] abroad and XLore [8], Zhishi.me [9], AliCoCo [10] in domestic. In view of the huge research value of KG, various technology companies and research institutions are accelerating to construct their knowledge graphs [1,2].

SCHOLAT[1] is a large comprehensive teaching and research collaboration platform, and its course platform has a huge amount of course information data. Faced with such a huge amount of data, there must be an efficient data organization method to model and represent it and knowledge graph is one exactly such technology. The construction of knowledge graph for our course platform can help to fully explore the potential information association and also can be used as the data foundation for many data analysis and data mining applications in the course platform, such as link prediction, prerequisite course determination, course recommendation, etc. Because of the natural intuitiveness of graph-based knowledge graphs, building an application system based on KG can enhance the interpretability of the system and thus improve the user's acceptance of the results given by such application, and also improve user's experience in terms of system transparency, trustworthiness, legibility, effectiveness and satisfaction [11]. In this paper, we extract entities, properties and relationship to construct domain knowledge graph for the course platform. After all information have been extracted we store them in Neo4j, one of the most popular graph database which is purpose-built to work with highly connected data, and created 16 indexes in total to speed up query.

2 Related Work

Many research works about the construction and application of Knowledge graph have been published in recent years. Liu et al. [1]introduced two ways of building knowledge graphs, top-down and bottom-up, and divided the construction of KG into three steps as information acquisition, knowledge fusion, and knowledge processing. Yang et al. [12] proposed a four-step approach for building domain knowledge graphs, namely domain ontology construction, crowdsourcing semi-automatic semantic annotation, exogenous data complementation, as well as information extraction and they took the construction of geographical knowledge graph as an example to describe the process of using the "four-step" method to build a domain knowledge graph. Buscald et al. [13] leveraged some state-of-the-art NLP models and text mining tools for extracting entities and relationships from Microsoft Academic Graph and built a knowledge graph of academic publications. MOOCCube [14], a data repository that integrated information about courses, student behavior, relationships, and external resources, which was built via extracting massive data from XuetangX[2]. It provided the

[1] https://www.scholat.com/.
[2] https://www.xuetangx.com/.

data foundation for course concept extraction, prerequisite course determination and course recommendation tasks. There are also some competitions based on MOOCCube, such as student dropout and answers correctness prediction which presented by Chain Dream[3].

Some researchers [15,16] has constructed course knowledge graph for MOOC, Table 1 below shows how SCKG compares to other similar jobs. However, their knowledge graphs were only course-centric and ignored students, which are the significant course study groups. Our knowledge graph for course platform is designed to focus on students(also called scholar in SCHOLAT) and courses as well so we named it Scholar-Course Knowledge Graph(SCKG), which brings a large number of learning behaviors (attendance, homework submission, etc.) and social relationships(follow, discussion, etc.) into it, making SCKG closer to the real situation and enriching its applications further. Not only the construction of Scholar-Course Knowledge Graph in this paper can serve our course platform, but also provide some reference for other researchers to develop similar study. Meanwhile, we will integrate SCKG into the development of course platform on next version after it was built so as to provide big data support for the new course platform while extracting more data from it to expand SCKG at the same time, making the course platform and SCKG flourish together.

Table 1. Comparison of SCKG with other similar researches.

Research	Major nodes	No. of relationships	Indexes	Storage	DataSources
HEKG [15]	Courses (481)	Unknown	–	MongoDB	Xuetangx
CKGWE [16]	Courses (1,225)	Unknown	–	RelationalDB	MOOC Wikipedia
SCKG	courses (1,207) students (36,219)	1,674,961	b-tree indexes (13) full-text indexes (3)	Neo4j	SCHOLAT BaiduScholar

3 Knowledge Graph Construction

In general, there are two ways to build a knowledge graph, top-down and bottom-up [2]. Top-down strategy firstly defines the data schema for knowledge graph from top-level concept, refines it down to a well-structured conceptual model gradually, and then adds entities to the concept. The schema represents the structure of nodes and relationships in database. This way is suitable for the construction of domain knowledge graphs with clear entity concepts usually. Bottom-up strategy analyzes and summarizes all involved entities and relationships to extract bottom concept, and then abstracts upward to form top-level concept gradually so as to generate the data schema for ontology construction. The construction of KG involves various techniques such as knowledge modeling, knowledge extraction, knowledge linking, graph storage and so forth [17].

[3] https://www.biendata.xyz/competition/chaindream_mooccube_task1/.

Most modern knowledge graphs are usually constructed by transforming existing structured data resources like relational database to form a basic knowledge set, then extend the knowledge graph from multiple data sources with automated knowledge extraction and knowledge graph complementation techniques, and finally further improving the quality of the knowledge graph through manual crowdsourcing.

SCKG is built in top-down method. We first construct the domain ontology of SCKG in ontology model software and then extract information from structured data (relational database of course platform, util April 15, 2021), semi-structured data (web pages) and unstructured data (raw text) with the help of Database-to-RDF (D2R) technology, web crawler and BiLSTM-CRF models respectively. After all data is extracted we form SCKG via refining them into entities and relationships in the form of RDF, and finally store it in Neo4j. Figure 1 illustrates the whole construction process of SCKG.

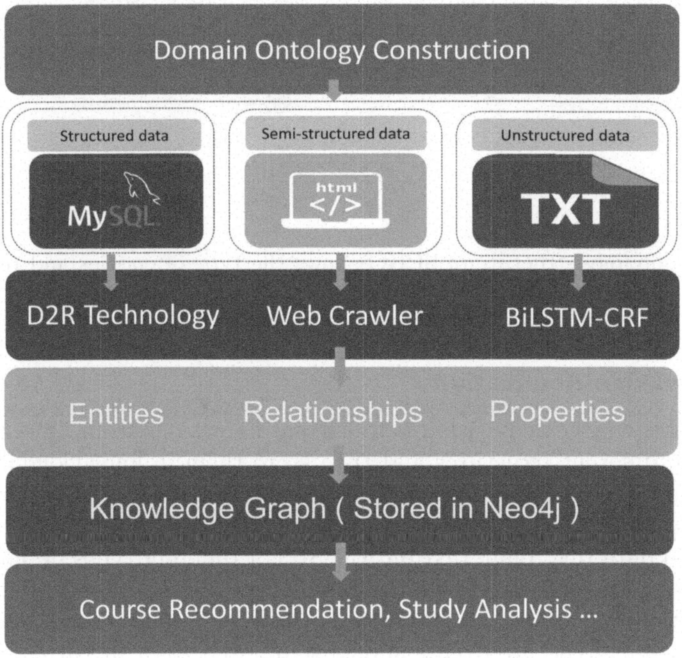

Fig. 1. The procedure of building SCKG in top-down way.

3.1 Domain Ontology Construction

Ontology structure can be understood as the basic framework of KG [12], which is equivalent to the table structure definition of a relational database. In order to define the data schema of SCKG, we first discuss in detail with the developers and users of the course platform to clarify the entity types, properties and relationship types of SCKG, and then construct the ontology. There are several tools available to accomplish this task such as protégé[4], Hozo[5], etc., and protégé is the one we chose. Figure 2 shows the conceptual of the ontology we build. After we accomplish the data schema entities properties and relationships are integrated to SCKG in strict accordance with the schema specification.

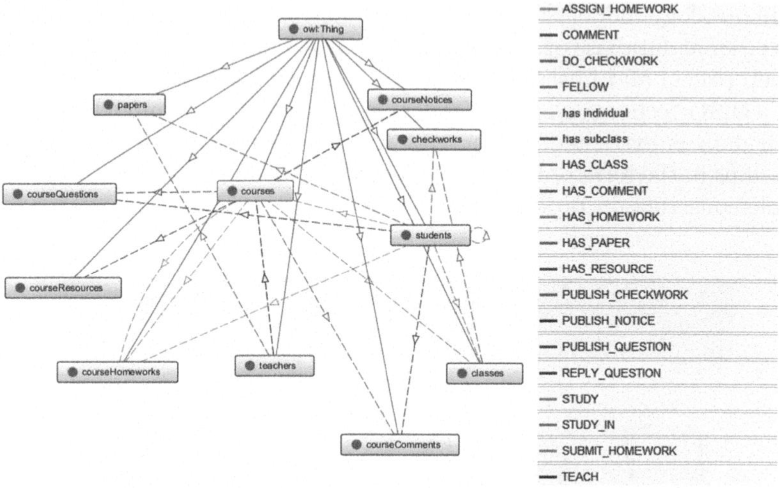

Fig. 2. The ontology structure of SCKG shows the type of entities and relationships in it.

3.2 Knowledge Acquisition

The aim of knowledge acquisition is to extract knowledge from different sources of data with different structures and then store them in knowledge graph. The data sources for knowledge extraction can be structured data (e.g. linked data, relational databases), semi-structured data (e.g. tables and lists in web pages) or unstructured data (e.g. plain text data) [18]. For different types of data sources, key technologies involved and technical difficulties needed to be solved in knowledge extraction may differ. The following section describes how we obtain structured data, semi-structured data and unstructured data in turn. In the data cleaning process, we remove some low-value data and test data with no effect. In terms of overall, SCKG contains 110,856 entities, 1,674,961 pairs of relationships, and the following figure is a brief view of the distribution of partial data in it for better understanding. Figure 3(a) shows the distribution of courses within a specific range of student numbers, Fig. 3(b) illustrates the number of students for different numbers of study courses, Fig. 3(c) depicts the distribution of the number of students whose homework submissions fall within a particular range.

[4] https://protege.stanford.edu/.
[5] http://www.hozo.jp/.

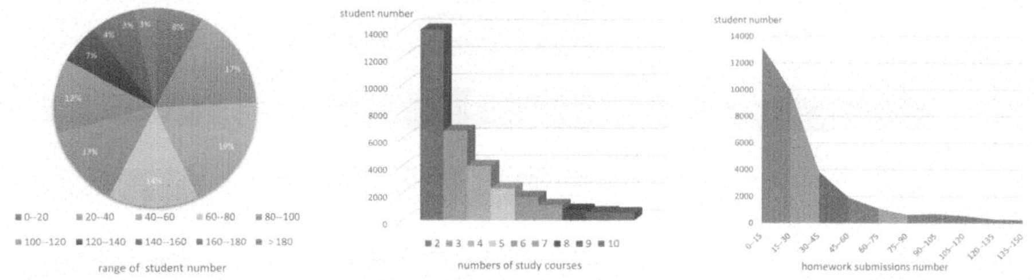

(a) (b) (c)

Fig. 3. Partial data distribution of SCKG. (a) shows courses distribution for different number of students, (b) illustrates number of students taking courses, (c) depicts student submission of homework.

Structured Data Processing. Structured databases such as relational databases are the main data source for the vast majority of knowledge in KG [19]. The existing structured databases usually cannot be used directly as knowledge graphs, so it is necessary to make semantic mapping between structured data and ontology models [20], and then realise the transformation of structured data to KG through semantic translation tools. In addition, a combination of data fusion, knowledge linking and other techniques are needed to improve the normalisation of data and enhance the association between data.

D2RQ[6], a powerful D2R tool, is used to achieve the transformation from relational data to RDF. Accessing relational databases as virtual RDF graphs is one of the most important features of D2RQ [21]. The mapping of it defined a virtual RDF graph that contained information from the database. This is similar to the concept of views in SQL, except that the virtual data structure is an RDF graph instead of a virtual relational table. Its mechanism can be outlined as a mapping file that translates operations such as queries on RDF into SQL statements, and ultimately implemented the corresponding operations on the relational database. Figure 4 shows the mapping structure of our relational database. d2rq:ClassMaps and d2rq:PropertyBridges are used to map database to RDF terms. ClassMaps, which represents a class or a group of similar classes of the ontology, are the most important objects within the mapping, class map specifies how URIs (or blank nodes) are generated for the instances of a class. It has a set of property bridges, which specify how the properties of an instance are created.

The key to transforming structured data into RDF is semantic mapping. Mapping language is used to define various rules for how data in relational database can be transformed into RDF data, specifically the generation of URIs, the definition of RDF classes and properties, the handling of blank nodes, and the expression of association relationships between data. We use D2RQ mapping language to transform data from relational databases to RDF graph. We use JDBC as a connection bridge between D2RQ and MySQL during the map-

[6] https://github.com/d2rq.

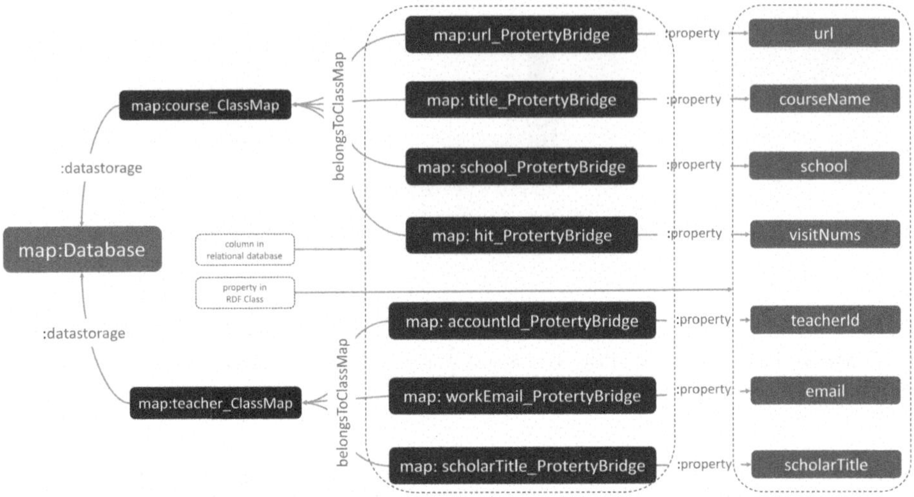

Fig. 4. Mapping structure for relational database to RDF

ping, the tables in the database are mapped to RDF classes, the columns in the database are mapped to RDF properties, and each row in the database is mapped to a entity, the value of each cell in the database is mapped to a literal value, if the value of a cell corresponds to a foreign key, it will be replaced by the IRI of the entity to which the foreign key value refers. The mapping can automatically generate a predefined mapping file based on relational database, and can also be modified by user to map data to their own ontology. After we complete the semantic mapping, dump-rdf tool is used to convert relational database into RDF graph.

Semi-Structured Data Processing. Semi-structured data is a special form of structured data that does not conform to the structure of a relational database or other form of data table, but contains tags or other markup to separate semantic elements and maintain a hierarchy of data fields [22]. With the booming development of Internet, semi-structured data is becoming more and more abundant and databases are no longer the only form of data, and semi-structured data has also become an important source of knowledge acquisition [5]. Currently, encyclopaedic data and web data are important semi-structured data that can be used for knowledge acquisition, web crawlers are the most common and effective way of acquiring semi-structured information. In the process of KG construction, it is common that the data of some nodes are not sufficient. In SCHOLAT, scholars can upload and display their academic papers, but part of scholars do not fill in their academic information fully, for example, when filling in the paper information, they just simply write the title and author of their paper, but not the keyword and abstract and other information, which leads to the lack of property data of the paper nodes in SCKG. We program web crawler to crawl the data from Baidu Scholar[7] to solve this problem. In short, the crawler carries the features of a paper such as title and author in HTTP request, and then parses the returned response body to get the information which we want. The original HTML document retrieved from Baidu Scholar contains very little data, and the rest data is presented after loading asynchronously, which leads to our crawler returning only the frame of the page without specific data in the response body. To solve this problem, we use HtmlUnit[8] to simulate the execution of JavaScript code to send asynchronous requests so as to get a page with complete information, and then extract useful information for our paper nodes such as keywords, abstract, DOI number through Xpath expressions and CSS selectors. The information is used to complement the properties of paper nodes, and the paper url in Baidu Scholar can also be used as the URI of the corresponding paper node.

Unstructured Data Processing. Named entity recognition(NER) technology, which aims to extract entity information elements from text, including names of people, organization names, geographic locations, time, etc. [23], to extract information from unstructured raw text. We build BiLSTM-CRF model [24,25], which had become the most dominant model in the current deep learning-based NER approaches and used it to accomplish the NER task. The model use a long shot-term memory neural network (LSTM) combined with CRF for named entity recognition. Formulas (1)–(6) describes the data flow calculation procedure of LSTM. Briefly, a LSTM cell is computed from the current network input value x_t, the previous moment LSTM output value h_{t-1}, and the previous moment cell state c_{t-1} to get the LSTM output value h_t and the current moment cell state c_t in current moment t. f_t, i_t and o_t denotes forget-gate, input-gate and output-gate respectively, and h_t are the final output at the current moment, where symbol W is the weight matrix, b denotes the bias term, $\sigma()$ and tanh() represents the activation function sigmoid and tanh, $\odot$ denotes the Hamiltonian product.

$$f_t = \sigma(W_f \cdot [h_{t-1}, x_t] + b_f) \tag{1}$$

$$i_t = \sigma(W_i \cdot [h_{t-1}, x_t] + b_i) \tag{2}$$

$$\tilde{c} = \tanh(W_c \cdot [h_{t-1}, x_t] + b_{\tilde{c}}) \tag{3}$$

$$c_t = c_{t-1} \odot f_t + \tilde{c} \odot i_t \tag{4}$$

$$o_t = \sigma(W_o \cdot [h_{t-1}, x_t] + b_o) \tag{5}$$

$$h_t = \tanh(c_t) \odot o_t \tag{6}$$

[7] https://xueshu.baidu.com/.
[8] https://github.com/HtmlUnit.

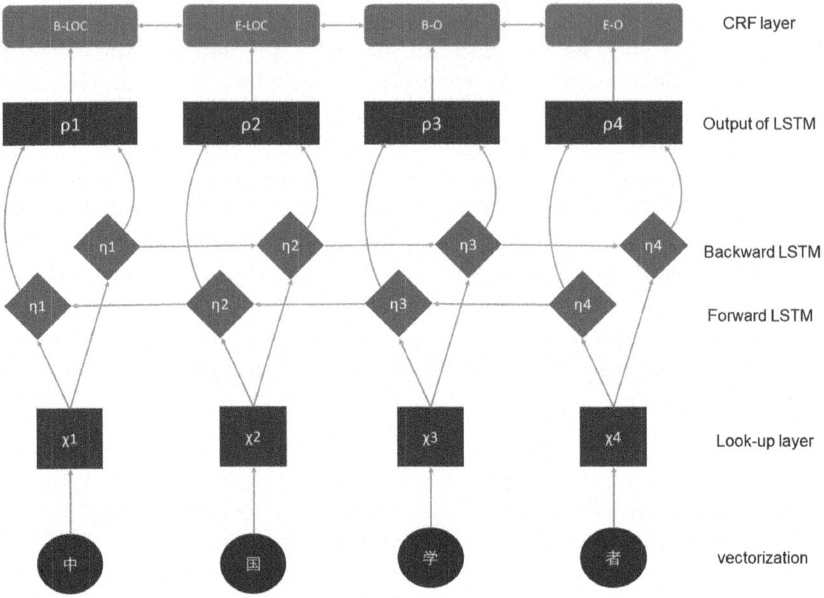

Fig. 5. The structure of BiLSTM-CRF model

The model shown in Fig. 5 is bottom-up with Embedding layer, bidirectional LSTM layer and CRF layer. Embedding layer represents words in the sentence as vectors, and we use the commonly used one-hot vectorization method to achieve vectorized representation of words as input to bidirectional LSTM. BiLSTM layer takes char embedding sequence of each word of a sentence as input for every time step, and then join implicit state sequence of forward LSTM output with implicit state of backward LSTM output at each position to obtain full implicit state sequence, subsequently calculate the vectors corresponding to each word by considering the left and right words, finally join two vectors of each word to form the vector output of word. The CRF layer takes the vector output from bidirectional LSTM as input and performs sequence tagging on named entities in the sentence. The final output of model shown in formula (7) is the result of the probabilistic scoring function, where $X = (x_1, x_2, ..., x_n)$ represents word vector generated from input sentence, and $Y = (y_1, y_2, ..., y_n)$ denotes the output label after prediction. We employ this model in our NER task, after it was built and trained, the test accuracy can up to 88.6%.

$$S(X,Y) = \sum_{i=0}^{n} A_{y_i y_{i+1}} + \sum_{i=0}^{n} P_{i,yi} \tag{7}$$

4 The Storage of SCKG

In terms of data model, there are RDF graph model and property graph model for graph databases generally [26]. The former is compatible with traditional structured data storage and has good commonality, but suffers from low query performance when facing large-scale KGs; the latter has built-in support for vertex properties and edge attributes as well as rich query language support, and is the most widely adopted data model for graph databases. Neo4j[9], the most popular graph database products currently [27], which owns a very active community. Neo4j is based on the property graph model, and its storage management layer designs a targeted storage scheme for nodes, node attributes, edge and edge attributes [28], making it much more efficient than relational database in accessing graph data at the storage layer.

Considering the above advantages of Neo4j, the RDF data exported from relational databases was stored in it, which is shown in Fig. 6. Native Neo4j does not support importing RDF data, we use NeoSemantic[10] tool to achieve this goal. With it, we can use Cypher(a query language of graph) to import RDF data into Neo4j and store it as a graph. Since Neo4j is developed in Java, it can be integrated with Java naturally. For example, we can use “`"MATCH(teacher:teachers)-[relation1:TEACH]->(course:courses)<-[relation2:STUDY]-(student:students) WHERE teacher.teacherName = '汤庸' Return student`” to find out all the students who have taken the courses taught by Professor Tang, and then use returned results for subsequent processing in Java. In order to make better use of graph algorithms in SCKG and speed up queries, b-tree indexes on some key properties were created, we also created full-text indexes to tokenize the string values, so it can match terms anywhere within the strings properties of nodes, which allows us to retrieve text properties more quickly.

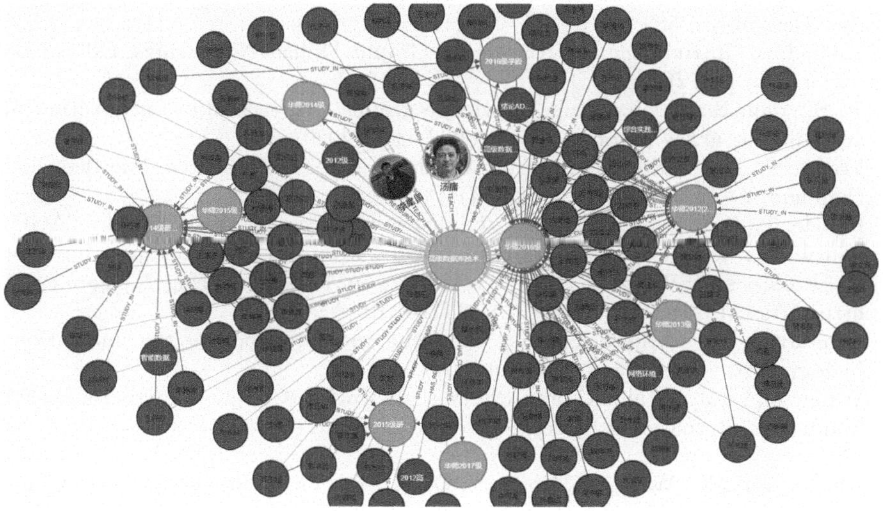

Fig. 6. SCKG stored in Neo4j, different colors for different types of nodes and relationships

[9] https://neo4j.com/.
[10] https://github.com/neo4j-labs/neosemantics.

5 Conclusions

In this paper, we build the scholar-course knowledge graph with relational data as the main source and the rest semi-structured and unstructured data as the supplement. Different processing techniques were used for different types of data sources, such as D2R, web crawlers, and BiLSTM-CRF deep learning models. The article describes in detail the whole process of SCKG's construction from ontology construction, knowledge acquisition to knowledge storage.

SCKG is rich in terms of data volume relatively, but there is still room for improvement. Our course platform generates a large amount of data every day, such as course information data and user behavior data. In next step, we will dedicate to update the new data generated by the course platform to SCKG in real time automatically, so that it can play a greater value in the big data analysis and application of the course platform. SCKG not only includes course information but also rich information about scholars and social relationships, which is what makes it different from other similar work, and in the future we will use these rich data to develop more practical applications, such as intelligent question and answer system, student learning behavior analysis, course recommendation, etc.

References

1. Li, J., Hou, L.: Review on knowledge graph research. J. Shanxi Univ. (Nat. Sci. Edn.) 454–459 (2017)
2. Liu, Q., Yang, L., et al.: Knowledge graph construction techniques. J. Comput. Res. Dev. **53**(3), 582 (2016)
3. Singhal, A.: Introducing the Knowledge Graph: Things, Not Strings, Official Blog (of Google) (2012)
4. Ji, S., Pan, S.: A survey on knowledge graphs: representation, acquisition and applications. arXiv preprint arXiv:2002.00388 (2020)
5. Vrandecic, D., Markus, K., et al.: Wikidata: a free collaborative knowledgebase. Commun. ACM **57**(10), 78–85 (2014)
6. Rebele, T., Suchanek, F., Hoffart, J., Biega, J., Kuzey, E., Weikum, G.: YAGO: a multilingual knowledge base from Wikipedia, wordnet, and geonames. In: Groth, P., et al. (eds.) ISWC 2016. LNCS, vol. 9982, pp. 177–185. Springer, Cham (2016). https://doi.org/10.1007/978-3-319-46547-0_19
7. Ashburner, M., Catherine, A., et al.: Gene ontology: tool for the unification of biology. Nat. Genet. **25**(1), 25–29 (2000)
8. Wang, Z., Li, J., et al.: XLore: a large-scale English-Chinese bilingual knowledge graph. In: International Semantic Web Conference (Posters & Demos), vol. 1035 (2013)
9. Niu, X., Sun, X., Wang, H., Rong, S., Qi, G., Yu, Y.: Zhishi.me - weaving Chinese linking open data. In: Aroyo, L., et al. (eds.) ISWC 2011. LNCS, vol. 7032, pp. 205–220. Springer, Heidelberg (2011). https://doi.org/10.1007/978-3-642-25093-4_14
10. Luo, X., Liu, L., et al.: AliCoCo: alibaba e-commerce cognitive concept net. In: Proceedings of the 2020 ACM SIGMOD International Conference on Management of Data (2020)

11. Huang, L., Jiang, B., et al.: Survey on deep learning based recommender systems. Chin. J. Comput. **41**(7), 1619–1647 (2018)
12. Yang, Y., Xu, B., et al.: Accurate and efficient method for constructing domain knowledge graph. J. Softw. **29**(10), 2931–2947 (2018)
13. Buscaldi, D., Dessì, D., Motta, E., Osborne, F., Reforgiato Recupero, D.: Mining scholarly publications for scientific knowledge graph construction. In: Hitzler, P., et al. (eds.) ESWC 2019. LNCS, vol. 11762, pp. 8–12. Springer, Cham (2019). https://doi.org/10.1007/978-3-030-32327-1_2
14. Yu, J., Luo, G., et al.: MOOCCube: a large-scale data repository for NLP applications in MOOCs. In: Proceedings of the 58th Annual Meeting of the Association for Computational Linguistics (2020)
15. Hou, J.: Constructing higher education knowledge graph for MOOC using data mining methods. Beijing University of Posts and Telecommunications (2017)
16. Huang, C.: Research on the method of extracting course knowledge graph for wisdom education. Harbin Institute of Technology (2020)
17. Zhao, Z., Han, S., et al.: Architecture of knowledge graph construction techniques. Int. J. Pure Appl. Math. **118**(19), 1869–1883 (2018)
18. Aidan, H., Michael, C., et al.: Knowledge graphs. arXiv preprint arXiv:2003.02320 (2020)
19. Yan, J., Wang, C., Cheng, W., Gao, M., Zhou, A.: A retrospective of knowledge graphs. Front. Comp. Sci. **12**(1), 55–74 (2018). https://doi.org/10.1007/s11704-016-5228-9
20. Bizer, C.: D2R map-a database to RDF mapping language (2003)
21. Bizer, C., Seaborne, A.: D2RQ-treating non-RDF databases as virtual RDF graphs. In: Proceedings of the 3rd International Semantic Web Conference (ISWC2004), Proceedings of ISWC2004, vol. 2004 (2004)
22. Lin, Y., Zhou, J., et al.: A method of extracting the semi-structured data implication rules. Proc. Comput. Sci. **131**, 706–716 (2018)
23. Goyal, A., Gupta, V.: Recent named entity recognition and classification techniques: a systematic review. Comput. Sci. Rev. **29**, 21–43 (2018)
24. Huang, Z., Xu, W., et al.: Bidirectional LSTM-CRF models for sequence tagging [J/OL]. CoRR, abs/1508.01991 (2015). http://arxiv.org/abs/1508.01991
25. Lample, G., Ballesteros, M., et al.: Neural architectures for named entity recognition In: Proceedings of the 2016 Conference of the North American Chapter of the Association for Computational Linguistics, pp. 260–270 (2016)
26. Wang, X., Zou, L., et al.: Research on knowledge graph data management: a survey. J. Softw. **30**(7), 2140 (2019)
27. Fernandes, D., Bernardino, J.: Graph databases comparison: AllegroGraph, ArangoDB, InfiniteGraph, Neo4J, and OrientDB. DATA 373–380 (2018)
28. Baton, J., Van Bruggen, R.: Learning Neo4j 3. x: Effective Data Modeling, Performance Tuning and Data Visualization Techniques in Neo4j. Packt Publishing Ltd. (2017)
29. Guo, Q., Zhuang, F., et al.: A survey on knowledge graph-based recommender systems. IEEE Trans. Knowl. Data Eng. (2020)
30. Lal, M.: Neo4j Graph Data Modeling. Packt Publishing Ltd. (2015)

Game-Based Learning Models for Building Chinese College Students' Disciplinary English Literacy in Mathematics

Nana Jin[1], Zili Chen[2], and Chenxu Tian[3](✉)

[1] School of Foreign Languages, Shenzhen University, Shenzhen, China
[2] Division of Languages and Communication, The College of Professional and Continuing Education, The Hong Kong Polytechnic University, Hong Kong, China
val.chen@cpce-polyu.edu.hk
[3] Department of Foreign Languages, Bozhou University, Bozhou, Anhui, China

Abstract. This study focuses on designing a game-based learning model for disciplinary English in mathematics, and it is exclusively designed for college students learning English as a second language. Disciplinary literacy is highly related to disciplinary knowledge, and usually they develop side by side for a native speaker. For Chinese college students, their disciplinary English literacy has not developed due to the lack of disciplinary language training in high school and college. This research takes mathematics as an example, analyzing the linguistic features of this discipline, and furthermore designs a game-based and mobile-assisted learning model. Four mobile Apps are used in the model for various learning purposes: *Quizlet*, *Padlet*, *Edpuzzle* and *Kahoot*. Disciplinary English learning could be monotonous, but the engaging learning model moves students' attention from disciplinary English learning to solving disciplinary questions. The feedback from our pretest shows that the game-based learning model helps students maintain interests and curiosity in developing disciplinary English literacy.

Keywords: Disciplinary English literacy · Game-based learning models · Chinese college students · Mathematics

1 Introduction

Disciplinary literacy here refers to the reading and writing abilities in the fields of various disciplines, such as mathematics, science, biology, history, chemistry. In view of recent 40 years of China's tertiary education history and the reality that college graduates confront literacy difficulties in their first jobs due to disciplinary barriers, it is a necessity to offer students multiple disciplinary knowledge in tertiary education. Education policies on knowledge fusing were released [1], for example in the advocate of the construction of New Liberal Arts. The New Liberal Arts construction requires universities and colleges to enlarge the number of science and technology related courses for students of arts, which leads to a new demand for disciplinary literacy.

W. Jia et al. (Eds.): SETE 2021, LNCS 13089, pp. 460–468, 2021.
https://doi.org/10.1007/978-3-030-92836-0_41

With the current social environment and market needs, universities and colleges are encouraged to break down the barriers of disciplines in hope to promote a deep integration of liberal arts majors, and an integration of liberal arts with science, engineering, agriculture, and medicine, with the goal of integrating modern information technology to empower liberal arts education [2]. For English education, the challenges are no different. With a gradual popularization of English education, people's awareness of learning English continues to increase. Many entrepreneurs or managers have mastered English to a high level and no longer need specialized English translators to help them. The market demand for purely language and literature graduates is gradually decreasing. Therefore, a change in teaching is on the way and this research aims to design joyful and game-based learning models to build language students' disciplinary literacy. Once language students are equipped with various basic disciplinary knowledge, they will be able to perform discipline-related tasks more effectively and efficiently at workplace.

2 Methodology

Before we go further in this study, there are two key concepts to be clarified: disciplinary English literacy, and game-based learning models. First, this study focuses on building Chinese college students' English disciplinary literacy. Since the construction of the New Liberal Arts has new demand for current tertiary education, the previous teaching syllabuses need to be revamped. Universities and colleges in China are required to change and rearrange current majors and disciplines, to rewrite syllabuses and to design more suitable courses. Take English major at Shenzhen University as an example, the new course *Disciplinary English Reading* was born within this background, and its predecessor course was called *English Reading*, which was one of the elective courses for English majors. The aim of this new course is to enable English major students to understand how basic knowledge of various disciplines is conveyed in English. The basic knowledge of various disciplines is not 'new' to college students, because they already mastered it at high school. However, when they were learning the disciplinary knowledge in high school, they learned it in Chinese and the knowledge now is stored in their mind in Chinese as well. What we need to do now and here is to help students switch the code from Chinese to English and 'activate' the same disciplinary knowledge expressed in English. That is to say, students are not supposed to learn new disciplinary knowledge in this course, but to learn how the familiar disciplinary knowledge is expressed in English. This is not an easy job, since the lack of the disciplinary English literacy education exists all the way from public primary school to high school in China. Students in public schools are used to thinking in Chinese, and they do not have the English vocabulary for various disciplines, let alone the featured sentence patterns in each discipline. In fact, a sophomore English major student who can read Shakespeare in English class might not be able to master the English expressions in basic algebra books. Even for English native students, disciplinary literacy does not naturally develop side by side with their basic literacy [3, 4]. Disciplinary literacy development stands always at the top of one's literacy pyramid, and students need to go through a disciplinary training to develop this literacy. Shanahan &

Shanahan [5] drew the pyramid shown in Fig. 1 to illustrate how the development of literacy progresses. As they claimed, "the base of the pyramid represents the highly generalizable basic skills that are entailed in all or most reading tasks… Basic Literacy: literacy skills such as decoding and knowledge of high-frequency words that underlie virtually all reading tasks. Intermediate Literacy: literacy skills common to many tasks, including generic comprehension strategies, common word meanings, and basic fluency. Disciplinary Literacy: literacy skills specialized to history, science, mathematics, literature, or other subject matter".

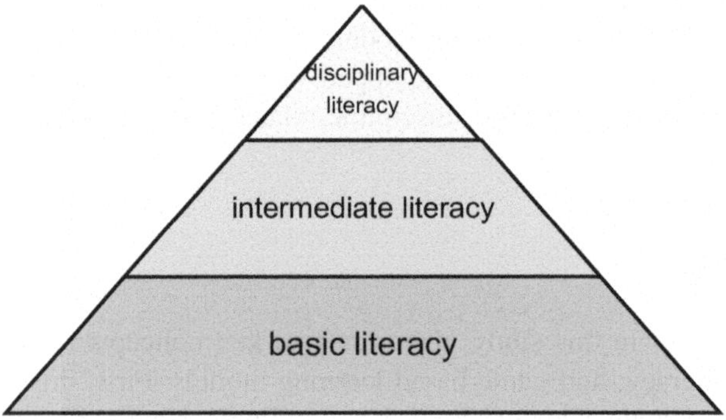

Fig. 1. The increasing specialization of literacy development

What Fig. 1 shows is native language students' literacy development. For English as a second language (hereinafter L2) college students, the English literacy development is another picture, as shown in Fig. 2. L2 college students' English literacy develops slowly and unevenly due to a lack of cognitive language environment. Currently in China, most of college students have no problem in English daily conversation and reading simple story books (but still have difficulties in stories embedded with historical events, regional customs and cultural events), some of them could develop the English literacy of intermediate arts and literature, but very few of them could reach the top of the pyramid: English literacy of science disciplines.

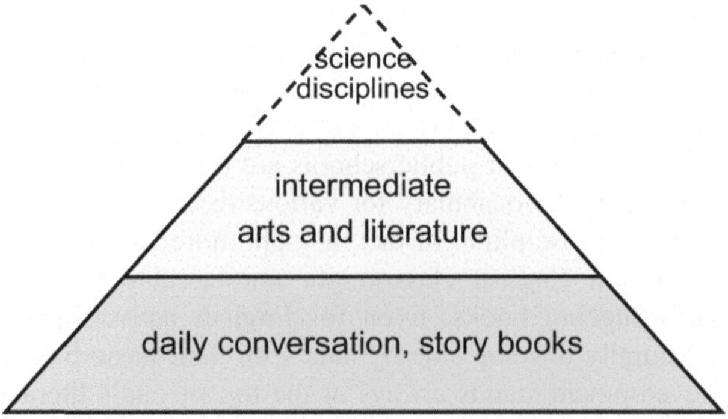

Fig. 2. A hierarchy illustration of English literacy for non-English college students in China

Since L2 college students' disciplinary literacy has not been developed under the current teaching syllabus, how to improve the situation and build their English disciplinary literacy is one of the focuses in this study. This is a breakthrough for language related major students, though there are similar teaching trials at some colleges, especially at technology universities. For students of certain majors such as Information Technology, Computer Science, Economics, International Law, their disciplinary English literacy is built through *Professional English* Courses. However, their disciplinary English literacy is usually limited within one discipline – their own major. What we are trying to develop here is the English literacy across multiple disciplines at basic levels.

Second, to prompt students' curiosity of disciplinary knowledge in English, game-based learning models are supposed to be desirable [6–8]. We will focus on building the linkage from Chinese to English toward basic disciplinary knowledge, instead of introducing or explaining complicated and advanced disciplinary knowledge. Since knowledge learning is not the focus, how to design game-based and joyful learning models for the new course *English Disciplinary Reading* is the key to the success of the new course and the teaching reform. There are numerous educational Apps in use to make teaching and learning more fun and joyful, such as *Padlet, Quizlet, Kahoot, Edpuzzle,* etc. Mobile-assisted learning models are well received among students too [9]. To design a suitable learning model for disciplinary literacy, it is a must to consider each discipline's linguistic characteristics.

3 Linguistic Features Analysis of Mathematics

As we all know, language usage varies on different occasions. Teaching language is different from daily language, and the vocabulary in literature is different from the vocabulary in mathematics, history, geography, etc. [10]. What are the linguistic features of each discipline? This study takes mathematics as an example to explore its linguistic features, and furthermore designs suitable learning models for this discipline.

Example 1. *Add 5 to the product of 4 and 6.*

Example 2. *To reduce a fraction, we can divide both its numerator and denominator by their common factor. After reducing a fraction, the value of the fraction is unchanged.*

Example 3. *In the figure, a square paper with side 8 cm is put inside a square frame with side x cm. Suppose the area of the frame is A cm^2. Write down the formula for calculating the area (A) of the frame.*

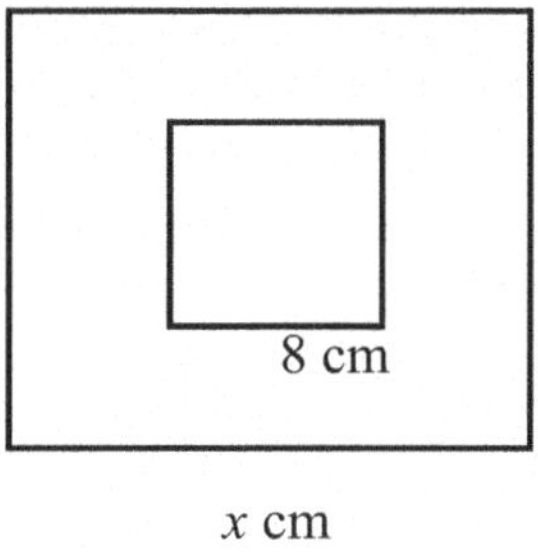

Examples 1, 2, and 3 are from mathematics books, and they are ranging from the simplest calculation level to a more difficult level of algebra. The disciplinary knowledge here is at three different levels respectively: basic arithmetic operation, fraction, and algebraic operation. For L2 college students, the disciplinary knowledge involved here is not a problem, but almost no students would understand what these three examples mean. They tried hard to translate these sentences with the strategies that they learned in literature reading, but in vain. In Example 1, there isn't any new word, but students misunderstood the word 'product' for 'commodities offered for sale'. In their previous English literature study, they've never read such a sentence in English literature books, and thus couldn't understand that the word 'product' refers to 'the result of multiplication'. A common word 'product' in daily English could have a specific and very different referential meaning in mathematics. In Example 2, there are two kinds of literacy difficulties for students: one is similar to the previous case, a common word with special referential meaning in mathematics – 'common factor'; another kind of difficulty rests on exclusive words and phrases in mathematics that L2 college students have not learned – 'fraction', 'numerator', 'denominator', 'reduce a fraction'. Example 3 is more difficult than Example 2 in terms of disciplinary knowledge, since Example 3 involves algebraic operation and is more abstract. But both Example 2 and Example 3 are at the same level to L2 college students in terms of English language comprehension. Once students understand the mathematic expression 'a square with side 8 cm', they will have no difficulty in working out the operation in Example 3. Based on the analyses of mathematic disciplinary English, a summary of linguistic features of mathematics is shown in Table 1.

Table 1. A brief summary of linguistic features in mathematics

No.	Types of linguistic features	Examples
1	Common words and phrases with special referential meaning	*Product, difference, factor, term, operation*
2	Exclusive words and phrases	*Fraction, decimal, numerator, denominator, arithmetic sequence, geometric sequence*
3	Exclusive expressions	*Reduce a fraction, expand a fraction,*
4	Abbreviations	*H.C.F., L.C.M.*

Besides the linguistic features that L2 college students should pay attention to, there are other reading strategies as well in building disciplinary mathematics literacy. Examples 4, 5, and 6 are word phrases for algebraic expressions.

Example 4. *Subtract a from b and then divide the difference by 2.*

Example 5. *a minus b and then divide the difference by 2.*

Example 6. *Divide the product of a and b by 2.*

The word phrases in Examples 4, 5, and 6 are similar. With a quick glance on 'subtract' and 'minus' in Examples 4 and 5, it is likely to be assumed that they refer to the same algebraic expression: $\frac{a-b}{2}$. They refer to different algebraic expressions respectively: $\frac{b-a}{2}$, $\frac{a-b}{2}$, $\frac{ab}{2}$. Although 'subtract' means the same as 'minus', 'subtract a from b' is contrary to 'a minus b'. This might be clear to native speakers, but it will pose a language trick to L2 students. Thus, building disciplinary English in mathematics requires one to be very careful with words and extremely precise in logic, which indicates that one needs to reread some words and phrases in one sentence to guarantee a right understanding. Furthermore, these examples also tell us that one algebraic expression may have more than one word phrase, and thus L2 college students are supposed to master various kinds of word phrases toward an algebraic expression.

4 Course Design Experiment and Results

To design a suitable teaching plan for the new course *Disciplinary English Reading,* we conducted a case study to observe the efficiency of two different teaching models for mathematics, shown in Table 2.

Table 2. A comparison of two different teaching models of building disciplinary literacy

	Student A	Student B
Teaching step 1	Give the student a list of vocabulary with Chinese translation and require the student to memorize the words and their Chinese translation	Use the mobile App *Quizlet* for the student to learn the mathematics vocabulary. (*Quizlet* contains various vocabulary exercises and games, such as flash cards, words match, group competition)
Teaching step 2	Give the student an English article in mathematics and ask her to translate it; give the student the word dictation to check whether she has mastered the vocabulary	Use the App *Padlet* to ask the student to finish a worksheet. (*Padlet* allows students to see each other's progress and self-check their own answers)
Teaching step 3	Play an English video clip of related disciplinary knowledge and help the student get information input from various media	Use the App *Edpuzzle* in an English video clip of related disciplinary knowledge. (*Edpuzzle* will pop out questions at any designed time in the course of video playing and thus ongoingly check whether students understand the content)
Teaching step 4	Give the student a quiz, mainly focusing on reading comprehension and translating the mathematic expressions	Use the App *Kahoot* to give the student quizzes while competing with the teacher. (*Kahoot* is good at organizing quizzes in a competing mode)
Students' feedbacks	Vocabulary learning is difficult and one easily gets bored. Translating work is challenging, but one gets a little satisfaction after translating it. Not much interest in further studying the discipline	Vocabulary learning is difficult but fun and efficient with *Quizlet* App. Finishing English worksheets in *Padlet* App makes oneself satisfied not only with disciplinary English literacy, but also disciplinary knowledge. A video clip playing with *Edpuzzle* App keeps one's attention from distracting. The most fun part is *Kahoot* App used to compete with others as everyone is eager to win a game

In Table 2, Student A received a traditional learning model, which is quite similar to the way of learning English literature, while Student B, on the contrary, was given a game-based learning model. Both of them were given the same vocabulary and the same disciplinary English article, and the only difference is learning models. Considering the special linguistic features of mathematics English, we began with vocabulary learning, and then passage reading, video clip watching and a quiz. As students' feedback shown in Table 2, a game-based and mobile-assisted learning model was more attractive and made the learning more efficient. When the student was given worksheets to finish at *Quizlet* and *Padlet*, she was dealing with two tasks of disciplinary language and disciplinary knowledge sequentially. For these two tasks, the disciplinary questions in a worksheet attracted her more, since the disciplinary knowledge involved was not a big challenge. Once she understood the disciplinary language correctly, she quickly moved her attention to the mathematic content and tried to solve the questions. When she figured out the correct answers, she had a satisfaction of acquiring both disciplinary language and disciplinary knowledge, which helped maintain interests and curiosity toward the disciplinary literacy. It is observed that a game-based and joyful learning model is a better and more efficient way to help students build a bilingual literacy toward a disciplinary knowledge by putting the emphasis on question solution instead of language learning only. Some snapshots of the vocabulary learning models are shown in Figs. 3 and 4. Example 7 is part of a sample worksheet for basic mixed operations. All 5 questions are quite similar, which require students to read them carefully and be precise in operation.

Fig. 3. Bilingual flash cards of mathematic vocabulary in *Quizlet* app

Fig. 4. Mathematic vocabulary games in *Quizlet* app

Example 7.
Write the algebraic expressions of the following word phrases and find the value. (a = 6, b = 2 c = 3).

i. *a times the sum of b and c.*
ii. *Subtract the product of a and b from c.*
iii. *Multiply a by b and then add c to the result.*
iv. *Divide the square of a by the product of b and c.*
v. *Add b to a and then subtract c from the sum.*
*(**Keys**: i. a(b + c) = 30; ii. C – ab = −9; iii. Ab + c = 15; iv. $a^2 \div bc = 6$; v. a + b – c = 5).*

5 Conclusion

Disciplinary English literacy does not develop simultaneously with one's English literacy development. It requires an exclusive training for each discipline. For Chinese college students, basic disciplinary knowledge poses no challenge, and thus the emphasis of their learning models should focus on linguistic features of English disciplines. Traditional disciplinary language learning can be tedious and thus this study designed a game-based and mobile-assisted learning model based on linguistic features of mathematics. Based on the analyses results of the linguistic features of mathematics, four mobile Apps *Quizlet*, *Padlet*, *Edpuzzle,* and *Kahoot* were used for different learning purposes in the learning model. In comparison with a traditional learning model, the game-based and joyful learning model helps students maintain their curiosity of disciplinary English literacy and receive more learning satisfaction. This learning model is customized for learning disciplinary English in mathematics to suit mathematics' linguistic features. Its suitability for learning other disciplinary literacy needs to be further studied.

Acknowledgement. This study is supported by the 2018 Anhui Province University Outstanding Young Talents Support Program Key Project (gxyqZD2018086), China.

References

1. CCTV news website. http://news.cctv.com/2019/02/26/ARTIlnODaBP6AQFFV8AKcrRp190226.shtml. Accessed 25 Aug 2021
2. Research Institute of Higher Education Website. http://gjs.njit.edu.cn/info/1064/1599.htm. Accessed 25 Aug 2021
3. Fang, Z.H.: Language correlates of disciplinary literacy. Top Lang Disord. **32**(1), 19–34 (2012)
4. Howell, E., Barlow, W., Dyches, J.: Disciplinary literacy: successes and challenges of professional development. J. Lang. Lit. Educ. **17**(1), 1–26 (2021)
5. Shanahan, T., Shanahan, C.: Teaching disciplinary literacy to adolescents: rethinking content-area literacy. Harv. Educ. Rev. **78**(1), 40–59 (2008)

6. Zou, D., Wang, F.L., Xie, H., Kohnke, L.: Game-based vocabulary learning in China and Hong Kong: students' evaluation of different word learning APPs. In: Cheung, S., Lam, J., Li, K., Au, O., Ma, W., Ho, W. (eds.) ICTE 2018. Communications in Computer and Information Science, vol. 843, pp. 44–55. Springer, Singapore (2018). https://doi.org/10.1007/978-981-13-0008-0_5
7. Zou, D., Xie, H.R.: Personalized word-learning based on technique feature analysis and learning analytics. J. Educ. Technol. Soc. **21**(2), 233–244 (2018)
8. Kim, D., et al.: Mobile assisted language learning experiences. Int. J. Mob. Blended Learn. **9** (1), 49–60 (2017)
9. Hsu, C.K., Hwang, G.J., Chang, C.K.: A personalized recommendation-based mobile learning approach to improving the reading performance of EFL students. Comput. Educ. **63** (1), 327–336 (2013)
10. Shreiner, T.L., David, E.Z.: It's just different: identifying features of disciplinary literacy unique to world history. Hist. Teach. **53**(3), 441–469 (2020)

The Effect Analysis of Mind Mapping Technique on Chinese EFL Undergraduates' Writing Skills

Meng-lian Liu(✉)

Laboratory of Language and Artificial Intelligence, Guangdong University of Foreign Studies, Guangzhou 510420, China
Lmenglian@gdufs.edu.cn

Abstract. The purpose of this research was to examine the effect of employing mind mapping as a pre-writing strategy on English as a Foreign Language (EFL) students to generate better writing essays. Non-equivalent groups pre- and posttest design was used in this study. A questionnaire is also carried out to get the writing attitude of the participants'. Two classes (A and B) participated the experience in College English Reading and Writing. Both groups had the same teacher. The control group received instruction as required in the textbook only, and the experimental group were additionally required to construct mind maps at the pre-writing stage and compose essays based on the constructed maps. All participants were required to have pre- and post-tests to track their writing performance before and after the experimental group took a tutorial on how to create mind maps. After the implementation of the intervention, comparison of the students' mean scores of the pre- and post-tests showed a statistically significant improvement in the experimental students' ability to generate better argumentative essays in terms of point of view, unity and coherence, development, organization, and thinking. The results highlight the effectiveness of employing min mapping as a focused instructional strategy at the pre-writing stage in developing EFL students' writing skill. Pedagogical implications for using mind mapping in EFL writing classes are considered.

Keywords: Mind mapping · EFL · Learning effect · Learning analysis · Pre-writing

1 Introduction

Writing is the act or process of one who writes, such as the act or art of forming visible letters or characters, or something written, such as letters or characters that serve as visible signs of ideas, words, or symbols et al. [1]. This means writing is both a product and a process. Nunan [2] thinks that EFL writing is an extremely complex cognitive activity in which the writer is required to demonstrate control of variables simultaneously. At the sentence level, these include control of contents, format, sentence structure, vocabulary, spelling and letter formation. Beyond the sentence, the writer must be able to structure and integrate information into cohesive and coherent paragraph and text. So, EFL writing is a demanding cognitive process. There is more to this

W. Jia et al. (Eds.): SETE 2021, LNCS 13089, pp. 469–478, 2021.
https://doi.org/10.1007/978-3-030-92836-0_42

process than just putting language units together. It requires a lot of preparation, brainstorming, planning, drafting, editing, and modifying [3]. The writing processes of planning, thinking, and organizing are just as important as the final product. This stresses the need for dealing with writing as a process rather than as a product [4]. Actually, writing difficulties arise when the writer is trying to gather ideas on a particular subject. Problems in strategic issues such as the process of organizing ideas, the ability to generate and organize relevant important ideas (whether the prose is grammatically correct or not), the use of correct punctuation tools, the accurate spelling of what is written, and some rhetorical and linguistic tasks in drafting, are all dependent on writing skills [5]. Usually, the process of writing can be divided into pre-writing and actual writing activities. The pre-writing stage is important because at this stage ideas and thoughts are generated, which is vital to writing. Yet, EFL learners struggle mostly at the pre-writing stage for their writing task.

Focusing on the pre-writing activities is an important way for EFL students. Proper prior planning promotes positive writing performance, and insufficient planning may lead to poor writing performance [6]. Some researchers even believe that good writing is indicative of good thinking [7].

For promoting writing skills, it is necessary to consider the writing strategies used in students' planning process. Planning the process before writing has been taken as a baseline for setting goals, organizing ideas and brainstorming [8]. So, writing preparation and strategy using are important for EFL students' writing learning and instruction. EFL students need more planning and organizing strategies as well as techniques so as to organize their ideas in a coherent and unified way before writing. Students must be aware of writing as a practical and productive process, as well as abide by writing rules and conventions such as knowledge, management, and control of techniques [9].

Mind map can be utilized as a writing strategy for the satisfaction of the requirements. A good mind map can function as a graphic organizer visualizing not only a writer's ideas for a specific writing topic, but also the connected relationships among the ideas. Writers can examine what ideas are missing or irrelevant with the assistance of mind maps. With the rapid development of technology, mind mapping software is used and welcomed in language learning and teaching field. Computerized concept maps can facilitate the modification of nodes and links and make it easier to draw and revise. Computerized maps can be easily retrieved and manipulated, which makes pre-writing brainstorming work convenient and effective.

This paper focuses on effect of computerized mind mapping-based pre-writing activities in Chinese EFL undergraduates' writing. The class with computerized mind mapping-based pre-writing activities is called Class A, while the one without is called Class B. The research questions are:

a. Does Class A do better than Class B in terms of being pertinent to the topic?
b. Does Class A do better than Class B in terms of essay's structure organization?
c. Does Class A do better than Class B in terms of language use and lexical diversity?

2 Literature Review

2.1 Mind Mapping

Mind mapping was first proposed by Tony Buzan in the late 1960s and later was further developed by Joseph Novak and his research team at Cornell University in the early 1970s [10]. According to Buzan, a "Mind Map" is an associative network of images and words which "harnesses the full range of cortical skills: word, image, number, logic, rhythm, colour and spatial awareness in a single, uniquely powerful technique" [11]. He claims that a "Mind Map" can unleash the mind′s potential because it mirrors the associative functioning of the brain which is radiant and holistic. Mind map uses color symbols and pictures to help students not only study in a pleasant and good way but also help the students to use their brains to encourage their beliefs in a method that masters' vocabulary knowledge [12].

Here "mind mapping" means a graphic software which can create electric mind maps easily. It is a non-linear visual tool for expressing ideas and the association between the ideas [13]. A mind map contains a central key word or image and sub-ideas that radiate from the central idea as branches. The key idea crystallizes the subject of attention while the branches represent the connections established with the central idea, which forms a connected nodal structure.

Mind maps can help users to simplify any information on a page because they are composed of keywords which is easier and faster to process. The structured style is helpful to categorize and sub-categorize information in a way that makes it easier to understand and navigate. The tree-structure of a mind map shows the connection of information to at least one other piece of information. Connections include a higher level (parent) topic, and potentially the same level (siblings) topics, or lower-level (child) topics, which can help users to understand concepts by breaking them down into their component parts.

To summarize, mind mapping can help students deal with the structural and conceptual elements of writing paragraphs. It can also help students organize, store and recall knowledge and information needed for the writing task.

2.2 Mind Mapping and EFL Writing Teaching

It is important and challenging to propose learning tools and strategies to provide supports to EFL learners and to improve their learning motivation in English writing classrooms [14]. There are some studies which use mind mapping tools as pre-writing planning strategies to help EFL writing.

Sundeen [15] examined the effects of an organizational strategy (mind mapping) on the writing of high school students with learning disabilities. The results indicated an improvement in the quality of data from a writing pre- and post-test. Nurlaila [16] conducted a study on the use of mind mapping technique in writing a descriptive text. The results showed a significant improvement of the writing ability. Saed & Al-Omari [10] studied the effectiveness of a mind mapping program to develop writing achievement skills among Jordanian high school students. The results showed statistically significant differences in the mean scores of students in their academic achievement and their attitudes towards writing. Bukhari [17] studies mind mapping techniques to enhance the EFL learners' writing ability and the results manifested that the hierarchical structure of the Mind mapping techniques used in the pre-writing process enhanced the EFL learners' writings. Nodoushan [18] investigated the effect of mind mapping strategy on vocabulary use in the writings of Iranian EFL learners, and the results showed that with a greater focus mind mapping strategy of vocabulary can be very effective in teaching writing especially for EFL students even at the pre-intermediate levels. Mohammad [19] studies the effect of using mind maps to enhance EFL learners' writing achievement and students' attitudes towards writing and got the results that students positively perceived the strategy of mind mapping which helped them to better writing in English. Naghmeh-Abbaspour [20] analyzed the effect of mind mapping technique on the Iranian English as Foreign Language learning' writing skills, and the results indicated that an application of mind mapping in writing classes would help the learners to organize their writings in more effective ways.

To summarize, EFL writing is a highly complex skill as it includes several cognitive processes. Mind mapping, as a proposed strategy, supported by theoretical and empirical evidence, has the potential to be a successful method in enhancing L2 and EFL writing. The aforementioned studies led to insights that the pre-writing implementation of mind mapping in the Chinese EFL undergraduates' writing instruction may be desirable.

3 Method and Procedure

3.1 Participants

A group of 74 Chinese EFL students participated in this study. They are sophomore university students. 37 students served as the experimental group (Class A) and another 37 as the control group (Class B). The major of Class A is Digital Media and Class B is Network Engineering.

3.2 Methodology

Cognitive Theory as Guiding Theory. Leonard [21] states that "the focus of cognitivism on learning is how learners process inputs and outputs mentally in order to understand how people think, learn, transmit information, and solve problems". Especially the cognitive theory of multimedia learning, which assumes that active learning involves managing several coordinated cognitive processes, and the aim of instructional design is to use instructional tools as well as learning strategies designed to help students process, store and recall information. Cognitive theory is the theoretical basis of the study.

A Mixed Method Approach. This research is a quasi-experimental as well as a correlational study. The effect of using the strategy of mind mapping on the writing achievement and attitudes towards writing is reported. A mixed method approach is used to collect and analyze data, check compatibility results, and integrate results and conclusions.

There are three phases in this study: the pre-experimental phase, which took place during the first week; the experimental phase, which started in the 2nd week and ended on the 14th week, and the post-experimental phase, which took place during the 15–16th week. The instruments employed to collect the necessary data were the pre-test initially and writing attitude questionnaire. At the end of the experiment a post-test and a final term-test of paragraph writing, similar to the pre-test, were administered to the students of group A and B. Here is also a writing attitude questionnaire during the post-experimental phase.

Writing Assessment Criteria. The study chooses CET-4 writing scoring rubric as the writing assessment criteria. The CET-4 essay scoring rubric includes the following four major criteria for each essay: a. being pertinent to the topic; b. clear expression of ideas; c. coherent; d. free of grammatical errors.

3.3 Procedures and Data Collection

This study is undertaken in three phases and the procedures are like the followings.

Do Writing Achievement Pre-test and Writing Attitudes Questionnaire in Pre-experimental Phase. Carry out writing achievement pre-test and writing attitudes questionnaire to both Class A and B. The pre-test gives the beginning level of all the students. Writing attitudes questionnaire addresses the constructs of enjoyment, confidence (ease), competence/ability, and strategy used to write. The total is 22 Likert-scale items. Choices on the scale ranged from 1 (strongly disagree) to 5 (strongly agree). The questionnaire is used to investigate the students' attitudes towards writing in EFL before the treatment. Distributed 74 questionnaires and received 73 valid ones.

Do mind Mapping Pre-writing Activities to Help Students' EFL Writing in Experimental Phase. The experiment lasts 12 weeks. For Class A, do mind mapping pre-writing activities to help students learn how to catch the characteristics of different genres of essays, how to organize an essay, how to use the writing style, how to brainstorming the words, expressions, patterns and sentences that can be used in the required essays to be written to broaden lexical range and improve their language using ability. Students should do the following mind maps: the analysis of writing style of the essay, the organization of the essay, the possible words and phrases can be used. Students in Class A are also asked to do mind maps of synonyms, antonyms, homonyms, cognates, phrases and connected idioms of some words that can be used in the essays to be written later. They also asked to exchange the basic words with advanced ones as much as possible. Mind maps will be shown in class and shared in WeChat group with classmates after class. Figure 1 and Fig. 2 are some mind maps that students made for the structure organization and possibly-used words in writing a topic-required essay.

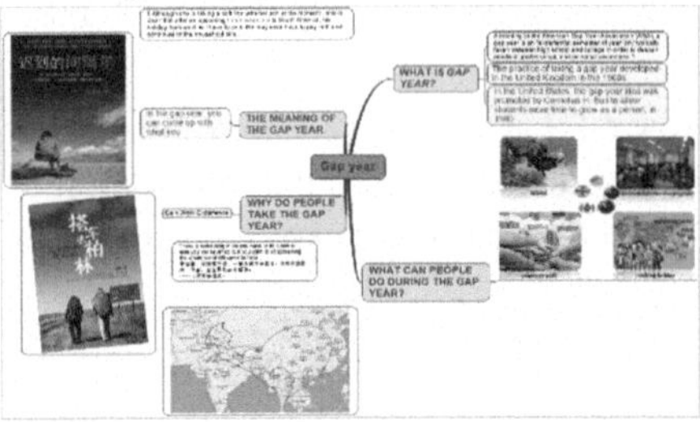

Fig. 1. Mind map of structure organization

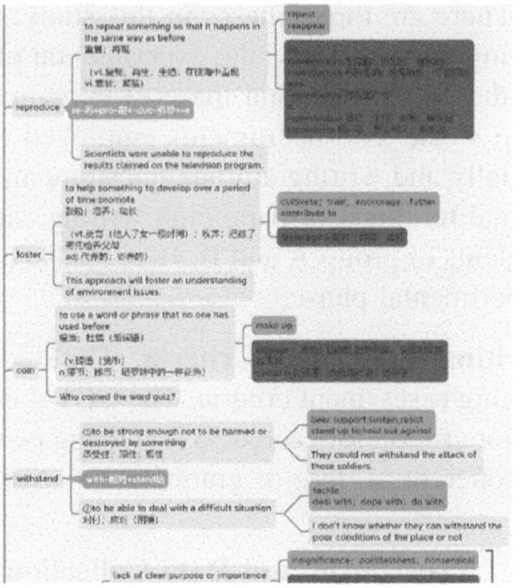

Fig. 2. Mind map of possibly-used vocabulary

The genre types of the training essays to be written are mainly expository and argumentative. For Class B, just do traditional writing instruction only in class.

Do Writing Achievement Post-test And Writing Attitudes Questionnaire in Post-experimental Phase. Do writing achievement post-test in both Class A and B. Also have writing attitudes questionnaire in the two classes. Distributed 74 questionnaires and received 74 valid ones. The questionnaire return rate was 100%.

4 Results

4.1 For Being Pertinent to the Topic

The Comparison of the Two Classes in Pre- and Post-test in Terms of Being Pertinent to the Topic that Class A do Better than Class B. The result of the pre-test shows that there are 25 students in Class A (experimental group) whose essays are pertinent to the topic, while in Class B, there are 26 students. It shows, in terms of being pertinent to the topic while writing English essays, the students in Class B (control group) do better than those in Class A. For the post-test, the number in terms of being pertinent to the topic in Class A is 36, while in Class B is 29. The number in Class A is more than that in Class B, which shows that the students in Class A do better than Class B after the experiment in terms of being pertinent to the topic in EFL writing. It answers the first research question. Table 1 shows the comparison of the two classes in pre-test and post-test in terms of being pertinent to the topic.

Table 1. Being pertinent to the topic

Number and percentage of being pertinent to the topic		
	Pre-test	Post-test
Class A	25(67.6%)	36(97.3%)
Class B	26(70.3%)	29(78.4%)

4.2 For essay's Genre Understanding and Structure Organization

The Comparison of the Two Classes in Pre- and Post-test Shows Class A Do Better than Class B in Terms of Essay's Genre Understanding and Structure Organization. The result in pre-test shows there are only 20 students in Class A who can understand essay's genres and pay attention to the structure, while the number is Class B is 22 students. There are several students in both classes who even write essays just in one paragraph. After the mind-map-based pre-writing doing experiment, from the result in post-test that there are 34 students who can understand essay's genres and pay attention to the structure organization while writing English essays. The percentage is from 54.1% to 91.2%. For Class B, there are 22 students whose writings show that they can understand the essay's genre as well as being aware of the structure in the pre-test. In the post-test, the number in Class B is 26. The percentage is from 59.5% to 70.3%. The growth rate is 37.1% in Class A and 10.8% in Class B. The growth rate in Class A is much bigger than that in Class B, which answers the second research question that Class A do better than Class B in terms of essay's genre understanding and structure organization. Table 2 shows the comparison of the two classes in pre- and post-test in terms of essay's genre understanding and structure organization. It shows that Class A do better than Class B.

Table 2. Table of essay's genre understanding and structure organization

Number and percentage of essay's genre understanding and structure organization		
	Pre-test	Post-test
Class A	20(54.1%)	35(94.6%)
Class B	22(59.5%)	28(75.7%)

4.3 For Lexical Diversity and Language Usage

Comparison Between Pre-test and Post-test in Experimental and Control Groups. The Pre-test of both Class A and Class B shows that there are about 20 students in each class who can be aware of lexical problem and pay attention to the language usage. This means the two classes are at the same level in terms of lexical diversity and language usage at the beginning of the experiment. While 12 weeks' later, the post-test shows there are 33 students in Class A and 26 students in Class B who can do well in lexical diversity and language usage. The increasing number in Class A is more than that in Class B. Table 3 shows the comparison result of the two classes in pre- and post-test in terms of lexical diversity and language usage.

Table 3. Table of lexical diversity and language usage

Number and percentage of lexical diversity and language usage		
	Pre-test	Post-test
Class A	20 (54.1%)	33 (89.2%)
Class B	20 (54.1%)	26 (70.3%)

Within-Group comparison of Pre-test and Post-test in Experimental Group. There are great changes within-group comparison of pre-test and post-test in the experimental class. The result of pre-test shows that nearly 47% of the students in Class A can only use basic, simple and general words in their writings such as "get", "say", "beautiful", etc. About 7 students can only use informal even chatty words in their writing. The result of post-test shows that nearly 90% of the students in the same class can use advanced and specific words and even phrases in their writing. About 17 students are familiar with using different words to express same meaning. For example, they can use "vital", "critical", "essential", "significant" instead of "important" to show the importance of something. Some can use "take … into consideration", "take… into account" instead of "consider", and "take… advantage of", "make use of" instead of the word "use". Some can use different sentence structure such as emphatic, and inverted sentences and Some can even use attributive clause, adverbial clause and rhetoric questions to show their ideas. The writing performance in post-test is much better than that in pre-test in Class A.

For lexical diversity and language usage, both the comparison between Pre-test and Post-test in Experimental and Control Groups and within-group comparison of Pre-test and Post-test in the Experimental Group show that the experimental group (Class A) do better than the control group (Class B).

4.4 Students with Mind Maps Pre-writing Activities Show More Positive Writing Attitude Than Those Students Without

The writing attitude in this study includes four categories which are enjoyment, confidence (ease), competence/ability, and strategy use in writing. As designed as Likert-scale items, the writing attitude questionnaire were distributed and data were accumulated. Table 4 shows the EFL writing confidence results in Likert Scale& Five-Scale questionnaire.

Table 4. Table of EFL writing confidence Likert scale& five-scale

Pre-test			Post-test		
	Score	Mean		Score	Mean
Class A (N = 37)	74	2	Class A (N = 37)	131	3.54
Class B (N = 36)	74	2.06	Class B (N = 37)	102	2.86

The scale ranged from 1 (strongly disagree) to 5 (strongly agree) in Likert Scale& Five-Scale questionnaire, so the average score is 3. The pre-test result shows the Mean is 2 in Class A and 2.06 in Class B, which explain that both of the two classes are not confident in EFL writing. The Mean in Class A is 3.54 and Class B is 2.86 in the post-test, which indicates that the students in Class A are more confident than those in Class B.

5 Conclusion and Discussion

The present study set out to evaluate the effectiveness employing mind mapping as a pre-writing strategy on Chines EFL students to create better English essays. A quasi-experiment is carried out and data are collected and analyzed. It can be concluded that Class A do better than Class B in terms of being pertinent to the topic, understanding essay's genre and structure organization, lexical diversity and language usage in EFL writing after computerized mind mapping-based pre-writing activities. It can also be concluded that Class A are more confident than Class B for EFL writing. The results answer the research questions.

There are still some questions to be discussed for the future study such as enhancing the accuracy of pre-test and post-test result. Much work should be done to improve the test. For EFL writing attitude analysis, it need to study deeply on it. The study sample also needs to be expanded.

References

1. Merriam-Webster Homepage. https://www.merriam-webster.com/dictionary/writing. Accessed 26 Aug 2021
2. Nunan, D.: Language Teaching Methodology: A Textbook for Teachers. Edinburgh (1991)
3. Brodney, B., Reeves, C., Kazelskis, R.: Selected prewriting treatments: effects on expository written by fifth-grade students. J. Exp. Educ. **68**(1), 5–20 (1999)
4. Peregoy, S.F., Boyle, O.F.: Reading, Writing, and Learning in ESL. Longman, New York (1997)
5. Myles, J.: Second language writing and research: the writing process and error analysis in student texts. Teach. Engl. Second Foreign Lang. **6**(2), 1–19 (2002)
6. Bourdin, B., Fayol, M.: Is graphic activity cognitively costly? A developmental approach. Read. Writ.: Interdisc. J. **13**, 183–196 (2000)
7. Rao, Z.: Training in brainstorming and developing writing skills. ELT J. **61**(2), 100–106 (2007)

8. Flower, L.S., Hayes, J.R.: Plans that guide the composing process. In: Frederiksen, C.H., Whiteman, M.F., Dominic, J.F. (eds.) Writing: The Nature of Development, and Teaching of Written Communication, vol. 2. Erbaum Associates, Hillsdale (1981)
9. Anwar, I.: The effect of using peer review groups in teaching essay writing to fourth year English majors, faculty of education, on their writing performance, apprehension, revising and attitudes. J. Res. Educ. Psychol. (Issued: Fac. Educ. Minia Univ.) **14**(1), 94–129 (2000)
10. Saed, H., Al-Omari, H.: The effectiveness of a proposed program based on a mind mapping strategy in developing the writing achievement of eleventh grade EFL students in Jordan and their attitudes towards writing. J. Educ. Pract. **5**, 88–109 (2014)
11. Buzan, T., Buzan, B.: The Mind Map Book: How to Use Radiant Thinking to Maximize Your Brain's Untapped Potential. Plume (1996)
12. Trianto: Design Model Learning Innovative-Progressive. Jakarta: Kencana Prenada Media Group (2009)
13. Biktimirov, E.N., Nilson, L.B.: Show them the money: using mind mapping in the introductory finance course. J. Financ. Educ. **32**, 72–86 (2006)
14. Hyland, K.: Teaching and researching writing. Int. J. Inf. Educ. Technol. **7**(5), 357 (2002)
15. Sundeen, T.: Explicit prewriting instruction: effect on writing quality of adolescents with learning disabilities. Learn. Disabil. **18**(1), 23–33 (2012)
16. Nurlaila, A.: The use of mind mapping technique in writing descriptive text. J. Engl. Educ. **1** (2), 9–15 (2013)
17. Bukhari, S.S.F.: Mind mapping technique to enhance EFL writing skill. Int. J. Linguist. Commun. **4**(1), 58–77 (2016)
18. Nodoushan, T.J., Maibodi, A.H.: The Impact of mind mapping strategy on vocabulary use in the writing of Iranian EFL learners (2017)
19. Al Kamli, H.M.: The effect of using mind maps to enhance EFL learners' writing achievement and students' attitudes towards writing at Taif University. Arab World Engl. J. Theses ID, 232 (2019)
20. Naghmeh-Abbaspour, B., Rastgoo, V.: Analysis for finding the effect of mind mapping technique on the Iranian English as foreign language learning' writing skills. Texto Livre: Linguagem Tecnol. **13**(2), 102–116 (2020)
21. Leonard, D.: Learning theories A to Z. Oryx Press, Westport (2002)

"Gold Course" in Higher Vocational Colleges Construction Standards: Connotation, Principles, Paths and Evaluation

Yan Zengxian[1] and Nie Zhe[2](✉)

[1] Guangxi Modern Polytechnic College, Hechi 547000, Guangxi, China
[2] Shezhen Polytechnic, Shenzhen 518055, Guangdong, China

Abstract. Based on "gold course" construction in higher vocational colleges, the paper has been to clarify the "gold course" connotation: suitability of the course objectives, advantage of the course content, effectiveness of the teaching process, and achievement of learning degrees, has been clear about the "gold course" construction principle: course education, value guidance; build between colleges, work-integrated learning; digital technology, comprehensive integration; to student center, continuous improvement, and put forward the "gold course" development path and paradigm from construction contents, construction path and evaluation standard.

Keywords: "Gold course" in higher vocational colleges · Construction standards · Connotation · Principle · Evaluation

Course is embodied the concept of "all-round development as the center on the students" main body, students benefit from the university of the most direct, the most core, is of course had marked effect, the implementation of the "take high moral values establishment and people cultivation" fundamental task is the key to curriculum. Since 2003, the Ministry of Education has issued the measures for the implementation of the national fine course construction, the measures for the implementation of "high-quality goods resource sharing class construction, the Ministry of Education about strengthening the construction of institutions of higher learning online open courses application and management opinion" and the Ministry of Education of the construction of first-class undergraduate courses of the implementation opinions "and other documents, and advance the course construction. In August 2018, the Ministry of Education about vigorously promotes the new era of national institutions of higher learning of undergraduate education work conference spirit to carry out the circular letter [2018] no. 8 (superior) pointed out that "universities will comprehensively comb all courses teaching content, to eliminate 'water class', create 'gold course', promote comprehensive academic challenge degree, increase the difficulty of the class, expand course depth, effectively raise the quality of teaching" [1].

At present, the job of undergraduate gold course building the class has formed the relative system, complete system of classification of curriculum construction and construction standards, but vocational education building the course and the research work is still in its infancy. Conducting higher vocational "gold course" construction

W. Jia et al. (Eds.): SETE 2021, LNCS 13089, pp. 479–485, 2021.
https://doi.org/10.1007/978-3-030-92836-0_43

research, development of higher vocational "gold course" construction standard and evaluation index system, build the path of the development of higher vocational curriculum and paradigm, "gold course" in higher vocational education curriculum construction and the development practice provide strong support, the practice of higher vocational colleges in order to speed up the course construction and development provides new ideas and new thinking [1].

1 "Gold Course" in Higher Vocational Colleges

Fine course construction goal is to create the first-class teaching staff, teaching contents, teaching methods, teaching material and teaching management; Boutique lesson resource sharing and online boutique resources for the construction of the open class goal is to teach (architect) and learning (raw) provide sharing high quality teaching resources, is on the basis of the fine course construction, pay attention to resource sharing, and focus on the learner's experience.

In class boutique resources sharing and boutique resources online open classes, on the basis of course how to realize the value guidance and education, advanced content, process, effect, promote students' all-round development [3], is the target of higher vocational "gold course". Therefore, higher vocational "gold course" refers to the teaching goal clear, advanced teaching contents, teaching effectiveness, learning effective, of unity of knowledge, ability and quality, promote students' all-round development.

1.1 Suitability of the Course Objectives

Course is committed to open the potential students and learning motivation, pay attention to the knowledge, skills training, improve quality, support for the professional training objectives to achieve plays an important role.

1.2 Curriculum Content of Advanced Nature

Course content follow the production technological frontier, focusing on the core knowledge and skills, to the professional knowledge, skill and quality organic course, in a timely manner will industry industry of new technology, new knowledge, new technology, new specification into teaching. Rich variety, high quality teaching resources, can effectively support and promote between the teachers and students, students to resource sharing, communication and collaborative learning problem.

1.3 Effectiveness of the Teaching Process

According to characteristics of students' cognitive regularity and learn, through inquiry, the application of the teaching methods such as heuristic, hybrid, promote interaction between teachers and students, resources sharing, highlights the learning process of students and teachers, build wisdom education students and teachers can assign the learning community.

1.4 Achievement of Learning Degrees

Learning outcomes docking jobs work comprehensively, fully develop the students' professional skills and innovative consciousness, innovative spirit and the sustainable development ability, etc.

2 "Gold Course" Construction Principle in Vocational Colleges

"Gold course" in vocational colleges should be to uphold the party's education policy, with students as the center, for the purpose of service, follow the demand orientation, problem orientation and goal oriented [4], optimize course structure, rich resources, deepen the reform of the curriculum, course management, constantly improving the quality of curriculum construction, improve the teaching quality of education in an all-round way.

2.1 Course Education, Value Guidance

Mining, combing contained in the course of ideological education elements, clarify the course ideological education the main line, the value guidance and develop organic way of thinking, strengthen the "catalyst" role of emotion in education, realize the whole process of education course.

2.2 Build Between Colleges, Work-Integrated Learning

Refined typical work tasks, together with the industry enterprise analysis to complete the task should have professional ability and quality requirements, according to the typical task integration refactoring, the content of the course and teaching, with work-integrated learning, cultivate the students' post competency project driving.

2.3 Digital Technology, Comprehensive Integration

Combining with the social development of the digital transformation, to complete the tasks using the digital technology of organic blend in teaching content, give full play to the advantages of the digital technology such as information technology, artificial intelligence, construction can meet the students, social learning teaching resources, realize the personalized, differentiated learning, and in the planning and study plan, record students' progress and evaluate the results of learning to carry out accurate teaching exploration.

2.4 Student Center, Continuous Improvement

Take the student as the center, give full play to the peer mutual aid, group learning, such as social learning advantages, real-time strategy of teaching and the effect of reflection, the relationship between curriculum innovation, constantly improve students all-round development.

3 "Gold Course" Construction Principle in Vocational Colleges

3.1 Curriculum Standard

Course education, guide enterprises to proselytize" as the gripper, based on the professional ability and professional teaching standards, focusing on the professional ability training, university-enterprise joint establishment curriculum standard.

3.2 Curriculum Content

We should follow the basic rules of students' vocational ability training, based on real work tasks and work process, "class facilities, teaching facilities" organic combination, integration and reconstruction of teaching content, scientific design of learning tasks, to realize the integration of do, learn, teach; Want to strengthen the students' comprehensive application ability as the goal, according to the core competence of the specifications of the constituent elements of professional requirements, building modular teaching content.

3.3 Curriculum Resources

We should attach great importance to the diversity of curriculum resources, versatility, and generic in nature. Curriculum resources to include multiple forms and media form, for the students of different learning style suitable form. Processing of resources to support learning before class, class, and after-school learning. To adopt or write depth docking industry enterprise standards, meet the requirement of "documentary evidence accommodation, teaching facilities", rich form, content, update teaching materials.

3.4 Curriculum Teaching

Around the goal, teaching content, organization, implementation and evaluation of the overall planning, the growth pattern conforms to the students in the teaching strategies, teaching methods, teaching process, teaching evaluation and so on, exploring the flip classroom, hybrid, exploratory, participatory, personalized teaching mode, a variety of applications such as innovating the mode of teaching and learning, build wisdom classroom, let the students grow in knowledge acquisition and skill training.

3.5 Curriculum Evaluation

To diagnostic evaluation, process evaluation, summative evaluation organic combination, from the aspect of knowledge, skills, quality and so on to multiple evaluation of learning outcomes, promote the all-round development of students.

3.6 Curriculum Teaching Team

We must strengthen the double structure of teachers team construction, the introduction of industry company as part-time teachers, researchers pay more attention to teacher echelon construction, promote the teachers' ability to transition.

4 "Gold Course" Building Path in Vocational Colleges

4.1 Comprehensive Research and Comb, Clear Course Construction Goal and Mission

Comprehensive research course docking post specific professional ability request, the curriculum goal, content, such as students and evaluation for comprehensive combing, give attention to both the future society and personal development appeals to the talented person demand, analyze the gap between ideal and the current course, clear objectives and key construction tasks. To implement course construction to each teaching unit, to the list and assign task, guarantee the course group all members to reach consensus, to each teacher's individual responsibilities and tasks.

4.2 Obtain the Build for the Gripper, Reconstruction and Optimization of Teaching Design and Teaching Resources

Stick to build between colleges, combining with the industry in the future change, reconstruction and optimization of the teaching content, form new teaching design. To gradually form systematic curriculum education in the curriculum system, and the industry standard, X certificate, skills competitions, new technologies such as organic course.

4.3 To Aim at Learning Outcomes, Fully Stimulate Students Learning Motivation

We must adhere to in the teaching implementation project driven and task-oriented teaching mode, extensive use of digital technology, insist on creating learning situation, adhere to the enterprise moved to classroom practice, change the course of the implementation of the pattern, course content, teaching method and teaching mode innovation, create active classroom, pay attention to students' learning outcomes, fully stimulate students learning motivation.

4.4 Real-Time Assessment and Iteration, Make High Quality Courses

We should constantly practice in curriculum implementation, evaluation and reflection effect of curriculum construction, real-time adjust course construction and iteration, the curriculum construction into high quality "gold Course".

5 "Gold Course" Evaluation Standard in Vocational Colleges

5.1 Overall Design to Rot Two Level

One is rot course education, to dig, combing contained in the course of ideological education elements, and integrate the value guidance and thinking training courses, course education in the curriculum goal, curriculum standards, lesson plans, teaching file, course education through classroom teaching, training seminars and so on each link of teaching activities; 2 it is rot: curriculum standard to the positioning of the course has an important support role, the target of profession fostering, subsequent courses before cohesion is proper, and industry demand for organic fit, docking vocational skills standard, the competition and 1 + X certificate, etc., from the perspectives of knowledge, skills, experience, clear teaching goal, pay attention to cultivate the students' ability of sustainable development.

5.2 Teaching Content Should be Advanced and Practical

We should insist university-enterprise cooperation development course, according to the project curriculum design, with the actual project (case, activities, etc.) for the teaching carrier, reflect the latest technology and achievement, effective support to achieve the goals of teaching; "Class facilities, teaching facilities" organic combination, integration and reconstruction of teaching content, scientific design of learning tasks, to realize the integration of do, learn, teach; To attach importance to learning tasks and activity design, course design, teaching arrangement and presentation in accordance with students' cognitive regularity; To adopt or write depth docking industry enterprise standards, meet the requirement of "documentary evidence accommodation, teaching facilities", rich in form, content, update teaching materials; Curriculum resources rich variety, there is a certain redundancy, forming around the knowledge skill points spread knowledge framework, clear expression of curriculum resources, scientific and comprehensive annotation resource property, convenient for teacher to carry out online teaching, effective support students before class, class, and the whole process of learning after class.

5.3 Teaching Implementation Should be Comprehensive and Efficient

We should adhere to the "student" as the center of the problem of lead, task driven teaching methods, such as exploring flip classroom, hybrid, exploratory, participatory, personalized teaching mode, a variety of applications such as innovating the mode of teaching and learning, build wisdom classroom, let the students grow in knowledge acquisition and skill training; High student online learning response, and the interaction between teachers and students fully, can effectively promote between the teachers and students, resource sharing, interactive communication between students and autonomous and collaborative learning; Diversification of evaluation, pay attention to students' self-evaluation and peer evaluation, teacher evaluation, evaluation and comprehensive evaluation of enterprise, the diagnostic evaluation, process evaluation, summative evaluation organic combination, from the aspect of knowledge, skills, quality and so on to multiple evaluation of learning outcomes, promote the all-round development of students.

5.4 Teaching Effect to Achieve Objective

We should pay attention to the teacher echelon construction, advancing teachers' ability to transition, form a reasonable structure, Professional teachers and enterprise combination with research and development ability, teaching and application of comprehensive development teaching team; Students' course acceptance, a strong interest in learning; Outstanding academic achievements and learning outcomes of jointing the professional work, comprehensive technical skills, to cultivate the students' innovation consciousness, innovation spirit and the sustainable development ability.

References

1. The Ministry of Education of the People's Republic of China. About vigorously promotes the new times spirit of the national conference of job of undergraduate course education of institutions of higher learning, adopt notice. Teach high letter, no. 8, 22 August 2018 (2018)
2. Wang, Z., Wang, G.: Research on reconstruction strategy of "golden course" in higher vocational colleges based on structural reform. Vocat. Tech. Educ. (29), 23–26 (2019)
3. Zhang, X.: The ideas and action of creating 'golden course' in higher vocational education. Chin. Vocat. Tech. Educ. (2), 8–10 (2019)
4. Wang, W., Zhou, C., Gu, Z.: Construction of "golden course" in higher vocational colleges: elements, characteristics and paths. Vocat. Tech. Educ. **41**(5), 19–22 (2020)

Author Index

The manufacturer's authorised representative in the EU is Springer Nature Customer Service Centre GmbH, Europaplatz 3, 69115 Heidelberg, Germany. If you have any concerns regarding our products, please contact ProductSafety@springernature.com

Printed and bound by CPI Group (UK) Ltd, Croydon, CR0 4YY
02/10/2026
02227135-0007